DIMENSIONS OF
NATURAL OBJECTS IN MILES

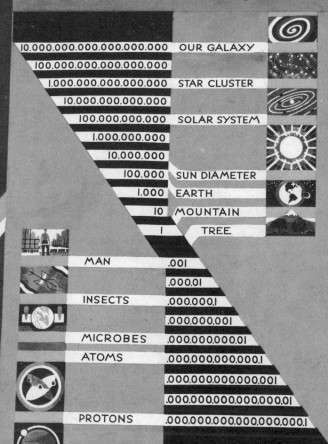

10,000,000,000,000,000,000	OUR GALAXY
100,000,000,000,000,000	
1,000,000,000,000,000	STAR CLUSTER
10,000,000,000,000	
100,000,000,000	SOLAR SYSTEM
1,000,000,000	
10,000,000	
100,000	SUN DIAMETER
1,000	EARTH
10	MOUNTAIN
1	TREE

MAN	.001
	.000,01
INSECTS	.000,000,1
	.000,000,001
MICROBES	.000,000,000,01
ATOMS	.000,000,000,000,1
	.000,000,000,000,001
	.000,000,000,000,000,01
PROTONS	.000,000,000,000,000,000,1

CAPITOL BUILDING, WILLIAMSBURG, VA.

This restoration of the old capitol building of Virginia Colony is on the site of the original structure. At the close of the seventeenth century, the charming colonial town of Williamsburg replaced Jamestown as the capital of Virginia. It remained the seat of government until 1779. In the years that followed, many of the fine old buildings of Williamsburg fell into decay or were torn down. Through the generosity of John D. Rockefeller, Jr., scores of authentic colonial structures have been rebuilt—living symbols of the past. Portions of the town have been included in Colonial National Historical Park. [See Williamsburg.]

The
AMERICAN
EDUCATOR
Encyclopedia

*A Thoroughly Modern Work Designed to
Meet the Needs of Every Age*

ELLSWORTH D. FOSTER, LL.B.
ORIGINAL EDITOR IN CHIEF
Former Managing Editor, The World Book

LORIMER V. CAVINS, Ph.D.
EDITOR IN CHIEF
*Research Director, Technical Adviser in Education.
Associated with The General Education Board
and The Brookings Institution*

JAMES LAUGHLIN HUGHES
EDITOR FOR CANADA
Former Chief Inspector of Schools, Toronto

BERTHA MAUDE WHITE, A.B.
MANAGING EDITOR

EUNICE W. THOMPSON, M.A.

*Assisted by a Large Number of Contributors in all
Fields of Knowledge*

1943

THE UNITED EDUCATORS, INC.
E. C. B. & S. CO.   *Publishers*   W. K. CORP.
CHICAGO
M. S. S. INC.

PRONUNCIATION

The pronunciation of titles is indicated by accenting the word or by respelling it phonetically in italics. In the phonetic spelling, letters are used to indicate the sounds which they most commonly represent.

A vowel is *short* when followed by a consonant in the same syllable, unless the syllable ends in silent *e*.

A vowel is *long* when standing alone or in a syllable which ends in silent *e* or when ending an accented syllable.

S is always soft, and never has the sound of *z*.

The foreign sounds which have no equivalent in the English language are represented as follows:

K for the German *ch*, as in Bach: (**Bach**, *baK*).

N for the French *n*, as in Breton: (**Breton**, *bre toN'*).

ö for the German *ö*, as in Göttingen: (**Göttingen**, *gö'ting en*).

ü for the German *ü*, as in Blücher: (**Blücher**, *blüK'ur*).

Copyright

1919, 1922, 1923, 1924,
1925, 1926, 1928, 1930,
1932, 1933, 1934, 1935,
1936, 1937, 1939, 1941,
1942, 1943

•

THE UNITED EDUCATORS, INC.
PUBLISHERS
CHICAGO
Printed in U.S.A.

TURKEY, the name that for centuries was borne by one of the world's mightiest empires, when it bestrode three continents and from its throne of beauty at Constantinople swayed the destinies not only of millions of Turks but of many subject peoples held to an unwilling allegiance by the power of the sword. Under the white heat of religious zeal and fanaticism which taught that to kill an infidel or to die in a "holy" war was rewarded gloriously in the hereafter, the empire expanded until North Africa, Southwest Asia and much of Southern Europe lay at the feet of the Mohammedan power.

It could not govern well. It despised the infidel—anyone not a follower of Mohammed. Tyranny, despotism, repression and bloodshed in the course of time wrought its doom. As its alien peoples desperately began to free themselves from this overlordship, the empire started to shrink. How it lost its African domain in Egypt and Tripoli, the manner in which it was forced step by step out of Europe until only a tenuous foothold was retained along the Dardanelles and the Sea of Marmora, and its Asiatic realm was reduced until there remained only its old fertile stronghold on the Anatolian plateau (old Asia Minor)—these moving facts this article records, and more. The empire itself has disappeared, and on its ruins was erected a modern government, republican in form, liberal in outlook, known as the National State of Turkey. Population, 1935, 16,158,018.

A Look Backward. While the generation now coming to knowledge of world affairs sees a new Turkey trying to get in step with Western ideals and modern standards—and succeeding very well—the Turkey with which the passing generation is familiar was popularly known as the Ottoman Empire, so called from Othman, or Osman, its founder. About the year 1300, by martial ability and valor, to which he added deceitful wiles, he reared an independent kingdom on the ruins of the Seljuk Turks, whom Christian Europe had come to know as its foe during the Crusades. Othman's followers were a tribe that had swarmed out of the unknown in Central Asia about fifty years before.

The spirit of conquest was strong in these early Ottoman Turks, and gradually they subjugated the Armenian peoples, absorbed the dependencies of the Eastern Roman or Byzantine Empire, and fought their way into South Central Europe and Africa. In the sixteenth century, when the power of the Ottoman Turk was at its height, the empire included Arabia, and the Asiatic possessions of the fallen Byzantine Empire, including Constantinople; Macedonia, Greece, Albania, Serbia, the provinces that became modern Rumania, Bulgaria, the Greek Mediterranean islands, Syria, Tripoli and Egypt. The Ottomans even gained a foothold in Hungary and in Italy, but after 1683 they were gradually pushed out of Europe. One by one the European provinces of Turkey gained their independence. In 1912 Italy by a successful war wrested Tripoli from Turkey, and at the close of the Balkan Wars, in 1913, the empire was shorn of all its European holdings except Constantinople, Adrianople, a small section adjoining these cities and a few islands in the Mediterranean.

Then came the World War. The interests of Germany and Turkey were closely related. The former had projected the Berlin-to-Baghdad Railway, and a part of it had been constructed through Turkish territory. Turkey reasoned with considerable assurance that the Germanic powers would win the war, and at its close, with Turkish participation on the side of the Central Powers, its world position would be greatly strengthened. It could be of material assistance to Germany, for even with the losses it had recently suffered, the empire covered more than 760,000 square miles, exclusive of Egypt, where it still exercised nominal authority. Hostilities were begun by Turkish bombardment of Odessa, and Russia declared war on Turkey on November 3, 1914. Two days later, France and Great Britain declared war, and Italy followed in August, 1915. Early in 1915, the French and British began an unsuccessful attack on the Dardanelles.

For the Allies, the Dardanelles campaign was one of the most disastrous movements of the World War. Consequently, when Britain and France again became involved in war with Germany, in 1939, they realized the importance of retaining the friendship of Turkey, which again was guardian of the strategic gateway to the East. Both countries concluded an alliance with Turkey early in the conflict. In the World War, however, the Allies suffered a diplomatic defeat by having Turkey an enemy allied with Germany. This alliance was one of the factors that delayed the final victory. Moreover, it cost the Allies severe losses in men and supplies.

Changes During the World War. Early in the World War the British annexed the island of Cyprus, and in 1915 declared Egypt a British protectorate. In 1916 the people of Hedjaz, a narrow strip of territory in Arabia, bordering on the Red Sea, revolted and set up an independent kingdom; this state has an area of 96,500 square miles and a population of 300,000. In 1917 Palestine was captured by the British, and by the end of the war all of Syria was under allied control. Mesopotamia fell into British hands in 1917, and when Turkey surrendered in

France and Great Britain with mandates to govern and prepare them for statehood.

Turkey and Its People. The discussion which follows is restricted to the genuinely Turkish portion of the old empire, namely, Anatolia, or Asia Minor. (For descriptive matter on the various parts of the former domain, see ARMENIA, ARABIA, PALESTINE, SYRIA, MESOPOTAMIA, EGYPT, etc.) *Anatolia* is derived from Greek words meaning *to rise,* a word chosen with reference to the elevated surface, and is the modern name for Asia Minor. The country includes the

TURKEY AND ITS ASIATIC NEIGHBORS

The area with boundary heavily shaded marks the limits of the present National State of Turkey. All that part of Asia west of Persia and south of Soviet Transcaucasia was a part of the Turkish Empire until after the World War.

the fall of 1918 practically Constantinople only was left to the Turk in Europe.

Turkey Dismembered. The part of the old empire that was predominantly Turkish was Anatolia, or Asia Minor. This the Allies determined should constitute the new Turkey, with the addition of the area surrounding Constantinople, on the European mainland, and a few small adjacent islands in the Aegean Sea. All other possessions were swept away; Palestine, Syria, and Mesopotamia (now Iraq) were given hope of eventual independence, but placed temporarily under

peninsula bounded by the Armenian highlands on the east, Syria and the Mediterranean on the south, the Aegean Sea on the west, and the Black Sea and Sea of Marmora on the north. In the interior the land is a series of plateaus, having an average elevation of 3,000 feet. Near the Mediterranean seacoast these uplands suddenly sink to the narrow belt of level land called the *Levant.* The plateaus are nearly bare of trees and are interspersed with salt plains, marshes and salty lakes. The land is here best adapted for grazing. Under irrigation, however, the soil is productive. The strips of seacoast on the west, north and south are fertile and bear a luxuriant vegetation, including such fruits as prunes, olives and figs. Farming is practiced in the interior with considerable toil, and grains, cotton and tobacco are raised. Silk culture also receives attention.

The plateau is bordered on the north by a series of parallel mountains which run the whole length of the Black Sea. The greatest elevation, in the extreme east, is 12,000 feet. On the south is the Taurus range, following the Mediterranean coast, and having many peaks over 10,000 feet in height. These mountains are rich in minerals, but the mines have as yet been little developed. The mineral deposits of Anatolia include coal, lead, manganese, iron, gold, salt and petroleum, and they offer a promising field for capitalists when normal conditions return.

In Anatolia, as in other parts of the old Turkish domain, industry has long been in a backward state. The rural population which lives chiefly by farming and sheep raising, has suffered from misgovernment, lack of transportation facilities ignorance and extortion of tax officials. Manufacturing in the modern sense is almost unknown, but Turkish artisans show great skill in producing copper and brass utensils, and, especially, hand-woven rugs. Cloth, olive oil and soap are made in limited quantities.

The Turkish peasants are naturally patient, hospitable and kind-hearted; it is the unscrupulous deeds of the ruling classes that have given rise to the feeling in Western nations expressed in the term, the "Unspeakable Turk." The Turkish people are all Mohammedans in religion, and are devoted followers of the Prophet. They are found in all parts of the old empire, both in Europe and Asia, but are nowhere numerically dominant except in Asia Minor. In the cities Greeks, Jews and Armenians are important in commercial life, but Turks have political control. Nomadic Turkomans, who are racially akin to the Turks, are found in the rural districts in large numbers. The chief cities include Smyrna, Scutari, Brussa, Adana, Trebizond and Adalia.

History of the Empire. The Ottoman Turks came originally from the region of the Altai Mountains, in central Asia, and in the sixth century A. D. they pushed onward to the west, in connection with other Turkish tribes. Early in the eighth century they came in contact with the Saracens, from whom they took their religion, and of whom they were at first the slaves and mercenaries. In the thirteenth century they appeared as allies of the Seljukian Turks against the Mongols, and for their aid they received a grant of lands in Asia Minor. Othman or Osman, the son of their leader, Ertogrul, became the most powerful emir of Western Asia, and after the death of the Seljuk sultan of Iconium in the year 1300, he proclaimed himself sultan. Thus was founded, upon the ruins of the Saracen, Seljuk and Mongol power, the Empire of the Osman, or Ottoman Turks, in Asia. After Osman, the courage, policy and enterprise of eight great princes, whom the dignity of caliph placed in possession of the standard of the prophet, and who were animated by religious fanaticism and a passion for military glory, raised the Empire to the rank of the first military power, in both Europe and Asia (1300–1566).

Period of Expansion. The first of these princes was Orkhan, son of Osman. He subdued all Asia Minor to the Hellespont and was the first to organize the Turkish power. Orkhan's son, Soliman, first invaded Europe in 1355. In 1361 Orkhan's second son and successor, Amurath I, took Adrianople, which became the seat of the empire in Europe, and he later conquered Macedonia, Albania and Serbia and defeated a great Slav confederation, under the Bosnian king Stephen, at Kossovo. Bajazet (ruler from 1389 to 1402) invaded Thessaly and advanced toward Constantinople. In 1396 he defeated the Western Christians under Sigismund, king of Hungary, at Nicopolis, in Bulgaria; but at Angora, in 1402, he was himself conquered and taken prisoner by Timur, who divided the provinces between the sons of Bajazet. Finally, in 1413, the fourth son of Bajazet, Mohammed I, seated himself upon the throne of Osman. Mohammed was succeeded by his son, Amurath II (1421–1451), who defeated Ladislas, king of Hungary and Poland, at Varna in 1444. Mohammed II, the son of Amurath, completed the work of conquest (1451–1481). He attacked Constantinople, which was taken on May 29, 1453, and the Byzantine Empire came to an end. After that time Constantinople was the seat of the Sublime Porte, or Turkish government. Mohammed added Serbia, Bosnia, Albania and Greece to the Ottoman Empire, and threatened Italy, which was freed from danger by his death. His grandson, Selim I (Sultan from 1512 to 1520), conquered Egypt and Syria. Under Solyman II (1520–1566), the Ottoman Empire reached the highest pitch of power and splendor, but after his time, the race of Osman degenerated, and the power of the Porte declined.

Period of Decline. During the latter part of the sixteenth century and most of the seventeenth century, the chief wars which Turkey waged were with Venice and with Austria. The Battle of Lepanto in 1571, in which the Ottoman fleet was overthrown by the combined fleets of Venice and Spain, was the first great Ottoman reverse at sea; and the Battle of Saint Gotthard, in 1664, in which Montecuccoli defeated the Vizier Kiuprili, the first great Ottoman reverse on land. In 1683 Vienna was besieged by the Turks, but it was relieved by John Sobieski, and in 1697 the Turks were defeated at Zenta by the Austrians under Prince Eugene. Two years after this defeat, the Peace of Karlowitz was signed, by which Turkey agreed to renounce its claims upon Transylvania and a large part of Hungary, to give up the Morea to the Venetians, to restore the Ukraine to Poland and to leave Azov to the Russians. Eugene's subsequent victories at Peterwardein and Belgrade obliged the Porte, by the Treaty of Passarowitz, in 1718, to give up Belgrade, with a part of Serbia and Wallachia; but the Turks, on the other hand, took the Morea from Venice, and by the Treaty of Belgrade, in 1739, they regained Belgrade, Serbia and Little Wallachia, while for a time they also regained Azov.

Russia, which had been making steady advances under Peter the Great and subsequently, now became the great opponent of Turkey. In the middle of the eighteenth century, the Ottoman Empire still embraced a large part of southern Russia. The victories of the Russians in the war between 1736 and 1744 determined the political superiority of Russia, and compelled Turkey to renounce all sovereignty over the Crimea, to yield to Russia the country between the Bog and the Dnieper and to open its seas to the Russian merchant ships. By the Peace of Jassy, 1792, which closed the war of 1787–1791, Russia retained Tauride and the country between the Bug and the Dniester and gained some accessions in the Caucasus.

In the long series of wars which followed the French Revolution, the Ottoman Empire was first opposed to France, in consequence of Bonaparte's campaign in Egypt, and later to Russia, which demanded a more distinct recognition of its protectorate over the Christians. By the Peace of Bucharest in 1812, Turkey ceded to Russia the country between the Dniester and the Pruth. Further disputes ended in the Porte making additional concessions, which tended toward loosening the connection of Serbia, Moldavia and Wallachia with Turkey. In 1821 the war of Greek independence broke out. In 1826 the massacre of the Janizaries took place at Constantinople, after a revolt. In 1828 the Russians crossed the Balkans and took Adrianople, the war being terminated by the Peace of Adrianople in 1829. In 1831 Mehemet Ali, nominally pasha of Egypt, but real ruler both of Egypt and Syria, levied war against his sovereign and threatened Constantinople; but the Russians, who had been called on for aid by the sultan, forced the invaders to desist. In 1839 Mehemet Ali again rose against his sovereign; but through the active intervention of Austria, Great Britain and Russia, he was compelled to evacuate Syria, though he was recognized as hereditary viceroy of Egypt.

The next important event in the history of the Ottoman Empire was the Crimean War. In 1875 the people of Herzegovina, unable to endure longer the misgovernment of the Turks, broke into rebellion. A year later the Serbians and Montenegrins likewise took up arms, and though the former were unsuccessful and obliged to abandon the war, the Montenegrins still held out. Meantime, the great powers of Europe were pressing reforms on Turkey, and at the end of 1876 a conference met at Constantinople, with the view of making a fresh settlement of the relations between Turkey and the Christian provinces. All the recommendations of the conference were, however, rejected by Turkey; and in April following, Russia, which had been coming more and more prominently forward as the champion of the oppressed provinces and had for months been massing troops on both the Asiatic and the European frontier of Turkey, issued a warlike manifesto and commenced hostile operations in both parts of the Turkish Empire. The final settlement of this war was effected by the Treaty of Berlin.

SANTA SOPHIA, NOW A MOHAMMEDAN EDIFICE, ISTANBUL, TURKEY

It stands today as the most famous example of Byzantine architecture. Built for a Christian Church by the Roman Emperor Justinian the Great, it was completed in 538. The dome is the most impressive feature of the structure. It is 180 feet high and 107 feet in diameter, and is supported on four arches, each having a span of about 100 feet. The interior is finished with marble and beautiful mosaic.

THE OLD AND THE NEW IN TURKEY

Above: A picturesque street scene in the ancient city of Ankara, the capital of modern Turkey.

Below: Old and new costumes of Turkish women; the two at the right in modern costumes without veils, permitted under the present régime.

The main events in the history of the Ottoman Empire from the Treaty of Berlin to the year 1890 were the treaty with Greece, executed under pressure of the great powers in 1881, by which Turkey ceded to Greece almost the whole of Thessaly and a strip of Epirus; the occupation of Egypt by Great Britain in 1882; and the revolution at Philippopolis in 1885, when the government of Eastern Rumelia was overthrown and the union of that province with Bulgaria was proclaimed. In July, 1894, Constantinople was visited by a series of earthquakes, which lasted eight days, two or more occurring each day. Great damage was done to the city and surrounding country.

For several decades the Turkish government was faced with revolts within its borders and with attacks by neighboring countries. In July, 1908, by a successful revolution, the Young Turks, a reform party, compelled the sultan to grant a Constitution. Another revolt in 1909 forced Abd-ul-Hamid II to abdicate; his younger brother ascended the throne as Mohammed V. Italy, in 1912, waged war on Turkey, which was forced to yield Tripoli to the aggressor. On the close of this conflict, the allied Balkan states declared war on Turkey. The European powers interfered after several months of this warfare, and Turkey, by the Treaty of London in 1913, lost all its European territory except Constantinople, Adrianople and a small adjacent area. Turkey entered the World War in 1914 on the side of the Central Powers (see WORLD WAR for military operations.) In 1915 came a recurrence of Turkey's persecution of the Armenians.

After the World War. With Turkey's surrender to the Allies in October, 1918, the Ottoman Empire came to an end. The Allies occupied Constantinople (now Istanbul), where the new Sultan, Mohammed VI, remained in power. The rest of Turkey, until November, 1922, was under the *de facto* Nationalist government at Angora (Ankara), set up in 1920 by Mustapha Kemal Pasha.

The humiliating terms of the Sèvres Treaty, signed by the sultan's government in 1920, ceded considerable territory to Greece and designated areas of Italian and French influence. In November, 1922, Turkish forces under Kemal Pasha captured Smyrna (which see) and recovered the section of Asia Minor that had been awarded to Greece. In the same month the National assembly abolished the sultanate and took over the Constantinople government. The Treaty of Lausanne in 1923 revoked the Sèvres Treaty, returned Constantinople and Adrianople to Turkey and decreed the internationalization of the Dardanelles; Turkey, however, again fortified the straits in 1936. The present area of Turkey is about 296,000 square miles.

In 1923 the Turkish Republic was proclaimed. Kemal Pasha, who took the name Kemal Atatürk, was elected its first President. By the next year, when the caliphate was abolished, the old order was definitely over. Ankara was declared the national capital and Turkey instituted, under Kemal Atatürk's leadership, reforms leading to the modernizing of the new republic.

Kemal Atatürk was unanimously reëlected in 1927. On his death, in 1938, General Ismet Inönü, for twelve years Prime Minister of Turkey, was elected to succeed him. In 1939 Turkey concluded with France and Great Britain a treaty of mutual assistance. Hatay, formerly the Sanjak of Alexandretta, was ceded by France to Turkey.

Related Articles. Consult the following titles for additional information:

CITIES

Adrianople	Constantinople
Ankara	Smyrna

HISTORY

Abd-ul-Hamid II	Gallipoli
Balance of Power	Kemal Pasha,
Balkan Wars	Mustapha
Berlin, Congress of	Mohammed V
Bosporus	Russia
Byzantine Empire	Russo-Turkish War
Crimean War	Seljuks
Dardanelles	World War

TURKEY, a large game bird of the pheasant family, native to North America. There are only two species; one is found in Yucatan and Central America, and the other is the common wild turkey of Mexico and the United States. The wild turkey is a tall, handsome bird, the full-grown male weighing from ten to twenty-five pounds. The brilliant plumage has copper, bronze and green reflections. The head and neck are bare of feathers. The male, which is larger than the female, has a tuft of bristly feathers hanging from its breast. These birds feed on insects, seeds, berries and other small fruits. The nests are placed on the ground, and the eggs, twice the size of a hen's egg, are creamy white. One brood, usually consisting of about twelve, is reared a season. A second brood is raised only in case the first comes to grief. The birds are becoming rapidly exterminated. The domestic turkey, which is derived from the Mexican wild turkey, is less brilliantly colored. Turkeys require about the same care as chickens. See GAME, color plate.

TURKEY BUZ'ZARD, or TURKEY VULTURE, the commonest of American vultures, so named because at a distance it resembles a turkey in appearance. The turkey buzzard is about two and a half feet long, and its wings extend to about six feet in breadth. It lives in most of the warmer regions of the United States and extends its habitat through Mexico and South America.

TURKMENISTAN. See TURKESTAN.

TURKS, a race of Mongolo-Talei origin, widely disseminated throughout Western and Northwestern, Asia and Southeastern Europe. They are divided into the Ottoman Turks, Turkomans, Kirghizes, Usbecks, Yakuts and other tribes. The Ottoman Turks developed in the Middle Ages to commanding military and political power, but have since greatly declined.

TUR'MERIC, an aromatic plant, native to Southern Asia; also a yellow dye prepared from its roots. Turmeric is used as a condiment in the Orient, being an important ingredient in curry powder. It is also useful in chemistry, in making test papers.

TURN'ER, JOSEPH MALLARD WILLIAM (1775–1851), an English landscape painter, member of the Royal Academy, first celebrated as a landscape painter in water colors and later in oils. In the first half of the nineteenth century he exhibited at the Academy more than two hundred pictures, easily becoming the most popular landscape painter of the English school. His works claim special merit because of their fine coloring effects. Details are often wanting, and drawing is imperfect, but the idealistic effect is unsurpassed. During the latter period of his work, however, he fell into a vague trifling with effects of light and shade and color, which somewhat lessened his great reputation. He bequeathed most of his pictures and sketches to the nation, on condition that a suitable building be erected for their reception. They have been placed in the Turner Gallery, occupying two rooms in the National Gallery in London. Some of his most noted paintings are *Slave Ship; The Fighting Temeraire; Rain, Steam and Speed on the Great Western Railway; Hannibal and His Army Crossing the Alps,* and *The Garden of the Hesperides.*

TURNER, NAT (about 1800–1831), an American negro slave, born in Southampton County, Va., who from earliest childhood claimed to be chosen and inspired for the accomplishment of a great purpose. In 1828, he declared that at a certain sign he would lead an insurrection against his enemies. In 1831, at an eclipse of the sun, he began carrying out this plan by killing five members of his master's family. Joined by other slave recruits, he continued the massacre until every person in the neighborhood had been murdered. On the following day the insurrection was broken up by a band of white men and by the arrival of Federal troops. Turner was captured October 30 and executed within a few days. The insurrection, known as the Nat Turner Insurrection, resulted in the passage of stringent laws for the management and punishment of slaves in most of the Southern states.

TUR'NIP, a biennial plant of the mustard family, much cultivated on account of its fleshy root. It was well known to the Greeks and Romans, and has been used as a vegetable in all temperate climates, being cultivated on a large scale in some countries as food for stock. Turnips may be planted succeeding the harvest of a crop of wheat or oats.

TURN'STONE, a shore bird of the plover family, with pied black and white plumage,

TURNSTONE

varied with rufous and ash, taking its name from its habit of turning up small stones in search for marine worms, minute crustaceans, etc., for food. It is found in almost every part of the globe during migrations, and breeds on rocky coasts in the Arctic regions, cunningly concealing its eggs, four in number, among the sparse Arctic vegetation.

TURNVEREIN, *toorn' fer ine,* German athletic organizations first established by Friedrich Ludwig Jahn about the beginning of the nineteenth century, and exerting an enormous influence in building up a vigorous and hardy German population after the Napoleonic wars. In America turnvereins were first organized by German refugees in Philadelphia and Cincinnati, in 1848. They were subsequently extended to other cities with large German populations, the total membership attaining to about 40,000.

TUR'PENTINE, the distilled gum of the pine tree. Turpentine is manufactured by collecting the gum, or crude turpentine, from the trees and distilling it in copper vessels. The season begins when the first spring sap rises, and it ends when winter checks the flow of the sap. In January or February the trees are hacked. The hacks are about six inches deep; they are cut near the roots of the tree, and as close together, to the height of a man's head, as can be done without killing the pine. The hacker leaves a width of bark between each cut, so as to preserve the vitality of the tree. The sap or gum, fills the cuts with a clear, sticky, thick fluid, and this is removed with a dipper. The sap is deposited in barrels, which are scattered through the woods. The first sap which flows in the spring makes the best resin, and the poorest is the product of the hardened gum which is left on the sides of the cuts. This is removed by the *scraper*, who moves through the woods gathering the leavings.

The still is a copper vat, hooded, with a close-fitting, air-tight cover, in which is a funnel, which, in turn, is connected with the *worm* of the still (see DISTILLATION). This worm runs down into another vat, near at hand, and in this vat the fumes, or vapor, of the heated gum are distilled into turpentine. Fire under the copper vat heats the gum, and the volatile parts rise to the funnel, pass into the still and are condensed by the water in the second vat into spirits of turpentine. The residuum left in the vat is the rosin of commerce, which is passed through a series of strainers and sieves to the barrels, which are made on the spot. The turpentine cannot be barreled so easily, for it will work through an ordinary barrel. It is placed in white pine barrels, which have been coated inside with several coats of strong, hot glue, which keeps the turpentine from soaking into the wood. The trees are worked for five or six seasons. All the turpentines dissolve in pure alcohol, and by distillation they yield oils, which are termed *spirits of turpentine*. Oil, or spirits, of turpentine is used to a limited extent in medicine. It is also much used in the arts, for dissolving resins and oils in making varnishes. See RESINS; ROSIN.

TURQUOISE, *tur'koiz*, a precious stone, of beautiful blue or green color due to the presence of copper. It is capable of taking a high polish, and has long been a favorite gem in the East, especially in Persia, where the finest specimens are found. When exposed to fatty acids, the turquoise loses its color and turns greenish, thus leading to the Oriental superstition that its dullness foretells misfortune. *Bone turquoise* is an imitation turquoise, composed of fossil bone.

TURTLE, a name given to reptiles that differ but little from tortoise; in fact, *turtle* is the name commonly given to both forms. The shell which encloses the body of the turtle is in two parts, the upper portion called the *carapace*, the lower, the *plastron*. Turtles have no teeth, but the jaws have a tough, horny skin. The food of some turtles is marine plants; others feed on insect larvæ, fish and mollusks. They deposit their eggs usually in holes in sandy places, cover them with sand, and leave them to be hatched by the warmth of the sun. The young begin to crawl on leaving the egg, and soon find water. Turtles are found in the seas of warm climates, and in many inland lakes and rivers. The most important species is the *green turtle,* which is from six to seven feet long and weighs from 700 to 800 pounds. It is found in the West Indies, and is brought to the United States for its food value. See GALAPAGOS, for reference to turtles.

Mud Turtle, the name commonly applied to small turtles of aquatic habits which prowl about the muddy bottoms of rivers and ponds in search of food. The common mud turtle is about four inches long, dull olive or brown above and yellow or pale brown below. Other species include the *Louisiana,* the *yellow-necked* and the *Mexican.*

Related Articles. Consult the following titles for additional information:
Leatherback   Terrapin   Tortoise
Snapping Turtle

TURTLE DOVE, *duv*, a small European pigeon, pale grayish-brown in color, marked with a darker hue above and with a purple tinge on the feathers of its breast. Its cooing note is plaintive and tender. Its nest is loosely built in the crotch of a low tree or bush. The eggs are creamy-white, and are two in number. The similar North American species is known as the *mourning dove.*

TUSCALOOSA, *tus ka loo'sah,* ALA., the county seat of Tuscaloosa County, fifty-six miles southwest of Birmingham, on the Southern, the Mobile & Ohio and the Louisville & Nashville railroads. The principal industries are the manufacturing of kraft paper, cast-iron pipe, condensed milk, lumber, veneer, fertilizers, cottonseed-oil products and coal, and cotton ginning. Located here are Stillman Institute (for Negroes), a state hospital for the insane and a home for the feeble-minded. Tuscaloosa was the capital of the state from 1826 to 1846. The place was settled in 1812 and incorporated in 1816. The commission form of government was adopted in 1912. Population, 1940, 27,493.

TUSCANY, *tus' ka ni,* a small department or province of Northern Italy. It comprised ancient Etruria, and the Etrurians (Etruscans) were the earliest known inhabitants of the peninsula. They became subject to Rome in the fourth century B. C. During the period of barbarian migrations they were overcome in turn by the Ostrogoths, the emperors of Constantinople and the Lombards. In the Middle Ages several of the cities of Etruria, notably Florence, Pisa and Genoa, became independent and prosperous, and in the latter half of the sixteenth century the Florentine possessions were formed into the Grand Duchy of Tuscany. From 1745 to 1859 Tuscany was under the rule of Germany; in 1861 it became by vote of its population a part of the kingdom of Italy.

Among the noted names of natives of Tuscany are the Medici, Giotto, Boccaccio, Dante and Petrarch. The dialect of Tuscany became the classical language of Italy.

TUSCARORA, *tus ka ro' rah,* a migrating Iroquoian tribe, which finally settled in New York and was received as a sixth member in the confederacy. See FIVE NATIONS, THE.

TUSKEGEE, *tus ke'ge,* **INSTITUTE,** a school for Negroes founded in 1881 by Booker T. Washington in Tuskegee, Ala., with an appropriation of $2,000 from the state legislature. It opened in a borrowed church, with thirty pupils and Booker T. Washington as the only teacher. Tuskegee was world-famous for its practical training and synonymous with industrial education at the time of the founder's death in 1915. His successors increased the endowment (now approximately $7,000,000), improved the physical plant and raised the curriculum from secondary to college level. Tuskegee now has over 3,500 acres of land and 132 buildings. The faculty and staff (all Negroes) total about 225, and the student enrollment is 2,800. The Institute grants diplomas in trades and nurses' training; bachelor of science degrees in education, agriculture, mechanical industries, home economics and commercial dietetics; and certificates in aviation (Civil Aeronautics Administration). See WASHINGTON, BOOKER T.

TUS'SOCK MOTH, a family of moths named from the tufts of hairs, often bright-colored, appearing in the caterpillars. The moths are dull-colored, and the females of some species are wingless. Several varieties of this moth are very destructive to fruit, shade and forest trees, the most notable among these being the *gypsy moth,* the *browntail moth* and the *white-marked tussock moth.* Of the latter there are two or three generations each summer, and the young caterpillars are extremely voracious. Trees are protected against these moths by winter pruning and burning of the cocoons, and by summer spraying and banding of trees. See GYPSY MOTH.

TUT-ANKH-AMEN, a pharaoh (or king) of ancient Egypt, who reigned about 1,400 B. C. The finding of his tomb in the Valley of Kings, near Thebes, is called the greatest archeological exploit of modern times. The expedition which discovered and opened this tomb was led by Lord Carnarvon of England, and Howard Carter, an American archeologist. The tomb and contents were opened and revealed to the world in 1923. Rare and priceless relics were disclosed.

TWAIN, MARK. See CLEMENS, SAMUEL LANGHORNE.

TWEED, a twilled wool or wool-and-cotton fabric for men's wear, with an unfinished surface and of two colors, usually combined in the yarn. It is largely manufactured in Southern Scotland and takes its name from the Tweed River, along which it was first made.

TWEED, a river of Great Britain, ninety-five miles in length, rising in the southeastern part of Scotland and flowing easterly and northeasterly into the North Sea. The lower part of its course forms a part of the boundary between Scotland and England.

TWEED, WILLIAM MARCY (1823-1878), an American politician, notorious as the leader of the famous "Tweed Ring" in New York City. As a member of the famous

Tammany Hall, he gained immense influence and with the help of several unscrupulous supporters formed a combination for the political control of New York City. By the bribery of legislators and judges, bills were passed and decisions rendered which allowed the ring to carry out vast schemes of improvement, through which, by the padding of pay rolls and the auditing of fraudulent bills, they gained immense wealth. The régime lasted for more than six years, during which time the debt of the city was increased from $20,000,000 to $101,000,000. Finally, in 1871, through an exposure by the New York *Times* and a vigorous prosecution under a committee led by Samuel J. Tilden, the ring was broken up. Tweed was twice tried, finally convicted and sentenced to twelve years' confinement in the penitentiary and a fine of more than $12,000. He was released two years later on a legal technicality, but was immediately rearrested on a suit for damages to the amount of more than $6,000,-000. While confined in jail awaiting trial, he escaped and fled to Spain. Finally, being captured, he died in jail.

TWEEDSMUIR. See BUCHAN, JOHN.

TWELVE TABLES, LAW OF THE, the earliest written code of law among the Romans. According to tradition it was drawn up to appease the plebeians, who had complained that they were not getting justice from the patrician judges. In 451 B. C., ten magistrates, called *decemvirs,* were elected to draft the laws, and the following year they submitted these to the people. The laws were afterwards written on brass tablets and placed in the Forum, over the orator's platform, where everyone might read them. These laws formed the basis of Roman legislation for centuries.

TWILIGHT, *twi'lite,* the glow in the sky before sunrise and after sunset. Twilight is caused by the refraction of the sun's rays as they pass through the atmosphere. The evening twilight is brightest immediately after sunset and continues to fade until the sun reaches 18° below the horizon, when twilight ceases. The time required for the sun to reach this point varies in different latitudes. In the torrid zone, where the sun's path throughout the year takes nearly the same direction as the parallels, twilight is of short duration, but in summer its duration increases toward the Poles, and near the Arctic Circle it lasts all night.

TWILIGHT SLEEP, the name commonly applied to a method of applying anesthetics during childbirth. It originated at the hospital at Freiburg, Germany, and has been attempted, with varying success, in other countries. The Freiburg method consists in the administration of measured doses of morphine and scopolamine, these being given at specified intervals. Under ideal conditions, and when the method operates successfully, the patient comes out of the ordeal with no recollection of pain. Undoubtedly in successful cases the mother is greatly benefited by the method, as the elements of shock and exhaustion are reduced to a minimum. Twilight sleep has been tried in the best hospitals in America, but the results have not always been satisfactory, though it is practicable in certain selected cases. Few physicians recommend methods of delivery which preclude all possible assistance from the mother. Promiscuous adoption of twilight sleep might result in great harm.

TYCHO BRAHE, *te'ko brah'eh,* or *brah.* See BRAHE, TYCHO.

Grave, Richmond, Virginia.

TYLER, JOHN, (1790-1862), the tenth President of the United States, and the first "accidental" President, so-called because as Vice-President he succeeded automatically to the higher office through the death of the duly-elected executive.

Early Career. Tyler was a Virginian, born at Greenway, March 20, 1790, the son of John Tyler, Sr., who was at various times judge of state and Federal courts, speaker of the Virginia house of delegates and governor of the state. The future President was fortunate in his ancestry. By the time young Tyler was nineteen years of age he was a practicing attorney, and when twenty-one was a member of the state legislature, where he served for five consecutive terms, leaving that post only to go to Congress, to which he was elected in 1816, as a Democrat.

After two terms in Congress, he was returned to the state legislature in 1823, and two years later became governor of Virginia, the state promoting the son to the post with which it had once honored his father. After two terms as governor, Tyler was elected to the United States Senate, in which body he took his seat in 1828.

Independence had been his chief characteristic in political life; though he was a Democrat, not always did he support the Democratic program. In the Senate the nation found him to be a stubborn man, who could not be moved from a position once deliberately taken. He came prominently into notice by opposing the tariff measurers of 1832 and 1833, and was the only Senator to oppose the Force Bill of 1832. He had supported Jackson for the Presidency, but in 1834 made a report censuring the President for removing deposits from United States banks. The Virginia legislature ordered him to vote to expunge the vote of censure, but this Tyler refused to do, and soon he resigned from the Senate and retired to private life.

He became a leading member of the new Whig party, and sought to have the party name him for the Vice-Presidency in 1836. This effort failed, but in 1840 a chain of circumstances gave this former Democrat the coveted office. He was nominated on the Whig ticket with William Henry Harrison, the choice of Tyler being largely attributed to the Whig desire to secure the votes of Democrats who were dissatisfied with the two preceding administrations, which had brought upon the country the panic of 1837. Harrison and Tyler received 234 electoral votes; the opposition, 60. On March 4, 1841, the new administration assumed control of the government, and on April 4 President Harrison died.

Tyler as President. There was a stronger man than Tyler in official Washington; this was Henry Clay, the acknowledged leader of the Whigs. Clay looked upon the Presidential election as a vindication of his course in politics; Tyler considered the result to be merely a rebuke of the preceding administration. There was soon a clash of factions, and Tyler, the President and nominal leader, broke with the party.

The incident which caused the breach was legislation respecting a second United States Bank. Tyler approved the abolition of the sub-treasury system, but would not consent to another United States bank, which Congress favored. Twice he vetoed a bank bill; after this second refusal to carry out the wishes of the party all the Cabinet resigned, with the exception of Daniel Webster, who

Administration of John Tyler, 1841-1845.

I. JOHN TYLER
  (1) Birth
  (2) Parentage
  (3) Education
  (4) Early career
  (5) Public life after breach with Jackson
  (6) Career after end of his term
  (7) Character
  (8) Death

II. GOVERNMENTAL AFFAIRS
  (1) Domestic
    (a) President's quarrel with Whigs
  (2) Results
    (a) Resignation of Cabinet
    (b) Tyler read out of his party
  (3) Foreign
    (a) Webster - Ashburton Treaty
      (1) Negotiators
      (2) Settled Maine boundary dispute
      (3) Other settlements

III. INTERNAL AFFAIRS.
  (1) Dorr's Rebellion
  (2) Patroon War
  (3) The Mormons
    (a) At Nauvoo
    (b) In Utah
  (4) Dedication of Bunker Hill Monument
  (5) Construction of first telegraph line
  (6) Discovery of copper

Questions on Tyler

When and where was John Tyler born?

What public offices did he hold before his inauguration as President?

What were Tyler's views on internal improvements?

Why did the Whigs resign from the Cabinet?

Why was the South anxious to annex Texas?

Who was Lord Ashburton?

What disputes did the Webster-Ashburton Treaty settle?

Explain Dorr's Rebellion.

ADMINISTRATIONS OF HARRISON AND TYLER
1841 1845

DEDICATION OF BUNKER HILL MONUMENT. 1843.

FLORIDA ADMITTED 1845

COPPER DISCOVERED IN MICHIGAN 1844

H·M·HAINES

FIRST TELEGRAPH LINE 1844

IMPORTANT EVENTS
DORR'S REBELLION – 1842.
SCREW PROPELLER INTRODUCED INTO U.S. NAVY–1844
TROUBLE WITH MORMONS–1844.

WEBSTER-ASHBURTON BOUNDARY TREATY. 1842

MAINE

VER

N.H.

NEW YORK

CANADA

MICHIGAN

MINNESOTA

MICHIGAN

WISCONSIN

LOG CABIN CAMPAIGN

HARRISON SERVED ONE MONTH MARCH 4 TO APRIL 4

HARD CIDER

TIPPECANOE AND TYLER TOO

NATIONAL BANK BILL 1841

wished to conclude the Webster-Ashburton Treaty, then the subject of negotiation.

Most of the Whigs thereafter refused to recognize Tyler as a party leader. The Democrats rallied to his support, however, and in the Congressional elections of 1842 they overthrew the Whig majority and established themselves in the House by a majority of sixty-one—a change of eighty-six votes.

Legislation for the remainder of the Presidential term was in part a matter of compromises; the Whigs did not again press the bank act, and on some measures they acted with the President. A protective tariff bill was passed. Two river and harbor bills were presented, one for the eastern part of the country and another for the western section, the former being vetoed. The other was signed by Tyler because it contained appropriations for the Mississippi River, which he believed would be a national, not a sectional, benefit. The Webster-Ashburton Treaty, defining the northeastern boundary between the United States and Canada, was concluded in 1842. In 1844 the State Department negotiated a treaty providing for the annexation of Texas, but the Senate refused to confirm it, owing to powerful Whig opposition. A year later the sentiment had changed enough to bring about the admission of Texas as a state on March 3, 1845, the day before Tyler's term ended. Florida was also admitted in 1845. Of economic importance were the construction of the first telegraph line and the discovery of copper in Michigan.

After his retirement from office Tyler spent several quiet years on his estate, three miles from his birthplace. The threat of civil war called him again into public life, and in February, 1861, he presided over a convention of the border states, held in Washington, D. C., and called to consider the situation presented by the session of South Carolina. When Congress refused to accept the recommendations of the convention Tyler urged his own state to secede, and in the fall of 1861 he was elected to the Confederate Congress. In January, 1862, he died, and was buried in Hollywood Cemetery, Richmond. In 1914 Congress appropriated $10,000 for the erection of a monument in his memory.

Related Articles. Consult the following titles for additional information:
Force Bills　　　　　Webster-Ashburton
Harrison, William H.　　Treaty

TYLER, Tex., the county seat of Smith County, about 100 miles southeast of Dallas, on the Saint Louis Southwestern and Missouri Pacific railroads. There is an airport. The city is the center of fruit-growing in Eastern Texas. It ships large quantities of cotton, fruit and garden products. Industrial establishments include railway shops, fruit and vegetable canneries and manufactories of work clothing, soil pipe and fittings, crates and baskets, milk products and petroleum products. A large part of the nation's supply of rose bushes is grown in Tyler. There are two junior colleges (one colored) and a Negro college. The place was settled in 1846 and was chartered as a city in 1875. It is governed by a city manager and a commission. Population, 1940, 28,279.

TYLER, Wat, an English soldier, in 1381 a leader of what is known as *Wat Tyler's Rebellion.* When a poll tax was levied on the already overburdened English people, riots broke out, and a mob, led by Tyler, marched on London, pillaging as it went. The young king, Richard II, rode out to meet the rebels. He promised to grant them charters of freedom and amnesty and many of them, satisfied, dispersed. But Tyler, growing bold and insolent, made further demands, and William Walworth, mayor of London, stabbed him. The liberties granted were soon revoked, but the movement had the effect of hastening the general tendency toward the abolition of villenage.

TYNDALE, tin'dal, William (?-1536), an English reformer and translator of the Bible. He studied at Oxford and Cambridge and was ordained priest about 1521. Having made himself unpopular by the expression of certain heretical sentiments, he left England for the continent in 1524. After a visit to Luther at Wittenberg, he settled at Cologne, where he completed a translation of the New Testament; and on his expulsion from Cologne he took refuge in Worms, where, in 1525, his translation was published. He translated the *Pentateuch* and the book of *Jonah.* When he openly opposed the divorce of Henry VIII from Catharine of Aragon, he was imprisoned in the castle of Vilvorde, near Brussels, and after a trial for heresy, he was strangled and his body was burned. In addition to the works mentioned, he wrote *The Obedience of a Christian Man* and *How Christian Rulers Ought to Govern.*

TYN'DALL, John (1820-1893), an Englishman and one of the world's greatest physicists, was born at Leighlin Bridge. He was largely self-taught, gaining his first scientific training as an ordnance surveyor and railway engineer. After teaching mathematics at Queenwood College, he went to Germany for study and received a doctor's degree from the University of Marburg. He became a professor of natural philosophy at the Royal Institution in 1853, and on the death of Faraday was appointed director. Tyndall studied natural phenomena minutely and with open mind, and he made valuable contributions to scientific knowledge through his investigations of magnetism, electricity, heat, light and sound. Particularly important were his discoveries in regard to the transmission of radiant heat and its absorption by vapors and gases. In 1872 and 1873 he lectured in America. The large sums he earned were placed in a trust fund, to be devoted to original research in the United States. He made an extensive study of the Swiss glaciers.

Especially noteworthy was his effort to popularize science—to bring it within the reach of ordinary men. *Fragments of Science for Unscientific People, The Glaciers of the Alps* and *Hours of Exercise in the Alps* are among his "popular" writings. Other noteworthy books are *Heat as a Mode of Motion, Lectures on Light, On Sound* and *Contributions to Molecular Physics in the Domain of Radiant Heat.*

TYPE, a piece of metal, wood or other material, on one end of which is cast or engraved a letter, figure or other character. The earliest types were made of wood, and in style they resembled the script letters used in copying books before the invention of the art of printing. The parts of a type are (1) the body, (2) the face, (3) the shoulder, (4) the nick and (5) the groove. The *face* is that part that does the printing; the *nick* is to show the right side of the type when set, and the *groove* is to make it stand firmly on its base. In the early days of printing, each printer made his own type, but with the extension of the industry, type casting, or founding, became a business by itself. A few of the large types used in printing are still made of wood, but all others are of type metal, which is an alloy, consisting of three

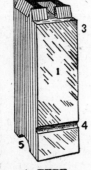

A TYPE

parts of lead to one part of antimony, with a small quantity of tin and copper added.

Type are cast by machinery. A steel die, which is an exact pattern of the letter, is first made. This is driven into a piece of soft copper, so as to form a perfect impression of the letter. This is called the *matrix*. The matrix is then placed in a metallic box, called the *mold*. This is placed in the type-casting machine, which opens and closes the mold and fills it with type metal. The metal hardens instantly, and when the mold opens the type drops out. The face is then smoothed on a stone, and the body is nicked and grooved. The type are then tied up in packages, each of which contains only one kind of letter, and are ready for use. All types are ninety-two hundredths of an inch high.

A complete assortment of type is called a *font* and contains large and small capitals, small letters and italics, marks of punctuation and figures; in all, there are about 225 characters for English printing. The size of a font varies according to the work to be done with it. Small fonts contain from 500 to 800 pounds, and large ones have from 20,000 to 50,000 pounds. Type founders have a rule for determining the number of different letters necessary to make each font complete. Z requires the smallest number. For every *z* there will be 46 *a*'s, 60 *e*'s, 32 *h*'s, 15 *m*'s, and so on.

There are thirteen sizes of type in ordinary use in printing books and newspapers. These are designated by special names and by the number of points they measure, a point being $\frac{1}{72}$ of an inch. Both methods of naming are given in the illustration.

Nonpareil 6-point
Minion ....….........7-point
Brevier........................ . 8-point
Bourgeois 9-point
Long Primer............10-point
Small Pica 11-point
Pica 12-point
English ······ 14-point

The smaller sizes are not used in general printing, although sometimes small Bibles are printed from $5\frac{1}{2}$ point, or agate, and still smaller sizes are used for marginal references in Bibles and other works. The type used in job printing is of various sizes, to suit the taste and conditions of the advertiser. See PRINTING.

TYPE'SETTING MACHINES. See LINOTYPE; MONOTYPE.

TYPEWRITER, a machine for the rapid transcribing of letters, manuscripts, etc., as a substitute for handwriting. It was first successfully put into operation in 1875, and since that date has made its way into every kind of business house, court of law and governmental department where speed, accuracy and system in correspondence, the making of reports and tabulating of statistics are required. An average typewriter operator writes sixty words a minute, a rate three times that of a good penman, and the characters are much more legible. As women are the best operators of typewriters, the effect has been to bring thousands of them into the business world, where they have found opportunity to advance to responsible secretarial and executive positions.

The essential parts of the typewriter mechanism are a set of types; an arrangement of keys, for bringing the types in contact with the paper; a paper carrier, or carriage; a platen, or roller, against which the types strike, and an inking device. While there are many patterns of typewriters, from the earliest "Remington" to the latest make, full of new devices, all belong to two classes, those known as the *basket* machines and those known as *cylinder* machines. In the basket machines, each type is on the end of a bar, hung on a pivot and joined to its respective key by a lever attachment. These type bars are attached to a frame which was formerly circular, forming the basket from which the machine takes its name. In modern machines the frame is an arc of a circle. The bars are of such length that the type on each strikes the platen at the same point. When a key is depressed, the bar strikes the inking ribbon against the paper, making the impression of the character. As the bar drops back to its position, the carriage moves forward one space, thus putting the paper in position for the next letter.

The cylinder machines have the type arranged on a cylinder, and the depression of the key causes the cylinder to revolve to a point which allows the character desired to be pressed upon the paper by a little hammer. The arrangement of keys on all makes of typewriters is practically the same; the so-called universal keyboard is in use with but slight modifications on over ninety per cent of all models.

TYPHOID, *ti foid'*, **FEVER,** a germ disease caused by the presence of a bacillus which lodges in the intestines, spleen and mesenteric lymph nodes. The multiplication of the bacilli causes ulceration of the intestines, and when the ulcers perforate the intestinal membranes the disease is fatal. Typhoid germs enter the system through the mouth, from whence they find their way to the intestinal tract. Food and drink are the most common vehicles which serve as conveyors of the bacillus, and polluted water and milk are the most common sources of infection. Water containing sewage is a particularly dangerous carrier of bacilli.

Symptoms and Treatment. It requires from eight to fourteen days for the disease to develop after the germs have entered the system. The attack usually comes on slowly, and the patient may continue his regular work for a few days, but ultimately he will have to go to bed. The first symptoms are nausea, headache, pains in the back and limbs and sometimes nosebleed and chills. During the first week the fever rises about one degree a day, until the temperature reaches 103° or 104°. The fever remains stationary the second week; during the third week it should begin to subside, and convalescence should begin the fourth week, unless the case is one of unusual severity. Sometimes the ulcers penetrate the blood vessels of the intestines and cause hemorrhages, which may prove fatal. When the fever begins to decline the patient is in grave danger; he suffers from weakness, tremors of the muscles and possibly delirium, and he may die from weakness.

The treatment for typhoid fever is largely hygienic. The fever is kept down by sponging, and by cold packs and baths. Liquid nourishment, consisting of milk and broths, is given at intervals of about three hours to keep up the patient's strength, and medicines to counteract the effects of the germs are administered. Proper nursing is the most important part of the treatment.

Prevention. Excretions from the bowels and the urine of one affected with typhoid fever contain millions of germs, and all bodily discharges should be disinfected by strong solutions of corrosive sublimate, carbolic acid or chloride of lime. The bedding and clothing should be immersed in boiling water. All dishes, thermometers or other appliances used about the patient should be thoroughly disinfected every time they are used. Flies, when they have access to infected substances, gather the germs on their feet and carry them to other households. They are one of the prolific causes of the spread of the disease.

Typhoid is not contagious by the breath or by touch; it is conveyed only by carrying the germs. Vaccination with three hypodermic injections of a special vaccine is considered to render one immune for three years; army surgeons attribute the protection of the allied forces during the World War to this method of prevention. There have been widespread educational campaigns to teach people how to prevent typhoid fever, and as a result of this work there has been a marked decline in the number of cases since the beginning of the present century. The following directions issued by the New York City Department of Health should be observed by every family and community:

Keep yourself in good health. Do not use alcoholic drinks. Keep your home and your body clean. Always wash your hands before eating. Drink only the best milk; if in doubt, boil it. Drink only pure water; if in doubt, boil it. Eat only pure, good food. Fresh-cooked food is safest; heat kills the germs. Avoid salads, raw vegetables and raw oysters, unless you know they come from a clean place. Wash ice when it comes and keep the ice-box clean. Do not put ice in drinking water or on food. Deal only with good, clean food stores. Don't eat at dirty restaurants. Keep flies out of your rooms and away from your food. Be careful when you go to the country; be sure of what you eat and do not drink from a strange spring or stream. Never visit where there is a case of typhoid fever. Be careful about friends who have had typhoid fever; they may be carriers. Where there is an outbreak of typhoid fever use only boiled water for drinking, and also boil milk just before it is used. If typhoid fever is in your house or neighborhood, or you are exposed to the disease in any way, or are likely to be, have yourself immunized.

TYPHOON, *ti foon'*, the name applied to the hurricanes that sweep over the coast of China, and Japan and the neighboring archipelagoes from May to November. The storms are most frequent and disastrous in July, August and September. The typhoons are cyclonic storms, which originate somewhat farther south than Manila and move towards Indies. See HURRICANE.

TYPHUS, *ti' fus*, **FEVER,** known, also, from the place where it occurs, as *hospital fever, jail fever* and by other names, is essentially a fever of the poor, ill-fed and badly-housed inhabitants of large cities. It is infectious, and is carried by both body lice and head lice. A period of from five to twelve days passes after infection, before the first symptoms show themselves. Then the disease comes on suddenly, with a chill, followed by a high fever, sharp rheumatic pains and headache. Generally about the seventh day, a rash, of irregular spots of dusky hue, appears over the chest and back, and this has given to the disease the common name of *spotted fever*. Delirium is almost always present during the second week, and after a marked crisis, followed by a sound sleep, the person awakes with the fever gone. Thereafter recovery is rapid. The disease is often fatal, especially where the best of care is not given the patient.

The treatment consists in keeping the sufferer in a well-ventilated room, and in preventing exhaustion by light, wholesome diet. One of the worst epidemics of typhus fever known in recent times occurred in Serbia in 1914–1915. Several cases were carried to New York by passenger steamers, and during the study of these cases Dr. Plotz discovered the germ which causes the disease.

TYRE, *tire,* one of the most celebrated cities of ancient Phoenicia, on the Mediterranean Sea, fifty miles south of Beirut and twenty-four miles southwest of Sidon. From 1200 to 850 B. C., it was a wealthy and magnificent city, the chief commercial center of the world, famous for its dyes and glassware. The original city occupied an island three-fourths of a mile from the mainland. In 332 B. C., when Alexander the Great besieged the city, he built a causeway out to the island, and the sands deposited by the sea upon this structure transformed the island into a peninsula. The modern town, called Sur, has a population of about 6,000.

TYROL, or **TIROL,** *tir'ol,* before the dissolution of the Austro-Hungarian monarchy in 1918, a crownland of Austria, comprising the greater part of the political district of Tyrol and Vorarlberg. It lies in the heart of the Alpine region, and is noted for the charm and variety of its scenery, which is much like that of Switzerland. After the World War, Italy claimed this region, but was awarded only the section south of the Brenner Pass. The Italian Tyrol was divided into the provinces of Bolzano and Trento. Their combined area is 5,371 square miles. Austrian Tyrol, now a part of Germany, has an area of 4,882 square miles.

ADDED BY GREEKS

V Circa 500 B.C. GREEK
V 50 B.C. ROMAN
U 6th Century ANGLO-SAXON

8th Century IRISH U
8th Century ROMAN UNCIAL u
14th Century LOMBARDIC u
16th Century GERMAN GOTHIC Uu

U, the twenty-first letter and the fifth vowel in the English alphabet. It comes from the Greek alphabet, as the Phoenician had no such character, and it was, until comparatively recent times, used interchangeably with *v.* In time, *v* came to be used for the consonant sound and *u* for the vowel sound, as in the case of *j* and *i.* The true primary sound of *u* was that which it still retains in most of the languages in Europe, that of *oo* in *cool,* the sound being sometimes short, sometimes long. The so-called "long *u*" in English, however, has a distinct *y* sound prefixed to the *oo* sound, as in *use, abuse.*

U'DALL, NICHOLAS (1506–1556), the author of *Ralph Roister Doister,* the earliest English comedy. He was master of Eton School from 1534 to 1541, and the play was originally written for performance by the scholars. Udall was in favor at court as a writer of pageants and interludes.

UFFIZI, *oof feet' se,* a famous palace in Florence, containing one of the most extensive and valuable art collections in the world. This gallery was founded by the Medici family in the fifteenth century, and valuable additions have been made from time to time. In the collection are the statues *Venus de' Medici, The Dancing Faun* and *The Wrestlers,* and the works of great masters, such as Raphael, Michelangelo, Titian, Correggio, Holbein and Rembrandt. The Uffizi also contains the Biblioteca Nazionale, a collection of 300,000 volumes and 14,000 manuscripts. It is connected by covered passageway with the Pitti Palace (which see).

UGANDA, *oo gahn'da,* the administrative division of British East Africa that forms the western part of the colony. It consists of the former native kingdom of Uganda and a number of adjacent states. Its area is 109,-119 square miles, practically that of the state of Nevada. Of this area, 16,377 square

miles are water, for within the boundaries lie portions of Victoria Nyanza, Lake Edward, Lake Albert and Lake Rudolph, and all of lakes George, Kioga and Salisbury. The region around Lake Rudolph is low and generally unproductive. The western and southwestern parts of the protectorate consist of rolling country and plateaus, varying in altitude from 2,000 to 4,000 feet, upon which mountain peaks rise to the height of 12,000 to 16,000 feet. Here are some of the most prominent mountains of Africa including the Ruwenzori, whose highest summit, Alexandra, has an altitude of 16,794 feet.

Gold is mined, and there is an abundance of iron throughout the country. Although the natives are quite skilful in working the ore, there is but little mining. With the exception of the Lake Rudolph region, the soil is generally fertile. The climate in the highland region of the southwest is pleasant and inviting, and this part of the protectorate holds great possibilities. Commercially, cotton is the most important crop, and its cultivation is being rapidly extended. Coffee, peanuts and cacao are among the other leading crops. Ivory and hides are exported.

In 1934 there were 3,630,000 inhabitants, and about 3,604,000 of these were natives. The Bantus, who are agriculturists, and the Baganda are the most important tribes. The Baganda, who number about 874,000, are noted for their intelligence. Most of them have embraced Christianity, and they are rapidly adopting the ways of civilization. They build permanent homes, and have done much in constructing roads and in developing the country since it was opened to Europeans. The country has railway, steamboat and telegraph communication.

The protectorate is divided into five provinces for the purpose of local administration. The native tribes maintain their own form of control in all local measures, and some of these governments are very efficient. Entebbe is the seat of government and British headquarters, and Mengo is the native capital.

Uganda was first visited by Captain Speke in 1862. It was again visited in 1875 by Stanley, who wrote an extended description of the country and its people for his *Through the Dark Continent.*

UHLANS, *oo'lahnz,* bodies of mounted lancers, chiefly employed in reconnoitering, skirmishing and outpost duty. They were of Eastern European origin, and formerly wore a semi-Oriental uniform with flowing sleeves and baggy trousers. Later, Uhlans became a part of several western armies. In the World War (1914-1919) the term was particularly applied to the Prussian light cavalry troops.

UINTA, *u in' tah*, **MOUNTAINS**, a mountain range in Northeastern Utah, a part of the Rocky Mountain system, jutting at right angles from the Wasatch range. Its highest peaks are Gilbert Peak, 13,687 feet above sea level; Emmons Peak, 13,624 feet, and Wilson Peak, 13,300 feet. The Green River gorge cuts across the Uinta range.

UKRAINE, The, or **UKRAINIA**, a rich agricultural region in Central Europe, originally a part of the old Polish Kingdom. Most of the Ukraine was absorbed by the former Russian Empire in 1667 and 1793. In the territorial adjustments following the World War, the greater part of the region became the Ukrainian Socialist Soviet Republic. As finally established, it occupied 170,998 square miles in the southwestern part of European Russia, having Poland and Rumania on the west and southwest and the Black Sea on the south. In 1933 it had a population of 31,901,400. A considerable portion of Western Ukrainia was incorporated in the new Polish Republic. In 1939, after the Russians invaded Poland, the Soviet Union proclaimed the Polish Western Ukraine a part of the Ukrainian Socialist Soviet Republic. In 1940 the Soviet Union forced Rumania to cede Bessarabia and Northern Bukowina to the U.S.S.R. Part of Bessarabia and the Bukowinian area were then added to the Ukrainian S.S.R.

Ukrainia is a part of the fertile black-earth region of Russia, and it produces large crops of wheat and other grains, sugar beets and oil seeds. Stock breeding also is important. About three-fourths of the people are engaged in agriculture, and there are over 27,000 collective farms. The government has introduced mechanized farming and electrification on a large scale. The Ukraine has valuable deposits of coal, iron ores and manganese, and several salt mines. Fifty per cent of the steel output of the Soviet Union (U.S.S.R.) comes from the Ukrainian Republic. The territory acquired from Poland has oil deposits and is an important grain area.

The capital of the Ukrainian Republic is Kiev. Kharkov is the largest city, and Odessa is the chief port on the Black Sea.

In 1941 the Ukraine was invaded by the Germans, and a large part of the territory was brought under German control.

ULCER, *ul' ser,* an open sore on the skin or any of the mucous membranes, both external and internal. The tendency of an ulcer is to eat away the underlying tissues. An abscess, on the other hand, usually begins in the tissues and works outward (see ABSCESS). Ulcers may be caused by constitutional disorders or through infection. Treatment consists in giving the patient fresh air, proper diet and hygienic surroundings, and providing local treatment for the sore.

ULTRAMARINE, *ul trah ma reen',* a beautiful and durable sky-blue pigment, a color formed of the mineral called lapis lazuli. This substance is much valued by painters, on account of the beauty and permanence of its color, both for oil and water painting.

ULYSSES, *u lis'eez,* called by the Greeks ODYSSEUS, one of the most famous of their legendary heroes, an important character in the *Iliad.* Rejected by Helen, Ulysses married Penelope and settled down with her to a happy life. Shortly after the birth of his son Telemachus, the Trojan War broke out, and Ulysses, in spite of a vow to help Menelaus, was unwilling to leave home and engage in the struggle. In order to escape, he feigned madness, but Palamedes visited him and, becoming convinced of his sanity, made use of a stratagem. While Ulysses was plowing up the seashore and sowing it with salt, Palamedes placed the boy Telemachus in front of his father's plow, and Ulysses, carefully turning aside his team, unwittingly revealed that his madness was merely feigned.

He was compelled to join the expedition and at Troy proved himself one of the bravest of the Greek heroes. The chief interest in Ulysses, however, attaches to his adventures while he was returning from Troy. Driven to the country of the Lotus-eaters, he with difficulty broke the spell cast upon his companions and induced them to continue the voyage. Meeting with Polyphemus the Cyclops, he put him to death, thus offending Neptune, who constantly pursued him with his wrath. He was driven upon the island of Circe; he was placed in danger between Scylla and Charybdis, and he was borne, after the death of all of his companions, to the island of the nymph Calypso, where he remained for seven years. Returning at last to Ithaca, after wandering twenty years, he found Penelope in great trouble, but with the aid of Telemachus overcame her annoying suitors and made himself powerful again.

Related Articles. Consult the following titles for additional information:

Calypso　　　　　Penelope
Circe　　　　　　Polyphemus

UMBELLIFERAE, *um bel if'ur ee,* the parsley family of flowering plants, containing about 2,000 species, among which are the familiar garden varieties, carrot, parsnip, celery, anise, parsley, fennel and caraway. The flowers, usually inconspicuous and individual, are arranged in large umbrellalike groups, called umbels. The leaves contain oil and a resinous matter, sometimes of a poisonous character. The umbelliferae are distributed throughout the world, but are most abundant in the north temperate zone.

UM'BER, a mineral pigment resembling ochre, yielding a brown paint when raw and a reddish paint when burnt. It is found in many localities in Europe, notably the island of Cyprus, and takes its name from Umbria, Italy, where it was first discovered. There are veins of umber in Illinois, Pennsylvania and several other states.

UMBREL'LA BIRD, a black South American bird, related to the crows and remarkable for its handsome drooping crest of blueblack feathers. It lives in the deep woods, depositing its eggs on a platform of sticks in the top of a high tree. Its cries are described as "lowings."

UNALASKA, *oo nah lahs'kah,* one of the largest of the Aleutian Islands, about seventy-five miles long and twenty miles wide at its widest point. The chief settlement is Unalaska, or Iluliuk, on the north side of the island. Population, 225, gradually decreasing. See ALEUTIAN ISLANDS.

UNCAS, *un'kahz* (?–about 1683), an American Indian chief, born in the Pequot settlement in Connecticut. In 1635 he re-

belled against the head chief of the Pequots and founded a tribe of his own known as the Mohegan. In 1637 he combined with the colonists for the destruction of the Pequots and was given a portion of the conquered territory. His friendly intercourse with the colonists aroused the jealousy of the Narragansetts, who made war upon the Mohegans, and for the next few years Uncas was almost continually defending his territory from invasion. A monument has been erected in Norwich, Conn., in his honor.

UNC'TION, or **EXTREME UNCTION,** a sacrament of the Roman Catholic Church, administered to the dying to give them strength and grace physically and spiritually in the hour of death. In this sacrament, the priest, dipping his thumb in the oil, anoints the sick person in the form of the cross upon the eyes, ears, mouth, nose, hands and feet, saying, "Through this Holy Unction and His most tender mercy, may the Lord pardon thee whatever sins thou hast committed by seeing. Amen." He repeats the same, adapting it to the part anointed. The oil used in this sacrament must be blessed by the bishop, a ceremony performed each year on Maundy Thursday.

UN'DERGROUND RAIL'ROAD, the name applied to a method used by Northern abolitionists before the Civil War in assisting slaves from the South to escape from their masters. Regular routes were laid out, and certain houses at convenient intervals were designated as stations. Fleeing negroes were conducted secretly from one of these points to the next, given rest and food and prepared for the next stage in their journey. The most common routes were through Ohio and Pennsylvania, the goal of each being Canada. Among the prominent promoters of the underground railroad were Gerrit Smith, Theodore Parker and Levi Coffin. It is believed that fully 25,000 negroes were thus given liberty during the quarter century preceding the Civil War, fines inflicted on detection for violation of the Fugitive Slave Law having little effect on the abolitionists. An interesting account of the system occurs in Mrs. Stowe's *Uncle Tom's Cabin.*

UNDERGROUND RAILWAY. See SUBWAY.

UNDERWOOD, OSCAR W. (1862–1929), an American statesman, one of the prominent Democrats in Congress of a former decade. He was born in Louisville, Ky., and was educated in that city and at the University of Virginia. After completing a law course, he was admitted to the bar in 1884 and began practice in Birmingham, Ala. Entering politics, he was elected to Congress and took his seat in the lower house in 1895 as Representative of the Ninth Alabama district. This office he held until 1915. In the special session of Congress called by President Wilson in 1913 to revise the tariff, Underwood, who was chairman of the Ways and Means Committee and majority leader in the House, took a prominent part in framing the tariff law that bears his name (see TARIFF). He was elected to the Senate in 1914 and reëlected in 1920.

UNEMPLOYMENT. In the days when people depended for their livelihood on agriculture and home crafts, unemployment was considered a personal problem. Those who were mentally or physically unfit for work were cared for in almshouses; the other unemployed were punished—often being indentured, or forced to labor, for a term of years. With the Industrial Revolution, unemployment came to be looked upon as a problem in industrial organization, those idle because unwilling or unable to work being considered problems for social rather than economic adjustment.

Causes of Unemployment. The following are some of the causes of unemployment:

1. **Change of Season.** Some occupations depend upon the seasons. Among those affected are the migratory workers who follow the harvest season from north to south.

2. **Fluctuation of Demand.** A number of industries have their dull seasons and their busy seasons. Clothing and millinery are good illustrations of industries of this class.

3. **New Inventions and Discoveries.** The introduction of new machinery and of new processes of manufacture always throw a number of workmen out of employment, temporarily, but men thrown out in this way are usually given employment in some other occupation, if they are willing to make the change.

4. **Change of Location.** Occasionally an industry is removed to a distant locality, and some of the workmen are unable or unwilling to remove to the new location and are left without employment. This condition is frequently brought about by combining firms under one ownership. For economic reasons some of the plants thereafter might be closed.

5. **Congestion of Labor.** Every year thousands of men and women flock to the great cities for the purpose, as they suppose, of bettering their condition. To these, others may

be added by immigration. Usually there are more laborers in large cities than the regular industries can profitably employ.

6. **Industrial Depression.** During periods of prosperity there is a tendency to produce commodities in excess of the demand for them. In course of time the market becomes overstocked, manufacturers have their capital invested in products that they cannot sell and production is greatly restricted or entirely suspended. When this occurs, large numbers of workmen are without jobs.

7. **Labor Troubles.** Disagreements between employers and employes over wages and other conditions all too frequently lead to strikes and lockouts, causing large numbers to be thrown out of employment for indefinite periods. In these contests both parties generally lose. See Labor Organizations; Strike.

Means of Prevention. From the nature of the problem statistics of unemployment are incomplete, and consequently are of little value. Much time and effort have been expended in trying to solve the problem, yet it is found that from five to fifteen per cent of the laboring population in the United States are unemployed. This means that at all times there are several million idle workmen, regardless of economic conditions. The following measures have been taken or suggested to remedy this condition:

1. **Labor Bureaus.** The establishing of labor bureaus, which register applications for positions and calls for workmen, has been found an excellent means of bringing the workman and the employer together. The United States Department of Labor through branch bureaus located in different parts of the country is serving as a general clearing house for the unemployed, and its services are very beneficial. A number of states also have established free employment bureaus. In addition to these there are many private bureaus that operate on a commission basis.

2. **Publishing Labor Condition.** It is the opinion of those who have devoted much study to this problem that regular publication by responsible authorities, state or national, of the condition of the labor market in great cities might check the influx of laborers to these centers.

3. **Shorter Days.** Some recommend the adopting of a shorter day so that it would require more workmen to keep production up to the standard. However, the results of this method are debatable.

4. **Restriction of Immigration.** A large proportion of immigrants remain in the ports where they land; the balance go to other cities or to mining regions, where there is usually a congestion of labor.

5. **Agricultural Colonies.** With rare exceptions there is a scarcity of labor in the country. Could many of these workmen who are out of employment be induced to remove

to farms, they might become prosperous, but special inducements are necessary to lead them to make this change. States having large areas of vacant land, philanthropic organizations and the United States government are interested in establishing farm colonies.

UNGAVA, *ung gah' va,* formerly a territory of Canada, but united to Quebec in 1912, the year in which so many provincial boundaries in the Dominion were changed. In the same year the province of Quebec formed a new territory under its jurisdiction, called the Territory of New Quebec. In this Ungava was included. It has an area of 351,780 square miles. The population is about 14,300; of these 8,800 are white people, 3,500 are Indians and 2,000 are Eskimos. See LABRADOR.

UN'GULATES, an order of mammals including the buffalo, camel, cow, deer, elephant, pig, goat, sheep, and related animals, generally characterized by strong molar teeth for the chewing of vegetable food; horny hoofs, which enclose their toes; and, in many cases, by the ability to run with speed. Ungulates are the only animals that have horns. They are important in human economy, funishing man with food, clothing, working power and means of transportation.

Related Articles. Consult the following titles for additional information:

Antelope	Elephant	Ibex
Boar	Giraffe	Peccary
Camel	Goat	Rhinoceros
Cattle	Hippopotamus	Sheep
Deer	Horse	Tapir

U'NICORN, a fabulous animal of Greek and Roman mythology, similar to a horse but having a horn on its forehead. With the lion it forms a part of the British coat of arms.

UNIFORMS, MILITARY AND NAVAL. A uniform is a distinguishing dress worn by members of armies, navies and other organizations. This article treats of military and naval uniforms only. Since the beginning of the present century, the military uniforms of the leading nations have been radically changed. The display dress of former times has been replaced by one designed especially for comfort and service. The change was inaugurated by Great Britain, because at the beginning of the South African War the uniforms of the British soldiers were too heavy for service in a hot country.

The old uniforms were replaced by those of khaki. The color adopted was the same as that of the khaki-colored uniforms used in India. The cut was loose; the coat had patch pockets and the trousers were tight at the knee. The lower leg was protected by boots, leather leggings, or strips of strong woolen material called *puttees,* which were wound around the leg. This type of uniform proved to be so comfortable and serviceable that it has been practically copied by all the leading nations, each making such modifications in color and minor particulars as would distinguish its uniform from that of other nations. The service uniform of the German army was a greenish-gray, and that of Italy is a brownish-gray. The French, however, still retain the blue and red color scheme of former days.

United States. The service dress of the United States army is of khaki; the cut is similar to that of the British uniform described above. A cap of the same material and color is worn, but when the soldier is in battle this cap is replaced by a metal helmet.

Branch and Line Badges. Each branch is distinguished by a badge. Members of the general staff wear the United States coat of arms of gold and enamel on a silver star. A shield marks the department of the adjutant-general, and the inspector-general is designated by a crossed sword and fasces with a wreath. A sword and key crossed on a wheel and surmounted by a spread eagle is the badge of the quarter-master-general. Members of the medical staff wear the caduceus, or wand of mercury; engineers are indicated by a metal castle, and members of the signal corps by two crossed signal flags and a torch in gold and silver. The badges for officers are as follows: infantry, two crossed rifles with the number of the regiment above the intersection; for cavalry, two crossed sabers, and for artillery, two crossed guns.

Distinctions in Rank. A brigadier-general is designated by one star on the shoulder straps, and a major-general by two stars. On shoulder knot and shoulder loop the general wears a coat of arms between two stars; lieutenant-general, one large star between two small ones; major-general, two silver stars; brigadier-general, one silver star; colonel, a silver eagle; lieutenant-colonel, a silver leaf; major, a gold leaf; captain, two silver bars; first lieutenant, one silver bar; second lieutenant, one gold bar. The rank of noncommissioned officers is indicated by chevrons on the coat. All officers, without distinction of rank, wear the letters *U. S.* in Gothic design on the collar.

Gold chevrons on the lower part of the sleeve of soldiers returning from the World War indicated the length of service abroad, there being one chevron for every six months of service.

The Navy. The uniforms worn in the United States navy may be considered typical of those in other navies, since naval uniforms are similar throughout the world. Three uniforms—dress, undress and service—are furnished to every member of the navy. The dress uniform consists of a double-breasted blue broadcloth coat with a high collar and gilt buttons; blue trousers with a strip of gold lace along the seam; epaulets, hat and sword. The service uniform includes a blue or white blouse, with white braid. This or the undress uniform is worn during hot weather and in the tropics.

Officers and cadets wear on the cap a silver shield surmounted by a spread eagle, the design being mounted on two gold anchors crossed. Rank is indicated by special emblems on collar, epaulet and shoulder strap. An admiral wears on the sleeve two strips of two-inch gold lace with a one-inch strip between; a rear-admiral wears a half-inch strip of gold lace above a two-inch strip; captain, four half-inch strips; commander, three strips; lieutenant-commander, two half-inch strips with a quarter-inch strip between; lieutenant, two half-inch strips; lieutenant (junior grade) one half-inch strip with one quarter-inch strip above; ensign, one half-inch strip; cadet, one quarter-inch strip.

UNION, Act of, an act of the British Parliament in 1841 for uniting Upper and Lower Canada. It was the result of the Earl of Durham's famous *Report on the Affairs of British North America,* and was favored at the time by the legislatures of both Upper and Lower Canada. Under the Act of Union, Canada was governed by a legislative council of not more than twenty members, appointed by the Crown, and a legislative assembly in which the provinces had equal representation. It was never entirely satisfactory in its operation, however, and was succeded, in 1867, by the organization of the Dominion of Canada.

UNION OF SOUTH AFRICA, a self-governing state of the British Empire, widely known for its mineral wealth and consisting of the provinces of the Cape of Good Hope, Natal, Orange Free State and the Transvaal. It was established by an act of Parliament in 1910, and became a member of the British Commonwealth of Nations in 1926. Its area is 472,550 square miles; its population, about 8,000,000, one-fifth white.

Agriculture. The country consists of plateaus and rolling plains, or *veldts,* which are almost treeless and afford excellent pasturage. The climate is temperate, and the soil is fertile. Wherever there is sufficient rainfall excellent crops can be grown, but stock raising is the chief agricultural occupation. Millions of sheep are pastured on the prairies, and wool is the staple of wealth among the farmers. Angora goats and cattle are also raised in large numbers, and ostrich farming has become an important industry. Sugar cane and tea are successfully cultivated in the warmest regions. Wheat and fruits are important products of the Cape Province. It is claimed that the Union of South Africa has such a variety of climate as to admit of the successful cultivation of all crops within its borders.

Mineral Resources. The mines constitute the greatest source of wealth, and the discovery of the vast deposits of gold and rich diamond fields brought the country into universal notice. The principal gold mines are in the Witwatersrand in the Transvaal, and the output of these mines is about $250,000,000 each year. The most valuable diamond mines are around Kimberley, and the yearly output of diamonds has exceeded $50,000,000. There are valuable copper mines in Namaqualand, and extensive deposits of coal and iron have been discovered in the Cape Province and Natal. Silver, graphite and manganese occur in paying quantities, and marble and other building stone are found.

Transportation and Communication. The roads are fair in the settled districts, and mail carts and other wagons connect large towns off the railways with these lines of transportation. All the important ports of the south and east coast are connected by railway, and these lines are joined to the Cape-to-Cario Railway, extending from Cape Town into the interior of the continent. At the end of 1934 there were 13,000 miles of railways in the South African railway system. There were about 36,000 miles of telegraph line, and the telephone lines carried over 400,000 miles of wire. The country has over 3,200 post-offices and an efficient mail service.

Government. The government is organized on the same plan as the governments of Canada and Australia. The chief executive is the Governor-General, who is appointed by the Crown. He is aided by an Executive Council of his own selection. The Parliament consists of a Senate of forty members (eight appointive and thirty-two elective) and a House of Assembly of 150 members elected by the people. Each province has its local government, consisting of a lieutenant-governor and a legislative assembly. The courts are guided by Dutch law in settling civil suits, and both Dutch and English languages are used. Both of these languages are taught in the schools.

History. The early history of the provinces is given under their respective titles. Before the South African War there was a constant struggle between the Dutch and English settlers. The war gave the English the ascendency, and the ablest of the Dutch leaders soon joined the English leaders in an effort to establish a permanent government that would be satisfactory to all parties; their efforts resulted in establishing a federated state including the five provinces. Several clashes with the natives have occurred, and soon after the outbreak of the World War the country was threatened with a serious rebellion, but the rebels were defeated.

The Union gave notable assistance to the Allies in that war. British and Union soldiers took German Southwest Africa early in the war, and at its conclusion the Union was given the mandate to govern it.

In 1926 the Union sent delegates to the Imperial Conference in London, that historic meeting which made the six leading colonial outposts of the Empire free members of the British Commonwealth of Nations. Statesmen of the Union were prominent in these deliberations. In 1939 South Africa again supported Britain in war against Germany.

Related Articles. Consult the following titles for additional information:

Cape of Good Hope, Province of the
Cape Town
Johannesburg
Kimberley
Natal
Orange Free State
Pretoria
South African War
Transvaal, The

UNION OF SOVIET SOCIALIST REPUBLICS. See RUSSIA.

U'NIT, a single thing regard as an undivided whole. In arithmetic the term is also used to denote the least whole number, *one* or *unity*, represented by the figure 1. In mathematics and physics, a unit is any known determinate quantity, by which any other quantity of the same kind is measured, as a foot, a second, a degree, a square yard (see WEIGHTS AND MEASURES). Below are given the more important special units used in physics.

The *unit of specific gravity*, for solids or liquids, is the specific gravity of one cubic foot of distilled water at 62° F.; for air and gases, of one cubic foot of atmospheric air at 62° F. The *unit* of *heat*, or the *thermal unit*, is the quantity of heat required to raise one pound of pure water from a temperature of 39°F. to a temperature of 40°F., or, in the metric system, the amount of heat required to raise a gram of pure water from a temperature of 3.94° C. to 4.94° C.

In electricity the *unit of quantity* is that quantity of electricity, which, with an electromotive force of one volt, will flow through a resistance of 1,000,000 ohms in one second; it is called a *farad*. The *unit of electric current* is a current of one farad a second. The *unit of physical work* is that amount of work which will produce a velocity of one meter per second in a mass weighing one gram, after acting upon it a second of time. The *dynamic unit* is the unit expressing the quantity of force or the amount of work done, as the *footpound*.

In physical calculations the system of units now in general use is that known as the *C. G. S. System*, based upon the metric system of weights and measures, in which the centimeter is the *unit of length*, the gram is the *unit of mass* and the second the *unit of time*. Consequently, the *unit of area* is the square centimeter; the *unit of volume*, the cubic centimeter; the *unit of velocity*, a velocity of one centimeter per second. The *unit of momentum* is the momentum of a gram moving with a unit velocity.

For definitions of units of measurement in other fields of work, see articles on those units, as FOOT POUND; DOLLAR.

UNITA'RIANS, a religious denomination believing in one God, the Father, and not in a Trinity of Father, Son and Holy Spirit. They accept Christ as a divinely appointed teacher, to be followed, but not worshiped, and regard the Bible as an endeavor of the religion of the spirit to express itself in literature. The Unitarians have no creed; their faith may be summed up in the words of James Freeman Clarke, "the fatherhood of God, the brotherhood of man, the leadership of Jesus, salvation by character and the progress of mankind upward and onward forever." In 1819, Dr. Channing of Boston led a movement which turned 150 of the New England churches to Unitarianism. See CHANNING, WILLIAM ELLERY.

UNITED CHURCH OF CANADA, a union of the Methodist, Congregational, and certain Presbyterian churches of Canada, effected in 1925. It was brought about partly by decreasing emphasis on doctrinal differences among Protestant bodies, but quite as much by realization of unnecessary expenditure of effort and waste of resources through overlapping of activities. In the newer sections of Western Canada especially, the maintenance of separate church bodies had become a problem.

The movement in the direction of unity began in 1889. By 1912 the Methodists and Congregationalists had expressed themselves favorably; action by the Presbyterian General Assembly was deferred until the end of World War I. In 1924 the Canadian Parliament passed the permissive act of union, effective in one year. In this act doctrinal points to guide the new Church and rules for organization were set forth in detail. A large group of Presbyterians, however, remained out of the union.

UNITED DAUGHTERS OF THE CONFEDERACY. See CONFEDERACY, UNITED DAUGHTERS OF THE.

UNITED EMPIRE LOYALISTS, the name given to those British colonists in America who remained loyal to the King, and refused to join the majority who in 1776 declared their independence of Great Britain. About 40,000 of these colonists left New England and other colonies to the south, crossed the border into Canada, and made new homes there. Many moved to Nova Scotia and Quebec, but most of them settled in New Brunswick and Southern Ontario and were an important element in the creation of these provinces. It was said that this great migration "was the saving of British interest in the great region which England still retained in North America."

UNITED KINGDOM, THE, officially THE UNITED KINGDOM OF GREAT BRITAIN AND IRELAND, a term formally adopted in 1801 to indicate the political union of England, Ire-

land, Scotland and Wales. When recognition was given in 1922 to the new status of a large part of Ireland as the Irish Free State, the old official designation was no longer justified by the facts. No immediate steps were taken to change the name, but in 1927 the British Parliament decreed that the term thenceforth should be THE UNITED KINGDOM OF GREAT BRITAIN AND NORTHERN IRELAND.

UNITED METHODIST CHURCH, a sect known also as United Methodists, was organized in England in 1907 by religionists who refused to conform to the established Methodist usages. Three branches of Methodism joined to form the new Church, namely, the United Methodist Free Churches, the Bible Christians and the Methodist New Connection. This new organization was further augmented in 1932 by union with the Wesleyan Methodists and the Primitive Methodists. Thus in England the various Methodist bodies sought and secured a degree of unity such as the American Methodists achieved later. See METHODISTS.

UNITED STATES COAST GUARD. See COAST GUARD.

UNITED STATES COURTS. See COURT, subhead *United States Courts.*

UNITED STATES OF AMERICA, one of the world's great powers, the oldest of the great republics, although one of the youngest nations. It occupies the central part of North America, having Canada for its northern neighbor and Mexico on its southwestern border. The United States lies between two oceans, the Atlantic bordering it on the east and the Pacific on the west. The Gulf of Mexico extends along its southern boundary between the peninsulas of Texas and Florida. From east to west its greatest extent is 3,100 miles; from north to south it extends 1,700 miles. In 1940 the area of continental United States was 3,022,387 square miles. The area of the outlying possessions (including the Philippine Islands) was 712,836 square miles, the total area under the American flag being 3,735,223 square miles. The British Empire and China are larger than the United States, including all the outer possessions, and

Brazil is larger than continental United States. The British Empire and China have each about four times the population of the United States, but Brazil has only about one-fourth as many inhabitants.

Geographic Advantages. Human development has always been influenced by geographic conditions, chief among which are climate, soil and relative location. When these conditions are applied to the United States, it is seen that it is more highly favored geographically than most other nations. The country lies wholly within the north temperate zone, which has been the home of the great civilizations of history; it lies between two great oceans, almost equally distant from the other great land masses of the earth, with which it has easy communication; mountain and valley, hill and plain are so interspersed as to adapt the country as a whole to all lines of industry; while the great interior, with its broad plains, fertile soil and abundant rainfall is the richest agricultural region of the world. Great rivers furnish natural waterways leading far into the interior and affording inexpensive transportation, while thousands of mountain streams turn the wheels of industry. The ease with which railways can be constructed has caused all parts of the country to be bound together with bands of steel, and commodious harbors on the seaboards accommodate ships laden with the products of all climes. These conditions, combined with the energy, intelligence and genius of the American people, have placed the United States in the foremost position among the great nations of the world.

Boundaries and Coastal Features. West of the 95th meridian the northern boundary is formed by the 49th parallel of north latitude until the Pacific coast is reached; then it extends southward to the Strait of Juan de Fuca, thus placing Vancouver Island within the Dominion of Canada. East of the 95th meridian the northern boundary is very irregular. That portion of it between the meridian and Lake Superior is formed by the Rainy and Pigeon rivers. Through the Great Lakes the boundary line follows the deepest channel, which divides Lakes Huron, Erie and Ontario nearly equally between the two nations, but gives the larger part of Lake Superior to the United States. Following Lake Ontario the boundary is formed for a short distance by the St. Lawrence River, then across New York and Vermont by the 45th parallel;

thence it follows the Height of Land in an irregular course to the northeast, until the northerly point of Maine is reached. From there the boundary is completed by the Saint Johns River, a short, arbitrary line and the Saint Croix River. A portion of the southern boundary is formed by the Rio Grande.

The northern boundary affords the finest example in the world of international faith. By mutual agreement between the United States and Great Britain there has never been a fortification erected along its entire length nor has either nation ever placed a warship or even a gunboat on the Great Lakes. The integrity of the boundary has never been violated.

The prominent projections are, on the Atlantic coast, Cape Cod, Cape Hatteras and the peninsula of Florida; on the Gulf coast, Cape San Blas and the delta of the Mississippi, and on the Pacific coast, Cape Mendocino. The important coast waters are, on the Atlantic, Massachusetts Bay, Long Island Sound, Delaware Bay, Chesapeake Bay, Albemarle Sound and Pamlico Sound; on the Gulf, Apalachee Bay and Mobile Bay, and on the Pacific, San Francisco Bay and Puget Sound. The coast line of the entire country, exclusive of the Great Lakes, is 12,101 miles. The Atlantic coast is 6,017 miles; the Gulf, 3,551, and the Pacific, 2,533.

The chief islands on the Atlantic coast are Nantucket, Martha's Vineyard, Long, Manhattan, Staten, Roanoke and Florida Keys; in the Gulf of Mexico, Tortugas, Saint George's, Santa Rosa, the Chandeleur group, Galveston and Padre; on the Pacific, Santa Catalina, the Santa Barbara group and San Juan.

Surface and Drainage

The vast extent of territory embraced within the United States contains a great variety of surface, but this is naturally divided into five regions—the Atlantic Slope, the Appalachian Highlands, the Central Plain, the Rocky Mountain Highlands and the Pacific Slope.

The Atlantic Slope. This region embraces a narrow strip of land extending from the northeastern corner of Maine to Florida. In the northern part it is extremely narrow, and the slope is steep. The irregularity of the coast line produces numerous good harbors, upon which some of the largest cities of the country are located. Chief among these indentations are Boston Bay, New York

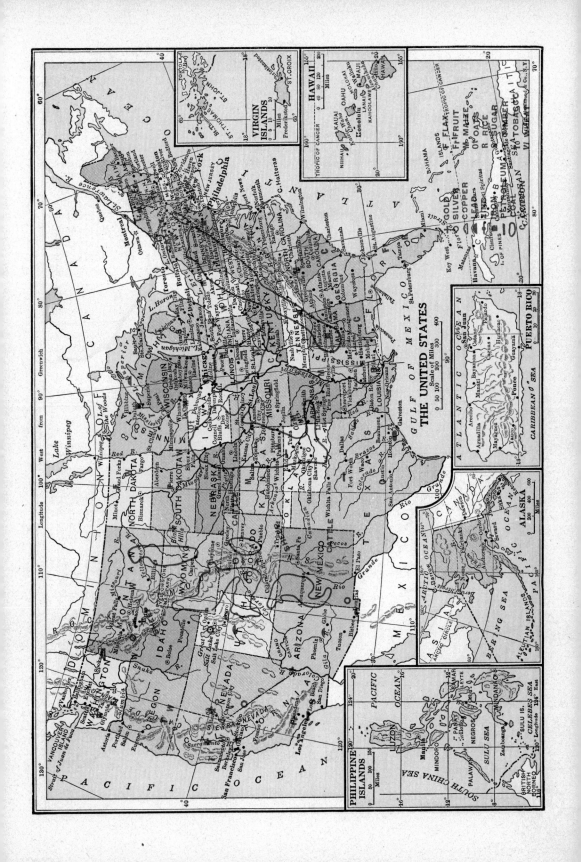

THE UNITED STATES
Scale of Miles

VIRGIN ISLANDS

HAWAII

PUERTO RICO

ALASKA

PHILIPPINE ISLANDS

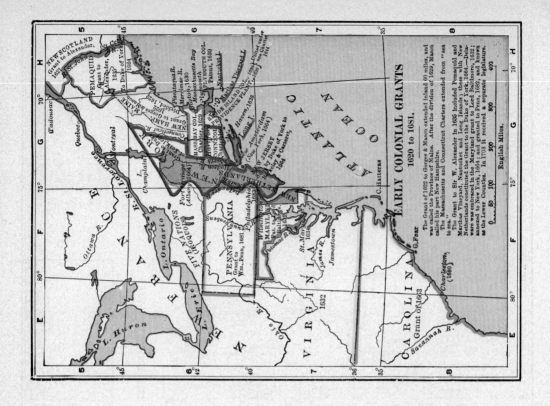

EARLY COLONIAL GRANTS
1620 to 1651.

The Grant of 1622 to Gorges & Mason extended inland 60 miles, and was called the Province of Maine. After the division of 1629, Mason called his part New Hampshire.

The Massachusetts and Connecticut Charters extended from "sea to sea."

The Grant to Sir W. Alexander in 1635 included Pemaquid and Martha's Vineyard, Nantucket and Long Islands; these with New Netherland constituted the Grant to the Duke of York, 1664. Delaware was annexed in 1682; New Jersey in 1664, 1682; Delaware was annexed to New York, 1664; and granted to Penn, 1682, and known as the Lower Counties. In 1703 it received a separate legislature.

English Miles.
0   50   100   200   300   400

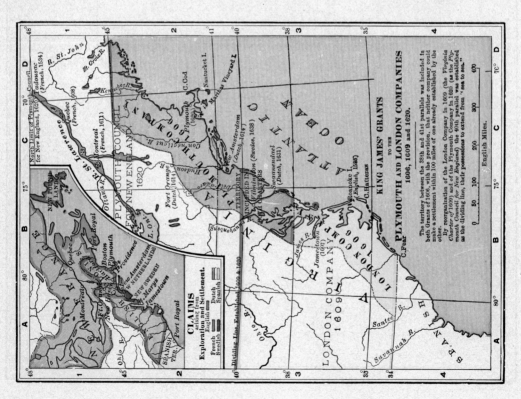

KING JAMES' GRANTS
TO THE
PLYMOUTH AND LONDON COMPANIES
1606, 1609 and 1620.

The territory between the 38th and 41st parallels was included in both Grants of 1606, with the provision, that neither company could make a settlement within 100 miles of one already established by the other.

By reorganization of the London Company in 1609 (the Virginia Charter) 1600 square miles of the Plymouth Grant and the Plymouth Council in 1620, the latter having its southern limit at the 40th parallel, was established as the dividing line, their possessions to extend from "sea to sea."

English Miles.
0   50   100   200   300   400

CLAIMS
arising from
Exploration and Settlement.

French	Dutch
Swedish	Spanish

Dividing Line Established 1609 & 1620

RELIEF MAP OF THE UNITED STATES

Bay, Delaware Bay and Chesapeake Bay. South of Long Island the coast region consists of a tract of level land, varying from 75 to 300 miles in width, known as the Atlantic coastal plain. Along the shore and for a short distance inland the surface is low, level and, in many places, marshy. The land then rises gradually until it meets the Piedmont region, or foothills of the Appalachians, which consist of the remains of an old, worn-down mountain system, formed previous to the present Appalachian system. Where the plain joins the Piedmont region, there is a marked elevation, known as the Fall Line because the rivers reaching the Atlantic fall over this uplift, producing numerous rapids and affording excellent water power.

Appalachian Highlands. This region constitutes the eastern continental barrier and extends from the Gulf of Saint Lawrence to within about 300 miles of the Gulf of Mexico. The trend of the mountains is from the northeast to the southwest. The region consists of a low plateau, from 1,500 to 3,000 feet in altitude, upon which are a number of parallel ranges of mountains. The northern part of the plateau is quite broken, and the mountains are disconnected, forming separate ranges or groups, as the Green Mountains, the White Mountains and the Adirondacks. South of this division, however, the plateau is continuous and is surmounted by a number of parallel ranges of low mountains, such as the Blue Ridge, the Alleghanies and others. The highest peaks in these highlands are Mount Washington (6,293 feet), in the White Mountains, and Mount Mitchell (6,711 feet), in the Black Mountains of North Carolina. On their western slope these highlands descend by a series of foothills to the prairie region in the central plain.

Central Plain. This occupies the vast interior of the country, and embraces that portion of the great central plain of North America included within the boundaries of the United States. It is naturally divided into three regions, the great plain, the lake region and the gulf region.

The Great Plain. East of the Mississippi, this plain occupies that portion of the interior between the Ohio River and the lake region. Here it descends from the western foothills of the Appalachians to the broad, level prairies which compose most of the

states bordering on the Mississippi. This stretch of level or slightly rolling land continues westward, until it rises in gradual swells to meet the foothills of the Rocky Mountain highlands, where it attains an elevation of from 3,000 to 6,000 feet. With the exception of the Black Hills in South Dakota and Wyoming, the Ozark Plateau, which extends eastward from the southern boundary of Kansas, crossing Arkansas, the southern part of Missouri and the southern part of Illinois, this level tract of land extends southward into Texas and westward until it joins the Staked Plains in the northwestern part of that state. With the exception of the forests in Northern Minnesota and in the Ozark Region, this entire portion of the country is nearly treeless. Timber is found only along streams and in regions where trees have been planted by settlers. These vast tracts of level, treeless land are generally known as *prairies*. Their deep, rich soil, abundant rainfall and salubrious climate make the prairies the most valuable agricultural region in the world.

Lake Region. The Lake region constitutes that portion of the United States which drains into the Great Lakes, and thence through the Saint Lawrence River into the Atlantic. The Height of Land, forming the southern boundary of this region, is nearly parallel with the southern shores of Lakes Ontario and Erie. It extends across the northern part of Ohio, Indiana and Illinois, thence turns northward, to include the eastern portion of Wisconsin, all of Michigan and the northwestern part of Minnesota. The region within the United States is not large. It is either level or rolling, nowhere having high altitudes and much of it was formerly heavily timbered, but the lumbering interests have greatly reduced the forest area. The most distinctive feature of this region is the presence of the great inland seas, which lie wholly or partially within its boundaries.

Gulf Region. The Gulf region includes the lowlands bordering on the Gulf of Mexico and extending inland until they meet the foothills of the Appalachian Highlands. In the valley of the Mississippi, this plain extends northward to the Ohio River, and west of the Mississippi it extends northward to the Ozark Mountains. Along the coast the land is low, level and swampy, but with the exception of that immediately in the vicinity of the Mississippi River, it rises gradually toward the interior, until it reaches a height of 300 to 500 feet. The plain includes all of the southern and southeastern parts of Texas, and in that state it is from 150 to 200 miles in width.

Rocky Mountain Highlands. This region occupies nearly one-third of the area of the country, and consists of a great plateau, upon which rise several ranges of mountains. This plateau reaches its greatest height and width in Colorado and Wyoming. Here it is nearly 1,000 miles wide and from 7,000 to 8,000 feet in altitude. On its eastern slope it rises from the plain in a series of elevations, until the Rocky Mountains, which form its eastern boundary, are reached. These extend entirely across the country and contain numerous peaks, with altitudes of 14,000 feet or more. The western border of the plateau is formed by the Cascade Mountains, in the north, and their southern continuation, the Sierra Nevadas. These mountains contain some peaks higher than those found in the Rocky Mountains. Their eastern slope, since they rise from the plateau, is less abrupt than the western, which descends to the valley between them and the low ranges.

Between these mountain barriers, the surface of the great plateau is widely diversified by lesser ranges, extending in various directions. These ranges divide this vast inland region into three well-marked divisions, the Columbia Plateau, in the north; the Great Basin, and the Colorado Plateau. The first occupies the mountain regions of Washington, Oregon and Idaho. The Great Basin includes nearly all Nevada and Utah and a small portion of Oregon and California; it is entirely surrounded by mountains, and its rivers find no outlet, hence it contains a number of salt lakes and marshes, the most noted among which is Great Salt Lake. South of this, and occupying a small part of Nevada, nearly all of Colorado, a part of Utah, most of Arizona and New Mexico and the southern part of California, is the Colorado Plateau, marked by many high peaks and the deep gorges of its streams. Within the Rocky Mountain Highlands are located several of the great national parks.

The Pacific Slope. Between the Sierra Nevada and Cascade mountains and the coast are low parallel ranges, known as the Coast Ranges. West of these is the narrow strip of land bordering upon the ocean. This low land is much narrower than that bordering

upon the Atlantic, but between the mountains are several valleys noted for their fertility. Chief among these are the valleys of the San Joaquin and Sacramento rivers, the region around San Francisco Bay and that around Puget Sound. Farther inland, in the southeastern part of California, is Death Valley, a remarkable depression, 276 feet below sea level.

Rivers. The United States is drained by five river systems—the Lake system, the Atlantic system, the Gulf system, the Pacific system and the Great Basin system. The portion of the country drained by the Lake system is comparatively small, and the streams flowing into it are generally short and of little importance, though the Saint Lawrence River, forming the outlet of this drainage area, is one of the most important streams in North America.

Owing to the position of the Appalachian Highlands, the rivers of the Atlantic system are short and many of them are rapid. However, the largest of these streams enter the ocean by broad estuaries, which afford excellent harbors, and some of them, particularly the Hudson, the Delaware and the Potomac, cut their way through the mountains, forming deep gorges remarkable for their beautiful scenery. The most important of these rivers, in order, beginning at the north, are the Penobscot, the Kennebec, the Merrimac, the Connecticut, the Hudson, the Delaware, the Potomac, the James, the Pedee, the Santee, the Savannah and the Altamaha. Most of these streams afford excellent water power and the banks of the Merrimac and many others are lined with factories.

The rivers of the Gulf system include the Appalachicola, the Alabama, the Pearl, the Sabine, the Trinity, the Brazos, the Colorado of Texas, the Nueces, the Red, the Rio Grande and the Mississippi, which drains by far the largest part of the country.

The rivers of the Pacific system are few, and with the exception of the Columbia, draining the northwestern part of the country, and the Colorado, flowing into the Gulf of California, they are all short and small. Proceeding southward from the Columbia, those worthy of mention are the Klamath, the Sacramento, the San Joaquin and the Salinas. The Colorado, formed far up in Utah, with the Green as a tributary, drains a portion of the plateau between the Rocky and the Sierra Nevada mountains.

This stream is remarkable for the gorges which it has formed in the middle and lower parts of its course.

The Great Basin system consists of a number of small streams which flow into Great Salt Lake and a few smaller lakes, or those which lose themselves in salt marshes in the desert. The Humboldt is the only important river that loses itself in the sands.

Lakes. Fully one-half of the area of lakes Superior, Huron, Erie and Ontario belongs to the United States, and all of Lake Michigan is within her boundaries. In addition to these great bodies of water, the northern part of the Appalachian Highlands contains many lakes noted for their clear waters and beautiful scenery. Chief among these is Moosehead, in Maine; Winnepesaukee, in New Hampshire, and Champlain, between Vermont and New York. The northern parts of Michigan, Wisconsin and Minnesota are also studded with lakes, and in the Rocky Mountain region are found numerous lakes, some of which, like Lake Tahoe, are noted for their high altitude, others for their great depth, abundance of fish and beautiful surroundings. The Great Basin has Great Salt Lake and numerous other smaller bodies of salt water.

Scenery. For variety, beauty and grandeur, the scenery of the United States is unequaled by that of any other country. The Appalachian Highlands are noted for their mountain lakes, sparkling streams and deep gorges, through which rivers find their way to the sea. Notable among the last are the Crawford Notch, in the White Mountains; the Palisades of the Hudson, and the Delaware Water Gap. The central plain presents to view vast areas of fertile fields. The expanse of fresh water afforded by the Great Lakes is nowhere equaled and is approached only by the great lakes in the equatorial regions of Africa. The only cataract comparable with Niagara is Victoria Falls, on the Zambezi, while the Shoshone Falls, Yosemite Falls, the Falls of the Yellowstone and many others in the Rocky Mountain region are unsurpassed in beauty. The extent and grandeur of mountain scenery found in the Rocky Mountains exceed that of any other single country; the Royal Gorge, Yosemite Valley and the canyons of the Colorado and Yellowstone are features of unusual interest, and the geysers and hot springs of Yellowstone National Park have caused that region to be termed the "World's Wonderland."

Climate

Within the boundaries of the United States may be found every range of temperate climate, and the extreme southern and southwestern sections are semitropical. This great diversity of climate is due to the wide range of latitude (24°), the position and extent of the mountain systems and differences in altitude.

Temperature. On the northern boundary, the average temperature for January is 12°, and for July, 60°. The contrast between the winter temperature on the Pacific and Atlantic coasts in the northern part of the country is very marked, the mean temperature on the Pacific coast being 41°, and on the Atlantic coast, 14°. Toward the south the average temperature rises, and it also becomes more nearly equal at the eastern and western extremities; at the 30th parallel of latitude the difference between the average temperature of the two regions for January is only 2°, and for July, only 9°, while at the extreme southern boundary the January difference is 3°, and the July difference, but 1°. The central plain is open to the passage of air currents with little or no obstruction; consequently alternating north and south winds sweep over this region, causing sudden and marked changes in temperature. The northern part of the Appalachian Highlands has a cool temperate climate. The winters are usually long and severe, and in New England, New York, some parts of Pennsylvania and northern Ohio, there is a heavy fall of snow. Toward the south the mean temperature rises, and south of Pennsylvania little snow falls, except on the highest mountains. Near the Gulf the temperature seldom falls below freezing point, and the Gulf states, with South Carolina and Georgia, verge upon a subtropical climate. The Rocky Mountain region is cooler than other regions in the same latitude, because of its high altitude. The northern part of this region, as well as the northern portion of the central plain, is subject to intensely cold waves during winter, the thermometer occasionally falling as low as 40° below zero; yet, owing to the dryness of the atmosphere, these extremes produce little discomfort. The Pacific coast has a mild climate throughout the year, with a remarkably equable temperature. At sea level the thermometer seldom falls below freezing point, even in the northwestern part of the country, and during summer it seldom rises above 80° or 85°. In the southern part of California, the temperature in summer may be higher than this, though hot waves, even there, last but a short time.

Rainfall. The position of the mountains causes a very unequal distribution of rain. In general, all that portion of the country

western part of Utah, the western part of Arizona and the southeastern part of California, is practically rainless. This is because the winds are robbed of their moisture as they pass inland from the Sierras. The moisture brought by the winds from the Pacific is precipitated on the western slopes of these mountains. The valleys between them and the coast ranges are well watered, and along the coast through Washington,

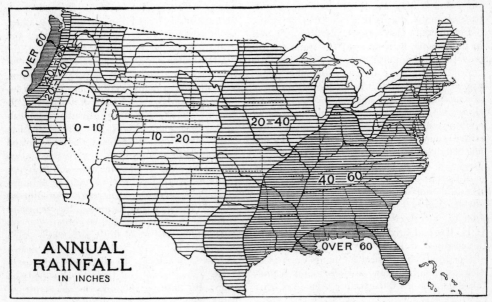

ANNUAL RAINFALL IN INCHES

east of the 100th meridian, crossing the middle of North and South Dakota and Nebraska, has sufficient rainfall for agriculture. In most of this region the annual precipitation varies from 40 to 60 inches, which is evenly distributed throughout the year, making this region well suited to agriculture.

A small region in the eastern part of North Carolina, and another area north of the Gulf of Mexico, have over 60 inches. The northern half of Illinois, Wisconsin, Minnesota, Iowa, most of Kansas, Missouri, Oklahoma and the eastern half of Texas have from 20 to 40 inches of rain, which assures crops; but west of this region the annual precipitation varies from 10 to 20 inches, and agriculture can be successfully prosecuted only by irrigation. However, large areas are well adapted to grazing, since there is sufficient moisture to produce a good growth of grass. The great plateau between the mountains is arid, and the southern half of it, including nearly all of Nevada, the

Oregon and the northern part of California, there is a region which receives over 60 inches of rain during the year.

Mineral Resources

The minerals of the United States constitute one of its chief sources of wealth, and in extent and variety they exceed those of any other country. With the exception of some coal and petroleum, most of the valuable minerals are found in the mountainous regions, and there the mining industry is most fully developed. The important mineral fuels are coal, petroleum and natural gas; the chief metals are iron, gold, silver, copper, lead, zinc and quicksilver.

Coal. The most extensive coal measures are found in the central part of the Appalachian highlands, including Pennsylvania and West Virginia and extending westward through the southern part of Ohio, Indiana and Illinois. There are also extensive coal measures in Missouri and Iowa, and areas of lesser extent occur in North Dakota, Montana, Wyoming, Colorado, Utah and New Mexico. There are also valuable coal measures in Alaska. In all, the area of coal measures is about 330,000 square miles. By far the greater portion of this area contains bituminous coal, but the anthracite variety is confined within the boundaries of Pennsylvania. The United States produces more coal than any other country, the output being nearly one-third the world's output; annually as great as 600,000,000 tons.

Petroleum. Petroleum ranks next to coal in importance as a mineral fuel, and the oil industry is becoming one of the gigantic businesses of the country. The chief fields are in Pennsylvania, West Virginia, Ohio, Michigan, Indiana, Kansas, Colorado, Texas, Oklahoma, Arkansas, southern California, and Wyoming. The annual output for the entire country has been as great as 900,-000,000 barrels, which exceeds the quantity produced by any other country.

Natural Gas. Natural gas occurs in usable quantities in Pennsylvania, Ohio, Indiana, Kentucky, Oklahoma, Texas, California, and a number of other states. It is of great advantage, since it furnishes the cheapest and most convenient fuel, especially for many manufacturing purposes, such as smelting iron and steel and manufacturing glass. Unfortunately much of this gas has been wasted.

Iron. Iron ranks first in value and importance among the metals produced within the country. The great deposits of ore are in Michigan and Minnesota, around Lake Superior; in eastern New York; in Pennsylvania; in Alabama, and Georgia and in southern Missouri, in the Ozark plateau. Deposits of less importance are quite widely distributed, especially in the Rocky Mountain region. Minnesota and Michigan are the leading states in the production of iron ore, and the great centers of iron manufacture are naturally where iron ore and coal can be most cheaply brought together. These are Pennsylvania, Ohio, Illinois, Indiana and Alabama. The United States now leads all other nations in the production of iron and steel, her average annual output of pig iron being 15 to 40 million tons.

Gold and Silver. All the important gold and silver mines are located in the Rocky Mountain region, throughout which the ores are quite generally distributed. Present methods of extracting the metals from the ore enable miners to work with profit at quantities of low grade ores that were formerly considered worthless, and this has increased the output of both metals. The annual production of gold, including Alaska, is about $50,000,000, and this amount is exceeded only by the mines in South Africa. The leading states in the production of gold are Colorado, California, Nevada, Utah, South Dakota, Idaho, Arizona and New Mexico, and these also contain the chief silver mines. In production of silver, the country is surpassed only by Mexico.

Other Metals. The United States produces two-thirds of the world's supply of copper. The most important mines are located in Michigan, on the shore of Lake Superior; in Montana, and in Arizona. Lead is mined in Colorado, Idaho, Illinois, Iowa, Kansas, Missouri, Utah and Wisconsin, and the United States produces more than any other country. Lead and copper ores are frequently found combined with silver ore. Zinc is also found in Illinois, Kansas, Missouri, New Jersey and Wisconsin, the Kansas, Missouri, and Wisconsin mines being the largest producers. Quicksilver, is found in California, which produces about all of that substance mined within the country. The United States produces about one-half of the world's supply of aluminum, the reduction works being at Pittsburgh and Niagara Falls.

Building Stones. Limestone is very generally distributed throughout the country and is used for a great many purposes, such as the manufacture of lime and the construction of foundations for buildings and of piers for bridges; the finer varieties, such as those obtained in Indiana, are often used for the exteriors of buildings, or when dressed, for trimmings in buildings constructed of other stone or brick. Granite is found in large quantities in the New England states, particularly Maine, New Hampshire and Vermont; there are also large quarries in Minnesota and other states. This is used extensively for building purposes and for tombstones. Granite is very widely distributed through the mountainous regions, and the Rocky Mountain plateau contains sufficient to supply large demands, whenever transportation facilities will warrant working the quarries. Marble is extensively quarried in Vermont and Georgia, and to some extent it is found in Tennessee and other states. The United

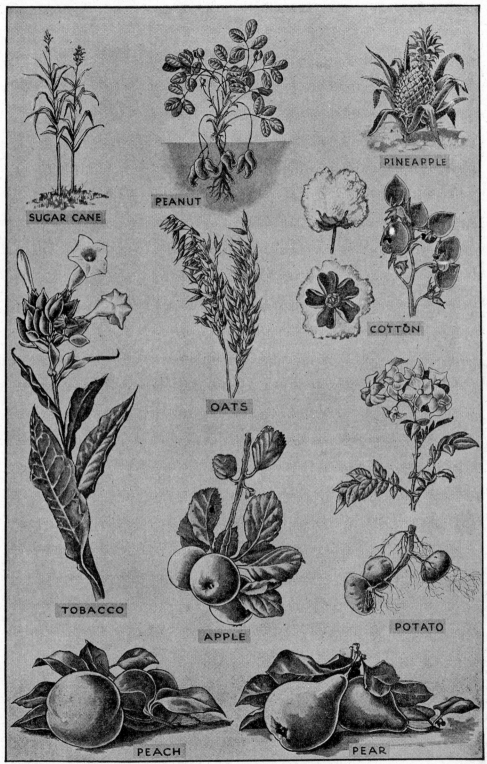

PLANT LIFE OF THE UNITED STATES
See, also, full-page illustration, Plant Life of North America, in article North America.

States produces more marble than any other country. There are large quarries of slate in Vermont, Pennsylvania and several other states. This stone is used for finishing interiors and for roofing. Clays of suitable quality for the manufacture of brick and tile and for pottery are widely distributed.

Miscellaneous Minerals. Gypsum is found in many localities, and salt is obtained from the waters of salt springs and wells, New York and Michigan being the leading states in its production. The manufacture of salt is an important industry in these states.

Vegetation. The plant life of the United States is characteristic of that of the temperate regions. Originally fully one-third of the country was covered with forests; but in the Appalachian Highlands and the Great Lake region, many sections have been almost wholly denuded, to supply the demand for lumber. In general, the forest areas include the Appalachian Highlands; the region bordering on the south of the Great Lakes and extending westward to the eastern boundary of the valley of the Red River of the North; the region along the Gulf of Mexico, including the eastern third of Texas and most of Arkansas, and the region occupied by the Cascade and Coast ranges of mountains, extending southward from the Dominion boundary as far as the central part of California.

The Appalachian forests are characterized by a great variety of hard wood, such as oak, maple, ash, beech and birch. There are also many cone-bearing trees, including spruce, hemlock and the white pine, in the north, and the yellow pine and the cypress, in the south. The forests in the lake region formerly had a great abundance of white pine, which was interspersed with some hard woods, and those of the Pacific coast are notable for peculiar species of cone-bearing trees, which attain great size, particularly the Douglas fir, the redwood, the yellow cedar and the sequoia.

In addition to its forests the Appalachian Highland region and Atlantic coast plain have a great variety of smaller plants, many of which are useful, while many are desirable only because of their beautiful flowers. Among the latter are the flowering plants of the mint family, a great number of grasses and a number of shrubs. The great central plain is characterized by the growth of herbaceous plants, most of which belong to the grass family. Many of these grasses are highly nutritious, and previous to the occupation of this region by white men they sustained vast herds of buffalo, which roamed over the prairies. Within the arid region of the Rocky Mountain plateau are found plants peculiar to desert areas. These consist almost wholly of species of sagebrush, bunch grass and buffalo grass, except in the southern portion of the plateau. Here many species of cactus are found, some of them growing to great size. The Pacific slope is characterized by vegetation peculiarly its own, containing a number of species which are tropical or semitropical in nature. Among these are several palms. The southern parts of Texas and Florida have a number of species belonging to the semitropical regions, and the vegetation of Florida very closely resembles that of the West Indies. Two plants discovered in America have become of great economic importance. These are maize, or Indian corn, and tobacco. The cultivated plants are described under their respective titles, and the areas that they occupy are more fully outlined under the subhead *Agriculture,* in the articles treating of the various states.

Animal Life

The native animals of the United States include a large number of species. Among these are 310 species of mammals, 756 species of birds, 816 species of fish, 257 species of reptiles and over 1,000 species of mollusks. Among the larger quadrupeds of the carnivorous order are bears, several varieties of wolf, the puma, or mountain lion, the wildcat, the lynx and the coyote. Among the ruminating animals, various species of deer, the buffalo, the mountain sheep and the pronghorn are the most important. Of these, the buffalo and the mountain sheep are peculiar to North America. Both are now protected in the game preserves of the national parks. There are many species of rodents, of which the beaver is the largest. This animal is also nearly extinct and is found only in the most unfrequented regions of the country. The prairies abound in gophers and prairie dogs, and various species of squirrels frequent nearly all parts of the country. Among the large birds of prey are the eagle, the hawk and various species of owls. The most important water fowl include the Canada goose, the pelican and ducks. Other game birds of

ANIMALS OF THE UNITED STATES
See, also, full-page illustration, Animals of North America, in article North America.

Porcupine	Hare	Coyote
Deer		Beaver
Raccoon	3681	Crane

importance are the wild turkey (now nearly extinct), various species of grouse and pigeons. Song birds exist in large numbers and are found in all parts of the country.

Furs and Fish. It was fish that first drew the French to America, and we might say that it was furs that kept them there. Lured by the profits to be derived from buying furs from the Indians, they explored all of Canada as far west as the head of Lake Superior and much of the northern part of the interior of the United States. From those early days to the present, the fur trade has been a source of income to the inhabitants of the forest and mountainous regions of the United States, as well as to those of Canada. So diligently have the hunters pursued the most valuable fur-bearing animals—the beaver, the otter and the fox—that these have nearly disappeared from the land. But the mink, the muskrat and the skunk are still found, and they furnish the greater part of the fur marketed in the United States. Alaska is valuable for its furs, especially the fur of the seal, but the seal fisheries have been greatly restricted by the government, to prevent the extermination of these valuable animals. Fur farms have been established in some of the islands off the Alaskan coast and in Prince Edward Island, and here the valuable silver and black fox are raised in captivity.

The fisheries of the United States give employment to over 220,000 persons, and the value of the yearly output is about $125,000,000. Cod, mackerel, lobsters and oysters are the chief products of the Atlantic coast fisheries, and salmon leads on the Pacific coast. The catch on the Great Lakes includes whitefish, lake trout and sturgeon.

Agriculture

General Survey. For more than a century the United States has been the leading agricultural country of the world, and not one-half of the agricultural resources have been developed. The mountains and large areas of arid land are not suited to the growing of crops, but some of these lands offer good pasturage, and upon them millions of cattle, horses and sheep are raised. In 1910 less than one-half of the land was in farms, and only a little more than one-half of that in farms was under cultivation. In 1934 there were in the country about 518,267,000 acres of unappropriated and unsurveyed land (see LANDS, PUBLIC). This is an

area more than two times the area of Texas, and much of it will yield the farmer good returns for his investment and labor.

The United States has the largest acreage of cultivated land of any country in the world except possibly, China, for which statistics are not obtainable. The crop acreage of the United States exceeds that of all the great countries of Europe combined, excluding Russia. Of still greater significance is the acreage per capita of population, which in the United States is 3.5 per person, while in European countries it is from 1.5 to 1, and in the United Kingdom only 0.4. In other words, there is 8.4 times as much land per person in crops in the United States as in the United Kingdom, and the improved land per person is much more than this.

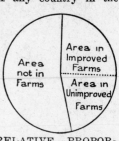

RELATIVE PROPORTIONS OF LAND, IMPROVED AND UNIMPROVED

With reference to the food supply of the United States, the Department of Agriculture at Washington makes the following statement:

The United States is practically independent of the rest of the World in the food supply, except for coffee, tea, sugar, cocoa, bananas and olive oil; and the principal source of supply of these food products, except tea and olive oil, is found in the western hemisphere.

Of all the cereals except rice, the United States produces more than it consumes. The United States produces and consumes about 70 per cent of the world's corn, over 25 per cent of the world's oats, between 15 and 20 per cent of the world's barley. Of the world's rye, the United States produces only about 2 per cent and of the world's rice less than 1 per cent.

Agricultural Regions. The great agricultural regions are the prairies of the Mississippi Basin, east of the 100th meridian; the land bordering on the Gulf of Mexico, and the valleys of the Pacific slope. The Appalachian region is not so fertile as the others. However, in the valleys and on other low lands there are many valuable farms. In this part of the country the raising of cereals is not profitable, and the region cannot compete with the Mississippi Basin; hence the region is characterized by small farms, whose occupants are engaged in a variety of inter-

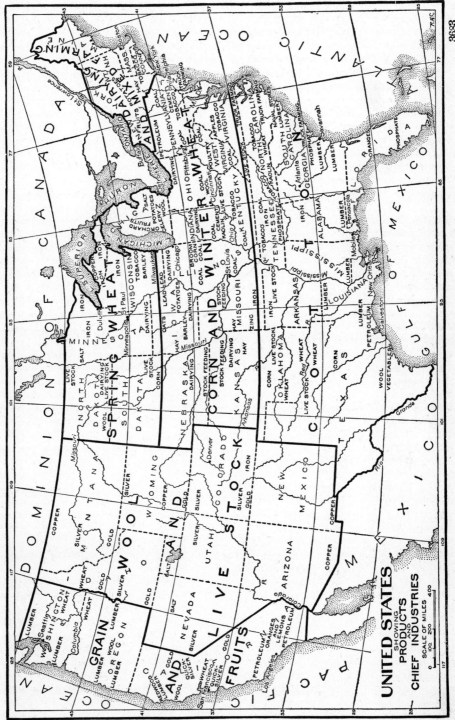

UNITED STATES
SHOWING
PRODUCTS
AND
CHIEF INDUSTRIES

SCALE OF MILES
0   100   200   300   400

ests. The arid region, including the states within the Rocky Mountain plateau and the southern part of California, embraces nearly one-third of the country. Over most of this the soil is fertile, and wherever water can be supplied for irrigation, abundant crops are raised. The national government has undertaken works of gigantic proportions, for the purpose of reclaiming as much as possible of this region. The valleys of the Pacific slope, where well watered, produce abundant crops of all plants which can be raised in that climate.

The product map on page 3683 shows that agriculturally the country is divided into six regions. The words in large type indicate the chief crop or industry in each region. Those in smaller type indicate other products and industries. A careful study of this map will show that the northern New England states and New York are chiefly engaged in mixed farming and dairying, and that each of the other regions is devoted to one or more principal crops or industries, each of which is worthy of special consideration. For the development of agriculture in the country, see AGRICULTURE, and for more particular accounts, see subhead *Agriculture*, under the articles treating of the different states.

Cereals. As a whole, cereals constitute the most important agricultural product of the country. The great region devoted to these crops comprises the states of the Mississippi Basin, portions of Pennsylvania and West Virginia, and portions of Oregon, Washington and California. The leading wheat-producing states are Montana, North Dakota, Kansas, Nebraska and Oklahoma. More than half the crop is winter wheat. The annual crop varies from 750,000,000 to about 850,000,000 bushels, but has reached 932,000,000 bushels. The leading corn-producing states are Illinois, Iowa, Missouri, Indiana, Nebraska and Kansas. The annual crop varies from about 2,500,000,000 bushels to 3,200,000,000 bushels. In 1935 it was 1,400,000,000 bushels. The leading states in oats production are Minnesota and Iowa. The crop amounts to about 1,200,000,000 bushels yearly. Rice is produced in Louisiana, South Carolina, Texas, Georgia, North Carolina and California. The annual crop is about 40,000,000 bushels. Considerable buckwheat is grown in some states, and some of the Northern states also produce more or less rye; but in the production of this grain the United States is far behind some of the European countries.

Cotton and Tobacco. Cotton is the chief product of the Southern states and the one from which they derive the greatest amount of money. The annual crop has reached 16,000,000 bales, but averages 10,000,000.

The leading states in its production are Texas, Mississippi, Georgia, Alabama, South Carolina and Arkansas. Tobacco is also an important crop, and it is generally distributed over the country. The amount grown yearly is about 1,200,000,000 pounds. The leading states in tobacco production, in the order of their importance, are North Carolina, Kentucky, Virginia, Tennessee, Georgia, Pennsylvania, Wisconsin and South Carolina. A number of other states also raise considerable quantities.

Fruit. Horticulture is an important branch of agriculture, and the raising of fruit is the leading occupation in Florida, Delaware, parts of New Jersey, the western part of New York and the southern and central parts of California, while its production engages the attention of a large number of farmers in Washington, Oregon, the mountainous part of Montana and a number of other states. In Florida pineapples and oranges are the chief fruits. In California oranges, lemons, apricots, grapes, prunes and almonds, among the larger fruits, are of greatest importance, while grapes and small fruits are raised in large quantities. Grapes and peaches are grown extensively in New York, and apples and peaches are produced in New York, Michigan, Colorado, Missouri and numerous other states. Small fruits, including raspberries, blackberries and strawberries, are found in nearly all parts of the country where there is sufficient rainfall for their growth.

Other Crops. In Minnesota, Wisconsin and some other Northern states, considerable flax is grown, mostly for the seed. Sugar cane is raised in Louisiana and a few other of the Gulf states, and the sugar beet is grown in many of the states. Potatoes are raised in large quantities in Wisconsin, Minnesota and New York. Sweet potatoes are grown in Virginia, in the southern part of Illinois and in a number of the Southern states. Vegetables are grown for market in Delaware and New Jersey and in nearly all states in which large cities are located. New

THE LIFE-GIVING LAND

From field, plantation and pasture come food and raiment,
industrial products and a multitude of human comforts.
The American farm provides bread for man, food for his
stock, fiber and wool for his clothing, and leather for his
shoes. The American farmer uses modern methods to build

Factory whistles and smokestacks throughout the land symbolize the progress of an industrial nation. Water power and steam operate powerful dynamos, which generate electricity. The electricity turns motors in steel plants and other factories, creating the myriad products of our modern life.

York and the states on the Pacific slope are noted for their production of hops.

Live Stock. Much of the arid region is well suited to grazing, and in this section of the country large herds of cattle and sheep are raised. Texas leads in the production of cattle, and Wyoming is first in the production of sheep. Some of the corn states, particularly Iowa and Illinois, are noted for their beef cattle and hogs. New York, the northern New England states, Iowa, Illinois and Wisconsin are extensively engaged in dairying, and the value of the dairy products is great. The annual production of milk in the United States has amounted to 48 billion quarts a year.

Poultry. The raising of poultry is an important branch of agricultural industry, and it engages many people in all parts of the country, though it has received less attention on the Pacific coast than in other regions. About 700,000,000 fowls are raised annually and 2,000,000,000 eggs are produced. The annual value of the poultry products is about $1,000,000,000. The leading poultry states are Illinois, Missouri, Iowa, Ohio, Indiana, California, and Texas.

Manufacturing Industries

Causes of Development. During the early period of existence as a nation everything was made by hand, and the clothing and other necessities for the family were produced in the home. The mother was housekeeper, spinner, weaver and tailoress; the father was farmer, carpenter, blacksmith and harnessmaker, and the traveling shoemaker came around once or twice a year and made shoes for the family. Gradually, these industries began to be separated. One family in the settlement made the cloth, one man did the carpenter work and another became a blacksmith. Shops were erected, and where there was water power simple machinery was installed. As the number of settlers increased, factories became more numerous and the distinction between trades more marked. Nevertheless, the growth of the manufacturing industries was slow until about 1860, and since that date, they have developed more rapidly than any other lines of industry. Now the United States is the leading manufacturing country of the world, producing more than one-third of the world's manufactured products.

The chief causes for this rapid development of the United States as a manufacturing nation are the country's abundant agricultural resources, its mineral resources, its extensive forests, the remarkable transportation facilities afforded, the inventive genius of the people and the opportunities for an extensive trade between the states. The extent and variety of agricultural products assure an abundance of food supplies for the people, and the methods of agriculture are such that a comparatively small proportion of the inhabitants can supply food for the entire nation and also for export to foreign lands. This leaves large numbers free to engage in other occupations, and this enables a larger proportion of the people to engage in manufacturing industries than would be possible were the agricultural conditions such that nearly all were dependent for support upon their own efforts in tilling the soil.

The abundant supply of coal, iron and other useful metals makes the manufacture of many products convenient and comparatively cheap. This is particularly true of iron and steel and their products, while the presence of clay and various forms of building stone is of equal advantage in the construction of factories and other establishments connected directly or indirectly with manufacturing industries. The great forest areas provide an abundance of lumber and timber for all articles made of wood; hence this line of manufactures has been developed on a very large scale.

In addition to the coal for fuel, thousands of streams furnish abundant water power, and the invention of the electric motor has brought into use many power sites so far from manufacturing centers that the location of factories on them formerly was impracticable. Since electric power can be carried distances without great loss, it may operate factories hundreds of miles from its source. The perfection of the gasoline engine has greatly increased the power for propelling machinery. While not adapted to large factories this engine supplies power to many small industries.

The American people have always been noted for their mechanical ingenuity, and they have produced a great number of machines and devices which have greatly influenced, and in some cases have revolutionized, the industries of the world. Chief among these are the cotton gin, the sewing machine, the steamboat, the reaping machine, the telegraph and the telephone. To these, many others of lesser importance might be added. Their combined effect has been to simplify and cheapen many processes of manufacturing, transportation and communication, all of which have aided in the development of manufacturing industry.

The freedom of commerce between the states is one of the greatest advantages enjoyed by the country. In no other region of the world is there such an extent of country entirely free from tariff barriers. In addition to this, the country embraces localities whose needs differ widely; consequently there is a demand for interchange of products among these sections, and these conditions have combined to build up a domestic commerce much greater than that known in any other country in the world. This has led to the development of various lines of manufactures. No other country has such extensive and numerous transportation lines, both by water and by rail; hence the carrying of commodities from one section to another is comparatively easy and cheap.

Location of Manufacturing Districts. The manufacturing districts are very unevenly distributed over the country. In general, those states east of the Mississippi River and north of the Ohio are the leading manufacturing states, and more than four-fifths of all the manufactures in the country are produced within this territory. Without this limit are a few important manufactures, and these are being rapidly developed. Among them are the iron industries of Alabama and Georgia and the cotton industries of Alabama, Georgia, North Carolina and South Carolina. Some of the large cities on the Mississippi are also important manufacturing centers. Chief among these are Saint Louis, Saint Paul and Minneapolis. On the Pacific coast, lumbering, the manufacture of furniture and some other industries are fully developed, while others are increasing in number and importance from year to year.

Leading Industries. Among the many manufactured products of the country the following are the most important: Food products, including flour and meat; iron and steel; textiles; automobiles; lumber and its allied products; leather and its finished products; metals other than iron and steel, with various allied products, and paper. To the manufacture of these commodities should be added printing and publishing, as another major industry.

Food Products. The time was when the farmer carried his wheat to the local mill, brought home the flour, and the wife cooked all the food for the household, but that time has passed, and now much of the food consumed in rural districts as well as the cities is prepared in large establishments. In addition to flour and cured meat, canned goods, breakfast foods, biscuits and numerous other articles are turned out in large quantities of an immense annual value.

The great fruit-growing regions of California, Florida and other States have developed a vast industry in the raising and marketing of citrus and other valuable fruits. Thanks to the development of improved methods of refrigeration in transport, oranges, grapefruit, grapes, and other varieties of succulent fruits are accessible practically everywhere in the country.

Iron and Steel. The United States produces more iron and steel than any other country. At the outbreak of the World War (1914) the output of pig iron and steel in the United States was nearly equal to the combined output of Germany, France and Great Britain, the next three largest producers. The leading states in the manufacture of iron and steel products are Pennsylvania, Illinois, Ohio and Indiana. Minnesota and Michigan lead in the production of iron ore.

Textiles. New England is the great center for the manufacture of cotton goods, and Massachusetts is the leading state in this industry. Outside of New England, North Carolina, South Carolina, Georgia and Alabama have established extensive cotton mills. In the output of her cotton goods, the United States is second only to Great Britain. Next in importance to the manufacture of cotton goods is the manufacture of woolens, including carpets and hats. Massachusetts, Pennsylvania and Rhode Island are the states in which this industry is principally located, Philadelphia being one of the greatest centers of carpet manufacture in the world. In the manufacture of silk goods the United States is the leading nation, followed by France. The great centers of the industry are in New Jersey and Pennsylvania. Extensive factories for the production of knit goods are also found throughout the New England and North Atlantic states.

Lumber. The lumbering industries naturally center in those states containing extensive forest areas. It is now largest in Oregon and Washington.

Leather. Pennsylvania ranks first in the tanning and finishing of leather, while Massachusetts is the leading state in the production of boots and shoes. Perhaps in no other industry is the effect of American invention and perfection of organization better seen than in the manufacture of boots and shoes. Owing to the invention of a number of ingenious machines, this industry has been highly organized, and the United States produces more boots and shoes than any other country.

Paper. In the manufacture of paper the United States also leads the world. Much of this product is now made from wood pulp, which is generally manufactured in the states that have large supplies of suitable timber for this purpose. The annual output of paper and wood pulp products is about 5,000,000 tons.

Automobiles. Although it is one of the youngest industries in the country, the manufacture of automobiles has reached third place among the manufacturing industries. In 1929, the best year of the industry, 5,358,414 automobiles and trucks were made; the value of all automobiles owned in the country was about $3,000,000,000, and of motor trucks about $600,000,000. Registrations numbered over 26,500,000.

The leading states in the industry are Michigan, Ohio, Wisconsin and New York.

Other Industries. Connecticut leads in the manufacture of small articles, such as needles, pins, buttons, clocks, and various kinds of hardware. The great watch factories of the country are at Waltham, Mass., and Elgin, Ill. The manufacture of electrical apparatus and appliances is extensive and still on the increase. Before the World War the United States depended upon Germany for most of its chemicals and dyestuffs, but the war prevented the exportation of these products from Germany, and this condition stimulated manufacturing chemists to supply the market with American-made goods. The war also caused a great advance in shipbuilding, placing the country second only to Great Britain in this industry. In the manufacture of agricultural implements and machinery the United States surpasses every other nation. This industry is most extensive in Illinois, Chicago being the leading center. Other states in which it is large are Ohio, New York and Wisconsin. The yearly output is about $600,000,000. Annual production of clay, glass and stone products is over $1,000,000,000. Besides these larger industries there are many smaller ones, considered as miscellaneous, whose annual output exceeds $1,000,000,000 in value, while the hand trades, or those occupations in which the articles are produced by the use of hand tools, have an annual output exceeding $1,184,000,000.

Transportation and Communication

Waterways. The United States has over 12,000 miles of seacoast and more than 18,000 miles of inland waterways. Formerly the inland waterways were of the greatest importance, since by their means the interior of the country found an outlet to the sea. The most important systems of these waterways are those of the Mississippi River and tributaries and the Great Lakes. Since the construction of railways, the river systems have become less valuable; but the completion of canals, by means of which steamers of deep draft can pass from the lakes to the ocean through the Saint Lawrence River has rendered this waterway of great importance. In connection with it, the construction of the Erie Canal, early in the nineteenth century, opened the way for the transportation of commodities between the Atlantic seaboard and the interior. The important canals are described under their titles.

Railroads. The first railroads of importance in the United States were constructed in 1830 and 1832, and at the close of the latter year there were 23 miles of railway in the country. In 1935 the mileage was over 250,000 or more than that of the entire continent of Europe. It is nearly one-third of all the mileage of the world. Naturally the older states contain the larger number of lines; the portion of the country east of the Mississippi River is fully supplied with railways, so that nearly all towns have convenient means of communication. In the Appalachian region, the longest lines extend approximately north and south; west of these mountains the general trend of the railways is east and west; in the Mississippi Valley there are a number of north and south lines, connecting Chicago and Saint

Louis with important commercial ports on the Gulf of Mexico. Some of these lines extend into Mexico.

Six transcontinental lines now extend to the Pacific coast, and the Canadian Pacific, the Canadian Northern and the Grand Trunk Pacific, only a short distance north of the international boundary line, also render some service to the inhabitants of the northern part of the country. Electric railways connect many towns situated within a few miles of one another, and these systems are being extended to the rural districts, especially in the eastern part of the country and the southern part of California. On the whole, the country is well supplied with water and rail transportation.

Roads. The development of railways and their importance in the industrial systems of the country has caused neglect of wagon roads, and in the construction of these important means of transportation the United States is far behind European countries. In most states the roads are poor, and in some states, during certain seasons of the year, they are well-nigh impassable.

In 1893 the United States Department of Agriculture inaugurated the Good Roads Movement, and since that time the national government has given some assistance in improving the public highways. In 1914 Congress appropriated $25,000,000 for the construction and improvement of roads, and in 1918 this amount was increased to $266,-750,000, to be spent within the next three years. This money was divided among the states on condition that each state must appropriate as much money as it received from the national government. Federal coöperation has been continued since on a generous scale, aided by state appropriations.

Air Service. There are about twenty-five companies of major importance engaged in transport service. They operate about 4,500 'planes, and cover nearly 50,000,000 miles a year. Passengers carried now number more than 250,000 yearly; mail carried has reached a total of more than 9,000,000 pounds a year, and express, more than 3,000,000 pounds. Passenger 'planes are increasing in capacity. The continent is spanned between daylight and darkness.

Commerce

Domestic Commerce. The domestic commerce of the United States is larger than that of any other country and far exceeds its trade with foreign nations. The widely separated sections of the country, differing from one another in climate, soil and products, create a great demand in each section for the products of the others, and in the supplying of this demand an extensive commerce has sprung up. The amount of this trade cannot be obtained, since no record is kept of the shipments of merchandise that are not entered at customhouses; but that it is very great is evident to all who are conversant with commercial systems.

Foreign Commerce. Before 1915, in its foreign commerce the United States was exceeded by Great Britain and Germany and ranked third among the great nations. But the World War created such a demand for American products that it advanced to first place. In 1920 it occupied first place, with imports and exports exceeding 13 billion dollars. This immense total gradually decreased until under normal conditions the totals were between 3 billion and 5 billion dollars. Under normal conditions the exports are divided among various products as follows: Agricultural products, 62 per cent; manufactures, 30 per cent; forest products, 4 per cent; mining products, 3 per cent. The imports have the following apportionment: Raw material, 38 per cent; food and domestic animals, 21 per cent; manufactures, 16.79 per cent; luxuries, 14.47 per cent.

Most of the foreign trade was carried on with the European nations in the following order of importance: The United Kingdom, Germany, France, Netherlands, Belgium. Italy and Russia also have a considerable share. Of Asiatic nations Japan has the first place and China the second. Europe takes about three-fourths of the exports and supplies one-half of the imports. Of the other foreign nations, Canada is the most important in North America, and Brazil, Argentina and Chile lead in South America. The great seaports engaged in European trade are New York, Boston, Philadelphia and Baltimore, while those engaged in trade with China, Japan and the Philippines are San Francisco, Seattle and Tacoma. The Panama Canal has also brought the Atlantic ports much nearer these far-eastern countries.

While American products are found in all countries of the world, the foreign commerce of the United States has until recently been crippled, from the fact that nearly all of it is carried in the ships of other nations, American vessels being engaged almost entirely in the coastwise trade. During the World War the number of American merchant ships was greatly increased, and most of the new ships were engaged in foreign trade, placing the country for a few years approximately in the position it held before the Civil War.

The People

Colonial Period. During the Colonial Period settlements were made by English, Scotch, Irish, Swedes, Dutch, French and Germans, but the people from the British

tion, by their force of character and superior education they impressed their ideals upon the others, and at the beginning of the Revolutionary War the 2,000,000 or more inhabitants of the English colonies were firmly united. Moreover, during this century and a half of their existence the political ideas of the colonies were developed and established so firmly that there was little danger of their being changed by immigration in the years that followed, and the country entered upon its national existence with a population firmly united as to nationality and social and political ideas.

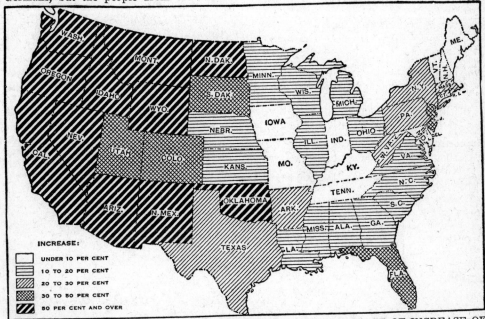

MAP CLASSIFYING STATES WITH RESPECT TO THE PERCENTAGE OF INCREASE OF POPULATION BETWEEN TWELFTH AND FOURTEENTH CENSUSES.

Isles far outnumbered all others. With the exception of the Germans, about 100,000 of whom settled in Pennsylvania, the other nationalities in time blended with the English, so that in language, customs, government and commercial methods the colonies were thoroughly Anglo-Saxon.

Many of the first settlers were people of exceptional character and ability, who were driven to the New World by civil or religious persecution. This applies to the Quakers and Germans in Pennsylvania and the Huguenots of South Carolina, as well as to the Puritans of New England. Although these people were fewer in number than those who came to better their condi-

Increase in Population. The first national census was taken in 1790. At that time the United States contained in round numbers 4,000,000 inhabitants. About one-fifth of these, or 750,000, were negroes. The growth in population by decades is shown in the table on page 3690.

The greatest growth has been in the central and western states, where the increase has been unusually large. This is due to the fertility of the soil in the Mississippi Valley and the opportunities and advantages offered by a new country. These attracted large numbers of immigrants.

Movement Westward. In 1790 the center of population was 23 miles east of Baltimore.

This center moved westward with varying degrees; the greatest movement took place during the decade from 1850 to 1860, when

CENSUS	POPULATION, excluding Alaska, etc.	INCREASE	
		NUMBER	PER CENT
1940........	131,669,275	8,894,229	7.2
1930........	122,775,046	17,064,426	16.1
1920........	105,710,620	13,738,354	14.9
1910........	91,972,266	15,977,691	21.0
1900........	75,568,686	12,946,436	20.7
1890........	62,622,250	12,466,467	24.9
1880........	50,155,783	11,597,412	30.1
1870........	38,558,371	7,115,050	22.6
1860........	31,443,321	8,251,445	35.6
1850........	23,191,876	6,122,423	35.9
1840........	17,069,453	4,203,433	32.7
1830........	12,866,020	3,227,567	33.5
1820........	9,638,453	2,398,572	33.1
1810........	7,239,881	1,931,398	36.4
1800........	5,308,483	1,379,269	35.1
1790........	3,929,214	....	.....

the center advanced 80.6 miles. The accompanying map shows the approximate location of the center of population at each census from 1790 to 1940.

Density. At the 1940 census the average density of population for the United States

168; Illinois, 141; Delaware, 134. All other states had fewer than 100 people to the square mile. Wyoming, with 2.6, and Nevada, with 1.0, were the least densely populated of the states.

Percentage Increase. The percentage increase for the country as a whole, from 1790 to 1940, is shown in the accompanying table, compiled by the Census Bureau.

The increase from 1930 to 1940 was largest in the District of Columbia—36.2 per cent. First of the states was Florida, 29.2 per cent. Then came New Mexico, 25.6 per cent; California, 21.7 per cent; Nevada, 21.1 per cent; Idaho, 17.9 per cent; Arizona, 14.6 per cent; and Oregon, with a percentage of 14.2.

Growth of Cities. Since the organization of the government, the population of cities and towns has increased far more, proportionately, than the population of the country at large, and this proportion has been constantly increasing. In 1790, 3.4 people out of every 100 lived in cities of 8,000 or more inhabitants. In 1840 this

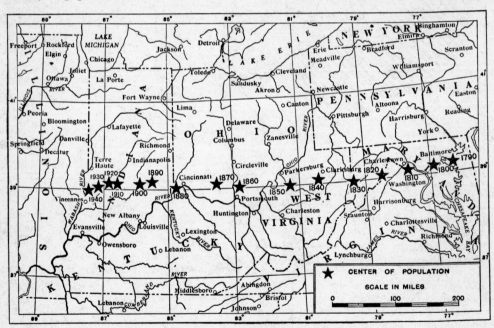

MOVEMENT OF THE CENTER OF POPULATION

was 44.2. Rhode Island, the smallest state, having 674.2 persons to the square mile, was the most densely populated; New Jersey, with 553.1, was second. Massachusetts had 545.9; Connecticut, 348; New York, 281; Pennsylvania, 219; Maryland, 184; Ohio,

proportion had increased to 8.5 per 100. In 1850, one-eighth of the people dwelt in cities of 8,000 or over; in 1890, over one-fourth, and by 1930, over one-third. In 1940, over half the population was classed as urban. This rapid growth of cities is due to the establishment of the factory system, necessitating the bringing together of a large number of operatives; to increased facilities of transportation; to immigration; and to a desire for better schools.

The following table gives the seventy largest cities of the United States. The population statistics are government census returns for 1940:

New York, N. Y. 7,454 995
Chicago, Ill. 3,396,808
Philadelphia, Pa. 1,931,334
Detroit, Mich. 1,623,452
Los Angeles, Calif. 1,504,277
Cleveland, Ohio 878,336
Baltimore, Md. 859,100
St. Louis, Mo. 816,048
Boston, Mass. 770,816
Pittsburgh, Pa. 671,659
Washington, D. C. 663,091
San Francisco, Calif. 634,536
Milwaukee, Wis. 587,472
Buffalo, N. Y. 575,901
New Orleans, La. 494,537
Minneapolis, Minn. 492,370
Cincinnati, Ohio 455,610
Newark, N. J. 429,760
Kansas City, Mo. 399,178
Indianapolis, Ind. 386,972
Houston, Texas 384,514
Seattle, Wash. 368,302
Rochester, N. Y. 324,975
Denver, Colo. 322,412
Louisville, Ky. 319,077
Columbus, Ohio 306,087
Portland, Ore. 305,394
Atlanta, Ga. 302,288
Oakland, Calif. 302,163
Jersey City, N. J. 301,173
Dallas, Texas 294,734
Memphis, Tenn. 292,942
St. Paul, Minn. 287,736
Toledo, Ohio 282,349
Birmingham, Ala 267,583
San Antonio, Texas 253,854
Providence, R. I. 253,504
Akron, Ohio 244,791
Omaha, Neb. 223,844
Dayton, Ohio 210,718
Syracuse, N. Y. 205,967
Oklahoma City, Okla. 204,424
San Diego, Calif. 203,341
Worcester, Mass. 193,694
Richmond, Va. 193,042
Fort Worth, Texas 177,662
Jacksonville, Fla. 173,065
Miami, Fla. 172,172
Youngstown, Ohio 167,720
Nashville, Tenn. 167,402
Hartford, Conn. 166,267
Grand Rapids, Mich. 164,292
Long Beach, Calif. 164,271
New Haven, Conn. 160,605
Des Moines, Iowa 159,819
Flint, Mich. 151,543
Salt Lake City, Utah 149,934
Springfield, Mass. 149,554

Bridgeport, Conn. 147,121
Norfolk, Va. 144,332
Yonkers, N. Y. 142,598
Tulsa, Okla. 142,157
Scranton, Pa. 140,404
Paterson, N. J. 139,656
Albany, N. Y. 130,577
Chattanooga, Tenn. 128,163
Trenton, N. J. 124,697
Spokane, Wash. 122,001
Kansas City, Kan. 121,458
Fort Wayne, Ind. 118,410

Immigration. Previous to 1800 no statistics of immigration were kept. Good authorities, however, estimate that at the beginning of the Revolutionary War about one-fifth of the people were immigrants and that from 1790 to 1800 about 5,000 people entered the country each year. During the first half-century following the adoption of the Constitution, immigration was small; and previous to the Civil War, only about 1,000,000 foreigners had settled in the United States. After 1870 immigrants began to come by the thousands, and by 1910 they had added nearly 30,000,000 to the population. Previous to 1895 most of the immigrants were from the northern countries of Europe, the majority coming from the British Isles, Germany, Norway and Sweden. Most of them settled in the new states, in the northern part of the Mississippi Valley, where their descendants now constitute a thrifty, law-abiding and industrious people. After that time, however, the character of immigration almost entirely changed, and by far the larger proportion of immigrants came from Italy and Austria-Hungary, with smaller numbers from other countries of Southern Europe. Since 1929 only about 153,900 immigrants are admitted per year.

In 1850 only 9.7 people in 100 among the population were foreign born, while in 1930 the proportion exceeded 12. For the year ending June 30, 1910, 1,041,570 aliens entered the United States, and each year thereafter until 1915 over 1,000,000 immigrants were received each year. Between 1820 and 1914 about 32,000,000 aliens entered the country, exclusive of temporary arrivals, a number equal to almost one-third the entire population. Immigration was greatly reduced during the World War. In 1914, the number of immigrants was 1,218,480; in 1915 it was 326,700, and for 1916 and 1917 less than 300,000. More than 38,000,000 immigrants have been admitted since 1870. In 1917 Congress passed a law restricting immigration to those who could read at least one language. For a fuller account of this subject, see the article IMMIGRATION.

Color. In 1790 the negroes constituted one-fifth of the population and in 1910, less than one-ninth; that is, of the entire population, 9,827,763 were negroes. In 1930 the number had increased to 11,891,000, according to the census of the United States government.

The great majority of negroes are found in the states south of the Ohio River, including Texas and Arkansas, though bordering states contain large numbers. In South Carolina and Mississippi, the negroes outnumber the white population. In 1930 there were also 74,954 Chinese and 138,834 Japanese in the United States. The greater pro-

Germany, Switzerland, Scotland, Holland, France and England. In large cities and in some rural communities immigrants settle in communities and for years maintain their language and many of the customs of the Old World; but in most instances the children educated in the public schools become Americanized.

With very few exceptions, English is the language spoken throughout the country, and everywhere it is the official language of the land. After the United States entered World War I, and for a period after the war ended, many states prohibited the teaching of languages of the opposing countries in the public schools.

In 1900 the population was 76,303,387, not reckoning the outlying possessions. In 1920

GREAT SEAL OF THE UNITED STATES (SEE PAGE 3241)

portion of oriental immigrants are confined to the Pacific states. There were also in the country 332,397 Indians, most of whom were on reservations. The Indian population, after a decrease, has begun to increase. The number of Japanese increased more than 25 per cent in ten years, mostly in California and Washington.

Present Character. The population of the United States comprises representatives of nearly every race and nation, and the large cities are probably more cosmopolitan than any others in the world. Because of this characteristic, the percentage of illiteracy in the country is higher than it is in some of the European countries, namely,

it was 105,710,620, and in 1930, 122,775,046. In 1940 the census reported a population of 131,669,275 for continental United States, and 2,595,956 for outlying possessions, excluding the Philippines.

Government

General Features. The national government began with the Continental Congress, which, after the Declaration of Independence, framed the first national constitution, known as the Articles of Confederation. This instrument, however, was soon found to be inadequate to the needs of the country and in 1787 the Constitution, establishing the present government, was framed. As organized under the Constitution, the government of the United States is a federal republic, in which the states are self-governing, each having a republican form of government.

The powers of the national government are defined by the Constitution, and all powers not specifically delegated to the United States are reserved to the states and to the people. However, the states are prohibited from the exercise of certain powers, among which are making treaties with foreign nations, declaring war and coining money. There are other powers, also, which they are forbidden to exercise except by permission of the national government.

The national government is organized in three coördinate departments, legislative, executive and judicial.

While these departments, within certain limits, are independent of one another, each is so related to the others as to form, with them, an organic whole. For instance, laws must originate in the legislative department, but the president has the power of veto, and the judicial department can render any law null and void by declaring it unconstitutional. The legislative department also has power to impeach and try United States officers, including the head of the executive department, and the president cannot appoint to certain offices except by the advice and consent of the Senate. The relation of these departments to each other is shown in the diagram accompanying the article CIVIL GOVERNMENT, and the government of each state is described in the article on that state.

Legislative Department. The legislative department consists of a Congress, comprising a House of Representatives and a Senate. The House of Representatives consists of members apportioned among the states according to population, the apportionment being made every ten years. Each state has at least one Representative, whatever its population. The members are chosen at a general election, on the first Tuesday after the first Monday of November, in even-numbered years, and they hold their offices for two years. The apportionment in 1911 was one Representative to every 211,430 inhabitants, and the number of Representatives according to this apportionment was 435. The House of Representatives elects one of its members as the presiding officer, entitled *speaker,* for a term of two years. All bills for raising revenue must originate in this branch of Congress, but in passing bills, the two houses must agree, and they have equal power to reject measures.

The Senate is composed of two members from each state, formerly chosen by the state legislature, but since the adoption of the Seventeenth Amendment, elected by popular vote for a term of six years. Members are so elected that the terms of one-third of the Senators expire every two years. The presiding officer is the Vice-President of the United States. The Senate has sole power to try cases of impeachment and to ratify treaties with foreign nations.

Executive Department. The executive department consists of the President, the Vice-President and such other officers as the President may select or as may be provided for by law. The President and the Vice-President are chosen by electors for a term of four years. In order that this branch of the government might be efficiently administered, Washington established, in 1789, the following departments: State, War and Navy, Treasury and Postoffice. Since then the following departments have been added: Interior, 1849; Justice, 1870; Agriculture, 1889; and Commerce and Labor, 1903, which in 1913 was divided into the Department of Commerce and the Department of Labor. With the exception of the Department of Justice and the Postoffice Department, the officers at the heads of the departments are styled Secretaries. The Attorney-General is the head of the Department of Justice, and the Postmaster-General is at the head of the Postoffice Department. These heads of the department, taken collectively, constitute the President's Cabinet. Each of the departments is explained under its title. The heads of departments and other important officers are appointed by the President, with the advice and consent of the Senate, while many minor officers are appointed by the President without consulting the Senate, or by the heads of departments.

The President is commander in chief of the army and navy, has the power to call Congress in special session, when necessary, and can veto any bill passed by Congress, though such a bill may be passed over his veto by a two-thirds vote of the members of each house. It is the President's duty to send a message to Congress at the beginning of each session, setting forth the condition of the country and recommending such legislation as he believes is necessary. He also has power to grant reprieves and pardons to persons who are sentenced by United States courts, and it is his duty to see that the laws are executed throughout the country and all of its dependencies.

The Judicial Department. The Judicial Department consists of the Supreme Court and such other courts as may from time to time be established by law. At present the United States courts consist of the Supreme Court, nine Circuit Courts of Appeals, 103

missioners appointed by the United States, and the inhabitants were given an active part in the management of government affairs as rapidly as they became competent. Now both of these possessions have their own legislatures. For a detailed statement, the reader is referred to the subhead *Government* in the articles describing each of these possessions. Alaska and Hawaii are organized territories. The Virgin Islands, acquired by purchase from Denmark in 1917, are under an appointed governor.

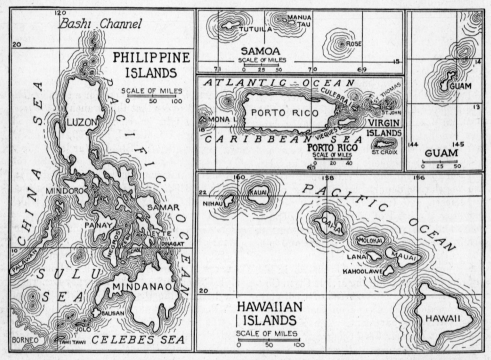

POSSESSIONS OF THE UNITED STATES NOT ON THE AMERICAN CONTINENT

District Courts, a Court of Claims, a Court of Private Land Claims, a Court of Appeals for the District of Columbia, the Supreme Court of the District of Columbia, the territorial courts and admiralty courts. The organization and jurisdiction of these courts are described in the article COURTS.

Outlying Possessions. The acquisition of the Philippine Islands and Porto Rico in 1898 entailed upon the United States a new problem in government. The inhabitants of these islands had never governed themselves, and they were not prepared to assume the responsibilities of government. They were at first governed by a governor-general and com-

State Governments. The government of each state is based upon a constitution, and in the main follows the plan of the national government. Nearly all states have a legislature of two branches, a Senate and a House of representatives. In many the members of the senate are elected for a longer term than the members of the house, and in some states the terms of only a part of the senators expire at one time, so that one-half of them are chosen at each general election. The executive officers of the state are usually a governor, a lieutenant-governor, a secretary of state, a treasurer, an attorney-general and a superintendent or commissioner of public instruction. To these some states add an auditor of public accounts and a comptroller.

The state government deals with all affairs pertaining to the interests of the state, such as laws governing marriage and divorce, the obligation of contracts, the settling of estates, the transference of real property and the regulation of loans, interests and mortgages.

In the matter of courts there is a greater divergence of plan. Almost every state has a supreme court, which has a limited original jurisdiction, and to which cases of certain importance may be appealed from the lower courts. Below this are circuit courts, which usually have jurisdiction over several coun-

township officers are chosen at an annual town meeting, in which all voters have a right to participate. All the public business of the local community is in the hands of these town officers. In the county system the township is not recognized, the county being the principal unit of government. The only subdivision is the parish. Under this plan nearly all matters of public interest are looked after by county officers, who are chosen at regular elections. In most states these are known as county commissioners, or county supervisors. Between New England and Virginia a third form of local government grew up. It was the outgrowth of the two systems described above and may be

THE DEVELOPMENT OF THE FLAG

ties, and in some states there are county courts. Almost all the states have county probate courts for the settlement of estates.

Local Government. The early colonists established two forms of local government, the *township* form in New England, and the *county* form in Virginia and other southern colonies. These shaped the local government in most of the original states. Under the former plan the township is the unit, and the

called the *mixed,* or *township-county,* system. Under this scheme certain minor duties devolve upon township officers, while more important local duties rest with county officers. The officers of the county include commissioners, representing the different towns of the county, an auditor, a register of deeds, a treasurer and a superintendent of schools, or school commissioner. Other officers are sometimes added. This system, on the whole,

STATE	POPULAR NAME	CAPITAL	TOTAL AREA SQUARE MILES	RANK	ADMITTED TO THE UNION	POPULATION CENSUS 1940
Alabama	Cotton State	Montgomery	51,609	28	1819	2,832,961
Arizona	Sunset State	Phoenix	113,909	5	1912	499,261
Arkansas	Wonder State	Little Rock	53,102	26	1836	1,949,387
California	Golden State	Sacramento	158,693	2	1850	6,907,387
Colorado	Centennial State	Denver	104,247	7	1876	1,123,296
Connecticut	Nutmeg State	Hartford	5,009	46	*	1,709,242
Delaware	Blue Hen State	Dover	2,057	47	*	266,505
Florida	Peninsula State	Tallahassee	58,560	21	1845	1,897,414
Georgia	Empire State of the South	Atlanta	58,876	20	*	3,123,723
Idaho	Gem of the Mountains	Boise	83,557	12	1890	524,873
Illinois	Prairie State	Springfield	56,400	23	1818	7,897,241
Indiana	Hoosier State	Indianapolis	36,291	37	1816	3,427,796
Iowa	Hawkeye State	Des Moines	56,280	24	1846	2,538,268
Kansas	Sunflower State	Topeka	82,276	13	1861	1,801,028
Kentucky	Blue Grass State	Frankfort	40,395	36	1792	2,845,627
Louisiana	Pelican State	Baton Rouge	48,523	30	1812	2,363,880
Maine	Pine Tree State	Augusta	33,215	38	1820	847,226
Maryland	Old Line State	Annapolis	10,577	41	*	1,821,244
Massachusetts	Old Bay State	Boston	8,257	44	*	4,316,721
Michigan	Wolverine State	Lansing	58,216	22	1837	5,256,106
Minnesota	Gopher State	St. Paul	84,068	11	1858	2,792,300
Mississippi	Magnolia State	Jackson	47,716	31	1817	2,183,796
Missouri	Bullion State	Jefferson City	69,674	18	1821	3,784,664
Montana	Treasure State	Helena	147,138	3	1889	559,456
Nebraska	Tree Planters' State	Lincoln	77,237	14	1867	1,315,834
Nevada	Silver State	Carson City	110,540	6	1864	110,247
New Hampshire	Granite State	Concord	9,304	43	*	491,524
New Jersey	Garden State	Trenton	7,836	45	*	4,160,165
New Mexico	Sunshine State	Santa Fe	121,666	4	1912	531,818
New York	Empire State	Albany	49,576	29	*	13,479,142
North Carolina	Old North State	Raleigh	52,712	27	*	3,571,623
North Dakota	Flickertail State	Bismarck	70,665	16	1889	641,935
Ohio	Buckeye State	Columbus	41,222	34	1803	6,907,612
Oklahoma	Boomer State	Oklahoma City	69,919	17	1907	2,336,434
Oregon	Beaver State	Salem	96,981	9	1859	1,089,684
Pennsylvania	Keystone State	Harrisburg	45,333	32	*	9,900,180
Rhode Island	Little Rhody	Providence	1,214	48	*	713,346
South Carolina	Palmetto State	Columbia	31,055	39	*	1,899,804
South Dakota	Sunshine State	Pierre	77,047	15	1889	642,961
Tennessee	Volunteer State	Nashville	42,246	33	1796	2,915,841
Texas	Lone Star State	Austin	267,339	1	1845	6,414,824
Utah	Salt Lake State	Salt Lake City	84,916	10	1896	550,310
Vermont	Green Mountain State	Montpelier	9,609	42	1791	359,231
Virginia	Old Dominion	Richmond	40,815	35	*	2,677,773
Washington	Evergreen State	Olympia	68,192	19	1889	1,736,191
West Virginia	Panhandle State	Charleston	24,181	40	1863	1,901,974
Wisconsin	Badger State	Madison	56,154	25	1848	3,137,587
Wyoming	Equality State	Cheyenne	97,914	8	1890	250,742

*Original State.

is more satisfactory than either of the others, and it has influenced the systems of local government in practically all of the western states. It combines sufficient local interest with an economy in management that is not possible under the old township system.

Territories. As the national domain was settled, territorial forms of government were organized to exercise control over such areas as would best meet the needs of the inhabitants. As the territories became more densely populated they were subdivided, and the subdivisions were in time admitted into the Union and became states. Under a territorial government the governor and territorial judges are appointed by the President with the advice and consent of the Senate; otherwise the territory administers its local affairs, the same as does a state, electing a legislature which enacts laws to meet the needs of the inhabitants. Alaska and Hawaii are territories.

Finance. The Constitution gives Congress power to levy and collect direct taxes, duties on imported goods and excise taxes. Direct taxation soon proved to be unpop-

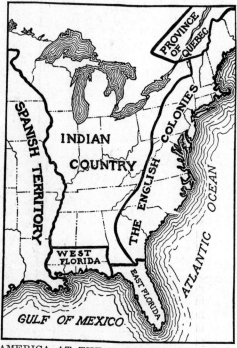

AMERICA AT THE TIME OF THE REVO-
LUTION

ular, and except in extreme cases, such as war, rebellion and famine, was rarely adopted until 1913, when an income tax law was passed. Most of the government's revenue, however, until 1920 was derived from import duties and excise taxes on spirituous liquors, tobacco and other articles of manufacture, particularly luxuries. In that year the nation lost its liquor revenue for 13 years through the prohibition amendment. In 1917 taxes were levied on many articles not ordinarily taxed, because of the expenses incurred on account of the World War.

The income is ample for the usual needs of the government. Loans are occasionally obtained through the sale of bonds. During the World War five such loans were made, aggregating $19,100,000,000. Four of them were designated as Liberty Loans, and the fifth as the Victory Loan. All were oversubscribed. United States bonds are usually payable after a long period, and while the interest is low, the permanency of the investment and the perfect security offered

by the government make them very desirable to capitalists.

The most important items of expenditure are pensions, the postoffice, the army, the navy and the interest on the public debt.

Political Divisions. Within the United States proper there are 48 states and 1 federal district. The external possessions consist of the territories of Alaska and Hawaii; Guam, the Philippines, Tutuila, Porto Rico, the Virgin Islands, formerly the Danish West Indies, and a few other small islands. At the adoption of the Constitution there were thirteen organized states, and these are known as the Original States. The first new state admitted was Vermont, in 1791, and the last were New Mexico and Arizona, which came into the Union in 1912. The outlying possessions are described under their titles. The table on page 3696 includes only the states within the United States proper. The figures given are taken from the United States Census of 1930. Arizona and New Mexico, the latest additions to the union of states, elect one Representative each. Each state will be found described under its title.

Territorial Expansion

At the organization of the government, the Mississippi River formed the western boundary of the United States, and the

UNITED STATES IN 1800

area of the country was 828,000 square miles. Only about 300,000 square miles, or a little over one-third of this area, was actually settled. In 1803 the first great addition of

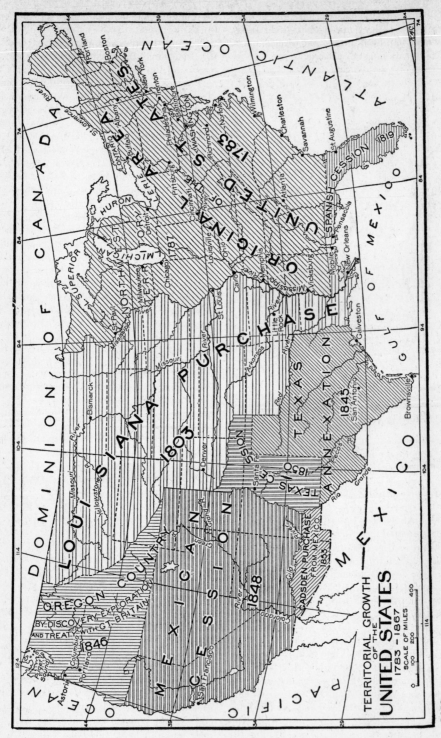

TERRITORIAL GROWTH
OF THE
UNITED STATES
1783-1867

SCALE OF MILES
0   100   200   300   400

3698

territory was made by the purchase of Louisiana. Sixteen years later, this was followed by the acquisition of Florida. With these accessions of territory, the country was openly committed to the policy of expanding her domains, so that in the admission of Texas and the taking over of the territory ceded by Mexico no new policy was established, except in the method pursued. Thus far all territory acquired had been adjoining the United States, but in 1867 Secretary Seward, in the purchase of Alaska, took a radical step, in acquiring territory somewhat remote from the country. A still more radical step was taken in the annexation of Hawaii and the acquisition of the Philippine Islands and Porto Rico. In 1917 the Danish West Indies were purchased and renamed the Virgin Islands. Each of these possessions is described under its title.

The following table contains data concerning the territory added to the United States:

TERRITORIAL DIVISION	YEAR	AREA ADDED (SQ. MI.)	PURCHASE PRICE
Louisiana	1803	875,025	$15,000,000
Florida	1819	70,107	5,499,768
Texas	1845	389,795	....
Oregon Territory	1846	288,689	....
Mexican Cession	1848	523,802	18,250,000†
Gadsden Purchase	1853	36,211	10,000,000
Alaska	1867	590,884	7,200,000
Hawaiian Islands	1897	6,449	....
Porto Rico	1898	3,435	....
Guam	1898	210	....
Philippine Islands	1898	114,958	20,000,000
Tutuila (Samoa Is.)	1899	77	....
Additional Philippines	1901	68	100,000
Panama Canal Strip	1904	474	10,000,000*
Virgin Islands	1917	134	25,000,000
Total		2,900,318	$102,039,768
Original Territory		827,844	
Total		3,900,162	

*Besides an annual rental of $250,000.
†This does not include $10,000,000 paid to Texas for territory outside of its present boundaries, but included in the state at the time of annexation.

Education

The United States has no national system of education, in the sense that there is an educational system administered by the Federal government. However, from the time of the Ordinance of 1787, in which certain sections of land in the Northwest Territory were reserved for educational purposes, the national government has assisted very materially in public education, by granting generous portions of the public domain for the support of universities, agricultural colleges and public schools, and in 1917 liberal appropriations were granted for vocational education below college grade. In addition to this it maintains the Office of Education, which is a division under the Department of the Interior. The chief officer, called the commissioner of education, collect statistics and publishes a biennial report, containing educational data of national importance. Further than this his duties are advisory only. However, under the able commissioners who have filled the office since the bureau was established, very much has been done to advance the educational interests of the country. The work of the Office is more fully explained in the article EDUCATION, OFFICE OF.

The administration of the public schools is left to the states, and each maintains its own system of public education. However, these systems so closely resemble one another that, taken together, they practically constitute a national system of education. The articles COMMON SCHOOLS, HIGH SCHOOLS, and those on the important universities of the country will furnish additional information.

Art and Literature

For information on American art see the articles PAINTING and SCULPTURE. American literature will be found in the article LITERATURE, subhead *American Literature.*

History

Discovery and Exploration. At the time of its discovery by Europeans, America was inhabited by savages belonging to the American, or Red, race. The origin and antiquity of these people and the degree of their civilization are still subjects of investigation and dispute. It is also uncertain at what time and place the American continents were first discovered. Norse seamen are said to have visited the North American coast about A. D. 1000, and it is probable that fishermen from Northern Europe had made voyages across the Atlantic before that date. But even if both these facts were true, the credit for the real discovery of America must still be given to those navigators who, at the close of the fifteenth century, crossed the Atlantic and explored the shores of the "New World."

The first of these navigators was Christopher Columbus, who in 1492 discovered the Bahama Islands and on later voyages explored the South and Central American coasts. John and Sebastian Cabot in 1497 and 1498, under the auspices of England, skirted the coast of Labrador and perhaps

THE PURITAN
St. Gaudens

FOUNTAIN OF THE GREAT LAKES
Taft

COLUMBUS
Bartlett

TWO NATURES
Barnard

MEMORY
French

ETHAN ALLEN
Mead

DEATH AND THE SCULPTOR.   French

GEORGE WASHINGTON
Ward

EXAMPLES OF AMERICAN SCULPTURE

New England, giving Britain the basis for her claim to the continent of North America. About the same time Americus Vespucius was exploring the coasts of South America, and in his honor America was named. In 1513 Balboa, a Spanish adventurer, discovered the Pacific, and in the same year Ponce de Leon discovered and explored Florida. Verrazano was the first to represent France in this new field, his voyage being made in 1524. Frenchmen and Spaniards then vied for the control of the new-found riches. Narvaez, Coronado and De Soto, in the south, set out to conquer for Spain the vast interior of the North American continent, while in the north, Cartier, and in Florida, Ribaut and the Huguenots attempted to establish the power of France, but without success.

Meantime, English enterprise had been dormant, but with the advent of Queen Elizabeth to the throne, in 1558, a group of distinguished mariners became anxious to extend English influence in the New World. Of these, Sir John Hawkins, Sir Francis Drake, Sir Humphrey Gilbert and Sir Walter Raleigh were the most important, but they accomplished little of permanent value. It was not till the opening of the seventeenth century that real progress was made toward subduing and colonizing America. At that time, France, under the leadership of such brilliant men as Champlain, Marquette, Joliet and La Salle, extended her influence throughout the region of Canada and into the Mississippi and Ohio valleys, establishing fur-trading posts throughout this territory. In 1565 Spain established a settlement at Saint Augustine, Florida, and made feeble efforts to extend her authority northward, but with little success.

Colonization. A detailed account of the development of each of the colonies, is given in articles upon the several states and also upon the leading discoveries and explorers of the period.

English Colonies. The chief fact in American history during the seventeenth century is the settlement of English colonies along the Atlantic coast. This was begun in 1607 at Jamestown, Virginia, under the auspices of the London Company, a trading and colonizing corporation similar to the East India Company. This colony was in large measure a commercial and political enterprise, and its settlers were drawn from all classes, but especially from the wealthy

and the adventurous. During its early life Jamestown witnessed some of the most important episodes of American history, among them the establishment of the first representative assembly in America (1619), and the institution of negro slavery (1619).

The second English settlement was at Plymouth, Massachusetts, in 1620, and was made by men who had fled from England to avoid religious persecution. In 1628 a settlement was made at Salem by English Puritans. This, too, was a religious movement. The early history of Plymouth and Salem, the latter called Massachusetts Bay Colony, was somewhat troubled. The colonists early manifested a desire for self-government, which led to bitter contests with the king, but at the same time brought about important progress toward political and religious liberty. However, in 1636 Roger Williams was exiled for his religious belief, and in 1651 a bitter persecution of the Quakers began in Boston. Meantime, Harvard College had been founded in 1638, and the first printing press had been set up in 1639.

The success of the early colonies led to other enterprises, and settlements in New Hampshire and Maine resulted. But even the freedom which was nominally established in Massachusetts did not satisfy that community, and in 1633 bodies of settlers from the coast began to travel inland and found settlements along the Connecticut River. These developed into the Colony of Connecticut, which in 1637 adopted the first written constitution in America, known as the "Fundamental Orders of Connecticut." New Haven was settled in this year and was united with Connecticut in 1682. Maryland was organized as a proprietary colony, under the Lords Baltimore, and its first settlement was at Saint Mary's, the original purpose being to found a haven of refuge for English Catholics. The territory of the Carolinas was first settled by Virginians, but in 1663 it was granted to eight English noblemen, who divided it into two colonies, which were again united in 1699, but governed separately after 1729.

Pennsylvania was a Quaker proprietary colony, founded by William Penn, Jr., in 1676 and colonized six years later. Its government was organized on an extremely liberal basis and exerted a powerful influence upon other American colonies. The settlement of Rhode Island was the outgrowth of the religious persecution in Massachusetts, being founded by two exiles, Roger Williams and Anne Hutchinson, the former settling at Providence, the latter at Portsmouth.

They eventually united their forces. Georgia was the last of the thirteen colonies to be settled; it was founded by James Oglethorpe in 1732, as a refuge for honest debtors. A village was settled at Savannah in the following year.

Other Colonies. New Jersey was first colonized by the Dutch at Fort Nassau, now Gloucester. This was subsequently conquered by the Swedes, restored to the Dutch in 1655 and finally transferred to the English in 1664, becoming a proprietary province under Lord Berkeley and Sir George Carteret. The Dutch were also the first to establish colonies within the territory of New York, by reason of the voyage of Henry Hudson in 1609. Albany was settled in 1623, and New Amsterdam (New York), the same year. The colony was conquered by the English in 1664. Delaware was long a fighting ground between the Dutch and the Swedes, the latter finally being compelled to relinquish their claim; but the English conquered in 1664.

Colonial Development. During the seventeenth century the scattering colonies of all the nations steadily advanced in strength and constantly extended their borders, until the Atlantic coast from Labrador to Mexico was dotted with prosperous villages and trading centers. During the first half of the eighteenth century, the interests of France and England began to come into conflict, as each attempted to extend its dominion over the fertile interior of the continent. This resulted in a series of wars, known, collectively, as the French and Indian wars, extending with but slight interruptions from 1689 to 1763. This long conflict had three great results from the standpoint of the colonies: (1) It practically drove France from America and decided that American Institutions should be organized chiefly upon British models; (2) it gave the colonists military experience and a feeling of independent power, which made them more willing to stand firmly for their rights against the mother country; (3) it disclosed the necessity for intercolonial union.

During this same time the colonies were developing politically and were manifesting more and more clearly their determination to govern themselves, at least in all local affairs.

The Development of Union. From the earliest times events in America had shaped themselves to the end that the colonies should become not independent units, but parts of a general system. By the middle of the eigthteenth century the necessity of such a result had become more evident, only because in the meantime minor issues of a local nature had been decided, and because recent events, in which all the colonies were united, had disclosed to the colonists their common interests and ideals. This development of the spirit of union culminated in 1754 in a congress, held at Albany for the purpose of framing a treaty of friendship with the Indians, and also of devising a plan for the union of all the colonies. The latter plan, prepared by Franklin, was adopted by the convention, but it was rejected by every colony and by the mother country. The reasons for its rejection disclosed a state of affairs which found its natural conclusion in the Revolutionary War. Says Franklin, "The Assembly did not adopt it, as they all thought there was too much *prerogative* in it, and in England, it was judged to have too much of the *democratic.*" Thus the issue was clearly drawn between England and the colonies; the former was set resolutely against the growing spirit of independence and democracy in America; the latter were determined to prevent interference in their affairs.

Revolutionary War. *Causes and Beginnings.* The fundamental cause of the Revolutionary War had both economic and political phases. It was laid in the theory of colonization held by every important country in the world at that time, namely, that colonies existed for the mother country and that they had no political or commercial rights except those specifically granted to them. This principle probably would not have been contested, if the tendency of all governments, and especially of England, had not been to repress the growing strength of their colonies and thus to cause distressing economic conditions, which the colonists themselves had no power to remedy.

This led to the demand for political self-government, which, when refused, roused a spirit of resistance and, finally, of revolution. This end was hastened by the passage of more and more repressive legislation, such as the enlargement of the Navigation Acts (which see), the establishment of British garrisons in America and the taxation of the colonies to

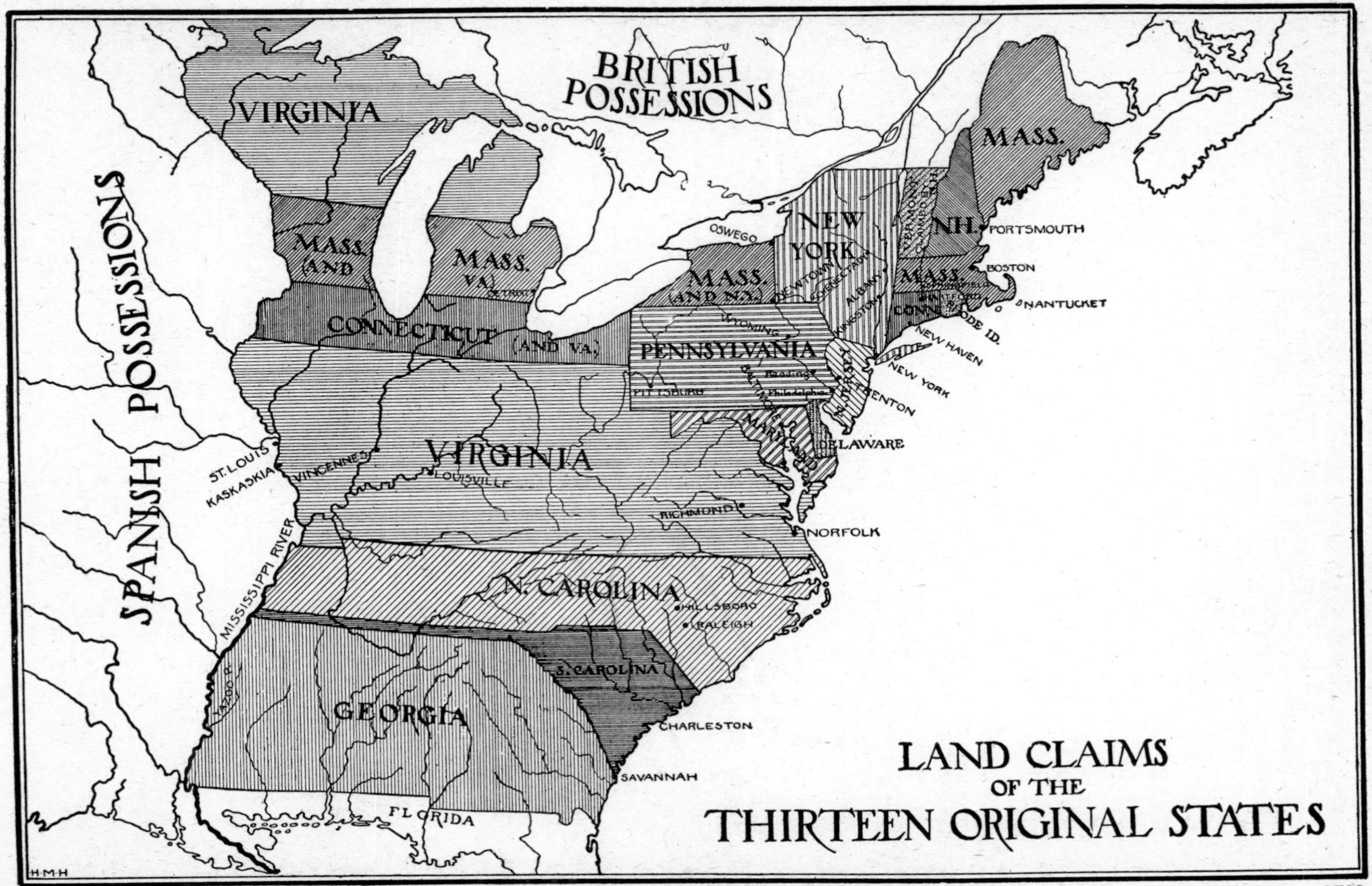

LAND CLAIMS
OF THE
THIRTEEN ORIGINAL STATES

3703

support these garrisons. To enforce the second policy, a stamp tax was inaugurated, which gave to every colonist a grievance and awakened the famous cry, "Taxation without representation is tyranny." The act repealing the Stamp Act was accompanied by a declaration that the Crown had the right to tax the Colonies, and thus it was of little benefit in appeasing the wrath of the Americans. When followed by the Townshend Acts the situation became serious and culminated in open violence in Boston, during which British soldiers in Boston killed a number of citizens.

It soon became evident to the leading men in the colonies that little was to be expected in the direction of conciliation, and an effort was made to unite the colonies more firmly in opposition to the mother country. One of the important means to this end was the formation of committees of correspondence, which kept the different colonies informed of the march of events throughout the country. The spirit of defiance became more widespread, as was indicated by the destruction of the *Gaspee*, a British man-of-war, stationed near Rhode Island to prevent violation of the customs laws, and by the Boston Tea Party. To punish this lawlessness, the British government passed, and attempted to enforce, laws clearly violating the English constitution, and striking at rights especially dear to the colonists. Among these were the Boston Port Bill, closing the port of Boston to all commerce, and acts allowing the trial in England of certain official offenders, permitting the quartering of soldiers upon the colonies and abolishing certain provisions of their charters. To enforce these laws, General Gage and a force of soldiers were sent to Massachusetts.

The colonies were thoroughly aroused, and in reply to a request of the Massachusetts assembly, they sent delegates to a congress at Philadelphia, September 1, 1774. This body, known as the First Continental Congress, passed resolutions of protest against the British policy and agreed not to import goods from England, then adjourned, to reassemble May 1, 1775. Their petition to Parliament was answered by still more oppressive acts; and before the second Congress met, the American cause had gone beyond the stage of discussion or compromise. The colonies, led by Massachusetts, collected military forces and supplies, and when General Gage attempted to seize the stores at Lexington and Concord, and to arrest Samuel Adams and John Hancock, his force was met by a body of minutemen, drawn up on Lexington Common. In the battle which followed the first blood in the Revolutionary War was shed. The government of the colonies was soon taken over by the patriots and, guided and inspired by the Second Continental Congress, measures of increasing defiance and independence were taken from time to time. (See articles upon the REVOLUTIONARY WAR IN AMERICA and the decisive battles, for brief outlines of the chief military campaigns; see also articles upon the great statesmen and soldiers of the period.)

Results of the War. At the opening of the struggle the people of the country were not united in the conviction that political independence of Great Britain was the end to be desired. They were still loyal to the mother country and were determined to fight to regain their rights as Englishmen. But the passage of events and the necessary assumption of the ordinary functions of government by Congress and the provisional governments of the colonies, brought the question of independence prominently forward and finally caused independence to be proclaimed. Meanwhile, foreign relations had been established by the appointment of a committee to correspond with foreign governments, and this resulted, in February, 1778, in the signing of a treaty of alliance with France. This treaty is generally considered the turning-point of the war, since it led to such active support by France that England was eventually compelled to make peace, the treaty being signed at Paris, September 3, 1783.

Articles of Confederation. The financial and internal affairs of the colonies were in a far from satisfactory state. The Continental Congress had assumed only the absolutely necessary functions and had no legal power to compel obedience to its decrees. Appreciating the importance of forming a stronger government to replace that which was being destroyed by the Revolution, Congress appointed a committee in the summer of 1776, to draw up articles for the confederation of the thirteen colonies. These articles, though a vast improvement over the organization which had previously existed, left much to be desired, since the same spirit

ABOVE, MAKERS OF THE CONSTITUTION. BELOW, SIGNERS OF THE DECLARATION OF INDEPENDENCE.

which had led the colonists to resist the encroachments of British power led them to fear the establishment of a strong power among themselves. The articles therefore provided for no executive head of the government, leaving all power with Congress, which could pass laws only with the consent of the representatives of nine states, a majority of the representatives of each state being necessary to cast its vote.

In spite of the apparent weakness of the government which was thus created, state jealousies prevented the adoption of the articles until almost the close of the war, in 1781. Meantime, the financial affairs of the government as a whole and of the several colonies had come to a serious state, since all the governments had been compelled to borrow vast sums of money and, besides, had issued paper notes in payment of debts. This paper money, coming from many sources without adequate security, rapidly depreciated in value, until at the close of the war it was practically worthless. The department of war was in a similarly disorganized state.

Adoption of the Constitution. Soon after the adoption of the Articles of Confederation a large faction in the states demanded that a stronger government be immediately organized, but it was several years before they were able to win public sentiment to their view. Finally, in 1786, a convention was proposed by several states, for the purpose of amending the Articles, in order to increase the power of the central government. This convention met in May, 1787, at Philadelphia, and contained in its membership the most able and distinguished statesmen in America, including George Washington, Alexander Hamilton, James Madison, Gouverneur Morris, Robert Morris, Roger Sherman and others. Its sessions were turbulent, owing to the presence of a strong minority party, who feared the centralization of authority, and it was only through compromise that the Constitution was finally produced and accepted. In its completed form it did not satisfy either party, and the discussion which had taken place in the convention was carried before the people in the contest for ratification. Through the efforts of Jay, Hamilton, Madison, Henry Lee, George Washington and others, it was finally adopted, however, being recognized as the most satisfactory constitution which could at that time be made.

Before its final adjournment, the old Congress of the Confederation performed its most notable work, in passing the famous Ordinance of 1787, for the government of the Northwest Territory.

Organization of the National Government. After the ratification of the Constitution by nine states, Congress proceeded to plan for the organization of the new government. The election, held in January, 1789, resulted in **the unanimous choice of George Washington** for President; John Adams, having the next highest number of votes, was made Vice-President. The inauguration of the government was delayed until April 30, 1789. Washington took the oath of office at New York, where the first national Congress was assembled.

This body already showed a tendency toward division. The Federalists, that is, those who had advocated the ratification of the Constitution, were opposed by the old Anti-Federalists, now styling themselves Democratic-Republicans, or Republicans, who desired the strict interpretation of the Constitution and a tendency toward decentralization of power. Washington chose for his advisers representatives of both of these factions, Hamilton being the acknowledged leader of the former, and Jefferson, of the latter. Hamilton became Secretary of the Treasury, and the first important action of the new government was the carrying into effect of principles suggested by him for the management of the finances of the country. These included the inauguration of the tariff duties; the establishment of a national bank; the assumption of debts contracted by the states during the Revolution; the institution of the excise tax; the establishment of a national mint, and a system of coinage. All of these measures aroused the greatest opposition, but all were passed, and all soon proved their value and efficacy. Washington set himself to organize the executive departments of the government, and he established precedents which have ever since been followed. During his first term, also, the judicial system was organized, and the first ten amendments to the Federal Constitution were adopted.

In spite of his opposition, Washington was nominated and reëlected unanimously in 1793. Adams was also reëlected Vice-President, but was opposed by George Clinton of New York, a Republican. The most important matter connected with Washington's second administration was the relation of the government to foreign nations, especially England and France. The Federalists sympathized with England, and the Republicans sympathized with France, in the war which had begun between them. The visit of Citizen Genet, Washington's refusal to recognize him and the later proclamation of neutrality, together with the signing of the very unsatisfactory treaty with England, known as the Jay Treaty, and the refusal of England to evacuate its posts in the Northwest Territory or to grant privileges to American commerce, all led to serious domestic disturbances and almost to war; but such an event was averted by Washington's tact and frankness. His second administration was also important for the suppression of the first rebellion against the government, the Whisky Insurrection in Pennsylvania; for the unsuccessful expedition of Saint Clair against the Indians and the successful expedition of General Wayne, resulting in the cession of a large tract of land by the Indians to the United States. A treaty was negotiated with Spain, by which the United States secured the free navigation of the Mississippi. In 1793 Eli Whitney invented the cotton gin, which was to be of greater political importance during the next century than any other single invention of history.

Washington positively refused to accept a third term as President, delivered a famous farewell address and retired to Mount Vernon. He was succeeded by John Adams, a Federalist, who received 71 votes, in opposition to Thomas Jefferson, a Republican, who received but 68. Adams' administration was at first highly popular, on account of the firm stand which it took against the insolent actions of France, but the passage in 1798 of the Alien and Sedition acts not only forfeited the popularity of the party, but led to its overthrow. The famous Kentucky and Virginia resolutions were passed at this time in relation to these laws. The seat of government was changed in 1800 from Philadelphia to Washington. Doubtless the most important appointment of Adams' administration was that of John Marshall to be Chief Justice of the United States Supreme Court.

At the election in 1800, Adams was defeated, but the two Republican candidates, Jefferson and Burr, had an equal number of electoral votes. The House of Representatives elected Jefferson after a long contest.

Supremacy of the Anti-Federalists. The ascendency of the Anti-Federalists marks an important change in American politics. At the close of the Revolutionary War there was a notable reaction from the extreme ideas of liberty which that struggle had expressed, and the Constitution placed far more power in the central government than pleased many of the more radical Democrats in the country. But after Adams' administration, another reaction set in, away from centralization, toward democracy. In spite of his theories of strict construction, Jefferson soon was compelled to take steps involving broader powers than either of his Federalist predecessors had assumed. First was the purchase of Louisiana in 1803, the constitutionality of which even he himself doubted. On the other hand, he attempted to reduce the importance of the national government by making but small appropriations for the army and navy; but he was compelled to abandon even this policy when a war with the Barbary powers broke out in 1801. During his first term the Twelfth Amendment to the Constitution was passed, changing the method of voting for President and Vice-President.

Jefferson was reëlected in 1804, with George Clinton of New York as Vice-President. The most important problem which confronted him during his second administration was the relation of the United States to the commercial war between France and England. He attempted to establish in law his theory that the United States could compel Europe to consider its rights by shutting American ports to the commerce of European nations. This was the cause of the Embargo Act of December, 1807, forbidding American vessels to leave for foreign ports (see EMBARGO). However, this measure did not accomplish its intended purpose, but instead it seriously injured American commerce. The relations between the United States and Great Britain became more and more strained, because of the persistent attempts of British vessels to impress seamen from American ships. This resulted in several small battles. During Jefferson's administration, also, Aaron Burr attempted to separate the western states from the Union; Lewis and Clark made their famous expedition to the Pacific coast (see LEWIS AND CLARK EXPEDITION); the Cumberland Road was authorized and begun; West Point Military Academy was established; Fulton succeeded in constructing the first successful steamboat, and the slave trade was abolished after 1808.

Jefferson declined a third election and was succeeded by his Secretary of State, James Madison, who defeated Charles C. Pinckney. The Embargo Act was replaced by the Non-Intercourse Act, before Madison's inauguration, but this did not relieve matters greatly. Madison attempted to carry out Jefferson's policy, but was finally compelled to take more stern measures, and the War of 1812 resulted. Meantime, Madison was reëlected, with Elbridge Gerry as Vice-President, defeating De Witt Clinton. The war was vigorously opposed by the Federalists, especially of New England, and they held a convention at Hartford, in December, 1814, which, it was rumored, threatened secession; but this movement did not gain sufficient strength to be a serious menace to the country. The treaty of peace was signed at Ghent, December 24, 1814.

The end of the war marked, also, the practical end of the Federalist party as an organization, for its unpatriotic stand during the war had won for it the derision of people in all parts of the country. However, the Anti-Federalist party had meantime so changed its position upon constitutional questions that many of the Federalist principles were already firmly incorporated in the government. During Madison's term, laws were passed granting a second charter to the United States Bank, establishing a protective tariff and appropriating large sums for internal improvements, all measures which the Anti-Federalists had formerly opposed. The Supreme Court, under Marshall's leadership, had also taken firm ground in favor of a strong national government.

The Era of Good Feeling. In 1816 James Monroe of Virginia, Madison's Secretary of State, was elected President, receiving the votes of all the states except Massachusetts, Connecticut and Delaware, which were cast for Rufus King of New York. Since the downfall of the Federalist party had removed many questions from controversy, Monroe's administrations are sometimes known as the "Era of Good Feeling;" but, in fact, just as sincere debate was carried on during this time as at any time before or after, the main questions being the tariff and the admission of Missouri, the latter of which involved the discussion of the rising issue of slavery. Monroe was reëlected in 1820, receiving all the elec-

toral votes but one, which was cast for John Quincy Adams. The most important incident of his second administration was the promulgation of the Monroe Doctrine. In 1824 a higher protective tariff was passed. The election of 1824 turned upon personal questions and resulted in a contest between Andrew Jackson, John Quincy Adams, William H. Crawford and Henry Clay, the House of Representatives finally electing John Quincy Adams.

Rise of the Whigs. This election marks another change in the political history of the United States. The Republican, or Democratic-Republican, party at this time took the name of Democratic, which it has since retained, and the Clay and Adams factions, consisting of the loose constructionists of the old party, took the name of National Republican, which eventually was changed to Whig. Adams' administration was marked by a long controversy between his followers and those of Jackson, who claimed that they had been deprived of the election by a corrupt compact between Adams and Clay. This helped to defeat the Adams faction in 1828 and to elect Jackson. The most important event of this period was the passage of the Tariff of Abominations of 1828, which led to the nullification controversy in the following administration. Adams' term also saw the extension of the policy of internal improvements at the expense of the national government, and the beginning of a vast immigration into the West.

Democracy Again in Power. Jackson was elected in 1828 by a vote of 178 to 83, with John C. Calhoun as Vice-President. This election marks the return of the radical Democratic party to power. The chief contests of Jackson's term were over the United States Bank and the tariff, the former being refused a continuance of its charter and the latter resulting in the nullification episode, which was firmly handled by President Jackson, secession being prevented by a compromise bill introduced by Henry Clay. During this controversy the famous debate between Daniel Webster and Robert Y. Hayne occurred. Jackson was reëlected in 1832 over Henry Clay, John Floyd and William Wirt, and Martin Van Buren was chosen Vice-President. His second administration was marked by Indian disturbances, in the South with the Cherokee and Seminole, and in the West with the Sacs and Foxes under Black Hawk.

The Senate took firm ground against the President, especially for his attitude toward the national bank, and this contest was bitter throughout his term. The question of the independence or annexation of Texas also arose during Jackson's second term and signalized the increasing importance of the slavery controversy, the Texas question resolving itself into a contest upon the part of the South for the extension of slavery territory, and resistance to this policy by the North. The first anti-slavery societies date from this time. President Jackson's terms were also notable for the first important contest over the spoils system, which he had introduced into the national government.

Jackson was succeeded by his follower, Martin Van Buren, who defeated the Whig candidate, William Henry Harrison of Indiana. Richard M. Johnson was elected Vice-President. The first year of Van Buren's term was marked by a terrible financial panic, which caused the failure of many banks and corporations and produced great suffering among the people. Van Buren continued the hostility of the Democratic party to the establishment of a national bank and replaced that institution by a system known as the independent treasury. Van Buren's plan, with modifications, has continued to the present.

A Whig Triumph. The financial depression and other issues led to the election of the popular Whig candidate, William Henry Harrison, in 1840, after a memorable campaign, known to history as the "log cabin and hard cider campaign." The anti-slavery party at this election for the first time nominated independent candidates, James G. Birney being the candidate of the Liberty party. Harrison died shortly after his inauguration, and was succeeded by John Tyler, formerly a Democrat. He immediately came into conflict with Congress over the proposed reestablishment of the national bank, and he vetoed two bills drawn to that end. The controversy became so heated that all of Tyler's Cabinet except Webster resigned, he remaining merely to complete the negotiation of the famous Webster-Ashburton Treaty, which fixed the northeastern boundary between the United States and Canada.

In 1843 President Tyler arranged a treaty with the Republic of Texas, providing for the future annexation of that country to the United States, but it was rejected by the Senate. The Texas question became the leading issue in the following campaign, however, which resulted in the election of James K. Polk, the Democratic candidate, over Henry Clay, the Whig, and James G. Birney, the candidate of the Liberty party. Before Tyler left office Congress had approved a resolution for the annexation of Texas.

Texas and the Mexican War. The administration of President Polk was chiefly notable for the precipitation of the Mexican War, as a result of his order to the United States troops under General Taylor to take possession of territory claimed by both Texas and Mexico. Texas was admitted as a state in June, 1845. The war resulted in an easy victory for the United States and by the treaty of Guadalupe Hidalgo the United States territory was greatly extended. The war is described in the article MEXICAN WAR.

The dispute over the territory of Oregon was also an issue in the campaign in 1844 and was settled by a treaty with England in 1846. During Polk's administration, the Walker tariff of 1846 was passed; it was a return to the principle of tariff for revenue only. The independent treasury was also firmly established. The slavery question again cropped out over the extension of the institution to the territory acquired from Mexico and in the formation of the Free-Soil party. Gold was discovered in California in 1848 and resulted in a vast immigration to that region.

The Liberty party had been fused with the Free-Soil party, and in 1848 it nominated Martin Van Buren as its candidate for President, against Lewis Cass, the Democratic nominee, and General Zachary Taylor, the Whig nominee. Taylor was elected, with Millard Fillmore as Vice-President.

Downfall of the Whigs. In spite of its triumph at this election, the Whig party soon showed signs of disintegration, being absorbed in part by the Free-Soil movement, which later took form in the Republican party. Meantime, the Democratic party came under the control of its pro-slavery faction, and the slavery issue was therefore brought to a crisis. For a time in 1850 the controversy seemed to be allayed through the compromise measures, which admitted California as a free state, but gave the South numerous concessions, in the form of the Fugitive Slave Law and the organization of New Mexico and Utah with the right to admit or prohibit slavery as they chose.

President Taylor died before the passage of these acts, and Millard Fillmore succeeded to the Presidency. The most important event of his administration was the signing of the Clayton-Bulwer Treaty, regarding the interoceanic canal. In the election of 1852 the Democrats were successful, Franklin Pierce of New Hampshire becoming President, and William R. King of Alabama, Vice-President. The Whig nominees were General Winfield Scott and William A Graham. The Free-Soil party nominated John P. Hale of New Hampshire and George W. Julian.

Slavery. In spite of the apparent cessation of the slavery controversy, the struggle soon revived over the organization of the territories of Kansas and Nebraska, and the doctrine proposed by Stephen A. Douglas for the regulation of these territories, known as "squatter sovereignty" (which see). This contest marked the final dissolution of the Whig party, most of the Southern members joining with the Democrats in favor of the extension of slavery, the Northerners, together with other anti-slavery factions, uniting to form the Republican party. During this time a fierce struggle for the possession of Kansas ensued between the anti-slavery and pro-slavery factions (see KANSAS, subhead *History*). It was during Pierce's administration that Commodore Perry negotiated his treaty with Japan.

The election of 1856 again resulted in a Democratic success, James Buchanan being elected President and John C. Breckinridge Vice-President, over John C. Fremont and William L. Dayton, the Republican candidates, and Millard Fillmore and A. J. Donelson, the nominees of a new party, known as the Know-Nothings or American party. It was during Buchanan's administration that the slavery struggle came to a head. It witnessed the Supreme Court decision in the Dred Scott case, declaring that Congress had no right to prohibit slavery in the territories; the attempts upon the part of Southern statesmen to gain possession of Cuba, for the extension of slavery, and the continuation of the bitter struggle in Kansas, which resulted, in the succeeding administration, in the admission of Kansas as a free state. In 1859 occurred John Brown's raid at Harper's Ferry, which roused the most bitter antagonism in the South. The Democratic party was now practically divided, and two sets of candidates were nominated, one by the North-

ern wing and the other by the Southern wing. The former was Stephen A. Douglas, of Illinois, and Herschel V. Johnson, of Georgia; the latter, John C. Breckinridge, of Kentucky, and Joseph Lane, of Oregon. The Republicans nominated Abraham Lincoln, of Illinois, and Hannibal Hamlin, of Maine, while a third party, the successor of the American party, now known as the Constitutional Union party, nominated John Bell, of Tennessee, and Edward Everett, of Massachusetts. Lincoln was elected by a comparatively small plurality and by far less than a majority of the popular vote.

Secession. The election of Lincoln was the signal for the South to take measures to overcome the overwhelming opposition to them in the United States government, and it resulted in the secession of South Carolina on December 20, 1860. Mississippi, Florida, Alabama, Georgia, Louisiana, Texas, Virginia, Arkansas, North Carolina and Tennessee followed within the next six months, and a new nation, known as the Confederate States of America, was organized at Montgomery, Ala., in February, 1861. President Buchanan opposed secession, but denied his right to coerce the seceding states to return to the Union, and therefore he made little effort to protect government property in the South, which was being taken over as rapidly as possible by the seceding states. Efforts at compromise were made during Buchanan's administration, but without effect. A resolution introduced into the Senate by Senator Crittenden proposed to divide the Union into a slave country and a free country.

Civil War. In his inaugural address President Lincoln urged all sections and classes to come to the support of the government, but expressed his determination to prevent secession. Accordingly, he soon called for volunteers. The Confederate government also called for volunteers and retaliated for Lincoln's proclamation of a blockade by licensing privateers to prey upon Northern commerce. The war began with the bombardment of Fort Sumter on April 14, and its surrender. In April, 1862, Congress purchased and emancipated all slaves in the District of Columbia; two months later it abolished slavery throughout the territories and the public domain, and on January 1, 1863, President Lincoln issued his famous Emancipation Proclamation, which he had announced in the previous September, after the Battle of Antietam. This proclamation set free all the slaves in states then in rebellion against the United States.

During the war the President did not have the undivided support of the North. His suspension of the writ of habeas corpus, the suppression of newspapers and of public gatherings, the Conscription Act of 1863 and the apparent failure of the Union armies in the field during the early years of the war, all led to serious opposition and criticism. The financial problems of the war also necessitated taxes and other extraordinary measures, which became exceedingly unpopular. However in the election of 1864 the Democratic party, in spite of the nomination of a popular general, George B. McClellan, was defeated, on a platform which declared that the war was a failure, and Lincoln was triumphantly reëlected. West Virginia, which had been separated from the old State of Virginia, soon after the beginning of the struggle, was admitted to the Union in December, 1862. The war practically came to a close on the surrender of General Lee in April, 1865, but the rejoicing which that event caused was soon overshadowed by universal sorrow at the assassination of President Lincoln, April 14. For a full account of the war, see the article CIVIL WAR IN AMERICA. See, also, articles on the important battles and the leading statesmen and military leaders of the period.

Reconstruction. The problems which the close of the war would bring were anticipated by Lincoln and by Congress, and steps were taken as early as 1863 to provide for the return of the seceded states to the Union and the reëstablishment of loyal state governments. President Johnson, who acceded to the presidency at the death of Lincoln, carried out as far as possible his predecessor's lenient policy of reconstruction, but in so doing he won the enmity of Congress and was impeached, being saved from conviction by a single vote. Meantime, Congress had passed the Thirteenth Amendment, abolishing slavery, and it had been ratified in December, 1865. It had also passed other laws, placing the Southern states in the position of conquered provinces. In 1868, Arkansas, Alabama, Florida, North and South Carolina, Georgia and Louisiana were readmitted to the Union.

The election of 1868 placed General U. S. Grant in the President's chair, with Schuyler Colfax of Indiana, as Vice-President. The Democratic candidates were Horatio Seymour of New York, and Francis P. Blair, Jr., of Missouri. Before Grant's inauguration, the Fourteenth and Fifteenth Amendments to the Constitution had been passed, granting suffrage to the negroes. The latter was ratified in March, 1870.

The most important event of Grant's first term was the settlement of the Alabama claims, which were claims of the United States against England for American ships destroyed by the *Alabama,* a Confederate privateer that was fitted out in England. The award was favorable to the United States. The Union Pacific Railroad was completed, giving the country its first transcontinental railway, but the construction was accompanied by a stock deal which involved several members of Congress and the Vice-President in a notorious scandal, fully described in the article CREDIT MOBILIER OF AMERICA.

The reconstruction policy of Congress led to serious difficulties in the South, which the President sought to remove, but with only partial success. Irresponsible demagogues from the North secured appointment to offices in the South, and were thus placed in positions which they were nowise qualified to fill. Their chief aim seemed to be to reap all possible benefit for themselves and then to leave the country when they could no longer hold office. They were styled *carpetbaggers,* because it was alleged that they could carry all their personal effects in a carpetbag.

This carpetbag régime and other abuses led to the formation of a secret organization among the men of the South, known as the *Ku-Klux Klan,* whose chief purpose was to resist the carpetbaggers and to prevent the execution of their orders. A fuller account of these events will be found in the articles RECONSTRUCTION and IMPEACHMENT, and in the articles on the various Southern states under the subhead *History.*

The Credit Mobilier scandal led to a demand for a reform in the civil service, which was made an important issue in the succeeding campaign. This issue, with that of reconstruction and the tendency of the Republicans to centralize power, led to the formation of a new party, the Liberal Republican party, whose candidates, Horace Greely and B. Gratz Brown, were endorsed by the Democratic convention. However, General Grant was reëlected, with Henry Wilson of Massachusetts as Vice-President, Greeley having died before the count of the electoral votes. In the same election the Prohibition party and a labor reform party first appeared.

Grant's second term was troublesome. Soon after his reëlection he was confronted by a difficulty with Spain. A Spanish warship seized the American merchantman *Virginius,* which was carrying munitions and other supplies to the rebels in Cuba. Four Cubans who were on the vessel, the captain and thirty-six of the crew, were executed by orders of the Spanish authorities. The affair came near leading the country into war with Spain, but it was finally settled by diplomacy. Another difficulty was caused by the alliance of several Federal revenue collectors with distillers for the purpose of defrauding the government of the excise tax on whisky. This *Whisky Ring,* as the combination was called, had influential friends in the Treasury Department at Washington, and it was a long time before the loss of revenue could be located. The "ring" was finally exposed, the officials implicated were dismissed from office and the distillers were prosecuted and convicted, but most of the prominent ones were pardoned. There was a controversy over the resumption of specie payments and a disastrous financial panic in 1873. Indian troubles culminated in a war with the Modocs and Sioux, during which General Custer and his entire force were massacred.

In 1876 the Centennial Exposition was held in Philadelphia to commemorate the first century of the nation's independence. It was the first great international exposition held in America, and all the leading nations of the world were represented.

Industrial and Economic Progress. Discontent with Grant's administration increased. The Democrats gained a majority in Congress and made a hard fight for the election of 1876. Their candidate, Samuel J. Tilden, received a majority of the popular vote, but was defeated by one electoral vote, as a result of an investigation by a specially constituted electoral commission, which considered the disputed returns from several states. The successful candidate, President Hayes, immediately withdrew United States troops from the South and thus paved the way for a return of good feeling between the two sections. His term was also notable for the rise of a party representing the laboring

classes, which demanded a bimetallic standard of money, the suppression of national bank notes, the institution of an income tax and the prohibition of Chinese immigration. This party became known as the Greenback party. In 1878 the Bland-Allison Bill, which required the government to purchase not less than $2,000,000 nor more than $4,000,000 of silver per month, was passed, and in the following year specie payments were resumed. In 1880 within the Republican party arose a fierce contest for control between the followers of Ulysses S. Grant who demanded for him a third term, and those of James G. Blaine and John Sherman. James A. Garfield, of Ohio, a compromise candidate, was finally chosen, however, and was victorious over General Winfield S. Hancock, the Democratic nominee, and James B. Weaver, the Greenback-Labor candidate.

The early part of Garfield's administration was marked by the continuation of the party contest and by the disclosure of frauds in the postal service. President Garfield was assassinated in July, 1881, and died in the following September, Chester A. Arthur becoming President. During his administration the Edmunds law against polygamy was passed; also a bill suspending Chinese immigration for ten years. Civil service reform was forced to the front by the Democratic party, and in 1884 their nominee, Grover Cleveland, of New York, was elected over James G. Blaine by a small popular plurality. The election disclosed an independent movement in the Republican party, which was led by some of the most prominent Republicans in the country. Benjamin F. Butler, of Massachusetts, was the candidate of the Greenback-Labor party, and John P. Saint John was the candidate of the Prohibition party.

President Cleveland proceeded to extend the civil-service reform to a vast number of offices, thus securing the antagonism of many of the political leaders in his own party. The death of Vice-President Hendricks made necessary the passage of a law governing the Presidential succession. During the same administration a new anti-polygamy law, the Interstate Commerce Act of 1887 and a law prohibiting Chinese immigration, were passed. The administration was characterized by an unprecedented use of the veto power, especially upon private pension bills. The campaign of 1888 turned upon the tariff,

EXPLORATIONS

1400 1500 1600 1700

SPANISH
- 92 Columbus discovers West Indies
- 98 Columbus discovers American Continent
- 99 Amerigo Vespucci visits America
- 12 Ponce De Leon visits Florida
- 13 Balboa reaches Pacific Coast
- 20 Cortez conquers Mexico
- 28 De Narvaez explores Florida
- 39 De Soto visits America
- 41 De Soto discovers Mississippi River
- 65 St. Augustine founded by Melendez

ENGLISH
- 97 John Cabot discovers Newfoundland
- 98 Sebastian Cabot explores American Coast
- 76 Frobisher visits Labrador
- 79 Drake explores Pacific Coast
- 83 Gilbert's voyage
- 84-87 Raleigh attempts to settle Roanoke Island
- 2 Gosnold's voyage
- 7 Settlement at Jamestown
- 20 Puritans settle at Plymouth
- 34 Maryland settled by Catholics

FRENCH
- 24 Verrazzani explores Atlantic Coast
- 34 Cartier explores St. Lawrence
- 42 Roberval visits Canada
- 64 Huguenots in Florida
- 98 La Roche in Nova Scotia
- 4 De Monts founds Port Royal
- 8 Champlain founds Quebec

DUTCH
- 9 Hudson explores Hudson R.
- 14 May and Block explorations
- 14 New Amsterdam founded

INDIANS

Nations — **Tribes**
- Catawbas
- Cherokees
- Sioux
- Uchees
- Natchez
- Huron-Iroquois { Hurons, Eries
- Mobilians { Creeks, Seminoles, Choctaws, Chickasaws
- Iroquois (Six Tribes) { Mohawks, Oneidas, Onandagas, Cayugas, Senecas, Tuscaroras
- Algonquins { Chippewas, Menomenees, Miamis, Sacs, Foxes, Kickapoos, Abenaquis, Narragansetts, Pequods, Massachusetts, Mohegans, Delawares, Powhattans, Shawnees

Contemporaneous History
- 15 John Huss burned
- 29 Joan Arc raises siege of Orleans
- 55 War of the Roses
- 56 Turks defeated at Belgrade
- 69 Ferdinand marries Isabella
- 80-84 Inquisition
- 92 Ferdinand takes Granada
- 20 Field of the Cloth of Gold
- 21 Diet at Worms
- 30 Augsburg Confession
- 40 Order of Jesuits founded
- 54 Siberia discovered
- 87 Mary of Scots beheaded
- 88 Spanish Armada
- 32 Battle of Lutzen
- 48 Treaty of Westphalia
- 66 London Fire
- 71 Cossacks subdued
- Peace of Ryswick 97
- Peace of Carlowitz 99

COLONIES

1600   1700   1775

VIRGINIA
7 Settlement at Jamestown
8 John Smith governor
19 Slavery introduced
19 Legislative Assembly
24 Overthrow of London Co.
29 Sir John Harvey
Gov. Berkeley 42
44 Indian Massacre
51 Navigation Acts
75 Bacon's Rebellion
77 Proprietary Government
15 Proprietary government
91 Royal Province
Livelihood - Agriculture and Manufacturing
Motive - Religion
Settlers - English Adventurers   Motive - Wealth   Livelihood - Agriculture

MARYLAND
34 First settlement at St. Marys
49 Toleration Act
Settlers - Roman Catholics

NORTH CAROLINA
33 First settlement from Virginia
63 Grant to Proprietors
Settlers - Refugees and Huguenots
90 Sother's Rebellion
11 Coree War
91 Union of Carolinas
29 Separation
Motive - Agriculture and Political Strife   Livelihood - Rice, Tar and Turpentine
32 Birth of Washington
Virginia Resolutions 65

NEW JERSEY
33 Settled by Dutch
33 Ft. Nassau destroyed by Ind.
64 Elizabethtown settled
65 Slavery introduced
73 Division East and West Jersey
85 Charter annulled
2 Reunion of Jerseys
38 Separated from New York
Settlers - Dutch and Quakers   Motive - Agriculture   Livelihood - Agriculture

NEW YORK
9 Hudson sails up Hudson River
23 New Amsterdam settled
15 Trading post at Manhattan Is.
21 Dutch West India Co. formed
29 Patroon system organized
38 Delaware settled by Swedes
47 Peter Stuyvesant
64 English Conquest
73 Reconquered by Dutch
74 English Colony
Andros' Administration 75
89 Charter hidden
Settlers - Dutch   Motive - Trade   Livelihood - Furs

DELAWARE
3 Becomes separate colony
82 Added to Pennsylvania
Settlers - Swedes and Quakers   Motive - Agriculture   Livelihood - Agriculture

CONNECTICUT
36 Hartford settled
43 New Haven Republic organized
62 New Charter Granted
1 Yale College founded
Pequo I War 36
Settlers - Puritans and Colonists   Motive - Agriculture and Religion   Livelihood - Agriculture and Manufacturing

RHODE ISLAND
36 Settled by Roger Williams
47 Code of laws enacted
Newport founded 39
87 Joined to New York
Settlers - Dissenters   Motive - Religion   Livelihood - Agriculture and Fishing

MASSACHUSETTS
20 Settlement at Plymouth
23 New Hampshire settled
32 Capital at Boston
Harvard College founded 36
47 Public Schools Est.
39 First printing press at Cambridge
75 King Philip's War
84 Lose Charter
89 King William's War
90 First paper money
92 Witchcraft
2 Queen Anne's War
97 Capt. Kidd Piracy
89 First Intercolonial Assembly
32 Gov. Crosby
44 Negro Plot
French and Indian War 54
First Colonial Congress 65
Settlers - Puritans   Motive - Religion   Livelihood - Farming and Fishing

NEW HAMPSHIRE
79 Separate Col.
98 Absorbed by Massachusetts
11 Finally separated
44 King George's War
Quebec captured 59
45 Capture of Louisburg
French and Indian War 54
Settlers - Colonists   Motive - Trade   Livelihood - Agriculture and Fishing

SOUTH CAROLINA
70 Settled by English
71 Slavery Intro.
80 Charleston founded
2 Expedition against St. Augustine
6 Spanish invasion
29 Royal Province
Settlers - Refugees   Motive - Agriculture and Religion   Livelihood - Cotton, Rice and Silk

PENNSYLVANIA
81 Settled
82 Ind. Treaty
1 Charter of Privileges
92 Penn dispossessed
18 Death of Penn
French and Indian War 54
Braddock's defeat 55
Settlers - Quakers   Motive - Religion   Livelihood - Agriculture, Mining and Manufacturing

GEORGIA
33 Settled at Savannah
39 War with Spaniards
43 Royal Province
Settlers - Scotch and Poor   Motive - Philanthropy   Livelihood - Cotton

REVOLUTION

1775	1776	1777	1778	1779	1780	1781
Lexington and Concord April 19 — Parker / Smith Pitcairn	Dorchester Heights March 4 — Washington	Princeton Jan. 3 — Washington / Mawhood	Naval Battle March 7 — Randolph Yarmouth	Kettle Creek Feb. 14 — Pickens / Tories	Monk's Corner April 14 — Huger / Tarleton	Cowpens Jan. 17 — Morgan / Tarleton
Ticonderoga May 10 — Allen Arnold	Sullivan's Island June 28 — Moultrie / Clinton Parker	Fort Schuyler Aug. 3 — Herkimer / St. Leger	Monmouth June 28 — Washington Clinton	Vincennes Feb. 25 — Clark / Hamilton	Capture of Charleston May 12 — Lincoln / Clinton Cornwallis	Guilford Courthouse March 15 — Greene / Cornwallis
Crown Point May 12 — Warner	Long Island August 27 — Putnam / Clinton	Bennington Aug. 16 — Stark Warner / Baum Breyman	Wyoming Massacre July 3 — Indians Butler	Brier Creek March 3 — Ashe / Prevost	Waxhaw Creek May 29 — Buford / Tarleton	Hobkirk's Hill April 25 — Greene / Rawdon
Bunker Hill June 17 — Prescott / Howe	Harlem Plains Sept. 16 — Knowlton Leitch	Brandywine Sept. 11 — Washington / Howe	Newport Aug. 29 — Greene	Stony Point July 16 — Wayne	Hanging Rock Aug. 6 — Sumter / American Loyalists	Fort Watson April 26 — Marion Lee
Capture of Montreal Nov. 13 — Montgomery / Prescott	White Plains Oct. 28 — Washington / Howe	Bemis Heights Sept. 19 — Gates / Burgoyne	Light Horse captured Sept. 28 — Baylor / Grey	Elmira Aug. 29 — Sullivan / Indians	Camden Aug. 16 — Gates / Cornwallis	Jamestown Ford July 4 — Wayne / Cornwallis
Great Bridge Dec. 9 — Dunmore	Fort Washington Nov. 16 — Magaw / Howe	Germantown Oct. 4 — Washington / Howe	Massacre Oct. 15 — Pulaski's Infantry / Ferguson	Paul Jones' Victory Sept. 23 — Richard / Serapis	Fishing Creek Aug. 18 — Sumter / Tarleton	Fort Griswold Sept. 6 — Ledyard / Arnold
Quebec Dec. 31 — Arnold Montgomery	Trenton Dec. 26 — Washington / Donop Rall	Saratoga Oct. 7 — Gates / Burgoyne	Cherry Val. Massacre Nov. 10 — Indians Butler	Savannah Oct. 9 — Lincoln D'Estaing / Prevost	King's Mountain Oct. 7 — Campbell / Ferguson	Eutaw Springs Sept. 8 — Greene / Stewart
		Fort Mercer Oct. 23 — Greene / Donop	Savannah Seized Dec. 29 — Campbell		Blackstock Nov. 20 — Sumter / Tarleton	Siege of Yorktown Sept. 8 to Oct. 19 — Washington / Cornwallis

Troops Enlisted

1775	1776	1777	1778	1779	1780	1781
37,363	89,761	68,720	51,046	44,275	43,079	29,340

Miscellany

1775	1776	1777	1778	1779	1780	1781
Washington Commander in Chief / First Continental Currency	Evacuation of Boston / Declaration of Independence	Congress adopts Flag / Articles of Confederation	Alliance with France / Charleston Burned	Depreciation of Federal Money	First Bank Chartered / England Declares War with Holland	Federal Union Established / Bank of North America Chartered

AMERICANS ☐ BRITISH ▨ INDECISIVE ☐

ADMINISTRATIONS

Section	Category	WASHINGTON (1789)	ADAMS (1797)	JEFFERSON (1801)	MADISON (1809–1817)
EXECUTIVE	President	WASHINGTON	ADAMS	JEFFERSON	MADISON
	Leaders in Cabinet	Jefferson Hamilton	Pickering Wolcott	Madison Dearborn	Gallatin Dallas
	Important Messages & Papers	Farewell Address		First Written Message	
JUDICIAL	Chief Justice	Jay	Ellsworth Marshall		
	Decisions			Marbury and Madison	
LEGISLATIVE	Pres. of Senate	Adams	Jefferson	Burr Clinton	Clinton Gerry
	Speaker of House	Muhlenberg Trumbull Dayton	Sedgwick	Macon Varnum	Clay Cheves
	Number of Members	Senate 26 House 65	Senate 32 House 105	Senate 32 House 141	Senate 34 House 181
	Leaders	Madison Gerry	Clay	J. Q. Adams	Calhoun Webster
	Laws	Revenue Bill Naturalization Law	Alien and Sedition Acts	Embargo Act	Non Intercourse Act
IMPORTANT EVENTS	Wars	Indian Whisky Rebellion	Quasi	Tripoli	Indian War of 1812
	Inventions	Cotton Gin Nail Cutter	Locomotive Plow	Steamboat Blow Pipe Steam Dredge	Breech-loading Rifle Printing of Cotton Goods
	Acquisition Territories			Louisiana	
	Foreign Relations	Treaty with England Treaty with Spain	Treaty with France		Treaty of Ghent
	Slavery	Petition to Abolish sent to Congress		Slave Trade Abolished	
	Deaths	Allen Franklin Hancock Jones	Henry Washington	Hamilton Sam'l Adams Moultrie	Clinton Gerry
	States Admitted	Vermont Kentucky Tennessee		Ohio	Louisiana Indiana
	Miscellany	Census Capitol Moved		Lewis & Clark Expedition West Point Academy	Washington Burned
	Foreign Events	French Revolution		Milan Decree	Revolution in Venezuela Mexican Uprising

ADMINISTRATIONS

	MONROE (1817)	ADAMS (1825)	JACKSON (1829)	VAN BUREN (1837)	HARRISON / TYLER (1841)	POLK (1845–1849)
Pres.	Monroe		Jackson	Van Buren	Harrison / Tyler	Polk
Cab'n't	Adams, Calhoun	Clay, Rush	Van Buren, Berrien, Livingston	Forsyth	Webster, Calhoun	Buchanan
Messages	Monroe Doctrine		Bank Message			
Chief Just.			Taney			
Decisions	Dartmouth College					
Pres. Senate	Tompkins	Calhoun	Calhoun, Van Buren	Johnson	White, Jones	Dallas
Speak. House	Clay, Taylor, Barbour	Taylor, Stevenson	Bell, Polk	Hunter		Davis, Winthrop
No. Mems	Senate 42, House 213	Senate 48, House 213	Senate 48, House 240	Senate 52, House 240	Senate 52, House 223	Senate 58, House 223
Leaders	Clay, Webster, Jackson	Van Buren, Buchanan	Webster, Hayne, Clay, Benton	Wright, Adams		Wilmot, Corwin
Laws	Tenure of Office Act		U. S. Bank Bill Vetoed, Force Act	Sub-Treasury Bill	Annexation Bill	Wilmot Proviso
Wars	Seminole		Black Hawk, Seminole	Seminole	Dorr Rebellion	Mexican
Acquisitions	Florida					
Inventions	Shoe Pegs, Velocipede	Planing Mach., Passenger Train	Colt's Revolver, Chloroform used, Typewriter used	Friction Match, Elec. Telegraph	Telegraph Line, Use of Ether	Sewing Machine, Hoe Ptg. Press
For'n Rel.	Treaty with Canada		Treaty with Brazil		Webster-Ashburton	Treaty of Hidalgo
Slavery	Missouri Compromise	Slavery abolished in N. Y.	Anti-Slavery in New England	Anti-Slavery Party	Growth of Abolition	Wilmot Proviso
Deaths	Decatur, Boone, Stark	Adams, Jefferson	Jay, Monroe, Marshall, Madison	Black Hawk	Channing, Jackson	J. Q. Adams
States Admitted	Mississippi, Illinois, Alabama, Maine, Missouri		Michigan, Arkansas		Texas, Florida	Iowa, Wisconsin
Miscellany	First Steam Voyage across the Atlantic	First Threshing Machine	Rise of American Literature	Indians removed to Indian Ter.	Postage Stamps	Discovery of Gold in Calif.
Events for'n or	Mexican Revolution		Independence of Mexico, Independence of Texas	Canadian Reb., Victoria Crown	Federal Union in C. A. Dissolved	

ADMINISTRATIONS

	1849 TAYLOR / FILLMORE	1853 PIERCE	1857 BUCHANAN	1861 LINCOLN	JOHNSON	1869 GRANT	1877 HAYES	1881 GARFIELD / ARTHUR	1885
Pres't	Taylor Fillmore	Pierce	Buchanan	Lincoln	Johnson	Grant	Hayes	Garfield Arthur	
Cab't	Webster Meredith	Marcy Davis	Cass Dix	Seward	McCulloch	Fish Sherman Brewster	Evarts Sherman	Blaine Sherman	Lincoln
Mes-sages			Revolutionary Message	Emancipation Proc.	Proc. Amnesty				
Chief Just.					Chase	Waite			
Decl-sions									
Speak House	Cobb	Boyd Banks	Orr Pennington	Grow	Colfax	Blaine Kerr	Randall	Keifer	Carlisle
Pres. Sen'te	Boyd		Breckenridge	Hamlin		Colfax Wilson	Wheeler		
No. Mems House / Senate	Senate 62 House 237	Senate 62 House 237	Senate 66 House 243	Senate 50 House 243	House 243	Senate 74 House 293	Senate 76 House 293	Senate 76 House 332	House 332
Lead-ers		Douglas Cass Stephens	Seward Cameron	Stevens Sumner	Morrell Crittenden	Morton Wilson Schurz Trumbull	Edmunds	Pendleton Conklin	Bland
Laws	Omnibus Bill	Kansas-Nebr. Bill		Income Tax Law Civil Rights Bill	Civil Rights Bill	Salary Act			
Wars		Border Warfare	J. Brown's Raid Mormon Insur'n	Civil War	Civil War	Modoc Sioux	Nez Perce	Apaches Captured	
Inven-tions		Type Setting Machine	Sleeping Car Atlantic Cable	Repeating Rifle	Gatling Gun	Fire Extinguisher Telephone Crematory	Steam Heating Phonograph	Flying Machine	
Acqui-sitions		Gadsden			Alaska				
For'n Rel.	Clayton-Bulwer Treaty	Treaty with Japan	Treaty with China	Burlingame Treaty		Treaty of Washington	New Chinese Treaty	Treaty with China	
Slav-ery	Fugitive Slave Law	Underground Railway	Dred Scott Decision	Secession of States 13th Amendment		Ku Klux Klan Colored Senator	Anti-Chinese Bill Negro Exodus	Civil Service Chinese Bill	
Death	Calhoun Webster Clay		Irving Mann	Tyler Jackson Van Buren Buchanan		Greeley Prentice Pierce Farragut	Bryant	Garfield Emerson Longfellow	Young
Miscel-lany / States Admit.	California	Lopez Expedition	Minnesota Kansas Oregon / Secession	West Virginia Nevada Nebraska / Atlantic Cable Laid	Nevada	Colorado / Pacific R.R. Chicago Fire Weather Bureau	Electric Light Life Sav. Station	Washington Monument	
For'n Events	Cuban Revolution	Ostend Manifesto	Three Year War in Mexico	Fenian Raid in Canada Wars in South America		Franco-German War	Famine in Brazil		

ADMINISTRATIONS

	1885 CLEVELAND	1889 HARRISON	1893 CLEVELAND	1897 McKINLEY	1901 ROOSEVELT	1905 ROOSEVELT	1909 TAFT	1913 WILSON 1921
Pres.	Cleveland	Harrison	Cleveland	McKinley	Roosevelt	Roosevelt	Taft	Wilson
Cab't	Bayard, Fairchild	Blaine, Elkins	Olney, Carlisle	Root, Day, Wilson, Hay	Hay, Root	Taft, Root	Knox, MacVeagh	Bryan, Lansing, Lane, McAdoo
Messages			Venezuela	Panama Canal	Trusts	Trusts	Trusts	Tariff and Currency, Peace Treaty
Chief Just.	Fuller						White	
Decl'sions			Income Tax		Northern Securities		Standard Oil, Tobacco	Prohibition, Volstead Act
V. Pres.	Hendricks	Morton	Stevenson	Hobart	Roosevelt	Fairbanks	Sherman	Marshall
Speaker	Carlisle	Reed	Crisp	Reed	Henderson	Cannon	Cannon, Clark	Clark, Gillette
No. Mems. Senate / House	Senate 76, House 332	Senate 88, House 357	Senate 88, House 357	Senate 90, House 357	Senate 90, House 386	Senate 90, House 386	Senate 92, House 391	Senate 96, House 435
Leaders	Logan, Gorman	McKinley, Sherman	Wilson, Hill	Dingley, Hanna	Williams, Hoar	Lodge, Tillman	LaFollette, Underwood	Martin, Mann, Underwood
Laws	Interstate Com. Act, Dawes' Bill	International Copyright Law	Sherman Law, Wilson Bill	Chinese Exclusion Bill		Pure Food Law, Meat Insp. Bill	Payne-Aldrich Tariff	Tariff, Banking and Currency
Wars	Anarchist Riots	Sioux War	Coal Strikes, Railroad Strikes	Spanish American, Philippines		Springfield Riot		World War, U.S. Entered 1917
Inventions		Natural Gas used	Niagara Falls Harnessed	Liquefied Air, Wireless Telegraphy		Aeroplane		Wireless Telephone
For'n Acquisitions				Hawaii, Porto Rico, Guam, Philippines, Samoa				
For'n Rel.	Extrad. Treaty, C-Bayard Treaty	Samoan Treaty, Recip. Treaty		Arbitration Treaty, Hay-Pauncefote Treaty		Hay-Varilla Treaty		Freedom of the Sea, Mexican troubles
Death	Sheridan, Seymour, Arthur, Grant	Fremont		Jos. Jefferson, Harrison	McKinley	Harper, Hoar, Cleveland	Harlan, Dolliver	J. P. Morgan, Roosevelt
States Adm'd		Wash., Mont., N. and S. Dakota; Idaho, Wyoming	Utah			Oklahoma	Arizona, New Mexico	
Miscel.	Earthquake in Charleston	Johnstown Flood	World's Fair at Chicago			Baltimore Fire, Hague Peace Conference	Postal Banks, Parcel Post	16th, 17th, 18th, 19th Amendments
Events For'n	Chinese Exclusion Act	Brazil Republic, Boxer Rebellion	Cuban Rev., Hawaiian Rev.	Cuba under protection of U.S., Boer War		Russo-Japanese War	Turko-Italian War	Peace Treaty, League of Nations

ADMINISTRATIONS

	HARDING 1921	COOLIDGE 1923	HOOVER 1929	ROOSEVELT 1933
Pres.	Harding	Coolidge	Hoover	Roosevelt
Cab't	Hughes Weeks / Hoover Mellon	Kellogg Hoover / Mellon Davis	Stimson Hurley / Mellon Adams	Hull Ickes / Morgenthau Wickard
Mes-sages	Budget Reform Post-War Problems	Economy, Tax Re-vision	Farm Relief, Tax and Tariff Revision	Recovery, Relief, Banking Declarations of War
Chief Just.	Taft	Taft	Hughes	Stone
Deci-sions	Income Tax		Railroad Revaluation	Upheld Wagner Labor Act and Social Security Act
Pres.	Coolidge	Dawes	Curtis	Garner Wallace
Speak	Gillette	Gillette—Longworth	Longworth Garner	Bankhead Rayburn
Sen'te	Senate 96	Senate 96	Senate 96	Senate 96
House Mems	House 435	House 435	House 435	House 435
Lead-ers	Lodge Underwood	Lodge Capper Underwood	Smoot Moses Robinson	Glass Barkley Vandenberg Wheeler
Laws	Budget Reform Tax Revision	Tax Revision Immigration Law	Tariff Agricultural Relief	Banks, Stock Exchange, Labor, TVA, Lend-Lease
Wars				World War II
Inven-tions	Radio Telephony	Television	Talking Pictures	Synthetic Products
Insti-tutions				
Rel. Acqui-sitions				
For'n Rel.	Limit. Arms Conference	Military forces in China and Nicaragua	Moratorium on Germany's Debt	Reciprocal Trade Pacts Pan American Conferences
Slav-ery				
Death	Champ Clark Card. Gibbons	Woodrow Wilson Cummins Lodge	Edison Coolidge Taft Longworth	Robinson Swanson Borah Brandeis Card. Mundelein
Admin.				
Miscel-lany States		Navy Airplane crossed Pacific Ocean	Economic Depression	Roosevelt Elected to Third Term
For'n Events		Civil War—China Civil War—Mexico	Revolutions, S. Amer. Sino-Jap Conflict	Axis Nations Attack the United States

which President Cleveland had brought forward as an issue by a late message in December, 1887. Cleveland was nominated by the Democrats in that year, but was defeated by the Republican candidate, Benjamin Harrison, though Cleveland received a majority of the popular vote.

Harrison's administration was notable for the remarkable diplomacy of James G. Blaine, for the extension of the policy of reciprocity, for the passage of the McKinley Tariff Bill, the extension of the pension system by a dependent pension law, passed in 1890, by the repeal of the Bland-Allison law and the substitution of the Sherman Silver Purchase Act, requiring the Secretary of the Treasury to purchase 4,500,000 ounces of silver each month and to coin 2,000,000 ounces into dollars monthly. The monarchy in the Hawaiian Islands was overthrown, and a bill favoring annexation to the United States was passed by Congress. In 1892 the Democratic party returned to power, with Grover Cleveland and Adlai E. Stevenson as its candidates, the Republicans having nominated President Harrison and Whitelaw Reid. The People's party, or Populists, the successor of the Greenback-Labor party, nominated James B. Weaver of Iowa and received 22 electoral votes.

Financial Depression. The second administration of Cleveland opened with a terrible financial panic, with which most of the early important events of his term were connected, especially his efforts to repeal the Sherman law, his issuance of bonds to replenish the treasury gold reserve and the passage of the Wilson Tariff Law. The treaty of annexation of Hawaii was also withdrawn from the Senate, and the United States government made an effort to reëstablish the monarchy over the islands. Cleveland's term was also marked by the successful intervention of the United States in a boundary dispute between Venezuela and Great Britain; by a great world's fair at Chicago; by the settlement of the Bering Sea controversy over the seal fisheries; by the extension of the civil service reform and by a great strike of railroad employes, which necessitated the calling out of Federal troops. The Democratic party failed to support the President in his financial policy, and at its convention in 1896 it nominated William Jennings Bryan of Nebraska for President, upon a platform demanding the free and unlimited coinage of

silver on the ratio of 16 ounces of silver to one ounce of gold. The Republicans nominated William McKinley of Ohio. A faction of the Democratic party formed a new organization, known as the National Democratic party, favoring the gold standard, and nominated John M. Palmer of Illinois. The Prohibitionist candidate was Joshua Levering; the Socialist Labor standard bearer was Charles H. Matchett. The Populist party endorsed Bryan and the Free Silver Prohibition party nominated Charles E. Bentley. McKinley was elected by a large electoral and popular majority.

Spanish-American War and its Effects. The most important episode of McKinley's term was the Spanish-American War (which see). It resulted in the abolition of Spanish rule in Cuba and the establishment of military government under the United States, which continued until 1902, when the Republic of Cuba was organized. The war also brought into the possession of the United States the Philippine Islands and Porto Rico. In 1898 Hawaii was annexed to the United States, and in 1900 it was made a territory.

A law establishing the gold dollar as the standard of currency was adopted in 1900, and bills reorganizing the army and abolishing the army canteen were passed in 1901. The United States participated in a joint international military expedition to China, to assist in the suppression of the Boxer rebellion, in 1900. The diplomatic events following this expedition emphasized the change in the position of the United States in international affairs, and showed its new rank as a world power.

The chief issues in the campaign of 1900 were imperialism, that is, the question of the retention of the Philippine Islands, and the trust problem. McKinley was again the Republican nominee, and Bryan was the Democratic candidate. McKinley was elected by an increased majority. Soon after his inauguration, President McKinley was assassinated, while attending the Pan-American Exposition at Buffalo, and he was succeeded by Theodore Roosevelt, who retained McKinley's Cabinet and furthered his policy.

Commercial and Economic Expansion. During Roosevelt's administration, the important events were the passage of the Chinese Exclusion Bill; a law providing for the irrigation of the arid lands of the West; the conclusion of a reciprocity treaty with

Cuba; the creation of a department of Commerce and Labor, which in 1913 was reorganized into the Department of Commerce and the Department of Labor, the passage of the bills for the reorganization of the militia, the increase of the navy and the creation of a general staff for the army; the passage of an anti-trust law in 1903; the ratification of a treaty between the United States and Great Britain, giving the United States the right to construct and maintain a canal across the Isthmus. In 1904 a treaty was concluded with the new Republic of Panama providing for the construction of the Panama Canal. Roosevelt's administration was also marked by the successful conclusion of a treaty fixing the boundary between Alaska and the Northwest Territories of the Dominion of Canada, the result being generally favorable to the United States. The campaign of 1904 turned on the personalities of the candidates and on the questions raised by the policy of the Roosevelt administrations. Roosevelt was elected by a large majority over Alton B. Parker, the Democratic candidate. The successful intervention of President Roosevelt to end the Russo-Japanese War, the prosecution of several large corporations for violation of the anti-trust law, the agitation for regulation of railroad rates, the rigid investigations of insurance corporations, and the movement for the conservation of natural resources are important in Roosevelt's second administration.

Republican Defeat. In the election of 1908, William Howard Taft, the Republican candidate, was successful over Bryan. In the spring of 1909 the President called Congress in special session to revise the tariff. But the new tariff was unpopular, and was one of the strongest factors in causing the election of a majority of Democrats to the House of Representatives in 1910. This Congress passed acts for the admission of Arizona and New Mexico as states, and considered a reciprocity treaty with Canada which was finally rejected by the Canadians.

The election of 1912 was marked by a split in the Republican party. The regular Republicans renominated Taft and Sherman, but the supporters of Roosevelt, charging that they had been defrauded of their rights in the convention, withdrew, held a convention of their own and formed the national Progressive party, which nominated Roosevelt for President and Hiram Johnson of California for Vice-President. The Democratic candidates, Woodrow Wilson and Thomas R. Marshall, were elected by a plurality of more than 2,000,000 votes.

Wilson's Administration. Immediately after his inauguration President Wilson called Congress in special session to revise the tariff; the Underwood-Simmons Tariff Act was the result. Other important legislation included the Federal Reserve Act of 1913, establishing the Federal Reserve Banks, the Clayton Anti-Trust Act, the Trade Commission Act, and the repeal of the clause exempting American ships from paying toll for passing through the Panama Canal, in 1914. The opening of the Panama Canal to commerce, the international expositions at San Francisco and San Diego, Calif., the Bryan arbitration treaties with most of the world's civilized nations, and the proclamation of the seventeenth amendment to the Constitution were other important events of Wilson's first term.

Foreign relations occupied the attention of the President and of Congress to an unusual extent. During Taft's administration a revolution occurred in Mexico. Madero, the President, was assassinated, and Huerta, who was considered responsible for Madero's death, had assumed the Presidency. Wilson refused to recognize Huerta, but maintained a strictly neutral policy towards Mexican affairs, notwithstanding many insults were offered to American citizens and the government of the United States.

Affairs came to a crisis in April 1914, when a number of marines from a United States warship stationed at Tampico were arrested by Huerta's soldiers, while they went ashore peaceably to purchase supplies. Rear-Admiral Mayo demanded the release of the men, an apology and a salute to the United States flag. Huerta refused to salute the flag, and the President applied to Congress for permission to employ the military and naval forces to enforce his demands. His request was granted, and United States forces occupied Vera Cruz. There was a strong demand for intervention, but the President continued his policy of "watchful waiting", in the belief that the forces under Carranza would soon overthrow Huerta, and this they finally accomplished.

After Carranza became President, Villa, his chief aid in the overthrow of Huerta, rebelled and gained control over a number of the northern states of Mexico. In 1916 Villa's forces made a number of marauding raids into Texas, Arizona and New Mexico, and a punitive expedition under command of General Pershing, in conjunction with the forces of Carranza, attempted to capture Villa, but he escaped to the mountains, and in course of time the United States force was withdrawn.

The embargoes and blockades established by the belligerent nations in World War I complicated American relations with these nations, especially with Great Britain and Germany, because of the effect of these measures upon American commerce. The sinking of the *Lusitania,* May 7, 1915, by a German submarine, came near severing diplomatic relations between the United States and Germany, but the Imperial government made promises that partially satisfied the President, and the breach was avoided. Germany's acts aroused intense feeling against the country in the United States, and many Americans expected and desired war.

In the campaign of 1916 the nominees of the Republican party for President and Vice-President were Charles Evans Hughes of New York and Charles W. Fairbanks of Indiana. President Wilson and Vice-President Marshall were the Democratic nominees. The Republicans attacked the President's foreign policies, such as his "watchful waiting" in regard to Mexico and his long drawn-out diplomatic contest with Germany, and they opposed the economic theories of the Democrats. The Democrats asked for an endorsement of Wilson's record for constructive statesmanship in domestic affairs and approval of his forbearance and patience in the handling of intricate international problems. One of the rallying cries of the Democrats was "Wilson kept us out of war." The election was very close, for the country was plainly confused as to the exact attitude of both parties toward Germany. Wilson and Marshall secured 277 electoral votes and Hughes and Fairbanks 254. The Republicans carried the East and several Middle West states; the Democrats carried most of the West, part of the Middle West, and the South solidly. In general, the President ran ahead of his party, but the Democratic majority in Congress was considerably reduced.

The Approach of War. In spite of his record as a peace President, Wilson was forced to lead the country into World War I early in his new administration. On January 31, 1917, the German government made known its decision to begin unrestricted submarine warfare. The President was informed that American ships of any kind whatsoever violating certain specified regulations would be sunk without warning. This decision was the culmination of a long series of aggressive acts on the part of Germany, including the indefensible activities of a well-organized spy system.

With the approval of the majority of the people, the President on February 3 broke off diplomatic relations with Germany and handed Count Bernstorff, the German ambassador, his passports. After several weeks of uncertainty, during which German aggressions continued unchecked, the President (April 2, 1917) appeared before a special session of the Sixty-fifth Congress, and in a speech of moving eloquence asked that body to declare that a state of war existed between the Imperial German government and the United States. The next day the Foreign Affairs Committees of both houses agreed upon a resolution formally declaring this fact. On April 4 the Senate passed the resolution by a vote of 86 to 6 and the House took similar action on April 6 by a vote of 373 to 50. On the afternoon of that day the resolution was signed by the President.

In World War I. Measures relating to the prosecution of the war were given immediate consideration. As emergencies arose, laws conferring extraordinary powers upon the President, providing for regulating the distribution of food and fuel, placing the operation of the railroads and finally of the telegraph and telephone lines under control of the government, were passed. Regardless of party, Congress and the nation supported the President in the prosecution of the war. Taxes were increased, and five government loans aggregating over $19,000,000,000 were authorized and oversubscribed. Never before had a nation accomplished a task of such magnitude within the allotted time as did the United States in prosecuting the war with Germany.

At the declaration of war America had an army of less than 200,000 men. The nation was insufficiently supplied with arms, munitions and other equipment for a large army, and was without sufficient ships for transporting men and supplies to Europe. Through the coöperation and help of its

Outline on the United States

I. LOCATION AND EXTENT
  (a) Latitude
  (b) Longitude
  (c) Boundaries
  (d) Area
  (e) Comparison with other countries

II. SURFACE AND DRAINAGE
  (a) Atlantic slope
  (b) Appalachian highlands
  (c) Great central plain
  (d) Rocky Mountain highlands
  (e) Pacific slope
  (f) River systems
  (g) Lakes

III. CLIMATE
  (a) Conditions expected, due to latitude
  (b) Changes wrought by physical conditions
  (c) Average temperature in various sections
  (d) Average rainfall in various sections
  (e) Need for irrigation

IV. INDUSTRIES
  (a) Mineral resources
    (1) Where each is found
    (2) Annual output and value
    (3) States leading in production
  (b) Agricultural products
    (1) Cereals
    (2) Fruits
    (3) Market gardening
    (4) Live stock and dairy products
  (c) Manufactures
    (1) Natural locations of districts
    (2) Leading industries
      (a) Iron and steel
      (b) Textiles
      (c) Boots and shoes
      (d) Others of note
      (e) Rank with other nations in production
  (d) Commerce
    (1) Domestic commerce
      (a) By rail
      (b) By water
      (c) Coasting trade
    (2) Foreign commerce
      (a) Leading countries included in
      (b) Exports and imports
      (c) Principal countries engaged in carrying trade

V. POPULATION
  (a) Per cent of annual increase
  (b) Center and density of population
  (c) Comparative growth of cities and rural communities
  (d) Immigration

VI. GOVERNMENT
  (a) General character
  (b) Departments
    (1) Executive
      (a) President
      (b) Vice-President
    (2) Legislative
      (a) Congress
        (1) Senate
        (2) House of Representatives
    (3) Judicial
      (a) Supreme Court
      (b) Inferior courts
        (1) Circuit courts
        (2) District courts
        (3) Courts of appeals
  (c) State governments
  (d) Government of dependencies
  (e) Territories

VII. EDUCATION IN UNITED STATES

VIII. CITIES
  (a) List of twenty-five largest

IX. HISTORY
  (a) Periods
    (1) Discovery and exploration
    (2) Colonization
    (3) Development of colonies
    (4) War for independence
    (5) Organization of republic
    (6) National growth

(a) Development of resources

(b) Annexation of territory

(7) Mexican war

(8) Slavery issue

(9) Civil war

(10) Reconstruction

(11) Industrial progress

(12) Spanish-American war

(13) World War

(14) Prohibition era

(15) Stock-market crash

(16) Bank failures

(17) "New Deal" Policies

Questions on the United States

How does the United States compare in area with the other-great countries of the world?

What change does a ship have to make in its dates in going from San Francisco to the Philippine Islands?

What geographic conditions exert the greatest influence upon human development?

What effect does the geographic position of the United States have upon her industrial development?

How does this location affect her relations to other countries?

Why were the English colonies confined to a narrow strip of land along the Atlantic Coast?

What is the most remarkable feature of the boundary line between the United States and Canada?

Why is the Atlantic coast line so much longer than that on the Pacific?

Which coast has the larger number of good harbors? Why?

What is the Fall Line? Why is it so called?

What part of the United States is the greatest agricultural region in the world? What conditions have made it so?

Account for the location and growth of the following cities: New York, Chicago, Galveston, Seattle.

How many railroads extend across the United States from the Mississippi River to the Pacific Coast?

What effect have these so-called transcontinental lines had upon the development of the country west of the Mississippi River?

How does the Constitution of the United States differ from the Articles of Confederation?

What political party supported the ratification of the Constitution? From what circumstance was this party named?

What American inventions have exerted the greatest influence upon the industries and commerce of the world?

What regions in the United States are widely known for their scenery?

What has the National government done to preserve these regions for the people?

What island possession of the United States is about two-thirds the area of Connecticut? How does it compare with Connecticut in population?

From what nations did the United States receive the largest number of immigrants in the years just preceding the World War?

What effect did the World War have upon immigration?

How do you account for the rapid growth of cities since 1890?

What effect did the entrance of the United States into the World War have upon the American merchant marine?

What precedents of long standing did President Wilson set aside?

Why does not the United States have a national system of education?

How many hours apart by air are New York and Los Angeles?

How many Americans were killed in the World War? How many died of disease? How many were wounded?

How important are the new oil fields in Texas?

What cities in the United States are almost directly north of the city of Panama, at the western terminus of the Panama Canal?

What is the official status of child labor in the United States?

What is the status of Porto Rico?

What is the "Galveston plan" in the government of cities?

allies, the unstinted devotion and loyalty of the American people and a speeding up of all war activities, the United States placed on the battlefields of France over 2,225,000 soldiers, trained and equipped, including needed men back of the lines. The American army played an important part in the operations of the summer of 1918, and contributed materially to bringing about an armistice on November 11, 1918. (For a full account of the nation's war activities, see the article WORLD WAR.)

The Way to Peace. President Wilson had, during the war, issued a statement summarizing the objects for which America was fighting. These were grouped in fourteen paragraphs, the last one calling for a general association of nations. He led an American delegation to the peace conference in Paris in 1919. The conference finally drafted treaties between the warring nations, including the establishment of a league of nations. President Wilson submitted the treaty to the United States Senate in May, 1919, but the Senate refused to ratify it, and it was not until 1921 that separate treaties were made with Germany and its allies.

Constitutional Amendments. The eighteenth (prohibition) amendment to the Constitution, was ratified by the States and became effective January 16, 1920. The nineteenth amendment, extending suffrage rights to women, was ratified in 1920. The twentieth amendment, changing the time for sessions of Congress and inauguration of the President, was ratified in 1933. The twenty-first amendment, repealing the eighteenth, was ratified in 1933.

Later Events. In 1920 Warren G. Harding was elected President and Calvin Coolidge Vice President. Important events in Harding's administration were the Limitation of Arms Conference in Washington, which resulted in an agreement for a naval holiday; a law to restrict immigration; the enactment of a budget law, and an extension of the program of aid for veterans of the World War. President Harding died in 1923, and was succeeded as President by Vice President Coolidge. (See HARDING, WARREN G.)

The Coolidge administration was a period of peace and recovery from the effects of war. The budget system was continued, taxes were reduced and greater economy was exercised in government affairs. Congress passed a new income tax law, and passed a soldiers'

bonus law over the President's veto. (See COOLIDGE, CALVIN.)

In 1928, Herbert Hoover, Secretary of Commerce since 1920, was elected President by a record popular vote. To meet the demands of a depressed agriculture President Hoover advocated measures for farm relief. The Smoot-Hawley tariff act was passed in 1930; it increased duties on many farm products. To aid world recovery, President Hoover, in 1931, presented a plan, which was adopted, for a moratorium of one year on the payment of war debts. For other events in this administration, see HOOVER, HERBERT.

In 1932 the Democratic candidates, Franklin Delano Roosevelt and John Nance Garner, won the election. In 1936 they were reëlected by increased majorities. The Roosevelt administration was notable for reforms in the economic, financial and political fields. The President received wide powers to regulate credit, currency and banking. Legislation was passed placing the security and commodity exchanges under rigid control and restricting utility holding companies. Corporation income taxes were increased. Laws favorable to organized labor were enacted. Vast sums were voted for unemployment relief and public works and for the benefit of farmers and other depressed groups. Congress passed a Social Security Law authorizing old-age and other benefits.

Following the outbreak of war in Europe, in 1939, the United States adopted a policy of aid to Great Britain and other nations attacked by Germany. In 1940, President Roosevelt was elected to a third term and Henry A. Wallace was elected Vice-President. Congress voted billions of dollars for rearmament, passed the Lend-Lease and Selective Service acts and modified the Neutrality Act. On December 7, 1941, during negotiations with Japan for a settlement of Far Eastern problems, Japanese forces made surprise attacks on the Philippines and on Pearl Harbor, Hawaii. On December 8, Congress declared war on Japan. Within a week the United States was also at war with Germany and Italy and their allies.

Related Articles. The reader is referred to the following articles:

Alleghany Mountains	Missouri River
Appalachian Mountains	Niagara Falls and River
Cascade Range	Ohio River
Coast Range	Parks, National
Columbia River	Rocky Mountains
Grand Canyon	Saint Lawrence River
Great Lakes	Sierra Nevada Mountains
Mississippi River	

UNITED STATES STEEL CORPORA-TION, the largest business enterprise in the world, was organized in 1901, by the consolidation of a number of large corporations engaged in the manufacture of iron and steel. These included the Carnegie, the Federal Steel, the American Steel and Wire, the National Steel, the National Tube and the American Tin Plate companies. The United States Steel Corporation makes more steel than all of Great Britain or Germany, and one-fourth of the total amount made in all the countries of the world. Many of the employes have become stockholders, and the corporation has a commendable record in its dealings with its great army of workmen. In 1911 the United States government brought suit for the dissolution of the corporation on grounds of violating the Sherman Anti-Trust Law; in 1915 the courts sustained the corporation and an appeal was taken to the Supreme Court. This court decided that the corporation need not be dissolved.

The capital of the corporation is over $1,000,000,000; its gross revenues sometimes have exceeded a million dollars a day.

UNIVER'SALISTS, a religious body whose distinctive belief is that all men will ultimately be saved; in other words, that eternal progress is the lot of every created soul. This, they claim, is in harmony with the teachings of Jesus and early interpretations of the Bible, as well as with science and philosophy. As a faith universalism has a place in Christian thought far beyond the confines of the organized body, which was established late in the eighteenth century in Massachusetts by an English clergyman, John Murray. There are now about 55,000 Universalists in the United States and 2,000 in Canada.

UNIVERSAL LANGUAGE, a proposed medium of communication, for the use of all peoples of the earth which have commercial intercourse with each other. There have been two unsuccessful efforts in this direction within recent years, Esperanto and Volapuk (which see).

UNIVERSE, *u'ni vurs,* a term referring to all created things, embracing everything included in space, planets, suns, stars, considered as an orderly system. Man's idea of the universe has been an expanding one. At first he considered the earth the center about which sun, moon and stars revolved. Then he discovered that earth, asteroids and planets revolve about the sun and thought of our solar system as the universe. Now he knows that the system of which our earth is a part is but one among the millions whirling majestically in the immensity of space. The universe in its vastness is beyond the power of the mind to conceive.

Related Articles. Consult the following tites for additional information:

Astronomy	Planet
Earth	Stars
Moon	Solar System
Nebular Hypothesis	Sun

UNIVERSITY, an institution for advanced learning or for the examination of students who have c o m p l e t e d specified courses in the h i g h e r branches. Universities are maintained in nearly all countries, and they confer degrees which receive universal recognition. A study of the organization of the universities of different countries shows that there are some variations in plan and spirit, but everywhere the term *university* i m p l i e s a greater number of departments and courses of study than does *college* (which see).

Some universities and colleges with continuous existence since they were founded are among the oldest institutions of man. In the American Union, Harvard (1636), William and Mary (1693), Yale (1701), Moravian Seminary and College for Women (1742), Princeton (1746), University of Pennsylvania (1749), Washington and Lee (1749), Columbia, for many years King's College (1754), Brown University, (1764), Dartmouth (1769), Hampton-Sydney (1775), are older than the United States.

It is believed that the oldest university in the world with a continuous existence is El Azhar, in Cairo, Egypt; it was founded in 972 of the Christian Era, or 361 by Mohammedan calculation. The University of Pavia, Italy, was founded by Lothair, grandson of Charlemagne, in 825, but its history has not been continuous. The University of Bologna, Italy, was organized as a body of students in 1088; it reverted to the standard type in 1200. The oldest university in the New World is still in operation at Lima, Peru, dating from 1551.

In the United States. In the United States the term *university* has been used indiscriminately and is sometimes applied to degree-conferring institutions regardless of their provision for graduate work. Moreover, many schools established in the newer states, either by private or denominational enterprises, have been styled universities when they are really colleges offering courses given in the undergraduate department of the true university.

A university maintains a college of liberal arts, and faculties of law, medicine, engineering, agriculture, journalism, etc. In the universities of highest standard students entering the professional departments are required to have two or more years of college work.

According to the plan upon which they have been established, American universities can be grouped into the following classes:

(1) Those which have developed from older colleges, such as Harvard, Yale, Pennsylvania and Princeton.

(2) Those that have been established by act of legislature and are known as state universities, such as the universities of Michigan, Minnesota, Wisconsin and Illinois.

(3) Those that have been established by benefactions, such as Johns Hopkins and Cornell.

(4) Those established under the auspices of some religious denomination, such as the Catholic University, at Washington; the University of Chicago, and Northwestern University, at Evanston and Chicago.

All of these institutions maintain undergraduate, or college, departments, and in some of the newer states the state university is under the necessity of maintaining a preparatory school.

In Canada. Provincial and endowed universities and colleges are maintained in the Dominion in large numbers. The universities of British Columbia, Alberta, Saskatchewan and Manitoba correspond in a general way to the American state universities. In Ontario the University of Toronto is at the head of the school system. In Quebec the two leading universities, McGill and Laval, are at the head of the Protestant and Catholic schools, respectively.

(For more detailed information, consult the articles on the various institutions and provinces.)

Related Articles. The most important universities of the world are described in these volumes under their separate headings. They are listed at the end of the article Education. Each of the American state universities is given separate treatment in alphabetical order.

UNIVERSITY EXTEN'SION, a movement for extending the means of a higher education to persons of all classes, by a system of lectures and instruction, carried on by instructors of an established university. University extension originated with Cambridge University, England, in 1872, and it was taken up by the University of Oxford in 1885.

In the United States the movement was

systematically started by Doctor Melville Dewey in 1888. At that time Doctor Dewey was chief librarian of Columbia University, and he laid before the regents of the University of the State of New York a plan for university extension, in connection with public libraries. Two years later a committee of the New York colleges and universities urged the regents to establish such a system of teaching under state supervision, and in 1891 a bill passed the legislature, appropriating $10,000 for the expenses of organizing the movement. Previous to this, some extension work had been done by the professors of Johns Hopkins University, who, however, conducted it as an individual enterprise, and in 1891 the University of Pennsylvania organized a corps of lecturers, who were to lecture on literature, history, sociology and science in the surrounding towns, wherever local organizations for the study of any of these subjects could be formed. From these beginnings the larger universities took up the work, and it gradually extended over the country. The most successful work has been done by the universities of Pennsylvania, Cornell, Harvard, Yale, Chicago and Wisconsin.

The plan includes (1) the arrangement of lecture study courses with syllabi, by the faculties of the university; (2) the organization of local centers, these centers to include people who are interested in pursuing some one of the lecture courses; they decide upon the subject to be studied and engage the lecturer, whose salary and traveling expenses are paid by the center; (3) the lecture, with studies conducted either before or after it, the lecturer carrying on a quiz, in which he gives opportunity for free discussion, asking and answering questions; (4) traveling libraries, which are sent to the different centers; (5) the preparation of papers by members of the center, these papers being read and graded by the lecturer; (6) the giving of credits by the university, for satisfactory completion of the work. These credits are of limited value to those who are seeking degrees. Agricultural colleges in some states have extension departments which render very practical assistance to the farmer and his family. The extension department of the University of Wisconsin is intended to cover practically all lines of industry in the state. See CHAUTAUQUA INSTITUTION.

UNKNOWN SOLDIER TOMBS. After the World War, national commissions sought to identify and give burial in special war cemeteries to the honored dead of the allied nations. It was found impossible to identify or to locate the remains of many thousands of these. A sentimental gesture to honor collectively the unknown dead from each of the principal allied countries brought the highest patriotic response from all the people.

The United States took the body of an unidentified soldier of the American armies from his nameless grave in France, brought it home on a warship, and buried it impressively in Arlington National Cemetery. The body of a British unknown was solemnly interred within the precincts of Westminster Abbey. France's unknown hero was taken to Paris and buried beneath the Arc de Triomphe (Arch of Triumph), where burns an everlasting flame. Belgium selected one of its unknown dead and gave him a resting place in Brussels, at the base of the Colonnade of the Congress. Italy's selection for the honor of representing all of that country's unknown dead lies beneath a hilltop monument in Rome.

U'PAS, a tree belonging to the same family as the mulberry and breadfruit, common in the forests of Java and the Philippine Islands. The exaggerated stories formerly current concerning the deadly exhalations of this plant are now believed to have their origin in the presence of volcanic gases in the Javanese valleys. The sap, however, is poisonous and forms the principal element in a mixture used by the natives for tipping their arrowheads. The fiber of the bark is made into a kind of cloth.

U'RAL MOUNTAINS, a low mountain range in Russia extending southward from the Arctic Ocean, approximately along the 60th meridian of east longitude, and forming a portion of the boundary between Europe and Asia. The highest elevations are in the northern and southern sections and exceed 5,000 feet. The central section is low, and through a pass in this part of the range the Trans-Siberian Railway reaches Siberia. The lower slopes are covered with forests of evergreens, birch and beech. The Central Urals are rich in minerals, which include gold, silver, copper, iron, lead, zinc and platinum. There are also large deposits of coal.

URAL RIVER, a river of Russia, rising on the eastern slope of the Ural Mountains and flowing southward a distance of 1,400 miles into the Caspian Sea. Its chief tributaries are the Kizil and the Sak-Mara from the west, and the Sunduk, the Or and the Ilek from the east. Rainfall in the Ural basin is slight, and the river is shallow and unnavigable, except during the period of high water.

URA'NIA, in Greek mythology, the muse of astronomy, usually represented as holding in her left hand a celestial globe and in her right a staff or compass.

URA'NIUM, a rare, silvery-white metallic element, found chiefly as an oxide in pitchblende. It is the source of uranium yellow, used for painting on glass and porcelain, and in making the fluorescent yellow uranium glass. With its compounds, uranium is radioactive, undergoing slow disintegration with the formation of a new element, known as uranium X. See RADIOACTIVITY.

U'RANUS, the seventh planet from the sun, discovered by Sir William Herschel in 1781 and first called *Georgium Sidus,* in honor of George III, and afterwards *Herschel,* in honor of the discoverer. Both these names falling into disuse, the name *Uranus,* suggested by Bode, was adopted. Its mean distance from the sun is more than 1,750,000,000 miles. The length of its year is equal to about eighty-four of our years; the length of its day is thought to be about ten hours. Its mean diameter is estimated at about 33,000 miles. Its volume is about seventy-four times that of the earth, but its mean density is so much less that the mass of Uranus is only about twelve and one-half times as great as that of the earth.

Uranus has four satellites, which differ from those of all but one of the other planets, in that their orbits are nearly perpendicular to that of the planet, while the satellites of the other planets revolve in nearly the same plane as the planet to which they belong. Through the telescope, Uranus is merely a pale, greenish disk, with no certain markings; but the spectroscope seems to indicate that it differs materially from the other planets in composition. To the naked eye it appears like a star of the sixth magnitude. See PLANET.

URANUS, in Greek mythology, the husband of Gaea, the earth, and father of her children, the Titans and Cyclops. Uranus hated his children and confined them in Tartarus, but on the instigation of Gaea, Saturn, the youngest of the Titans, overthrew and dethroned him. From the part of his blood which fell upon the earth sprang Gigantes, father of the giants, and from the part which fell into the sea sprang the goddess Aphrodite.

UR'BAN, the name of eight Roman Popes, three of whom made notable contribution to history.

Urban I, SAINT, was bishop of Rome from 222 to 230. He was a strong pontiff, setting himself firmly against the schismatic movement of Hippolytus, which he kept in check.

Urban II was Pope from 1088 to 1099. He successfully prosecuted the struggle of the Papacy against Henry IV, and in 1094 he excommunicated Philip I of France for his matrimonial infidelity. In 1095 he presided at the famous Council of Clermont, which gave the impulse to the Crusades. He died before the success of the First Crusade, which he had organized.

Urban VIII, Pope from 1624 to 1644, supported Richelieu's policy against Austria and Spain. He was the founder of the College of the Propaganda and was a patron of Galileo.

URBAN'A, ILL., the county seat of Champaign County, 128 miles nearly south of Chicago, on the Wabash, the Cleveland, Cincinnati, Chicago & Saint Louis and the Illinois Central railroads. It shares its railroad facilities and the University of Illinois campus (see ILLINOIS, UNIVERSITY OF) with Champaign, which adjoins it on the west. Urbana is the trade center for a rich agricultural and coal-mining region. Railroad shops of the Cleveland, Cincinnati, Chicago & Saint Louis (New York Central) are here. Chanute Field, a United States Army training field, is at Rantoul, twelve miles to the north. Urbana's largest park is the 102-acre Crystal Lake Park, a woodland resort and recreational area. The place was settled in 1824 and was chartered as a city in 1860. The government is by mayor and council. Population, 1940, 14,064.

URINE, *u'rin,* the fluid waste separated from the blood by the kidneys. It carries out of the system many of the wornout tissues, especially the nitrogenous waste. Its composition varies in different animals. Human urine, of a healthy individual, is a clear, amber-colored fluid, slightly acid, and it weighs one and fifteen-thousandths to one and twenty-five thousandths times as much as water. The average quantity discharged in twenty-four hours is about two and a half pints, but the amount varies greatly, being diminished during excessive perspiration, thirst and fever, and being increased by cold, by drinking large quantities of water, by exercise, by certain foods, as salt or sugar, and by certain drugs. The principal solid and the most important ingredient found in urine is urea, the amount of which varies, being greater when animal food is used freely than when the diet is vegetable. The condition of the urine is an index to the state of health, and physicians often analyze it as a part of their diagnosis. The presence of albumin indicates Bright's disease, and the presence of sugar indicates diabetes.

URSA MAJOR and **URSA MINOR** (greater bear and lesser bear), two constellations of the northern hemisphere always visible and wheeling about the Polar Star, which at present is that star in the extremity of the little bear's tail. In the larger constellation are seven bright stars which outline the Great Dipper.

UR'SO, CAMILLA (1842–1902), a famous violinist, born in Nantes, France, who came to America at the age of ten. She appeared in concert with immense success, becoming the most noted female violinist in the world.

URSULA, SAINT, a legendary saint and martyr in the Roman Catholic Church, whose story has been given various forms. She is supposed to have suffered death about the year 237. By repute the daughter of a British king, she was desired by the son of another king for his wife; if his suit were denied, her father's lands would be devastated. Ursula had vowed to remain a virgin, so she succeeded in securing a three-years' delay before deciding. During this time she was to visit holy places, and she chose 11,000 virgins to accompany her. When Cologne was reached in a voyage down the Rhine the Huns murdered all of them; a church was later built over their remains.

URSULINES, ur'su linz, or **NUNS OF SAINT URSULA,** a sisterhood founded by Saint Angela Merici, at Brescia, Italy, in 1537, especially for the education of girls. They had many houses in France during the seventeenth century. The Canadian Ursulines date from 1639; the Irish, from 1771. There are now four houses in Ireland, four in England and twenty-four in the United States, with thousands of pupils. The whole number is 300 convents and 7,000 nuns.

Theater in Montevideo

URUGUAY, u'roo gwa, or oo'roo gwi, officially THE EASTERN REPUBLIC OF URUGUAY, is the smallest republic of South America. It is separated from Argentina on the west of the Uruguay River, and is bounded on the northeast and east by Brazil; the great estuary of the Rio de La Plata washes its southern shore. The country is nearly triangular in outline; its greatest length and breadth, 350 miles, are about equal; its area is 72,153 square miles, making it about one-half the size of Montana, or equal to the combined areas of North Dakota and Delaware. Population, 1934, 1,993,234.

The People. The population is about equally divided between the white and colored peoples, the latter including Paraguay Indians, or *Guarani,* and mixed breeds. Spaniards and Italians constitute the great majority of the whites, though the Germans and French are numerous. The speech, manners and customs are Spanish. The color line is drawn in the names of the political parties which are designated as *Blancos* and *Colorados* (whites and colored), but in political practice these names have lost much of their former significance. The chief cities are Montevideo (which see), the capital, with a population of 667,212, 1934. Paysandu, on the Uruguay River; Salto, Mercedes, San José, Agosto and Maldonado.

The Roman Catholic Church has by far the largest number of adherents, and until 1916 it was the state Church. In that year the state Church was abolished, and all religious denominations were placed on an equal footing before the government.

Surface and Drainage. In the north and west there are ranges of low mountains, or hills, which attain an altitude of about 2,000 feet, and along the Uruguay River are tablelands, somewhat higher than those in Argentina; but the southeastern part of the country is low and marshy, and the interior is composed of rolling plains. The chief rivers are the Uruguay, which forms the western boundary, and its largest tributary, the Negro, which flows across the country in a southwesterly direction, dividing it into two nearly equal parts. Lake Mirim, situated on the northeastern border, is partly in Uruguay and partly in Brazil. The plains in the interior and the hills in the north and northwest are covered with dense forests, and the southeastern portion of the country is overgrown with grass.

Resources and Industries. The chief minerals are iron, zinc, lead, antimony, sulphur and coal, and some gold has been found. There are also quarries of marble and other building stone, but the mineral resources of the country have not been extensively exploited. The rich soil and salubrious climate, accompanied by an abundance of moisture, make the country favorable for agriculture, yet only small areas are under tillage. The chief crops are wheat, corn, barley, millet, oats, rye and flaxseed. Stockraising is the most important industry of the country, and large numbers of horses, mules, cattle and sheep are reared.

There is a yearly average of more than 7,-250,000 cattle and about 21,000,000 sheep. Wool and meat are the principal exports.

Transportation and Trade. Many of the rivers are navigable, and are used for inland transportation. There are over 1,700 miles of railway connecting the chief centers of trade within the country with those of Argentina, besides 170 miles of tramways. In proportion to its size, Uruguay has more miles of good roads than most other South American countries. All the important towns have telegraph and telephone service.

The imports consist of foodstuffs, cotton and woolen goods, clothing, machinery and other manufactured products. The exports include meats, hides, tallow, cattle, wool and a few other agricultural products.

Education. The University of Uruguay, at Montevideo, is the leading educational institution. It has departments of law, medicine, mathematics, agriculture, commerce, social service and veterinary science. There are also a preparatory school and other institutions for secondary education and normal schools for both sexes. Its library and museum are of considerable value. The public schools are poor. There is a compulsory education law, but it is not enforced, and the proportion of illiteracy is very large.

Government and History. Uruguay has a republican form of government, at the head of which is a President. This official was originally elected by the national legislative body, consisting of a Senate and a Chamber of Representatives. In 1934 a new Constitution was adopted; this provides for a President, elected by the legislature, and a Council of Ministers composed of nine members from the two leading political parties.

Uruguay was a source of dispute between Spain and Portugal in early times, but finally became a Spanish possession, forming a part of the Viceroyalty of Rio de la Plata. It was later, for a short time, a province of Brazil, becoming independent in 1828. Until the close of the first decade of the twentieth century, Uruguay was torn by revolution and political strife. Then it prospered until the depression of 1929 affected its foreign markets; political unrest followed but civil war was averted. The increase in the export of livestock products, caused by the outbreak of war in Europe in 1939, somewhat eased the economic stress of the country. Uruguay participates, with the rest of the Americas, in Pan American affairs.

URUGUAY RIVER, a South American river which rises in the southeastern part of Brazil, flows westward, then southward, and enters the estuary of the Rio de la Plata. It forms a part of the boundary between Brazil and Argentina and the entire boundary between Argentina and Uruguay. Its length is about 950 miles, and in the lower part of its course it is from six to nine miles wide. It is navigable for large vessels as far as Paysandu, about 150 miles, and for smaller vessels for 300 miles farther.

USURY, u' zhu ry, originally, money paid for the use of money, or interest; according to present usage, interest in excess of the legal rate. In most states a maximum rate of interest is fixed by law, and penalties of greater or less severity, imposed for charging a higher rate. The table below gives the legal rate of interest in each of the states, and also the rate permitted if both parties agree. See INTEREST.

STATES	Legal Rate Per Cent	Contract Rate Per Cent	STATES	Legal Rate Per Cent	Contract Rate Per Cent
Alabama ...	8	8	Florida	8	10
Alaska	8	12	Georgia	7	8
Arizona	6	8	Idaho	6	8
Arkansas ..	6	10	Illinois	5	7
California ..	7	12	Indiana	6	8
Colorado ...	8	*	Iowa	6	8
Connecticut	6	12	Kansas	6	10
Delaware ...	6	6	Kentucky ..	6	6
D. of Col. ..	6	8	Louisiana ..	5	8

STATES	Legal Rate Per Cent	Contract Rate Per Cent	STATES	Legal Rate Per Cent	Contract Rate Per Cent
Maine	6	*	Ohio	6	8
Maryland	6	6	Oklahoma	6	10
Mass.	6	*	Oregon	6	10
Michigan	7	7	Penn.	6	6
Minnesota	6	8	R. Island	6	*
Mississippi	6	8	S. Carolina	7	8
Missouri	6	8	S. Dakota	6	8
Montana	8	*	Tennessee	6	6
Nebraska	6	9	Texas	6	10
Nevada	7	*	Utah	8	12
New Hamp.	6	*	Vermont	6	6
New Jersey	6	6	Virginia	6	6
New Mexico	6	10	Wash.	6	12
New York	6	6	W. Virginia	6	6
N. Carolina	6	6	Wisconsin	6	10
N. Dakota	8	8	Wyoming	7	10

*Any rate on which both parties may agree.

UTAH, one of the Rocky Mountain states, originally settled by the Mormons. The name of the state is the designation of the Ute, or Utah, a tribe of Indians, and means *highlanders*. Because of the extensive salt lake within its borders, Utah is popularly called THE SALT LAKE STATE; other popular names are BEEHIVE STATE and MORMON STATE. The motto is *Deseret,* a word meaning *Industry* in the Book of Mormon. The state flower is the sego lily.

Location and Area. The state is bounded on the north by Idaho and Wyoming, on the east by Colorado and Wyoming, on the south by Arizona and on the west by Nevada. It has straight boundary lines on all sides, and is regularly oblong in shape, except in the northeastern corner, where the southwestern corner of Wyoming cuts off several square miles.

The state is tenth in the Union in size, with an area of 84,916 square miles, of which 2,570 square miles are water; it is more than twice as large as Virginia, and about one-third the size of Texas.

People and Cities. The population of Utah in 1940 was 550,310, giving it the rank of forty-first among the states in number of inhabitants. The average density was 6.7 persons to the square mile; only six other states are less densely settled. About eight per cent of the whole population is foreign-born; of these, the principal nationalities are the English, Danish, Swedish, Greek, German, Italian, Scotch, Welsh and Norwegian. There are about 2,200 Indians on reservations, and about 1,100 Negroes.

About sixty-five per cent of the inhabitants are adherents of the Church of Jesus Christ of Latter Day Saints (Mormon). Roman Catholics, Methodists and Presbyterians are well represented, and other sects are found in small numbers.

About 55.5 per cent of the inhabitants are urban. Only four cities have populations of 10,000 or over: Salt Lake City (the capital), 149,934; Ogden, 43,688; Provo, 18,071; and Logan, 11,868.

Surface and Drainage. The surface is greatly diversified, containing high mountains, broad, arid valleys and desert plateaus. Near the middle of the northern boundary, the Wasatch Mountains enter the state and extend southward along the middle line, finally degenerating into plateaus. This is the principal mountain range of the state, and its position marks the highest land, from which, as a watershed, the streams flow eastward and westward, the former to the Colorado, the latter to sink in the Great Basin. Eastward from the Wasatch, along the northern boundary of Utah, stretches a broad, massive range known as the Uinta. It has many high peaks, including Gilbert, Kings, Emmons and Lovenia.

Great Salt Lake, with its extraordinary percentage of saline matter in solution, is but the remnant of a vast body of fresh water, which once covered Western Utah. The principal stream of Eastern Utah is the Colorado. This is formed by the junction of Green River, which rises in the Wind River Mountains of Wyoming and the Grand, whose sources are in the snow fields on Long's Peak, in Colorado. The Green and the Colorado receive numerous branches from the Uinta and Wasatch ranges, among them the Uinta, the Price, the Fremont, the San Rafael and the Virgin. The scenery is varied, including fertile valleys, snow-capped mountains, the Great American Desert (an area as large as Connecticut), deep canyons, dashing Cascades and the greatest natural bridges in the world. In the southern part are the Zion and Bryce Canyon National Parks. See PARKS, NATIONAL.

Climate. The mean annual temperature ranges from 48°, in the north, to 51°, in the south. The mean temperature at Frisco is 51°. The average rainfall is 16 inches. If the snow chances to fall early in the winter, it becomes compact, and the melting is retarded. A fall of snow late in the season lies loosely on the mountain sides, and the water reaches the valleys before the crops are ready to receive its full benefit.

Mineral Resources. Next to agriculture, mining is the chief industry. Utah has 210 useful minerals. Silver is found in nearly all the mountains, and Utah is second among the states in production. The gold product is over $4,000,000. Utah ranks second in the production of copper and third in lead. Other important metals are iron and zinc. There are extensive coal fields in Emery, Carbon and Summit counties, the largest sulphur deposits in the world are in Millard and Washington counties, and a superior quality of onyx is found on the west shore of Utah Lake. Salt is mined in Juab County and is obtained from Great Salt Lake. Other mineral products are asphalt, building stone, mica, graphite and gypsum. The state also has a natural gas area.

Agriculture. The agricultural districts of the state are chiefly in the valleys immediately west of the Wasatch Mountains, in the Great Basin. Elsewhere, except in a few favored spots, the altitude or the insufficient water supply east of the Wasatch range, prevents successful farming. This vast area is used for grazing, and large herds of sheep and cattle are raised. Many sheep are exported, and the production of wool exceeded 17,-000,000 pounds in 1933.

Irrigation in the Great Basin of Utah was the first important enterprise of the kind by Anglo-Saxons in the arid west. In 1847, the Mormon pioneers turned the waters of City Creek upon the parched soil of Salt Lake Valley, and now, out of 1,250,000 acres of improved land, over 1,000,000 acres are irrigated. The wheat, oats, barley, hay and rye are of superior quality, and the yield is large. In most localities the heights are too cool for successful corn-growing. Potatoes, beets and other vegetables are profitably

raised. Utah is the fourth state in the production of sugar beets. Fruits are abundant. Among these are apples, peaches, plums, apricots, cherries and grapes; and in the south, oranges, lemons and figs are grown.

Manufactures. Utah is rapidly forging ahead in industry, the larger cities being extensively engaged in both manufacturing and distributing activities. The industrial plants of Salt Lake City number 263. The leading manufacturing industry is the smelting and refining of copper and lead ores. Other industries, in the order of their importance, are the manufacture of beet sugar, flour and grist milling, construction and repair of railroad equipment, and preparation of salt.

Transportation. The state has railway communication with all the great cities, east and west. The principal roads are the Union Pacific, the Southern Pacific, the Denver & Rio Grande, the San Pedro, Los Angeles & Salt Lake and the Western Pacific. Short lines connect the mining towns with the principal cities. In all, the state has about 2,200 miles of railway lines. Utah has a considerable local commerce. The state exports, however, a large proportion of the products of the mines and ranges.

Government. The state senate has 23 members; the house of representatives, 60. The number of senators can never exceed thirty and the number of representatives cannot exceed three times, or fall below twice, the number of senators. Both senators and representatives are apportioned by districts, one-half of the senators being elected every two years, for a term of four years, and the representatives being elected for two years. The executive department consists of the governor, secretary of state, auditor, treasurer, attorney-general and superintendent of public instruction, elected for four years. The state courts comprise a supreme court, consisting of five judges, elected for ten years, and such inferior courts as may be established by law. The judges of the district courts are elected for four years. The state constitution provides for woman suffrage.

Education. The present educational system of Utah dates from 1890, when a superior grade of public schools was established by the legislature of the territory which superceded the more primitive pioneer educational facilities. High schools are sup-

UTAH
THE SALT LAKE STATE

(1) Bonneville Salt Flats. (2) A canyon in the Rockies. (3) Where the two sections of the Union Pacific were joined, at Promontory, Utah, May 10, 1869. (4) In Bryce Canyon National Park. (5) Mormon Temple, Salt Lake City. (6) Valley farms. (7) World's largest open-cut copper mine.

ported in all of the larger towns and cities, and there is a state university at Salt Lake City, with which the state normal school is connected. The state agricultural college is at Logan, with experiment stations in the Saint George region and at Nephi. The Mormon Church maintains Brigham Young University at Provo, and numerous seminaries giving special religious instruction. Schools are also maintained by other denominations. Only four states show a better record for literacy than Utah.

Institutions. Penal and charitable institutions are under the control of boards appointed by the governor. They include an industrial school at Ogden, a hospital for the insane at Provo City, a school for the deaf and blind at Ogden and a state penitentiary at Salt Lake City.

History. The first white visitors to this region were the members of the Coronado Expedition in 1540. In 1824 James Bridger discovered Great Salt Lake. The real history of Utah, however, begins with the coming of the Mormons in 1847. In the following year the United States gained possession under the Treaty of Guadalupe Hidalgo, and in 1849 a constitution for the "State of Deseret" was adopted. Though Congress refused admission to the new state, it organized the Territory of Utah, including a much greater area than the state now has. Federal troops entered Utah in 1857-1858, because of misunderstandings and the inadequacy of communication facilities. In 1862 Congress passed a law making polygamy a crime, but it was not seriously enforced; twenty years later the Edmunds Bill, disfranchising polygamists and placing the territory under a commission of five men, was passed. Six separate efforts to acquire statehood, between 1849 and 1887, were unsuccessful because of objections to the practice of polygamy in the territory. The Mormon Church declared in 1890 that it no longer countenanced polygamy. In 1895 a constitution was adopted and a year later Utah was admitted to statehood.

UTAH, UNIVERSITY OF, a state university established at Salt Lake City in 1850, as the University of the State of Deseret. For years a weak school, it functioned feebly until 1867, owing to lack of funds. The present charter was secured in 1891, when a grant of sixty acres of land and a state appropriation of $300,000 for buildings were made. At that time the present name was adopted. The university maintains a lower division, a graduate division and schools of arts and science, mines and engineering, education (including the state normal school), medicine, law, business and social work. The faculty numbers about 200, and the student enrollment is about 4,500. The library contains over 150,000 volumes and 37,000 pamphlets. The legislature provides a state tax to insure a regular income.

UTAH LAKE, a fresh-water lake in the north-central part of Utah, about twenty-four miles in length and eight miles in width. It is situated in a valley bordered by mountains, and it discharges into Great Salt Lake through the Jordan River.

UTAMARO, KITAGAWA (1754–1806), famous Japanese color-print artist, born at Kawayoye. His father was a painter of the classic Kano school, which followed the Chinese style; in this tradition Utamaro himself painted until the popularity of the artist Kigonaga turned him to the designing of color prints. His subjects were usually women, although he painted some landscapes. In style his composition and draughtsmanship and his effective use of color, especially red and black, made him popular among his contemporaries and won for him the title "great master of the popular school." Utamaro's prints were among the first to reach the attention of the Western World, as they were imported into Europe in the eighteenth century by Dutch exporters from the port of Nagasaki (which see).

UTE, a tribe of Indians of the Shoshonean family, formerly scattered throughout New Mexico, Utah and Colorado. They give their name to the state of Utah, where seven of the original thirteen or so Ute tribes were banded in a confederacy. A restless and warlike tribe, they lived by hunting and fishing and rarely engaged in agriculture. They made their first treaty with the United States in 1848. At present they are confined to Indian reservations in Colorado and Utah and number about 2,000.

U'TICA, an ancient Phoenician city of North Africa, located on the Gulf of Tunis. Though subject to Carthage, it for a long time resisted that authority successfully, and was never contented under Carthaginian rule. In the third Punic War, Utica submitted to Rome, and after the fall of Carthage was made the capital of the province of Africa. It was at Utica that Cato killed himself, after Caesar's victory at Thapsus. The Arabs destroyed the city in the seventh century. It was excavated by the French engineer, Daux, in 1869.

UTICA, N. Y., the county seat of Oneida County, ninety-five miles west of Albany, on the Mohawk River and the Erie Canal, and on the New York Central, the West Shore, the Delaware, Lackawanna & Western and the New York, Ontario & Western railroads. It is the gateway to the Adirondack region and a center for tourists. It is situated 500 feet above sea level; its water supply comes from the Adirondack Mountains, and its hydro-electric power from Trenton Falls, fifteen miles north of the city.

Utica has a state hospital for the insane, the State Masonic Home and the Masonic Soldiers and Sailors Memorial Hospital. The principal manufactures of the city are rayon yarn, cotton and woolen goods, clothing, heating and ventilating equipment, machine-shop and lumber products and steel products.

During the French and Indian War a fort was erected on this site to control the fording place on the Mohawk. It was named in honor of Philip Schuyler, and, when the fort at Rome was renamed Fort Schuyler, it became known as Old Fort Schuyler. After the Revolution, a settlement grew up at this point, which was incorporated as the village of Utica in 1798. The city was chartered in 1832. Population, 1940, 100,518.

UTILITA'RIANISM, a term given to that system of ethics and philosophy whose fundamental principle is that the standard of right and wrong is the happiness of mankind; that is, that an act is good only to the extent that it proves itself serviceable in promoting the welfare or happiness of society. This theory is of modern origin, having been first definitely stated by John Stuart Mill and accepted by such later philosophers as Spencer and Sir Leslie Stephen. However, it is the natural outgrowth of the philosophy of such men as Hume, Locke, Bentham and Hobbes. See PHILOSOPHY.

UTO'PIA, from a Greek word meaning *no place,* is an ideal country where all things are perfect. The term is taken from the title of a political romance written by Sir Thomas More, in 1516, describing the state of society on an imaginary island where all the property belonged to the commonwealth, to which every one contributed by his labor and from which he received his supplies. Its mild penal code was in striking contrast to that which prevailed at that period in England. The people had learned to tolerate diversity of opinion in religious matters. Promotion was according to merit, and the citizens rose through all the gradations of their existence, from form to form, as in a great public school. *Utopia* was published in Latin in 1516, and was later translated into English by Bishop Burnet. It attained a wide popularity, its name furnishing the familiar epithet *Utopian,* which is commonly applied to idealistic projects of reform in religion, government or society.

UTRECHT, *u' trekt,* NETHERLANDS, capital of the province of the same name, situated on the Rhine, where it branches into the Old Rhine and the canalized Vecht. It lies twenty-three miles southeast of Amsterdam, and is the chief railway center of the Netherlands. It is strongly fortified, according to belief prior to 1914, for it was the outpost of defense for Amsterdam. The University of Utrecht, dating from early in the seventeenth century, is located here. Its library contains over 250,000 volumes. The city also has a number of learned societies, a museum of paintings by the old masters and an archiepiscopal museum, which contains a collection of sacred relics. The Gothic Cathedral of Saint Martin, rising in the center of the city, is the most prominent edifice.

The principal industries are the manufacture of carpets, velvets, floor cloths, cottons, linens, cigars, chemicals, musical instruments and machinery. The trade is important. In this city, in 1579, the Union of Utrecht was formed, establishing the Dutch Republic. In 1713 the Peace of Utrecht was concluded here, terminating the War of the Spanish Succession. Population, 1933, 157,925.

UTRECHT, PEACE OF, a series of treaties agreed upon at Utrecht, between the years 1713 and 1715, by the powers that had been engaged in the War of the Spanish Succession. This was the most important political adjustment between the Peace of Westphalia (1648) and the Congress of Vienna (1815).

By its provisions, Austria and Holland on the north, Prussia on the east and Savoy on the southwest were secured from French aggression. A treaty between France and England recognized the Hanoverian line of kings, engaged never to unite the crowns of France and Spain, and ceded to England Nova Scotia, Newfoundland and Hudson Bay and Strait. Gibraltar and Minorca were ceded to England by Spain, which also transferred Naples, Milan, Sardinia and the Spanish Netherlands to Austria. The Dutch were allowed to garrison eight frontier towns in the Austrian Netherlands as protection against France, and were given important trade privileges. France surrendered Lorraine and certain cities on the right bank of the Rhine, retaining Alsace, with Strassburg. The Prussian king received confirmation of royal title and the Duke of Savoy was raised to kingly dignity. England received trade concessions which laid the basis of a lucrative slave trade with Spanish America.

It is from the Treaty of Utrecht that England dates its commercial and colonial expansion. See SUCCESSION WARS, subhead *War of the Spanish Succession.*

UZ, in the Old Testament, the scene of the story of Job, a region probably lying east or southeast of Palestine, the exact location remaining undetermined.

UZ'BEK, a Soviet republic, since 1925 a member of the Union of Socialist Soviet Republics. It is located almost at the southwest corner of old Siberia, directly north of Afghanistan, and has an area estimated at 75,000 square miles. The most recent estimate of population is 4,447,600. Askabad is the capital; Bokhara and Samarkand are the largest cities.

Agriculture is the principal industry, though irrigation is necessary; in this half-desert country every drop of water must be utilized. The great crop is cotton, and this product makes Uzbek of immense value to the Soviet government in Russia, for more than 40 per cent of the cotton mills of the Soviet Union draw their supplies of raw cotton from here. Uzbek also has cotton mills. There are many vineyards; industry is opening up silk culture, coal mining, and oil fields.

Uzbek has had a modern historical relation with Russia since about 1550, when Uzbekians enjoyed independence. Russian influence in time rendered it a vassal state, and under the later czars it was reduced to a deplorable condition. The country was free after the 1917 revolution, but its people soon found their future would be more secure if they joined the Soviet Union.

V, the twenty-second letter of the English alphabet, was used interchangeably with *u* in Latin, and in English until the seventeenth century. The sound of *v* is always the same, and the letter which is most closely allied to it is *f*, with which it is often interchanged in related languages. In English this close connection of the two letters is shown by the plural of such words as wi*f*e, wives; hal*f*, halves.

As a Roman numeral, V means five; with a line above it, it stand for 5,000.

VACATION SCHOOLS. The long summer vacation for public school pupils, especially in the congested sections of cities where there are no playgrounds, has been found to be anything but beneficial to the children. Many of the large cities now maintain schools in such centers for a portion of the vacation, and these are known as vacation schools. Some of the branches taught are the same as those in the regular course of study, but usually more time is given to industrial training and to recreation. The girls are taught sewing and cooking; the boys, woodwork or some other occupation. Some schools offer work of the regular term for pupils who failed of promotion. In schools having a large number of pupils of foreign parentage, special emphasis is placed upon English. Vacation schools are popular, and usually the number of applicants for admission far exceeds the capacity of the buildings.

VACCINATION, *vak se na'shun,* inoculation with the cowpox—a disease akin to, but much less severe than, smallpox—in order to prevent a person from catching the latter, or to make the attack much less severe. The principle upon which vaccination is based is that if one acquires the disease in a mild form, antitoxins for the cure of the disease will be manufactured in the blood and render that person immune from the attacks of smallpox for several years. The practice of vaccination was introduced by Edward Jenner, an English physician, and it soon came into common use.

The usual method in vaccination is to make, upon the upper part of the arm, a few scratches across one another, with a clean lancet point. The virus from cowpox eruptions is then rubbed on the skin where the scratches have been made. If the vaccination proves successful, a small inflamed sore appears about the third day and increases in size until the tenth day. On the eighth day the constitutional effects manifest themselves by a slight pain in the part, headache, shivering and loss of appetite. These subside in one or two days. Afterward the fluid in the pustule dries up, and a scab forms, which disappears about the twentieth day, leaving a scar in the skin. Few things have been more definitely proved in medicine than that vaccination is a preventive of smallpox. To secure perfect immunity, repeated vaccinations at intervals of several years are necessary in most cases.

There is no danger in vaccination if pure virus is used and if the wound is kept free from infection. The wise plan is to have the vaccination made by a good physician, who will treat the wound properly and prevent any injurious results.

VACCINE THERAPY, *vak'seen ther'a pi,* a method of medical treatment for combating diseases caused by bacteria. The treatment is based upon the principle that injection into the system of killed bacteria that produce the disease will develop in the blood another sort of bacteria that will destroy the disease-producing bacteria. The vaccines are usually prepared by placing some fluid of the body containing the disease-producing bacteria in some substance in which the bacteria will grow rapidly, then purifying this "culture" and treating it with a preservative. The vaccine is injected hypodermically, and works in a few hours. This method of treatment is successful in such diseases as carbuncle, ulcers, typhoid fever, tuberculosis and asthma. See SERUM THERAPY.

VAC'UUM, a term usually applied to a space from which air or other gases have been exhausted. An absolute vacuum is impossible, since however completely the gases may be exhausted, the space will still be filled with ether (see ETHER). However, in the ordinary use of the term, a vacuum is said to be produced when the air is removed from space as completely as possible by means of an air pump. Such vacuums are sufficiently perfect for common experiments. The most perfect vacuum formed in practice is that above the mercury in a barometer tube, produced by filling the tube with mercury and allowing it to settle until the column sustained is equal to the weight of an equal column of atmosphere (see BAROMETER). Other practical applications of the vacuum are found in the vacuum brake and the vacuum pan. See AIR BRAKE; VACUUM PAN.

VACUUM CLEANER, a device for removing dust from floors, walls and hangings by means of rolling brushes and air suction. Small cleaners propelled by hand or capable of being attached for power to electric sockets are in use in individual households. For larger buildings an air pump mounted on a truck and run by a gasoline engine may go from door to door, carrying the dust to a box in the truck by means of a large hose. Office buildings are commonly equipped with stationary engines, run by gasoline or electricity and operating a pump connected with a system of pipes leading to the different floors.

The use of the vacuum cleaner is a distinct advance in the matter of sanitation, as the former method of sweeping with brooms scattered the dust and was a means of spreading contagion.

VALDAI, *val dī',* **HILLS,** a group of hills in West Central Russia, forming the chief watershed of that part of Europe. They consist of hills and plateaus, with an average altitude of from 8,000 to 9,000 feet. Formerly covered with forests, they are now cleared and cultivated. They contain the sources of the Volga, the Dnieper and the Duna.

VALENCIA, *val len'she ah,* SPAIN, the third city in population in the country, situ-

ated on the Guadalaviar River, three miles from the Mediterranean. Its history dates to 138 B. C. It was destroyed by Pompey of Rome, and was captured by the Visigoths in 413 and by the Moors in 714. From 1021 to 1238 it was the capital of an independent Moorish kingdom. In its modern aspect it is a picturesque mixture of Moorish architecture and modern streets and plazas. The University of Valencia, founded in 1411, is one of the foremost in Spain. The harbor is secure and well equipped to accommodate commerce and the city is an important railway center. The leading industry is the manufacture of silk, and the place is also noted for the making of colored tiles. Fruit raising is extensively carried on in the surrounding country. Population, 1934, 341,322.

VA'LENS (328–378), Roman emperor of the East, associated in power with his brother Valentinian I. The chief event of Valens' reign was a war with the Goths, who, driven southward by the Huns, had received permission to settle on Roman territory. Irritated, however, by the treatment they received at the hands of the Roman officials, they soon took up arms and destroyed Valens and the greater part of his army.

VAL'ENTINE, SAINT, a saint of the Roman calendar, said to have been martyred in A. D. 306. The custom of choosing valentines on his day (February 14) has been accidentally associated with his name. On the eve of Saint Valentine's day, young people of both sexes used to meet, and each of the men drew from a number of names of the opposite sex. Each gentleman thus got a lady for his valentine, and he became the valentine of a lady, to whom he was bound to be faithful for a year. A similar custom prevailed in the Roman Lupercalia, to which the modern custom has, with probability, been traced. The day is now celebrated by sending through the post, sentimental or ludicrous missives, specially prepared for the purpose.

VALENTIN'IAN I (321–375), on the death of Jovian, in 364, chosen emperor of Rome by the army, therefore one of the "barracks emperors." He shared the empire with his brother Valens, who ruled in the East. Although chiefly occupied throughout his reign in repelling invasions of the barbarians, he proved himself a firm and just ruler, instituting many political and social reforms. His sons, Gratianus and Valentinian II, succeeded him.

VALENTINIAN III, Roman emperor from 425 to 455. He was made emperor by Theodosius II, his grandfather, but never really exercised the imperial power, leaving it in the hands of his mother, Placidia, until her death in 450, and then largely in the hands of the eunuch Heraclius. Although the barbarians who were constantly harassing the empire were repeatedly defeated by Aëtius, general of the army, Spain, Africa, Gaul and other provinces were lost to Rome during Valentinian's reign, and the empire grew steadily weaker. Valentinian was assassinated.

VALE'RIAN, a medicinal plant, native to Europe and Northern Asia, growing abundantly by the sides of rivers and in ditches and moist weeds. The aromatic, volatile oil obtained from its roots is used as a stimulant in the treatment of nervous and circulatory disorders.

VALHAL'LA, in Old Norse mythology, the palace of immortality, inhabited by the souls of heroes slain in battle, and carried hither by the swift Valkyries. Here they spent their time in drinking and feasting and fighting furious battles; their wounds, though often serious, were healed every night. The name Valhalla is applied figuratively to any edifice which is the final resting place of many heroes. See VALKYRIES.

VALKYRIES, *val kir'eez,* in Old Norse mythology, the maiden attendants of Odin, who, at his command, rode over battlefields and bore the souls of the bravest of the slain to Valhalla, Odin's great hall. Here the Valkyries waited upon the heroes, serving them mead in vessels made from skulls. The Valkyries were sometimes regarded as the personification of clouds, especially of storm clouds. See VALHALLA.

VALLADOLID, *vahl ya do leed',* MEXICO. See MORELIA, MEXICO.

VALLEJO, *val ya'ho,* CALIF., a city of Solano County, situated on the northeastern shore of San Pablo Bay, twenty-three miles northeast of San Francisco, on the Southern Pacific railroad. It has a fine, deep harbor, which admits the largest ocean ships, and is an important shipping point for grain. Its leading establishment is the Mare Island Navy Yard. There are also flour mills and tanning yards. The city is built on the slopes of a hill, and the surrounding country is devoted to the raising of fruit. The public institutions include an orphans' home, Saint Vincent's Academy, a sailors' clubhouse, a Carnegie Library and a city hall. The city was founded in 1851 with the intention of making it the capital of the state. The legislature met here in 1851, in 1852 and for a time in 1853. The commission form of government was adopted in 1911. Population, 1920, 16,845; in 1930, 16,072; and in 1940, 20,072.

VAL'LEY, low land between mountains, hills or bluffs. The largest and most important valleys have been formed by the upheaval and folding of the earth's crust. Such valleys are found among mountain systems, and are called *intermontane* valleys. They are long and narrow, and their floor may have an elevation several hundred or several thousand feet above the sea level. The simplest valleys of this sort are found in the Jura Mountains, where the strata were not broken in folding and where the slopes are remarkably uniform and even. Many of the so-called basins in the Rocky Mountain plateau are also valleys formed by the folding of strata, but most of these are irregular and are caused by transverse ranges, show-

A VALKYRIE

ing that the movements by which they were formed were very complex.

Valleys running parallel to the mountain ranges are known as *longitudinal* valleys, those running across the ranges are *trans-*

verse valleys. Transverse valleys may be due to breaks in the folded strata, but most of them have been formed by erosion. They are usually narrow, with very steep sides, and the floor is only wide enough for the stream which flows in it. When of high altitude these valleys are known as *passes*. Among the most celebrated of these passes are the Khyber Pass in the Himalayas and the Simplon Pass. When of low altitude, transverse valleys are frequently known as *water gaps,* as the Delaware Water Gap.

Valleys in volcanic regions are usually due to volcanic action and are found in the side or on the summit of mountains, around the crater. They are small and of comparatively little importance. *River* valleys are formed by erosion, but their location was first determined by the formation of mountains and valleys by folding. Glacial valleys are those which have been formed or modified by the action of glaciers. They are found in mountainous regions, and most of them were undoubtedly river gorges, previous to the glacial period. The lochs and firths of Scotland are good illustrations.

Drowned valleys are those partially under the sea, and are formed by the lowering of the coast. The fiords of Norway, Delaware Bay and the Gulf of Saint Lawrence are good examples.

Related Articles. Consult the following titles for additional information:

Canyon	Glaciers
Fiord	Mountain

VALLEYFIELD, QUE., on the Canadian National and the Saint Lawrence & Adirondacks railways, is the western terminus of the Beauharnois Canal. The town has large cotton and flour mills, paper, biscuit, gasoline motor, glove, clothing and cigar factories. It is the seat of a Roman Catholic bishop. Considerable lumbering and iron mining are done in the vicinity. Population, 1941, 16,968.

VALLEY FORGE, a village in Chester County, Pa., famous as the site of the quarters of the American colonial army under George Washington in the winter of 1777 and 1778. The army was 11,000 strong when it went into camp, December 17, but owing to mismanagement on the part of the quartermaster-general and the commissary department the supplies were totally inadequate, and fully half the men were soon unfit for duty. The suffering of the soldiers during the winter and following spring was almost incredible and tried the patriotism of even the most loyal

friends of the colonial cause. Washington remained with his men throughout this period and with the aid of Baron Steuben finally reorganized the army and restored its morale. Camp was broken June 18, 1778.

Part of Valley Forge camping ground is now included in a state memorial park. The tract of rolling wooded country is about twenty miles northwest of Philadelphia, on the Schuylkill River. The old stone house which Washington made his headquarters contains many interesting war relics, and there has been erected an impressive Washington Memorial, consisting of a beautiful chapel, a tower with a carillon, and the Cloister of the Colonies. The stained glass windows of the chapel commemorate persons and events of the Revolution. Other interesting features of the park include an equestrian statue of Anthony Wayne and a memorial arch dedicated to the soldiers who perished at Valley Forge.

VALOIS, *val wah',* a dynasty ruling in France from 1328 to 1589, having its origin in the circumstances by which Philip III, in 1285, gave the county of Valois to his younger son, Charles. Upon the extinction of the Capet dynasty, in 1328, the eldest son of this Charles of Valois ascended the French throne as Philip VI. The elevation of the House of Valois to the throne of France gave rise to the series of long and bloody conflicts with England known as the Hundred Years' War.

VALPARAISO, *val pa ri'zo,* CHILE, the capital of the province of Valparaiso and the chief port of the country, situated on the Pacific Ocean, sixty-eight miles northwest of Santiago. It has a commodious harbor, protected by a newly-constructed breakwater, and is connected by regular lines of steamers with leading American and European ports. It is strongly fortified, and has a large naval arsenal.

Back of the harbor rise hills and mountains, on the lower slopes of which is the newer residence portion of the city. The lower town contains the business section and city park. The buildings are mostly constructed of stone and are of a substantial character. The educational institutions include a naval school, a number of colleges and a school for marines. The city maintains a hydrographic bureau and a museum of natural history. The industrial establishments include foundries, machine shops, bottling works, distilleries, sugar refineries and railroad shops. The principal exports are grain, wool, leather, guano, saltpeter and copper; the imports are textile and other manufactured and mineral products.

Valparaiso was founded by Juan de Saavedra in 1536. It has been visited by several disastrous earthquakes, the latest being that of August 16 and 17, 1906. Population, 1932, 189,119.

VALPARAISO UNIVERSITY, an educational institution at Valparaiso, Ind. It was founded in 1873 as the revival of the Valparaiso Male and Female College (Methodist, 1859–69), and has been under the control of the Lutheran University Association since 1925. The university is composed of a college of arts and sciences, a school of law and a summer session. Under a coöperative arrangement with Purdue University, Valparaiso offers the first two years of civil, electrical, mechanical and chemical engineering. A five-year coöperative plan in journalism is in effect with the Medill School of Journalism. The average enrollment is 500, and the faculty numbers over forty. The libraries contain about 45,000 volumes.

VALUE. See SUPPLY AND DEMAND.

VALVE, a device, as a cap, ball or slide, for the purpose of controlling the flow of liquids, steam, gas or loose material through pipes, tubes or chutes. As to the method of their operation, most valves may be included in this general classification: (1) valves opened and closed by hand; (2) those operated by independent mechanism; (3) those operated by mechanisms connected with the machine whose operation they control; and (4) those opened and closed by the motion of the fluid whose flow they control. Valves may rotate, rise and fall from their seats or open and close by sliding on and parallel to their seats. In the human anatomy the loose flap or fold of lining membrane which regulates the flow of the blood and other bodily fluids is called a valve. See PUMP; STEAM ENGINE.

VAM'PIRE, in Slavic folklore, a corpse which leaves its grave during the night and sucks the blood of living human beings, particularly of young people and children. The victims gradually lose strength and finally die from no apparent malady, while the corpse retains the appearance of a living being. The belief in vampires is an ancient one, fostered by the medieval Greek church as a means of terrifying the people into

godly behavior. It still persists in the locality of the lower Danube, where heretics, outcasts and criminals are still supposed to become vampires at death.

Figuratively, a vampire is a person who in any way preys on another. Kipling's poem, *The Vampire,* characterizes the parasitic woman.

VAMPIRE BAT, a Central and South American bat which takes its name from the habit of some of the species of sucking the blood of the cows, horses, and even men, attacking them in their sleep. These bats are of small size, are tailless, and have a pair of upper incisors elongated and sharpened to pierce the skin of their victims. They have gullets so small that only a liquid diet is possible, and the intestinal canal is modified to accommodate a diet of blood. The destructive qualities of these bats, however, have been greatly exaggerated.

VANA'DIUM, a silvery-white metallic element, extracted by difficult processes from a number of minerals. It is of value as an alloy in the manufacture of steel, especially that used in automobile construction, because it increases elasticity and tensile strength. Certain vanadium salts yield compounds that produce intense, permanently black pigments that are combined with aniline in the manufacture of dyes and also as the basis of black writing fluids.

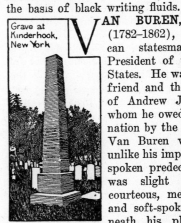

Grave at Kinderhook, New York

VAN BUREN, MARTIN (1782–1862), an American statesman, eighth President of the United States. He was the close friend and the successor of Andrew Jackson, to whom he owed his nomination by the Democrats. Van Buren was totally unlike his imperious, outspoken predecessor. He was slight of figure, courteous, mellow-voiced and soft-spoken, yet beneath his placidity of manner there lay individuality, a firm will and strength of character. Tactful and conciliating as he was, Van Buren could fight doggedly for principle, and notwithstanding his strong sense of party loyalty, he could break with his party when his conscience so dictated. His administration is noteworthy chiefly for the establishment of the independent treasury system, the result of his own tireless efforts. At the time he gained little credit for this achievement, but historians of to-day find this the outstanding feature of his career as President.

Early Life. Martin Van Buren was born at Kinderhook, Columbia County, New York, on December 5, 1782. He was the son of a small farmer. He attended the local schools until he was fourteen, after which he became office boy for a neighborhood lawyer, rising to the positions of clerk, copyist of pleas and special pleader in the constables' courts. After six years of such training he entered a New York law office, and in 1803 was admitted to the bar. He then entered into a partnership with his half brother, James Van Allen, in Kinderhook, where he was soon a conspicuous figure in local Democratic (then called Democratic-Republican) politics. Within the next few years Van Buren advanced rapidly in his profession, becoming probate judge in Columbia County, in 1808, and holding that position until 1813.

Political Advancement. In 1812 Van Buren was elected to the state senate of New York, and in 1815, while still a member of that body, was appointed attorney-general. He was reëlected to the senate for the term 1816–1820, but lost his position as attorney-general in 1819 because of a political disagreement with Governor De Witt Clinton. Throughout this period he was steadily gaining in power of leadership, and in 1820 was successful in securing the reëlection of Rufus King to the United States Senate. The following year he himself won a seat in that body.

Van Buren remained in the Senate until 1828, when he was elected governor of New York. In the Senate he had favored strict construction of the Constitution on all questions, and as a member of the finance committee and chairman of the judiciary committee he had made a good impression by his sincerity and moderation. His career as governor is of special interest to-day, in that he advocated two principles whose wisdom is more appreciated at present than in his time. In the first place he opposed free banking, and advocated a system whereby all the state banks would become "mutual insurers of each other's soundness." This plan is a feature of the present Federal Reserve system. Secondly, he recommended that state and national elections be separated.

While this principle has not been extensively adopted, its soundness is generally accepted.

In the Presidential election of 1828, Van Buren effectively supported Andrew Jackson, whom he warmly admired, and in 1829 the latter rewarded him with the most important place in his first Cabinet, that of Secretary of State. Van Buren retained this office long enough to settle a disagreement between England and the United States with respect to the trade of the West Indies.

He resigned in 1831 and soon accepted the post of minister to England, but as a bit of party politics the Senate Whigs succeeded in holding up the nomination after the appointee had sailed. It was known in political circles that Van Buren had resigned in order not to jeopardize his chances for the Presidential nomination in 1836, to which he was looking forward. The Whigs hoped to discredit him by their maneuver, but the pretext which they used was so feeble that their act served only to increase Van Buren's popularity. In 1832 he was elected Vice-President on the ticket with Jackson, and was in line for the nomination for President on the expiration of Jackson's second term. The Whigs were badly split, and in the electoral college in 1836 the party vote was divided among William Henry Harrison, Hugh L. White of Tennessee, Daniel Webster and W. P. Mangum of South Carolina. Van Buren had 170 votes against seventy-three for his nearest rival, Harrison.

Administration. As Vice-President, Van Buren consistently supported Jackson and his policies, and on taking over the Presidential office he reappointed most of Jackson's Cabinet. In his inaugural address he gave an indication of his attitude on the slavery question when he stated that he would oppose abolition of slavery in the District of Columbia if the slave states opposed it; and he promised not to interfere with slavery where it was practiced. Early in his administration he had to meet a serious financial crisis. President Jackson, in 1833, had removed the funds of the government from the United States Bank, practically putting an end to the institution, which he regarded as a symbol of the "money power." The funds had been distributed among certain "pet banks," which used them in unsound speculation. Subsequently, Jackson issued a "specie circular" requiring that gold and

Administration of Martin Van Buren, 1837-1841

I. THE PRESIDENT
 (1) Birth
 (2) Education
 (3) Early career
 (4) Later life
 (5) Character
 (6) Death

II. THE PANIC OF 1837
 (1) Causes
  (a) Over-speculation in land
  (b) Expenditures for internal improvements
  (c) Panic in England
  (d) Failure of the wheat crop
  (e) Wild-cat banking
 (2) Effects
  (a) High prices of necessaries
  (b) Bank and brokerage failures
  (c) Business failures
  (d) Distress among the poor
  (e) Suspension of specie payments
 (3) Led to independent treasury

III. DOMESTIC AFFAIRS
 (1) Slavery agitation
  (a) Riots and demonstrations
   (1) Murder of Lovejoy
   (2) Garrison mobbed in Boston
 (2) Second Seminole War
  (a) Skirmishes and raids
  (b) Capture of Osceola and other chiefs
  (c) Zachary Taylor's force defeats Indians at Okechobee swamp
 (3) Oregon settlements
  (a) Mostly by Hudson Bay Company
  (b) Americans were missionaries
 (4) The Mormons in Missouri
  (a) Control of the government by the Mormon church
  (b) Troubles at Kirtland
  (c) Driven out of Missouri
 (5) Riots and disorder
  (a) The "buckshot" war
  (b) The "broad seal" war
  (c) Anti-rent or "patroon" war
  (d) Canadian rebellion
   (1) Attempts to enlist American aid
   (2) Strict neutrality of the United States
   (3) The Caroline affair
 (6) Great inventions and discoveries
  (a) Friction matches, 1838
  (b) Magnetic telegraph
  (c) First photograph taken
  (d) Vulcanized rubber

IV. QUARREL WITH MEXICO
 (1) Causes
  (a) Property of Americans in danger
  (b) United States vessels seized
  (c) United States citizens imprisoned and executed
 (2) Mexico resented recognition of Texan independence

V. ELECTION OF 1840
 (1) Issues
 (2) Candidates

Questions on Van Buren

When was Martin Van Buren born? In what state?

What profession did he adopt?

What public offices did he hold before 1837?

What can you say of his abilities and character?

What were the principal causes of the panic of 1837? Give details of each as far as you can.

What were some of the immediate effects of the panic?

What is meant by the independent treasury or subtreasury system?

Who was Elijah Lovejoy? Where did he live?

Give a brief summary of the career of William Lloyd Garrison.

What future President took a prominent part in the second Seminole War?

Who was the founder of the Mormon sect?

Name three inventions perfected during Van Buren's administration.

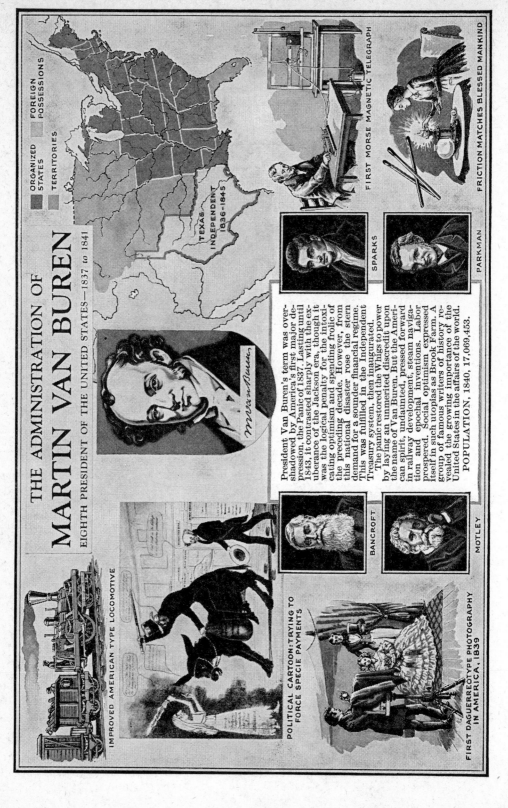

THE ADMINISTRATION OF
MARTIN VAN BUREN
EIGHTH PRESIDENT OF THE UNITED STATES—1837 to 1841

ORGANIZED STATES
FOREIGN POSSESSIONS
TERRITORIES

TEXAS INDEPENDENT 1836-1845

FIRST MORSE MAGNETIC TELEGRAPH

FRICTION MATCHES BLESSED MANKIND

SPARKS

PARKMAN

President Van Buren's term was overshadowed by America's first major depression, the Panic of 1837. Lasting until 1843, it contrasted sharply with the exuberance of the Jackson era, though it was the logical penalty for the intoxicating optimism and spending frolic of the preceding decade. However, from this national disaster rose the stern demand for a sounder financial regime. This was fulfilled in the Independent Treasury system, then inaugurated.

The panic restored the Whigs to power by laying an unmerited discredit upon the name of Van Buren. But the American spirit, undaunted, pressed forward in railway development, steam navigation and epochal inventions. Labor prospered. Social optimism expressed itself in such utopias as Brook Farm. A group of famous writers of history revealed the growing importance of the United States in the affairs of the world.

POPULATION, 1840, 17,069,453.

IMPROVED AMERICAN TYPE LOCOMOTIVE

BANCROFT

MOTLEY

POLITICAL CARTOON - TRYING TO FORCE SPECIE PAYMENTS

FIRST DAGUERREOTYPE PHOTOGRAPHY IN AMERICA, 1839

silver be paid for public lands, which drained the banks of their reserves and caused many failures. It was a period of credit inflation, reckless issuance of paper money and extravagant expenditures for public improvements, and in 1837, shortly after Van Buren began his term, a disastrous panic overwhelmed the nation.

The President called Congress in special session, and in his first message, September 1, 1837, outlined his policy. After explaining the causes of the panic, he presented his plan for an independent treasury, whereby the control of national finances would be divorced from private banking and the government would be the custodian of its own funds, as it is to-day. For three years he labored to have this policy adopted; not until July, 1840, did he succeed in persuading a reluctant Congress to pass the law which he regarded as a sort of "second Declaration of Independence." Except for a short interval under the Whig régime, the independent treasury has remained a permanent national institution.

Though the financial issue overshadowed all others, it is not true that Van Buren's term was in other respects uneventful. The slavery issue, becoming yearly more entangled with politics, was the cause of such disturbances as the murder of Elijah Lovejoy at Alton, Ill., and the mobbing of the great abolitionist, William Lloyd Garrison. There were outbreaks in New York against the landlords, or patroons, and in Missouri against the Mormons; in Florida a desperate war with the Seminoles was waged. A rebellion in Canada and the establishment of the republic of Texas caused disturbances along the international boundaries, north and south.

Van Buren was not responsible for these conditions, but they reacted against him, and with the prevalent hard times served to make his administration and the Democratic party extremely unpopular. He also alienated many voters by refusing to aid the Canadian rebels, though time has vindicated his attitude of strict neutrality. Considerable material progress is recorded of the period. In 1837 the magnetic telegraph was invented; friction matches were first used in 1838; in 1839 the first photograph was taken in America. In 1839, too, the process of vulcanizing rubber was invented by Charles Goodyear.

Van Buren was a candidate for reëlection, but his administration was connected with too much that was disagreeable, and he was defeated. He secured but sixty electoral votes, to 234 for the Whig candidate, William Henry Harrison. Calmly accepting his defeat, he retired to his country seat of Lindenwald in his native county.

As Ex-President. Van Buren by no means disappeared from the public eye during the last two decades of his life. In 1844 he took a firm stand against the annexation of Texas, thus losing the Democratic nomination for the Presidency, and within the next three years he came out definitely against the extension of slavery. In 1848 the faction of the Democratic party which upheld the Wilmot Proviso (which see) nominated him, against his wishes, for the Presidency, and the nomination was confirmed by a convention of "Free-Soilers." The regular Democrats nominated Lewis Cass, from whom Van Buren pulled enough votes to give the election to Zachary Taylor. Van Buren received about 300,000 popular votes, but he carried no state. He remained a Democrat to the end of his life, but his sympathy for the anti-slavery cause made him a firm supporter of Lincoln after the outbreak of the Civil War. He died in the second year of the struggle, and was buried at Kinderhook, N. Y.

Related Articles. Consult the following titles for additional information:

Garrison, William Lloyd	Seminole
Lovejoy, Elijah P.	Texas (history)
Political Parties in the United States	Treasury Department

VANCOUVER, *van koo'ver,* B. C., the third largest city of Canada and the metropolis of the province, is situated on Burrard Inlet, an arm of the Strait of Georgia. Vancouver is the western terminus of the Canadian Pacific Railway, and it was laid out by that railway corporation in 1885. It is now also the terminus of two other great trans-continental railway systems, the Canadian National Railways, and the Pacific Great Eastern. It is also the western terminus of the British Columbia Electric Railway, which extends to Chilliwack and New Westminster. The city is on one of the best harbors in the world, and has regular steamship connection with China, Japan and other ports of the Orient. It also has a coastwise trade with Alaska and the Pacific ports of the United States.

The prominent buildings include the Vancouver Block, the Standard Bank Building, Rogers Building, Vancouver Hotel, the custom-house, public library and courthouse. The University of British Columbia, the leading

VANCOUVER ISLAND AND CITY

educational institution of the province, is located here. Stanley Park, having an area of 600 acres, mostly in the natural state, adds much to the beauty of the city.

Vancouver is next to Prince Rupert the nearest North American port to the Orient, and it has a large export trade exceeding $100,000,000 a year. It is also an important manufacturing center. The principal manufactures include lumber and lumber products, structural steel, wooden and steel ships, furniture, machinery and refined sugar. Population, 1941, 271,597.

VANCOUVER, George (1758–1798), an explorer and discoverer. He accompanied Cook on several of his voyages, and later was in command of an expedition to explore Australia and New Zealand. From there he sailed by way of the Hawaiian Islands to North America, where he surveyed, in a period of two years, the coast from 35° to 56° North latitude. Vancouver Island was named after him. He sailed for England via Cape Horn and Saint Helena, and died shortly after his arrival at his home in Surrey.

VANCOUVER, Wash., the county seat of Clarke County, five miles north of Portland, Ore., on the Columbia River and on the Northern Pacific, the Great Northern, Union Pacific, and the Spokane, Portland & Seattle railroads. There are two airports, one a Federal field. It is the United States military headquarters for the department of Columbia. Vancouver lies in a section of large forests and farming lands. The leading industrial plants include a paper mill, flour mills, an ice plant, creameries, canneries, car-repair shops, brickyards, box factories and fruit-packing plants. The state schools for the blind and the deaf and Saint Joseph's Hospital are located here. Notable buildings are a Carnegie Library, the United States National Bank Building, and a courthouse and postoffice. An Interstate bridge spans the Columbia River at this point. Vancouver was first settled as a post of the Hudson's Bay Company in 1828, and was incorporated as a city in 1858. Population, 1920, 12,637. In 1930 it was 15,766; and in 1940, 18,788.

VANCOUVER ISLAND, an island in the Pacific Ocean, off the coast of British Columbia, of which it is politically a part. It is separated from the mainland of Canada by the Gulf of Georgia and Queen Charlotte Sound and from the United States by the Strait of Juan de Fuca. Its length is 275 miles; its greatest breadth, sixty-five miles; and its area, about 12,000 square miles. The island is generally mountainous, being a continuation of the Coast Ranges formation. It has a mild, moist climate, and in the south and east its soil is fertile and well suited to agriculture and fruit growing. The mountains are generally covered with heavy coniferous and deciduous forests. The interior is well adapted to grazing, and large numbers of horses, cattle, sheep and swine are raised. Fishing interests along the shores of the streams and lakes are of considerable importance. Mineral resources include coal, gold and copper. The coal mines are extensively worked and supply the greater part of the coal used on the Pacific coast. The chief town is Victoria, the capital of British Columbia. The island was visited by Vancouver, an officer of the British navy, in 1792, and was named for him. The United States claimed it, but when the Oregon boundary question was settled in 1846, it became a possession of Great Britain.

VAN'DALS, an ancient Teutonic people, inhabiting the region between the Vistula and the Oder, whence they moved southward and settled in Pannonia, becoming Christians of the Arian faith. At the beginning of the

VANDALS IN ROME

fifth century they entered Gaul and crossed the Pyrenees into Spain. One section settled in Galicia and were almost entirely destroyed in a struggle with the Goths and Suevi; the other settled in a part of Baetica, which received from them the name *Andalusia*. In 429 they crossed the Strait of Gibraltar, under their dreaded leader, Genseric, carrying devastation and ruin from the shores of the Atlantic to the frontiers of Cyrene. In 455 Genseric and his soldiers sacked Rome, plundering and ruining temples, beautiful buildings and works of art. The word *vandal* is still applied to the wilfully destructive.

VAN'DERBILT, CORNELIUS (1794-1877), American capitalist and financier, born on Staten Island, N. Y. At the age of sixteen he bought a boat and ferried passengers and goods across to the city. Gradually extending his enterprise, by the age of forty he had become the owner of a fleet of steamers running to Boston and up the Hudson. In 1849 he founded a steamship and transfer line by way of Lake Nicaragua to California. Because of the large fleet of boats he owned he was popularly known as "Commodore." Later he transferred his capital from steamships to railroads, obtaining a controlling interest in a large number of Eastern roads, and extending his system to Chicago by securing the Lake Shore & Michigan Southern and Canada Southern roads. His philanthropies included a gift of a million dollars for the founding of Vanderbilt University.

VANDERBILT, CORNELIUS (1843–1899), son of William Henry Vanderbilt, first vice-president of the New York Central Railroad when his father succeeded to its presidency, on the death of his grandfather, Cornelius Vanderbilt, in 1877. He was a contributor to Vanderbilt and Yale universities and presented to the Metropolitan Museum, New York, Rosa Bonheur's famous painting, *Horse Fair*.

VANDERBILT, WILLIAM HENRY (1821–1885), son of "Commodore" Vanderbilt and his successor in the management of the Vanderbilt system of railroads, which he extended till he controlled the Michigan Central, the Lake Shore & Michigan Southern, the Canada Southern, the Chicago & North Western, the Nickel Plate and the West Shore railroads. He was considered one of the greatest authorities on transportation in his day. He gave large sums to Vanderbilt University and Columbia University.

VANDERBILT, WILLIAM KISSAM (1849–1920), son of William Henry Vanderbilt, was entrusted by his father with the management of numerous responsible offices connected with the New York Central Railroad and became a director in fourteen different lines. With his brothers, Frederick William and George Washington Vanderbilt, he founded the Vanderbilt Clinic in New York City, and erected Kissam Hall at Vanderbilt University, in memory of their mother.

VANDERBILT UNIVERSITY, a coeducational institution, established at Nashville, Tenn., in 1872, under the auspices of the Methodist Church. It was named in honor of Cornelius Vanderbilt, who gave $1,000,000 for establishing the school. However, the university is not now under sectarian management. There are maintained a graduate school, a college of arts and sciences and schools of law, religion, medicine, nursing and engineering. Vanderbilt University has been a strong influence in the South in keeping educational standards high. It has a student enrollment of over 1,800 and a faculty of about 400. There are nearly 243,000 volumes in the library. The university has received generous gifts from the Vanderbilt and Rockefeller families, Andrew Carnegie and the General Education Board.

VAN DYCK, or **VANDYKE**, *van dike'*, ANTHONY, Sir (1599–1641), next to Rubens his teacher, the most famous portrait painter of the Flemish school. He was born at Antwerp, where his father was a merchant and his mother a skilled worker in tapestry. He studied under Van Balen and Rubens and also in Genoa, Venice and Rome. Having acquired a great reputation in Antwerp as a fashionable portrait painter, he was invited to England by Charles I, who bestowed upon him knighthood and a considerable annuity. While in England he painted more than 300 portraits, his patrons including almost every distinguished person of the court. His portraits are characterized by delicacy and refinement. Those best known are *Portrait of Charles I* and *Children of Charles I*, now in Munich; and *Portrait of a Lady and Child,* in the Morgan Collection, Metropolitan Museum. Among his sacred pictures are *Elevation of the Cross* (Courtrai, Belgium), *Christ on the Cross* (Antwerp) and *Crucifixion* (Mechlin, Belgium). Van Dyck married Lady Mary Ruthven, of the English nobility, and executed several portraits of her. The best of these, showing her playing the 'cello, is in Munich. Van Dyck was also an expert in the art of portrait etching, and made his own drawings as well as the engravings. He was buried in Saint Paul's, London.

VAN DYKE, HENRY (1852-1933), American poet, essayist and educator. He was born at Germantown, Pa., and graduated at Princeton and at Princeton Theological Seminary. In 1878 he became pastor of the United Congregational Church of Newport, R. I., and five years later was called to the Brick Presbyterian Church of New York. Here he remained as pastor until 1900, when he became professor of English literature in Princeton University. Van Dyke wrote extensively, and always attractively, in various fields. *The Builders and Other Poems* and *Music and Other Poems* are among his volumes of poetry. *The Gospel for an Age of Doubt* and *Sermons to Young Men* are examples of his religious work; *The Blue Flower* and *The Ruling Passion* are some of his charming works of fiction, and *Fisherman's Luck* and *Little Rivers* include his best work in the field of essays. In 1913 Dr. Van Dyke was appointed minister to the Netherlands by President Wilson, a position which he held with honor throughout the greater part of the World War. This post he resigned in 1917 before the United States entered the war. After America became a belligerent he was appointed supervisory chaplain in the navy.

VAN HISE', CHARLES RICHARD (1857-1918), an American geologist and educator, born at Fulton, Wisconsin, educated in the University of Wisconsin. Soon after graduation he became connected with the faculty of his alma mater, serving successively as instructor in chemistry, assistant professor of mineralogy, professor of geology and president of the university, to which position he was elevated in 1903. Under his administration the institution became one of the most progressive and useful schools in the United States. He was particularly effective in making extension courses available to all classes of people throughout the state.

Professor Van Hise was made a member of the United States Geological Survey in 1883. He won recognition as the highest authority on rocks of the Algonkian and Archaean Systems and especially on the ore-bearing rocks of the Lake Superior region. He was the author of a series of books on geological subjects and of *The Conservation of Natural Resources in the United States.*

VAN HORNE, WILLIAM CORNELIUS, Sir (1843-1915), railway official and expert, best known for his connection with the Canadian Pacific Railway, which was completed under his energetic and efficient management. He served that railway from 1882 to 1910 as general manager, vice-president, president and chairman of the board of directors, successively. Van Horne was born in the United States and served several mid-western railroads in that country before being called to Canada.

VANIL'LA, a genus of plants belonging to the orchid family, source of the well-known vanilla of commerce. The plants are common in Mexico, and are also found in Central and South America and the East Indies. The vanilla plant climbs by means of aerial roots and has large white, red or greenish flowers. The fruit is a long, brown, shiny bean, filled with a dark, oily, odorous pulp. This bean is gathered before it is fully ripe, and the oil is extracted by a slow process which brings out its peculiar odor and flavor. Vanilla is used in medicine as a

VANILLA

stimulant, but its chief use is in the preparation of liquors and perfumery and in flavoring candy and other confections. The vanilla plant is propagated by cuttings, produces a crop every three years and continues bearing for thirty or forty years. Vanilla is produced artificially by several methods; the artificial product is very common.

VAN· LOON, HENDRIK WILLEM (1882–). Born in Rotterdam, Holland, and educated in universities in Europe and America, he became a reporter, editor, professor of history, then one of the most notable authors of his generation. Van Loon came to public attention when he published *The Story of Mankind;* he wrote it in 1921 solely for his son, but was induced to publish it. Another volume, *Van Loon's Geography,* proved equally popular. *The Story of the Bible, Ancient Man, America, The Fall of the Dutch Republic, The Rise of the Dutch Kingdom, A Short History of Discovery, Tolerance, Ships and How They Sailed the Seven Seas,* and *Air-Storming* followed. He illustrates his works with his own pen-drawings.

VA'POR, in physics, the gaseous state into which solids and liquids pass when heated. In their structure and physical properties, there is practically no difference between vapors and gases (see GAS), but in ordinary usage the term *vapor* is applied to those gases that are formed by the action of heat on liquids and solids, while the term *gas* is applied to those substances which remain in gaseous form under ordinary conditions of temperature and pressure. We speak of steam as a vapor and of oxygen as a gas. Water vapor formed by the action of the heat of the sun on the surface of the land is always present in the atmosphere and has an important effect on climate. See RAIN.

VARICOSE, *var e kose'*, **VEINS**, dilated veins, which are marked by knotty swellings at the valves. The disease commonly affects the lower limbs and sometimes becomes very painful and even dangerous, from the bursting of the veins, though it often is merely an inconvenience. Rest and support in an elevated position and the application of proper bandages are elements in the treatment.

VARI'ETY, in plant and animal classification, a subdivision of a species, including an individual or group of individuals differing in some nonessential way from the rest of the species. Varieties are believed to result from differences in climate, nourishment, cultivation and the like, and to be less permanent than species.

In naming plants and animals, the name of the variety is placed third, following the name of the species; as *Ranunculus multifidus,* variety, *terrestris.* Here, *Ranunculus multifidus* is the common, yellow, water crowfoot, and the variety *terrestris* is a form growing on the ground.

VA'RIOLOID, a mild form of smallpox, induced by inoculation. See SMALLPOX.

VAR'NISH, a transparent liquid made by dissolving gums in alcohol, turpentine or oil. It is used to form a transparent coat over surfaces to protect them from air and moisture or to make them more beautiful. The resinous substances most commonly employed for varnishes are mastic, lac, copal, amber and asphalt; and the solvents are fixed oil, volatile oil and alcohol. Varnishes are colored with arnotto, gamboge, saffron, dragon's blood and other substances.

The base of varnish is gum copal, or the fossil gum found in Zanzibar, Sierra Leone, New Zealand and the Philippine Islands. The best gum is found in Zanzibar. When the gum is received in the varnish factory, it is broken up into pieces about the size of small egg coal. As it is being broken up, it is selected, for in one chunk of the amberlike material there may be both transparent and almost opaque streaks; the white transparent gum goes into the making of the best grades of varnish, and the dark-colored gum goes into the poorer grades. After the gum copal is broken, it is run through a series of hand sieves, which divide it into block, nut, chip and dust, for convenience in handling. The gum is then ready for the kettle.

For first-class varnish, Calcutta linseed oil ·is preferred. This oil is made from the flaxseed of India. The turpentine used for thinning the varnish is of the best and purest grade. The copper kettles in which the melting and mixing are done are on truck wheels, so that they can be rolled over a fire or taken off easily. The melting gum is constantly stirred. When the oil has been mixed with the liquid gum, the kettle is run back over the fire once more, and the gum and oil are boiled again. Then it is set away to cool, after which a quantity of turpentine is mixed with the gum and oil and the varnish is made. The varnish is strained through cotton before it is pumped into the storage tanks, where it is left to age for at least six months and often for two years.

Shellac varnish is made in churns, or barrels, revolving on journals. The shellac as it comes from India looks like amber-colored mica, for it is in thin sheets and is almost transparent. This shellac is mixed with the proper amount of alcohol, to dissolve it and form the varnish.

VAS'CO DA GAM'A. See GAMA, VASCO DA.

VASE, a vessel of an ornamental character, generally of pottery but frequently of stone, glass, metal or other materials. Those which have come down to us from ancient times in greatest numbers are the so-called Etruscan vases, made of terra cotta and adorned with painted figures (see ETRURIA, subhead *Etruscan Vases*). The Greek vases of the oldest style come chiefly from Corinth and the islands of Thera and Melos. Those of the late rich style have been almost exclusively discovered in Lower Italy, Apulia and Lucania. They were probably manufactured there, chiefly in the fourth and third centuries B. C.

Italy, France and Germany in the sixteenth and seventeenth centuries produced many vases which are the perfection of artistic form and execution, and since the fifteenth century the Venetian vases have been masterpieces of art. From India, China and Japan also have been obtained vases of various materials, especially of porcelain, which are distinguished for their elegance of form and beauty of ornamentation. Vases have been produced in the potteries of the United States which compare favorably with those made in other lands.

VASELINE, *vas'e lin*, or *vas'e leen*, a registered trade-mark used on products of the Chesebrough Manufacturing Company, Consolidated. The chief product is petroleum jelly, a semisolid mixture of hydrocarbons, distilled from petroleum and purified. It is used largely as an unguent and lubricant. See PETROLEUM.

VAS'SAR COLLEGE, one of the leading American colleges for women, founded near Poughkeepsie, N. Y., in 1861, and named in honor of Matthew Vassar, whose generosity made its establishment possible. Besides residence houses, students' building, chapel,

library, observatory and classroom building, there are separate buildings for music, art, chemisty, physics, social sciences and physical education; a new infirmary building was completed in 1940. The campus and farm, on which is maintained a model dairy, include 900 acres. Flower gardens, an open-air theater and athletic grounds are other interesting features. Vassar maintains high standards of scholarship and provides courses leading to the degrees of bachelor of arts and master of arts. There is a faculty of nearly 200, and a student enrollment of about 1,200. The library contains over 225,-000 volumes.

Matthew Vassar (1792–1868), founder of the college, was born at Norfolk, England, but was brought to America when four years old. His boyhood was passed near Poughkeepsie, where his father built up a prosperous brewing business. Besides contributing funds to establish the college which bears his name, he gave generously to other causes.

VATICAN CITY, the smallest independent state in the world, the domain of the Pope. It is also the center of the Roman Catholic religion; therefore the Pope is a temporal ruler as well as the spiritual head of his Church. Before 1870 the Papal States, about 16,000 square miles in Northern Italy, were controlled by the Church, and in them the Pope exercised temporal power. When modern Italy was organized, the Papal States were seized; the Pope was given the Vatican Palace and the Lateran palaces in Rome, in which he secluded himself a voluntary prisoner, and from which his successors never ventured.

Continued protest against loss of temporal power led to an agreement in 1929 by which 108.7 acres within Rome were ceded to the Church, an area once more assigned to the temporal power of the Pope. In addition, 750,000,000 lire in cash and 1,000,000,000 lire in Italian bonds were given to the Pope as added recompense for the loss of the old Papal States. The civil rule of the Pope embraces all legal, executive and judicial powers, but he entrusts his authority to a governor, who is responsible solely to him. Vatican City possesses its own postal system and coinage. Population, 1932, 1,025.

See PAPAL STATES; POPE.

Vatican Palace, the residence of the Pope, the chief building in Vatican City, no less famed than St. Peter's Church. Its construction was begun about 1150; it has been many times enlarged, and is said to contain 1,100 rooms. On the walls and ceilings are renowned works of art by Michelangelo, Raphael, and others. The library contains priceless collections of manuscripts and rare books, many of them hundreds of years old. The total number of volumes is not less than 250,000.

VATICAN COUNCIL, the Ecumenical Council of the Church of Rome, which met in the Vatican under Pope Pius IX, Dec. 8, 1869, and adjourned July 18, 1870. No council had ever been attended by so large a number of ecclesiastics. It declared the personal infallibility of the Pope, when speaking *ex cathedra*, to be a doctrine of the Church, a declaration yet maintained.

VAUDEVILLE, *vode'vil*, in the French sense, a kind of farcical comedy in which dialogue is interspersed with dancing, comic acting and songs of the day, a name originally given to a popular humorous drinking song, first composed in the valley of *Vau-de-Vire*. In the United States, vaudeville is merely a series of singing, acting and dancing numbers, pretending to no unity and having no relation to the drama.

VAULT, in architecture, a continued arch, or an arched roof, so constructed that the stones, bricks or other materials of which it is composed, sustain and keep one another in place. Vaults may be cylindrical, elliptical, single, double, cross, diagonal or Gothic.

VEDAS, *va'das*, from a Sanskrit word meaning *know*, the oldest sacred writings of India, written in Sanskrit and supposed to have been produced by a series of authors between 1500 and 1000 B. C. The Vedas are four in number, called respectively, the *Rig-Veda, Yajur-Veda, Sama-Veda* and *Atharva-Veda*. Of these the *Rig-Veda* is the oldest and most important. Its name means *stanzas of praise*, and it consists of more than a thousand hymns, most of them celebrating the deeds and begging the blessing of the greater gods. The other three seem to have been drawn largely from the first one. The latest of the four is sometimes questioned as to authenticity, being concerned rather with superstition than with religion. It reflects the development of the Brahmanical system with its departure from the earlier monotheistic system and its polytheistic rites.

All the Vedas are believed by the Brahmans to be inspired, and are held by them in the highest respect.

VEGA CARPIO, *va'ga kahr'pe o*, FELIX LOPE DE (1562–1635), a dramatic poet of Spain, best known as Lope de Vega, the most prolific imaginative writer in the annals of literature. Born in Madrid, in 1562, he joined the army, and in 1588 accompanied the Invincible Armada on its ill-fated expedition against England. After being twice married and twice a widower, he became a priest and subsequently entered the order of Saint Francis. He had already published various poems, but his dramatic and poetical productions now multiplied with extraordinary rapidity. For many years there was scarcely a week when he did not produce a play, and he himself declared that he often wrote, rehearsed and produced a play in twenty-four hours. He enjoyed an immense popularity and received marks of distinction from the king of Spain and from Pope Urban VIII. About three hundred of his dramatic works have been printed. They reveal an inexhaustible, though ill-regulated, imagination, a strong mixture of the sublime and the ridiculous and extraordinary facility in versification.

VEGETABLE, *vej'e ta b'l*, I'VORY. See IVORY PALM.

VEGETABLES, in the sense in which the term is generally used, those parts of plants, exclusive of fruits, which are used for food. In some, as the turnip, the roots are the parts used; in others, as the onion, the bulbs. The tubers of the potato and artichoke; the stems of asparagus; the leaves of the lettuce and cabbage; the flower buds of the cauliflower; the green fruit of the cucumber; the ripe fruit of the tomato; the seeds of corn, peas and beans, are common vegetable foods.

The principal components of vegetables are water, protein, fat, nitrogen, starch and certain indigestible refuse, like fiber and ash. The proportions of these constituents vary among different vegetables, but in all, the principal element is water. The amount of water varies from 58.9 per cent, in green beans, to 95.4 per cent, in the cucumber. The per cent of protein varies from .4 per cent, in the watermelon, to 9.4 per cent, in green beans. The amount of fat varies from .1 per cent, in the pumpkin, the radish, the potato, celery and the beet, to 1.1 per cent in green corn. The amount of nitrogen varies from 2.2, in lettuce, to 26.1, in the sweet potato.

Of fresh vegetables, green shelled beans have the highest fuel value, and the cucumber has the lowest, the value of the latter being about one-ninth that of the former. Others which contain a high fuel value are sweet potatoes, green peas, green corn, sugar peas and parsnips. In the cooking of vegetables, besides the loss of water content, there are chemical changes which often detract materially from the food value. Vegetables form an important part of the diet; in addition to their nutritive value, they contain many of the vitamins and other elements essential to the health of the body.

Related Articles. For descriptions of the vegetables in common use consult the following titles:

Artichoke	Corn	Pea
Asparagus	Cress	Potato
Bean	Cucumber	Pumpkin
Beet	Eggplant	Radish
Brussels	Kohl-rabi	Rhubarb
Sprouts	Lentil	Spinach
Cabbage	Lettuce	Squash
Carrot	Onion	Tomato
Cauliflower	Oyster Plant	Turnip
Celery	Parsley	Sweet Potato
Chard	Parsnip	Yam
Chicory		

VEGETA′RIANISM, the belief and practice of subsisting on a vegetable diet to the exclusion of animal food, a doctrine held in ancient times by such men as Pythagoras, Plato and Plutarch and later by Rousseau, Shelley and Swedenborg. At present vegetarian societies exist in considerable numbers in the United States, Canada and several European countries. A vegetable diet, it is claimed, is more healthful, economical and ethically effective than a diet mixed with animal food. Vegetarians differ among themselves, however, as to the degree to which they exclude animal products, some excluding only flesh, others fish and fowl, and others milk, eggs and cheese, as well. While scientific investigations on the whole show the superior efficacy of a mixed diet on the human mechanism, the vegetarians have without doubt done society a service in calling attention to the prevailing custom of eating too much meat.

VEII, *ve′yi,* an ancient Etruscan town, in early times the most formidable rival of Rome. The Romans and the Veientines were constantly at war, and because the latter were uniformly unsuccessful in pitched battle, they adopted the plan of shutting themselves up in the city when the Romans

approached and of going out to plunder when they were safe from attack. The family of Fabius, to whom had been entrusted the defense of Roman territory against the Veientines, were decoyed into ambush and put to death in this manner. About 396 B. C. Camillus took the city, after which it declined to an insignificant village.

VEIN, *vane,* in geology, a formation of igneous rock, occupying a fissure in other rock, as represented by the nearly perpendicular l a y e r s in t h e figure. They often extend into t h e earth hundreds of feet. Veins are u s u a l l y formed by rock in molten condition, forced into

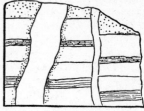

VEINS

the crevice by pressure, but may also be the result of mineral deposits left by underground waters. They often contain ore deposits, as gold, silver and other metals. Miners call a metal-bearing vein a *lode.* Small veins are often seen in boulders and pebbles, where they can be easily studied. See DIKE; GEOLOGY.

VEINS, a system of canals, or tubes, distributed throughout the bodies of animals, for the purpose of returning the impure blood to the heart and lungs, after it has been carried to the various parts by the arteries. Veins originate in the capillaries as tiny tubes, and as they unite they decrease in number and increase in size, till all those from the head, neck and upper extremities form the *superior vena cava* and those from the other parts of the body form the *inferior vena cava.* Both these large veins empty into the right auricle of the heart. The position of the veins in the circulatory system is shown in the color plate accompanying the article CIRCULATION.

The walls of the veins, like those of the arteries, are composed of three coats, but they are less elastic and have no pulsation. They collapse readily when empty. The distinguishing parts of a vein are the valves, which are made of folds in the internal coat and are arranged in pairs. They lie against the walls when the blood is flowing onward, but if from any cause the flow is obstructed, the valves are forced upward till they meet in the middle of the vein, and so prevent the blood from flowing backward. The action of the valves may be shown by pressing on some vein near the surface, thus preventing the flow of the blood toward the heart, when the valves will make little elevations in the vein. Valves are not found in the very smallest veins, nor in those of the abdomen, lungs and brain.

The blood flowing from a wounded vein is dark in color and comes out in an even stream. To check the flow, press on the vein below the wound or between it and the extremity.

Related Articles. Consult the following titles for additional information:

Arteries	Circulation
Capillaries	Wound

VELAZQUEZ, or VELASQUEZ, *va lahs' kaith,* Diego Rodriguez de Silva y (1599-1660), the most famous master of Spanish painting. He was born at Seville, of Portuguese parents, and studied first under Francisco Herrera the Elder, and afterward under Francisco Pacheco. Velazquez was fortunate in having so admirable a teacher as Pacheco at a formative period in his career. Less talented than his pupil, Pacheco had a remarkable gift for imparting basic principles concretely, and from him Velazquez gained a thorough knowledge of proportion, perspective, color and light and shade. In 1622 he went to Madrid, and as the result of this visit received an appointment as principal painter to Philip IV. Through the advice and intercession of Rubens, Velazquez went later to Italy, where he closely studied the works of Michelangelo, Raphael and Titian and the contemporary painters, especially Guido Reni, whose influence is evident to a marked degree in his works. On his return to Spain, in 1631, Velazquez was received with great distinction, and in 1658 the king raised him to the dignity of a noble.

Velazquez' chief characteristic in painting is naturalism. He was never imaginative, but painted exactly what he saw, combining this power of realism with a mastery of light, shade, coloring and composition. Among his finest works are the *Aguador,* or *Water Carrier;* a *Nativity,* or *Adoration of the Shepherds;* the *Brothers of Joseph; Moses Taken from the Nile; The Surrender of Breda;* portraits of Philip IV and of Elizabeth, his queen, Pope Innocent X and other dignitaries, and many pictures from common life.

VELOCIPEDE, *ve los'e peed,* a light vehicle or carriage propelled by the feet of its rider. One of the older forms of this carriage was constructed of two wheels of nearly equal size, placed one before the other and connected by a beam, on which the driver's seat was fixed. The rider, sitting astride the machine, propelled it by the thrust of each foot on the ground. This form dates from the early part of the nineteenth century. It was about half a century later that treadles, operating cranks on the axle of the front wheel, came into use. See BICYCLE.

VELOCITY, *ve los'e ty,* the rate at which a body changes its position in space. Velocity is popularly expressed as so many miles per hour or as so many feet per second. The velocity of a body is *uniform,* when it passes through equal spaces in equal times; it is *variable,* when the spaces passed through in equal times are unequal; it is *accelerated,* when during each portion of time it passes through a greater space than during the preceding equal portion; it is *retarded,* when a less space is passed through in each successive portion of time. Linear velocity is speed forward in a straight line; angular velocity is speed about an axis.

VEL'VET, the most familiar of the fabrics woven with a pile, produced by adding to the usual threads of the warp and weft an additional row of warp yarns, woven into the ground of the cloth and passed over wires on the surface. In the case of a loop pile, the wires are drawn out, without cutting, but for velvet or other cut pile, a knife is passed along a groove on the top of each wire before the wire is withdrawn. Real velvet is made entirely of silk. Cotton and woolen goods, woven in this manner, are called *velveteen* and *plush,* respectively.

Some of the richest and most artistic of the textiles woven on Italian looms in the fifteenth and sixteenth centuries were made, in part at least, of velvet. Similar stuffs were also made in Spain and Flanders. Many of these were for ecclesiastical vestments and altar cloths, and for hangings. The effect of a raised pattern in velvet, on a plain or figured silk ground, is very beautiful. Sometimes a design is formed of a long, upon a short, pile, called *velvet upon velvet,* and this, too, has a fine effect. Velvet is believed to have been made first in China.

VELVET LEAF. See INDIAN MALLOW.

VENATION, *ve na'shun,* the arrangement of veins in leaves, related to the shape of the leaf and its mode of germination, an important characteristic in the classification of plants. Most leaves are netted-veined, parallel-veined or fork-veined. The netted-veined are the most numerous, and are divided into several groups. True netted leaves have a single midrib from which branch primary veins terminating in delicate veinlets that curve upward just within the margin of the leaf. If the primary veins extend directly to the edge of the leaf they are said to be feather-veined. For illustrations of venation, see the article LEAVES.

VENDET'TA, an Italian word taken from the Latin *vindicta,* meaning *revenge.* It is applied to a blood feud in which the next of kin assumes responsibility for avenging a murdered person, probably a survival of methods of enforcing justice practiced before the organization of public courts. In Corsica the vendetta was held to be one of the most binding of family obligations, and the custom is held to a greater or less degree among the Albanians, Druses, Bedouins and other isolated and primitive peoples. The *feuds* among the mountaineers of Eastern Kentucky and Tennessee and Western Virginia in America are analogous to the vendetta. See BLOOD, AVENGER OF.

VENDOME, *vahN'dohm',* **COLUMN,** 142 feet high, stands in Paris, in the Place de la Vendome. It was built in 1806–1810 by Napoleon's order, to commemorate his 1805 victories in Russia. The column was later thrown down by the communists, but the preserved pieces were re-erected on the same spot in 1875. The masonry column is set with 900 feet of bronze, made from 1,200 melted captured cannon, depicting memorable scenes in the Napoleonic campaigns. The Place Vendome was named for the Duke of Vendome, who as a member of a noble house of the old French kingdom served his country in many wars.

VENEER', a thin layer of hard wood, as mahogany, rosewood or maple, glued to the surface of other woods to enhance the appearance of furniture and some interior finishings. Owing to recent improvements in sawing machinery, layers can be obtained that are almost as thin as paper. A good piece of veneer, contrary to popular belief, may be more serviceable than solid wood, for the reason that it is less likely to warp.

VENETIAN, *ve ne'shan,* **SCHOOL OF PAINTING.** See TINTORETTO; TITIAN; VERONESE, PAUL.

VENEZUELA, *ven e zwe'la,* a republic of South America, officially known as the United States of Venezuela. It is the most northerly country of the South American continent, and its much-indented coast line borders on the Caribbean Sea for about 1,750 miles. British Guiana lies to the east of Venezuela, Brazil is on the southeast, and Colombia is west and southwest. In Caribbean waters offshore are more than seventy islands belonging to Venezuela. The largest are Margarita (400 square miles) and Tortuga (85 square miles). In 1941, Great Britain ceded to Venezuela the island of Patos, three miles off the coast. It is 170 acres in area. The area of Venezuela is given officially as 352,143 square miles. The country is a union of twenty states, two territories, a Federal Dependency and the Federal District, which contains the capital and largest city, Caracas.

The People. The population consists of whites, mestizos (mixed white and Indian blood) and Indians. Most of the whites are of Spanish descent. They constitute the ruling class, although they form only ten per cent of the population. At the census of 1936, the total population was 3,491,159; Indians then numbered 100,670.

Venezuela is a Roman Catholic country, but religious tolerance prevails. In the elementary schools religious instruction is given only to those children whose parents request such instruction.

Public education is under the control of the Federal government. Attendance in primary (elementary) schools is compulsory for children between the ages of seven and fourteen years. In the rural schools special vocational courses are given. About 245,000 pupils are enrolled in the public urban and rural schools.

Completion of the six-year elementary course is required for entrance to the secondary schools, which number forty-eight. The National Pedagogical Institute in Caracas, founded in 1936, offers a three-year course for elementary teachers and two-year advanced courses for teachers preparing for high-school service. National universities have been established in Caracas and Merida and there is a School of Geology in Maracaibo. In Caracas there are special schools of agriculture, commerce and modern languages. Museums, libraries and academies of learning are maintained at government expense in different cities.

Surface and Drainage. Venezuela is naturally divided into four surface regions—the Guayana Highlands, the central plains, or *llanos,* the mountain areas of the north and west, and the Maracaibo lowlands.

The Guayana Highlands, comprising the state of Bolivar and the territory of Amazonas, occupy the southern half of the country. This area is an elevated plateau of dense forests and is largely unexplored. It rises from the right bank of the Orinoco River to the border ranges of the Parima and Pacaraima mountains, its highest points being Mount Maraguaca (10,500 feet) and Roraima Peak (8,661 feet). The latter is near the point where the borders of Brazil, Venezuela and British Guiana meet.

The central plains are a tract of level grasslands containing the principal grazing areas of Venezuela. They extend for 700 miles between the Colombia boundary and the Carribean Sea, and lie chiefly north of the Orinoco.

The greater part of Venezuela's population is found in the mountain district of the north and west, as this region contains fertile valleys and is near the sea. Farthest west is the Sierra Nevada de Merida, a range of the Andes which enters the country from Colombia and divides into two parallel ranges. Extending eastward along the coast are two parallel ranges known as the Maritime Andes or Caribbean Hills. In the valley of this chain the capital city of Caracas is situated. The highest peaks of Venezuela are found in the Sierra Nevada de Merida. This range reaches an altitude of 16,410 feet in La Columna, and has numerous other peaks over 15,000 feet high, eternally crowned with snow.

The fourth region, comprising the Maracaibo lowlands, lies in the northwest corner of Venezuela. Its principal feature is Lake Maracaibo, which has direct connection with the sea. Many rivers traverse the lowland region, which contains rich deposits of oil.

About four-fifths of Venezuela is drained by the Orinoco River and its 436 tributaries. This great river system is the third largest in Venezuela, being surpassed only by the Amazon and the Parana-Plata systems (see ORINOCO).

Climate. Venezuela lies wholly within the torrid zone, but it has three climatic zones, based principally on differences in altitude. The hottest zone, with temperatures ranging from 75° to 97° F., comprises territory less than 1,800 feet above sea level. The central plains and coastal areas make up the greater part of this zone, in which are situated the cities of Maracaibo and La Guaira, the port of Caracas. The second (temperate) zone includes the regions that are from 1,800 to 6,000 feet in altitude. Temperatures range between 50° and 77° F. The chief city in this zone is Caracas, situated at an altitude of about 3,000 feet. The third zone takes in all territory above 6,000 feet. Temperatures in the lower cities in this zone go as low as 14° F., and on the mountain peaks Arctic cold prevails.

Venezuela, like other tropical countries, has only two seasons—the wet and the dry. The former, lasting from May through November, is a period of torrential rains. Parts of the lowlands and interior plains experience flood conditions during this season, and the days are hot and humid. From December through April the weather is fairly pleasant, and the heat is tempered by dry, refreshing winds from the north.

Mineral Resources. Venezuela is rich in minerals, but a lack of transportation facilities and of modern machinery, and scarcity of capital have delayed the exploitation of many of these resources. An exception is petroleum, which is found abundantly in the Lake Maracaibo district and in the eastern part of the country. Foreign companies have been granted rights to exploit the wells, with the proviso that a considerable number of native laborers must be hired. Profits from the oil wells give Venezuela a higher per capita income than any other South American country. Venezuela usually ranks third in world production, being surpassed by the United States and the Soviet Union. Most of the crude oil is refined on the Dutch islands of Aruba and Curaçao.

Venezuela also has one of the world's most important sources of asphalt in Bermudez Lake, 1,000 acres in extent. It is located in the northeastern part of the country, in the same geographic area as the island of Trinidad, another source of asphalt. The island, however, is a British possession. Other minerals of Venezuela now being developed are gold, copper ore, coal, iron, tin, asbestos and mica. Salt mines are worked by the government. In the waters about the island of Margarita there are important pearl fisheries.

Agriculture. About one-fifth of the population is engaged in agriculture, comprising three-fourths of all persons gainfully employed. Coffee, the most important product, is grown generally over the country but flourishes best in the higher altitudes of the states of Tachira, Merida and Trujillo. Cacao, for the production of cocoa, is second to coffee in value. Both products are exported and both are of excellent quality. Sugar, corn, cotton, wheat, rice, oats, tobacco, bananas and truck crops are raised for home consumption and the country also produces a variety of tropical products, including copaiba, caoutchouc, tonka beans and vanilla. Venezuela's forest wealth is yet to be developed. The country's grazing lands support large herds of cattle. Other livestock includes sheep, goats, horses, mules and hogs.

Industry and Commerce. Because of a lack of raw materials, Venezuela has few manufacturing industries. The most important is wood-working. Cotton mills in several cities produce calico, denim, knit goods and hosiery. Products of less importance include carbonated beverages, straw hats, glass, cement, cordage and candles. Closely related to agriculture are tanneries using native skins, meat-packing plants, creameries and dairies, sugar mills and tobacco factories. Manufacturing equipment has to be imported.

Venezuela has several good natural harbors, as well as a man-made port at La Guaira, gateway to Caracas. Other active ports are Maracaibo, Puerto Cabello, Cristobal Colon and Ciudad Bolivar. In peacetime, Venezuela's most important foreign customers are the United States, the United Kingdom, Germany, the Netherlands, Canada and France. Petroleum, coffee and cacao are the leading exports. There is a thriving coastal trade.

Transportation. Inland transportation routes include 6,500 miles of navigable rivers, nearly 600 miles of commercial railways, and about 5,900 miles of roadways. There are twelve main lines of railway, of which five are owned by foreign capitalists. The Great Railway of Venezuela, 112 miles in extent, connects Valencia and Caracas. The twenty-three-mile La Guaira-Caracas Railway, extending from the capital to the sea, is the country's most scenic railroad. Venezuela is building a modern highway system through the populated northern districts. Some of the newer motor roads traverse the lofty Andean ranges. The country is also served by a network of airlines.

Government. Venezuela is governed under a Constitution which went into effect in 1936. Legislative authority is vested in a Congress of two houses—the Chamber of Deputies and the Senate. One-half the members in each house are elected every two years for a four-year term. The Deputies are chosen by conventions representing the municipalities, which elect one Deputy for each 35,000 inhabitants of the state, but every state must be represented by at least one Deputy. Senators are elected, two for each state, by the state legislatures. All candidates must be native-born Venezuelans.

The President of the union is elected by Congress for a five-year term and is ineligible for reëlection to the term immediately following. He must be a Venezuelan by birth and must be at least thirty years old. He may not be a cleric. The President is assisted by a Council of Ministers, or Cabinet.

The states are autonomous and reserve to themselves all powers not granted to the Federal government by the Constitution.

History. The coast of Venezuela was first seen by Columbus in 1498. The following year an expedition including Americus Vespucius gave the region the name it now bears, which means *Little Venice;* it was applied because of the discovery of Indian villages built on piles along the swampy shores of Lake Maracaibo. The first permanent white settlement in South America was founded by the Spanish in 1522, on the site of Cumana. Venezuela was under Spanish rule until 1821, when it was united with Colombia. In 1829 it became independent.

In spite of social uprisings and boundary disputes, Venezuela has made great progress toward political stability. A dispute with Great Britain over the boundary between Venezuela and British Guiana (1895) was settled by arbitration after President Cleveland had intervened. In 1903, President Theodore Roosevelt protested a blockade of Venezuelan ports by Italy, Great Britain and Germany and the difficulty was referred to The Hague. Under the dictatorship of General Juan Vicente Gomez, the country paid off its foreign debts. The Presidents since 1936 have been General Eleasar Lopez Contreras and General Isaias Medina Angarita.

Venezuela maintained a state of neutrality in World War I; in 1920 it joined the League of Nations. In World War II it supported the United States in its program for Western Hemisphere defense and it broke off diplomatic relations with the Axis powers after the Japanese attack on Pearl Harbor. See WORLD WAR.

Related Articles. Consult the following titles for additional information:

Bolivar, Simon
Caracas

Maracaibo
Trinidad

VENICE, *ven'is,* ITALY (in Italian, Venezia), a city famed for its unique character and splendid art treasures. Venice, built on a cluster of islands, has canals for its principal streets, and more bridges than any other city in the world. Gondolas and other boats take the place of cabs, street cars and automobiles. The city lies in a sheltered lagoon on the northwestern shore of the Adriatic Sea, 164 miles by rail east of Milan. The islands on which it is built number 120, and are divided into two main groups, between which flows the celebrated Grand Canal. This canal, which is the principal thoroughfare, passes through the city in the form of a letter *S* and divides it into two nearly equal parts. The canal is crossed by four bridges, the chief of which is the Rialto. There are 146 smaller canals, by means of which all parts of the city can be reached by boat.

In amount of ship tonnage entering its harbor, Venice is the fourth Italian seaport. A new port on the mainland, called Marghera, was built by Mussolini, the Italian dictator. A long sandbank, the Lido, separates the island waters from the Adriatic, and is a fashionable beach resort. It is protected by a sea wall.

The Piazza, or Square of Saint Mark's, is the center of interest. This is the great center of business and amusement. It is 576 feet long, 269 feet wide on one side and 185 feet wide on the other. The east side is faced by the Cathedral of Saint Mark's, one of the most renowned structures of its kind in the world. On the north and south sides of the square are the palaces formerly occupied by the procurators of the cathedral, and they now form a part of the royal palace. These buildings contain many rare paintings by some of the most celebrated artists of Venice, including Tintoretto and Paul Veronese. The famous Campanile, which fell in 1902, and was rebuilt, also faces the square. Another object of interest facing

the square is the clock tower, built in 1496 and surmounted by two bronze figures, which strike the hours on a large bell.

Among the churches of special interest is that of Santa Maria della Salute, which contains excellent paintings of Titian, including

VENICE

his masterpiece, *The Assumption of the Virgin,* and *The Presentation in the Temple.* The Church of San Sebastiano is celebrated for its altarpieces by Paul Veronese, and the Friari, a church built for the friars, is interesting for its size and because it is a good representation of the Italian Gothic style of architecture. It contains many monuments and pictures. The palaces are of no less interest than the churches. Of these the palace of the Doges, originally built in 800, but several times destroyed and rebuilt, is the most important. During the time of Venice's greatest prosperity, this was the residence of its rulers. It now contains many treasures of art. From the rear of this palace the celebrated "Bridge of Sighs" leads to the prison, which is still in use. Many of the palaces are now used for other purposes, serving as hotels, museums and office buildings. The Academy of Fine Arts is also of great interest, because it contains one of the most valuable collections of paintings found in Europe. The Rialto is the principal commercial street and typically represents the life of the city. The bridge of this name crosses the Grand Canal at the point where the first settlement was made.

Modern Venice is of considerable commercial importance. The manufactures include lace, tapestries, mosaics, bronzes, jewelry and wood-carvings among its finer wares, and cotton and woolen goods, chemicals, heavy machinery and clocks among its larger industries. There is also some shipbuilding, and glassware is manufactured.

The islands occupied by the city were formerly a refuge from the hordes of barbarians which invaded Italy from the north. It is supposed that the first settlement was made about the middle of the fifth century, but there is no authentic record of the fact. In the sixth century Venice was independent, though it was tributary to the Eastern Empire. It was obliged to defend itself from pirates and from the Lombards of Italy, and because of this an organized government was formed and the leader or ruler, entitled *doge,* was selected. The Crusades gave the city a great impetus, because it became a commercial center for these military movements.

During the Middle Ages Venice had increased in commercial importance and power until considerable surrounding territory of the mainland was under its control, and just previous to the discovery of America it was the leading commercial city of Europe. From that time its influence began to wane. The Turks captured Constantinople and cut off much of the trade from the East. A route to India around the Cape of Good Hope also brought much of that trade to Portugal, and the commerce which had entered Europe through Venetian harbors now came through Genoa and other cities to the west. In 1797 the Venetian Republic was deprived of its independence by Napoleon, and most of the possessions were given to Austria. Within a few years the Austrians ceded Venice to Italy. Between this time and 1866, the city was alternately under the rule of Austria and Italy, until finally by vote of the inhabitants it was joined to Italy.

The proximity of Venice to the war zone during the World War, especially after the Austro-German drive of 1917, caused great anxiety as to its fate, but it was never captured. However, the uncertain conditions caused thousands of its inhabitants to flee, and until the close of the war it retained only the memories of its former glory and activity. Time and peace have restored its prosperity and made it again the mecca of art lovers and tourists. In 1921 the population was 171,665; ten years later it had increased to 260,250.

Related Articles. Consult the following titles for additional information:

Adriatic Sea	Doge
Bridge of Sighs	Saint Mark's,
Campanile	Cathedral of

VENIZELOS, *ven e za′ lohs,* ELEUTHERIOS (1864–1936), an eminent Greek lawyer and statesman, through whose influence Greece was brought into the World War on the side of the entente allies, was born of humble parentage on the island of Crete. He was educated in Canea, Crete and the University of Athens. After completing his education Venizelos returned to Crete, and at the age of twenty-three was elected to the assembly, where he soon became the leader of the liberal party. In 1910 he removed to Athens to become the leader of a party founded by the Military League, which was working for constitutional reform. Within a year he was chosen Prime Minister.

In 1913 King Constantine, whose wife was a sister of Emperor William II, ascended the throne of Greece. At the outbreak of the World War, Venizelos led the movement to unite Greece with the entente allies, but Constantine advocated strict neutrality. Venizelos resigned in March, 1915, since he and the king could not work together. He was, however, persuaded to form a new Ministry; when Bulgaria entered the war against Serbia, he insisted that the Greek forces be mobilized, and accomplished his purpose in spite of the king's opposition. Since Greece was bound by treaty to go to the aid of Serbia if it were attacked by Bulgaria, Venizelos insisted that this aggreement be fulfilled. Constantine refused his consent, and the Prime Minister again resigned.

In September, 1916, Venizelos and his followers set up a provisional government at Canea, but later transferred it to Saloniki. When Constantine was forced to abdicate in 1917, Venizelos was returned to power and Greece joined the forces against the Central Powers. He represented his country at the peace conference at Versailles in 1919. In 1935 Venizelos inspired a revolution against the government, which failed, and he sought refuge in Paris.

VENTILATION, *ven ti la′shun.* See HEATING AND VENTILATION.

VENTRILOQUISM, *ven tril′ o kwiz′m,* the art of speaking in such a way that the voice seems to come not from the speaker but from another source. Long practice is necessary to develop the art to perfection. The ventriloquist is able to "throw his voice," or produce the illusion of distance chiefly by proper control of his larynx. He draws a full breath, speaks without moving the muscles of his face, neck or chest, expelling the air through a narrow glottis. The ventriloquist's success depends largely on his skill in directing the imagination of his audience. The human ear is not quick to detect the direction from which a sound comes, and if a listener's attention is directed to a particular location his imagination is apt to associate it with the sound he hears.

VEN'UE, CHANGE OF, a change in the county or judicial district in which a case in law is brought to trial. It is made for the convenience of witnesses or on motion of the defense because prejudice on the part of the court or community precludes a fair trial in the jurisdiction where the action is brought. Change of venue is regulated by statute.

VE'NUS, the Roman name for the goddess of love. The Greeks called her APHRODITE. By some accounts she was the daughter of Jupiter, but according to the most popular legend she was born from the sea foam, near the island of Cythera. She was brought up by the nymphs in their ocean caves, and when she had attained the fulness of her size and beauty, she was conducted to Olympus, where she excited the greatest admiration. All of the gods wished to marry her, but she scorned them all, and as a punishment she was compelled by Jupiter to marry Vulcan, the ugliest of the gods. He gained no great happiness from the union, for Venus always despised him and bestowed her love on Mars and on the mortals Adonis and Anchises. Cupid was her son by Mars, and Aeneas was her son by Anchises. Venus was the special protectress of all young people who were in love, but she does not seem to have continued her interest in their affairs after they were once married. She was consequently chiefly worshiped by young people.

VENUS, one of the smallest but the most brilliant and conspicuous of the planets, second from the sun, its orbit lying between Mercury and the Earth. To the ancients, Venus was known as *Lucifer,* morning star, and *Hesperus,* evening star, according as it was seen after sunset or before sunrise. As evening star on clear moonless nights it may be observed to cast a shadow, its reflecting power being three times as great as that of the moon, due probably to a dense atmosphere and the presence of many clouds. The diameter of Venus is 7,700 miles, and it is 67,200,000 miles distant from the sun. Its sidereal revolution is performed in 225 days; its rotation period remains in doubt, because of difficulty of observation. It has various phases, according to the position it occupies, appearing as a thin crescent, gradually increasing to a full circle and then decreasing until it disappears.

Transit of Venus, the passage of the planet Venus across the disk of the sun, an occurrence of unsurpassed interest to astronomers and the entire scientific world. A full transit of Venus across the center of the sun's disk occupies about eight hours, the time being shortened when it occurs nearer the edge of the disk. Transits of Venus were observed in 1874 and 1882, and will occur again in 2004 and 2012.

VENUS DE MILO. See SCULPTURE.

VENUS'S FLOWER BASKET, a beautiful sponge, whose skeleton looks like spun glass, woven into an exquisite pattern, so delicate and white that one can scarcely believe it to be a natural skeleton. It is found in the deep sea near the Philippine Islands.

VENUS'S FLY'TRAP, or **DIONAEA,** *di o ne'a,* a plant of the sundew family, the leaves of which serve as traps for insects, upon which the plant feeds. It grows in the sandy soil of the North Carolina coast, and the insects it entraps are necessary to supply it with the nitrogen lacking in the earth. A flower stalk bearing a cluster of small white flowers rises from a rosette of leaves which spring directly from the ground. Each leaf is divided into two parts, the lower, flat and bladelike in ap-

VENUS'S FLYTRAP

pearance, and the upper, a roundish portion, consisting of two lobes, divided by a midrib. On the surfaces of the lobes are sensitive, hairlike processes, and along the edges are sharp bristles. When an insect alights on one of these sensitive hairs, the two lobes come together like a trap. A fluid is secreted by means of which the plant assimilates the juices of the animal. When the food is exhausted the leaf opens. After a leaf has captured several insects it loses its vitality and dies. See SUNDEW.

VERA CRUZ, *va'rah krooz,* MEXICO, the chief seaport of the republic, situated on an arm of the Gulf of Mexico, about 190 miles east of Mexico City. Though the site is low and sandy and the climate somewhat un-healthful, the construction of sanitation and port works has greatly improved conditions and has prevented the recurrence of periodic outbreaks of yellow fever. At the entrance of the fine harbor is the picturesque old fortress of San Juan de Ulloa, formerly used as a prison, but now only an interesting relic of colonial days. The city itself, with its encircling wall built of coral, is very attractive. Buildings of recent construc-tion include a customhouse and a post and telegraph office, both constructed of cement, and the handsome building of the general lighthouse board, erected on land reclaimed from the sea. The dwelling houses of Vera Cruz are built of coral limestone in Span-ish style.

The streets of the city are narrow, but are straight and well-kept, and are paved with asphalt over a wide area. Liberty Boulevard is the handsomest thoroughfare, and there are two public gardens. Prom-inent institutions include Vera Cruz Insti-tute (a high school), the naval school, the only one of the kind in Mexico, the public library and a hospital. There are several factories, and fishing is an important occu-pation. Vera Cruz has a large, commodious harbor, with modern docks and other im-provements, and enjoys a large general trade. Regular lines of steamers from the United States, the West Indies and Europe visit the port, and four railway lines meet here.

The city was founded by Cortez in 1520. During the Mexican War it was captured by Americans, and in 1914 it was temporarily occupied by United States marines as a re-sult of Huerta's insult to the flag (see MEX-ICO, subhead *History*). To the Americans chief credit is due for making the city sanitary, for during their occupation they cleaned it thoroughly. Population, 1930, 71,883.

VERB. The verb is that part of speech which expresses action or that tells what some object is or does, as, "The boy *runs,*" "The man *lifts* the stone," "Fishes *swim,*" "He *suffers* much," "The leaves *are* green." Verbs usually have the power of indicating time and mode, by means of tenses and moods,

these varying in the different languages, as does also the conjugation, or system of verbal inflections and forms as a whole.

According to their relation to objects, verbs are classed as *transitive* and *intransitive.* A transitive does or may take an object, as "John *struck* Harry." An intransitive verb may not or cannot take an object, as "The tree *falls.*" Some verbs are used both transi-tively and intransitively, as "The boy *studies*" and "The boy *studies his lesson.*" According to their form in different tenses, verbs are *regular* or *irregular.* A regular verb forms its past tense and past participle by adding *d* or *ed* to the present tense form, as *live, lived.* Irregular verbs form their past tense and past participle otherwise, as *give, gave.*

Transitive verbs are in the *active* or *pas-sive voice,* according to their representation of the subject as *acting* or as *being acted* upon, as "The sun *attracts* the earth," "The earth *is attracted* by the sun." *Auxiliary* verbs are those used with principal verbs to indicate mood and tense, as "The man *is* here," "The man *was here* yesterday," I *will* go tomorrow." *Inflection* of a verb is giving the changes in form to denote person, num-ber and tense. *Conjugation* is the process of systematically carrying a verb through all its different moods, tenses, persons and num-bers, in both active and passive voices, if it is a transitive verb.

VERBENA, *vur be' nah,* a genus of tropi-cal and subtropical American plants of the vervain family, several species of which are cultivated for the beauty of their flowers. The cultivated varieties have creeping or spreading stems and bear their blossoms in dense, showy spikes, of almost every color except yellow. The wild varieties are often troublesome as weeds. The verbena of the perfumers is the lemon grass, from which the oil of verbena is extracted.

VERDI, *ver'de,* GIUSEPPE (1813–1901), the greatest composer of opera Italy has produced. He was born at Roncole, near Parma, the son of a poor storekeeper. He early showed a fondness for music, and at the age of eight began his studies with the village organist. Later he was taught for three years by the organist of a neighboring village. Verdi then went to Milan and placed himself under the conductor of the famous Scala Theater. In 1839 an opera of his was accepted by the Scala manage-ment, and the price paid for it—about four hundred dollars—was more money than the composer had ever before possessed in all the combined years of his life. Verdi had married some years previously, and the struggle with poverty had been a hard one.

After the production of his first opera, Verdi received commissions for others, and in 1842 he enjoyed a substantial success with *Nabucodonosor*. Two other successes followed in 1843 and 1844, *I Lombardi* and *Ernani*. The latter, with a libretto based on Victor Hugo's *Hernani*, was a triumph for its composer in England and other European countries. There followed a period of too many undertakings and too rapid composing; the operas produced during the next few years are unknown to-day. Then, in 1851, Verdi scored an instantaneous success with *Rigoletto*, one of the most popular operas in modern repertoires. Equally popular have been his *Il Trovatore* and *La Traviata*, both produced in 1853.

Even greater triumphs were in store for him. In 1870 the khedive of Egypt invited the composer to write an opera for the opening of the Grand Opera House in Cairo, and in 1871 *Aida* was presented before an audience that was captivated, as are present-day audiences, by its stirring music and colorful, dramatic story. *Otello* and *Falstaff*, composed in Verdi's old age, reveal a further ripening of his powers. He also composed sacred pieces—a *Requiem* and a *Te Deum*.

VERDIGRIS, *vur' de grees,* a greenish substance that forms on copper when exposed to acetic acid. It is used principally in the composition of paints and Paris Green, in the manufacture of dyes and as an ointment, or liniment. Taken internally, it is poisonous. White of egg and milk are antidotes.

VERDUN, *vair duN',* FRANCE, a fortified city, on an almost direct line between Paris and Metz, 175 miles from the former, and on the Meuse River. Its fame is not derived from its size or from its industrial importance, but because it has been "a rock of history, around which the storms of battle have raged repeatedly." It had a population of about 21,000 in 1914; its industrial activity included a few factories which produced hardware, leather goods, and confections, and liquor was distilled. In 1933, fifteen years after the devastation wrought by the World War, its people had not recovered from the disaster, for the population

was then only 13,000. Other sieges had the city withstood, but between 1914 and 1918, Verdun was the center of the German offensive in its attempts to reach Paris, and its destruction was almost complete. But the long siege failed. (See below.)

Battle of Verdun. After the war of 1870–1871 Verdun was made a first-class fortress, having about it a thirty-mile ring of sixteen large forts and twenty smaller works. The great attack on the outer defenses was begun in February, 1916. General Pétain commanded the French forces. During seven months of the most sanguinary fighting, from February to September, the Germans gained 130 square miles of territory, but failed to capture the heart of the fortress; had they succeeded they would have made a breach in the allied defense of Paris. In October a counter-attack under General Nivelle was begun, which was followed by a second offensive in December. The French succeeded in reaching the second line of defenses by February, 1917, and, after a period of inactivity, began a third offensive in August. A succession of smashing blows drove the Germans back until all the dominating positions were in French hands. The Battle of Verdun is counted a great allied victory. The losses were exceedingly heavy on both sides; it is believed the Germans lost over half a million men.

VERESTCHAGIN, *vyeh reh shchah'gin,* VASILI (1842–1904), a Russian painter, noted especially for his pictures of war scenes. He was born at Novgorod, and was educated in Saint Petersburg (Petrograd) and in France and Germany. Among his productions are a series of paintings based on the expedition of 1867 against the Central Asian provinces, *The Departure of Napoleon from Moscow* and *Roosevelt at the Head of the Rough Riders.* Verestchagin depicted the cruel side of war with remarkable realism. He was killed in the Russo-Japanese War, while on a battleship which was sunk by the Japanese.

VERGIL, *vur' jil* (70-19 B. C.), the common designation of Publius Vergilius Maro, a great Roman poet, author of the *Aeneid*. He was born near Mantua, in northern Italy, and was the son of a small land-owner. His education, which was careful and thorough, was received at Cremona, Milan, Naples and Rome, where he became thoroughly acquainted with the Epicurean philosophy. **A**

naturally retiring disposition and a delicate constitution, together with the fact of his not being by birth a Roman citizen, would have checked any aspirations he might have had to the calling of the soldier, the orator or the statesman. He retired to his father's estate, with the intention of passing his life in the pursuit of poetry and agriculture, but was rudely disturbed by the allotment of his farm to the soldiers of Octavius, after the Battle of Philippi (42 B. C.). He recovered it through the aid of Asinius Pollio, the Roman governor; but further troubles arose, and he abandoned it, going at the instance of friends to Rome, where soon afterward he became acquainted with Maecenas and Octavius, to whom Pollio had recommended him. Through these powerful friends he received an estate in Campania and was enabled to devote his life to his favorite pursuits.

Vergil had become a great favorite of Octavius, and when, after the Battle of Actium (31 B. C.), the latter became Augustus, the poet was not forgotten. It was under the encouragement and patronage of the emperor that Vergil's greatest work, the *Aeneid,* was written; and indeed only the firm establishment of the Empire and the glorious achievements of Augustus in war and peace could have produced such an epic. During the years of its composition the poet recited selections before the imperial household. When the *Aeneid* was brought to a close, Vergil went to Athens, intending to spend a few years in revising the poem and completing certain unfinished parts. Soon afterward Augustus arrived in Athens from the East, and he induced Vergil to accompany him to Italy. Under the strain of seasickness and exposure to the strong sea air, his delicate constitution broke down, and he barely lived to reach Italy, dying at Brundusium, Sept. 21, 19 B. C. Rather than leave his life-work, the *Aeneid,* imperfect and incomplete, he ordered it burned, but finally yielded to the request of Augustus, that its revision might be entrusted to his friends Tucca and Varius, who edited it with the utmost care. The first of Vergil's poems of which the authorship is certain are the *Bucolics,* or *Eclogues.* While based on the model of the *Idyls* of Theocritus, these ten poems are by no means solely pastoral in character. Many contain allusions or are entirely devoted to current political events or to matters concerning the poet, the background and language alone

being pastoral. The *Georgics* comprise four books of didactic poems on agricultural subjects. Book I deals with the tilling of the soil; Book II, with the cultivation of fruit trees; Book III tells of horses and cattle, and Book IV treats of bees. The *Georgics* are addressed to Maecenas and were said by some to have been written at his patron's request; the work is the most finished of all Vergil's poetry.

The *Aeneid,* the composition of which probably occupied most of the twelve years between the beginning of Augustus's reign and the poet's death, is Vergil's greatest work, although it is not as highly polished as some of his other poems. In general treatment of character and incident, it is inferior to its Greek models, the *Iliad* and the *Odyssey*; but certain parts are very successfully handled; and the whole poem is conceived in a spirit of delicacy, true culture and noble patriotism. In refinement of expression and elegant metrical construction, Vergil has not been surpassed. For an outline of the poem, see AENEID.

VERMES, *vur'meez,* or **WORMS,** that branch of the animal kingdom formerly including all invertebrate creatures (those without backbones) except the insects, but now restricted to such forms as earthworms, sea-worms and leeches. Most of the animals of this division have long, flat or cylindrical bodies, which are divided more or less distinctly into segments which have no limbs. Many of the Vermes are parasites, and some live in the intestines of human beings, where they cause great discomfort. See ZOÖLOGY.

VERMICELLI, *vur me chel'le* or *vur me sel'le.* See MACARONI.

VERMIFORM, *vur'me form,* **APPEN'-DIX,** a long, slender, wormlike organ, which opens from the colon near its lower end. It is normally from three to four inches in length and is hollow to its tip. It is in the right side of the lower abdomen and projects upward in most cases. It performs no bodily function, but is the source of appendicitis (which see).

VERMIL'ION, a bright red pigment, named from a French word meaning *little worm,* because formerly crimson, or carmine, was obtained from a small red worm. The vermilion of commerce is obtained by mixing together in a revolving drum, mercury, sulphur and a solution of potash in water, and heating the mixture to about 115°, when it gradually assumes a red color. Vermilion is a permanent color and can be used with water or oil, but volatilizes at red heat and cannot be used for enamels. Cinnabar, a sulphide of mercury which occurs in large quantities in California, Brazil, Spain, China and other countries, is also a valuable source of vermilion.

VERMONT', the second largest of the New England states, popularly called THE GREEN MOUNTAIN STATE, *green mountains* being an English translation of the French words *verts* and *monts,* from which *Vermont* is derived. The state is appropriately named, for its picturesque mountains with their wooded slopes are among the most charming phases of New England scenery. The flower emblem of the state is the red clover.

Location and Area. Vermont lies directly south of the Canadian province of Quebec, and its southern boundary follows the northern Massachusetts line. It is bounded on the east by New Hampshire, from which it is separated by the Connecticut River, and on the west by New York. It is therefore the only New England state having no coast line. The western boundary, however, follows the deepest channels of Lake Champlain for more than one hundred miles, and over half the lake belongs to Vermont. Along the northern boundary the state is ninety miles wide; along the southern, but forty. From north to south it is about 150 miles in extent. Its area is 9,609 square miles, of which 331 square miles are water. Maine, the largest New England state, is over three times as large as Vermont, which ranks forty-second in size among the states of the American Union.

People and Cities. In 1940, with a population of 359,231, Vermont was the forty-sixth state in number of inhabitants. At the same time there was an average of 38.7 persons to the square mile, ranking Vermont twenty-eighth among the states in density of population; the average density for the entire United States was 44.2 in 1940. The rural population of the state comprises 65.7 per cent of the people.

About two-fifths of the foreign-born inhabitants, who number about 50,000, are French-Canadians, and consequently the Roman Catholic Church claims the largest number of adherents of any one denomination. Among Protestant bodies, the Congregational, Methodist, Baptist and Episcopal are the most important.

Fourteen municipalities in 1940 had populations exceeding 2,500. Of these only three had 10,000 or more inhabitants: Burlington, 27,686; Rutland, 17,082; and Barre, 10,909. Montpelier, with a population in 1940 of 8,006, is the capital.

Surface and Drainage. The entire state is mountainous, owing to the presence of the Green Mountain range, which extends from the Canadian border into Massachusetts, and to numerous parallel ranges, which extend in a nearly north and south direction. The Taconic range lies in the southwestern part of the state and is parallel to the main range. There are also several short ranges in the northern and eastern sections. The highest peaks of the main range from north to south are Jay, Sterling, Mansfield, Camel's Hump, Lincoln, Pico, Killington, Shrewsbury, Stratton and Haystack, of which Mount Mansfield, with an altitude of 4,406 feet, is the highest. There are forty-one peaks having an altitude of 3,500 feet or more. All of the mountains of the parallel ranges are comparatively low, have rounded summits and are well timbered. These various ranges are separated by low, broad valleys, through which one or more streams flow and which have fairly fertile soil. The lowest point in the state is the valley of Lake Champlain. In general the surface is a combination of forest-clad hills and mountains, beautiful valleys and sparkling lakes and streams.

The eastern half of the state is drained by the Connecticut River and its tributaries, the most important of these being the Passumpsic, the Waits, the White, the Ottaquechee, the Williams, the Saxtons and the West. The western part of the state is drained into Lake Champlain and thence into the Saint Lawrence River. The most important streams flowing into the lake are the Missisquoi, the Lamoille, the Winooski and the Otter Creek, the last being the largest river wholly within the state. The southwestern section is drained into the Hudson River by the Battenkill and the Hoosic.

The most important lake is Lake Champlain, more than half of which belongs to Vermont. Other lakes in the Champlain Valley are Bomoseen, Saint Catherine and Dunmore. In the northeastern part of the state is Lake Memphremagog, a portion of which is in Vermont and the remainder in Canada. Southeast of this is Willoughby Lake, renowned for its peculiar surroundings. The lake is about six miles long and lies between two mountains which seem to have been rent asunder in some past geologic age. This region also contains numerous other smaller lakes, frequently known as ponds. All of these bodies of water have become favorite summer resorts.

Climate. The climate of Vermont is subject to extreme and sudden changes. In summer the temperature varies from 65° to 90° in winter it ranges from 18° to 45°. At Burlington the mean annual temperature is 45°. The climate is milder in the Champlain Valley than east of the Green Mountains. During the winter there is often much snow, which in the colder parts of the state covers the ground for three months. The average annual rainfall is thirty-seven inches. The air is clear and pure.

Mineral Resources. The chief mineral wealth of the state is in its quarries. No other state in the Union produces so great a variety or quantity of marble and granite, and Vermont has practically become the center of the marble and granite industries. The value of the annual output of granite exceeds $3,000,000; the largest quarries are at Barre and Woodbury. The marble industry is chiefly in Rutland County. Roofing and other slate are obtained in large quantities, and the output is of fine quality.

Agriculture. The soil in the valleys along the streams and at the foot of the mountains and hills is usually fertile, though but very little of it compares favorably in this respect with the soils of the great prairie states in the Mississippi Valley. Agriculture is the leading industry of the state. The farms are comparatively small, averaging less than 200 acres, and most of them are tilled by their owners. Formerly Vermont was known for its production of wheat, oats, corn and potatoes, but since the development of the great agricultural states in the Missippi Valley, the New England states have been unable to compete in the markets which the Western producers could reach; consequently, in recent years methods and products have been radically changed. Now intensified farming is generally practiced and the raising of wheat has given way to the raising of corn, which is very generally used as ensilage. Dairying is the chief agricultural industry. Excellent qualities of butter and cheese are made, and these find ready market in Boston and other Eastern cities. In the output of these products the state ranks among the first ten. Vermont has always been famed for the excellent breeds of horses produced there, and horses are still raised in large numbers. In some sections the raising of garden vegetables and apples for market is also a profitable industry, and Vermont is unsurpassed in the United States in the quality and quantity of maple sugar produced.

Manufactures. The chief manufacturing industries include dressing stone particularly marble and granite; the manufacture of scales, centered in Saint Johnsbury and in Rutland; the production of flour and other grist mill products; the manufacture of lumber products, and the manufacture of textiles, particularly woolen goods. Since the introduction of electrical power, many small factories have been established within the state, obtaining their power from mountain streams which were previously useless. This has increased the output of manufactures very materially since 1890.

Transportation. The northwestern part of the state finds a ready outlet by water through Lake Champlain and the Richelieu River, but these are closed to navigation during the winter season. Lines of railway traverse the state from north to south, both on the eastern and western sides. There are also numerous cross lines so that every county has good railway facilities, and nearly every town is on a line of railway or within ready access of it. The railways of the state are under the control of the Rutland, the Canadian National and the Vermont Central systems; the total mileage is about 1,075. A number of electric lines connect near-by towns.

Government. The legislature consists of a senate of thirty members and a house

VERMONT·
THE GREEN MOUNTAIN STATE

VERMONT
FREEDOM AND UNITY

STATE FLOWER
RED CLOVER

Courtesy Vermont Department of Agriculture

(1) Modern dairy farm; (2) thoroughbred dairy cows; (3) seed potatoes; (4) house for evaporating maple sap; (5) collecting the sap; (6) Bennington Monument.

of representatives of 246 members, the latter containing one representative for each town and city within the state. Both senators and representatives are elected every two years. The legislature meets biennially. The executive department consists of a governor, lieutenant-governor, secretary of state, treasurer and auditor, elected by the people for two years. The judiciary consists of a state supreme court of five judges, a superior court of six judges, a chancery court and county courts. The judges of the supreme court, the superior judges and some other officers are elected by the legislature. The state sends one Representative to Congress.

Education. The commissioner of education is at the head of the public-school system. The township system is in vogue, in which the town constitutes the smallest unit for school purposes. Supervision is by districts in which several adjoining towns are united. A superintendent who devotes his entire time to the work is appointed for each district. Graded schools are maintained in all the larger towns and villages, most of which have high schools.

The higher institutions of learning are the University of Vermont, at Burlington, with which is connected the State Agricultural College; Middlebury College, at Middlebury; and Norwich University at Northfield. Montpelier Seminary, at Montpelier; Goddard Ladies Seminary, at Barre; Saint Johnsbury Academy, at Saint Johnsbury; Vermont Academy, at Saxton's River, and Brigham Academy, at Bakersfield, are among the most prominent academies.

There are several teacher-training institutions in Vermont. They are as follows: the University of Vermont—a four-year course; state normal schools at Castleton and Lyndon—two-year and three-year courses; state normal school at Johnson—two-year course.

Institutions. The charitable and correctional institutions of the state include the state penitentiary for men at Windsor, the woman's reformatory at Rutland, the industrial school at Vergennes, the state asylums for the insane at Waterbury and Brattleboro, the soldiers' home at Bennington and the state sanatorium at Pittsford. There are also ten hospitals under the control of the state authorities.

History. The first white man to enter the territory of Vermont was probably Champlain (1609), but no settlements were made until 1665, when French trading posts were established on the western border. Vermont was the scene of numerous expeditions by both French and English during the French and Indian Wars. After the middle of the eighteenth century, the territory was a cause of dispute between New Hampshire and New York, each claiming jurisdiction over it, by reason of charters and royal grants. On account of the grants of lands made there by New Hampshire, Vermont came to be known as the *Hampshire Grants*. It was finally decided by England that New York had jurisdiction, but the settlers of Vermont, by means of organized militia, known as "Green Mountain Boys," resisted the establishment of the authority of New York. Several skirmishes followed.

During the Revolution, Vermont organized its own forces and fought effectively against the Indians and British in the north. Meantime it set up a claim of independent statehood, and existed as an independent commonwealth for fourteen years, until it was admitted into the Union, March 4, 1791. Its progress during the nineteenth century was consistent. Its government in most respects was rather more democratic than that of other New England states. During the Civil War it furnished its full quota of troops and it was the scene of the operations of the Fenians in 1864 and 1870. In 1852 an amendment prohibiting the sale of intoxicating liquors was adopted, but was repealed in 1902, local option being substituted.

In proportion to its population Vermont has been second to none in the number of eminent men it has furnished the nation. President Calvin Coolidge was her most distinguished son. Admiral George Dewey and Captain Charles E. Clark of the *Oregon* were noted Vermonters; President Chester A. Arthur, Vice-Presidents Levi P. Morton and William A. Wheeler and Justin S. Morrill were also Vermont citizens.

Related Articles. Consult the following titles for additional information:

CITIES

Barre	Montpelier
Bennington	Rutland
Burlington	

PHYSICAL FEATURES

Champlain, Lake	Memphremagog
Connecticut River	(lake)
Green Mountains	Taconic Mountains

HISTORY

Allen, Ethan	Green Mountain Boys
Champlain, Samuel	Revolutionary War
Coolidge, Calvin	Ticonderoga

VERMONT, UNIVERSITY OF, a coeducational institution of learning, founded in 1791 at Burlington. In 1862 the university was assured a share in the benefits of the land-grant act passed by Congress, and three years later the Vermont Agricultural College was incorporated with it. The full title of the institution is The University of Vermont and State Agricultural College; it comprises the colleges of arts and sciences, engineering, agriculture and medicine. There is a student enrollment of about 1,450, and a faculty of about 250. The library contains more than 160,000 volumes.

VERNE, *vairn,* JULES (1828–1905), a popular French romancer. He studied law for some time, but afterward began writing short pieces for the stage. He then began to write stories of adventure. The highly imaginative and fantastic exploits he recounted were given an air of plausibility by the author's manner of presenting them as scientifically possible. He wrote narratives of voyages on and under the sea, of travel on earth and flights in the air, foretelling, in the guise of fiction, some of the modern achievements of men who have traveled in submarines, automobiles and airships. His first essay in the vein of the marvelous was *Five Weeks in a Balloon.* This was followed by *Twenty Thousand Leagues under the Sea, From the Earth to the Moon, Around the World in Eighty Days, Michael Strogoff* and *The Mysterious Island.* Most of his books have been translated into the various European languages, and some even into Arabic and Japanese. They will long remain popular for their ingenuity and their lively style. *Michael Strogoff,* a story of Russian adventure, was a great stage success, and was also presented as a talking picture.

VERONA, *va ro'nah,* ITALY, next to Venice the most famous city in the Venetian plain. The city is so old that an old Roman amphitheater built by the emperor Diocletian still stands, for many years a ruin, eloquent of the dead past, but now restored. This building is over 500 feet long and is 106 feet high; it was built to seat 20,000 people. In the vicinity of the busiest part of the town is a marble tablet marking the spot where the people believe Juliet lived, and to whose house came Romeo. Through the town runs the swiftly-flowing Adige River, which is spanned by seven bridges. Population, 1931, 154,000.

VERONESE, *va ro nay' zah,* PAUL (1528–1588), the popular name of Paolo Cagliari, an eminent Italian artist, born at Verona. He studied painting under his uncle, Antonio Badile, and worked successively in Venice, Rome and other cities of Italy; but Venice was his chief residence. Some idea of his talent may be gained from the fact that he was soon recognized as a rival of Titian and Tintoretto. He was an excellent colorist, as were most of the Venetian school, and he was distinguished by the richness and fertility of his imagination. His pictures are exceedingly numerous and varied in subject. Among his masterpieces are *The Marriage at Cana* (now in the Louvre), *The Calling of Saint Andrew to the Apostleship, The Rape of Europa, The Family of Darius at the Feet of Alexander, Adoration of the Magi, Consecration of Saint Nicholas and Saint Helena* and *The Vision of the Invention of the Cross.* The last five mentioned are in the National Gallery. Veronese died at Venice in the full maturity of his genius.

VERON'ICA, SAINT, a female saint, who, according to legend, met Jesus Christ bending under the weight of the cross and offered him her veil to wipe the sweat from his brow. The divine features were found miraculously impressed on the cloth, and this veil was brought from Palestine to Rome, where it is still preserved by the canons of Saint Peter's. Milan and other places claim they have the genuine veil.

VERRAZANO, *ver a tsah' no,* GIOVANNI DA (1480?–1527), a Florentine navigator, about whose life little is known. About 1523 he made his first voyage of discovery, and in 1524 he voyaged to America, probably touching the coast of North Carolina. He wrote a letter to Francis I, describing this voyage, and this letter is almost the only source of information concerning his discoveries. Some accounts relate that Verrazano was hanged as a corsair; others state that he died while preparing for another expedition to America. The exact truth may never be known.

VERSAILLES, *ver sah'y',* FRANCE, the capital of the department of the Seine-et-Oise, situated twelve miles southwest of Paris. The town is noted as the location of the magnificent Palace of Versailles, erected in 1661 by Louis XIV and since that time the scene of a number of important and dramatic events in the history of France and of the world. Here, in 1871, the French signed the hard treaty terms which concluded the Franco-German War; in July, 1919, the victorious allies concluded in the same palace peace terms with Germany at the close of the World War (see VERSAILLES, PALACE OF; VERSAILLES, TREATY OF). From 1871 to 1879 Versailles, was the seat of government of the republic of France. Population, 1931, 66,859.

VERSAILLES, PALACE OF, the famous residence of the Bourbon court and subsequent place of meeting of many important conferences for the adjustment of national and international affairs, including that following the World War. The palace was built as a residence by Louis XIV in 1661, at a cost of $100,000,000. It was permanently occupied by the court about 1682 and remained its center for a hundred years, or until the overthrow of the Bourbons at the opening of the French Revolution. Since that time it has been used principally as a vast museum, its collections representing the development of French history and art from the time of Clovis to the present day. Especially interesting is a collection representing the era of the Crusades.

The Versailles palace is three stories high, in form a great square with wings at either side and at the back projecting into its surrounding park. It has an imposing façade a quarter of a mile long, above which are inscribed the words, *A toutes les gloires de la France* ("To all the glories of France"). The extensive Versailles gardens are filled with terraces, fountains, decorative ponds and artificially arranged trees and plants.

With the palace are associated the names of Mme. de Pompadour, Mme. du Barry and Marie Antoinette. Here was signed the Treaty of 1783 between England, France and Spain on the same day that England recognized the independence of the United States. Here, in 1789, was held the meeting of the States-General which formed the opening act of the French Revolution. During the Siege of Paris, 1870–71, King William of Prussia made his headquarters here, and there he was proclaimed Emperor William I of Germany. Again, in 1919, the interest of the world centered on Versailles, as the conference of the powers adjusted anew the affairs of a world shaken by the four years of the World War, this time with a new diplomacy based on the principles of a League of Nations.

Hall of Mirrors, Where Treaty Was Signed

VERSAILLES, TREATY OF, the name of the treaty which formally concluded the World War, negotiated by representatives of the allied powers on the one hand, and those of the central powers, including Turkey, on the other. There were four separate treaty agreements, made with Germany, Austria, Bulgaria and Turkey, respectively. The preliminary work on the agreements was carried on in Paris, but the name Versailles is applied to the treaty because the actual signing of the agreement with Germany, the head of the Teutonic alliance, took place in Versailles, a suburb of Paris. The German treaty was the first one negotiated, and was signed in the famous Hall of Mirrors, in the Palace of Versailles, in the same room where, in 1871, William I was crowned emperor of Germany at the close of the Franco-German War.

The peace conference began sessions at Paris on January 18, 1919. The United States, the British Empire, France, Italy and Japan were represented by five delegates each; Brazil, Belgium and Serbia were represented by three each, and there were two each from China, Greece, Poland, Portugal, the Czecho-Slovak Republic, Rumania and the kingdom of Hedjaz. Two delegates were allotted respectively to Australia, Canada, South Africa and India, and one to New Zealand, as these British possessions had made great sacrifices for the allied cause. Other minor nations were allowed one delegate each, namely, Siam, Cuba, Guatemala, Haiti, Honduras, Siberia, Nicaragua, Panama and Montenegro. Each delegation acted as a unit. The most influential group consisted of the heads of the American, British, French and Italian commissions—President Woodrow Wilson and Premiers Lloyd-George, Clemenceau and Orlando. They were termed "the big four."

The conference held its sessions in the building of the Ministry of Foreign Affairs, meeting in a splendid reception room originally called Salle d'Horloge (Hall of the Clock). It required nearly six months to ne-

PALACE OF VERSAILLES

Above is a view of the Marble Court of the Grand Palace. The building is set in the midst of beautiful gardens, adorned with statues and fountains. The largest fountain is the Basin of Neptune, a portion of which is pictured at the right. At night, when colored lights are turned on the playing waters, the fountains are a magnificent spectacle.

IN VERSAILLES PARK

Above, peristyle of the Grand Trianon, one of the architectural treasures of the great park extending beyond the grounds of the Grand Palace. The Grand Trianon, a smaller palace, was built by Louis XIV in 1685, as a residence for Madame de Maintenon. At left, a distant view of the Grand Palace, with avenue of statues.

gotiate a treaty with Germany. On May 7, 1919, 109 days after the associated powers had begun their deliberations, German envoys received the terms on which the victorious powers were willing to m a k e peace. The head of the German commission was Count von Brockdorff-Rantzau. A period of fifteen days was allotted the German envoys in which to reply to the terms. An extension of this period was granted, however, and German counter proposals were not delivered until May 29. On June 16, a revised version of the treaty, which had been slightly modified, was tendered the Germans, and on that date the delegation started for Germany. The German National Assembly at Weimar ratified the revised treaty on June 22, and on June 28 the terms were signed in Versailles. It was found necessary to appoint a new commission, the original envoys refusing to sign. A summary of the terms follows:

How Germany Paid. G e r m a n y was stripped of all colonial possessions, required to cede certain portions of its European domain, and forced to agree to the payment of heavy indemnities.

Territorial Changes. The following changes in Europe were authorized:

To France—Alsace-Lorraine, 5,600 square miles.

To Belgium—Two small districts (Eupen and Malmedy) between Holland and Luxembourg, 382 square miles.

To Poland—Part of Silesia and most of Posen and West Prussia, 12,504 square miles.

To league of nations—Mouth of Memel River and internationalized area around Danzig, 729 square miles; basin of the Saar (internationalized temporarily), 738 square miles.

Southeastern third of East Prussia, and Vistula River district, 5,785 square miles, voted to join Poland and Czechoslovakia. North half of Schleswig-Holstein peninsula, 2,787 square miles, voted to join Denmark.

France was given the right to use the output of the Saar coal mines for fifteen years. A vote is to be taken at the end of that period to decide the future status of the Saar valley. (In January, 1935, the people voted to return to German sovereignty.)

The following changes in colonial possessions were authorized.

Togoland and Kamerun—Divided between France and Great Britain.

German East Africa—under the mandate of Great Britain.

German Southwest Africa—under the mandate of Union of South Africa.

German Samoan Islands—under the mandate of New Zealand.

Caroline, Marshall and Ladrone Islands— under the mandate of Japan.

New Guinea—under the mandate of Australia.

Total, about 1,139,800 square miles.

German concessions in China, notably Kiaochau and the Shantung peninsula, were transferred to Japan.

Other Conditions. Germany lost most of its navy and most of its merchant marine, and the army was ordered reduced to 100,000 men. Possession of f o u r t e e n submarine cables was ordered relinquished, and sovereignty over the Kiel Canal, the Rhine and other important rivers was lost. Reparation for the damage done by the war thirty-one billion dollars (later reduced; only a little paid, with balance in doubt 15 years later). Luxembourg was freed from the German customs-union. Germany was required to recognize the independence of German Austria and Czecho-Slovakia, French control in Morocco and the British protectorate in Egypt. Though not admitted as a member, Germany was required to recognize the principle of the league of nations, the provisions for which occupied the first section of the treaty.

Austrian Settlement. The complete text of the Austrian treaty was handed to the Austrian delegation at Saint Germain, France, on July 20, the first section having been tendered on June 2.

There were boundary disputes with Jugo-Slavia, Czecho-Slovakia and Italy, but eventually Austria was reduced to the following territories:

PROVINCE	AREA (Sq.m.)	POPULATION AT THE TIME
Lower Austria	7,569	3,298,661
Upper Austria	4,628	858,795
Salzburg	2,763	214,200
Styria	6,327	953,684
Carinthia	3,684	366,589
Tyrol	4,790	306,304
Vorarlburg	1,005	133,212
Burgenland	1,586	296,891
Total	32,352	6,428,336

Austria's army was limited to 30,000 men, and the country was required to guarantee reparations for damages and to assume a portion of the debt of the old empire.

Turkish Settlement. It was the general opinion that the Turkish Empire should be dismembered; such an act would end the Turkish question that had vexed Europe for more than half a century. Some of the powers desired that the Turks should be forced out of Europe altogether, but finally they were permitted to retain Constantinople and Adrianople, with a small surrounding area

(9,257 square miles). In Asia Turkey was reduced in size practically to the peninsula of Anatolia, ancient Asia Minor. It lost Palestine, Syria, Mesopotamia (Iraq), the Lebanons, and all of Arabia. Besides Anatolia, it holds only a few small islands in adjacent Mediterranean waters.

Bulgarian Settlement. The little country of Bulgaria had received acquisitions of territory at the conclusion of the Balkan Wars of 1912-1913, but most of these gains were surrendered after its defeat as an ally of Germany in the World War. The Treaty of Neuilly gave the Southern Dobrudja to Rumania; an area on the south went to Greece and deprived Bulgaria of a sea front on the Aegean; to Jugo-Slavia it lost territory on the west. Its only outlet by water is on the Black Sea.

Later History. It was the determination of the Allied powers to force Germany to pay for the war, in addition to imposing territorial losses. Beyond the tentative $33,-000,000,000 in indemnities, interest charges would increase the payments to an incredible sum. It was a sullen country that faced its almost impossible task. By 1923 its protests were heeded. A commission headed by Gen. Charles G. Dawes reported in 1924 that payments must not be pressed beyond Germany's ability to pay, which was estimated at about $600,000,000 a year.

By 1929 a crisis impended in connection with payment of war debts to the United States by European powers; the latter contended that they could pay only as German reparations payments continued, and that Germany could not meet its obligations. Another commission headed by Owen D. Young, fixed the total payments at $8,800,000,000, installments to run for fifty-eight years. With the rise of Hitlerism, Germany gave notice of repudiation of the entire debt and made a demand for a revision of the Versailles treaty. Between 1935 and 1939, Hitler reoccupied the Rhineland and annexed Memel, German Poland, Austria, Bohemia and Moravia, thus nullifying much of the treaty.

VERSE, *vurs,* a line of poetry, or, more commonly but less correctly, a stanza composed of several lines. The term is also used, in its broader sense, to mean the measured and cadenced form of speech or composition adopted in poetry. Verse, as simply cadenced lines, is of great antiquity, but the use of rhymed cadences is comparatively modern.

Blank verse is verse in which the lines do not end in rhymes. For the classifications of verse on the basis of meter, see METER.

VER'TEBRATES, or **VERTEBRA'TA,** the highest branch of the animal kingdom, comprising all creatures having backbones. Vertebrates are classified as fishes, amphibians, reptiles, birds and mammals. Their bodies are capable of division into head, trunk and tail, and they have typically four limbs (fins in fishes) and an outer skin that consists of more than one layer of cells. The skeleton is internal, and the central nervous system consists of a nerve cord and brain, to which latter the sense organs are connected. Vertebrates also possess a system of sympathetic nerves, a digestive tract, respiratory organs (gills or lungs), special excretory organs, and reproductive organs, usually with separate sexes.

In the long process of evolution these anatomical essentials have been highly developed and variously differentiated. Not till the Tertiary Period, far down the line of the geological ages, did the mammals appear, while man, the youngest of creatures, is the development of the Pleistocene Age. As man advances in scientific knowledge and mechanical skill, penetrating to every part of the world, the other vertebrates become fewer and fewer, except as he domesticates them and raises them in numbers for use as food, the manufacture of clothing or means of transportation.

Related Articles. Consult the following titles for additional information:

Amphibians	Fish and	Reptiles
Birds	Fisheries	Rodents
Carnivora	Mammals	Ungulates
Cetacea	Marsupialia	Zoölogy
	Primates	

VERTIGO, *vur' te go,* an attack of giddiness, in which stationary objects appear to move in various directions, the person affected finding it difficult to maintain an erect position. It is a common symptom of excessive or defective supply of blood to the brain, as well as of nervous and general debility, though it also frequently arises from the disturbance of the digestive organs. Rapidly whirling the body will produce a severe form of vertigo.

VESPASIAN, *vez pa' zhe an* (9-79), emperor of Rome. After serving with distinction in Germany and in Britain, as commander of a legion, he was made consul. He afterward became proconsul of Africa; and on the rebellion of the Jews, he was sent with an army into Judea. He reduced nearly all Galilee and was preparing to attack Jerusalem when he received news of Nero's death (A. D. 68). Then followed the emperors Galba, Otho and Vitellius, and in A. D. 69. Vespasian was himself elected emperor by the army. He left the siege of Jerusalem to his son Titus and returned to Rome. He immediately reformed the discipline of the army, purified the senatorial and equestrian orders and improved the administration of justice. He was the patron of learned men, particularly Quintilian, Pliny and Josephus. He rebuilt a part of the city, restored the capitol and erected the gigantic amphitheater, the ruins of which are still celebrated under the name of the *Colosseum.*

VESPUCCI, *ves poot' che,* AMERIGO. See AMERICUS VESPUCIUS.

VES'TA, a Roman divinity, the goddess of the hearth. She was worshiped, along with the Penates, at every family meal, when the household assembled round the hearth, which was in the center of the room. Her public sanctuary was in the Forum, and the sacred fire was kept constantly burning in it by the vestal virgins, her priestesses. A special building, near the temple, was set aside as the dwelling of the vestals. Each community had a hearth, on which was kept constantly alight the sacred fire of Vesta, and colonists setting out from a city took with them some of the old fire to kindle a flame in their new home. Few legends are connected with Vesta.

VESUVIUS, *ve su' vi us,* the only active volcano in Europe, situated on the Bay of Naples, in Italy. Its first recorded eruption took place in A. D. 79, when the city of Pompeii was buried under twenty feet of loose ashes and Herculaneum was covered by a torrent of mud. The elder Pliny, in command of the Roman fleet at Misenum, sailed to the relief of the distracted inhabitants, but was suffocated with them by volcanic vapors. The catastrophe is graphically described by his son, the younger Pliny, in two letters written to Tacitus, long after the event.

Another eruption of Vesuvius occurred in the year of 472, when ashes were carried as far as Constantinople. In 1794 and in 1822 there were also violent eruptions, and a series of lesser eruptions took place in the latter part of the last century, beginning with 1865. The latest eruption occurred in 1906. The mountain is a state of constant activity, and, being of easy access, has been studied by more scientists and visited by more tourists than any other volcano in the world. An electric railway takes passengers from Naples to within 450 feet of the crater, and under direction of a guide visitors may descend some distance into the crater. An observatory is located on the west shoulder of the mountain, at an elevation of 2,200 feet.

Geologically, Vesuvius is thought to be of recent origin. It is a solitary mountain, with a base about thirty miles in circumference and is surmounted by two summits. The higher one, Vesuvius proper, is the cone from which are emitted the streams of lava. The lower one, known as Mount Somma, partly encloses the active cone. The mountain varies in height according to the amount of material thrown out or carried away by eruptions, averaging about 4,000 feet above the sea level.

Related Articles. Consult the following titles for additional information:

Herculaneum	Pompeii
Naples	Volcano

VETCH, a common name, rather loosely applied to several genera of climbing plants that are natives of the temperate zones. Many of them have been cultivated as forage plants for ages, and some yield edible seeds. Recently several species have been introduced into the United States for winter forage; the *hairy vetch* makes a good crop yielding from two to four tons of hay an acre. In Europe *spring vetch,* or *tare,* is more common. The plant has bluish-pink flowers resembling those of the pea, and compound leaves composed of twenty or thirty leaflets.

VET'ERINARY MEDICINE, the art which deals with the nature, causes and treatment of the disorders of the domestic animals. The first veterinary school was instituted in 1762 at Lyons, France; in 1766 that at Alfort, near Paris, was opened. A similar institution was established at London in 1791, and in the year following, one in Berlin. In the United States veterinary chairs have been added to the University of Pennsylvania, Cornell University and to several other leading universities, as well as to many of the schools of agriculture. Besides these, there are many private schools that give thorough instruction. Recently the requirements of admission to veterinary courses have been materially advanced, and in the better schools four-year courses of study are required.

The veterinarian must have a thorough knowledge of the anatomy and physiology of domestic animals, and of the causes and effects of the diseases common to them. Moreover, he must be a keen observer, for he must rely solely upon his observation in making a diagnosis; the horse or the cow cannot tell him how it feels or where pain is located. All states and the Canadian provinces require every veterinarian to possess a diploma from an approved school, or to take a rigid examination before he is allowed to practice.

One of the most valuable services that the veterinarian renders is the detection and prevention of contagious diseases among domestic animals, and his services for this purpose are usually authorized by the state, which maintains a board or commission, whose duty it is to see that the laws for preventing the spread of contagious diseases among domestic animals are enforced.

The Bureau of Animal Industry, in the United States Department of Agriculture, takes care of veterinary questions that come before the government, and the states and large cities have veterinarians who investigate diseases and attend to the enforcement of the veterinary laws of the districts in which they have power. Important documents are issued for public circulation by the Bureau of Animal Industry and by the experiment stations and boards of agriculture in the several states. In its progress veterinary medicine has kept pace with human medicine.

VE'TO, from the Latin, meaning *I forbid,* refers to the power of a chief executive to negative any legal measure originating in a lawmaking body. There are several forms of veto power, which may all be included in two main classes—*absolute* and *limited*. In the case of the former the executive action is final; in the case of the latter the legislature may override the executive decision, if an extraordinary majority is in favor of the bill. In Great Britain the veto of the ruler is absolute, but the power has not been exercised since 1708. In France the veto is limited, of the form known as suspensive; that is, the President may suspend the operation of a law and demand its reconsideration. A similar form of limited veto is in effect in the United States, where the Presidential veto may be overriden by a two-thirds vote of the members of each house of Congress.

VI'ADUCT, a structure for carrying a waterway or roadway across a valley or low-land or over a public highway. Viaducts of the older type usually consist of a series of arches of brick work, masonry or spans of steel, but of late they have been largely constructed of reinforced concrete. The viaduct crossing the Kaw River valley, connecting Kansas City, Mo., and Kansas City, Kan., has a length of 8,400 feet. The viaduct at Des Moines, Iowa, used by the Chicago & North Western Railroad, is 2,685 feet in length. Other notable viaducts are those over Tunkhannock Creek and Martin's Creek on the Lackawanna road, the one across the Pecos River in Texas, the viaduct over the White Elster at Goltsch, Saxony, and that at Gokteik, Burma. See BRIDGE.

VIC'AR, in a general sense, a representative or deputy authorized to perform the duties of another. In the Church of England a vicar is the priest of a parish, who receives only the smaller tithes, or a salary. In the United States the large city parishes which support two or more churches maintain a vicar for the clerical duties of the chapels.

In the Roman Catholic Church *vicar apostolic* is a bishop who possesses no diocese, but who exercises jurisdiction over a certain district by direct authority of the pope; *vicar-general* is the official assistant of a bishop or archbishop. The Pope calls himself the *Vicar of Christ on earth.*

VICE-ADMIRAL. See ADMIRAL.

VICE-PRESIDENT, the official of the United States government who is second in executive authority to the President. The Vice-President is chosen in the same way and for the same length of term as the President. A candidate for Vice-President must be a natural-born citizen of the United States, must have reached the age of thirty-five years and must have been for fourteen years a resident of the United States. He is inaugurated in the Senate chamber at Washington on the same day and immediately preceding the inauguration of the President. His chief duty is to preside over the sessions of the Senate. He is not allowed to vote, except in case of a tie. He becomes President if the President dies or is permanently incapacitated from performing the duties of his office; Tyler, Fillmore, Johnson, Arthur, Roosevelt and Coolidge succeeded to the Presidency in this manner. The salary of the Vice-President is $15,000 a year.

VICE'ROY, an official who rules a province or colony in the name of a sovereign, therefore, a vice-king. The Governor-General of British India is unofficially called a viceroy, and this title was given in 1936 to Italy's chief in Ethiopia.

VICKS'BURG, Miss., third largest city in the state and the county seat of Warren County, forty-three miles west of Jackson, on the Mississippi River at the mouth of the Yazoo, on two lines of the Illinois Central System. It is served by the Federal Barge Lines on the Mississippi River. The city is built on a range of hills about 350 feet above sea level, and is surrounded on three sides by the Vicksburg National Military Park, which is adjoined on its northern boundary by the National Cemetery. A state charity hospital is located here; here also is the United States Waterways Experiment Station, one of the largest hydraulic laboratories in the world.

Vicksburg is the commercial center for a large agricultural area that produces cotton, corn, hay and truck and fruit crops. It is also a cotton and hardwood market, and has numerous cotton-manufacturing industries, as well as lumber milling, foundry and sheet-metal manufacturing and oil refining. Repair shops of the Yazoo & Mississippi Valley Railroad are located here.

Settlement here began in 1811 with Reverend Newitt Vick. In 1824 the town was laid out on part of his plantation; it was incorporated in 1825 and chartered as a city in 1836. During the early part of the Civil War it was strongly fortified; and after a long siege it was surrendered to General Grant on July 4, 1863. Population, 1940, 24,460.

VIC'TOR EMMAN'UEL II (1820–1878), king of Sardinia, the son of Charles Albert. His aptitude for a military career became evident when he commanded the Savoy brigades against Austria (1848–1849), and he distinguished himself in the Battle of Goito by his reckless valor. After the Battle of Novara his father abdicated, and Victor Emmanuel ascended the throne of Sardinia. He had then to negotiate with Austria under most unfavorable circumstances, but he steadily refused to give up the principle of representative government in the Sardinian constitution, and this gained for him the good will of the Italian people. Under the advice of his celebrated minister, Cavour, he regulated the finances, reorganized the army and secularized the church property, for which he was excommunicated by the Pope.

Victor Emmanuel took part in the Crimean War against Russia, and in 1859, assisted by France, he renewed the contest with Austria, winning the battles of Magenta and Solferino. By the Treaty of Villafranca and the Peace of Zurich, which followed these successes, Lombardy was added to his dominions, but he had to cede Savoy and Nice to France. Parma, Modena and Tuscany now became united to Sardinia, and Garibaldi's successes in Sicily and Naples brought the whole of Southern Italy over to Victor Emmanuel. Early in 1861, he assumed the title of king of Italy. By the Peace of Vienna (1866) Austria ceded Venetia, and on the withdrawal of the French garrison from Rome in 1870 that city annexed itself to Italy. The king entered Rome on July 2, 1871, and took up his residence in the Quirinal. He was succeeded by his son Humbert.

Related Articles. Consult the following titles for additional information:

Cavour, Count	Humbert I
Crimean War	Italy (history)
Garibaldi, Giuseppe	Sardinia, Kingdom of

VICTOR EMMANUEL III (1869–   ), king of Italy and Albania and emperor of Ethiopia. The only son of King Humbert I, he entered the army at the age of eighteen and advanced from the rank of second lieutenant to that of general because of his record. In 1896, at the coronation of Nicholas II of Russia, and at Queen Victoria's golden and diamond jubilee, he represented his father, whom he succeeded in 1900. Victor Emmanuel married Princess Helena, daughter of Nicholas, king of Montenegro, in 1896. The Crown Prince, Humbert, was born in 1904, and in 1930 married Princess Marie Jose of Belgium. There are four princesses of the Italian royal house—Yolanda, Mafalda, Giovanna (queen of Bulgaria) and Maria. Victor Emmanuel has been a popular ruler. He assumed active command of the Italian armies on the Austrian front in the World War, and shirked neither hardship nor danger. Since the rise of the Fascists under Mussolini, the king has been something of a figurehead, but he has subordinated his personal feelings to the welfare of his people. In May, 1936, the Italian Parliament approved bills proclaiming him emperor of Ethiopia. In 1939 he added "Albania" to his title.

VICTO'RIA (1819–1901), a beloved Queen of the United Kingdom of Great Britain and Ireland, and Empress of India. She was the only child of Edward, Duke of Kent, fourth son of George III, and was born at Kensington Palace. The duke died when Victoria was only eight months old, and she was brought up by her mother with exceptional prudence and care. Upon the death of her uncle William IV, June 20, 1837, she ascended the throne and was crowned at Westminster, June 28, 1838. The English people knew little of their young queen, who had been brought up in seclusion, but she soon proved herself possessed of the clear judgment and moderation which a sovereign needs, and of a thorough goodness which won the hearts of her subjects.

During the reign of Victoria there were eighteen changes of government, the following Premiers taking office at the dates given: 1835, Melbourne; 1841, Peel; 1846, Russell; 1852, Derby; 1852, Aberdeen; 1855, Palmerston; 1858, D e r b y; 1859, Palmerston; 1865, R u s s e l l; 1866, D e r b y; 1 8 6 8, Disraeli; 1868, Gladstone; 1 8 7 4, Disraeli; 1880, Gladstone;

VICTORIA

1885, Salisbury; 1886, Gladstone; 1886, Salisbury; 1892, Gladstone; 1895, Salisbury.

The leading events of the reign were the confederation of Canada; the Opium War in China; the abolition of the Corn Laws, under the administration of Sir Robert Peel; the successive steps in parliamentary reform; the enfranchisement of the Jews; the Catholic Emancipation act; the assumption of the government of India by the Crown; the Crimean War; the wars with Afghanistan, Abyssinia the Zulu tribes and Egypt; the long struggle on the Irish home-rule question the beginning of the South African War, and the Australian federation.

In February, 1840, Victoria was married to her cousin, Prince Albert of Saxe-Coburg-Gotha, and the marriage proved an unusually happy one. Four sons and five daughters were born to the royal couple. Victoria, Princess Royal, born in 1840, married in 1858 to Frederick William, afterward German Emperor, died in 1901; Albert Edward, Prince of Wales, born in 1841, married

to Alexandra, daughter of the king of Denmark, succeeded to the throne on the death of his mother; Alice, born in 1843, married in 1862 to Prince Frederick William of Hesse, died in 1878; Alfred, born in 1844, married in 1874 to Marie, daughter of the Czar of Russia, died in 1901; Helena, born in 1846, was married in 1866 to Prince Christian of Denmark; Louise, born in 1848, was married in 1871 to the Marquis of Lorne; Arthur, born in 1850, was married in 1879 to Princess Louise Marguerite of Prussia; Leopold, born in 1853, married in 1882 to Princess Helen of Waldeck, died in 1884; Princess Beatrice, born in 1857, was married in 1885 to Prince Henry of Battenberg. In 1861 the Prince Consort died, and the queen withdrew from social life.

During the reign of Queen Victoria, Great Britain enjoyed a long era of uninterrupted prosperity; peace and contentment prevailed at home, and, with very rare exceptions, relations of amity were maintained with foreign powers. In length her reign was unprecedented in the world's history. It is true that Louis XIV of France ruled over a longer period than she, but subtracting the years during which he was under a regent, his responsible tenure of the crown was shorter than hers. Although George III nominally ruled sixty years, owing to his insanity a part of his reign was also under a regent.

In 1887 the people of Great Britain and the colonies celebrated the golden jubilee, or fiftieth year of Queen Victoria's reign. In 1897 they celebrated the diamond jubilee, with ceremonies more imposing than had ever attended any similar event. Representatives of all the colonies were present, and a grand procession, viewed by millions, moved through the streets of London. Victoria died January 22, 1901.

Related Articles. Consult the following titles for additional information:

Corn Laws	India (history)
Crimean War	South African War
Great Britain (history)	

VICTORIA, a state of the Australian Commonwealth, situated in the southeastern part of the continent. Victoria is next to the smallest state of the Commonwealth, but is second in population. Only Tasmania has a smaller area, and New South Wales is the only state with more inhabitants. It is bounded on the north by New South Wales, on the south and southeast by the Indian

Ocean and on the west by South Australia. Its area is 87,884 square miles, or a little less than the areas of Virginia and North Carolina combined. It has about 600 miles of sea coast, with a considerable number of bays and indentations, especially about the middle, where Port Phillip Bay, with an area of 875 square miles and an entrance barely two miles wide, affords shelter sufficient for the largest fleet.

Surface and Drainage. The interior, though diversified by mountains, is chiefly distinguished by vast, unwooded plains, mostly occupied as pasture. There is one principal mountain range, a portion of the Great Dividing Range of Eastern Australia, running from east to west through the state, with various offshoots. The eastern portion of it, called the Australian Alps, with numerous northern and western ramifications, rises to 6,500 feet in Mount Bogong and to 6,100 feet in Mount Hotham, and has several other peaks exceeding 5,000 feet in height. The most westerly portion, called the Grampians, runs north and south, and in Mount William reaches a height of 5,600 feet. The Grampians and the Australian Alps are connected by such ranges as the Pyrenees and Hume Range, containing numerous cones and extinct craters. This is the region of the gold fields. The rivers are numerous, but they are generally small and dry up in summer, leaving the country parched. The chief is the Murray, which rises in the Australian Alps and forms the northern boundary of the state for 980 miles. It is 1,300 miles long and is navigable for several hundred miles.

The climate of Victoria is temperate, but liable to sudden changes, and hot winds blow at intervals from November to February, causing great discomfort. The hottest period is in January and February, when the thermometer sometimes rises to 108° in the shade.

Industry and Trade. Victoria has produced more gold than any other Australian state, but at present she is far outrivalled in that respect by Western Australia. Tin, antimony, copper and coal are also worked.

General farming is quite extensively followed. The chief crops among the cereals are wheat, oats and barley. Hay is grown, and forage crops are also raised. Among fruits, grapes take the lead, and considerable attention is given to the manufacture of wine. Stock raising is important, and wool growing is the chief branch of agricultural industry. The state has over 17,000,000 sheep, and the annual output of wool averages over 145,000,000 pounds.

The manufacturing industries are quite generally distributed, and include the manufacture of textiles, machinery, food preparations, butter and cheese and malt and spirituous liquors.

Most of the commerce is with Great Britain, and in its foreign trade Victoria is the second state of the commonwealth. The chief exports are wool, gold, dairy products and wheat. Railway lines extend to all the most important trade centers and connect these directly or indirectly with Melbourne, the chief city and commercial port. In all, there are about 4,600 miles of railway in the state.

Government. The governor, who is the chief executive officer, is appointed by the British sovereign. The legislature consists of a council of thirty-four members, who are chosen for six years, and an assembly of sixty-five members, elected for three years. Suffrage is granted to men and women on equal terms. Melbourne, the capital, is the second largest city of Australia, following Sydney. Population of the state, 1927, 1,696,670; in 1933, 1,820,360.

Related Articles. Consult the following titles for additional information:
Australia
Ballarat
Melbourne
Murray River

VICTORIA, B. C., capital of the province, is situated on the southeastern extremity of Vancouver Island, on the Strait of San Juan de Fuca, seventy-five miles northwest of Seattle, Wash. It is within three miles of Esquimault, a naval base with one of the finest harbors on the Pacific coast. The city is well laid out and has good streets; excellent roads connect it with the surrounding country. The public buildings include the parliament house, the government offices and the provincial museum and library, the city hall, the courthouse, a marine hospital, the Anglican Cathedral and exposition buildings. Victoria is a favorite residential city. It has lumber mills, and is also the lumber distributing center for Vancouver Island. It also has a large trade in salmon. Originally a post of the Hudson's Bay Company, it was incorporated as a city in 1862, and until the founding of Vancouver was the largest Canadian city on the Pacific coast. Its foreign trade is large; great steamships connect with the Orient in regular sailings. Population in 1941, 42,907.

VICTORIA CROSS, the most highly-prized British military and naval decoration, instituted as a recognition of valor in the presence of the enemy at the close of the Crimean War in 1856. It is granted to soldiers and sailors of any rank, including native officers and men of the Indian army. Up to 1913 only 522 crosses had been awarded; this number was considerably increased during the World War. The cross is the more valuable because it is awarded sparingly, and only for the most conspicuous acts of bravery and devotion to the Empire.

VICTORIA FALLS, a celebrated cataract in the Zambezi River, in Rhodesia, South Africa, discovered by Livingstone in 1855 and named by him in honor of Queen Victoria. After flowing for a long distance over a rough and broken plateau, covered with brush and stunted trees, the Zambezi plunges suddenly into a chasm nearly 400 feet deep. The falls, 3,000 feet in width and 360 feet in height, are the most magnificent in the world. At low water the fall is broken by projecting rocks and is described by an observer as resembling a film of delicate lace, but when the river is swollen during the rainy season, an unbroken sheet of water is hurled over the ledge, forming a cataract unequaled elsewhere in the world. The roar of the falls can be heard for twenty miles, and the cloud of spray thrown into the air is visible for ten miles. Because of this cloud, the natives named the cataract *Mosi-oa-tuni,* which means *roaring smoke.*

Below the cataract the Zambezi flows for a long distance through a narrow gorge, with nearly perpendicular walls of basalt. Just below the falls the Cape-to-Cairo Railway crosses the river on a magnificent steel bridge, 600 feet long and 420 feet above the water; it is the highest structure of the kind in the world. From this bridge a magnificent view of the falls is obtained.

VICTORIA NYAN'ZA, the largest lake in Africa, having a surface area of 26,000 square miles and after Lake Superior the largest body of fresh water in the world. It was discovered in 1858 by Captain Speke and named for Queen Victoria (*nyanze* is the local word for *lake*). It lies about 600 miles from the eastern coast and is crossed by the equator. It is fed by several streams, the most important being the Kagera to the west, and drains an area of 92,000 square miles, where there is an annual rainfall of seventy-five inches. It is the principal source of the Nile River. As the Nile issues from the lake it forms the Ripon Falls, which are about 1,200 feet across. The lake is rocky and shallow and is dotted with islands. Port Bell, Entebbe and Jinja are the principal ports.

VICUNA, *ve koo'nyah,* a small animal of the camel family, somewhat resembling a wild goat or an antelope, which inhabits the Andes Mountains in South America. It is economically valuable because of its soft, silky, brown wool, which is of better quality even than that of the alpaca. It is commonly seen in herds of from six to fifteen females and one male. The animals are very timid, and have never been domesticated.

VIENNA, *ve en'ah* (in German, Wien). Before the World War, Vienna was the capital and largest city of the Austrian Empire. At the close of the war it became the capital of the Austrian Republic. The new state was greatly reduced in area, its population being less than 7,000,000. In the republic, Vienna had the status of a Federal province, and its area was 107 square miles. After a precarious existence of about twenty years, Austria was annexed by Adolf Hitler (March, 1938), and Vienna became a German city in the Federal State of Austria (Ostmark). Its area was increased to over 466 square miles.

As a center of art, education and music, Vienna was one of the most distinguished cities of pre-war Europe. Here originated some of the world's gayest and most tuneful light operas; here was carried on some of the most significant research in medicine and psychology. And as a center of social life, Vienna was the delight of tourists from all over the world. In spite of the depressed condition of Austria, Vienna carried out an admirable housing program after the war.

General Description. The city is situated on the south bank of the Danube, 330 miles south-southeast of Berlin and 630 miles east of Paris. The site is picturesque, for the plain on which the city was built is bordered by mountains, whose bases are covered with magnificent forests. A branch of the Danube, known as the Danube Canal, traverses the city from northwest to southeast. This canal is spanned by many bridges, and by the construction of a lock a section of it has been made into a capacious harbor.

Vienna is built upon the plan of the old European cities, containing an inner, or central city, surrounded by suburbs, which are now incorporated in the city and divided into districts. The old town, or Innere Stadt, occupying the center of the city, was formerly enclosed by a wall and fortifications. In 1858 these were removed, and a magnificent boulevard, the Ringstrasse, was erected upon their site. This is one of the finest streets in Europe, and upon it are found most of the important public buildings of the city. In the newer parts the streets are broad, and there are a number of boulevards and parks. Chief among these is the Prater, in the southeastern quarter, having an area of over 4,000 acres. The streets, parks and bridges are decorated with numerous statues and monuments. The buildings are noted for their beauty and elegant ornamentation, making Vienna, from the standpoint of architecture, one of the finest cities of the world.

Buildings and Monuments. In the center of the Innere Stadt is the Cathedral of Saint Stephen, which dates from the thirteenth century and is one of the finest Gothic structures in Europe. Other buildings of importance in and about the Ringstrasse are the imperial palace, in the southeastern quarter, noted for its age and size, rather than for its beauty; the townhall, a magnificent building adorned with many statues; the imperial museums of natural history and of art, with a monument of Maria Theresa between them; houses of parliament; the palace of justice; the imperial opera house; a number of churches, noted for their statuary and paintings and the University of Vienna, with its numerous structures. Among the noted monuments not already mentioned are the monument to Mozart, the equestrian statues of Archduke Charles and Prince Eugene of Savoy and the monument to the Archduchess Christine.

Institutions. The educational institutions include the University of Vienna, a polytechnic institute, an agricultural college, a geological institute, the academy of sciences, the conservatory of music and the military geographical institute, besides a large number of trade schools, which prepare their students for such occupations as printing, bookbinding and other mechanic arts. The imperial library contains 900,000 volumes, besides a large number of manuscripts and engravings, and the library of the university has 650,000 volumes. These are supplemented by other libraries in the various institutions. The collections in the academy of art and the museums are among the best in the world, while the armory contains a large collection of weapons and other instruments of war. The chief charitable institution is the general hospital, one of the largest and most famous institutions of its kind in the world; before the war medical students were drawn to it from all over Europe and America. There are also an asylum of the insane, and a number of smaller hospitals and homes for the blind and the deaf and dumb.

Industries. Vienna is situated at the crossing of the great commercial routes from London, Berlin and Paris to Constantinople and from Petrograd to Rome. Its situation made it an important industrial and commercial center. Among the leading industries were the manufacture of silks, woolens and other textiles, clothing, machinery, railway cars, locomotives and supplies, musical instruments, furniture, scientific and surgical instruments, pottery, jewelry, leather goods, malt liquors and numerous other products. Before the war the city had an extensive trade with the surrounding country and with the leading commercial centers of Europe, but during the war this trade was almost entirely cut off.

History. Vienna occupies the site of an ancient Roman camp, known as Vindobona. It first became prominent as the capital of the duchy of Austria, and for about 150 years from the middle of the sixteenth century it was the capital of the German Empire. It was the seat of the celebrated Congress of Vienna that reorganized Europe after the fall of Napoleon. Population in 1911, 2,031,498; by the official census of 1934 it was given as 1,874,581. See AUSTRIA; AUSTRIA-HUNGARY; WORLD WAR; VERSAILLES, TREATY OF.

VIENNA, CONGRESS OF, a convention of representatives of European powers which assembled late in 1814 to reorganize the political system of Europe after the close of the Napoleonic wars. It was a brilliant assemblage of crowned heads, prominent diplomats and statesmen, of whom Czar Alexander I of Russia, Prince Metternich, the Austrian Minister of State, Prince Talleyrand of France, Castlereagh and Wellington of Great Britain and Hardenberg and Humboldt of Prussia were among the most powerful.

By the provisions of the Congress of Vienna, France was deprived of the territory conquered by Napoleon; Holland and Belgium were united into a single kingdom under the House of Orange; Norway and Sweden were joined under a single ruler, one of Napoleon's generals, and the independence and neutrality of Switzerland were guaranteed. The German states were loosely confederated under a diet at Frankfort. In Italy the old governments, consolidated under Napoleon, were restored. Poland was reëstablished as a constitutional kingdom dependent upon Russia. Great Britain found compensation in the extension of its colonial possessions.

The Congress of Vienna is criticized for its blindness to the spirit of nationalism that had been awakened throughout Europe by the events of the French Revolution. It defined boundaries arbitrarily, without consulting the peoples concerned, thus laying the basis of many disputes and future wars. The diplomatic method known as the balance of power, brought into prominence by this Congress, led to unending international complications that finally resulted in the bursting forth, in 1914, of the World War, the most widespread and violent conflict in all history.

VI'KINGS. See NORTHMEN.

VILLA, *veel' ya*, FRANCISCO, or PANCHO (1877–1923), a Mexican revolutionist and bandit, born at Las Nieves. His real name is DOROTEO ARANGO; he called himself *Villa* after joining the Madero revolution. He had no education, and became a bandit and outlaw at a early age; long before the Madero uprising President Diaz had offered a reward for his capture. In 1914 he joined Carranza in a revolution against Huerta, and the next year he started a revolution against Carranza, gaining control of parts of the states of Sonora, Chihuahua and Sinaloa. In March, 1916, Villa invaded New Mexico, and raided the town of Columbus. United States troops under Pershing made an expedition of 500 miles into Mexico to capture Villa, but he fled to the mountains and escaped. After the troops were withdrawn, in 1917, he resumed his depredations, but did not invade the United States again during the period of the World War. In the summer of 1919, however, his attitude became very threatening, and an American patrol crossed the border. In 1920, after the deposal of Carranza, Villa came to terms with the new government, which gave him a money allowance and a military command. SEE MEXICO; UNITED STATES; CARRANZA.

VILLEINS, *vil' linz*, a class of feudal serfs, who were allowed to hold portions of land at the will of their lord, on condition of performing menial and non-military services. It frequently happened that lands held in villeinage descended in uninterrupted succession from father to son, until at length the occupiers or villeins became entitled, by prescription or custom, to hold their lands so long as they performed the required services. And although the villeins themselves acquired freedom, the villein services were still the condition of the tenure. These customs were preserved and evidenced by the rolls of the several courts in which they were entered, or by the immemorial usage of the several manors in which the lands lay. And as such tenants had nothing to show for their estates but the entries into those rolls, or copies of them, they at last came to be called *tenants by copy of court roll*, and their tenure was known as a *copy-hold*. See FEUDAL SYSTEM.

VIL'LI, minute projections covering the mucous lining of the small intestine. Each villus contains an artery, a vein, a capillary, or a network of capillaries, and lacteal. The function of the villi is to absorb the nutritious matter from the digested food in the intestines, after which the digested fats are carried to the thoracic duct, and the sugars, water, proteids and inorganic salts are carried by the portal vein to the liver. In constipation the villi are submerged by waste matter, and the absorption of food matter by them is made difficult or impossible.

VILLON, *ve-yawN'*, FRANÇOIS (1431– about 1484), a French lyric poet. Born near Paris of a poor family named de Montcorbier, he was befriended and educated by a priest, whose name he adopted. After leaving school, Villon was banished for killing a priest in a street quarrel, but was pardoned when he proved that the act was done in self-defense. He continued to lead the life of a dissolute vagabond, was often in prison and more than once barely escaped hanging. Nothing is known of Villon after 1462. His poems, consisting of songs and ballads, give a vivid picture of his times. They have been translated by Swinburne, Andrew Lang and others. Villon's exploits are the basis of an operetta, *The Vagabond King*, and of a popular screen play.

VIL'NA, or **WIL'NO**, Lithuania, a city of over 200,000 population, situated at the confluence of the Vileika and Viliya rivers, about 245 miles northeast of Warsaw. Vilna is an old city, dating from the tenth century. Before the annexation of Lithuania by Russia, in 1795, it was the Lithuanian capital. After the World War, Lithuania became an independent republic, but Vilna was seized by Poland. In 1939, after Eastern Poland was annexed by Russia, the Soviet Union restored the city to Lithuania, together with the surrounding district.

VINCENNES, *vin senz'*, Ind., one of the oldest towns in the United States, the county seat of Knox county, 117 miles southwest of Indianapolis, on the Wabash River and on the Baltimore & Ohio, the Chicago & Eastern Illinois, the Pennsylvania and the New York Central railroads. It is in an agricultural region producing fruit, sweet potatoes, grain and livestock. Leading manufactures include glass, paper products, structural steel, foundry products, packed foods, carbonated beverages, shoes and creamery products.

The town is the seat of Vincennes University, a junior college. Other interesting features include the old house occupied by William Henry Harrison when he was governor of the territory; Harrison Park, and George Rogers Clark Memorial. Vincennes is located on the site of an Indian village called Chip-kaw-kay. The first permanent settlement developed around a fort built by the French in 1702. Originally called The Post, the settlement was named Vincennes in honor of the founder, François Morgan de Vinsenne. The place was captured from the British by Virginia troops under George Rogers Clark in 1779, and was acquired by the United States in 1783. It was the capital of Indiana Territory from 1801 to 1816, and became a city in 1856. Population, 1940, 18,228.

VINCENT, George Edgar (1864-1941), an American educator and sociologist, son of Bishop John H. Vincent, born at Rockford, Ill. After his graduation from Yale University in 1885 he traveled in Europe and the Orient and then engaged for a time in journalistic and literary work. In 1888 he became vice-president of the Chautauqua system and in 1907 president of the Chautauqua Institution. At the same time he was a member of the faculty of the University of Chicago, having been appointed in 1894. In 1911 Professor Vincent became president of the University of Minnesota, and in 1917 resigned from that post to accept the presidency of the Rockefeller Foundation (which see), from which post he retired in 1929. He wrote voluminously on educational topics for many years.

VINCENT, *vin'sent*, John Heyl (1832–1920), a Methodist Episcopal bishop, best known as one of the founders of the Chautauqua Assembly movement. He was born at Tuscaloosa, Ala., and was educated at Lewisburg (Pa.) Academy and at Wesleyan Institute, Newark, N. J. Entering the New Jersey Conference in 1853, he preached four years in the East, and was then transferred to the Rock River Conference, in Northern Illinois. In 1865 he established the *Northwest Sunday-School Quarterly*, and the following year *The Sunday-School Teacher*. From 1868 to 1884 he was corresponding secretary of the Sunday-School Union of his denomination and editor of its publications. Ten years previous to the latter date he had helped to lay the foundations of Chautauqua Institution and in 1878 had become its chancellor. He was elected bishop in 1888, and twelve years later was appointed resident bishop in Europe, remaining abroad four years and then retiring from the active episcopate in 1904. His publications include *The Chautauqua Movement, The Church School and Its Officers, Studies in Young Life, A Study in Pedagogy* and *Family Worship for Every Day in the Year*. See Chautauqua Institution.

VINCI, *vin' che*, Leonardo da (1452-1519), one of the foremost scholars of the Italian Renaissance and one of the greatest artists of all time. His place in history is unique, not only because of the high quality of his art, but because of the versatility of his genius and his intellectual influence on his contemporaries. Such a combination of artistic and scientific capacities has not been known in any other man. Leonardo was distinguished not only as a painter, but as a sculptor, an architect, a musician and an engineer. As a philosopher and man of science he was the forerunner of Galileo, Bacon and Descartes. He was acknowledged the greatest physicist of the fifteenth century. He "united a remarkable knowledge of mathematics with the most admirable intuition of nature," and he "anticipated the grandest discoveries of modern science," says a modern scholar.

Leonardo was born at the small town of Vinci, near Florence, the son of a Florentine notary. In his youth he was distinguished for his great personal beauty, physical strength and eagerness for knowledge. After studies with the celebrated painter and sculptor Verrocchio he became an independent artist, and from the age of twenty onward enjoyed the most distinguished patronage; Lorenzo de' Medici, Ludovico the Duke of Milan and Francis I of France treated him with the highest honor. As architect, engineer, painter sculptor and decorator, he received numerous commissions, and in everything he undertook he aimed at perfection.

His supreme masterpiece, *The Last Supper,* painted on a wall of the monastery of Santa Maria delle Grazie, at Milan, represents Christ, seated with his disciples, at the dramatic instant following His announcement that one of the twelve should betray Him. In characterization and dramatic and spiritual significance it surpasses all other treatments of the same subject. Unfortunately, the picture has been exposed to dampness and smoke, and these elements, together with clumsy attempts to restore it, have obliterated much of its original beauty. The most celebrated of Leonardo's easel pictures, that known as *Mona Lisa,* is the portrait of a prominent Florentine lady, perhaps the most famous portrait in the world (see PAINTING). *The Virgin of the Rocks, The Virgin, Saint Anne and Christ* and *John the Baptist,* all in the Louvre, are his other chief masterpieces. Leonardo spent his last years in France in the service of Francis I. He wrote a celebrated treatise on painting.

VIN'EGAR, a sour liquid whose active principle is acetic acid, is made from the juices of fruits and vegetables and from almost any other liquid that will ferment. It is used as a condiment and in the pickling and preserving of foods. The vinegar of commerce is made from wine, cider or malt exposed to the air, usually at a heightened temperature until the alcohol which it contains turns into acetic acid. By far the largest part of the vinegar used in the United States is made from cider. Ohio, New York, Michigan and Missouri lead in the industry.

Cheap grades of vinegar are usually given their sour taste by the addition of sulphuric acid. This adulterated product is very unhealthful, and should not be purchased. The presence of the acid can be detected by boiling a mixture of vinegar and potato starch, and when this becomes cool, adding a small quantity of iodine. If the vinegar is pure, the mixture will turn blue on the addition of the iodine; if sulphuric acid is present, the color will remain unchanged.

VIN'LAND, the name given to that part of North America which was visited by Norsemen several centuries before Columbus made his famous voyage. As early as the tenth century a Norwegian viking, Bjarni Herjulfson, was driven by storms to the mainland near Greenland, and in the year 1000 Lief Ericson landed on the continent, probably somewhere between Delaware and Labrador. He named the region *Vinland* (also spelled *Vineland*) because of the numerous wild grapevines there. It is believed, however, that the Norsemen did settle at some point in America and that they built homes, which they deserted because of the hostility of Indians. The former popular belief that the old mill at Newport and the Dighton Rock are evidences of their visit has long since been discarded, the former having been erected by an early governor of Rhode Island and the latter being the work of Algonquin Indians.

VI'OL, a class of ancient musical instruments, which may be regarded as the precursors of the modern violins. They were fretted instruments, with three to six strings, and were played with a bow. There were three instruments in a set, differing in pitch; these were the treble, tenor and bass viols, and in concerts they were commonly played in pairs—two treble, two tenor and two bass. The bass viol, or *viol da gamba,* developed into the modern *violoncello.*

VI'OLET, the popular name given to a genus of plants, of which there are many species. They are favorite flowers in all northern and temperate climates, and many of them are among the first to make their appearance in the spring. The greatest favorites are the common sweet violet and the heart's-ease, the former being especially esteemed for its fragrance. The well-known pansies, so common as garden flowers, are but varieties of one species, produced by cultivation. In different localities, various species are called johnny-jump-ups. The so-called dog-tooth violet belongs to the lily family.

VIOLIN', a musical instrument, consisting of four catgut strings, the lowest of which is covered with silvered copper wire, stretched, by means of a bridge, over a hollow wooden body, and played with a bow. It is considered the most perfect of musical instruments, on account of its capabilities of fine tone and expression and of producing all the tones in any scale in perfect tune. It forms, with the viola, the violoncello, or bass violin, and the double bass, the main element of all orchestras.

The principal parts of the violin are the *scroll,* or *head,* in which are placed the pins for tuning the strings; the *neck,* which connects the scroll with the body, and to which is attached the *fingerboard,* upon which the strings are stopped by the fingers of the left hand, as it holds the neck in playing; the *belly,* over which the strings are stretched, and which has two *f*-shaped sound holes, one on each side; the *back,* or under side; the *sides,* or *ribs,* uniting the back and belly; the *tailpiece,* to which the strings are fastened, and the *bridge.* The back, neck and sides are generally of sycamore, the belly of deal, the fingerboard and tailpiece of ebony. Almost all the pieces are put together with glue.

The four strings of the violin are tuned at G, on the upper space of the base staff, D, A, E, reckoning upward. Every intermediate semitone in a compass of $3\frac{1}{2}$ octaves may be produced by stopping the strings with the fingers, and the compass may be almost indefinitely extended upward by touching the strings lightly. The *viola,* or tenor violin, has four strings, tuned to C (in the second space of the base staff), D, A, G, reckoning upward; it is an octave higher than the violoncello and a fifth lower than the violin.

The art of violin-making reached its highest development in the sixteenth, seventeenth and eighteenth centuries. The greatest of the world's violin makers, Stradivarius, Amati and Guarneri worked at Cremona, Italy. Very fine instruments were also made at the same time in France and Germany.

VIOLONCELLO, *vi o lon chel' lo,* also called CELLO (*chel'o*), a large musical instrument of the violin class, intermediate between the violin and the double bass. The performer rests one end of the instrument on the floor between his knees, and supports the neck with his left hand. There are four gut strings, the two lowest covered with silver wire. They are tuned in fifths—C, G, D, A. The instrument has a compass from C to $A_\flat$.

The higher notes are in the treble clef, the lower in the bass. Although the instrument is much larger than the violin, the cello bow is shorter. Comparatively little solo music has been written for the cello.

VI'PER, the name applied to a family of venomous reptiles found in tropical and temperate regions of Europe, Asia and Africa. This snake has a flat, triangular head, which in most species is covered with scales. The pupil of the eye is like a cat's eye. The *common viper* is rarely more than two feet long, is usually brownish-yellow, with black triangular spots on its sides and zigzag lines on its back. Its bite, as a rule, is not fatal, but may cause pain and fever. It is the only poisonous snake in Great Britain. Another species, called the *sand viper,* having a small fleshy horn on its nose, is found along the shores of Mediterranean countries. In Africa occur the *death adder, puff adder* and *saw viper.* The *horned viper* of the Egyptian desert which preys at night and burrows in the sand during the day, is much feared on account of its bite, which is usually fatal. The largest and most deadly of all vipers is *Russell's viper* of India. It is five feet long, and its poison is invariably fatal.

VIRCHOW, *veer'Ko,* RUDOLF (1821–1902), a German physician and pathologist, born in Pomerania. He studied medicine at Berlin and early became famous as a lecturer on pathological anatomy at Berlin University. His advanced liberal opinions during the movement of 1848 induced the government to deprive him, temporarily, of his appointment. In 1849 he accepted a chair at Wurzburg, where he remained seven years, at the end of which time he returned to Berlin as professor in the university and director of the pathological institute attached to it. In 1858 he published *Cellular Pathology,* in which he showed that pathological tissues are a collection of cells. Virchow rendered immense service to medical science by his discoveries in regard to inflammation, ulceration, tuberculosis and other diseases, and he has had great influence on the whole of modern medicine, including hospital reform and sanitary science. He was a voluminous writer, not only on scientific, but also on political subjects, and many of his works have been translated into the English and other European languages.

VIR'EO, a common name of a small family of birds, whose plumage is generally of a greenish shade. They are sometimes called greenlets, and about a dozen species are found in the United States. Many of the birds are singers, the songs of the several species varying considerably. The birds feed exclusively upon insects, and thus render a distinct service to the farmer. The nests of all are similar, being cup-shaped and constructed of ribbonlike materials.

The best-known species in the United States is the *red-eyed vireo*. It is about six inches long, has bright olive-green back and tail, and a double line of ash and white over the eye, the iris of which is red. The *yellow-throated vireo* has a bright, olive-green back and yellow throat and breast. The *warbling vireo* is of plain plumage, but has a charming song.

VIRGIL, *vur' jil*. See VERGIL.

VIRGIN ISLANDS OF THE UNITED STATES, a group of islands purchased by the United States from Denmark in 1917 for $25,000,000. Before the change of ownership they were known as the DANISH WEST INDIES. Geographically the Virgin Islands are a part of the Leeward Islands, which, with the Windward Islands to the south of them, constitute the Lesser Antilles, stretching southward from Porto Rico in a great semicircle nearly to the coast of South America.

The Virgin Islands consist of three main islands—Saint Croix, Saint John and Saint Thomas—and about fifty smaller ones, only five of which are inhabited. The total population of the three larger islands is about 22,000, and the combined area is about 132 square miles. Saint Croix has an approximate area of eighty-four square miles and a population of 11,413. Saint Thomas is twenty-eight square miles in extent, and is inhabited by 9,834 persons; Saint John, with an area of twenty square miles, has 765 inhabitants. (The population statistics are from the official census report of 1930.) The great majority of the people are of negro or of mixed white and negro blood.

These islands are of volcanic and coral origin, and are of slight importance industrially, but because of their strategic value as outposts for the protection of the Panama Canal their purchase by the United States was highly approved by all Americans. The harbor of Saint Thomas, the chief town on Saint Thomas, is one of the best in the West Indies, and the town is an important

calling station for vessels plying between Europe and the Americas, especially for those bound for the Panama Canal. Vessels not only may secure coal, oil and other supplies, but find in the harbor a safe refuge from storms. The Virgin Islands carry on a small import and export trade, almost entirely with the United States. They export hides, skins, and valuable woods, and import foodstuffs, boots and shoes, principally. In 1936 Congress voted them universal suffrage and a considerable measure of home rule. See SAINT THOMAS.

In the fall of 1940 the Virgin Islands came into prominence as an important link in the chain of naval and air bases established in the Caribbean as part of the United States Defense Program.

VIRGINIA, *vur jin'e ah,* one of the thirteen original states of the American Union, belonging to the South Atlantic group. In colonial days it was referred to in official documents as the "Dominion of Virginia," a name that survives in its popular designation, THE OLD DOMINION. Virginia is the picturesque name given the colony by Sir Walter Raleigh, who bestowed it in honor of Elizabeth, the "Virgin Queen" of England. As colony and state Virginia has had a unique and honored place in American history. On its soil in 1607 was planted the first permanent English settlement in the New World. A leader in the struggle for independence, it gave the American nation its first President and seven others, besides Patrick Henry, John Marshall, Richard Henry Lee, John Randolph and other distinguished orators and statesmen. Virginia's honorary title, "Mother of Presidents," is well deserved.

Location and Area. The state is the most northerly of the South Atlantic group. It has the shape of an irregular triangle, with the apex pointing northward, and Tennessee and North Carolina lying along the base, on the south. The sloping western boundary lies adjacent to West Virginia and Kentucky; Maryland is at the extreme north and along the northeast; Chesapeake Bay and the Atlantic Ocean bound the state on the east. With an area of 40,815 square miles, Virginia is the thirty-fifth commonwealth in the Union in size. Of its area, 916 square miles are water surface, as the state has numerous landlocked harbors and rivers. The states nearest it in size are Ohio, with an area of 41,222 square miles, and Kentucky, which covers 40,395 square miles.

People and Cities. In 1940 Virginia had a population of 2,677,773 and an average density of 67.1 persons to the square mile; it was nineteenth in rank in the United States in the number of inhabitants and seventeenth in the density of the population.

About one-fourth of the people are of Negro blood. Russians, Germans, English, Irish and Scotch are the most prominent of the foreign-born groups, which account for about one per cent of the people. The principal religious bodies are the Baptist, Methodist, Presbyterian, Roman Catholic and Episcopalian.

Sixteen cities had populations of 10,000 or over in 1940. Of these Richmond, with a population of 193,042, is the capital and largest city. The cities next in size were Norfolk, 144,332; Roanoke, 69,287; Portsmouth, 50,745; Lynchburg, 44,541; Newport News, 37,067; Alexandria, 33,523; Danville, 32,749; and Petersburg, 30,631.

Surface and Drainage. There are five natural divisions of Virginia, which differ greatly in scenery, soil, and productions. Named in their order, from east to west, they are the Coastal Plain (or the Tidewater), the Piedmont section, the Blue Ridge, the Appalachian Valley, and Appalachian Plateau. The Tidewater country extends about 100 miles westward from the ocean; it is divided by Chesapeake Bay and deeply cut by smaller bays, estuaries and rivers. The Piedmont section, extending from Tidewater to the Blue Ridge, is an undulating plain, increasing in elevation toward its western limits. The Blue Ridge, from three to twenty miles wide, broken by gorges and a series of beautiful peaks and expanding into an elevated plateau toward the south, is a prominent range. Its mountains and hills enclose picturesque valleys and coves.

The highest peak is Mt. Rogers (5,719 feet), in the Blue Ridge Plateau near the Tennessee line. The Valley of Virginia, between the Blue Ridge and the "Alleghenies," is a garden spot of the state. The limestone formations in the central part of this valley contain several noted caverns, besides the famous Natural Bridge and Natural Tunnel, considered wonders of the world. The "Alleghenies" are a mountainous region of narrow ridges, inclosing troughlike valleys, and trending southwest.

The Potomac, which forms a portion of the boundary between Virginia and Maryland, drains the northern and eastern parts of the state. Its chief tributaries are the South Branch (West Virginia) and the Shenandoah. The important streams flowing into Chesapeake Bay, from north to south, are the Rappahannock, the York, and the James. The Roanoke rises west of Roanoke and flows southeast into North Carolina, southwest of Emporia. This, with its tributaries, drains the south-central region. The southwestern part is drained into the Tennessee, and the northwestern, into the Potomac. The two counties, Accomac and Northampton, forming a peninsula between Chesapeake Bay and the Atlantic are lowlands, without notable streams. This area is indented by many estuaries and bays which provide safe and convenient harbors for small boats.

Climate. The climate is diversified according to the natural divisions of surface. In general, the state is free from intense heat and severe cold, although sudden changes are common in most localities. The mean annual temperature is 56°. The average annual rainfall ranges from about forty to forty-five inches. The climate is healthful the year round.

Mineral Resources. Virginia has a wide variety of minerals, and the annual output of all products was valued at about $42,000,000 in 1929 and about $17,000,000 in 1933. In the southwestern part, there are valuable coal mines now yielding 8,000,000 to 9,000,000 tons a year. Coal is the most important of the minerals, and is followed by stone products, notably cement materials, granite, limestone, sand and gravel, slate, and soapstone. Virginia is the first state in the production of soapstone. Clay products and lime are next in order of importance; among the former brick constitutes about eighty per cent of the total product.

Other minerals of commercial value include feldspar, gypsum, lead and zinc, manganese, mica, salt brine, silica, and titanium minerals. There are numerous mineral springs distributed over the state, some of which are frequented as health resorts because of their medicinal properties. Hot Springs, seventy-five miles north of Roanoke, is one of the best known.

Agriculture. Formerly cash crops furnished the major farm income, but more recently livestock, livestock products, and poultry have greatly increased in importance, and in recent years have contributed approximately one-half of the farm income.

Tobacco and potatoes alternate for the lead as the principal cash crop. Peanuts and cotton are important sources of income in about twelve counties in the southeastern part of the state. Bright tobacco is raised extensively in the central and southern sections, whereas the Burley variety is increasing in importance in the southwestern part of the state.

Virginia ranks third in the production of apples, with extensive orchards in the Shenandoah Valley and the Piedmont district. Corn is the most important crop in point of acreage and value, being largely used on the farms. Wheat is an important cash crop in the Shenandoah Valley.

Truck crops are grown extensively in Eastern Shore and Tidewater counties.

Fisheries. Virginia is one of the leading states in value of oyster fisheries, as the tidal waters contain immensely profitable beds of that mollusk; about two-thirds of the value of the entire fishery output is represented by the oyster catch. Other products of the fisheries include shad, menhaden, alewives, clams, crabs and bluefish.

Manufactures. The leading manufacturing enterprises are those connected with the making of lumber and lumber products. Second in importance is the manufacture of smoking and chewing tobacco. Richmond, which is the great center of this interest, has one of the largest tobacco factories in the United States. Flour milling, car construction and repair, leather tanning, the manufacture of fertilizer, paper making, the manufacture of cotton goods and of boots, shoes and the roasting of peanuts are other profitable lines of manufacture. Shipbuilding has developed extensively of late years, especially at Newport News, on Hampton Roads. Here is one of the largest shipyards in the country. Good water power, a wealth of raw materials and ready means of transportation are all favorable factors in the industrial growth of the state.

Transportation. There are over 4,700 miles of railroad in operation. Some of the main lines are the Chesapeake & Ohio, the Southern, the Norfolk & Western, the Baltimore & Ohio, the Atlantic Coast Line, the Virginian Railroad, and the Seaboard Railroad. Coastwise steamers run regularly between Virginia ports and New York, Philadelphia, Baltimore and Boston, and a line of freighters plies between Newport News and Liverpool. Hampton Roads, at the mouth of the James River, is one of the finest harbors along the Atlantic coast. There is a large interstate traffic, both by rail and water. The exports consist of tobacco and its manufactured products, lumber, grain, cotton, fruit, vegetables, coal, iron and naval stores, and the imports are manufactured goods and food products. Norfolk is the chief cotton shipping port and Newport News the principal city for coal shipment.

Government. The legislature consists of a senate, which cannot exceed forty members or have less than thirty-three members, and a house of delegates of not less than ninety, nor more than 100, members. The senators are elected for four years and the delegates for two. The executive department consists of a governor, a lieutenant-governor, a secretary of the commonwealth, an auditor, a treasurer, a superintendent of public instruction, an adjutant-general and commissioners of agriculture and insurance. The state courts consist of a supreme court of appeals, of five judges, chosen by the legislature for twelve years, and circuit courts, which are held in twenty-four judicial districts, each of which has a judge, elected by the legislature for eight years. Lower courts are established for cities and towns.

Education. The public school system is under the general supervision of a State Board of Education of seven members appointed for four years by the Governor, subject to confirmation by the General Assembly, and a State Superintendent of Public Instruction appointed by the Governor, subject to confirmation of the General Assembly for a term of four years coincident with that of the Governor making the appointment. The revenue for school purposes is provided almost wholly by state and local taxation. Separate schools are maintained for the white and colored children, and the law requires that each district must have an annual school term of at least one hundred and sixty school days.

The state supports the University of Virginia, the Virginia Polytechnic Institute, the Virginia Military Institute, College of William and Mary (the second oldest college in the United States), the Medical College of Virginia, at Richmond, four state teachers colleges, one each at Farmville, Fredericksburg, Harrisonburg, and Radford, Virginia School for the Deaf and Blind at Staunton, Virginia State College for Negroes at Petersburg, Virginia State School for the Colored Deaf and Blind at Newport News. The University of Virginia, at Charlottesville, was founded by Thomas Jefferson; the Virginia Military Institute, at Lexington, is called the "West Point of the South."

Other institutions of higher learning in the State consist of the following: Sullins College, at Bristol, Virginia Intermont College, at Bristol, Southern College, at Petersburg, Emory and Henry College, at Emory, Bridgewater College, at Bridgewater, Hampden-Sydney College, at Hampden-Sydney, Lynchburg College at Lynchburg, Randolph-Macon College, at Ashland, Randolph-Macon Woman's College, Lynchburg, Roanoke College at Salem, Sweet Briar College, at Sweet Briar, University of Richmond at Richmond, Washington and Lee University, at Lexington, Averett College, at Danville, Blackstone College, at Blackstone, Bluefield College, at Bluefield, Marion College, at Marion, Mary Baldwin College, at Staunton, and Shenandoah College, at Dayton. Also Hampton Normal and Industrial School for Colored, at Hampton.

The State through its Department of Health maintains the Blue Ridge Sanatorium, at Charlottesville; the Catawba Sanatorium, near Salem; the Piedmont Sanatorium, at Burkeville. Through its Department of Public Welfare it provides for the Virginia Commission for the Blind, Central State Hospital, at Petersburg; Eastern State Hospital, at Williamsburg; Southwestern State Hospital, at Marion; Western State Hospital, at Staunton; State Colony for Epileptics and Feeble-Minded, at Colony; R. E. Lee Camp Soldiers' Home, at Richmond; State Penitentiary Farm, at State Farm; State Penitentiary Farm for

Defective and Misdemeanant Women, at Goochland; State Penitentiary, at Richmond; Virginia Industrial School for Boys, at Maidens; Virginia Home and Industrial School for Girls, at Bon Air; Virginia Industrial School for Colored Girls, at Peaks Turnout, and Virginia Manual Labor School for Colored Boys, at Hanover.

History. The shores of Virginia were probably first visited by Sebastian Cabot in 1498, but no attempt at settlement was made until late in the following century, when Sir Walter Raleigh sent out several expeditions without success. The London Company was formed in 1606, and in the following spring a colony was established at Jamestown. Its leading spirit was Captain John Smith, whose energy and ability saved the settlement from early destruction by famine and Indian attacks. In 1610 Lord Delaware was sent to the colony as governor, and under his wise administration the settlement prospered. The year 1619 witnessed the introduction of negro slavery by Dutch traders, as well as the establishment of the first representative assembly in America. From this time on many immigrants, driven from England by the persecution of the Puritans, arrived in Virginia; but at the outbreak of the Puritan revolution, in 1642, William Berkeley, a stanch royalist, became governor and promptly suppressed the rebellious spirit. At this time an influx of royalists also began, which led to serious opposition to the Cromwell régime in England and to the joyful recognition of the return of the Stuarts to the throne. However, within the next few years discontent with economic conditions and the policy of the administration led to a serious insurrection, known as Bacon's Rebellion.

The eighteenth century in Virginia was marked by remarkable development, especially in the westward districts of the colony. During the French and Indian Wars, Virginia took an exceptionally prominent part, but it was also a leader in the resistance to Parliamentary taxation, its Assembly passing some of the earliest and most important measures of the period. Virginia also furnished some of the most conspicuous figures of the time, such as Washington, Jefferson, Patrick Henry, the Lees and Madison. The state took a prominent part in the Revolution, and the war ended on Virginia soil, in the surrender of Cornwallis. During the early years of the Republic, the state was

VIRGINIA
THE OLD DOMINION

(1) Blue Ridge Mountains. (2) Corn and tobacco, (3, 4) peanuts and cotton, products of Virginia's diversified agriculture. (5) Coal pier on Hampton Roads. (6) Rayon factory. (7) William and Mary College. (8) Virginia Colonial architecture.

Items of Interest on Virginia

The present state constitution was adopted in 1902.

The first white child born in the New World was born in Virginia and was named Virginia Dare.

The first exports of iron ore were sent from Virginia in 1608.

Twenty thousand pounds of tobacco were exported in 1619.

The first representative assembly in North America was the Virginia House of Burgesses, which met for the first time in 1619.

In 1648 the population of the colony was 15,000.

Seven states have been formed from territory which was formerly Virginia.

During the Civil War, of the six great campaigns in the East, four were on Virginia soil; the first Manassas Campaign (1861), the Peninsular battles (1862), the second Manassas, Fredericksburg and Chancellorsville (1862–63), and the great Battles of the Wilderness and campaigns around Petersburg (1864–65).

Questions on Virginia

What is the area of Virginia?

Name and describe the physical divisions.

Describe the drainage.

What is the character of the coast line?

What is the most valuable product of the fisheries?

How does Virginia rank as a tobacco-growing state?

Name four other important crops.

What is the most valuable mineral product?

Name two minerals in which Virginia leads all other states.

What are the leading manufactured products?

How many miles of railroad are there in the state?

What natural advantages has Richmond? What are its leading industries? What buildings of historical interest still stand in Richmond?

Name five prominent educational institutions.

stanchly Anti-Federalist, but six of the first ten Presidents were Virginians.

The state was at first favorable to the liberation of the slaves, but under the influence of states' rights theories and of agricultural conditions, it finally adhered to the policies of the lower South, and in the Civil War Virginia not only furnished the ablest generals in the Confederate armies, but became the battle ground of the great struggle. The state at first opposed secession, but finally passed the resolution, April 17, and from that time forward it was a continuous fighting ground between the two armies, many of the most important actions of the war, including Lee's surrender at Appomattox, taking place within its borders. A new constitution, framed in 1863, was adopted, but the state was not re-admitted until 1870. In 1902 a constitutional provision was adopted, limiting suffrage. After 1928 a gift of about $5,000,000 from John D. Rockefeller, Jr., restored Williamsburg (settled in 1632) to its pre-Revolutionary appearance. There has been recent coördination of transportation facilities.

Related Articles. Consult the following titles for additional information:

CITIES

Alexandria	Petersburg
Danville	Portsmouth
Lynchburg	Richmond
Newport News	Roanoke
Norfolk	Staunton

HISTORY

Bacon's Rebellion	Jamestown
Bull Run, Battles of	Revolutionary War in
Chancellorsville,	America
Battle of	Smith, John
Fredericksburg,	West Virginia, sub-
Battle of	head History
Harper's Ferry	

RIVERS

James	Roanoke
Potomac	Shenandoah
Rappahannock	

TOPOGRAPHIC FEATURES

Alleghany Mountains	Natural Bridge
Blue Ridge	Piedmont Region
Luray Caverns	

VIRGINIA, Minn., a mining community in Saint Louis County, seventy-five miles northwest of Duluth, on the Great Northern, the Canadian National and the Duluth, Missabe & Iron Range railroads. It is one of the most important distributing points for ores from the famous Vermilion and Mesabi ranges, one of the largest and richest iron-producing regions of the world. Saw mills, once famous here, are reduced to one small mill of slight capacity. There is an extensive dairy industry. Two miles north of town is the Laurentian Highland Divide, from which all waters of the area flow north and south.

The town was settled in 1892 and became a city in 1905. Twice burned by forest fires, the city has ordained that all buildings in its central part be constructed of non-inflammable material. Population, 1940, 12,-264.

VIRGINIA, UNIVERSITY OF, a state institution of higher learning, located near Charlottesville, four miles from Monticello, the old home of Thomas Jefferson. The university was founded by the state of Virginia through the influence of Jefferson, in 1819, and it owes much of its efficiency to his interest and care. In October, 1903, the government board created the office of president, prior to which time the executive officer of the university was called rector. The institution is organized into academic, engineering, law and medical departments. There are over 400 instructors and about 3,000 students. The library contains nearly 339,000 volumes; the endowment is approximately $12,000,000. The state of Virginia makes an annual appropriation for the maintenance of the university. Among the interesting buildings is the Rotunda, modeled upon the Pantheon at Rome; it formerly housed the library.

VIRGINIA CITY, NEV., an unincorporated town, the county seat of Storey County, twenty-three miles southeast of Reno and served by the Virginia & Truckee Railroad. It came into existence with the discovery in 1859 of the famous Comstock lode, the world's richest silver and gold mine, which subsequently had a consolidated output of approximately a billion dollars. In 1864 the city was incorporated. First known as Ophir and later as Silver City, it received its present name from an early settler who was familiarly known as "Old Virginia." In 1880 it had a population of 10,917, its decline after that date being largely due to exhaustion of the lode and a decline in the price of silver. Population, 1940, 488.

VIRGINIA CREEPER, a shrubby, hardy climbing plant of the grape family. It is much grown on walls on the continent of Europe, in the British Isles and in America as an ornamental vine. The stem develops tiny rootlets along its entire length, and by means of these the vines, which often attain a great size and weight are upheld. The foliage is compound, five leaflets to a stem, and in autumn is brilliantly colored. The wild Virginia creeper is sometimes mistaken for poison ivy, though the latter has three leaflets on a stem. Because of the little bunches of dark blue berries which appear in the fall the creeper is sometimes called *false grape.*

VIRGINIA RESOLUTIONS. See KENTUCKY AND VIRGINIA RESOLUTIONS.

VIRGO, *vur'go* (the virgin), the sixth sign of the zodiac, represented by the sign ♍. The principal star of this constellation is Spica, one of the lesser first-magnitude stars. The sun enters the constellation of Virgo about August 20th.

VIRUS. As the term is used in medicine, *virus* means disease poison, particularly the poison by which disease is conveyed from one person to another by contact. Formerly the application of the term was restricted to such diseases as measles, scarlet fever and smallpox, but the culture of any bacteria may be called a virus. The term is also applied to the vaccine used in vaccination.

Related Articles. Consult the following titles for additional information:

Antitoxin	Medicine
Bacteria	Vaccination
Germ Theory	Vaccine Therapy

VISCOUNT, *vi'kount,* originally, in English usage, the officer who acted as deputy to a count or earl. As a hereditary title, it was first granted to John Beaumont, in 1440. A viscount is "Right Honorable" and is styled "My Lord." His wife is a *viscountess,* and his children are addressed as "Honorable."

VISH'NU, the second of the three great Hindu gods, by his special worshipers considered to be the greatest. In the early Vedas he was not regarded as the most exalted deity, but this rank was accorded to him by the later writers. The myths relating to Vishnu are characterized by the idea that whenever a great physical or moral disorder affected the world, Vishnu descended to set it right. He is generally represented as having four hands, in which he holds a conch-shell, blown in battle; a disk, the symbol of supreme power; a mace, the emblem of punishment, and a lotus, the sign of the creative power. Often he is shown as riding on a being, half man and half bird. See BRAHMA; SIVA.

VISIBLE SPEECH, a term applied by Prof. A. Melville Bell, its inventor, to a system of alphabetical characters, designed to represent every possible articulate utterance of the organs of speech. The system is based or an exhaustive classification of the possible actions of the speech organs, each organ and every mode of action having its appropriate symbol. It is said that this invention is of great utility in teaching the deaf and dumb to comprehend spoken words and in aiding students of foreign languages to acquire their pronunciation from books.

VISIGOTHS, *viz' e goths.* See GOTHS.

VISION, *vizh' un,* or **SIGHT,** the act of perceiving objects through the eye. As an optical instrument, the eye closely resembles a camera, the cornea and crystalline lens

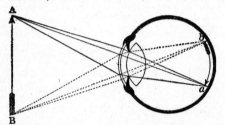

corresponding to the lens of a camera, and the retina corresponding to the screen. The rods and cones of the retina are sensitive only to the light, and their great number and variety enables the perfect eye to respond to light waves producing all colors. Rays of light entering the eye through the pupil are refracted, and they cross just back of the lens, the rays from *A* coming to a focus on the retina at *a,* and those at *B* coming to a focus at *b,* thus forming an inverted image on the retina. This may be observed by carefully cutting away the sclerotic coat from around the optic nerve of an eye taken from one of the lower animals, exposing the retina over an area about the size of a dime, and holding the eye towards a lighted lamp in a darkened room. An image of the lamp inverted on the retina can be plainly seen.

Physiology of Vision. Though the image may fall on the retina of a dead eye, there can be no vision in such case, as vision must depend upon the action of the living optic nerve.

The sensory fibers of the optic nerve originate in the optic centers of the brain. These fibers meet and cross at the base of the brain, forming the *optic commissure,* from which the optic nerves extend to each eye. In the commissure, half of the fibers cross, so that each optic nerve consists of half of the fibers from its own optic center and half of the fibers from the optic center on the opposite side of the brain. On reaching the eye, these

fibers are so distributed that those from the right optic center form the right half of the retina in each eye, and those from the left center form the left half. When the rods and cones are stimulated, impulses are transmitted along the optic nerves and optic tracks to the centers of unconscious sight in the brain. From these centers, other nerves extend to the centers of vision, and when the stimuli are strong enough to cause impulses to be transmitted to these centers, the person becomes conscious of them and sees the object. This is completed vision, and the image is retained in memory for a greater or less length of time, depending upon the strength of the stimuli and mental condition at the time the vision occurs. Consciousness and memory are mental activities, so that complete, intelligent vision depends upon mental, as well as physical action.

Related Articles. Consult the following titles for additional information:

Camera	Eye	Light
Color	Lens	Memory

VITAMINS, *vi' ta minz,* essential elements in food. Until the twentieth century, these elements were unrecognized, and much remains to be discovered about them. Having no direct food values in themselves, they are necessary to nutrition; unless the proper vitamins are present in the required amounts, the diet will not promote health and well-being. Absence or serious lack of any of the vitamins may lead to a so-called "deficiency disease."

Vitamin requirements vary according to the age, size, health and occupation of the individual. Vitamins are not cures, but rather preventives; they are indispensable to health, as they affect vitally every organ in the body and their lack may cause or contribute to diseases and even deformities.

More vitamins have been discovered than were originally thought to exist, resulting in temporary confusion. Most of them are referred to by alphabetical names for convenience. From time to time, new discoveries of vitamins are reported. The following are the chief known ones.

Vitamin A is essential for normal growth, good tooth and bone formation in children, and for healthy skin and good eyesight. Usually, Vitamin A will prevent or relieve night blindness, unless it is too far advanced. It aids in preventing infections, especially in the respiratory tract, kidneys and bladder. It is found in the liver and yellow body fat of most animals, in cod-liver oil, butter, cheese, eggs, milk, green and green leafy vegetables such as green beans and spinach, and in yellow fruits and vegetables such as apricots and carrots.

Vitamin B was originally thought to be a single element, but has been proved to be instead a complex containing a group. It includes the former Vitamins F (now B_1) and G (now B_2). Of the group, B_1, B_2 and B_6 are the most important.

B_1, or thiamin, is the preventive of beri-beri, a deficiency disease, and can correct certain forms of it. It is also of aid in treating certain forms of neuritis. A lack of B_1 results in a retardation of growth of children. It is present in seeds but not in highly refined cereal products, such as polished rice. Yeast and wheat germ are richest in B_1, which occurs also in whole-grain cereals and flours, in pork, fresh ham, liver, soy beans, green peas, nuts, egg yolk and lima beans.

B_2, or riboflavin, is essential for normal nutrition; its lack results in lesions around the mouth, and on the tongue and ears. It is so widely distributed that there should never be a lack of it. Important sources are yeast, liver (beef, calf, lamb, pork), whole cereals, milk, eggs, cheese, many green leafy vegetables, fruits, peanuts, and fish such as halibut, haddock, canned sardines and mackerel.

Nicotinic acid (renamed niacin) is the pellagra-preventive factor of the B complex. Even acute cases of pellagra respond with astonishing rapidity to this vitamin. Liver, lean meats, salmon, yeast, green vegetables, whole grains, tomato juice, eggs and milk are good sources of niacin, which can also be produced in pure chemical form and thus given directly to the pellagra victim.

Vitamin C is ascorbic and can be chemically produced. Deficiency in this vitamin results in scurvy, which may be avoided or cured by a rich Vitamin C diet. Vitamin C aids in normal development of bones, cartilages, teeth and gums. It exists widely in almost all raw fruits and vegetables, but especially in citrus fruits, green salad leaves and shoots, tomatoes, raw vegetables such as brussels sprouts and golden bantam corn, and baked potatoes or potatoes boiled in their skins. Vitamin C deteriorates in most foods canned or stored; they should be eaten while fresh.

Vitamin D aids in bone development, and prevents rickets and bone deformities. It is necessary for the body to utilize properly the calcium and phosphorus essential to growth. It has been produced in crystalline form. Few foods contain much of it. The best source is fish liver, such as halibut, tuna and cod. It also is present in canned salmon, sardines, eggs and butter, and in small amounts in liver, cream, milk and oysters. However, when the skin is exposed to the sun or to ultraviolet rays, Vitamin D is formed in the body.

Vitamin E is little known, but it has proved to be essential to normal reproduction in animals, although its relation to the human body is not yet clearly defined. The richest sources include wheat-germ oil, seeds of legumes, muscle meats, egg yolk, milk and milk products. It is, however, so widely distributed among common foods and so difficult to destroy that it is believed any ordinary diet will contain a sufficient amount of it.

Vitamin K is the coagulation factor, essential in enabling the blood to clot, and therefore a preventive of hemorrhage. It has not been proved of value in treating hemophilia (hereditary bleeding), but is useful in surgery where certain types of blood coagulate too slowly for safety. It is widely distributed, occurring especially in green leafy vegetables and in hog liver. Deficiencies in this vitamin come usually from faulty absorption rather than improper diet.

Enriched Foods. It has been found possible to "enrich" or "fortify" certain foods with additional vitamins. Milk, one of the most valuable foods, is frequently sold with added Vitamin D, either put into the milk in concentrated form or by means of ultraviolet rays (called irradiated milk), or by feeding the cows feeds which are rich in Vitamin D. The term "enriched" is used particularly for flour and bread. Enriched flour is white or nearly so, and contains specified amounts of Vitamin B_1, B_2, niacin and iron, with sometimes certain amounts of Vitamin D and calcium. Sometimes certain methods of milling insure the retention of those valuable elements in the discarded coarse outer portions of the grains; more often the vitamins and minerals are added to plain white flour. Enriched bread is made from such flour; or from plain white flour leavened with yeast enriched with those elements; or by adding the vitamins and minerals directly to the mixture. Oleomargarine is often sold with added Vitamin A, in which butter is naturally rich.

Vitamin Concentrates may be secured in tablet or capsule form. The average individual, however, can secure an adequate supply of vitamins from an ordinary diet and does not need such concentrates, which should be taken only on advice of a physician.

Conservation of Vitamins. Vitamins C, B_1, B_2 and niacin dissolve readily in water. Thus, when foods are cooked, considerable vitamin value is lost unless the water is used to make gravies or soups. Vitamin A is lost and C deteriorates in food storage or wilting of vegetables, while C escapes more quickly if fresh fruits and vegetables are bruised, peeled, cut or chopped. Slow drying causes loss of Vitamins A and C. Thus, fruits and vegetables should be secured as fresh as possible and served as quickly as possible. Very little water should be used in cooking, and long cooking processes such as stewing should be avoided. Food canned properly compares favorably with fresh food. The quick-freezing process retains all the vitamins and nutritional values.

In Wartime. Vitamins are essential in wartime, to keep the health of the soldiers and guard against disease in change of climate and fresh food supplies; to keep the health of civilians working long hours under the strain of war conditions; and to guard against "war nerves" for men in service and civilians alike.

VITAL STATISTICS. See POPULATION, subhead *Vital Statistics.*

VIT'RIOL, OIL OF, the common name given to strong sulphuric acid. See SULPHURIC ACID.

VIVISECTION, *viv i sek' shun,* physiological investigation on living animals for the purpose of discovering or demonstrating some fact of physiology. The term, which literally means *the cutting of the living,* was formerly employed to designate only cutting operations upon living animals for purposes of experiment. Today it has a broader application and includes inoculation with disease germs, experimentation with drugs, medicines and foods and with the effects of temperature upon living organisms, as well as cutting operations involving nerves, arteries and vital organs.

Vivisection has been generally regarded as the necessary means of acquiring physiological knowledge. Practically our entire knowledge of bacteriology and of the effects of drugs and medicines has been gained through this method of investigation, and nearly every operation and appliance to relieve pain or save life has been made possible through it.

VIZIER, *vi zeer',* a high official in Mohammedan countries, particularly the Prime Minister to the sultan, known as the grand vizier and possessing powers second only to the ruler himself.

VLADIVOSTOK, *vlah dye vohs tohk',* SIBERIA, the chief commercial and naval port of the country on the Pacific, the eastern terminus of the Trans-Siberian Railway. The city lies at the southern end of a peninsula, on an arm of the Sea of Japan. It has a fine harbor, ice-free nine months of the year, and is connected by steamship lines with Japanese, Korean, North Siberian and North American ports. The city is impressive in appearance when viewed from the magnificent bay, but on closer inspection is disappointing. During World War I, it was an Allied base and port of entry to Russia. The city declined in the period following the war. Later, Soviet Russia's economic development of its Eastern regions and Japan's military activity in Northern China gave it renewed importance. It was especially important to Russia in World War II. Population, 1933, 206,000. See SIBERIA.

VOCA'TIONAL EDUCATION, that type of education designed to prepare young people for their life work. Vocational education trains in the skills and social understanding necessary for a specific occupation; vocational guidance helps the individual choose his occupation. Since the beginning of the present century, vocational education has made rapid progress.

When the United States entered World War I in 1917, the government at once discovered the dearth of skilled workmen. Especially was there a scarcity of mechanics, carpenters and shipbuilders, and to supply the demand, the government entered upon a campaign of industrial training on a scale never before undertaken. The progress in vocational education in the two years following the declaration of war exceeded that during the ten years preceding that date.

The development of techniques and subject matter in the period that followed and the almost doubling of the number of pupils finishing grade school confirm the government's earlier contention—that, if the course of study could be changed so as to relate it more vitally to the occupations of life, most of these pupils could be retained in school. Under the leadership of the United States Bureau of Education, the leading educators made such revisions of the courses of study as enabled them to provide more liberally for vocational subjects and vocational guidance.

Vocational Guidance precedes and accompanies vocational education, as it provides the individual with the knowledge and experience necessary to best choose his life work. The increasing complexity and specialization in business, professional life and industry require assistance beyond what the parents can give in the home. Within the school system, the individual and the occupation can be studied, group and individual counseling given, and classes conducted with supplementary aids. Counselors aid in final placement. Often, the school coöperates with local business and employment offices toward the occupational adjustment of out-of-school youth, extending its influence even after graduation. A good vocational library is a decided asset, and, frequently, students can make visits to learn more about desired life works and careers. In some schools, actual experience is given through a system of free hours for employment during school hours, permitting youth to try out his chosen career and know whether he will be a misfit or whether he can handle the work and will find it enjoyable.

Vocational Schools. About eighty-five per cent of the pupils trained in the public schools earn their living through industrial processes, and vocational schools are designed to fit young people for useful occupations.

Vocational schools are elementary in character, but they do not receive pupils under fourteen years of age. The courses are usually two years in length; a few schools have three-year courses. In most of the schools the time is about equally divided between book-work and shop-work. The school work includes English, mechanical drawing, mathematics and other closely related subjects. Many evening schools are largely vocational.

Technical High Schools. Technical high schools have become a feature in the school systems of most large cities. Such schools aim to prepare trained workers for the industrial world. Cleveland and Chicago took the lead in introducing industrial courses in high school work, and these and other cities have such special schools.

The textile industry in the United States supports a number of schools which are closely allied to the high schools. Prominent among these are the Textile School of the Pennsylvania Museum at Philadelphia, and three schools in Massachusetts, at Fall River, New Bedford and Lowell, all three cities being great cloth manufacturing centers. Secondary schools, such as the Illinois Institute of Technology at Chicago, the Drexel Institute at Philadelphia and the Pratt Institute at Brooklyn, now offer similar courses.

Trade Schools. Trade schools have been developed to take the place of the apprenticeship system. The first important one in the United States, the New York Trade School, was founded in 1881, and was intended primarily for the mechanics in the building trades. A number of other important schools were established in the next thirty years, but not until 1910 was there a notable increase in the number of trade schools. Many of the schools, like the Baron de Hirsch School in New York, are privately endowed. In Chicago, Milwaukee, Philadelphia, Indianapolis, Worcester and Portland, Oregon, are trade schools supported wholly or in part by the municipality.

United States Aid. The most important factor in promoting vocational education in the United States is the Smith-Hughes Act, which became effective in February, 1917. This law is explained under HIGH SCHOOL (which see). The passage of this bill, for which the National Society for the Promotion of Industrial Education had labored for ten years, marked the beginning of a new educational policy, in granting Federal aid to schools below collegiate grade which are not state institutions. This act supplements the Morrill Act, which provided for the state agricultural colleges and experiment stations, and it makes provision for the training of a large group of the population that cannot be reached directly by the Federal government. The provision of the act requiring the state governments to coöperate with the Federal government in order to derive any benefit from the appropriation places vocational education on a permanent basis in every state.

Aid to Soldiers. In June, 1918, Congress passed a law providing for the vocational education of disabled soldiers and sailors on their return to civil life. The responsibility for this training is placed with the Federal Board of Vocational Education, and the plan provides for the coöperation of the War and Navy departments, the Bureau of War Risk Insurance and the labor exchanges in the Department of Labor. The scope of the work includes completion of the training for such occupation as the soldier may choose and placing him in industry.

Even before the United States entered World War II, and increasingly after, vocational education was fitted into the defense program for soldiers and civilians alike. The government encouraged an increase of vocational courses in schools with special emphasis on defense work and training needed for service. Defense courses sprang up everywhere during evening hours and on Saturday afternoons, for adults as well as youth. Such courses, both in and out of school, aimed to give training in actual defense services and also to train youth and adults to take the place of men gone into the service. Many openings were thus created and there was a lack of skilled workmen to fill them. This gave an opportunity for youth to choose and for adults to shift from one vocational field to another. Youth in school were trained to enter specific branches of the service, and soldiers in the army were given opportunity to fit themselves for vocations after their term of service would be ended. The program was remarkably successful.

VOD′KA, an alcoholic liquor distilled from corn, rye, or potatoes, or from barley mixed with potatoes and oats, or from potatoes and molasses. It is "hard liquor" of a most potent sort, for its natural alcoholic content varies from 60 to 90 per cent; before it is retailed the amount of alcohol is reduced by dilution to about 40 per cent. Vodka is strictly a Russian drink, and is the national beverage. During World War I, the czar prohibited its manufacture; in 1925 the Soviet government restored its sale as a state monopoly, and from it derives a very large revenue.

VOICE, *vois,* sound emitted by the vocal cords of persons and animals, by means of which they communicate to one another their thoughts or emotions. The organ of the voice is the larynx, a cartilaginous box at the top of the trachea, or windpipe, capable of more delicate adjustment than any musical instrument. Across its top are stretched highly-sensitive and delicate mucous membranes, the edges of which are specialized to form the vocal cords. Sound is produced by a blast of air forced from the lungs upward through the glottis, or opening between the cords.

The pitch of the voice depends upon the tension of the vocal cords; the greater the tension, the higher the note produced. During the emission of acute sounds, the glottis contracts to a mere line. A deep rumbling sound is made by relaxed cords. The strength or loudness of the voice depends on the energy of the expiratory blast. Its quality depends upon the form and thickness of the cords, and is modified by the varying position of tongue, teeth and lips.

In the speaking voice, the notes have nearly all the same pitch, variety being mainly achieved through articulation in the mouth. The musical voice makes use of a larger number of notes, and their vibrations correspond to the notes of the musical scale. In singing, the vocal cords are under greater tension than in speaking. The principal difference between male and female voices lies in their pitch. The female vocal cords are shorter than those of the male, therefore their pitch is correspondingly higher. The male singing voice is classed as tenor, or bass, according to quality, and the female as soprano or contralto. The combined range of both covers about four octaves. A boy's voice is alto or soprano, because the vocal cords are no longer than those of the female. Change of voice in the adolescent boy, when the voice cracks or breaks, is due to rapid change in the larynx and temporary imperfect muscular control. See LARYNX.

VO′LAPUK, an artificial language invented by Johann Martin Schleyer, a German priest, and published by him in 1879. It was intended for use as an international language, but the hope of its friends has never been realized. Volapük is extremely simple and regular in construction, and the orthography is entirely phonetic, the words being pronounced as they are written. The root words are derived from all the languages of Europe. Volapük at first attracted many students, and international congresses were held in 1884, 1887 and 1889. Disagreements among its adherents regarding reforms in the language retarded the movement and ultimately led to the development of new and rival systems. See ESPERANTO.

VOLCANO, *vol ka′no,* a mountain that has one or more openings through which heated matter is thrown from the interior. The parts of a volcano are shown in the illustration below. The base comprises the walls and often blends with the cone so completely that no line of separation can be discovered. The term *cone* is usually applied to the upper

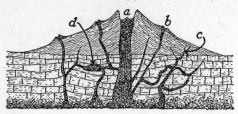

VOLCANO

(a) Crater; (b) Extinct crater; (c) Crevice; (d) Steam cavity.

and more recently formed portion of the volcano. In its summit is the opening called the *crater*. Leading from the crater down into the interior of the mountain is the *vent*, or *chimney*.

The form of the volcano depends quite largely upon the material thrown out. If this is ashes or thick viscid lava, that does not flow rapidly, the slopes of the mountain are steep and may be quite regular, as in the case of Vesuvius, Etna and many of the volcanoes of the Andes. If the material is of molten lava, that flows freely, a low, flat mountain, with gentle slopes, is formed. The volcanoes of Hawaii are the best illustrations of this type. In these volcanoes the flow of lava seldom takes place through an opening at the summit, but an outlet is forced through one or more crevices in the sides of the mountain. The crater is large and shallow and contains numerous vents, surrounded by small cones. Between these may also be found pools of molten lava.

In size, volcanoes vary from low mountains, comparatively small, like those in the vicinity of the Mediterranean, to great peaks, whose summits are from 17,000 to 20,000 feet above the sea, as is seen in the volcanoes of the Andes and the highest peaks of the Rocky Mountains, which are extinct volcanoes.

Volcanoes are classified as active, dormant and extinct. *Active* volcanoes are those either in continuous or frequent action. *Dormant* volcanoes are those which are active only at long intervals, and *extinct* volcanoes are those which have ceased action altogether. There is, however, no absolute division, as a volcano may pass from one class into another without warning, that is, a dormant or extinct volcano may become active, and an active volcano may become extinct.

Eruptions. The nature of the eruption is determined by the character of the material thrown out, and its violence is usually proportional to the length of time the mountain has been quiet. Volcanoes accustomed to throw out molten lava seldom eject ashes in large quantities. At the beginning, the lava flows rapidly, but as it cools it crusts over and flows more and more slowly until its motion ceases. The flow destroys everything in the path of the fiery stream, and the eruption often causes great devastation, suffering and loss of life. Some eruptions are characterized only by solid matter and steam. The solid matter is in the form of masses of rock, gravel, sand and dust, or ashes. These rise to a great height and are often carried through the atmosphere for many miles.

The causes of volcanic action are not well understood; but the chief cause is generally believed to be the contact of water with highly heated portions of the earth's interior. The violence of the action is supposed to be due to the expansive force of steam that has suddenly been released from great pressure. The steam forces out the ashes. The flow of lava is probably caused by its being squeezed into the fissure by the movements of the earth's crust. Some geologists believe that there are lakes of molten rock in various places in the interior of the earth, and that these are subject to tides like those on the ocean. They reason that the increased pressure caused by these tides may now and then force an opening in the earth's crust through which the heated matter is thrown out. An eruption is usually preceded by an increase in temperature of the land at the base and on the sides of the mountain, the drying up of springs and wells and frequently by local earthquakes. The most disastrous eruptions, as affecting loss of life, were the eruption of Vesuvius, A. D. 79; Krakatoa, in 1883, and Mont Pelee, on the island of Martinique, in 1902. At this eruption over thirty thousand people lost their lives within a few hours. The eruption of Mount Etna in 1911 was also very disastrous.

Related Articles. Consult the following titles for additional information:

VOLCANOES

Three of Java's many volcanoes. Cross section shows how subterranean forces effect an outlet in the earth's crust to release molten rock, ashes and gas. El Misti, a slumbering giant of Peru.

1-3 Ewing Galloway; 2 Publishers Photo Service

THREE FAMOUS VOLCANOES

Mount Vesuvius from across the Bay of Naples; Mount Lassen, California, last active in 1915; Fujiyama, Japan's sacred mountain.

VOLE, an English name applied to several species of the rat family. The voles are widely distributed, being found in Europe,

FIELD VOLE

Africa, Asia and in North and South America. The *water* vole is about the same size as the brown rat, and it is often called a rat. It has dark brown or black fur, a tail about half the length of the body, and very strong hind feet, with five rounded pads on the lower surfaces. It burrows by the banks of streams and feeds for the most part on vegetable food. The *field vole,* or *short-tailed field mouse,* is about the size of a common mouse, but the body is stouter and the tail shorter. It has brownish-gray fur; its hind feet have six pads. It lives in fields and woods, feeds on vegetable food, is very prolific and often does much damage to grain and other crops. The *bank vole* is like the field vole, but it has a rusty-colored back, larger ears and a longer tail.

VOL'GA, a river of Russia, the largest in Europe. It rises near the Valdai Hills, in the northwestern part of Russia, and flows in a circuitous course eastward and then southward, entering the Caspian Sea through a broad delta, a few miles below Astrakhan. The length of the river is about 2,200 miles, and it is navigable for nearly its entire course. The chief tributaries from the north and east are the Oka, the Sura and the Sarpa, and from the west, the Tvertsa, the Mologa, the Sheksna, the Kostroma, the Vetluga, the Kama and the Samara. The width of the river varies from 420 feet to 700 feet and exceeds even 2,400 feet, at Nijni Novgorod. During the spring it sometimes overflows, when its width varies from one and one-fourth miles to three miles. By means of canals the Volga is connected with the Black, the Baltic and the White seas, and with other important navigable rivers, so that it constitutes one of the most important inland waterways of Europe. With its tributaries it traverses a region inhabited by 50,000,000 people.

VOLT, the unit employed in measuring electric pressure, such a pressure as will produce a flow of one ampere per second against a resistance of one ohm.

VOLTA, *vohl' ta,* ALESSANDRO (1745–1827), an Italian scientist, famous for his researches and discoveries in physics and as the inventor of the voltaic battery, named after him. He was born at Como, Italy, where, in 1774, he became professor of physics in the Royal School. He previously made important investigations and discoveries in chemistry and physics, especially in electricity. In 1779 he became professor of physics in the University of Pavia, and remained there twenty-five years. He invented the electroscope, the electrical condenser, the voltaic pile and the voltaic cell, or battery. See ELECTRIC BATTERY.

VOLTA'IC CELL, or **VOLTAIC BATTERY.** See ELECTRIC BATTERY; ELECTRICITY, subhead *Voltaic Electricity.*

VOLTAIRE, *vol tair',* the assumed name of JEAN FRANÇOIS MARIE AROUET (1694–1778), a French writer and philosopher, was born at Paris. His father, a notary, gave him the best education possible, and the young man was early recognized as a scholar. In 1718 a tragedy named *Oedipus* was brought out by him and was most enthusiastically received. He soon became a fashionable poet, and resided mainly at Paris, in the midst of the most brilliant society.

In 1726 he was imprisoned in the Bastille for having sent a challenge to the Chevalier Rohan, by whom he had been insulted, but he was liberated within a month and allowed to go to England. Here he resided till 1729, in friendship with some of the chief literary men of the day, and he acquired a knowledge of English literature. His *Henriade,* an epic celebrating the exploits of Henry IV of France, was completed and published by subscription in England, and was widely read throughout Europe, except in France, from which country it was excluded by the government because of its forceful presentation of the idea of religious toleration.

After his return to France, Voltaire lived chiefly at Paris till 1734. During this period he raised himself from very moderate circumstances to a condition of affluence by successful monetary speculations. From 1734 to 1749 he resided with Madame du Châtelet at Cirey, in Lorraine, and he produced many plays during this period. After the death of Madame du Châtelet, Voltaire accepted the oft-repeated invitations of Frederick the Great to live at his court, at Potsdam. Here he was received with great honor, but a series of disagreements with the king ended in Voltaire's retirement from the Prussian court in 1753. After some unsettled years he fixed his residence with his niece, Madame Denis, at Ferney, near the boundary of the Republic of Geneva, and here he received a constant succession of distinguished visitors and maintained a correspondence which included in its range most of the rulers and savants of Europe. In February, 1778, he returned to Paris, but died soon afterwards.

Voltaire's works embrace almost every branch of literature—poetry, the drama, romance, history, philosophy and even science. He produced no single literary masterpiece; his greatness lay in his power to discern fanaticism and superstition, and nearly all his works are strongly animated by a spirit of hostility to the priests and the religion they represented. He was one of the foremost of that band of writers whose revolt against conventions, openly and most forcefully expressed, was preparing the way for the French Revolution. It is the commonly accepted opinion that he was an atheist, but this has never been proved. Voltaire's literary fame chiefly rests on his philosophical novels, *Zadig, Candide, L'Ingénu;* his histories, *The Age of Louis XIV, The History of Charles XII*; his correspondence, and more than all, perhaps, on his poetical epistles, satires and occasional light poems, all of which exhibit wit, gaiety, vivacity and grace.

VOLT'METER, an instrument for measuring the pressure of an electric current. It consists of a permanent steel horseshoe magnet, with a piece of soft iron attached to each pole. Between the poles, a soft iron cylinder is suspended, so that it can rotate vertically. Around this cylinder is a light rectangular frame of copper, wound with a coil of insulated wire. Spiral springs are attached at each end of this frame, and a needle, which moves over a graduated dial, is attached to the upper end of the axis. When an electric current passes through the coil or wire, it causes the copper frame to turn upon its axis. The springs furnish an amount of resistance that must be overcome by the current, and the position of the needle on the dial indicates the pressure. Volt-

meters are used with dynamo electric machines. See VOLT.

VOLUNTEERS', citizens who, of their own accord, offer the state their services in a military capacity. The oldest volunteer force in Great Britain is the Honorable Artillery Company of the city of London, which received its charter of incorporation from Henry VIII. Until the second year of the World War Great Britain depended upon a volunteer army to take care of territorial defense, and its volunteer forces in 1914 numbered over 251,000. Not until May, 1916, was conscription put in force in Great Britain. It was applied to England, Scotland and Wales, but not to Ireland, which, however, sent large numbers of volunteers to the front. Canada contributed a volunteer army of over 400,000, but adopted conscription in December, 1917. New Zealand, South Africa and Australia relied wholly on volunteering, and all contributed generously. In all of the other allied nations, as well as in the enemy countries, conscription had been a permanent policy before the war.

In the United States. The volunteers in American armies played an important part in all wars before America's entrance into the World War. Though conscription was resorted to in the Civil War, about 2,500,000 enrolled voluntarily on the Union side, and half as many on the Confederate. Volunteers and regulars made up the American army of the Spanish-American War. In the World War there were calls for volunteers in special branches of the service, and the state national guards were classed as volunteers, but the bulk of the great army that contributed so much to the defeat of Germany was made up of men enrolled through the selective draft. This was the first time that America ever enrolled all of its men under forty-six years of age for military service. Navies are usually recruited through volunteering, but this is a matter of custom and precedent. See CONSCRIPTION; WORLD WAR.

VOLUNTEERS OF AMERICA, a religious and philanthropic organization, formerly the American branch of the Salvation Army. In 1896 Ballington Booth, head of the Salvation Army in America, believing that the methods of his father, William Booth, were not perfectly suited to conditions in America, severed the connection of his branch which, thenceforth, has had an independent existence. The main purpose of the English and the American bodies, however, has remained the same.

The Volunteers are organized on a semi-military plan, and the officers bear military titles. They support various benevolent institutions. Lodging houses for destitute men and women and fresh-air camps for women and children are among their most important charities. A great quantity of Christian literature is distributed, and open-air religious services are conducted on the streets. A Volunteer Hospital has been established in New York City, where needy cases are taken care of. The official organ of the society is *The Volunteers' Gazette,* published at its headquarters in New York. General Ballington Booth and his wife, Maud Ballington Booth, are joint commanders. See SALVATION ARMY.

VOMITING, the forcible expulsion of matter from the stomach, through the oesophagus, or gullet. It is not a disease in itself, but it is a symptom common to numerous diseases, or as an accompaniment of extreme nervous sensitiveness. The treatment of vomiting depends upon its cause and upon the disease, if any, which accompanies it. Lying down, the application of mustard to the pit of the stomach, or small doses of soda, ice, whisky or coffee will sometimes relieve it. While sudden and violent vomiting in a healthy person is an indication of some poisonous substance in the stomach, yet very frequently vomiting is nature's method of relieving an overloaded stomach. See NAUSEA.

VORTICELLA, *vor te sel'lah,* or **BELL ANIMALCULE,** *an i mal'ku le,* a genus of infusoria, or one-celled animals characterized by a bell-shaped body, the opening of which is surrounded by tiny hairs, or cilia. These cilia are kept in constant and rapid motion, whereby they draw in particles of food. At the opposite end of the body is a slender stem, by means of which the animal attaches itself to objects in the water, such as rocks or weeds. This stem also moves, with a spiral springlike motion, and may be drawn up into the body when the animal wishes to detach itself from its moorings and swim freely about.

VOSGES, *vohzh,* **MOUNTAINS,** a chain of mountains about 100 miles long, extending in a north-northeast direction along the frontiers of Alsace in France, their course being nearly parallel with that of the Rhine. They are separated from the Jura Mountains by the valley of the Doubs on the south. The Vosges are composed chiefly of granite and are covered with forests of pine and beech to a height of about 3,600 feet, beyond which their summits, which are rounded in forms, are grassy. The highest peak is Ballon de Guebwiller, 4,067 feet. These mountains contain considerable silver, copper, lead and coal and large quantities of rock salt. Some of the bitter fighting of the World War took place in the Vosges region.

VOTE. See ELECTION; BALLOT.

VOTING MACHINE, a device for automatically registering and counting votes, having the advantages of secrecy, simplicity, rapidity of registration and counting and the avoidance of duplication.

In most patterns of voting machines, the voter enters the booth, and not till all the curtains are closed will the machine register his vote. The names of the candidates are arranged in order, either by parties or alphabetically. The voter can either vote a straight ticket or can vote for individual candidates. In the former case, either by the use of a key or by means of a lever, he registers a vote and thus locks the mechanism, so that he cannot vote further, unless, by turning back the lever, he cancels his first vote. If he wishes to split the ticket, he turns a lever or key for one candidate for each office, and is prevented thereby from voting for any other candidate. As he leaves the booth, by opening the curtains or doors at the exit he sets the machine for the next voter. Each vote cast for each office or for a straight ticket is registered by a patent device on a slip of paper, so that as soon as the last vote is cast, the final returns are ready to be announced. Many states have authorized the use of voting machines at the option of the local authorities.

VOWEL, an open sound made by the voice in speaking, distinguished from the consonant sounds, which are made with the organs of speech more or less closed. Vowels may be sounded by themselves, but consonants can be pronounced only in combination with vowels. In English, the vowel sounds are represented by the letters, *a, e, i, o, u,* and sometimes *w* and *y.* Each really represents several sounds, as the a-sounds in the words *father, flask, hall, what, any, preface, final* and *abound.* Most other languages have vowel sounds which the English does not possess. A more detailed discussion of vowels may be found in the article ORTHOGRAPHY.

VUL'CAN, called by the Greeks Hephaestus, in classical mythology, the god who presided over fire and the working of metals, and who patronized handicraftsmen of every kind. He was the son of Jupiter and Juno, but, unlike the other gods, he was seriously lame. By some writers he was said to have been born lame, and for that reason he was believed to have been thrown by his mother from Olympus; but by others his lameness is attributed to his having been thrown from Olympus by Jupiter, for interfering in Juno's behalf in a quarrel between her and Jupiter.

VUL'CANIZING. See RUBBER AND RUBBER MANUFACTURE.

VUL'GATE, the Latin translation of the Bible, which has, in the Roman Catholic Church, official authority, and which the Council of Trent, in its fourth session, on May 27, 1546, declared "shall be held as authentic in all public lectures, disputations, sermons and expositions; and that no one shall presume to reject it under any pretense whatsoever." Even in the early period of the Church, a Latin translation of the Old Testament existed, made not from the Hebrew, but from the Septuagint. Saint Jerome found that this translation was not always accurate, and between A. D. 385 and 405 he made a new Latin translation from the Hebrew, with the aid of the best Greek translations. This at first met with the greatest opposition, as the Septuagint was regarded as an inspired translation, and any deviation from it was considered sacrilegious. Before his death Jerome had justified himself and proved the purity of his intentions, but it was not until the ninth century that his version came to be used throughout the Church and not until centuries later that it was authorized. The version now in use is the edition published by Clement VIII in 1592.

VUL'TURE, the common name for a class of carrion-eating birds, characterized by necks destitute of feathers and by elongated beaks, with curved upper mandibles. Their talons are not relatively strong, and in tear-

VULTURE

ing their prey they make more use of their beaks than of their claws. Vultures are usually of a cowardly disposition and will not attack live animals, unless the latter are seriously wounded or dying, as they feed almost entirely on decaying animal flesh. They fly high in the air and detect their prey from great distances. They are valuable scavengers in all warm and tropical countries. The California vulture has a long, flat, orange-colored head and dull black plumage, with a grayish wing band. It builds a loose nest of sticks, in a hollow in a tree or cliff, and lays one round, greenish-white egg. The Egyptian species, called "Pharaoh's hen," is found in the countries bordering the Mediterranean. See CONDOR; TURKEY BUZZARD.

W, the twenty-third letter of the English alphabet. It is formed, as its name indicates, by doubling the *u* or *v*, and before it appeared as a separate character in English its sound was sometimes represented by *uu* or *vv*. At the end of words or syllables it is either silent, as in *low*, or it modifies the preceding vowel, as in *new, how,* having then the power of a vowel.

WABASH, *waw'bash*, IND., the county seat of Wabash County, forty-two miles southwest of Fort Wayne, on the Wabash River and on the Wabash and the Cleveland, Cincinnati, Chicago & Saint Louis (New York Central) and the Wabash railroads. It is the trade center for a rich agricultural and stock-raising region, and manufactures mineral wool, mechanical rubber goods, wood products and wood-working machinery, paper products and various metal products. Wabash was settled and incorporated in 1837, and was chartered as a city in 1866. It was one of the first cities in the world to be electrically lighted. Gene Stratton Porter was born here. Population, 1940, 9,653.

WABASH RIVER, a river 550 miles in length, rising in the western part of Ohio, flowing northwestward, westward then southward into the Ohio thirty miles below Evansville, Ind. It crosses Indiana, and in the latter part of its course forms a part of the boundary between Indiana and Illinois. It is navigable during high water as far as Lafayette, Ind., and at ordinary levels to Covington. Its chief tributary is the White River. Some of the principal towns on its banks are Wabash, Peru, Logansport, Lafayette, Covington, Terre Haute and Vincennes.

WACHT AM RHEIN, DIE ("the Watch on the Rhine"), a German patriotic song. The words were written by Max Schneckenburger in 1840, when the left bank of the Rhine seemed in danger of falling into the hands of France. The music, by Karl Wilhelm, was composed in 1854.

WA'CO, TEX., the county seat of McLennan County, ninety-seven miles south of Dallas, on the Brazos River and on the Missouri-Kansas-Texas, the Missouri Pacific, the Saint Louis Southwestern and the Southern Pacific railroads. There is regular air service from the well-equipped municipal airport, Rich Field. Lake Waco, with a storage capacity of 30,000 acre feet, provides the city's water supply. Industrially, Waco ranks about sixth among Texas cities, producing cotton and textiles, sash and doors, furniture, cement, dairy products, machine-shop products and other articles. It is also an important retail and wholesale trade center. Waco is the seat of Baylor University, the oldest institution of higher learning in Texas, and Paul Quinn College, for Negroes. A veterans' hospital and a state orphans' home are located here.

Waco derives its name from the Huaco Indians. It was laid out in 1849 and was incorporated the following year. It has adopted the city manager-commission form of government. Population, 1940, 55,982.

WADAI, *wah'di*, formerly a native state in the central part of Africa, annexed to the French Congo in 1909. The boundaries are indefinite, but the area is estimated at 170,-000 square miles. The surface is mostly of a desert character, but there are oases scattered through the region, and in some sections there are fertile tracts covered with forests. The population, estimated at 2,000,000, is composed chiefly of Negroes and Arabs, who are Mohammedans. The capital is Abeshr, and it is connected with Bengeazi by caravan route.

WAGER, *wa'jur*, a bet, also something staked on any uncertain outcome of an issue, such as the result of a contest, or the inevitable alternative in events, such as elections and the weather. The one whose opinion proves to be correct receives what has been staked by both. In some countries the laws provide that all contracts or agreements, whether oral or in writing, depending on wagers are null and void, and money due thereon cannot be recovered in any court of law. A wager is therefore called a *debt of honor*, since it cannot be collected except through the good faith of the parties.

WAGES, *wa'jez*. In modern industry production requires land, capital and labor. The payment for land is *rent;* the payment for capital is *interest,* and the payment for labor is *wages*. The United States government applies the term to compensation computed on an hourly, daily, piecework or similar basis, and defines *salary* as that which is computed on a weekly, monthly, annual or comparable basis. Wages may be classified as *nominal* and *real*. Nominal wages are the wages expressed in money, or as an absolute quantity, as five dollars a day. Real wages denote the purchasing value of the money received. To illustrate: If the cost of living advances and a laborer's wage remains the same, his real wage is lowered. If a bricklayer who received five dollars a day during a certain year received the same wage in a later year when living costs were fifty per cent greater, his real wage then was only two-thirds of what it was in the first instance. To enable him to maintain his standards, his later wage would have to be increased to seven and one-half dollars.

Difference in Wages. In economics, labor is considered as a commodity, the same as land, building material or wheat; and one of the chief causes in fixing wages is the law of supply and demand, other conditions being equal. When there are more laborers than production requires, wages will be low; when laborers are scarce, producers bid for their services, and wages are high. Wages in some occupations are higher than in others because of the nature of the occupation. Permanency of occupation, for instance, is an important factor in fixing wages. One can afford to work for a lower wage at an occupation which furnishes employment the year round than at an occupation which furnishes employment only part of the time. Skilled labor commands higher wages than unskilled labor, and dangerous occupations higher than those not considered as dangerous.

Wages and Profit Sharing. Many large firms distribute periodically among their employes a certain per cent of their profits. From the viewpoint of economics, their share of profit should not be considered as wages, but from the practical viewpoint of both employer and employe it is considered as so much additional compensation, or so much increase of the laborer's share of production.

Influence of Labor Organizations. As early as 1792, skilled workmen in America united to protect themselves against attempts by employers to lower wages. Trade unions, which since about 1830 have exerted increasing influence, have often secured for their members higher wages than could have been possible without a powerful organization. The power of labor organizations, keeping pace with the growing industrialization of the country, gave them an ever-greater political influence, which has resulted in Federal legislation bearing on wages. The National Labor Relations Act (1935), for instance, established the policy of collective bargaining, by which employers and labor representatives in joint conference adopt trade agreements affecting wages and other problems. In 1938 the Fair Labor Standards Act set maximum hours and a minimum wage which should be forty cents an hour after October 24, 1945, and until industrial committees should set minimum wages for each industry affected. See LABOR LEGISLATION.

Related Articles. Consult the following titles for additional information:

Capital	Profit Sharing
Labor Organizations	Socialism

WAGNER, *vagh'nur*, SIEGFRIED (1869–1930), a German operatic composer and orchestra leader, the son of Wilhelm Richard and Cosima Wagner. Beginning in 1893, he made several tours of Europe, presenting and interpreting his father's compositions. In 1896 he became co-director with his mother of the Bayreuth Wagner Festivals, and was general director of the playhouse after 1924.

WAGNER, WILHELM RICHARD (1813–1883), a German composer, poet and miscellaneous writer, born at Leipzig. He received his education at Leipzig and Dresden and after 1834 filled various musical engagements at Magdeburg, Riga and Königsberg. In 1839 he went to Paris and London and there composed his operas *Rienzi* and *The Flying Dutchman*. The brilliant success of the operas secured him the conductorship at the Royal Opera of Dresden in 1843. He joined the insurrectionary movement of 1848 and was compelled to exile himself. Until his return to Germany, in 1864, he spent most of his time in Switzerland, Italy, Paris and London. His *Tannhäuser* and *Lohengrin* appeared in 1845 and 1850, respectively. The king of Bavaria, Louis II, became an enthusiastic patron of Wagner, and the theater at Baireuth, especially built for Wagner by the contributions of Wagner societies throughout the world, was chiefly supported from the king's purse. Here the famous tetralogy *Der Ring des Nibelungen,* consisting of *Das Rheingold, Die Walküre, Siegfried* and *Götterdämmerung* was first performed in 1876. About a year before his death Wagner wrote *Parsifal,* which has since been produced with emphatic success. He gave to his works a national character by selecting his subjects from old German legends. His theory, founded upon the ideas of Gluck and Weber, was that in a perfect musical drama, the three arts, poetry, music and dramatic representation, should be welded together into one well-balanced whole. His particular views on music are embodied in a well-known work, entitled *Oper und Drama.* See OPERA.

WAG'ON, a four-wheeled vehicle drawn by one or more horses and used for carrying passengers or merchandise. In cities they have been almost entirely displaced by motor trucks. Wagons are constructed of a great variety of patterns, the body being adapted to the particular use for which the vehicle is intended. Farm wagons have long rectangular boxes, so made that they can be taken off or put on the gear at will. Most of these wagons may also have the running-gear extended or shortened to suit the purpose for which the wagon is needed. Road wagons have a light running-gear, springs and upholstered seats. For practically every purpose, even in rural districts, the motor vehicle is supplanting the wagon. See CARRIAGE.

WAG'TAIL, a group of birds so called from their habit of jerking their long tails when running or perching. Though several species are common in Europe, rarely is the bird seen in the United States. The wagtails frequent muddy lands and pastures, running rapidly along the edge of water and catching the insects they find there. A species of wagtail breeds on the coasts of Alaska in summer, making its nest of woven roots and grasses on or near the ground. The eggs are white with brown spots.

WAITE, MORRISON REMICK (1816–1888), an eminent American jurist, born at Lyme, Conn. He graduated at Yale in 1837 and was admitted to the bar two years later. He practiced successfully in Maumee City and Toledo, Ohio, was elected to the legislature and in 1871 was sent to Geneva as United States counsel in the Alabama case. President Grant appointed him to succeed Salmon P. Chase as Chief Justice of the Supreme Court of the United States in 1874. He held the position until his death, winning esteem for his impartiality and learning. Among the important questions presented to the Supreme Court and decided during Chief Justice Waite's term were those affecting polygamy, election laws, the civil rights of negroes, the Bell telephone case, the power of removal by the President and the Chicago anarchist cases.

WAKE, the name given to the custom of holding vigil over the dead during the night preceding burial. While it is a part of the practice of numerous religions, in America it is witnessed only among Roman Catholics. The wake originally was observed in the Church of England; it had nothing to do with death, but was observed with prayer and singing to commemorate the anniversary or consecration and dedication of the parish church.

WAKE ISLAND, a tiny coral island in the Pacific Ocean, which came into the possession of the United States in 1899. It lies about 2,400 miles west and south of Hawaii and about 2,950 miles north and east of Manila in latitude 19° 15' north, longitude 166° 38' east. The island is not attractive and was not regularly inhabited until it was made a station in the transpacific air route. The government reorganization of 1934 placed Wake Island under the control of the Navy Department; it was used as a communications depot, and a small garrison of marines was stationed there. In December, 1941, it was attacked by Japan and taken after heroic defense.

WAKE-ROBIN, another name for the trillium (which see).

WALDENSES, *wal den'seez,* a Christian sect founded in the twelfth century by Peter Waldo, a rich merchant of Lyons, France. About 1170 Waldo gave away his goods and his money to the poor and began preaching a life of poverty, chastity and obedience. While holding to the Roman Catholic faith, he believed the people should be preached to in their own dialects, that religious writings should be translated into their language, and that each man should be his own interpreter of the Bible. His followers, known as "the Poor Men of Lyons," suffered many persecutions, and in 1231 were excommunicated by the Pope. Their chief strongholds then as now, were the Cottian Alps, southwest of Turin. Since 1848 they have had the same religious and political rights as other religious sects in Italy, where they number about 12,000. Branches of the Church have been established in Argentina, Uruguay and the United States.

A typical costume

WALES, *waylz,* the smallest division of Great Britain, situated in the southwestern part of the island, forming a peninsula between Bristol Channel, on the south, and the Irish Sea, on the north. It has an area of 7,466 square miles, or a little less than that of New Jersey. Population, 1931, 2,158,374. Its surface is mountainous in the north, where the ranges are an extension of those of England. The country is rich in minerals, particularly coal, iron, copper and slate, and to these Wales owes its chief wealth. The coal trade is the most important and extensive, and the city of Cardiff on the Bristol Channel is one of the largest coal ports in the world. The presence of coal and iron ore has given rise to extensive iron and steel works, and there are also important copper plants. Other manufactures include woolen goods, especially flannel, coarse cloth and hosiery.

Previous to the Roman occupation, Wales appears to have been inhabited by a mixture of primitive Iberians and invading Celts. During the latter part of the Roman occupation one of the four provinces into which the entire island was divided included Wales and was called *Britannia Secunda.* After the invasion of the Saxons the country acquired a distinctly national character, becoming the refuge of the Celts, or early Britons, who were gradually driven to the west. The country was conquered in the thirteenth century by Edward I, who made his eldest son Prince of Wales, a title that has ever since been conferred upon the heir to the British crown. Succeeding this date there occurred a number of national uprisings, and the struggle for independence in Wales was not entirely suppressed till 1536, when the country became incorporated with England, and its inhabitants received all the privileges of English subjects. The language is Welsh, which is a branch of the Celtic, different from that used by the Irish and the Scotch Highlanders. The political and educational systems of Wales are identical with those of England. See ENGLAND; GREAT BRITAIN; CELTS.

WALES, PRINCE OF, a British title borne by the eldest son of the British monarch. It was first conferred by Edward I on his son, at the time of his conquest of the principality of Wales. Edward III was never Prince of Wales, but the title has been conferred on all the male heirs apparent to the English throne from the time of Edward the Black Prince, son of Edward III. The title is not hereditary, but is purely honorary; it does not pass to the holder automatically, but must be conferred with appropriate ceremony. It implies no power or authority, and the accompanying income is voted by Parliament.

As heir to the crown of Scotland, the Prince of Wales bears the titles of *Prince and High Steward of Scotland, Duke of Rothsay, Earl of Carrick, Baron of Renfrew, and Lord of the Isles.*

The last English prince to bear the title was the former Edward VIII, who received it in June, 1910, three months after his father ascended the throne as George V. Edward was unmarried while king, and his successor, George VI, has no son.

WALHALLA, *wahl hahl'a,* or TEMPLE OF FAME, a magnificent marble palace erected in 1830, near Ratisbon, Bavaria, by Ludwig I. The building, 115 by 246 feet in size, is in a style similar to Greek Doric. The pediments and frieze contain sculptures representing scenes from the early history of the Teutonic peoples, and inside are busts of noted Germans. The building is named for Walhalla, the mythological hall of the Norse deities.

WALKER, FRANCIS AMASA (1840–1897), an American economist and statistician, born at Boston, Mass., the son of Amasa Walker. He graduated at Amherst College and afterward studied law. He served in the Union army in the Civil War and was made brigadier general for gallantry at Chancellorsville, where he was wounded. From 1865 to 1867 he taught Latin and Greek at Williston Seminary, and in 1869 he was appointed chief of the bureau of statistics at Washington. As supervisor of the census of 1870, as United States Indian Commissioner in 1872 and (from 1873 to 1881) as professor of political economy in the Sheffield Scientific School of Yale College, he rendered distinguished service. In 1881 he became president of the Massachusetts Institute of Technology. He published many works, including volumes on the *Indian Question, Political Economy, The Wages Question, Money, International Bimetallism* and *The Making of the Nation.*

WALKER, WILLIAM (1824–1860), an American adventurer, notorious as a leader of several filibustering expeditions. He was born at Nashville, Tenn., and was graduated at the University of Nashville. After a course in law he was admitted to the bar, and later he studied medicine at the universities of Edinburgh and Heidelberg. On his return to America he engaged in journalism.

In the summer of 1853 Walker organized an expedition to conquer the state of Sonora, Mex. Forced to flee from Mexico on account of a lack of provisions and ammunition, he was arrested by United States authorities at San Diego, and was tried for violating neutrality, but was acquitted. He then conducted expeditions in Nicaragua and Costa Rica, and each time was driven out. After several attempts to conquer Honduras, he was compelled to surrender to the Honduran government, was condemned by court martial and executed. See FILIBUSTER.

WALKERVILLE, ONT., on the Canadian National, the Wabash, the Michigan Central and the Pere Marquette railways, one and one-half mile from Windsor, and directly across the river from Detroit. Steamship lines run to Fort William, Port Arthur, Montreal and intermediate points. The industries of the town are supplied by Niagara electric power; there are varnish and paint factories, wire fence works, bridge works, tobacco, clothing and chemical works, and manufactories of automobile bodies and trimmings, furnaces, castings and marine engines. It is now a part of Windsor city.

WALKING STICK, a name applied to a group of curiously-shaped insects, which closely resemble a small branch with twigs. In the southeastern part of the United States is found a typical species. The individuals have long, slender bodies and long, thin legs. They are green in summer, but turn brown in autumn; thus protected from detection they escape all but the closest scrutiny. The local names are *devil's horse* and *mule killer.* See LEAF INSECTS; PROTECTIVE COLORATION.

WALLACE, ALFRED RUSSEL (1823–1913), an English naturalist, born at Usk, Monmouthshire, and educated at Hertford Grammar School. While serving as English master at the Collegiate School of Leicester, Wallace became acquainted with Henry Walter Bates, the naturalist, and in 1848 the two departed on an exploring trip to the valley of the Amazon. This was the first of those scientific explorations that revealed to Wallace a wealth of new information in the field of plant and animal morphology. From 1854 to 1862 he was engaged in scientific study in the Malay Archipelago (which see). The material collected on these trips he embodied in *Travels on the Amazon and Rio Negro, The Malay Archipelago, Tropical Nature* and *The Geographical Distribution of Animals.* His observation of animal life and his philosophical nature led him to investigations which resulted in the formulation of a theory of natural selection and evolutionary development. Before Darwin gave his famous work to the world Wallace had published his *Speculation on the Origin of Species.* His share in establishing the theory of evolution has been acknowledged by Darwin. But while Darwin, in his later editions of the *Origin of Species,* somewhat modified his original conclusions, Wallace, in a late work, *Darwinism, an Exposition of the Theory of Natural Selection, with Some of its Applications,* strongly insists upon the complete controlling power of these primary laws and conditions. Moreover, he differs from Darwin on the subject of the intellectual, moral and spiritual nature of man. He contends that the higher faculties have been developed, not under the law of natural selection, but under a higher law, which has come in imperceptibly; and he maintains that the Darwinian theory, instead of opposing, "lends a decided support to a belief in the spiritual nature of man." His many essays entitle him to the claim of being a true Darwinian.

WALLACE, Edgar (1875–1932), an English newspaper man and novelist who issued his books with almost incredible rapidity. He was a war correspondent and special writer for London papers before turning exclusively to the more formal literary field. His novels, most of them mystery stories, were often written at the rate of one in ten days or two weeks, and in all they totalled more than 160. Though showing evidence of hurried composition, they found an immense sale in all English-speaking countries. Wallace was engaged to write for American moving-picture producers in 1931; in Hollywood, Calif., while engaged on scenarios, he died in the following year.

WALLACE, Lewis (1827–1905), an American soldier and novelist, generally known as Lew Wallace. He was born in Brooksville, Ind., received a common school education and began the study of law, which he practiced at intervals in Crawfordsville, Ind. He took part in the Mexican War, with rank of lieutenant, and was a member of the Indiana state legislature in 1848. At the outbreak of the Civil War he entered the service as colonel of an Indiana regiment, was appointed brigadier-general in 1861 and was made major-general for distinguished services at Fort Donelson in 1862. He was removed from command by Halleck, but was reinstated by Grant. He was sent to Mexico on secret diplomatic service in 1866, was elected governor of New Mexico in 1878 and was made minister to Turkey in 1881. His best-known works are *Ben Hur, The Fair God, The Prince of India* and *The Boyhood of Christ.*

WALLACE, William, Sir (about 1272–1305), the first of the great Scottish patriots, a man of herculean proportions and strength and possessing in a high degree those qualities of leadership which made his name famous. The king of England deposed the Scottish king in 1296 and placed over Scotland a guard of English soldiers. Wallace one day quarreled with and killed one of these soldiers, and escaped. He gathered a band of Highlanders and began a guerilla warfare on the English.

After collecting a considerable force, he was besieging the castle of Dundee when he heard that Surrey and Cressingham were advancing upon Stirling with a large army. He met them in the vicinity of that town and gained a complete victory (1297). After this Wallace gained the title of guardian of the kingdom and conducted a series of organized raids into England. In 1298 Edward I entered Scotland, and Wallace retired before him, wasting the country, but he was at length overtaken at Falkirk and was compelled to fight; after a gallant resistance, he was defeated. He succeeded in escaping, and little is known of his movements thenceforth. He was excluded from the peace granted by Edward to the Scots in 1304, and when he fell into the hands of the English he was conveyed to London and there executed as a traitor, though it was admitted that he had never sworn fealty to England.

WALLA WALLA, *wol'a wol'a*, Wash., commercial center of the southeastern part of the state, county seat of Walla Walla County, situated 159 miles southwest of Spokane on the Walla Walla River, and on the Northern Pacific and the Union Pacific railroads. There is regular air service at the municipal airport. The city is thirty miles east of the navigable Columbia River, and a hard-surfaced road, constructed from Walla Walla to Wallula, the nearest port, connects with boat lines. Walla Walla is located in a fertile valley which produces 5,000,000 bushels of wheat annually, besides extensive fruit, vegetables, livestock and dairy and poultry products. Whitman College, one of the oldest institutions of higher learning in the Northwest, and Walla Walla College are located here. The city has also the state prison and a veterans' hospital.

Walla Walla, a Nez Perce Indian term which means *many waters,* grew up about a military post which was established here in 1856; it was chartered as a town in 1859 under its present name, and was incorporated as a city in 1862. The commission form of government is in operation. The mission of Dr. Marcus Whitman was at Waiilatpu, six miles west of Walla Walla (see Whitman, Marcus). Population, 1940, 18,109.

WALLENSTEIN, *vahl'en stine,* or **WALDSTEIN**, Albrecht Eusebius Wenzel von, Duke of Friedland, Sagan and Mecklenburg (1583–1634), a famous leader in the Thirty Years' War, born at Hermanic, in Bohemia, of poor but noble parentage. He was educated in a Jesuit College and at the universities of Padua, Altdorf and Bologna. Through a wealthy marriage he became prominent in affairs in Bohemia. **For**

military service against Venice in 1617 he was made a count and commissioned a colonel. He took service in the Austrian army in the struggle against the Turks, and when the Thirty Years' War broke out in Bohemia (1618), he joined the imperial forces against his native country.

In September, 1630, owing to the jealousy of the nobles and the license of his followers, he was deprived of all command and retired to his duchy of Friedland, until the emperor was compelled to seek his aid against Gustavus Adolphus. Wallenstein then obtained almost absolute power, and his behavior thenceforth leaves no doubt that the emperor's interests were second to his own, and that he would not have hesitated to join the emperor's enemies, to secure his own independence and the crown of Bohemia. After some partial successes he encountered the king of Sweden at Lützen in 1632, and in the battle which took place Wallenstein was defeated and Gustavus was killed. Wallenstein had unsuccessfully treated on his own account with the Swedish king, and he now secretly reopened negotiations with France and the German princes, occasionally taking the field to display his military power. The court at Vienna was well aware of his double dealing, but the emperor was not strong enough to remove him, and he therefore had him assassinated. See THIRTY YEARS' WAR.

WALLFLOWER, a shrubby herb, belonging to the mustard family, native to Southern Europe, so called because it is often found growing among the stones of fallen walls. It thrives in dry soil and gravel and grows well on stony cliffs. The flowers in the wild state are invariably yellow; under cultivation they exhibit a variety of colors. A red specimen is known as bleeding heart. *Heartsease* and *gillyflower* are other names by which the plants are known. The fragrant, velvety flowers are much admired, and have gained for the plant a place in Northern hothouses.

WALL OF CHINA, THE GREAT. See GREAT WALL OF CHINA.

WALLOONS, *wal loonz'*, a Celtic race inhabiting Southern Belgium. They are the descendants of the ancient Belgae and resemble the French more than they do the Germans, being short and mostly of dark complexion. Their language, also called Walloon, is a French dialect, retaining numerous Gallic words, but it varies somewhat in the different provinces. There are about 2,750,000 Walloons now in Belgium.

WALL PAPER, paper used for decorating the walls and ceilings of rooms. It was invented by the Chinese about 2,000 years ago, but was unknown elsewhere until about the year 1350, when importations from China reached Europe. The first factory for its manufacture in Europe was built in France in 1750. The French still call it *papier paint*, because for many years in that country it was hand-painted. It came into quick popularity in Europe as a substitute for the expensive tapestries, brocades, and velvets that were the wall adornments of the wealthy. Today more wall paper is made in the United States than in any other country, its production there reaching 325,000,000 rolls a year, enough to put a belt almost sixty times around the world. European manufacturers still adhere quite largely in choice of patterns to copies of tapestries and historic and mythological designs, but American stylists specialize in new designs; one American manufacturer produces about 3,000 different styles of prints. The design in the sheet, which is printed on presses resembling printing presses, is repeated at intervals; and when the paper-hanger puts it on the wall he is careful to match the pattern.

WALL STREET, the center of financial operations in the United States, so called from the street in lower New York City, upon which are located the New York Stock Exchange, the Consolidated Exchange and numerous banking institutions that figure largely in the money market. The street itself extends from Broadway to East River, following the line of the old city wall built by Governor Peter Stuyvesant in 1653 to protect the town from possible attacks by the Indians. This wall, repaired and replaced from time to time, formed for fifty years the northern boundary of the future metropolis of the Western world.

WALNUT, *wawl'nut*, a genus including about twelve species of beautiful trees, mostly natives of North America and Asia. The three best-known species in America are the *English*, or *Persian* walnut, the *black* walnut and the *white* walnut, or *butternut*.

The English, or Persian walnut is a native of Persia and the Himalaya region, and is extensively cultivated on the California coast and in Southern Europe. It is a handsome tree, attaining a height of from sixty to ninety feet. It yields a sweet sap, somewhat like that of the sugar maple. The nut, which grows in a thin, wrinkled, two-valved shell, has a high food value, being a greater heat producer than almost any kind of meat. The unripe nuts are much used for making pickles and ketchups. The wood, called Circassian walnut, is valuable for cabinet work. It has been much used for interior finishing and for furniture, but is becoming rare. A beautiful brown dye is obtained from the bark.

WALPOLE, *wawl'pole,* HORACE, Sir, fourth Earl of Orford (1717-1797), an Englishman of letters, the son of Sir Robert Walpole. He received his education at Cambridge, and following his graduation spent several years in travel. In 1741 he entered Parliament. His first publication was *A Catalogue of Royal and Noble Authors.* It was followed in 1764 by *The Castle of Otranto,* a romance abounding in mystery, which at the time of its publication was very popular. Walpole is, however, chiefly remembered for his *Letters,* which give entertaining pictures of the society of his day.

WALPOLE, HUGH SEYMOUR (1884-1941), an English novelist, born in Auckland, New Zealand. He was educated at Cambridge University, where he wrote two novels. From 1910 on, his books met with general public favor, and he was in demand as a lecturer both in England and the United States. Walpole's novels picture his country's life and people in different periods of England's history. He wrote with vigor and with a true understanding of human character. *The Dark Forest* and *The Secret City* grew out of his experiences with the Russian Red Cross in the first World War. *The Cathedral* and *The Old Ladies* picture life in a cathedral town, somewhat in the manner of Anthony Trollope, whose biography he wrote. *Rogue Herries, Judith Paris, The Fortress, Vanessa* and *Bright Pavilions* are a series of novels forming the well-known "Herries Chronicles," which have been adapted for the stage, screen and radio. Walpole's other books include *The Young Enchanted, Portrait of a Man with Red Hair, Wintersmoon, Hans Frost, The Roman Fountain* and the *Jeremy* stories.

WALPOLE, ROBERT, Sir, first Earl of Orford (1676-1745), an English statesman. He was educated at Eton and at King's College, Cambridge, succeeded to his father's estate in 1700 and entered Parliament as member for Castle Rising. In 1702 he was elected for King's Lynn, became an active member of the Whig party and soon distinguished himself by his business capacity and by his ease in debate. As Chancellor of the Exchequer, First Lord of the Treasury and, from 1721 to 1742, head of the Cabinet, Walpole laid the foundation of England's political stability and later prosperity. His career covered parts of the reigns of the first two Georges.

THE WALRUS

WALRUS, a marine flesh-eating mammal, related to the seal, and inhabiting the colder climates. It is larger and heavier than the seal, and when full-grown will measure twelve feet in length and weigh about 2,000 pounds. When young, it is covered with thick, dull brown fur, but as it gets older this falls out, and when full-grown the walrus has practically no fur or hair on his wrinkled skin. The most characteristic feature of the walrus family is the pair of large pointed tusks (canine teeth) which project downward from the upper jaw. These tusks are of solid ivory, and are often from twenty to thirty inches in length. Walruses use them as tools and as weapons—to dig up clams and other food, to climb on ice and rocks, and to defend themselves from foes, especially from the polar bear, their chief enemy. Two species of walrus are found. The Atlantic walrus is found in the waters about Greenland and Labrador. The Pacific species occurs off the islands of the Bering Sea, but their numbers are diminishing rapidly. They are hunted for their hides and oil and for ivory, and by the natives on the Arctic coasts for food. They are either killed with the rifle or taken with harpoons.

WALTHAM, *wol'tham,* MASS., a city in Middlesex County, ten miles west of Boston, on the Charles River. It manufactures more watches than any other city in Massachusetts; its watch factories are among the largest in the world. It is well known also as a center for precision instruments and small machined parts, and is one of the largest salesbook manufacturing centers in New England. Middlesex University is located here. Waltham, originally a part of Watertown, became a separate town in 1738 and a city in 1884. Population, 1940, 40,020.

WALTON, *wawl'ton,* IZAAK (1593–1683), the author of the famous *Compleat Angler,* a treatise on fishing. For a number of years he was in business in London, as a linen draper according to some accounts; as an ironmonger according to others. He retired at the age of fifty and devoted his remaining forty years to a life of cultured ease and pleasure. His first edition of *The Compleat Angler* appeared in 1653. It is to his exquisite delineations of rural scenery, the ease and unaffected humor of his dialogue and the delightful simplicity of his style that *The Compleat Angler* owes its charm.

WALTZ, *wawlts,* a dance of Bohemian origin, executed with a rapid whirling motion, the gentleman having his arm round his partner's waist. The music is written in triple time and consists of phrases of eight or sixteen bars. Several of these phrases are now usually united, to prevent monotony. Johann Strauss and his son of the same name are the most noted composers of waltzes. The *valse à deux temps* is a form of waltz in which two steps are made to each bar of three beats. *Classical waltzes* are musical compositions in waltz form, not intended for dance tunes. Of this style the composer Chopin is the greatest master.

WAMPANOAG, *wom pa no'ag,* a tribe of Algonquian Indians who once occupied the lands east of Narragansett Bay, as far north as Massachusetts. Their number was reduced from 30,000 to barely 1,000 by a fearful epidemic, and a subsequent war with the whites resulted in their complete destruction. Massasoit and his son Philip were famous men of the tribe. See MASSASOIT; KING PHILIP.

WAMPUM, *wom'pum,* white and purple shell beads used for ornament and circulated in colonial days as money among Indian tribes east of the Mississippi. Because of the fixed value given to wampum strings, they came to be accepted by the New England colonists in exchange for their own coins. In some localities six wampum beads

equaled a penny. It was the custom of the Indians to weave wampum beads into belts, in such a manner that the figures formed permanent records. Few transactions of any sort were considered complete without the passing of the belts, and wampum records were invariably used in the ratification of treaties. Many wampum belts of historic importance are preserved in the state archives at Albany, New York.

WANAMAKER, *wahn'a ma kur,* JOHN (1838–1922), an American merchant, capitalist and philanthropist. He was born in Philadelphia, Pa., and there received a common school education and began his business career as errand boy in a book store; later he was a salesman, and in 1861 he established a clothing house, which he enlarged into a general department store in 1876. In 1896 he opened a branch in New York City.

He helped to organize the Christian Commission, which assisted the soldiers during the Civil War; was chairman of several relief committees, and was prominent in the management of the Centennial Exposition. Wanamaker was appointed Postmaster-General in 1889 and performed his duties with energy and administrative ability. He also took great interest in religious work and actively supported the Young Men's Christian Association. As one of the founders of the Presbyterian Hospital and Bethany Dispensary, as originator and president of the first Penny Savings Bank and as a donor to numerous charities he was one of the most influential men of his time.

WANDERING JEW. A legend, well known in almost all parts of the Christian world, says that while Christ was on his way to Calvary, bearing his cross, he was mocked by a Jew, who told him not to rest, but to hurry on with his burden. In reply, Christ said, "I go, but thou shalt tarry till I come." In consequence, the man has continued since to wander about the earth. He passes through his lifetime like any ordinary man, till he reaches one hundred years, and then he suffers a terrible sickness, after which he comes forth again young. This legend has been the subject of many literary works in prose, poetry and the drama. The most notable novel is *The Wandering Jew* by Eugene Sue.

WANDERING JEW, a creeping plant with glossy leaves having a silvery sheen and often a purplish cast. It grows in almost any soil, and even in water; and the persistency with which it lives and its manner of growth are responsible for the name. The plant grows and spreads rapidly and is used to advantage in hanging baskets and along the sides of window boxes. In the warmer of the temperate climates the plants live out of doors and often attain a length of several yards.

WAP'ITI. See ELK.

WAR, a contest between nations or states (international war), or between parties in the same state (civil war), carried on by force of arms. The causes of war are many. It may arise from disputes about territorial possessions and frontiers, unjust dealings with the subjects of one state by another, economic competition and oppression, questions of race, jealousy of military prestige or mere lust of conquest. Nearly all civil wars are due to the claims of rival contenders for supreme power in the state, or to attempts to establish some important point connected with civil, religious or political liberty. In all cases the aim of each contending party is to overthrow or weaken the enemy by the defeat or dispersion of his army or navy, by the occupation of important parts of his country, or by the ruin of his commerce, thus cutting off his resources of recuperation. In practically every instance, propaganda, much of it patently false, encourages the sentiment for war.

When war is carried into the territory of a hitherto friendly power, it is called an *aggressive,* or *offensive*, war; and when carried on to resist such aggression, it is called *defensive*. Previous to the outbreak of hostilities between states, the power taking the initiatory step may issue a *declaration of war,* which often takes the form of an explanatory manifesto, addressed to neutral governments (see WAR, DECLARATION OF).

During the progress of the struggle, certain laws, usages or rights of war have come to be generally recognized; such laws permit the destruction or capture of armed enemies, the destruction of property likely to be serviceable to them, the stoppage of their channels of traffic and the appropriation of everything in an enemy's country necessary for the support and subsistence of the invading army. On the other hand, though an enemy may be starved into surrender, wounding, except in battle, mutilation and all cruel and wanton devastation are contrary to the rules

of war, as also are bombarding an unprotected town, the use of poison and the employment of torture to extort information from an enemy. Works of art and the industries of peace should be exempt from destruction. The World War, however, showed that in actual conflict these rules may be disregarded. In that war, poison gas was first used by the Germans; the airplane and tank were introduced into modern warfare and the submarine for the first time became a significant tool of destruction in wartime. The war that began in Europe in 1939 was to an unprecedented degree a war against civilians. The use of powerful mechanized units and aerial bombing brought vast destruction to civilian life and property in the countries that were attacked.

When two warring nations must communicate, they customarily request the services of the embassies of some neutral powers, who make the preliminary arrangements before the belligerents themselves meet; in the Russo-Japanese War, for example, negotiations were carried on by the United States government. When the belligerents wish to meet to discuss peace terms or for any other reason, an *armistice* or *truce* is declared, during which hostilities cease.

If one nation completely conquers another, the war ceases, although many matters must subsequently be settled by a *treaty* or by *grant*. The World War peace treaty in 1919 was one of many notable agreements following the wars waged since civilization began. Treaties on the whole are based on the assumption that there will always be other wars, but some of their provisions usually recognize that war might be prevented.

Related Articles. Consult the following titles for additional information:

Airplane	Navy
Army	Neutrality
International Law	Tank

WAR, DECLARATION OF, a formal announcement by one nation of its intention to begin hostilities against another, or a statement recognizing the existence of a state of war between the two nations. With the modern facilities for rapid communication, actual warfare may be preceded by negotiations of longer or shorter duration. A common procedure is for one nation to send an ultimatum to the other, setting a definite time for a reply. On Sept. 3, 1939, for example, Great Britain sent an ultimatum to Germany, demanding the withdrawal of German troops from Poland within two hours; this it followed with a declaration of war when Germany failed to reply. It sometimes happens that hostilities begin without a formal declaration. What developed into a war between Japan and China began with Japan's unannounced invasion of North China in 1937. The United States, however, declared war against Japan when she attacked Pearl Harbor without warning on Dec. 7, 1941. In World War II Hitler did not declare war against the country attacked until December, 1941, when he declared war against the United States. See WAR.

WAR, DEPARTMENT OF, that one of the executive departments of a government which has to do primarily with military affairs. The chief of the department in the United States is the Secretary of War, who is a member of the President's Cabinet. He carries out the orders of the President, who is commander in chief of the army. The War Department consists of a number of different bureaus, over the chiefs of which the Secretary has general control. The affairs of the War Department, however, are not confined wholly to the national defense. It has authority over such nonmilitary functions as river and harbor development, river-flood control, the approval of bridge and pier plans and the maintenance and operation of the Panama Canal. The department also supervises the United States Military Academy and the Army General Service Schools. The War Department General Staff is headed by the Chief of Staff, who is charged with the planning, development and execution of the army program. The department was created by Congress in 1789. See ARMY.

WAR′BLERS, a family of tiny, insect-eating birds, found throughout the western continent, about seventy species of which reach the United States. Their migration northward is made with great regularity, and in May and early June they are commonly observed everywhere in the Northern states. In nesting, however, most species seek the deep woods, some penetrating as far northward as the Hudson Bay and Yukon regions. Nearly all spend the winter in the tropics.

Some of the better known species of warblers are the *yellow warbler,* or *summer yellow bird,* which remains about Northern homes and parks throughout the summer; the *black and white warbler,* which creeps about the branches of trees in early spring;

the *myrtle warbler,* marked with four yellow patches on head, rump and wing; the *black-throated green* and the *black-throated blue warblers,* the *chat,* the *American redstart* and the *oven bird.* Some warblers have fine singing voices, but the greater number have only weak, lisping notes. Their nests are usually cup-shaped, woven of twigs and grasses and placed in trees or bushes. The eggs are from three to five in number.

WARD, a minor who has been placed under a guardian appointed by the courts and who becomes legally responsible for the protection of his rights. The child must obey his guardian; he may not marry without his consent and may not bring suit against him, though in cases of unjust treatment he may file a complaint with the court. In most cases wardship ceases with marriage and always when the ward becomes of legal age. See GUARDIAN.

WARD. See MUNICIPAL GOVERNMENT.

WARD, ARTEMUS. See BROWNE, CHARLES FARRAR.

WARD, ELIZABETH STUART PHELPS (1844–1911), an American author and philanthropist, born at Andover, Mass. Besides lecturing and engaging in work for the advancement of women and for social reforms, she also wrote a number of stories, including *The Gates Ajar* (1868), which passed through twenty editions in the year of its publication, *Beyond the Gates, The Gates Between, Hedged In, The Silent Partner, The Story of Avis, A Singular Life* and, in conjunction with her husband, the Rev. Herbert D. Ward, *Come Forth* and *The Master of the Magicians.*

WARD, HENRY BALDWIN (1865–   ), an American zoölogist, born in Troy, N. Y., and educated at Williams College, Harvard and German universities. He was a member of the faculties of Michigan and Nebraska state universities before accepting the chair of zoölogy at the University of Illinois, in 1909. In 1933 he became professor emeritus. He is an authority on animal parasites.

WARD, MRS. HUMPHRY (1851–1920), one of the foremost woman novelists of twentieth-century England. She was born in Tasmania and was reared and educated in England. In 1872 she married Thomas Humphry Ward, a journalist. Matthew Arnold was her uncle. In 1888 she published *Robert Elsmere,* a novel which became immensely popular and which won the favorable notice of critics. Then followed *The History of David Grieve, Marcella, The Story of Bessie Costrell, Sir George Tressady, Helbeck of Bannisdale, Eleanor, Lady Rose's Daughter The Marriage of William Ashe, The Case of Richard Meynell, Eltham House, Missing, Elizabeth's Campaign* and *Helena* (1920). The principal criticism passed on Mrs. Ward's novels, especially on her earlier ones, is that the purpose is made too prominent and that in all there is too great similarity of leading characters. But her characters are clearly drawn, her literary execution is excellent and her topics are always vital and timely.

WARD, John Quincy Adams (1830–1910), one of the foremost American sculptors of his day, was born at Urbana, Ohio. Before the Civil War he established himself in New York, and became known for his portrait busts of notable people. His statuette *The Freedman,* made in 1865, was so popular that thousands of copies were sold; his *Indian Hunter,* which also makes a strong popular appeal, was the first piece of statuary erected in Central Park, New York City. *The Good Samaritan,* a group commemorating the discovery of the efficacy of ether as an anaesthetic, is in Boston. Ward's bronze bust of Shakespeare, a seated figure of Horace Greeley and statues of George Washington and Thomas Jefferson are among his finest portrait statuary. Ward was identified with the leading art organizations of his time and labored unremittingly to elevate national ideals in the field of art endeavor.

WARFIELD, David (1866–   ), an American actor who has achieved the highest success in several character portrayals. He was born at San Francisco and in that city began his stage career at a local theater at the age of twenty-two. He went to New York in 1890; in the ten years following he was connected with the Casino Theater and with Weber and Fields' Music Hall. Later attracting the attention of David Belasco, Warfield was starred in *The Auctioneer,* one of his greatest successes. He was equally successful in *The Music Master,* and this placed him in the front rank of American actors. His later performances have been in the leading rôle of *The Return of Peter Grimm* and as "Van der Decken" in the play of the same name, based on the legend of *The Flying Dutchman.* Warfield's impersonation of an eccentric but kindly old

gentleman, pathetic and courageous in misfortune, has never been excelled by any American actor.

WARNER, Charles Dudley (1829–1900), an American editor and critic, born at Plainfield, Mass. He received his degree at Hamilton College in 1852, was admitted to the bar and for a time practiced law in Chicago. Entering journalism, he became, in 1860, editor of the Hartford *Press* and later of the *Courant.* As correspondent of American papers he made an extensive tour of Europe, and on his return, in 1884, he became one of the editors of *Harper's Magazine,* to which he contributed until his death. The first book by which he attained prominence was *My Summer in a Garden,* a volume of sketches, which was followed by *Backlog Studies, Being a Boy* and *As We Were Saying.* Among his other works are *The Gilded Age,* a drama in which he collaborated with Samuel L. Clemens, and *A Little Journey in the World,* a novel with a moral purpose. He edited the "American Men of Letters" series and *A Library of the World's Best Literature.*

WARNER, Seth (1743–1784), an American soldier, one of the leaders of the Green Mountain Boys, who opposed New York's claim to the New Hampshire grants. He was elected lieutenant-colonel of the Green Mountain Boys in 1775, and the following year was appointed colonel of the continental regiment. He received a colonel's commission for the part he took in the capture of Crown Point. He was in command at the Battle of Hubbardton and rendered efficient service in the Battle of Bennington. In 1782 he retired on account of ill health.

WAR OF 1812, the name given to the struggle between the United States and Great Britain in the years 1812–1814. The general cause of the war was the attitude of Great Britain in relation to American shipping. Its claims to the right to board and search American vessels for the purpose of impressing British citizens, found in their crews, into the British service; its decrees and orders to the detriment of American commerce; its disregard of American protests, which had been a cause for grievance to the Americans for many years, at last compelled them to attempt to secure reparation by force. The same haughty actions regarding American commerce had been taken by France, and it was long a question as to which of the two powers the United States would fight first; but the proximity of Canada, which seemed to offer an attractive field for conquest, and the old ill-feeling toward England, resulting from the Revolution, finally caused the declaration of war against Great Britain, on June 18, 1812. Five days later the British government withdrew the "Orders in Council," which had been probably the most objectionable features of the British policy, since they established a paper blockade of European ports and practically excluded American commerce from the seas.

At the outset the land forces of the United States made little headway. Great Britain, with her vastly superior resources, was prepared for war, having been at war with France for many years, while the United States government had shown a shameful lack of appreciation of the dangers attending the new republic and had allowed the navy and war departments to deteriorate almost out of existence. The first military movement was that of General Hull, who invaded Canada with two thousand men, but soon retreated before an inferior force under General Brock and surrendered at Detroit, August 16. In October of the same year, General Van Rensselaer made another invasion of Canada near Niagara Falls, and after the Battle of Queenstown, in which the British general, Brock, was mortally wounded, the Americans were again driven back with great loss. Meantime, on the sea the United States vessels had some success. The *Constitution* had captured the British frigate *Guerriere* (August 19). The *Wasp,* after a sharp battle, took the *Frolic.* The *United States* captured the *Macedonian,* and in December the *Constitution* compelled the surrender of the frigate *Java.*

Of the American navy it can be said that at the beginning of the war there were practically no war vessels owned by the government. So badly in need of a naval arm was the country that privateers (which see) were licensed. A few naval vessels were assembled; these in 1812 and 1813 gave so good an account of themselves in action that the naval history of the war was remarkable. American valor on the sea made forever memorable such names as the *Constitution* ("Old Ironsides"), the *Wasp* and others scarcely less notable.

In the spring of 1813 General Dearborn, who had been placed at the head of affairs in the Northwest, invaded Canada for the third time, with an army of 1,700 men, and captured York (Toronto). He was relieved by Generals Wilkinson and Hampton, who made an attempt to take Montreal, but without success. In May an advance of the British into New York State was repulsed at Sackett's Harbor, and in September Commodore Perry fought the famous Battle of Lake Erie, by which he captured the most important British fleet upon the Great Lakes. This victory enabled General Harrison to invade Canada. There he defeated General Proctor, in the Battle of the Thames.

In 1814 General Jacob Brown again invaded Canada, captured the British Fort Erie and defeated the force under General Riall at Chippewa. Then followed the Battle of Lundy's Lane and the withdrawal of the Americans to Fort Erie, where they were

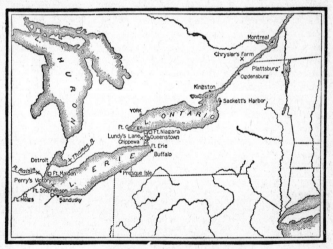

MAP OF MAIN OPERATIONS

besieged. In the following September, General Provost led 14,000 men in an invasion of New York, by way of Lake Champlain. The fleet which he had got together was defeated near Plattsburg by an American fleet under Commodore McDonough, while the land force was also repulsed. At about the same time, the British fleet ascended Chesapeake Bay, defeated the hastily summoned American militia at Bladensburg, entered Washington and sacked the government buildings, in retaliation for the sack of York at its capture.

Meanwhile, General Andrew Jackson had been fighting the Creek Indians in the extreme South and had gathered together an army of Kentucky and Tennessee frontiersmen. In January, 1815, this force was confronted by an army sent direct from England, under General Pakenham, and consisting of the veterans of Wellington's campaign against Napoleon. The result was the famous Battle of New Orleans.

On the sea the Americans continued to gain the upper hand, though the *Chesapeake* was captured by the *Shannon*, and other small American vessels were taken. Probably the most memorable event upon the sea during this period was the famous cruise of the American frigate *Essex*, which, after a long and brilliant career against British merchantmen, was compelled to surrender to the *Phoebe* and the *Cherub* in the Pacific Ocean, March 28, 1814. The very month in which the treaty of peace was signed, December, 1814, the Federalists of New England declared their opposition to the war. The Treaty of Ghent provided for the restoration of all lands captured by either side and for a commission to determine the boundary between the United States and Canada. It did not provide for the withdrawal of the British claims regarding right of search, the paper blockade and the laws of neutrality. These practices had already been discontinued by the British, on demand of their own merchants, and were never revived.

Related Articles. Consult the following titles for additional information:

Blockade	New Orleans, Battle
Brock, Sir Isaac	of
Champlain, Lake	Perry. Oliver H.
Constitution (ship)	Queenston Heights,
Continental System	Battle of
Embargo	Raisin River, Massa-
Erie, Lake, Battle of	cre of
Ghent, Treaty of	Star-Spangled Ban-
Hartford Convention	ner
Hull, William	Thames River, Bat-
Jackson, Andrew	tle of the
Lawrence, James	Tippecanoe, Battle of
Lundy's Lane, Battle	United States (his-
of	tory)

WARRANT, a writ issued by any qualified court officer directing a constable or sheriff to arrest the person named therein and bring him before the official issuing the warrant. A warrant is usually issued upon the oath of a complaining witness as to the guilt of the person concerned. Ar-

rests without a warrant are illegal, except in time of public danger, or when an overt act is witnessed by a peace officer.

WARREN, JOSEPH (1741-1775), an American patriot, born at Roxbury, Mass. He was graduated from Harvard College and became a physician at Boston and a leading figure in Massachusetts political movements, contributing with voice and pen to the cause of patriotism. He drew up the "Suffolk resolves," the most radical expression of the American position with respect to British oppression, and in the following year, 1775, was elected president of the provincial congress of Massachusetts. Although the rank of major-general of Massachusetts forces had been conferred on him, and he was offered chief command at Bunker Hill, he took his place as a volunteer and was killed in the fight of June 17. A monument in his memory, erected in 1794 on the spot where he fell, was later replaced by the Bunker Hill Monument. See BUNKER HILL.

WARREN, OHIO, the county seat of Trumbull County, fifty-two miles southeast of Cleveland, on the Erie, the Baltimore & Ohio and the Pennsylvania railroads. It is said to be the second city in the United States in the manufacture of electric lamps. Steel and other metal products, vitreous enamel products and rubber specialties are also important manufactures. John Packard was born in Warren, and the first Packard motor car was manufactured here. Warren was settled in 1799, and was incorporated as a town in 1834 and as a city in 1869. Population, 1940, 42,837.

WARREN, PA., the county seat of Warren County, sixty-six miles southeast of Erie, on the Allegheny River and on the Pennsylvania and the New York Central railroads. Warren is situated in a fertile region with abundant resources of wood, oil and natural gas, and receives water power from the Niagara Falls. The leading manufactures are furniture, iron and steel products and refined oil. Warren was laid out in 1795, and was incorporated as a borough in 1832. Population, 1940, 14,891.

WAR′SAW, a city of Central Europe, situated on the Vistula River, about 700 miles southwest of Moscow and 320 miles east of Berlin. Capital of the old kingdom of Poland and of the Polish Republic, Warsaw belonged to Russia at the beginning of the World War. It was occupied by the Germans in 1915 and restored to the Poles in 1918. As the capital and largest city of the reconstructed Polish nation, Warsaw enjoyed an era of political importance and industrial growth until the invasion of Poland by the Germans, in September, 1939. It withstood a siege of three weeks, during which it was partially destroyed. In the division of Poland between Germany and Russia, Warsaw was made a part of Greater Germany.

With its landmarks of the Middle Ages and its modern boulevards, parks and gardens, Warsaw became an attractive and interesting city. Notable structures associated with its historic past include the castle of the old Polish kings, the thirteenth-century Cathedral of Saint Johns and the fifteenth-century Church of the Holy Virgin. The University of Warsaw, founded in 1817, had an attendance of over 8,300 in 1938. Warsaw's musical conservatory, theaters, museum of fine arts, agricultural institute and radium institute and hospital contributed to the city's reputation as a center of culture. In the bombardment of 1939, the Warsaw Opera House, National Theater and Polytechnical School were demolished.

The city was built on a hill sloping toward the river, being connected with its suburb, Praga, by an iron bridge. In normal times it is a thriving industrial and trading center. The population in 1938 was about 1,265,700.

WARSHIP. See Navy; Submarine; Torpedo Boat.

WART, an excrescence of the skin caused by hardening of the papillae. Warts are usually the result of some form of irritation, and appear most commonly on the hands of children. They may disappear after a time, or may persist through life. There have been many superstitious beliefs as to methods of removing warts, but the only reliable way is that of having them cauterized by a physician, or treated with lactic acid or a similar chemical. Senile warts result from a breaking down of the skin, favored by irritation or lack of cleanliness, and are usually found on the back, neck and arms.

WART HOG, a wild pig, native to Africa. It stands about three feet high, having rather long legs. The face is rendered extremely hideous by large tusks and wart-like protuberances under the eyes and at each side of the huge snout. The coarse hair, short on the rest of the body, is long on the back and hangs in a mane on the neck. These hogs roam in small groups in search of food, and are destructive to crops. There are two principal species, one in Abyssinia and Somaliland, and the other in South Africa.

WARWICK, Richard Neville, Earl of, called the "king-maker" (1428–1471), an English soldier and statesman. He was the son of the Earl of Salisbury and became Earl of Warwick after marrying the heiress of the Warwick titles and estates. Taking the Yorkist side in the Wars of the Roses, he was the main instrument in placing Edward IV on the throne in 1461, in place of Henry VI, and he became the most powerful nobleman in the kingdom. He quarreled with Edward, however, on account of the latter's marriage, went over to Henry's side and was able to place him again on the throne, but was defeated and slain at the Battle of Barnet.

WASATCH, waw'satch, **MOUNTAINS,** a range belonging to the Rocky Mountain system. It extends from Southeastern Idaho to Southwestern Utah, forming the eastern boundary of the Great Basin in which lies the Great Salt Lake. The mountains rise abruptly from the plain and reach an average height of 10,000 feet. The highest peak, Mount Belknap, reaches 12,000 feet above sea level. The peaks, covered with perpetual snow, are the source of numerous streams, and the region is broken by canyons.

WASHBURN COLLEGE, a liberal arts college, with schools of law and music, founded in 1865 at Topeka, Kan., by the Kansas Congregational Conference. It is now a nonsectarian institution. The enrollment is about 1,100 and the faculty numbers 65. The library contains 40,000 volumes.

WASHING MACHINE, a mechanism of varied types and sizes for washing clothes, fabrics, etc., in the home and public laundries. The clothes are placed in a waterproof metal cylinder and agitated by an inner device containing cleansing solutions. The direction of rotation is reversed automatically every few revolutions, thus displacing dirt by forcing soap and water through the clothes. Most machines are electrically equipped. Many have roller attachments for wringing and mangling. All have safety features, the moving parts being covered to avoid accidental catching of clothes. Another feature is an automatic timer to turn off current when washing has continued the desired time.

Capitol Building

WASHINGTON, a state of the American Union, in the extreme northwestern part of the country, south of the international boundary and on the Pacific coast. Its popular name, THE EVERGREEN STATE, refers to its wealth of fir forests. About seventy per cent of the surface is forest-covered, and in the annual production of lumber Washington is the leading state in the Union. The rhododendron is its flower emblem.

Location and Area. The state is bounded on the north by the Canadian province of British Columbia, the forty-ninth parallel forming the line between the two divisions. Extending into the northwestern part of the state is the irregular, much-branching inlet, Puget Sound, which is connected with the open ocean by the straits of Juan de Fuca and Georgia. Between these straits lies the island of Vancouver, which is wholly Canadian territory, though it extends south of the international boundary. Washington touches the northern extension of Idaho on the east, and along most of its southern border it is separated from Oregon by the Columbia River.

With an area of 68,192 square miles, of which 1,215 square miles are water, the state is the nineteenth in size in the Union. It is more than two-thirds the size of Oregon, its neighbor to the south, and over twice the size of Maine, which is the largest state in the New England group.

People and Cities. In 1940 Washington ranked thirtieth in population, with 1,736,191 inhabitants, and thirty-fourth in density of population, with an average of 29.9 persons to the square mile. The census classified 53.1 per cent of the population as urban.

Of the foreign-born groups, who number in all about 244,000, the most prominent numerically are Canadians, Swedes, Germans, English and Irish. The state has twelve Indian reservations, with a total population of about 11,000. There are also large numbers of Japanese, Chinese and Negroes. Negroes numbered 6,840; Japanese, 17,800, and Chinese, 2,200, in 1930.

The largest religious bodies are the Roman Catholic, Methodist, Presbyterian, Lutheran, Baptist, Disciples and Congregationalist denominations.

According to the Federal census of 1940, Washington had fourteen cities with populations of 10,000 or over. There are three large cities—Seattle (368,302), Spokane (122,001) and Tacoma (109,408). Other important cities are Everett, Bellingham, Yakima, Walla Walla and Olympia, the capital.

Surface and Drainage. The Cascade Mountains cross the state from north to south about 120 miles east of the coast, and divide it into two unequal parts, Eastern Washington and Western Washington. These mountains form the chief physiographic feature of the state and have a mean elevation of about 8,000 feet. Their eastern slope rises gradually from the interior plateau, but the western slope is steep and broken. The range contains a number of lofty peaks whose summits are covered with perpetual snow. The most noted among these are Mount Rainier, 14,408 feet, now enclosed in a national park, Mount Adams, 12,307 feet, Mount Baker, 10,730 feet and Mount Saint Helens, 9,671 feet. Eastern Washington, which includes nearly two-thirds of the state, contains the Columbia River Basin, which is by far the largest natural division of surface within the state. Within this basin are the great irrigated and grain-growing districts and a number of fertile valleys famous for fruit products. In the southeastern part the Blue Mountains rise to an altitude of about 6,000 feet.

Western Washington is naturally divided into three physiographic regions—the Puget Sound Basin, including the territory between the Olympic and Cascade mountains, and surrounding the great inland sea, Puget Sound; the Olympic Peninsula, including that portion of the state containing the Olympic Mountains and the region extending from them to the Pacific, and the southwestern division, which occupies the region fronting on the Columbia River and Pacific Ocean and extending northward until meets the Olympic Peninsula. The Olympic

Mountains are the northern extension of the Coast Range.

The eastern section of the state, or Eastern Washington, is drained entirely by the Columbia River and its tributaries. This river enters the state near the northeastern corner and flows south by west then westward in an irregular course, then southward and southeastward until it reaches the southern boundary, when it makes a sharp turn to the west and pursues its course to the Pacific. These changes in direction form what is known as the Great Bend in the Columbia River, and this is for a part of the way the western boundary of the plateau. The chief tributaries of the Columbia are Clark Fork, from Idaho; the Snake, which flows through the southeastern corner of the state; the Spokane, the Okanogan, the Methow, the Wenatchee and the Yakima. Western Washington is drained into Puget Sound and the Pacific. In this section all of the rivers are short and comparatively unimportant, the most important being the Cowlitz, flowing southward into the Columbia, the Chehalis, flowing directly into the Pacific, and the Skagit, which enters Puget Sound. The state contains a number of mountain lakes, the largest being Lake Chelan.

Climate. The Cascade Mountains divide the state into two climatic regions. Eastern Washington is characterized by hot summers, cold though not severe winters and light rainfalls, the annual average being about sixteen inches. In many sections irrigation is necessary to successful agriculture. Except upon the high altitudes there are many hot days during the summer. During the winter there are heavy falls of snow, which are welcomed by the farmers, because as the snow on the lowlands melts, it is absorbed by the soil, and that upon the mountains during the summer feeds the streams which supply water for irrigation. The climate of Western Washington is mild and moist. The prevailing westerlies, blowing moisture-laden from the sea, strike the cool slopes of the mountains and have their moisture condensed. West of the Cascades the annual rainfall varies from twenty to 132 inches. The winters are mild and the summers are free from extreme heat.

Mineral Resources. There are extensive deposits of coal in the Puget Sound Basin, notably in King, Pierce, Lewis, Whatcom and Thurston counties, also in Kittitas county, east of the Cascade Range. About 1,625,000

tons of coal are mined annually. Both bituminous and lignite varieties are found. The coal deposits of Washington are the only ones of any great extent on the Pacific coast.

Veins of ore producing gold, silver, copper, lead, quicksilver and a number of rare metals occur throughout the mountainous regions. Gold and silver are mined in Whatcom, Skagit, Snohomish, King, Pierce, Lewis, Skamania, Cowlitz, Okanogan, Chelan, Kittitas, Yakima, Klickitat, Ferry and Stevens counties. Iron ore, and marble, granite, onyx, serpentine, limestone and sandstone occur in large quantities. Beds of fire clay, kaolin, talc and asbestos are among the valuable resources of the state. The value of the total annual output is about $12,000,000.

Fisheries. The waters of Puget Sound, the Columbia River and the indentations along the Pacific coast abound in excellent food-fish, and in the lakes and streams are found large quantities of fresh-water fish. The most important branch of the fisheries is catching and curing salmon (see SALMON). Second in point of value are the halibut fisheries. Large quantities of oysters, shrimps, clams and cod are also taken. In value of products of the fisheries Washington ranks fourth among the states.

Agriculture. Washington has a wide variety of soils. On the uplands of Eastern Washington wheat and other cereals are raised in large quantities. In the diked lands along Puget Sound oats are raised, and in the southeastern part barley constitutes the important crop. Rye, buckwheat and flax are also grown, and in some counties hops are a staple product. Many large irrigated areas east of the mountains are devoted to alfalfa; the state produces nearly 2,000,000 tons of hay annually. Potatoes, beets and other vegetables thrive and yield large returns.

Washington is one of the most important fruit-growing states of the Union. In the valleys of Eastern Washington there are thousands of orchards. This region is especially valuable for the raising of apples, pears, peaches, plums and cherries. In the western part of the state small fruits are raised in large quantities, and grapes are grown upon both sides of the mountains.

The mild winters and excellent pasturage make the raising of live stock profitable, and large numbers of cattle, horses, sheep and hogs are found. For all of these there is a ready market. Dairying is also profitable and can be practiced under ideal conditions.

Manufactures. Washington has abundant water power and a vast forest area. Because of these conditions, lumbering and its allied industries—the manufacture of doors, sash, shingles and furniture—constitute the leading manufacturing industry. Lumber mills are very generally distributed through the forest regions, but the most extensive establishments are found on the shores of Puget Sound, near the large forests of Western Washington.

The products of the flour and grist-mills are second in value, the most important commodity of the industry being white flour. Slaughtering and meat packing, the canning and curing of fish, printing and publishing and railroad-shop construction and repair are all prosperous lines of activity. Seattle, Tacoma and other ports are centers of shipbuilding. Seattle is the chief manufacturing city of the state, with Tacoma, Spokane, Everett, Bellingham, Aberdeen, Walla Walla and Yakima following.

The mineral resources have given rise to various other industries. In the Puget Sound Basin large quantities of lime are produced. Granite is quarried in Snohomish and Spokane counties. In other localities valuable sandstone occurs, and onyx of great variety and beauty is quarried in Stevens County. In King County are factories for the manufacture of brick, tile, terra cotta, stoneware and sewer pipe. The total value of all manufacturing output is over $400,000,000.

Transportation. Puget Sound and the Pacific Ocean have a Washington coast line exceeding 2,000 miles in extent. The largest ocean ships can sail on the Sound as far as Seattle and Tacoma, which are the chief harbors of the state. Three transcontinental lines of railway cross the state from east to west. Railway lines extend north and south from the great centers of trade on Puget Sound, and connect all important cities and towns in the state and maintain junction points for cities in British Columbia. The most important roads are the Northern Pacific, the Oregon & Washington, the Great Northern, the Chicago, Milwaukee, Saint Paul & Pacific, the Pacific Coast Railroad, the Union Pacific and the Southern Pacific. The total mileage of the state is about 5,500. There are 18 airports and three major air routes. Five bus companies operate on seven principal routes running both east and west and north and south. There are 900 miles of electric railway and 16,870 miles of surfaced roads.

Government. The legislature consists of a house of representatives, that cannot exceed ninety-nine members or be less than sixty-three, and a senate, whose number cannot exceed one-half, or be less than one-third of the number of representatives. The representatives are elected for two years, and the senators are elected for four years. The legislature meets biennially, and the regular sessions are limited to sixty days. The executive department consists of a governor, a lieutenant-governor, a secretary of state, a treasurer, an auditor, an attorney-general, a superintendent of public instruction, a comisioner of public lands, and an insurance commissioner, elected for four years. The courts consist of a supreme court of nine judges, elected for six years, and a superior court in each county, presided over by a judge elected for four years.

Education. The public schools are under the direction of the superintendent of public instruction and a board of education. The schools are organized on the district plan, and each district must maintain a school for at least five months in the year. Education is compulsory between the ages of eight and fifteen. The school fund is derived from state and local taxes and from income from the permanent fund derived from the sale and lease of school lands. The yearly cost of the public schools is about $33,000,000. The white population of Washington shows the lowest percentage of illiteracy of any state in the Union. The state university is at Seattle and teachers colleges are maintained at Bellingham, Cheney and Ellensburg. The state agricultural college is at Pullman. Other colleges are located as follows: at Spokane, Gozanga University, Whitworth College and Spokane University; the College of Puget Sound at Tacoma; Walla Walla College at College Place; Whitman College at Walla Walla; Seattle Pacific College at Seattle.

Other Institutions. The schools for the deaf and the blind are at Vancouver. The hospitals for the insane are at Fort Steilacoom, Sedro Woolley and Medical Lake, and there is a soldiers' home at Orting and a veterans' home at Port Orchard. The penal institutions consist of the penitentiary at Walla Walla and the reformatory at Monroe. The state training school is located at Chehalis

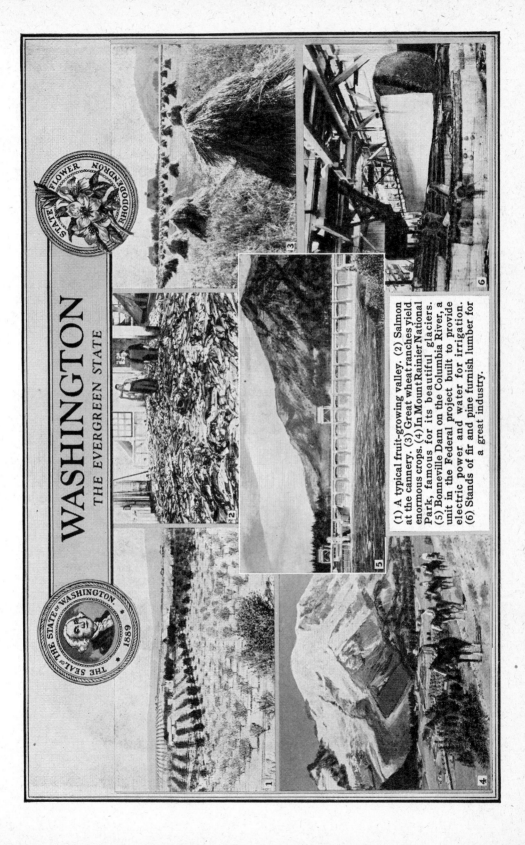

WASHINGTON
THE EVERGREEN STATE

(1) A typical fruit-growing valley. (2) Salmon at the cannery. (3) Great wheat ranches yield enormous crops. (4) In Mount Rainier National Park, famous for its beautiful glaciers. (5) Bonneville Dam on the Columbia River, a unit in the Federal project built to provide electric power and water for irrigation. (6) Stands of fir and pine furnish lumber for a great industry.

STATE FLOWER RHODODENDRON

THE SEAL OF THE STATE OF WASHINGTON. 1889

Items of Interest on Washington

The assessed valuation of taxable property is over a billion and a quarter dollars.

The lumber resources of the state will probably last for one hundred years.

The northern boundary of the state was fixed by treaty in 1846. "Fifty-four forty or fight" was a popular slogan in the presidential campaign of 1844, and represented the demands of citizens respecting this boundary.

Girls and boys between fifteen and sixteen who are unemployed are compelled to attend school.

Suffrage was granted to women in 1910.

Nearly 20 per cent of the potential hydro-electric power of the nation is credited to Washington.

The slopes of the Olympic Mountains have deep gorges and dense forests of fir, and are almost inaccessible.

The foreign-born make up 15.6 per cent of the population.

In a survey of the states made by the chief statistician of the Federal Office of Education, Washington stood first when measured by a ten-point scale.

Questions on Washington

Where are the Cascade Mountains?

Of what is the Columbia Plateau composed?

What is the principal drainage system in the state and which are the important tributaries?

How many acres in the national forest reserves?

How do the fisheries rank among the states of the Union?

What is the value of the annual output of minerals?

What are the leading crops?

What is the principal manufacturing industry?

How does the value of its products compare with that of other states?

Name four other important industries.

What will be the most startling sights when you visit Washington?

How does the state rank in matters of education?

History. For early history, see OREGON, subhead *History*. The territory of Washington was separated from Oregon in 1853, and soon afterward the discovery of gold led to an influx of settlers, which in turn induced the Indians to plan a massacre, known as the Washington-Oregon War, in 1855. Indian troubles continued to appear from time to time, but the constant increase of white population finally led to the acceptance of reservations by the Indians. After the Civil War, there were violent anti-Chinese agitations, which for a time retarded this territory's growth. Numerous attempts were made to secure statehood, and in 1889 the Omnibus Statehood Bill, admitting the two Dakotas, Montana and Washington, was signed by the President, and Washington became a state. The growth in the population and wealth of Washington since its admission has been uninterrupted. The Alaska-Yukon Exposition of 1909 at Seattle admirably celebrated the growth of the state. In 1922 the private sale of drugs for narcotic purposes was by law declared a felony. In 1932 the Wenatchee hydroelectric dam across the Columbia River was completed.

Related Articles. Consult the following titles for additional information:

CITIES

Aberdeen	Olympia	Vancouver
Bellingham	Seattle	Walla Walla
Everett	Spokane	Yakima
Hoquiam	Tacoma	

MOUNTAINS AND RIVERS

Cascade Range	Ranier, Mount
Coast Range	Snake River
Columbia River	

THE FIRST WHITE HOUSE

WASHINGTON, the capital of the United States of America, named for the first President of the republic and located on a site chosen by him. It lies on the Potomac River, 156 miles from Chesapeake Bay and 185 miles from the Atlantic. Washington is co-extensive with the District of Columbia, which covers an area of about seventy square miles. The southwestern border is formed by the Potomac, into which Rock Creek flows. The

Ewing Galloway

CENTERS OF ACTIVITY IN THE NATION'S CAPITAL

A new part of the City of Washington. Left to right, buildings for Department of Commerce; Department of Labor, and Interstate Commerce, with Postoffice Department at rear; Internal Revenue; Department of Justice; Archives Building. Below, the Capitol, from the air.

WHITE HOUSE, WASHINGTON

Showing western extension, containing President's business offices. A like extension has been added to the east side of the original building.

Anacostia River cuts through the city a mile and a half from the southeastern boundary and flows into the Potomac at the southernmost point of the city.

By the Federal census of 1940, Washington had a population of 663,091, ranking eleventh in size among American cities.

Plan of the City. Washington was laid out according to suggestions made by President Washington, who employed Pierre Charles L'Enfant, a French civil engineer, to prepare the plans for the proposed city. It is said that L'Enfant rode over the ground with the President and commissioners and grew enthusiastic over the location, deeming it a fit site for the capital of a "mighty empire." Jefferson furnished L'Enfant with plans of the great cities of Europe, but the French engineer, faithful to the inspiration he had received from Versailles, determined to have broad avenues, vistas, streets and parkings, which make Washington truly the "City of Magnificent Distances." The Capitol was located on a hill, which was then a thick wood; the lines of latitude and longitude which marked its center were carefully surveyed, and the streets and avenues were laid from this point with mathematical exactness. It was manifestly the intention that the chief front of the Capitol should be toward the east, and that the public buildings should be placed about that side; but many forces contributed to change this idea, and now the west front, with its great terraces topping the hill and with its magnificent stairways extending far down the side, is worthy to be called the main entrance.

From the middle of the four sides of the site of the Capitol extend four great streets, which separate the city into quarters, known as North West, North East, South West and South East. These four streets are known as North and South Capitol, East Capitol and the Mall. The last is a beautiful parked area, which takes the place of a West Capitol street. The streets running parallel to East Capitol and the Mall are named, both north and south, for the letters of the alphabet. The streets parallel to North and South Capitol are numbered consecutively east and west. Broad avenues, named for the states, traverse the city from northwest to southeast and from northeast to southwest. All of this will be clearly understood if the reader will study the accompanying map. In locating any place it is necessary, of course, to mention the quarter of the city. When this is done, the location is very definite; for instance, 1850 F Street N. W., would be known to lie between Eighteenth and Nineteenth streets on F Street, in the northwestern part of the city. In the addressing of mail to the North West section, it is customary to omit the letters N. W., but those for the other three sections should always be written.

The North West quarter of the city contains most of the business houses, the finest residence section and most of the government buildings. Pennsylvania Avenue extends northwest from the Capitol for about a mile to the Treasury building; there it bends sharply to the north and again to the west, here passing in front of the Executive Mansion and the State, War and Navy building; beyond that it turns again to the northwest. F, G, Seventh and Ninth streets North West are among the important business streets.

Washington is connected with all of the states by the Baltimore & Ohio, the Pennsylvania, the Chesapeake & Ohio, the Southern and other railroads. All trains enter the magnificent Union Station north of the Capitol. Seven principal bus and two air lines serve the city. The Washington-Hoover is a private airport; Boling Field belongs to the army; the navy maintains the Naval Air Station. Electric railways and motor buses afford easy transportation throughout the city and to Mount Vernon, Arlington and other points of interest.

Parks and Boulevards. The park surrounding the Capitol occupies sixteen city blocks, crowning a hill 58 feet high, overlooking the west half of the city. It is laid out with drives and walks, bordered by magnificent trees and beautiful shrubbery, interspersed with beds, in which blossom the flowers of the season. The small ornamental buildings, fountains and statuary lend a peculiar charm to the whole park.

From the west front of the Capitol a person looks down upon the broad Mall, which extends about a mile to the imposing Washington Monument, and then on to the Lincoln Memorial. In the Mall trees, shrubs and plants beautify the walks and drives. Along the north side of the Mall are grouped the great series of Federal buildings in the "triangle" area bounded by Pennsylvania and Constitution avenues on the north and south and by Fifteenth Street on the west. Running north from the west end of the Mall are the

Executive grounds, a magnificent tract which, with the private gardens of the White House, cover about twenty city squares. North of the White House and across Pennsylvania Avenue is Lafayette Square, another fine park adorned with fine statuary.

The intersections of the avenues and streets throughout the city form squares and circles

city filtration plant. In the spring, when the foliage is fresh and the flowers in the parks are in full bloom no more beautiful city is to be found.

A survey of the statues and memorials distributed over the city is both an extensive and a very instructive undertaking. Special mention should be made of the statues of George

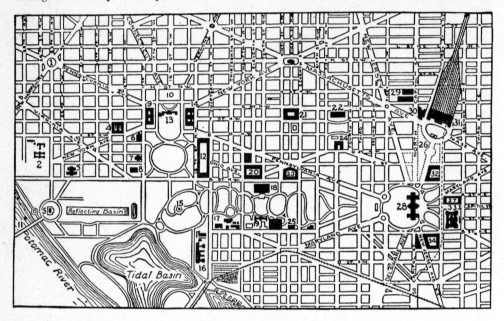

MAP AND KEY OF WASHINGTON, D. C.

1. Washington Circle.
2. U. S. Naval Hospital.
3. National Academy of Sciences.
4. Interior Department.
5. Lincoln Memorial.
6. Corcoran Art Gallery.
7. Continental Hall.
8. Pan-American Union.
9. State, War and Navy Building.
10. Lafayette Square.
11. Memorial Arlington Bridge.
12. Department of Commerce.
13. The White House.
14. Treasury Building.
15. Washington Monument.
16. Bureau of Engraving and Printing.
17. Department of Agriculture.
18. National Museum.
19. Smithsonian Institution.
20. Internal Revenue.
21. Patent Office.
22. Pension Office.
23. Archives Building.
24. Court House.
25. Army Medical Museum.
26. Capitol Park.
27. U. S. Supreme Court.
28. The Capitol.
29. Government Printing Office.
30. Post Office.
31. Union Station.
32. Senate Office Building.
33. Library of Congress.
34. House Office Building.

which are public gardens filled with statuary, flowers and shrubs. Out beyond Rock Creek is the great National Zoological Park, which in time will become one of the greatest in the world. North and south of this extends Rock Creek Park, a tract which is preserved in all its natural beauty.

Along the river is Potomac Park, a tract of 737 acres, adjacent to the west end of the Mall, made up of reclaimed land. The Soldiers' Home four miles north of the Capitol is in a beautiful park of 500 acres. To the south of it is McMillan Park, containing a

Washington, and statues of Andrew Jackson, Abraham Lincoln, Winfield S. Scott, John A. Rawlins, James B. McPherson, George H. Thomas, Joseph H. Henry, David S. Farragut and John Marshall. There are many others.

The memorials include the Emancipation Group, the Adams Memorial, Samuel Gompers and American Federation of Labor Memorial, among many others of equal or greater distinction.

Public Buildings and Institutions. Chief of all the public buildings is the Capitol which because of its towering dome is conspicuous from any direction in which one approaches the city. The original plans for the Capitol were drawn by Doctor Thornton, a native of the West Indies, but they were redrawn by Stephen H. Hallet; they were followed in the construction of the first building, which little resembled the Capitol of to-day. The north wing was finished in 1800, but the opposite wing was not ready until eleven years later. A wooden passageway then connected them. After the British burned the Capitol in 1814, the new central structure was planned, and the original building was completed in 1827, at a cost of not quite $2,500,-000. In 1851 the building was remodeled, and in 1856 the erection of the present iron dome was begun.

The Capitol as it now stands, together with its approaches, has cost about $26,000,000. The building is 751 feet long and 350 feet in its greatest width, and it covers nearly four acres of ground. Within this imposing building are the two chambers occupied by the Senate and the House of Representatives, and apartments for the various committees and officials who meet at the Capitol, and other rooms, made necessary by the great amount of business transacted there. The rotunda, the marble stairways and the dome are decorated with choice statuary and paintings by famous American artists. Most of the paintings depict great events in the nation's history. The famous doors, designed by Randolph Rogers, which guard the east entrance, are ornamented in high relief with historic scenes from the life of Columbus. The old Hall of Representatives is now called Statuary Hall. See STATUARY HALL.

To the north, and in a space adjoining the Capitol grounds, is a massive granite building, in which are located offices for the Senators, and to the south are two other buildings of white marble, which contain offices for the members of the House of Representatives. These great structures constitute a notable contribution to the splendid group of buildings which crown Capitol Hill.

Along the Mall are the buildings of the Fish Commission, the Medical Museum, the great National Museum, the Smithsonian Institution, the Agricultural Department and the Bureau of Engraving and Printing. The buildings on the north side of the Mall include those of the Commerce Department, the Interstate Commerce Commission, the Post Office Department, Internal Revenue and others. East of the White House is the low, massive Treasury Department building, while west of it rises the magnificent building of the State, War and Navy Departments. The government Printing Office, the Pension Office and the Interior Department are in different localities of the North West quarter. Near the Capitol, and east of it, is the Library of Congress. (See LIBRARY OF CONGRESS). The new Supreme Court building faces the Capitol on the east.

The Lincoln Memorial (1922), an imposing marble temple with Doric columns, is situated on the bank of the Potomac at the west end of the Mall; within is the colossal statue of Lincoln by Daniel Chester French. At this point the beautiful Memorial Bridge reaches across the Potomac to Arlington Cemetery.

The Navy Yard, the Arsenal and the War College occupy sites on the river at the south side of the city. Other buildings widely famous are the Corcoran Art Gallery, the Pan-American Union building, the Scottish Rite Temple, the Freer Gallery of Art, the National Academy of Sciences, the United States Chamber of Commerce building and the home of the National Geographic Society.

The Municipal Center is at John Marshall Place, north of Pennsylvania Avenue. The old Supreme Court building is the center of the group which includes accommodations for the municipal court, the police court, the recorder of deeds, the administration office of the District, offices of the public library and the Board of Education. The new buildings are limited to six stories in height.

Religious denominations have done their share in adding distinction to the city. Among famous church buildings is the Protestant Episcopal Cathedral of Saint Peter and Saint Paul. The project resulting in this magnificent structure was begun in 1891. It will be completed as funds are provided but is now so far advanced as to be a national shrine. It is situated on Mt. Saint Albans on a plot of 67 acres. The ground floor will accommodate 27,000 persons standing. It is built chiefly on Indiana limestone. Several institutions are housed in this edifice.

In the National Shrine of the Immaculate Conception, the dome is a distinctive architectural feature; there is also a triple apse with each part divided into five chapels. The Methodist Episcopal Church South, near Mount Vernon Square, cost $500,000. The

Baptist Memorial Church represents both the Northern and the Southern Baptists. President Lincoln worshipped at the famous New York Avenue Presbyterian Church.

The colored people own many churches, including the famous Asbury Memorial.

Government OF THE CAPITAL CITY. The city boundary is that of the District of Columbia; Congress governs the District through a commission appointed by the President. Government influences dominate all of the city's interests.

Residents in the District of Columbia even though citizens of the United States have no right of suffrage. It is left to voluntary organizations to consolidate public opinion in any effort to influence Congress in respect to civic affairs.

Educational Institutions. This is a great educational center. The public schools are excellent; the system was founded by a board of trustees of which Thomas Jefferson was the first president. Among the higher institutions of learning are Georgetown University, George Washington University, Catholic University of America, American University, National University, and Howard University for Negroes. More than 150 high grade private boarding schools and special schools give undergraduate instruction.

Supplementing the universities are the great scientific bureaus and institutions for research maintained by the government: these deal with problems of labor, education, fisheries, geological survey, health, scientific standards, forest conservation, weather and soil fertility. In fact there is scarcely a scientific area that is not investigated by government officials. There are 200 specialized libraries, some of them having large collections of valuable books.

The Smithsonian Institution, founded by James Smithson, an Englishman, who gave half a million dollars for its establishment, and the more recent Carnegie Institution, with an endowment of $10,000,000, are the leading private foundations for the advancement of knowledge.

History. Washington enjoys the distinction of having been designed and built for the capital of a great nation. Rome, London, Paris and Berlin grew out of the national conditions surrounding them and became the capitals of great empires, but the capital of the United States was located in a region sparsely populated and almost wholly wild; it was built from plans that were created before any city was in existence there. The site was selected by the great President whose name was given the city, and he watched over its early days with a personal care and interest.

Congress held its first session in the Capitol in 1800. The city grew until 1814, when, after a weak resistance by American troops at Bladensburg, it was captured by the British, who set fire to the public buildings and some private residences, with the expectation of destroying the entire city. A storm put out the conflagration, and the next day the British, in a panic of unnecessary fear, retreated, leaving Washington to be immediately rebuilt. At the breaking out of the Civil War it contained about 61,000 inhabitants. Beginning about 1900, following plans and designs by eminent architects and artists, vast improvements have been made in the appearance of the buildings erected by the Federal Government especially in the section between the Capitol and the White House.

Related Articles. Consult the following titles for additional information:

Corcoran Art Gallery
District of Columbia
Library of Congress
Washington
  Monument
Mount Vernon
National Museum
Potomac River
Smithsonian
  Institution
White House

WASHINGTON, BOOKER TALIAFERRO (about 1858–1915), an American negro educator. Freed from slavery by the Civil War, he began work in a salt furnace in West Virginia, attended a night school and obtained the rudiments of an education. He then went to Hampton Normal and Agricultural Institute, where he remained three years. After this he took a complete course at Wayland Seminary in Washington, D. C., and then became an instructor at Hampton, in charge of the work of the Indian pupils and of the night school.

His success was phenomenal, and in 1881 he was selected by General Armstrong, principal of the institute, to start a normal school at Tuskegee, Ala. He began his work in an old building, with thirty pupils, but in the course of the year purchased the plantation where the Tuskegee Normal and Industrial Institute is now located. Under his management this school developed into the largest and most influential industrial school for colored people in the world (see TUSKEGEE NORMAL AND INDUSTRIAL INSTITUTE).

He wrote *The Future of the American Negro, Up from Slavery* (his autobiography), *Character Building, The Story of My Life* and *Working with the Hands.*

WASHINGTON, George (1732-1799), an American soldier and statesman, the hero of American independence, and the first President of the nation which he helped to establish. There are two Americans of the generations now past who have won the undying love and reverence of their countrymen—Washington and Lincoln. Though they are equally honored, the one as founder and the other as preserver of the American nation, they are thought of as totally different types. Lincoln, so much nearer our own time, is by far the more human figure. His humanity, his rugged appearance, his humor and his kindliness are remembered as the characteristics of a very real man. Washington is more or less of a mythical personage. The idealized portrait painted by Charles Stuart, reproduced herewith in full page is in a way symbolic of the impression that Americans cherish of the "Father of His Country." He seems to them a lofty figure somewhat detached from everyday life; a great man, but one aloof from his fellowmen; a strong man, but without fire and vigor. The complete record of his life refutes these ideas. There is every reason to believe that if he were alive today he would be a virile and influential figure in American political affairs, a personality as vivid as in his own time.

Ancestry and Youth. The family of the first President came of a line of well-born Englishmen. They were the Washingtons of Sulgrave Manor, in Northamptonshire, who traced their ancestry to a Norman knight of the twelfth century. About the year 1657 John and Lawrence Washington, brothers, emigrated to America, and shortly afterwards purchased estates in Westmoreland County, Virginia. The eldest son of John was Lawrence Washington, the grandfather of the future President. His second son, Augustine, married Mary Ball as his second wife. Their first child, George, was born on February 22 (Old Calendar, 11th), 1732, at Bridges Creek, now Wakefield, in Westmoreland County. When George was three years old his parents removed to an estate on the Rappahannock River, in Stafford County, and there the boy's first school days were spent. George had as his first teacher the sexton of the parish. Under this man's guidance he learned to read and write.

At the age of eleven George lost his father, and his widowed mother sent him to the old homestead at Bridges Creek to live with his half brother, Augustine. There he attended school until he was nearly sixteen, geometry and surveying being included in his studies. While he was not an apt classical student, he made excellent progress in surveying, and throughout this school period he cultivated robust health by outdoor exercise, such as horseback riding and athletic games. It was when he was thirteen that he copied those rules of good behavior now so well known.

Soon after he left school George went to live with his eldest half brother, Lawrence, who was occupying that portion of the estate known as Mount Vernon. Lawrence Washington had married the daughter of William Fairfax, who was the manager of the great estate of his cousin, Lord Fairfax, the head of the family. Lord Fairfax conceived a great liking for young Washington, and presently entrusted to him the task of marking out the boundaries of the Fairfax estate. George began his duties in 1748, when he was but a few days past sixteen, and for many months he endured the hardships of a surveyor in the wilderness. His work was so well done that he was subsequently appointed public surveyor of Culpeper County, and his surveys were considered admirable examples of thoroughness and accuracy.

In 1751 George accompanied his brother Lawrence on a trip to the West Indies. The journey was undertaken in the hope of restoring the elder brother's health, undermined by service in the British navy. In 1752, a few months after the brothers returned to Virginia, Lawrence died, and George found himself the guardian of his niece and one of the executors of the estate. The death of this niece a few years later made him master of the Mount Vernon that is now cherished by all patriotic Americans. In later years, Washington enlarged the estate.

Early Military Career. Not long before he died Lawrence Washington had used his influence to have his brother appointed an adjutant-general over one of the several military districts into which Virginia colony was divided. This division was rendered necessary by the threatened encroachments of the Indians and of the French, who were establishing posts along the Ohio. Washington's eager pursuit of the study of military tactics was interrupted by the trip to the West Indies, but he resumed his duties as adjutant-general after his return, and late in 1753 was requested by Governor Dinwiddie to carry a message of warning to the French forces in the Ohio Valley. It was a hazardous mission for a young man of twenty-one, and the selection reflects favorably upon Washington's reputation for reliability and good judgment. In November, accompanied by an experienced frontiersman, he started on his 600-mile journey. After many narrow escapes from the Indians and the perils of the wilderness, he completed his mission and reported to Governor Dinwiddie on January 16, 1754, at Williamsburg, the capital of Virginia. Shortly afterwards he was appointed lieutenant-colonel of the Virginia regiment.

A skirmish with the French in the summer of 1754, which was not decisive, was followed by a reorganization of the Virginia troops and Washington's temporary retirement from things military. Early in 1755, however, General Braddock arrived from England with two regiments of British regulars, and offered the young colonial a place on his staff, with the rank of colonel. Promptly accepting, Washington entered eagerly into the preparation of the campaign, and on July 9 took part in the disastrous fight at Fort Duquesne. How the English regulars were mowed down by bullets fired from behind trees, and how the Virginians under Washington saved the little army from annihilation by fighting under cover, as did the French and Indians, is known to every American school boy. The troops succeeded in withdrawing from the field, but Braddock was fatally wounded, and died four days later. Washington later reorganized the colonial troops and was their chief commander until 1758, when he retired to Mount Vernon to rest. It was with great satisfaction, however, that, in November, 1758, he accompanied the British forces to the smoking ruins of Fort Duquesne, which was renamed Fort Pitt in honor of England's great Prime Minister.

At Mount Vernon. The period between the close of the French and Indian War and the outbreak of the Revolution brought to Washington some of the happiest years of his life. In January, 1759, he married Mrs. Martha Custis, an attractive and wealthy young widow with two children, John and Martha Parke Custis. The management of his own and his wife's property provided an outlet for his business instincts, and he entered whole-heartedly into the public affairs of Virginia colony as a delegate to the House of Burgesses, to which he had been elected before his marriage. These duties, with those of a good churchman and a hospitable colonial gentleman, rounded out a life completely wholesome and happy. The Mount Vernon mansion was always filled to overflowing during the hunting season, but none of its inmates enjoyed the pleasures of the chase more than the master himself.

As relations grew strained between the colonies and the mother country, Washington for a long time hoped that an agreement might be reached without resort to war, and he was very guarded in his utterances. In 1769, however, he drew up a nonimportation agreement which was adopted by the House of Burgesses, and from that time on he refused to permit any of the banned articles to be brought into his house.

As a member of the provincial convention, held in August, 1774, at Williamsburg, he vigorously upheld the right of the colonies to govern themselves, and, moved by reports about the effects of the Boston Port Bill, exclaimed in an impassioned speech, "I will raise a thousand men and march with them, at their head, for the relief of Boston." Virginia sent him as one of its six delegates to the First Continental Congress, and in this and the succeeding Congress, held in 1775, he made his influence felt through his personal contacts with individuals.

The Revolutionary War. On June 15, 1775, two months after the Battle of Lexington, Washington was unanimously chosen by Congress to be commander in chief of the Continental forces. Addressing the assembly the following day, he modestly accepted the honor, and assured the delegates that he would expect no remuneration except for his own expenses. He then departed on horseback for Boston, and on July 3, 1775, took command of the Continental army, in Cambridge. The old elm under which this cere-

GEORGE WASHINGTON
The unfinished portrait by Gilbert Stuart in the Athenaeum, Boston

MOUNT VERNON

It was Washington's great joy to return to Mount Vernon when the demands of his country permitted. He was a home-loving body. Here on his beautiful estate he "grew stronger, abler, and wiser in the happy years of rest and waiting which intervened" between his great periods of service.

WASHINGTON'S TOMB

mony took place was long preserved as a cherished relic.

The military events of the long struggle which the colonies waged for independence are told in these volumes in the article on the Revolutionary War. The personal share of Washington in the hard-won victory cannot be overestimated; from the perspective of a century and a half it seems almost incredible that he did succeed. Difficulties beset him that would have broken the courage of a weaker man. His little army of barely 14,000 was lacking in arms, supplies, discipline and organization. There was no uniform policy among the colonies on any matters essential to the prosecution of the war, and authority was vested in too many officials and organizations to bring about any semblance of unity. There were bickerings, quarrels and plots. Yet, somehow, Washington overrode all obstacles. For one thing, he was loved and trusted by his men, and because of that trust they endured terrible hardships to uphold him.

When the army went into winter quarters at Valley Forge, in December, 1777, Washington informed Congress that he had 2,898 men unfit for duty because they were "barefooted and otherwise naked." It is a matter of record that blood in the snow marked the path of those unshod troops as they marched into camp.

As a military leader Washington was superior to any of the field commanders sent over by England. In fact, his tactics in the movements on the Delaware River were characterized by Frederick the Great as the "most brilliant achievements recorded in military annals." Years later the old Prussian soldier sent his portrait to Washington, with this message: "From the oldest general in Europe to the greatest general in the world."

Coupled with his genius as a soldier was an abiding faith in the justice and ultimate triumph of the American cause. Toward the close of the struggle a movement was started to have Washington assume the title of king, but his repudiation of such a course was voiced in language as vigorous as he could make it. His great popularity never undermined his modest sense of his own worth or his deep-rooted conviction that the American nation was destined to be a democracy in which kings could have no part.

On November 2, 1783, he took final leave of his faithful army, and the following December appeared before Congress to resign the commission tendered him over seven years before. He said:

Having now finished the work assigned me, I retire from the great theatre of action, and, bidding an affectionate farewell to this august body, under whose orders I have long acted, I here offer my commission, and take my leave of all employments of public life." "You retire," replied the president of Congress, "from the theatre of action with the blessings of your fellow-citizens; but the glory of your virtues will not terminate with your military command: it will continue to animate remotest ages."

On Christmas Eve Washington arrived at Mount Vernon, where, during the interval before the organization of the government under the Constitution, he enjoyed once more the life of plantation owner and private citizen.

The Constitution and the First Administration. Five years after the signing of the peace treaty a new crisis called Washington again into public life. Under the Articles of Confederation affairs were steadily growing more chaotic, and in May, 1787, a convention was called to meet in Philadelphia to prepare a new form of union. To this body Washington was sent as head of the Virginia delegation; on its organization he was unanimously elected its president. In September the convention completed a new Constitution and gave it to the states for ratification. The influence that Washington exercised in the consummation of this great achievement is ably summarized in Woodrow Wilson's *History of the American People*:

"It gave the convention great dignity that Washington had presided over its counsels and was heart and soul for the adoption of the measures it proposed. His name and quiet force had steadied the convention on many an anxious day when disagreement threatened hopeless breach. His fame and influence infinitely strengthened also the measures proposed, now that they were completed. He supported them because they were thoroughgoing and courageous and cut to the root of the difficulties under which the country was laboring. Issue had been joined now, as he had wished to see it joined, between government or no government, and the country was to know at last where it stood in the most essential matters of its life."

It is not surprising that when the votes of the first Electoral College were counted it was found that Washington was the unanimous choice for President of the United States. John Adams was honored with the Vice-Presidency.

Washington was inaugurated in New York, which was then the national seat of government. Standing on the balcony in front of the old Federal Hall, whose site is now occupied by the imposing Subtreasury, he took the oath of office on April 30, 1789, though the legal day for the ceremony was March 4. Difficulties in setting the new machinery in motion were responsible for the delay.

From the first he displayed in civil affairs the same qualities of leadership and invariable good judgment which he had shown during his military career. He set about informing himself concerning all that had happened during the period of the Confederation—the relations of the new government to foreign nations, and the questions of internal administration and finance, which were soon to become pressing issues. He also chose a remarkably strong Cabinet, including Thomas Jefferson and Alexander Hamilton, who, though directly opposite in their political opinions, were acknowledged leaders in the political life of the country.

The selection of Alexander Hamilton as head of the Treasury Department was momentous in its results, for through his far-seeing statesmanship the country was put on a sound financial basis. In accordance with Hamilton's program the national government assumed the debts of the states incurred during the war; a national bank and a mint were established; and a national income was provided for by duties on imports and a system of internal revenue.

Other important events of the first four years under the Federal Constitution were the organization of the United States Supreme Court, the admission of Vermont (1791) and Kentucky (1792) as states, the adoption of a decimal system of coinage, and the incorporation into the Constitution of the first ten amendments. So profoundly impressed were the people with the results of Washington's first term that there was a spontaneous demand that he serve again. Against his personal wishes he consented, and was unanimously reëlected, being inaugurated in Philadelphia on March 4, 1793. The city of Washington did not become the national capital until 1800.

The Second Term. During this term international affairs for a time overshadowed domestic issues. A war between France and England vastly aroused the sympathies of a group friendly to France, and there were some extremists who demanded that the nation go to its assistance. Another faction as vehemently urged neutrality or support for England. Washington, who saw clearly that the United States was too weak and insecure to be implicated in European quarrels, issued a proclamation of neutrality and refused to take sides. An unfortunate incident of this affair was the activity of Edmond, or "Citizen," Genet, a Frenchman whose defiance of the proclamation caused the government considerable anxiety. The French sympathizers were also greatly exercised over the acceptance of the Jay Treaty (1794) with England. This treaty was not so favorable to America as its sponsors wished, but it was the best that could be obtained, and it served the purpose of averting war with England, which Washington felt would be a national calamity.

The power of the Federal government was vigorously exercised in this administration. In Pennsylvania in 1794 there occurred an insurrection in protest against the excise tax, to quell which Washington ordered out 15,000 militia. Trouble with the Indians was settled by Anthony Wayne's victory over them at Fallen Timbers in 1794 and by the negotiation of treaties. Other events include the invention of the cotton gin by Eli Whitney; the erection of the first woolen mill in Massachusetts; the admission of Tennessee into the Union, and the development of two great political parties, by followers of Hamilton and Jefferson, respectively.

The End of the Story. Washington declined a third election, delivered his famous farewell address and retired to Mount Vernon in 1797. Thereafter he devoted himself to agriculture, though in 1798, at the prospect of the war with France, he was chosen commander in chief of the United States army and accepted, though he was not called into the field. He died in December, 1799, from illness brought on by long exposure in the saddle. The news caused almost as widespread mourning in Europe as in America. The greatest statesmen and soldiers of every nation united in paying him tribute as a man, general, statesman and friend of humanity. The words of his old friend and companion, "Lighthorse Harry" Lee, "First in war, first in peace and first in the hearts of his countrymen," were without question literally true. He had avoided the snares of factional and partisan politics, had generously overlooked

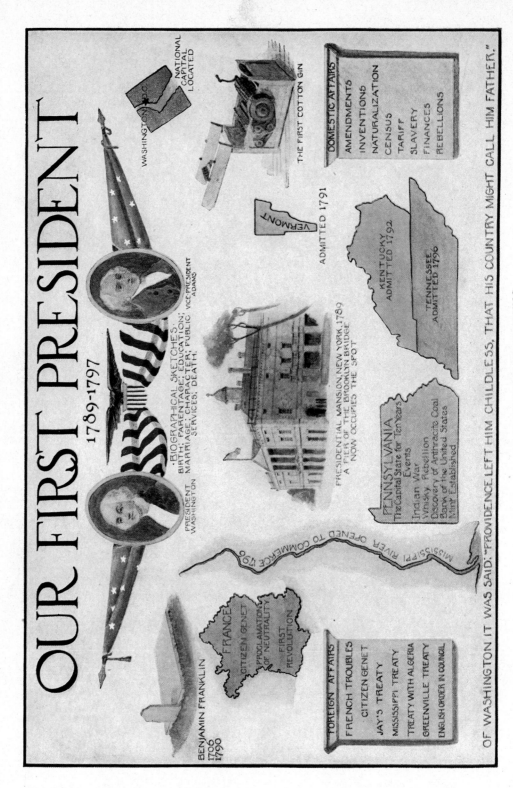

OUR FIRST PRESIDENT

1789-1797

NATIONAL CAPITAL LOCATED

WASHINGTON D.C.

THE FIRST COTTON GIN

DOMESTIC AFFAIRS
AMENDMENTS
INVENTIONS
NATURALIZATION
CENSUS
TARIFF
SLAVERY
FINANCES
REBELLIONS

·BIOGRAPHICAL·SKETCHES·
BIRTH; PARENTAGE; EDUCATION;
MARRIAGE; CHARACTER; PUBLIC
SERVICES; DEATH.

VICE PRESIDENT
ADAMS

PRESIDENT
WASHINGTON

ADMITTED 1791

VERMONT

KENTUCKY
ADMITTED 1792

TENNESSEE
ADMITTED 1796

PRESIDENTIAL MANSION, NEW YORK, 1789
A PIER OF THE BROOKLYN BRIDGE
NOW OCCUPIES THE SPOT

PENNSYLVANIA
The Capital State for Ten Years
Events
Indian War
Whisky Rebellion
Discovery of Anthracite Coal
Bank of the United States
Mint Established

MISSISSIPPI RIVER OPENED TO COMMERCE 1796

BENJAMIN FRANKLIN
1706
1790

FRANCE
CITIZEN GENET
PROCLAMATION
OF NEUTRALITY
FIRST
REVOLUTION

FOREIGN AFFAIRS
FRENCH TROUBLES
CITIZEN GENET
JAY'S TREATY
MISSISSIPPI TREATY
TREATY WITH ALGERIA
GREENVILLE TREATY
ENGLISH ORDER IN COUNCIL

OF WASHINGTON IT WAS SAID: "PROVIDENCE LEFT HIM CHILDLESS, THAT HIS COUNTRY MIGHT CALL HIM FATHER."

WHEN THE NATION WAS YOUNG

Administration of George Washington, 1789-1797

I. ELECTION AND INAUGURATION

II. THE PRESIDENT
- (1) Birth
- (2) Ancestry
- (3) Education
- (4) Previous public career
- (5) Character
- (6) Rank as a statesman
- (7) Death

III. ORGANIZATION OF THE GOVERNMENT
- (1) Strict and loose constructionists
  - (a) Followers of Hamilton
  - (b) Followers of Jefferson
- (2) Executive departments
  - (a) State
  - (b) Treasury
  - (c) War
  - (d) Attorney-General
- (3) Federal courts established, 1789
- (4) Financial measures
  - (a) The public debt
  - (b) The excise, 1791
  - (c) Bank of the United States
  - (d) The Mint
  - (e) Tariff on imports, 1789

IV. DOMESTIC AFFAIRS
- (1) Governmental
  - (a) Last state ratifies the Constitution
  - (b) Census of 1790
  - (c) Whisky Insurrection, 1794
  - (d) Admission of Vermont, Kentucky, Tennessee
  - (e) Site of Washington chosen
  - (f) Ten Amendments
  - (g) Campaigns against the Indians
- (2) General
  - (a) Invention of cotton gin
  - (b) Death of Franklin
  - (c) Slavery
  - (d) Settlement of Northwest Territory

V. FOREIGN AFFAIRS
- (1) Genet and quarrel with France
- (2) Jay Treaty
- (3) Treaty with Spain
  - (a) Opened the Mississippi
  - (b) Florida boundary

VI. ELECTION OF 1796
- (1) Political parties
  - (a) Federalists
  - (b) Republicans
- (2) Candidates
  - (a) John Adams
  - (b) Thomas Pinckney
  - (c) Thomas Jefferson
  - (d) Aaron Burr
- (3) Election of Adams

Questions on Washington

Where was Washington at the time of his election to the Presidency?

Where was he inaugurated?

What city was the capital during most of his administration?

How does he rank as a soldier and statesman?

In what way did Hamilton's ideas influence the organization of the government?

What were the original executive departments?

Was the Attorney-General the head of a department?

Who were the members of the first Cabinet?

When were the Federal courts established?

What compromise was necessary before Hamilton could secure the assumption of the state debts?

When was the Bank of the United States organized?

What were some of its powers?

When was the first tariff law passed?

What was its primary object?

When was the first census taken?

What states were admitted during Washington's term of office?

What caused the trouble with the Indians in the Northwest?

What battles were fought and with what result?

What party was friendly to France? Why?

Give an account of Genet's visit to the United States.

What was the Jay Treaty? What did it accomplish?

the harshest criticisms and had respected and used the abilities of his severest critics and opponents. Though a slave-holder at his death, he was in favor of the gradual abolition of slavery by legislation, and by his will he arranged that his one hundred twenty-five slaves should be emancipated at the death of his wife, so that the Negroes of the two estates who had intermarried might not be separated. Washington's body and that of his wife, who survived him nearly three years, rest in the family vault at Mount Vernon.

Consult Lodge's *George Washington*, in the American Statesmen Series, and Fiske's *Washington and His Country*, a condensed and simplified edition of Washington Irving's *Life of Washington*.

Related Articles. Consult the following titles for additional information:

Braddock, Edward
Constitution
French and Indian Wars
Genet, Edmond C.
Jay Treaty
Mount Vernon

Political Parties in the United States
Tariff
Revolutionary War
United States
Whisky Insurrection

WASHINGTON, MARTHA (1732-1802), the wife of George Washington, born in New Kent County, Va., the daughter of John Dandridge, a wealthy planter. Her first husband, to whom she was married in 1749, was Daniel Parke Custis. She was married to George Washington in 1759. As mistress of the White House she won a firm place in the hearts of the people. She died at Mount Vernon two years and a half after the death of President Washington.

WASHINGTON, PA., the county seat of Washington County, situated thirty-two miles southwest of Pittsburgh, on the Pennsylvania and the Baltimore & Ohio railroads. It is the seat of the Washington and Jefferson College, the oldest college west of the Alleghenies, and also of the Washington Seminary. Washington is said to have erected the first crematory in the United States. Bituminous coal and natural gas are produced in the vicinity. The manufacture of glass products is the chief industry; other products include fine steel, clay products, ferro alloys and iron castings. The vicinity of Washington was settled in 1768. The town was founded in 1781 by David Hoge, receiving its present name in 1784. It was incorporated as a borough in 1810 and as a city in 1924. Population, 1940, 26,166.

WASHINGTON, TREATY OF, the treaty between the United States and Great Britain, signed in 1871, providing for the settlement of several difficulties between the two countries, chief of which were the Alabama claims. A commission, which consisted of five representatives of Great Britain, headed by Earl de Grey and Sir John MacDonald, and five representatives of the United States, headed by Hamilton Fish and E. R. Hoar, began its meetings May 8 at Washington. It referred the Alabama Claims to a special court, which was to meet at Geneva (see ALABAMA, THE; GENEVA ARBITRATION). It provided for the establishment of a mixed commission to discuss and decide upon the northwestern fisheries question, and it submitted the northwest boundary dispute to the arbitration of the emperor of Germany. It also laid down certain rules regarding neutrality in war, which were to govern the Geneva Tribunal in deciding the Alabama question and which have since been considered the true principles of international law upon the subject.

WASHINGTON, UNIVERSITY OF, a coeducational state institution founded at Seattle. It was organized in 1861, but the regular four years' courses were not established until 1877. In 1889 it became the state university, as Washington entered the Union that year. It maintains the College of Arts and Sciences, which includes about ten semi-professional schools; the colleges of Economics and Business, Education, Engineering, Forestry, Mines and Pharmacy; the Graduate School, and the School of Law. The university has a faculty of about 560, and over 12,000 students in regular session. The libraries contain almost 469,000 volumes.

WASHINGTON AND LEE UNIVERSITY, an institution for men only located at Lexington, Va. It was established as the Augusta Academy in 1749 and afterwards renamed Washington Academy in recognition of a gift of money made to the institution by the "Father of his Country." This gift still yields an annual income of $3,000. In 1865 General Robert E. Lee was made president of the institution, a position which he held with great influence upon the students until his death in 1870. In 1871 the present name of the institution was adopted. The university has a Liberal Arts College, a School of Commerce and Administration and a School of Law; it offers B. A., B. S. and LL. B. degrees. It has a faculty of sixty-five members, about 925 students and property and endowments aggregating $5,000,000.

WASHINGTON ARCH, a beautiful memorial structure, erected to commemorate the first inauguration of George Washington as President of the United States. It stands at the foot of Fifth Avenue, New York, and was designed by Stanford White. It is of marble, seventy-seven feet high and sixty-two feet broad, with a single archway forty-seven feet high and thirty feet broad. Its cost of $128,000 was met by popular subscription.

WASHINGTON ELM, a famous elm, formerly standing near the northwest corner of the Common, in Cambridge, Mass. Near the base was a stone seat with the inscription: "Under this tree Washington took the command of the American Army July 3, 1775." Although carefully protected, the tree fell to the ground October 26, 1923.

WASHINGTON MONUMENT, an imposing marble obelisk in Washington, D. C., measuring 555 feet in height. It is situated in the Monument Gardens, south of the White House. It was begun in 1848, but was not dedicated until 1885, on Washington's birthday. The top, from which a magnificent view of the surrounding country is obtained, is reached by an elevator and by a wide, concrete interior stairway. The monument weighs over 43,600 tons and it cost $1,187,710.

WASHINGTON UNIVERSITY, a coeducational school at Saint Louis, Mo., founded in 1853 by Dr. William Greenleaf Eliot, on condition that it be kept nonsectarian and nonpartisan. Its activities were carried on in different parts of the city till 1905, when all were removed to the present location west of Forest Park. Ten new granite buildings on this site were occupied by the Louisiana Purchase Exposition in 1904. The departments of the university include those of liberal arts, engineering, architecture, business, law, medicine, dentistry, nursing, fine arts, evening classes, graduate school and summer school. The faculty numbers over 800; there are about 9,000 students. The library contains 300,000 volumes.

WASHITA, *wosh'e tah,* **RIVER,** or **OUACHITA RIVER,** a river that rises in the western part of Arkansas, flows southeast and then south into Louisiana and discharges into the Red River, about fifteen miles above the confluence of that stream with the Mississippi. The Washita is connected with the Mississippi by a series of bayous. Its length is 550 miles, and it is navigable for steamboats for about 350 miles.

WASP, *wahsp,* a winged insect resembling the bee in many respects. The body is bluish in color, with yellow markings, or black, marked with white or yellow. Common wasps live in societies, or colonies, composed of males, females and workers, or neuters (see BEE). The females are armed with an extremely powerful and venomous sting; the males do not sting.

The nest of the wasp is ingenious, both in material and construction. It is built in the ground or attached to a wall or tree, and is composed of a kind of chewed wood pulp or paper manufactured by the females. Within these nests the combs are enclosed completely, except for the small opening where the wasps enter. The cells of the comb, in which the larvae and pupae are reared, are six-sided and arranged in tiers, with the mouth downward or sidewise.

Wasp colonies multiply rapidly, and have been known to attain to 30,000 members in a favorable summer season. But in the fall all the members perish except a few females, which pass the winter under stones or in hollow trees. Wasps are voracious insects, living upon sugar, meat, fruit, honey or the juices of other insects. Certain species live solitary lives, each mother making its own nest and caring for its own eggs and larvae.

WATAU'GA ASSOCIATION, in American history a name given to an association of settlers, formed in 1772, in the eastern part of what is now Tennessee, just west of the Alleghany Mountains. Articles were drawn up for the purpose of creating a government for the district, and provision was made for five executive councilors, thirteen legislators, a sheriff and an attorney. The government had no jurisdiction over any but the signers of the compact, and the territory soon swarmed with outlaws and adventurers. In order to secure protection, the community, under the name of Washington District, asked for and secured representation in the North Carolina Assembly.

WATCH, a small, portable mechanism for measuring time, having about the same number of wheels as a clock, geared in the same manner, but differing from a clock in having a hairspring and a balance wheel, instead of a pendulum, and in having its parts much smaller and more delicately adjusted. It is attached to a chain and carried in the pocket, or to a bracelet and worn on the wrist.

Mechanism. A watch consists of two parts, the case and the works. The case is of metal, usually gold or silver, and it is made with one or two covers. The works consist of two plates, perforated for the purpose of holding the wheels in position, and so arranged that they contain, between them, all of the wheels except the balance wheel. The lower plate, known as the pillar plate, rests next to the dial. The upper plate may be in one or in several pieces, but in the best-made watches it is usually in one piece. These plates are bored and chiseled so that each wheel fits perfectly into its place. The perforations, in which the minute axles of the wheels rest, are usually set in jewels, which prevent wear. There are four wheels in the watch; these are (1) the barrel wheel, within which the mainspring is attached, (2) the first wheel, (3) the second wheel and (4) the third wheel, which is attached to the pinion of the escapement wheel. The motion is imparted by the uncoiling of the spring and is regulated by the escapement, which is kept in operation by the action of the mainspring and the hairspring combined, the two giving it an oscillating movement. The wheel which meshes into the pinion of the escapement wheel revolves once a minute and has sixty teeth upon its circumference. The pinion of this wheel meshes into the circumference of the wheel which gives the motion to the minute hand, and this meshes into the pinion of the center wheel, which gives the motion to the hour hand. The watch is regulated by a lever device, connected with the hairspring. By moving this to the right, or left, the tension is lessened or strengthened.

Watch Making. The works of a watch have for their foundation two plates of an alloy of brass and nickel. These plates are cut at the foundry, where the metal is cast, from dies furnished by the watch factory.

The rough plates are passed under trimming, or stripping, punches, which smooth off the roughness. Indentations absolutely exact are then made in the foundation plate, to allow room for the wheels. The plate is placed under the lathe portion of a machine, and a steel copy of what it is to be is fastened to another part. The machine follows the outline of the steel model, gradually cutting out the foundation plate, so that the various parts of the mechanism of the watch will be thrown into proper position. The thickness of the plate and the depth of the indentations are measured so as to be perfect, according to a gauge, two degrees of which equal the thousandth part of an inch. The necessary screw holes and apertures for the settings are then drilled into the plate. The work on the upper plate is done in the same manner. The plates are then polished and smoothed down, on an Ayr stone, a stone harder than a soapstone and softer than emery, capable of polishing without scratching.

The jewels used in watch making are garnets, rubies, sapphires and diamonds. Garnets are most common and are cut with diamond points into minute disks and then smoothed and pierced. These disks are set in larger disks of gold. The foundation plates are given an ordinary heavy plating of gold, by the battery process, and the jewels with their settings are fitted and fastened into the plate by exceedingly small screws.

The wheels of a watch are stamped out of sheets of brass, with the exception of one or two pieces. The screws and springs are made from sheet steel, the screws being cold-drawn from wire. In tempering some of the screws, the workman uses a thermometer of a peculiar sort, in order to regulate accurately the temperature to which they are to be heated and cooled. Others are regulated by a careful observation of their color. The figures are printed on the dial by a process resembling lithography (see LITHOGRAPHY). The base of the dial is of copper and is stamped out of a thin sheet of the metal, in such a manner that a rim is left turned up for a short distance all around. Powdered enamel is spread on the disk, and it is then fired, like pottery or china. Steel plates are engraved with the design to be executed, and the lines are filled with a mineral paint of the desired color. The plate is then passed under a roller, covered with sheet rubber, and the dial receives the impression from the rubber on the roller. It is again fired, and when fancy colors are employed, each color requires a separate impression and firing. The balance wheel requires forty different steps in its manufacture.

When all the parts are assembled, the watch is taken to a refrigerator and subjected to cold. This is followed by a period in a hot air compartment, the two tests ranging from 40° to 103° F. The making of watches by hand is thought to have originated in Germany about 1500. Since the advent of the machine-made watch, the United States has reached the foremost position as a watch-manufacturing country. The largest watch factory in the world is at Waltham, Mass., and another, nearly as large, is located at Elgin, Ill. See CLOCK.

WATER, the liquid that covers five-sevenths of the earth and is essential to all animal and vegetable life, is a chemical compound of hydrogen and oxygen in proportion of two atoms of the former to one of the latter. Its chemical symbol, therefore, is H_2O. Pure water is a colorless, tasteless, odorless liquid. It appears blue, like the atmosphere, when seen in mass.

Three Forms of Water. Water takes three forms, each depending upon temperature. It takes a solid form, that of ice or snow, at 32° Fahrenheit (0° Centigrade) and all lower temperatures; and it takes the form of vapor or steam at 212° F. (100° C.) under a pressure of 29.9 inches of mercury, and it retains that form at all higher temperatures. Under ordinary conditions, water possesses the liquid form only at temperatures lying between 32° and 212°. It is, however, possible to cool water very considerably below 32° F. and yet maintain it in the liquid form. Water may also be heated, under pressure in the laboratory, many degrees above 212° F., without passing into the state of steam.

The specific gravity of water is 1 at 39.2° F., (that is, one cubic centimeter of water weighs one gram), and it is the unit to which the specific gravities of all solids and liquids are referred, as a convenient standard; one cubic inch of water, at 62° F. and 29.9 inches barometrical pressure, weighs 252.458 grains. Distilled water is 815 times heavier than atmospheric air. Water is at its greatest density at 39.2° F. (4° C.), and in this respect it presents a singular exception to the general law of expansion by heat. If water at 39.2° F. be cooled, it expands as it cools, till reduced to 32°, when it solidifies; and if water at 39.2° F. be heated, it expands as the temperature increases, in accordance with the general law. Were it not for this peculiar property of water, ice would settle to the bottom of lakes and streams and they would become masses of solid ice, a condition which would soon destroy all life upon the earth.

So-called *heavy water* differs from ordinary water in having two atoms of heavy hydrogen and one atom of oxygen.

Water as a Solvent. From a chemical point of view, water is a neutral fluid and shows in itself neither acid nor basic properties; but it combines with both acids and bases, forming *hydrates,* and with neutral salts. Water also enters, as a liquid, into physical combination with the greater number of all known substances. Of all liquids, water is the most powerful and general solvent, and on this important property its use depends. In consequence of the great solvent power of water, it is never found pure in nature. Even in rain water, which is the purest, there are always traces of carbonic acid, ammonia and sea salt. Where the rain water has filtered through rocks and soils and reappears as spring or river water, it is always more or less charged with salts derived from the earth, such as sea salts, gypsum and chalk. When the proportion of these is small, the water is called *soft;* when larger, it is called *hard water.* The former dissolves soap better and is therefore preferred for washing; the latter is often pleasanter to drink. The only way to obtain perfectly pure water is to distill it, but matter simply held in suspension may be taken out by suitable filtration.

Sources of Water. The great reservoirs of water on the globe are the seas and lakes, which cover more than three-fifths of its surface, and from which water is raised by evaporation. Uniting with the air in the state of vapor, it is wafted over the earth, ready to be precipitated in the form of rain, snow or hail. Water, like air, is absolutely necessary to life, and healthy human life requires that it should be free from contamination; hence, an ample and pure water supply is considered as one of the first laws of sanitation.

Related Articles. Consult the following titles for additional information:

Boiling Point	Frost	River
Chemistry	Hail	Snow
Cloud	Humidity	Spring
Dew	Hydrogen	Steam
Distillation	Ice	Vapor
Erosion	Mineral Waters	Water Power
Evaporation	Ocean	Water Purification
Freezing	Rain	

WATER, ORDEAL BY. See ORDEAL.

WATER BEETLE, any representative of several families of beetles which live in or upon the water. Three of the families include beetles which live permanently in water; the rest include those species which live in the water only in the larvae (young) stage.

The *diving beetle* has a flat, oval body, over which the wings fit tight. The hind legs, which have a fringe of hairs, are flattened and adapted to swimming; the front legs are short. The common *water beetle* seen in summer darting over the surface of ponds has a water-tight compartment beneath the close-fitting wings for the storage of breathing air. In the evening these beetles leave the water and fly about. The larvae, called *water tigers*, are exceedingly rapacious, seizing in their sickle-like jaws small fish, tadpoles and other larvae, from which they suck the juices. Breathing is effected through tubes terminating in the tail, which is raised above the surface of the water.

The *whirligig beetles*, so called from their habit of moving in circles on the water, have long, clawed front legs and shorter, paddle-shaped hind legs. The body has an oily surface unaffected by water, and the compound eyes are adapted for vision in water and in air. One of the largest of the water beetles is the glossy *black beetle*, often seen on the wing at night. These insects can be transferred to an indoor aquarium, and their whole interesting life history may be studied in the school room. See BEETLE.

WATER BUG, a name applied to any insect belonging to one of six large families, including *water striders, water boatmen, water scorpions, toad bugs* and *fishkillers*. All have flat bodies, and are equipped with oar-shaped legs for swimming. They may be seen on summer days darting over the surface of ponds and lagoons or resting quietly on the surface, their bodies being buoyed up by the air stored in various parts of the insects. If alarmed, they may dive to the bottom and cling to plants or stones. About a dozen species are found in America. Some of them leave the water and fly around lights at night; the electric light bug is one of these. Some of the adults lie dormant in the mud of water bottoms in winter; others hibernate in rubbish on the banks, and here the eggs are deposited. When the young hatch they tumble into the water and feed on insects and other small animal food. The females of some species bore holes in aquatic plants and deposit their eggs there. In the United States the *croton bug,* a house pest resembling the cockroach, is incorrectly called water bug, because it is usually seen on or near warm-water pipes.

WAT'ERBURY, CONN., one of the county seats of New Haven County, about thirty miles southwest of Hartford, on the Naugatuck River and on the New York, New Haven & Hartford Railroad. It is an important manufacturing center; it leads the United States in brass and copper goods, and for this reason is sometimes known as the "Brass City." The famous Waterbury watches and clocks have been manufactured here in immense numbers since 1879. Buttons and buckles, tools, heavy machinery, chemicals, clothing and other articles are also manufactured. Grandfather clocks were made here in the late eighteenth century.

The place was settled in 1677, as part of Farmington township, and was known by the Indian name of Mattatuck until its incorporation as the township of Waterbury in 1686. In 1691 it suffered from a flood; in 1712 an epidemic proved fatal to about one-tenth of the population, and in 1902 a large portion of the business section was destroyed by fire. Waterbury was chartered as a city in 1853. The township and city of Waterbury were consolidated in 1901, and now cover an area of twenty-eight square miles. The Mattatuck Historical Society museum contains many interesting historical exhibits. The government of the city is by mayor and council. Population, 1940, 99,314.

WATER COLORS, pigments mixed and ground with gum size or some other adhesive substance, instead of oil. The water colors used in painting pictures are in the form of small, dry and hard cakes, while those used in coloring walls and the like are simply mixed up with glue or size. The quick drying of water colors is favorable to rapid execution, and a greater clearness and transparency is obtained than in an oil painting. Fresco, tempera, distemper, gouache and aquarelle (the modern method) are forms of water-color painting. See PAINTING.

WATER DOG. See MUD PUPPY.

WATERFALL. See CATARACT.

WATER LILY, a water plant with a gorgeous blossom, found in quiet waters of the temperate and torrid zones. From the oozy bottom the stems rise to the top of the water; there the leaves open out and lie flat upon the surface, and the buds unfold, disclosing numerous petals, stamens and carpels. The flowers may be pink, white or blue, and sometimes they are very fragrant. The most famous of water lilies is the Queen Victoria, a native of South America. The leaves, six feet or more in diameter, are flat, with upturned rim, and are often strong enough to support a man's weight. The blossoms, a foot in diameter, open on two successive nights; the first night they are white and fragrant, the second, pink and malodorous.

The Australian water lily is often as large and is usually blue. The Egyptian lotus is also a blue lily, famous since remote antiquity. The American pond lily is a lovely, creamy-white flower, with petals radiating in circles and a cluster of golden stamens. It expands to the sunshine and closes at dusk. The golden lily of Florida is a handsome flower, and the common yellow water lily of higher latitudes is less showy, but blooms all summer. A rose-colored variety is also found in North America. The seeds of the pond lily lie sunk in pits in the flattened top of a hemispherical pod. Those of several species are edible, and are sometimes called *water chinquapin.* They were an important article of food among the Indians.

WATERLOO, Battle of, the famous battle, fought June 18, 1815, near Waterloo, a village in Belgium about eleven miles south of Brussels, between Napoleon and the allied forces under Blücher and Wellington. It was Napoleon's last battle, and it put an end to his power (see Hundred Days). There had been two preliminary battles on the 16th, one at Quatre-Bras, by which Ney, although forced to retire, prevented Wellington from joining his Prussian allies, and one at Ligny, in which the Prussians under Blücher were defeated by Napoleon. On the morning of the eighteenth the main French army was drawn up near Waterloo, opposite the allied British, Dutch and German forces, under Wellington. Blücher, with the Prussian army, was absent at the opening of the fight. The French army numbered about 72,000, the allied army about 67,000, of which number many were untrained troops.

Napoleon's plan was to defeat Wellington before Blücher could come up with his troops, but the ground was in such a condition from the rain that had fallen all night that he was obliged to delay opening battle until almost noon. Wellington, on the contrary, simply aimed to hold out until the Prussians arrived, when a combined attack might be made on the French. In accordance with these plans the struggle throughout the day consisted chiefly of charges, brilliant but unsuccessful, on the part of the French, and firm resistance on the part of the English. The French

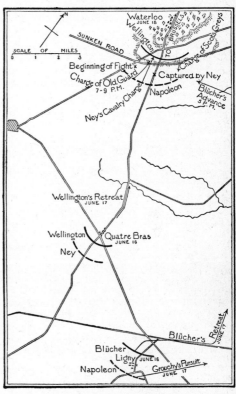

BATTLE OF WATERLOO

cavalry, charging during the afternoon, plunged into an unseen sunken road, and unable to check their rush, they filled the great ditch with troopers, over whom the remainder rode on. These repeated charges, although stubbornly resisted, had their effect, and the outcome of the battle remained doubtful until late in the day, when the arrival of the Prussians, at a time when both armies were about exhausted completely turned the tide against the French. Napoleon's last effort was the charge of the Old Guard, the picked veterans from the Imperial Guard, late in the evening. Its rout was complete, and many of its squares, refusing to surrender or retreat, fell to the last man. Wellington now gave the order for a general advance, and the French, utterly overpowered, gave way at every point. The army broke up in confusion, and the disastrous retreat, with the Prussians in pursuit, lasted through the night. Napoleon himself escaped by flight. The French lost in this battle probably thirty-one thousand in killed, wounded and missing, while the allies lost over twenty-two thousand.

The importance of the Battle of Waterloo as the means of finally crushing Napoleon has been somewhat exaggerated. Even had he been successful on that day, he could never have regained his old power. But the accomplishment of his overthrow that early in his campaign was fortunate for the allies and for the French, as it saved further bloodshed. See NAPOLEON I.

WATERLOO′, IOWA, the fifth city in the state in size, is the county seat of Black Hawk County, on the Red Cedar River and on the Chicago, Rock Island & Pacific, the Illinois Central and the Chicago Great Western railroads. Waterloo is one of the leading industrial cities in the state, deriving its principal income from meat packing and the manufacturing of farm machinery. The city produces about twenty per cent of the farm-type gasoline engines made in the United States; it is also one of the five leading meat-packing cities in Iowa, and has important manufactures of tractors, cream separators and cement mixers, as well as other products. Waterloo is the distributing center for northeastern Iowa—a farming and livestock-raising region—and is the headquarters for the Dairy Cattle Congress and the International Belgian Horse Show. Repair shops of the Illinois Central Railroad are here.

The city was settled about 1846. It was laid out in 1854 and chartered in 1868. The government is by mayor and council. Population, 1940, 51,743.

WATERLOO, ONT., on the Canadian National Ry., three miles northwest of Kitchener. It is an important center for manufacturing, furniture, boots and shoes, threshing machines, buttons, mattresses, washing machines, trunks and bags, bricks and tiles being the most important products. Niagara electric power is furnished to the factories. There are good public and separate schools and six churches. Population, 1941, 8,968.

WATERMELON, a creeping variety of gourd. The rind of the fruit is smooth and dark green when ripe; the inside of the melon is a coarse red or yellowish pulp, ninety per cent of which is water. Its native home was Africa, but it has been widely cultivated from remote times. It is very popular in the United States, where it has become a most important crop for the fruit-growers of the South Atlantic and Gulf states, in which sections thousands of acres are devoted to raising melons for the northern market. Watermelons in smaller quantities are raised as far north as Southern Ontario. The ideal soil for melon culture is light, sandy loam, which is naturally dry or else thoroughly drained. Most melons weigh from twenty to fifty pounds.

WATER PLANTS. See AQUATIC PLANTS.

WATER POLO, a ball game similar to hockey, played by swimmers, with a ball filled with air, which floats. It is a good game for swimming tanks, and is then played generally throughout the winter season. The object of the game, of course, is for one side to carry, push or throw the ball to the opponent's goal line, at the end of the tank.

WATER POWER. A waterfall capable of being "harnessed" to perform work has been appropriately referred to as "white coal." Much of the machinery of the world is operated directly or indirectly by water power. A great factory located where the power of falling water is available may be electrically operated, but water power may be utilized to generate the electric current. The installment of a water-power plant usually requires the construction of a dam, a canal or flume to conduct the water to the great paddle wheel, where the power of the water is applied. The original expense may be greater than that of a steam or electric plant, but the extra cost is soon recovered by the saving in operating expenses. See WATER WHEEL.

Classification. Water-power plants are divided into three classes—*low-head, medium-head,* and *high-head,* according to the height of the fall. Low-head plants have a fall not exceeding 100 feet; medium-head, not exceeding 350 feet, and the high-head class includes all plants having a fall of more than 350 feet. The fall of some plants in this class exceeds 5,000 feet. Most of the great plants are of low-head type, and they are located on the banks of large streams. They gain in volume what they lose in fall. The largest plants of this type are at the Wilson Dam in Alabama and one at Keokuk, Iowa. The most noted plant of the medium-head type is at Niagara Falls.

ANCIENT DEVICES

arly methods of raising water and of utilizing its
wer are in use today. The Archimedean screw, in-
nted 200 B. C., is still used in Egypt; the Oriental
sorts to foot-power; undershot and overshot
aterwheels generate power to operate machines.

Kaufmann-Fabry

WATER POWER AS DEVELOPED TODAY

Raging torrents and broad streams are harnessed, and giant turbines generate electricity to turn the wheels of industry. A high-head power plant utilizes a fall of water from extreme heights, while dammed streams provide the power for low-head plants.

Century of Progress Electric Power Exhibit

Plants of the high-head type are usually found on mountain streams having a rapid flow and small volume of water. A dam is constructed across a deep, narrow valley to impound the water, which is conducted to the power house through steel pipes. The power house may be two or three miles below the dam, so a high fall is secured. These plants are operated by a small volume of water under very high pressure and they require a special type of water wheel (see TURBINE WHEEL). Their principal use is in generating electric power, which is often carried long distances over wires. The power used in operating the street cars in San Francisco, for instance, is generated over 125 miles from the city.

Estimating Water Power. The power of water for operating machinery is derived from its weight or pressure. The pressure of a column of water of a given height is equal to the weight of the water. A cubic foot of water weighs 62.5 pounds; therefore a column of water one foot square and ten feet high weighs 625 pounds, and at its base exerts a pressure on a square foot equal to that weight. The rule for estimating the horse power of a water fall is as follows: Multiply the flow in cubic feet per second by the height of the fall and this product by .1134. A fall of 100 feet and 600 cubic feet flow will have a power equal to 100X600X .1134, or 6,804 horse power.

Government Ownership. In the United States all water power on government land is under control of the government, and since the beginning of the present century stringent laws for preventing great power sites from falling into the hands of monopolists have been passed. Unfortunately, however, before the conservation movement was started, many valuable sites had been appropriated by capitalists and a legal claim to them had been established. Since water, like air, is one of the great natural resources of a country, the theory of the most enlightened governments is that it belongs to all the people; therefore all water power should be under control of the government, and it should be leased, not sold. Canada is far ahead of the United States in this respect, for in Canada all water power is under government control. Power sites may be leased, but none can be purchased.

It is estimated that the total water power of the United States is 30,000,000 horse power, and that less than one-sixth of it has been developed. The water power of Canada is estimated at 43,000,000 horse power, only about fifteen per cent of which has been developed. Europe has 41,000,000 horse power, and utilizes only one-tenth of it. The water power of the other continents is not known.

WATERPROOFING, a process of rendering cloth and other articles proof against water. In the preparation of mackintoshes a solution of rubber is spread on the goods, and the cloth is doubled, pressed and finished with the waterproof layer in the middle. Such goods are impervious both to air and to water, but from a sanitary point of view they are not desirable for constant wear. A new process has been introduced, which renders the fabrics proof against water, but does not obstruct ventilation. The materials are saturated with soap and then dipped in an alum solution. Still another process, by which the same result is obtained, consists of treating the fibers of the cloth, instead of the manufactured, woven fabric, with the solution. Paraffin is often used as a substitute for rubber in waterproofing leather, wood and various other substances. Paper is made waterproof by immersing it in a solution of shellac in borax, a treatment which causes it to resemble parchment paper.

WATER PURIFICATION. Pure water is essential to health, and often one of the most perplexing problems connected with water supply is that of securing pure water. Because of its solvent power, all water obtained from natural sources contains more or less impurities, some of which may be highly injurious. Among the mineral impurities held in solution are usually found lime, iron, compounds of sulphur and sometimes compounds of lead. Impurities present but not held in solution are clay, particles of soil, animal and vegetable matter and bacteria.

Lime and sulphur are not injurious to health; neither is iron, unless it occurs in excess. The presence of clay, sand and organic matter makes the water turbid, and the organic matter renders the water dangerous to health. All these substances should be removed by purification processes.

The processes employed for purifying water on a large scale include settling or sedimentation, filtering and chemical treatment. Settling is secured by allowing the water to remain quietly in large tanks, from which it flows slowly from the top. Where the water contains a large quantity of solid matter two or three settling tanks may be necessary, but usually one is sufficient. The sand and gravel of the earth form a natural filter for spring water, and this sort of filter is used in water purification. The filters consist of large tanks with perforated bottoms, over which layers of gravel and sand are placed. As the water percolates through these layers the solid matter and most of the bacteria are removed. If the water contains a large proportion of lime, it may be treated with a solution of sulphate of alumina. The lime separates this compound into alumina and sulphuric acid. The acid unites with the lime or magnesia in the water and renders it harmless, and the alumina coagulates and deposits the organic matter.

Home Tests. Epidemics of typhoid, diphtheria and other contagious diseases are often traced to impure water. Because water is clear, it does not follow that it is pure. A glass of the most sparkling water imaginable may contain millions of death-dealing germs, and every household should know of simple means of testing water whose purity is suspected. The following tests can be applied by any one at practically no expense:

(1) Into a vial containing about two ounces of water put a quantity of granulated sugar equal in volume to a pea or small bean. When the sugar is dissolved, cork the vial and set it in a warm place for forty-eight hours. If, when the cork is removed, the water emits a disagreeable odor, it is unsafe.

(2) Makes a solution of permanganate of potash by dropping into an ounce of water a few crystals of this substance, which can be obtained at any drug store. Into a glass of the suspected water place a few drops of the solution. If the purple color disappears, the water is unsafe.

These tests are satisfactory within certain limits, but all water suspected of pollution should be tested by a chemist; any householder may have this done free of charge by sending a sample of the water to the State Department of Public Health. Water for household purposes should not be run through lead pipes, for it may attack the lead and form poisonous compounds. See LEAD POISONING.

Many cities impregnate their water with chlorine before it reaches the water mains.

WATERSHED, an elevation of land which separates the headwaters of natural drainage systems. Such a configuration of land is

sometimes called a *divide*. A watershed separating great river systems may be only a slight rise of ground, such as the divide between the waters flowing into Hudson Bay on the north and the Gulf of Mexico or the Atlantic on the south and east. Again it may be a range of lofty mountains, such as the Rockies, which separate the headwaters of streams flowing respectively into the Mississippi and the Pacific.

WATERSPOUT, a whirling column of water, extending from a cloud to the surface of a body of water, like the ocean or a lake. The presence of this column is marked by the cloud of vapor which it contains. This cloud is formed by the rapid condensation of the moisture in the atmosphere, due to expansion and rapid cooling, caused by the low pressure in the area occupied by the column. If the conditions continue a sufficient length of time, rain is produced and sometimes falls in such quantities as to constitute a small deluge. In waterspouts over the ocean, the lower part of the column may contain vapor from salt water, but usually the vapor is that of fresh water. Waterspouts are caused in the same way as whirlwinds. See WHIRL-WIND.

WATERTOWN, N. Y., the county seat of Jefferson County, seventy-three miles northeast of Syracuse, on the Black River and on the New York Central Railroad. The city is the center of one of the most productive dairying regions of the country. The river furnishes extensive water power, and there are large manufactories of paper-making machinery, air brakes, clothing, plumbing supplies, thermometers and paper specialties. The first American-made portable steam engine was manufactured in Watertown in 1847, and the first of the F. W. Woolworth chain of five-and-ten-cent stores was established here in 1878. Watertown is the commercial center for the Thousand Islands, Lake Ontario and western Adirondacks, and has an extensive summer tourist business because of its proximity to these resorts. Watertown was settled in 1800, was made the county seat in 1805 and was chartered as a city in 1869. It adopted the commission-manager form of government in 1920. Population, 1940, 33,385.

WATERTOWN, S. D., the county seat of Codington County, 214 miles west of Minneapolis, on the Big Sioux River and on the Chicago & North Western, the Chicago, Rock Island & Pacific, the Great Northern and the Minneapolis & Saint Louis railroads. It has regular air service. Watertown is in the lake region of northeastern South Dakota. It is an important shipping point for grain and livestock and a leading marketing center for poultry and certified seed potatoes. There are large grain elevators, warehouses and flour mills, and manufactories of millwork, agricultural implements and foundry and machine-shop products. It was incorporated in 1885 and is governed by a mayor and council. Population, 1940, 10,617.

WATERVILLE, MAINE, a city in Kennebec County, seventeen miles northeast of Augusta, on the Kennebec River and on four lines of the Maine Central Railroad. There is a modern municipal airport. The Belgrade Lakes resort country is ten miles west of Waterville. Railroad repair shops are here, and there are manufactories of cotton and woolen goods, pulp and paper products, men's shirts, canoes, traction engines and iron products. Colby College is here. Waterville was first settled about 1760, but it remained a part of Winslow until it became a town in 1802; it was incorporated as a city in 1883. Population, 1940, 16,688.

WATERVLIET, *waw tur vleet'*, N. Y., a city in Albany County, on the Hudson River, opposite Troy, near the terminals of the Erie and Champlain canals, and on the Delaware & Hudson railroad. A United States arsenal was established here in 1807 on a reservation of 109 acres, and has since been one of the largest permanent centers in the country for the manufacture of war materials. Other manufactures include steel, lumber products and precision instruments. Watervliet was first called West Troy. It was incorporated as a village in 1836 and as a city in 1897. The first Shaker settlement in America was here. Population, 1940, 16,114.

WATER WHEEL, a wheel constructed and set up for operating machinery by water power.

OVERSHOT WHEEL

The old style water wheels were large wooden structures, rotating upon a horizontal axis. They were constructed of two frames, from four to six feet apart, joined at their circumferences, with buckets or floats attached, as occasion required. They were known as *overshot or undershot* wheels, according to the method of operating, the overshot wheel receiving water at the top, and the undershot at the bottom. Each of these is described under its respective title. The *breast* wheel has the water admitted to the floats at a point horizontally opposite the axle.

A recent modification of the undershot wheel consists of a small iron wheel, with cups or buckets upon its circumference the whole enclosed in an iron box. This is often known as the *impact wheel* or, *water motor.* The water issues from a small nozzle under very high pressure, and as it strikes the box it causes the wheel to revolve

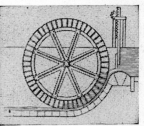

BREAST WHEEL

with great rapidity. These wheels are convenient, because of their small size and the ease with which they can be placed in almost any desired position, but they are of use only in cities where the waterworks enable a high pressure to be obtained. Another form of wheel in common use is the turbine. See TURBINE WHEEL; WATER POWER.

WATERWORKS, the system of reservoirs, pumps and mains arranged for supplying a community with water for domestic use, manufacturing purposes, fire protection and street and lawn sprinkling. The water supply of large cities is usually conducted from near-by lakes or rivers; small towns obtain their supply from springs or wells. The selection of a source of supply must be made with great care, in order that it may be free from decaying animal and vegetable matter and other organic impurities. It must also be free from sewage contamination. Cool water is considered better than warm, because it is less hospitable to the propagation of life.

Where the source of supply is a long distance from the city, a reservoir is usually constructed, which is connected with the city by an aqueduct emptying into one or more smaller reservoirs, as in the New York City plant. From these reservoirs the water is distributed through mains to different portions of the city, and from the mains to consumers. When a city is situated near a suitable source of supply, the water is pumped directly through the mains, as is the case in Chicago, which secures its water from Lake Michigan. Small cities commonly use standpipes for reservoirs. These are constructed of iron or steel, and are mounted on foundations of masonry.

WATSON, JOHN (1850–1907), an English author and clergyman, best known by his pen name, IAN MACLAREN. He was born at Manningtree, in Essex, of Scotch parents. He graduated in 1870 at the University of Edinburgh, and studied theology at New College, Edinburgh, and at Tübingen. His first charge was at Logiealmond, in Perthshire. In 1877 he became associate pastor of Saint Matthew's Church, Glasgow, and he took charge of the Sefton Park Presbyterian Church, Liverpool, in 1880. A number of sketches of humble Scottish life, which were published in the *British Weekly,* were in 1894 collected into a little volume called *Beside the Bonnie Brier Bush.* This has remained the author's most popular work. Among his other writings are *The Days of Auld Lang Syne, Kate Carnegie* and *A Doctor of the Old School.* Under the name John Watson, he wrote *The Mind of the Master* and other religious works.

WATSON, JOHN BROADUS (1878–   ), an American psychologist, leader of a school of psychology known as *behaviorism.* This is a movement that opposes the belief that consciousness or insight is the key to human actions, and asserts that a person's behavior should be described in terms of his physical response to stimuli. Watson was born in Greenville, S. C. He received the degree of Ph. D. at the University of Chicago in 1903, and from 1908 to 1920 was director of the psychological laboratory and professor of experimental and comparative psychology at Johns Hopkins. He edited the *Psychological Review* and *Journal of Experimental Psychology* and wrote a number of books setting forth his theories. These works include *Animal Education, Behavior, Suggestions of Modern Science Concerning Education, Behaviorism, Ways of the Child* and *Psychological Care of Infant and Child.*

WATSON, WILLIAM (1858–1935), an English poet, author of *Purple East,* containing his best sonnets; *The Year of Shame,* an indictment of England's policy in the Orient; *The Hope of the World; Studies in Poetry and Criticism,* and other works.

WATT, *wot,* in electricity the unit of power or measure of the rate of current, so named in recognition of James Watt (see below). The watt is equal to the pressure of one volt with a flow of one ampere per second. A volt is defined as the force or pressure that will drive a current of one ampere (unit of intensity) through a resistance of one ohm. Thus, by multiplying pressure by the current, or volts by amperes, we get watts, the measure of power. A thousand watts equal one kilowatt, the unit in common use. The energy consumed by an electrical device is measured by the watt-hour or kilowatt-hour meter. For a description of the meter in common use to measure electric current, see ELECTRIC METER.

WATT, JAMES (1736–1819), a Scottish engineer, celebrated for the improvements he made in the steam engine. He was born at Greenock, Scotland. Having determined to adopt the trade of making mathematical instruments, Watt went to London, at the age of eighteen, to learn the art; but ill health compelled him to return after only a year's apprenticeship. Shortly after his return he was appointed maker of mathematical instruments for the University of Glasgow. Resigning this position after a time, he worked as a civil engineer, making surveys for canals and harbors. In 1764, while repairing a Newcomen engine, Watt made experiments which resulted in the improvements that have made his name famous. In partnership with Matthew Boulton, a Birmingham manufacturer, he founded, at Soho, a factory where, in 1774, was completed the prototype, in principle, of the steam engine of today. See STEAM ENGINE.

Watt was a fellow of the Royal Societies of London and Edinburgh and a foreign member of the National Institute of France. Besides improving the steam engine, he invented or improved a variety of mechanical appliances, including a letter-copying press, a machine for reproducing sculpture and a fuel-saving furnace.

WATTEAU, *vah toh',* JEAN ANTOINE (1684–1721), one of the most celebrated painters of the eighteenth century, born of humble parents, in Flanders. At eighteen he went to Paris, where after years of struggle in obscurity he became a court favorite. In time his reputation extended throughout

Europe. His name is chiefly associated with a style characterized by ideal gardens and woodlands peopled with richly costumed men and women, who disport themselves with all the airs and formal graces of the times. In 1717 Watteau became a member of the Academy. He was a favorite of Frederick the Great, and to-day the finest collection of Watteaus in the world is owned by Germany.

WATTERSON, *wat' tur son*, HENRY (1840–1921), for nearly fifty years one of the most influential newspaper editors in the United States. He was born at Washington, D. C., was privately educated and at the age of twenty joined the staff of the Washington *Star*. He removed to Nashville in 1861, where he edited the *Republican Banner*, and during the Civil War he served in the Confederate army. The *Republican Banner* was revived after the close of the war; and in 1867 Watterson went to Louisville, where he founded the *Journal*, later consolidated with the *Courier*, and then known as the *Courier-Journal*. He steadily refused office, but in 1876 he accepted a seat in Congress, serving with distinction, but declining re-election. From 1872 to 1892 he was a delegate at large to every Democratic national convention, and he was until his retirement from active service in 1918 a power in national politics, through his editorials in the *Courier-Journal* and his strong personality. In 1919 he published *Looking Backward,* a series of sketches in which he reviewed in a personal vein his country's history for five decades.

WATTS, *wots*, GEORGE FREDERICK (1817–1904), an English artist, famous for his portraits, but chiefly for allegorical and symbolical pictures in which he attempted to show the power of love and the ugliness of greed. Watts was born in London, and at the age of thirty he married the actress Ellen Terry. The marriage was soon annulled. Among his more important pictures are *Love and Death,* now in Washington; *Life's Illusion, The Window Seat* and *Sir Galahad.* He is one of the most subtle and powerful of portrait painters, among his successful work in this line being portraits of Tennyson, Millais, Sir Frederick Leighton, Cardinal Manning and Browning.

More than almost any other artist, he devoted himself to the artistic interests of the nation, gratuitously decorating the din-

ing hall of Lincoln's Inn and giving the best of his work to form the nucleus of the National Gallery of British Art. The principles of his art are best summed up in his own words, "The end of art must be the expression of some weighty principle of spiritual significance, the illustration of great truth."

WATTS, ISAAC (1674–1748), an English clergyman and writer, noted for his hymns. He was born at Southampton. After tutoring six years, he became minister of the Independent Church in Mark Lane, in 1702. A severe illness ended this engagement and Watts spent the remainder of his life with Sir Thomas Abney, at Theobalds. Among his works are *Divine and Moral Songs for Children, Hymns and Spiritual Songs, Psalms of David Imitated and Horae Lyricae,* the last three containing nearly five hundred hymns and versions. "When I survey the wonderous cross" is said to be Watts's finest hymn, and with Ken's *Morning Hymn,* Charles Wesley's "Hark, the Herald Angels" and Toplady's "Rock of Ages," it stands at the head of all hymns in the English language.

WAUKEGAN, *waw ke'gon*, ILL., the county seat of Lake County, thirty-five miles north of Chicago, on Lake Michigan and on the Chicago & North Western, the Chicago North Shore & Milwaukee (electric) and the Elgin, Joliet & Eastern railroads. It has an excellent harbor, with docking facilities for the largest lake boats, and is the center of a large trade in farm and dairy products. Its proximity to the lakes region of northern Illinois makes it an active summer resort. The principal manufactures include asbestos products, building materials, wire and wire products, pharmaceuticals, leather goods, foundry and machine-shop products and envelopes. Sheridan Road, an automobile boulevard extending from Chicago to Milwaukee, passes through Waukegan; on this road just north of the city is the Bowen Country Club, the summer camp of Hull House in Chicago. The Great Lakes Naval Training Station is five miles south of the city.

Waukegan was settled in 1835 and was known as Little Fort until 1849, when it was incorporated as a town and the name changed to Waukegan, a Potawatomi word meaning "Little Fort." It became the county seat in 1841 and was chartered as a city in 1859. The first settlers found the ruins of an old stockade here, thought to be the site of a French trading post established as early as 1700. The government is by mayor and council. Population, 1940, 34,241.

WAUKESHA, *waw'ke shaw,* WIS., the county seat of Waukesha County, seventeen miles west of Milwaukee, on the Fox River and on the Chicago, Milwaukee, Saint Paul & Pacific, the Chicago & North Western and the "Soo Line" railroads. There is an airport. It has numerous mineral springs, and its principal industry is the bottling and shipping of water. There are also structural steel works, steel-bridge and malleable-iron works, plow and motor works and canning factories. Carroll College and the state industrial school for boys are located here. Other features of interest are the Rest Haven sanitarium, the courthouse, a public library and three parks. The place was settled in 1836, and incorporated in 1848. Population, 1920, 12,558; in 1930, 17,176; and in 1940, 19,242.

WAUSAU, *waw'saw,* WIS., the county seat of Marathon County, 180 miles northwest of Milwaukee, on the Wisconsin River and on the Chicago & North Western and the Chicago, Milwaukee, Saint Paul & Pacific railroads. It is surrounded by a lumbering, agricultural and dairying section, which also has extensive granite quarries. The river furnishes good water power, and the city maintains sawmills, sash and blind factories, machine shops, box and veneer factories, also paper and flour mills. A county training school for teachers, a county school of agriculture and domestic science, an asylum for the insane and a tuberculosis sanitarium are located here. The city also has a public library, a hospital, a fine courthouse and a city hall. The place was settled in 1842, and was at first known as Big Bull Falls. It was chartered as a city in 1872. Population, 1940, 27,268.

WAVES, *wayvz,* disturbances in matter, which result in carrying force from point to point, often to a great distance. The most familiar *visible* waves are those produced by the wind on the surface of a body of water. *Invisible* waves are those minute vibrations produced within a body, by striking it or by some other means of agitation. These waves are manifest through their results, as in sound, heat and light.

When waves are produced by the disturbance of a small quantity of liquid, as by throwing a pebble into a pool, they appear to advance from the point where the pebble strikes, in widening, concentric circles, the height of the wave decreasing gradually as the circle enlarges. There is, however, no progressive motion of the liquid itself, as may be seen by watching a body floating on its surface. This is true of large. as well as small, waves, and the waves of the ocean, which sometimes reach a height of forty feet or more, do not cause the water to move forward. Breakers are caused by the friction of the water on the bottom of the sea, which retards the motion at the wave base and causes the crest to break over it. They never occur in deep water. See SOUND.

WAX, a solid, fatty substance derived from animal and vegetable sources. A by-product of petroleum, paraffin, is a similar product, having a number of uses. The chief kinds of animal wax are *beeswax* and *spermaceti.* The first is secreted by bees to build their cells. It is used in the arts for modeling, and in making ointments, plasters and candles. Spermaceti, a constituent of whale oil, is used for making toilet creams and candles. A wax secreted by the pores of sheep and extracted from the cut wool is used in dressing leather. Myrtle wax, palm wax and Japanese wax are of vegetable origin. From myrtle wax bayberry candles are made. Vegetable wax is the basis of the finest Japanese lacquers.

WAX MYRTLE, or **WAX TREE.** See CANDLE-BERRY.

WAXWING, a handsome singing bird, distinguished by its high, pointed crest, yellow band across the end of the tail and red spots on the wings, which have the appearance of sealing w a x. The body plumage is reddish-brown above, yellowish underneath. The *cedar waxwing* is found in nearly every part of North America, and may be seen in summer as far north as Southern Alaska. It feeds on insects

WAXWING

and fruits, and nests in trees. The eggs are putty-colored, with black specks. The *Bohemian waxwing*, a familiar bird in both eastern and western hemispheres, also migrates to high latitudes in the nesting season, traveling, like the cedars, in small flocks.

WAY BILL. See BILL OF LADING.

WAY'CROSS, GA., the county seat of Ware County, ninety-seven miles southwest of Satilla River and on the Atlantic Coast Line, the Waycross & Southern, the Waycross & Western and the Atlanta & Birmingham railroads. It is the center of a fertile section, in which are gown cotton, fruit, live stock, pecans and sugar cane. There is abundant timber, and the city has large saw and planing mills. Other industrial establishments are railway shops, an overall factory, a packing plant, a turpentine plant, a cotton gin, a cold storage plant and a fireproof warehouse for cotton. There are a Federal building, a courthouse, a Y. M. C. A., Kings Daughters' Hospital and Baptist Institute. Population, 1920, 18,068; in 1930, 15,510; and in 1940, 16,763.

WAYNE, *wane*, ANTHONY (1745-1796), an American revolutionary leader, called "Mad Anthony" Wayne because of his brilliant bayonet charge on Stony Point in 1779, the most daring feat of the Revolutionary War. He was born at Easton, Pa., and was prominent in the patriotic movements before the Revolution. He served in the Pennsylvania legislature and in 1775, when the war broke out, he joined the army, was colonel of a volunteer regiment, and early in 1776 accompanied the expedition to Canada. For some time he was in command of a fort at Ticonderoga, and he afterward took part in the battles of Brandywine, Germantown and Monmouth. He captured Stony Point with a light infantry corps and became a popular idol; this was one of the romantic episodes of the war.

After the surrender of Cornwallis at Yorktown, at which he was present, he served for a time in Georgia and South Carolina. After the close of the war he held a number of civil offices in Pennsylvania and then removed to Georgia. In 1791 and 1792 he represented Georgia in Congress. In 1792 he was made general in chief of the United States army and was given command of an expedition against the Indians in the West. He defeated them at Fallen Timbers in August, 1794, and he concluded with them the Treaty of Greenville, by which the United States gained a large tract of land.

WEALTH, *welth*, a term used in economics to signify all material goods that have value. There are three essential qualities for objects classified as having value; they must be useful, must be limited in supply, and must be transferable. Gold, for example, comes under the category of wealth, for it has utility, it is produced in limited quantity, and it can be taken from one place to another. Health, while it is of priceless value to the possessor, is not wealth, for it is not a material thing. The possession of health is an aid to one who seeks to acquire wealth, but is not wealth itself, according to the terminology of economics. The same statement can be made of intelligence, physical strength, skill, education, and other intangible possessions that are in themselves of great value to man.

Circumstances alter the relative value of objects classified as wealth. On a desert island a shipwrecked sailor with a belt of money would consider food and drink of far greater value than his gold. If he were rescued and taken to a country where food was plentiful his money would be again classified as wealth. The four phases of wealth —production, exchange, distribution and consumption—are fundamental in the consideration of the economic structure of the world.

Related Articles. Consult the following titles for additional information:

Capital	Profit Sharing
Consumption	Socialism
Credit	Supply and
Economics	Demand
Money	Wages

WEASEL, *we'zel*, a small, carnivorous animal, a native of almost all the temperate and cold parts of the northern hemisphere. The body is extremely slender, the head small and flattened, the neck long and the legs short. It preys upon mice, birds and other small animals and is very destructive to poultry. The weasel is usually nocturnal in its habits. It is a fine hunter, having a very keen scent and sharp sight, and, being unwearying in pursuit of its victim, it often wears to exhaustion animals larger than itself. Several species are common in the United States, and others are found in most parts of the temperate zones. The *long-tailed*, or *New York*, *weasel* is one of the most familiar species in North America. It is dark brown above and white beneath, and in winter in cold climates it turns pure white, except for the tip of the tail, which is black.

Related Articles. Consult the following titles for additional information:

Ermine   Polecat
Ferret   Sable

A Weather Station

WEATHER BUREAU, *weth'ur bu'ro,* a government bureau maintained by all civilized countries for the purpose of studying weather conditions and giving useful information thereon to the people. Mark Twain once said, "People have been talking about the weather for years, but nothing has ever been done about it." As a matter of fact, considerable has been done about it by the weather bureaus. Nobody can ward off a storm sure to be destructive to crops, but the approach of such a storm can be foretold and precautions may be taken to lessen its menace. Warnings of floods, frost predictions, advice on rainfall, recommendations as to irrigation needs—these and many other practical suggestions come from the weather bureaus and help to moderate the tyranny of the weather, which it must be confessed, is a force for good and for ill in the life of nearly every person. The United States Weather Bureau is typical of those of other countries, and in efficiency and in the practical service it renders it is one of the best in the world.

United States Weather Bureau. Previous to the Civil War several attempts to maintain a systematic weather service were made, but on the breaking out of that conflict all these were abandoned. The United States Weather Bureau was organized in 1870 as a division of the signal service in the War Department. The organization was under the supervision of General Albert J. Myer, chief signal officer of the army, and it was adopted by Congress as a national service. Under General Myer's management, *signal stations,* as they were then called, were established throughout the country. In 1891 the Weather Bureau of the signal service was made a bureau of the Department of Agriculture. In 1940 the bureau was transferred to the Department of Commerce.

The Weather Bureau is organized into a number of divisions, each of which carries on its special line of work. The most important of these are the following:

(1) **The Forecast Division,** which receives twice a day reports from stations in the United States, the West Indies, Europe, Asia, Alaska and Hawaii, and makes charts showing the conditions embodied in these reports. These charts are the regular weather maps of the bureau and include forecasts for the entire northern hemisphere. Their predictions are for twenty-four or forty-eight hours.

(2) **The Division of River and Flood Service,** which obtains information concerning the amount of rainfall, ice and snow in the basins of the principal rivers, whether navigable or not. The information which this division gives is for facilitating commerce and especially for protecting river valleys from floods, of which it aims to give ample warning.

(3) **Aviation Service.** Information which is provided especially for airplane pilots has been a most important factor in making travel by air comparatively safe. Local conditions are sent by radio to all fliers, but the Weather Bureau by frequent reports, day and night, keep pilots informed of conditions far ahead on lines of flight. Many of these reporters are also air-line employes.

(4) **The Division of Climate and Crops.** This division maintains a staff of voluntary observers, who give reports of the temperature, rainfall and other important data pertaining to the welfare and growth of crops in different parts of the country. This information is published in weekly and monthly crop bulletins, which are regarded as the highest authority on crop conditions of the country and are of the greatest benefit to agricultural interests.

(5) **Other Divisions.** These include divisions which have charge of examining and testing all instruments used, a division of records and divisions of telegraphy, radio, publications and supplies.

Observing Stations. There are over 200 regular meteorological stations in the United States. Each of these is in charge of trained observers and is equipped with a full set

FIG. 1

of instruments. These observations are taken at 7:45 A. M. and 7:45 P. M. Washington time, and the results are telegraphed to the central station of the district and to the office at Washington, from each of which maps are issued and reports transmitted to the country. These stations and numerous other substations indicate the local weather conditions by the display of signals. A white flag (1 in Fig. 1) indicates fair weather. A flag with the upper half white and the lower half blue (2 in Fig. 1) indicates local rain or snow. A full blue flag (3 in Fig. 1) indicates general rain or snow. A triangular blue flag (4 in Fig. 1) indicates

triangle above indicates storm with wind from the northeast, and with the dark triangle below, storm with a wind from the southeast (see Fig. 3). The hurricane warning consits of two red flags with black centers, one above the other (see Fig. 4). Forecasts are also displayed in post offices and other public places, and in some sections of

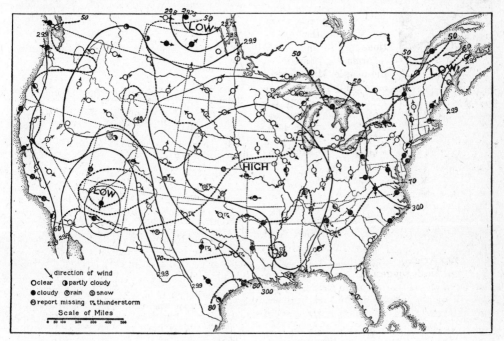

UNITED STATES WEATHER MAP

change of temperature. When placed below another flag it indicates colder, and when placed above, warmer. A white flag with a black square in the center (5 in Fig. 1) indicates a cold wave, which means a drop in temperature of from 15° to 20°.

The direction of winds is indicated by triangular flags, which are generally used in connection with storm warnings. The warning flag is red, with a black square in the center. When this is displayed with a triangular white

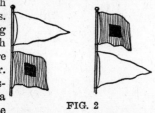

FIG. 2

flag above it, it indicates a storm with wind from the northwest. With the white flag below, it indicates a wind from the southwest (see Fig. 2). The warning flag with a dark

the country they are given by a series of signals by the whistles of locomotives.

Weather Charts. Through telegraphic reports received from all parts of the country

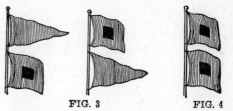

FIG. 3   FIG. 4

twice each day the United States Weather Bureau constructs, twice daily, weather charts showing areas of high and low barometric pressure, the former generally indicating centers of storm disturbance; the general temperature of the different sections of the country, those of equal temperatures being connected by lines called isotherms.

the direction of winds and the condition of the atmosphere, the latter being denoted as cloudy, partly cloudy or clear, and including presence of rain, snow or thunderstorms. By comparing the map under construction with previous maps and with the latest reports from the various stations, the forecaster is able to tell in what directions the areas of low pressure are moving, and at what speed, and can thus predict, with reasonable certainty, changes of weather in all parts of the country. As to changes in temperature and the velocity and the direction of winds, information furnished by the bureau is almost never far wrong, but so many influences affect the condition of the atmosphere that it is more difficult to predict

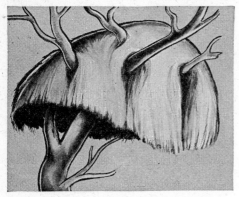

SOCIABLE WEAVER BIRD'S NEST

changes in this respect. The weather map shown here is an exact copy of one furnished by the government.

Canadian Bureau. In the Dominion of Canada the Meteorological Service, a division of the Department of Marine and Fisheries, performs the same tasks as the American Weather Bureau. The superintendent of the service has his headquarters at Toronto, Ont., and acts also as director of the Toronto Magnetic Observatory.

Related Articles. Consult the following titles for additional information:

Climate	Isobars	Rainbow
Cyclone	Isothermal	Snow
Frost	Lines	Storms
Hail	Meteorology	Tornado
Humidity	Rain	Wind
Hurricane		

WEAVER, *we'vur*, JAMES BAIRD (1833–1912), an American political leader, born at Dayton, Ohio. He graduated from the law school of Ohio University in 1854, served in the Civil War and was brevetted brigadier-general at its close. He removed to Iowa,

entered journalism, as editor of the Iowa *Tribune*, at Des Moines, and became a member of Congress in 1879 and again in 1885. In 1880 he was made the Greenback candidate for President of the United States and in 1892 was the candidate of the People's or Populist party, receiving twenty-two electoral votes.

WEAVER, *we'ver*, BIRD, a small bird resembling the finch, with pointed wings, a

WEAVER BIRD

sharp, conical bill and unusually long claws. The name has reference to the bird's manner of building its nest, which is a wonderful structure of woven vegetable substances. The form and workmanship of the nests vary with the several species. The *yellow weaver*, or *baya*, of India, builds a long, bottlelike nest, and hangs it from a slender branch of tree or shrub, often over the water, where it is impossible for anything but a bird to enter. The *sociable weaver birds* build a large dome-shaped structure, or roof, in the forks of branches, and underneath this common roof many families build their nests, each with a separate entrance. While all members of the community work on the roof, each pair works alone on its own nest. See BAYA.

BAYA'S NEST

WEAVING, *we'ving*, the art of making cloth by means of a loom, from threads or yarn. It is not known when weaving was first practiced, but it is certain that it is one of the earliest of the arts, and it seems probable that hand looms were invented independently by several of the ancient nations. The Greeks and Romans brought the weaving art to a high degree of perfection. Among modern countries Italy was the first to acquire fame for the manufacture of woolen

JACQUARD LOOM

and cotton cloths. France, England, Germany and the United States later developed extensive weaving industries. Since the fibers of wool are much more easily worked than are those of cotton or flax, woolen cloth has always been made among the more primitive peoples before they attempted fabrics of linen or cotton.

In weaving, two sets of threads are necessary, one running lengthwise of the cloth, and called the *warp*, the other running crosswise, and called the *weft*, or *woof*. The threads of the warp are arranged on the loom by being wound on a yarn beam, at the back, and stretched evenly to the front, where they are fastened to another beam, upon which the cloth is to be wound. In passing from one beam to the other, the warp threads are laid through the *heckles* and also through a comb on the batten. In laying the warp, every other thread passes through one heckle, and the alternate thread passes through the other. The weft is wound upon bobbins, which are placed in the shuttle, by means of which the weft is laid in position. Weaving by hand loom includes the following steps: (1) Pressing a treadle, which is connected with the heckles by a cord that passes over a pulley on the top of the loom. This spreads the

threads of the weft, raising one-half and lowering the others, so that they form an angle called the *shed*. (2) Throwing the shuttle across the warp and thus laying the thread of the weft in position. (3) Striking this thread with the batten, so as to drive it close up against the one previously laid. (4) Springing down the opposite treadle and thus preparing the web for the next thread of the weft.

Weaving in these times is almost exclusively done by power looms, operated by steam or electricity. Simple as the hand loom is, it contains the elements of all modern looms. The complexity of the pattern may be increased by placing more than two frames in the heckle and dividing the weft into more parts, also by inventions which raise certain threads in the warp at one time and certain others at another. An invention known as the *Jacquard* loom operates upon this plan. Any number of cords can be used, so that a pattern of any degree of complexity is possible, and since all cords are tied together in the form of an endless chain, the pattern may be repeated indefinitely.

WEBB CITY, Mo., a city in Jasper County, five miles northeast of Joplin, on the Frisco and the Missouri Pacific railroads. It is the center of the zinc and lead mining district of Southwestern Missouri. Mining plants in the vicinity number about two hundred, and there are in addition machine shops, foundries, a cement block factory and a brick and tile plant. The city has a Federal building, a hospital and a public library. It was settled in 1873 and incorporated in 1876. Population, 1920, 7,807; in 1930, 6,876; and in 1940, 7,033.

WEB′ER, KARL MARIA FRIEDRICH ERNST VON (1786–1826), a German composer, born at Eutin in Holstein. His father was a musician and gave him a good musical education. At the age of fourteen he wrote an opera, and in 1803 he visited Vienna, where he became acquainted with Haydn. He procured a musical directorship in Breslau, on which he entered in 1804, leaving it only to accept, successively, several more important positions. In 1820, at Berlin, he produced *Der Freischütz*, the most celebrated of his compositions. It was performed in London and Paris two years later. In 1822 *Euryanthe* was brought out, and in 1826 Weber visited London to superintend the production of *Oberon*, which he had composed for Covent Garden Theater. Shortly after its enthusiastic reception, the composer died in London. Besides the operas mentioned, Weber wrote a large number of works for the piano, notably the *Invitation to the Dance* and the *E flat major Polonaise.* He was the forerunner, in style, of Wagner, whom he strongly influenced.

WEBSTER, DANIEL (1782–1852), American orator and stateman, born in the township of Salisbury, N. H. His father was a backwoods f a r m e r, w h o had previously been a hunter and soldier, a n d Daniel owed his first education to his mother. Later, in the intervals of farm work, he attended village school, and when he h a d reached the age of fifteen, his father made

DANIEL WEBSTER

some generous sacrifices to send him to Dartmouth College, where he remained four years. After studying privately and in a Boston law office, he entered the law in 1804, settled at Portsmouth, N. H., and prospered.

Webster at first took little interest in politics, but in 1812, having already established a commanding reputation, he was elected to Congress by the anti-war party. He was placed on the committee of foreign affairs, and his maiden speech, delivered on June 10, 1813, upon the Berlin and Milan decrees, took the House and country by surprise by its display of rhetorical power and wealth of historical knowledge. His subsequent speeches on the increase of the navy, which he warmly recommended, and the repeal of the embargo, placed him in the first rank of debaters.

In 1816 Webster retired for a time from political life, removing to Boston to devote himself to his profession. For nearly seven years afterward, with a single exception, he filled no public office, but as an advocate and counselor achieved a preëminent position at the American bar. His strongest powers were displayed in arguing points of constitutional law, and his achievements in this direction drew upon him the attention of the whole country. In 1820, on the celebration of the bicentenary of the landing of the Pilgrim Fathers, he delivered an oration which added greatly to his fame as an orator,

and he continued to gain in public esteem through other great addresses, notably those at the laying of the cornerstone of Bunker Hill Monument in 1825 and at the memorial service for Adams and Jefferson in 1826.

In 1822 he was elected to Congress, and was reëlected in 1824 and 1826. At the end of his last term he was chosen Senator for Massachusetts. In January, 1830, he delivered a remarkable speech in favor of the nationalist view of the Constitution, in reply to a speech by Robert Y. Hayne of South Carolina. The address created a sensation throughout the Union and probably was more widely circulated throughout the country than any other in previous American history. Webster was strongly opposed to the nullification movement of Calhoun and the South Carolina school, and his eloquence in support of Jackson's energetic measures did much to prevent secession. In 1836 he was an unsuccessful candidate for the Presidency, and from 1841 to 1843 was Secretary of State under Harrison and Tyler. The chief event of this period was the negotiation of the famous Webster-Ashburton treaty with England, which was equally advantageous and honorable to both parties.

Webster generously supported Clay's candidacy for the Presidency in 1844; and was himself an unsuccessful aspirant for the Whig nomination in 1848. In 1845 he was reëlected to the Senate, and in the struggle over the admission of Texas and California he strongly favored the Northern, or anti-slavery, side. Afterward, however, when public excitement had reached a dangerous height, he supported a policy of compromise, and March 7, 1850, he made a speech in favor of obedience to the Fugitive Slave Law. The same year he was appointed a second time Secretary of State, which office he held till his death.

Webster's guiding principle in politics was the preservation of the Union, for which he was ready to make all sacrifices, opposing the nullifiers, on the one hand, and the abolitionists, on the other. One of his best remembered utterances is that from the *Reply to Hayne,* ending with the exclamation, "Liberty and Union, now and forever, one and inseparable!"

Related Articles. Consult the following titles for additional information:

Calhoun, John C. Webster-Ashburton
Clay, Henry   Treaty
Nullification

WEBSTER, HENRY KITCHELL (1875–1932), an American novelist, born at Evanston, Ill., and educated at Hamilton College. After graduation he taught English for a year in Union College and then began the publication of stories that soon gained for him a place as one of the most popular of American story writers. Among the stories that first brought him into prominence were *The Short Line War, Comrade John* and *Calumet K*, all written in collaboration with Samuel Merwin. Novels of which he is exclusively the author are *The Story of a Corner in Land, Roger Drake, The Sky Man, The Ghost Girl, The Butterfly, Real Adventure, The Thoroughbred, The Painted Scene* and *An American Family.*

WEBSTER, NOAH (1758–1843), an American lexicographer, author of the original *Webster's Dictionary* and of *Webster's Spelling Book.* He was educated at Yale and prepared for the law, but gave it up for teaching. His experience in schools led to the composition of his *Spelling Book*, which was published in 1784, and of which it is said that 62,000,000 copies have been sold. About 1807 he began work upon his *American Dictionary of the English Language.* In preparing this work he visited England and worked for some months at Cambridge. The first edition of the dictionary was finished in 1828, and a second edition was published by Webster in 1840. This work was the basis of the standard *Webster's International Dictionary.*

WEBSTER-ASHBURTON TREATY, a treaty concluded at Washington in 1842 by Daniel Webster, then Secretary of State, and Lord Ashburton, minister of Great Britain to the United States. It defined the northeastern boundary between the United States and Canada, which for years had been a source of irritation between the two countries.

WEDGE, *wej*, one of the so-called mechanical powers used in the construction of machines, formed of a combination of two inclined planes. Wedges of wood or metal are used for splitting various substances or for exerting strong pressure in a small space. The axe, with its thin and its broad edge, is one application of the principle of the wedge. See MECHANICAL POWERS.

WEDGWOOD, *wej'wood*, **WARE**, a superior kind of glazed pottery, capable of taking the most brilliant and delicate colors. It is usually decorated with classic designs, often in relief upon a solid ground. It is used not only for the table, but also for ornament; and, owing to its hardness and property of resisting the action of all corrosive substances, it is commonly used for mortars in laboratories. The ware was named after the inventor, Josiah Wedgwood. See POTTERY.

Josiah Wedgwood (1730–1795), one of the greatest of English potters, was born at Burslem, of a family of successful potters. At the age of eleven he began making pottery on a wheel. The loss of a leg compelled him to give up this work, and he afterwards became head of his own pottery works and the most famous of English potters. Wedgwood made many improvements in the manufacture of earthenwares, and all subsequent work in this field has reflected his powerful influence.

WEDNESDAY, *wenz'day* (Woden's day), the fourth day of the week.

WEED, THURLOW (1797–1882), an American journalist, born at Cairo, N. Y. At the age of twelve he began to learn the printer's trade in Catskill, N. Y., and ten years later he was editing. He founded the Onondaga County *Republican,* and in 1824 became editor and owner of the Rochester *Telegraph.* He was elected to the legislature in 1826, and at the close of his second term he established the Albany *Evening Journal,* a Whig paper, which he edited for thirty-three years. During the Civil War, at the instance of President Lincoln, he was sent to Europe on a semi-official mission, and he did much to remove the misapprehensions as to the war, and to induce foreign governments to refrain from interference. In 1867 he became editor of the New York *Commercial Advertiser,* which position he resigned on account of failing health. He was the author of *Letters from Europe and the West Indies* and an *Autobiography.*

WEEDS, a term applied to plants that are out of place—not wanted, and in most cases very troublesome. Many plants when grown and cultivated in gardens, as the goldenrod and the dandelion, are classed as flowers, while the same plants, running wild in uncultivated ground, are considered as weeds. The chief ways in which weeds are injurious are: (1) They increase the labor necessary to cultivate the soil; (2) they take up food from the soil, which should go to useful plants; (3) their foliage smothers the young plants; (4) they sometimes are poisonous to cattle. Care should be taken to eradicate them as soon as they begin to grow. There are various ways to prevent their growth, different weeds requiring different methods. Planting of pure seed, diligent tillage of the soil, rotation of crops, cultivation of all open land with crops, are some of the means used. Some weeds while young can be destroyed without injury to the crop, by spraying the field with certain chemicals, called *herbicides*. Weeds are often of service to a farmer, in aiding him to know the needs of his land, since many kinds grow only where the conditions are peculiarly adapted to them. See HERBICIDES.

Related Articles. On page 517, in the article Botany, is a further discussion of the subject of weeds. For descriptions of the common weeds, consult the following titles:

Abutilon	Dandelion	Mullein
Agrimony	Dock	Pigweed
Bindweed	Feverfew	Plantain
Botany	Fleabane	Ragweed
Burdock	Goosefoot	Sand Bur
Canada Thistle	Gromwell	Sow Thistle
Cocklebur	Indian Mallow	Stramonium
Cow Parsnip	Milkweed	Thistle

WEEK, a period of seven days, one of the conventional divisions of time, the origin of which is doubtful. Among the ancient nations who adopted the week as a division of time, are the Chinese, the Hindus, the Egyptians, the Chaldeans, the Jews, the Persians and the Peruvians. In some cases the name has been applied to cycles of time other than that of seven days. The nations with whom the weekly cycle has been traced with certainty to the greatest antiquity are the Egyptians and the Hebrews. The use of the week was introduced into the Roman Empire from Egypt, about the first or second century of the Christian Era, and it had been recognized independently of Christianity before the Emperor Constantine confirmed it by enjoining the observance of the Christian Sabbath.

WEEVIL, *we'v'l*, the name applied to a group of very small beetles, most of which have long snouts, slightly curved downward. They are very destructive to the products of agriculture, some of them injuring the plants, others ruining the fruit or seed. With the long snout the insects of some species bore into nuts, grain or fruit and eat out the interior. Sometimes they deposit their eggs in the fruit, or seeds, so that the larvae will have food when hatched. In this way weevils often hatch out in meal, flour, rice and such food stuffs, spoiling them.

The *boll weevil*, which attacks the cotton boll, is one of the worst pests in the United States, having caused enormous losses to Southern farmers. It is a grayish weevil one-fourth of an inch long. It lies torpid in winter, and when the cotton comes up feeds on the leaves and blossoms. The eggs are deposited in the cotton boll, which the maggots destroy. There are four or more generations each summer. The *alfalfa weevil* is another species of considerable economic importance, and the United States Department of Agriculture has employed stringent measures to have it checked. Peas and beans are among other crops subject to weevil attack. The insects breed in the growing pod and also in stored beans and peas. When infested, the beans float in water and should not be planted. See BOLL WEEVIL.

WEIGHING, *way'ing*, **SCALE**, a mechanical contrivance for ascertaining the weights of substances. The simplest form of the weighing machine is the balance formerly used by grocers. It consists of a horizontal beam pivoted in the middle and having at one end a deep pan, in which was placed the article to be weighed, and at the other a horizontal disk. Pieces of iron of graduated size and ranging in weight from an ounce or less to several pounds were used on the disk to balance the article to be weighed. A modification of this scale is the unequal beam balance; based on the principle of the lever. The horizontal beam is not pivoted at the middle point, but near one end; the weight to be determined is placed upon the shorter end and is balanced by a much smaller weight at the long end.

The *platform scale* is a typical example. It consists of a hinged platform, set above a stationary platform, which sinks under a weight and presses upon a lever underneath. The lever is connected with a vertical rod attached to the short end of the horizontally-pivoted beam already described. The longer end, or lever, of the beam is marked off in a graduated scale. The article to be weighed is placed on the platform, which sinks under the weight, pressing upon the lever, which conveys the pull to the vertical rod connected with the beam. The weight on the long end of the beam is moved along the scale until it balances with the weight on the platform. The weight of the article on the platform is indicated by the mark in pounds at which the weight balances. A weight of one pound on the lever may be made to balance with ten, a hundred or even a thousand pounds or more on the platform. Some of these scales are even built to weigh heavy guns and locomotives.

Among the most recent inventions of scales is a complicated device which not only weighs the goods but also computes the price of fractions of a pound.

WEIGHT, *wayt*, the measure of the force by which any body or a given portion of any substance gravitates or is attracted to the earth; in a more popular sense, the quantity of matter in a body, as estimated by the balance, or expressed numerically with reference to some standard unit. In determining weight in cases where very great precision is desired, due account must be taken of temperature, elevation and latitude. Hence, in fixing exact standards of weights, a particular temperature and pressure of air must be specified; thus the standard brass pound of Great Britain is directed to be used when the Fahrenheit thermometer stands at 62° and the barometer at thirty inches. See, also, Gravitation; Weights and Measures; Metric System.

WEIGHTS AND MEASURES, the standards used in measuring quantities. Most of the common standard units have been chosen arbitrarily, though efforts have always been made to have the units conform to some natural rule. Evidences of this fact remain in the names of both ancient and modern units, such as the *cubit* of the Egyptians and Hebrews, which was the length of the forearm, and the *foot* of the Greeks, which was the length of a man's foot.

The so-called *English* system of weights and measures, used in the British Empire and the United States, dates from a law passed in 1266 in England, which provided that an English penny should equal in weight 32 wheat corns, taken from the middle of the ear; that 20 pence should make an ounce, 12 ounces a pound, 8 pounds a gallon of wine and 8 gallons of wine a London bushel. Before this time, two pound units had grown up; one, the *Troy* pound, introduced into England by William the Conqueror, weighed considerably less than that before used in England, and its introduction created such dissatisfaction that an average pound of sixteen ounces, now known as the *avoirdupois* pound, was made the standard unit

for articles in common trade, while the **Troy** pound, of twelve ounces, was retained as the unit of weight for gold, silver, gems and apothecaries' supplies.

The units of length, capacity, weight and volume have often varied and are not yet entirely uniform, but the common standards of the English system are as follows: Of length, the *yard,* consisting of 3 *feet,* each foot containing 12 *inches;* 5½ yards equal 1 *rod;* 320 rods equal 1 *mile.* In England, the rod is called a *pole,* or a *perch.* The units of square and cubic measure are respectively the squares and cubes of the linear units, as *square yard, cubic inch,* etc. The *acre,* used in the measurement of land, contains 160 square rods. A *square mile* equals 640 acres.

There are two sets of measures of capacity, one for liquids and one for solids. The unit for liquid measure is the *gallon* of 231

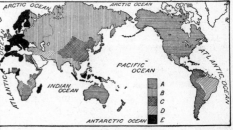

THE WORLD'S WEIGHTS AND MEASURES
Showing the commanding position of the English system
(A)   English weights and measures established and fundamental.
(B)   English basis for linear measurements.
(C)   Local and English prevail, and are closely identical. Metric also used.
(D)   Metric, local and English.
(E)   Metric prevails, with mixture of old and English.

cubic inches. The quart, one-fourth of a gallon, contains 57.75 cubic inches. The quart is divided into two pints and the pint into four gills. Standard gallon measures are maintained in England, Canada and the United States. The quart in dry measure contains 67.2 cubic inches; eight quarts make one peck and four pecks one bushel. The standard bushel contains 2130.42 cubic inches. The metric system (which see) is used in Europe.

There are numerous terms in use in special occupations, such as the *hand,* a unit used in measuring the height of an animal, and equivalent to about 4 inches; the *fathom* (2 yards), used in measuring the depth of water; the *knot,* or *geographical mile*

(6088.27 feet), used to designate distance at sea; the *chain* (4 rods), used in surveying; the *furlong* (10 chains); a *link* (.01 of a chain); the *ell* (3¾ feet); the *barrel* (31½ gallons); the *hogshead* (2 barrels). In England the barrel equals 36 gallons.

Making and keeping standards of the different units, weights and measures is in the hands of the governments of the respective nations. The work requires the greatest skill and care. In the United States these standards are prepared and kept by the United States National Bureau of Standards. In 1856 the British government sent to the United States two standards of length, which are still preserved. The same year the Treasury Department sent a complete set of weights and measures to the governor of each state. These sets are kept at the capitals of the respective states, and may be used for testing weights or measures whose accuracy is in doubt. Most states appoint inspectors whose duty it is to see that false weights and measures are not used by tradesmen.

Related Articles. Consult the following titles for additional information:

Acre	Furlong	Mile
Apothecaries' Weight	Gallon	Ohm
Avoirdupois	Gram	Ounce
Barrel	Hogshead	Pound
Bushel	Kilogram	Quart
Carat	Kilogrammeter	Scruple
Centimeter	Kilometer	Ton
Chain	Kilowatt	Troy Weight
Cubic Measure	Knot	Volt
Drachma	League	Watt
Fathom	Liter	Weighing
Foot	Mensuration	Scale
	Meter	

WEIMAR, *vi'mahr,* GERMANY, a quaint old city on the River Ilm, about fifty miles west-southwest of Leipzig, in the former grand duchy of Saxe-Weimar. The place is associated in a peculiarly interesting way with the new and with the old Germany. Here, in February, 1919, the first national assembly of the German republic met to establish a government based on democracy; here, in July of the same year, the Treaty of Versailles was ratified.

Weimar is famous, too, for its association with the classical epoch of German literature, and it has been called the "German Athens." Goethe, Schiller, Wieland and Herder lived here, and Goethe and Schiller are buried in the cemetery in the southern part of the town. Goethe's house is now the Goethe National Museum, and Schiller's house is also the property of the city and is open to the public. The Goethe-Schiller monument in bronze is in front of the famous court theater, in which the national assembly held its memorable sessions. Another striking building is the grand ducal palace, which was partially constructed under the supervision of Goethe. Weimar has an excellent school system, including an art school, an industrial school, a music school and other special schools. Stoves, straw hats, leather and cloth are manufactured, and the book trade is considerable. Population, 1933, 51,675.

WELD'ING, the process of uniting two pieces of a substance when softened by heat. In the arts the term is restricted to splicing such metals as iron and platinum, though glass and several other substances can be welded as readily as these metals. The simplest method of welding iron is that employed in the ordinary blacksmith shop. The smith hammers the ends of the bars to be welded into a wedgelike form, and heats them white hot, and just as they begin to soften, he covers them with borax or some other flux, to prevent the formation of oxide. The hot ends are then laid together and hammered, the soft surfaces unite, and the joint formed is usually as strong as any other portion of the bar. In most manufactories, electricity is now very generally used for welding, a current of sufficient power to heat and soften the metals being employed.

WELFARE ISLAND, formerly Blackwell's Island, in East River, New York City.

WELLAND, ONT., the county town of Welland County, on the Welland Canal and on the Canadian National, the Michigan Central, the Wabash, the Pere Marquette, the Canadian Pacific and other railways. Welland has become a railroad and manufacturing center. Especially important are iron and steel products of various kinds, agricultural implements, cordage, cotton goods, chemicals, stoves, tires, concrete and furniture. There is an abundance of water power and natural gas in the vicinity. Welland has a wireless station, two government docks, a court house, a registry office and a park. Population, 1941, 12,421.

WEL'LAND CANAL, a canal on the Canadian side of the Niagara River, connecting lakes Erie and Ontario, and constituting an important link in the chain of canals extending from Lake Superior to Montreal. It was opened in 1833 and in 1871 was considerably enlarged. It is 26¾ miles long, 160 feet wide and fifteen feet deep.

The growth of commercial transportation on the great lakes, and the increased size of ships, taxed the capacity of this, the only canal connection between the upper lakes and the ocean. As early as 1913 engineers reported a plan for a new and larger canal which would utilize in part the waterway of the old. The work was begun on the new canal, called the Welland Ship Canal, and was finally completed in 1930. The Ship Canal follows closely the old canal for about half its length, to Allanburg, and then follows a new and straighter course roughly parallel to the old, but east of it, entering Lake Ontario at Port Weller, about three miles east of Port Dalhousie. The total distance from lake to lake is 25 miles. The difference in level between the two lakes, 325½ feet, is overcome by seven lift locks, each having a lift of 46½ feet. Each lock is 800 feet long, 80 feet wide in the clear, and has a depth of 30 feet over the sills. The width of the Ship Canal at the water line is 310 feet, at the bottom 200 feet, and its depth is 25 feet.

The value and importance of such a waterway to the agricultural and industrial development of Canada and the United States can hardly be overstated.

WELLAND CANAL
1, New Canal; 2, Old Canal; 3, Feeders.

The cost of these improvements exceeded $125,000,000.

WELL BORING, a method of sinking wells of small diameter, for the purpose of obtaining water, petroleum or natural gas, or for discovering veins of ore.

Well boring is most frequently done by steam power. The machinery consists of a derrick, shaped like a square pyramid, about twenty feet across at the base and from seventy to seventy-five feet high; an engine for operating the machinery; a windlass for raising and lowering the drill; a walking beam, and bits and drills of different sizes and styles. The drill is attached to a rope, which runs over a pulley at the top of the derrick and down to a drum on the windlass. A few feet above the surface, this rope is grasped by a clamp, which is attached to a screw, called the *temper* screw, used to regulate the motion of the drill. The drill is attached to one end of the walking beam, which is operated by the engine and works the drill forcibly up and down. A rotary motion is given the drill by the operator's turning the handle slightly at every stroke. When the drill has descended the length of the temper screw, it is drawn out by the windlass. If the well is dry, water is run into it, and a bucket, called the *sandpipe,* is lowered, to draw out the mud and crushed rock. This bucket is a hollow cylinder, about sixteen feet long, with a bottom that opens upward. As it descends, the bottom opens and allows the cylinder to be filled. When the cylinder is drawn out, the weight of the mud closes the valve, and in this way the well is emptied. As fast as the hole is drilled, it is cased with a steel tube. Bored wells in the oil regions vary in size from five inches to eight inches in diameter. Artesian well bores are usually smaller.

Wells may be bored as deep as 4,000 or 5,000 feet. Difficulty in well boring increases with the depth, and deep wells are very expensive. See ARTESIAN WELL; PETROLEUM.

WELLES, *welz,* GIDEON (1802–1878), an American statesman, born at Glastonbury, Conn. He attended Norwich University, and on leaving there became editor of the Hartford *Times.* He was a member of the state legislature from 1827 to 1835, in the latter year becoming state comptroller. From 1846 to 1849 he was chief of the bureau of supplies of the United States navy. He joined the Republican party soon after its organization, and in 1861 was made Secretary of the Navy by President Lincoln. In this post he displayed remarkable executive ability, managing the navy with consummate skill and efficiency during the war. He also served throughout Johnson's administration. In 1872 he supported the Liberal Republican movement, and in 1876 he used his influence for Samuel J. Tilden.

WELLESLEY, *welz'ly,* RICHARD COLLEY WELLESLEY, Marquis (1760–1842), a British general and statesman, brother of the Duke of Wellington. He was educated at Harrow, Eton and Oxford and in 1784 entered the English House of Commons. In 1797 he was made governor-general of India, and for his suppression of the insurrection of Tippu Sahib of Mysore, and for the capture of Seringapatam, he was made Marquis Wellesley in the Irish peerage. He was also successful in the struggle with the Mahrattas in 1803–1805. His administration in India, which ended in 1805, was one of the most important in the history of British rule there, owing to his financial reforms and his military victories. In 1808, Wellesley was made minister to Spain, and in the following year he became secretary of state for foreign affairs. He was chosen prime minister in 1812, but was unsuccessful in his attempts to form a cabinet. From 1821 to 1828 and from 1830 to 1834 he was lord lieutenant of Ireland.

WELLESLEY COLLEGE, a nonsectarian institution for the higher education of women, founded in 1870 at Wellesley, Mass., twelve miles west of Boston. Until 1873, it was called Wellesley Female Seminary. The courses are largely elective, and lead to the degrees of Bachelor of Arts, Master of Arts, Master of Arts in Education and Master of Hygiene and Physical Education. The faculty includes about 200 instructors; the enrollment is about 1,500, and the library contains about 200,000 volumes. The endowment exceeds $9,000,000.

Henry Fowle Durant (1822–1881), the founder of Wellesley College, was born at Hanover, N. H., and educated at Harvard. After completing a law course he engaged in practice in Boston. Subsequently he became a lay preacher. Durant was officially treasurer of Wellesley College after founding the institution in 1870.

WELLINGTON, ARTHUR WELLESLEY, Duke of (1769–1852), a British general and statesman, the hero of the Battle of Waterloo. He was the son of the Earl of Mornington, and was educated at Eton, at Brighton and finally at the Military College of Angers, in France. In 1787 he received a commission as ensign in the army, and after a rapid series of changes and promotions he attained, by 1796, the rank of colonel. During 1794 and 1795 he served with his regiment under the Duke of York in Flanders, and in 1797 his regiment was dispatched to Bengal. War had just been declared against Tippu Sahib, and Colonel Wellesley's regiment had an important part in the Battle of Malavelly and

the storming of Seringapatum. He was then appointed civil and military governor of Mysore, which was invaded in 1800 by the robber chieftain, Dhundiah Waugh, with an army of 40,000. Wellesley attacked with vigor and pursued him into Mahratta territory, where he was forced to surrender. In 1803 Wellesley took command of the British forces in the war against the Mahrattas and secured their submission, drawing up his own terms of peace. In his contacts with the native chiefs, he displayed a remarkable understanding of Oriental psychology. For his service in restoring British control in the territory he received the thanks of Parliament and was made Knight Commander of the Bath. In 1805 he returned to England, was shortly afterward elected to Parliament for Rye, and in 1807 was appointed secretary of state for Ireland. In August, 1807, he received the command of a division in the expedition to Copenhagen, and he directed the only land operation of importance. In 1808 he attained the rank of lieutenant-general and received the command of a force destined to operate in the north of Spain and Portugal. He was subsequently superseded; but before giving up the command he gained the Battle of Vimeiro over Junot, the campaign being brought to a close with the Convention of Cintra, by which the French agreed to evacuate Portugal. In 1809 Wellesley was appointed to take the chief command in the peninsula, which had been overrun by the French. The passage of the Douro, and the defeat of Soult, which followed, fittingly opened this masterly campaign. For the victory at Talavera (July 28), the first of many which he won in the peninsula, the government raised Wellesley to the peerage, as Viscount Wellington.

Toward the end of 1810 he fought the Battle of Busaco, which was followed by the famous fortification and defense of the lines of Torres Vedras. Before these fortifications the French encamped for months, but they were finally compelled, by lack of supplies, to evacuate Portugal. A little later (in 1811) occurred the victory of Fuentes de Onoro. Early in 1812 Wellington took Ciudad Rodrigo and Badajoz by storm, fought the Battle of Salamanca, accounted one of his most famous victories, and in August entered Madrid. For his brilliant conduct of the campaign, he received the thanks of Parliament and was raised to the dignity of marquis. Next followed the Battle of Vittoria (1813), battles in the Pyrenees, the capture of San Sebastian and the forced retreat of Soult.

In 1814 a victory over Soult was gained, and in the same year the Battle of Toulouse, in which Soult's best troops were routed, opened the way for the British troops to the heart of France. Napoleon abdicated on April 12, and a few days later the war was brought to a close by the signing of conventions with Soult and Berthier. The triumphant general was created Marquis of Douro and Duke of Wellington and was given the thanks of both houses of Parliament. In July he went as ambassador to France and succeeded Lord Castlereagh as British representative in the Congress of Vienna, and when Napoleon returned, Wellington took command of the army assembled in the Netherlands to oppose him, winning the great victory of Waterloo. On his return to England, after the restoration of peace, he accepted the post of master-general of the ordnance, with a seat in the cabinet of Lord Liverpool. In 1822 he represented Great Britain in the Congress of Verona, and six years later he accepted the premiership, resigning the command of the forces to Lord Hill. The growing discontent throughout the country on the subject of Parliamentary reform, which Wellington steadily opposed, caused the resignation of the government in 1830. He held office under Sir Robert Peel as secretary of state, and in 1846 he helped to carry the repeal of the corn laws, which till then he had opposed. He died September 14, 1852, and was buried in Saint Paul's Cathedral. See WATERLOO, BATTLE OF.

WELLINGTON, NEW ZEALAND, the capital of the dominion of New Zealand, a seaport situated on Port Nicholson, on North Island, 1,280 miles southeast of Sydney, the nearest Australian port. It has a fine harbor and an extensive export and import trade. Manufacturing establishments include flour mills, saw mills, tanneries, foundries, soap and candle works, brick kilns, etc. Important buildings are a government building, a museum, buildings of Victoria University College, and the Wellington branch of the New Zealand Institute. Population, 1931, with suburbs, 138,510.

WELLS, HERBERT GEORGE (1866–   ), one of the most forceful and original of the modern group of English novelists. He was born at Bromley, Kent, of middle-class parents, and was educated at London University. After teaching for several years he began writing for magazines, and in 1895 produced a fantastic romance called *The Time Machine,* which met with instantaneous success. Other stories of a like character followed, including *The War of the Worlds, When the Sleeper Wakes* and *In the Days of the Comet.* In another series of novels of everyday life he finds opportunities to set forth his belief in Socialism, as in *The Research Magnificent* and *The Passionate Friends. Tono Bungay* is much admired for its excellent character drawing, and *History of Mr. Polly* for its näive humor. In *Mr. Britling Sees It Through* Wells produced one of the outstanding books based on the World War. In 1921 appeared *Russia in the Shadows* and *The Outline of History,* followed by *The Science of Life* and other volumes.

WELSBACH, *vels'bahk,* **BURNER,** an incandescent gas burner composed of a cone-shaped cotton-gauze mantle of oxides of thorium and cerium. When first lighted the cotton burns away, leaving a skeleton of the oxides. By means of this burner a strong, clear light is obtained with the use of a minimum amount of gas, smoke and unsteadiness of the flame being eliminated.

Karl Welsbach (1858-1929), inventor of the Welsbach burner, a native of Austria and pupil of Bunsen at the University of Heidelberg. He is the discoverer of the rare elements praseodymium, neodymium and lutecium.

WELWITSCHIA, *wel wich'e a,* a remarkable plant, growing in the dry regions of southern Africa. It consists of a stem, which forms a woody mass, rising not more than a foot above the ground and having a diameter of from four inches to as many feet. From this mass grow two enormous leaves, which become dry and are often split up into shreds, but which do not fall off. Every year several short flower stalks grow up from the base of these leaves, but no other leaves are ever produced.

WENTWORTH, *went'wurth,* THOMAS, Earl of Strafford. See STRAFFORD, THOMAS WENTWORTH, Earl of.

WESLEY, *wes'li,* the family name of two brothers famous as the founders of the religious sect from which the Methodist Church developed. John Wesley, the elder, was the leader of the movement.

John Wesley (1703–1791) was born at Epworth, England, June 17, 1703, a son of the village rector. His mother was a woman of intelligence and piety. The boy attended the Charter-House School and later Christ Church, Oxford, from which he was graduated in 1724. A year after his graduation he was ordained to the ministry, and for a time acted as his father's curate. When in 1729 he returned to Oxford he became associated with his brother Charles and a few other undergraduates in what was derisively called the "Holy Club."

In 1735 he and his brother Charles went with General Oglethorpe to America and for three years the brothers did missionary work among the Indians. John Wesley's preaching was not particularly successful, but the trip marked the turning point in his life, for on the journey over he made the acquaintance of some Moravian Brethren whose simple piety made a deep impression on him. On returning to London he sought the Brethren, and from Peter Böhler, one of their preachers, learned the doctrine of "saving faith." In the summer of 1738 he visited the Moravian leaders on the continent, and this experience confirmed him in his new faith in the saving power of Christ. Returning to England he became associated with George Whitefield, and his real life work as an evangelistic preacher began.

His new methods aroused much opposition, and churches were closed to him. He then began preaching in the open air, gaining a large number of followers. In 1740 an important step was taken when Wesley organized his first society and appointed lay preachers, who were communicants of the Church of England, to take charge of small groups of converts. The small meetings thus provided for caused the movement to spread rapidly. In 1744 the first conference of lay preachers was held. These remained members of the Established Church; it was not until 1784 that Wesley's organization became a new denomination, separate from the Church of England. Wesley was a prodigious worker, traveling long distances and preaching three or four times a day. At the same time he produced a large volume of religious literature. In 1750 he was married to Mrs. Vazeille, a widow with four children, but incompatibility soon led to a separation. At the time of his death Wesley's followers numbered 120,000.

A man of much charm of personality, kindly wit and humor, Wesley was admired even by those who opposed his doctrines. He retained his sprightliness and interest in all about him to the last. See METHODISTS.

Charles Wesley (1707–1788), a noted English evangelist, brother of John Wesley, aided his brother in founding the Methodist Church. He was born in Epworth, England, and was educated at Westminster School and at Christ Church, Oxford. In 1735 he went with his brother John to America and preached in the Georgia colony. His preaching was not successful, owing to his extreme views; and in 1738, influenced by his brother, he modified his doctrines and methods and became an itinerant preacher. He then began to attract large audiences. His chief service to the Methodist movement, however, was as a writer of hymns. He produced about 6,000, some of which remain favorites in the denomination.

WESLEYAN METHODISTS, an offshoot of the original Methodist Church, which preserved the form of church government originated by John Wesley. It is chiefly represented in the British Isles. The other important branch of the denomination, distributed chiefly in America, early adopted the Episcopal form of church organization and became known as the Methodist Episcopal Church. The Wesleyan Methodists joined the United Methodist Church (which see) in 1932.

WEST, BENJAMIN (1738–1820), an American painter, who made his way up from humble beginnings to a place of highest distinction in the world of his day. Painting and drawing he taught himself, making his colors of leaves and berries and his brushes of hair from his cat's tail. At the age of eighteen he established himself as a portrait painter in Philadelphia. In 1760 he went to Rome, where his *Cimon and Iphigenia* and *Angelica and Medora* received favorable comment. Three years later he went to England; and so cordial was his reception that he decided to make London his home. For King George III, his patron for more than thirty years, he executed a series of historical and religious paintings for Windsor Castle. On the death of Sir Joshua Reynolds, in 1792, he became president of the Royal Academy. The best of his historical paintings are *The Death of General Wolfe*, *Penn's Treaty with the Indians*, *The Battle of La Hogue* and *The Black Prince at Poitiers*. Among his religious pieces, the most notable is *Christ Healing the Sick*. Though not a great genius, West was a talented and painstaking painter, and is given credit for improvements he made in the manner of treating historical subjects.

WEST CHES′TER, PA., the county seat of Chester County, twenty miles west of Philadelphia, on the Pennsylvania and the Philadelphia, Baltimore & Wilmington railroads. It is surrounded by an agricultural region, and large cream separator works and extensive nurseries are the most notable industries. The city is the seat of the West Chester State Normal School, one of the largest normal schools in the country, and of Darlington Seminary for young ladies and Saint Anthony's Boys' College. The Battle of the Brandywine was fought within four miles of West Chester, and the battlefields of Chadd's Ford and Valley Forge are within driving distance. The Old Turk's Head Hotel dates from pre-Revolutionary days. Population, 1920, 11,717; in 1930, 12,325; and in 1940, 13,289.

WESTERN AUSTRA′LIA, a state of the Australian Commonwealth, occupying all of that portion of the continent west of the 129th meridian, east longitude. Its greatest extent from north to south is 1,480 miles, and from east to west, 1,000 miles. The area is estimated at 975,920 square miles, making it the largest of the Australian states. In this vast region there are less than three inhabitants to the square mile, as the population in 1933 (official census) was only 438,948. No other state of the Commonwealth is so sparsely populated.

The interior is a low plateau, varying in altitude from 700 to 1,000 feet and occasionally rising to greater height. It is mostly sterile, with little or no vegetation. Most of the eastern part of this division belongs to the great Victorian Desert. The western coast line is bordered by highlands or mountains, which are from 50 to 100 miles from the coast. These mountains also extend into the rorthern or Kimberley division. They are low, and their highest summits do not exceed 3,580 feet. The productive regions of the colony are in the west and southwest. Here there is sufficient rainfall to sustain vegetation, and extensive forests of eucalyptus, sandalwood and other Australian trees occur.

The lands are also well suited to grazing and agriculture. and wheat, barley, corn, oats,

potatoes and hay are raised in paying quantities. Apples, peaches, oranges, lemons, grapes and other fruits are also cultivated. Considerable livestock is raised and wool growing is an important branch of agricultural industry. Other resources of the state are timber, and mineral wealth, consisting largely of gold.

The government is similar to that of other Australian states. The governor is appointed by the British sovereign and the legislature consists of a legislative council of thirty members and an assembly of fifty members. The members of the council are chosen for six years, and of the assembly, for three years. Women vote on equal terms with men. Perth is the capital; with its port, Fremantle, its population is 208,000. See AUSTRALIA.

WESTERN RESERVE. In 1786, when Connecticut ceded to the United States government the western lands covered by its original charter of 1662, it retained a strip of land extending westward from the Pennsylvania boundary 120 miles, and called it the Western Reserve. Most of this tract was sold in 1795 and 1796 to the Connecticut Land Company, and the sum paid ($1,200,-000) was used for Connecticut public schools. The new company surveyed the land, and settlers began to take homesteads and to develop it. Later the district became a part of the state of Ohio. The name of the reservation disappeared from geography, but survives in a university at Cleveland, which is situated in the district (see below).

WESTERN RESERVE UNIVERSITY, a nonsectarian institution of higher learning, founded in 1826 and located in Cleveland, Ohio. The university comprises thirteen colleges and a summer session. Undergraduate liberal arts, science and business administration are offered in Adelbert College for men, the Flora Stone Mather College for women and Cleveland College, the downtown coeducational school. Graduate work in arts and science and business administration is offered in the graduate school and in Cleveland College. Other graduate schools are the schools of medicine, law, applied social sciences, library science and nursing. Undergraduate professional work is offered in the schools of education, architecture, pharmacy and dentistry. The university library contains about 520,000 bound volumes. Including the summer session, the students number about 12,000; the faculty numbers about 750.

WEST INDIES, *in'diz*, or **ANTILLES**, *an til' leez*, an archipelago lying between North America and South America, and between the Gulf of Mexico and Caribbean Sea on the west and the Atlantic on the east. The islands cover a total area of about 92,000 square miles, but their surface area comprises only about 300 square miles. They are believed to be the summits of a subterranean mountain chain. Cuba, the largest island of the group, is independent; the Dominican Republic (formerly Santo Domingo) and Haiti, both on the same island, are self-governed states sometimes advised financially by the United States.

In 1940 the United States secured leases of sites for eight naval bases from Great Britain, in exchange for fifty destroyers. Five of these were in the West Indies: one each in the Bahamas, Jamaica, Trinidad, Saint Lucia and Antigua (in the Leeward Islands).

The islands belong to the following governments:

Great Britain: The Bahamas (twenty inhabited and many uninhabited islands); the Barbados; Jamaica and its dependencies, the Cayman Islands and the Guano Islands (Morant Cays and Pedro Cays); Turks and the Caicos Islands; Trinidad; the Leeward Islands, including Antigua, Saint Christopher (or Saint Kitts), Montserrat, Sombrero and the British Virgin Islands (about thirty in all); and the Windward Islands, including Grenada, Saint Vincent and the Grenadines (half under each of the two former), Saint Lucia and Dominica.

United States: Porto Rico, ceded from Spain in 1898; and the Virgin Islands, formerly the Danish West Indies, purchased from Denmark in 1917, and comprising Saint Thomas, Saint John, and Saint Croix (Santa Cruz).

France: Martinique; Guadeloupe, consisting of Guadeloupe and Grand-Terre, with five dependencies (Marie Galante, Les Saintes, Désirade, Saint Barthélemy, and Saint Martin, northern section).

Netherlands: Surinam or Netherlands Guiana; Curaçao, consisting of two groups of islands about 500 miles apart: (1) Curaçao, Aruba and Bonaire; and (2) Saint Martin (southern), Saint Eustatius and Saba.

Venezuela: Margarita and neighboring islands.

Independent: Cuba and Isle of Pines, Haiti and the Dominican Republic. The island groups are described under their own titles.

Related Articles. Consult the following titles for additional information:

WEST'INGHOUSE, George (1846-1914), an American inventor and engineer, the inventor of the air brake. He was born in Schoharie County, N. Y., and was educated in the public schools of Schenectady. His inventions include a device for replacing railroad cars on the track; the air brake, which he invented in 1868 and subsequently improved; and a number of signaling devices. Alternating-current machinery was introduced in America largely through his efforts. See Air Brake.

WESTMINSTER ABBEY, a famous church in London, called "Abbey" because up to the time of Henry VIII it was a Benedictine monastery, presided over by an abbot. It is situated near the Thames, adjoining the Houses of Parliament. In 1065 a church was built on the site, in the Norman style, by

WESTMINSTER ABBEY

Edward the Confessor, but the main building, as it now stands, was begun in 1220 by Henry III and was practically completed by Edward I. Various additions were made down to the time of Henry VII, who built the chapel which bears his name. The upper parts of the two towers were designed by Sir Christopher Wren. The extreme length of the church is 423 feet, the roof is 102 feet high, and the towers are 225 feet. The coronation

Ewing Galloway

THE CHOIR OF WESTMINSTER ABBEY

THE CORONATION CHAIR

The oaken chair made to order of Edward I, to hold the famous "stone of destiny," on which the kings of Scotland had been crowned for centuries. The kings of England sit in this chair when crowned.

Ewing Galloway

STATELY BUILDINGS AND PARADE GROUNDS OF WEST POINT

Here, after years of severe training, second lieutenants are graduated for future service in the Army of the United States. The inset shows cadets marching with a precision that defies criticism.

of English kings takes place in the choir of Westminster Abbey, where the coronation stone brought by Edward I from Scotland, is placed beside the coronation chairs of the English sovereigns.

Burial in the Abbey is one of the greatest honors the nation can bestow, and not only sovereigns but some of the most celebrated men of science, soldiers, statesmen and men of letters are interred there. Some of the great men who have not been buried there are honored with tablets or portrait busts. In the *Poet's Corner* are monuments to most of England's great poets, from Chaucer to Robert Browning, and a memorial to Longfellow, the only American who is represented.

WESTMINSTER HALL, the hall of the old palace of Westminster, erected by Richard II on the foundations of a structure built by William Rufus. It is 290 feet long, sixty-eight feet wide and ninety feet high, and it has a fine porch, and a roof of carved timber which is considered the most notable of its kind. This building is closely associated with many stirring events in English History. Here Chancellor More, Lady Jane Grey, the Earl of Strafford, King Charles I and Warren Hastings were brought to trial. The hall was the center of the highest English courts of law until these were removed to the new buildings recently erected for their accommodation. It escaped the fire of 1834, and to-day serves as a vestibule to the Houses of Parliament.

WEST ORANGE, N. J. See ORANGE.

WESTPHALIA, *west fa' li ah*, a small province of Prussia, mountainous as to its surface, rich in iron, coal, zinc and copper. The iron and coal areas are extensions of the great Ruhr mines. Westphalia leads all Germany in coal. There is also a large stone and salt industry. Plants for the manufacture of metal wares and machinery abound. Westphalia also manufactures quantities of linen, woolen and cotton goods. About forty per cent of the area is under cultivation, producing crops of rye, oats, flax, potatoes and wheat. Münster is the principal city of the province.

Westphalia was retained as a part of Prussia in the formation of the new Republic of Germany. In 1923, France occupied the Ruhr district in this province, in an attempt to secure from Germany reparation payments guaranteed by treaty.

WESTPHALIA, PEACE OF, the treaty which closed the Thirty Years' War. Many states had been involved in this contest and two separate conventions were held to decide upon terms of peace. The representatives of the Empire, France and Spain and the Catholic electors and princes of the Empire met at Münster, and the representatives of Sweden, the Empire and the German Protestants at Osnabrück. Each of these conventions signed a treaty in 1648 and in October of that year the general treaty was signed at Westphalia, by the representatives of all the powers.

One of the important provisions of the treaty was the extension to the Calvinists of the religious liberty which had by the Peace of Augsburg been allowed only to the Lutherans. It was provided, also, that all territory which, in the Palatinate, Württemberg and Baden in 1618 and in the other states in 1624, had been held by Catholics, was to remain Catholic, and that all which at that time had been held by Protestants was to remain Protestant. A prince might make his religion compulsory with his subjects, but the latter had the right to emigrate if dissatisfied. The Upper Palatinate was added to the duchy of Bavaria; the Lower Palatinate was given to the son of the Elector Palatine, and Western Pomerania was ceded to Sweden. Brandenburg received certain cessions of territory to make up for the loss of Pomerania; France was given Alsace, with Metz, Toul and Verdun; Spain recognized the independence of the United Provinces of the Netherlands, and Austria recognized the independence of Switzerland. See THIRTY YEARS' WAR.

WEST POINT', N. Y., a village in Orange County, on the west bank of the Hudson, fifty-five miles north of New York City, at the opening of the Highlands. The village is beautifully situated on an elevated plateau and is chiefly noted as the seat of the United States Military Academy, which occupies a site covering 2,300 acres (see MILITARY ACADEMY, UNITED STATES).

In the early history of the country West Point was of considerable strategic importance, and during the Revolution it was fortified under the direction of the Polish engineer Kosciusko. It was given into the command of Benedict Arnold (see ARNOLD, BENEDICT), who treacherously attempted to surrender it to the British. It was selected as the site of the academy by Congress in 1802.

WEST VIRGINIA, a state in the eastern mountainous region of the United States, belonging to the South Central group of states. It lies west of Virginia, of which it was originally a part, and is one of the foremost mining states in the Union. Its popular names are PANHANDLE STATE and MOUNTAIN STATE. The rhododendron is the state flower.

Location and Size. The state is irregularly oval in shape, with extensions to the north and northeast; it has no seacoast. Ohio, Pennsylvania and Maryland are to the north, and Kentucky and Virginia lie along its curving southern boundary. Ohio and Kentucky border it on the west. With an area of 24,181 square miles, of which ninety-one square miles are inland water, West Virginia is the fortieth state in size.

People and Cities. The population in 1940 was 1,901,974, ranking the state twenty-fifth in number of inhabitants; it ranked thirteenth in density of population, with an average of seventy-nine persons to the square mile. More than ninety-five per cent of the people are native-born; of the foreign-born groups the most prominent are the Italians, Poles, Hungarians, English, Germans, Czechoslovakians, Greeks, Jugoslavs and Austrians. There are over 115,000 of Negro blood. The population in 1940 was 28.1 per cent urban. The chief religious denominations are the Northern Baptists, the Roman Catholics and the Methodists.

According to the Federal Census for 1940 there were twelve cities in West Virginia with populations of 10,000 or over. The first five, in order of size, are Huntington, 78,836; Charleston (the capital), 67,914; Wheeling, 61,099; Clarksburg, 30,579; and Parkersburg, 30,103. Over thirty-three others had populations exceeding 2,500.

Surface and Drainage. The surface as a whole is very uneven and in the eastern portion it is mountainous. The mountain region occupies more than one-third of the state, and the ranges extend in a northeast-southwest direction. Between the mountain ranges on the eastern and western sides are broad valleys, narrowing into ravines as they approach the hill region. The ridges in the eastern part are cut by numerous transverse valleys, and in the southern part these valleys are so numerous as to cut the mountain ranges into broad domes with spurs running in various directions, leaving but few definite ridges. The average elevation of the state, 1,500 feet, is the highest average of any state east of the Mississippi River. The highest point is Spruce Knob, in Pendleton County, which has an elevation of 4,860 feet, and the lowest point is Harper's Ferry, with an elevation of 260 feet. Some of the other prominent peaks are Bald Knob, 4,800 feet, and High Knob, 4,170 feet. West of the mountains there is a belt of broad, flat hills, ranging from 1,000 to 2,000 feet in elevation. These hills are followed by a more gently rolling country, sloping toward the Ohio River.

The Ohio River furnishes steam navigation along the whole western boundary and receives all the principal streams of the state, except the Potomac and its affluents. The largest rivers flowing into the Ohio are the Guyandot, the Kanawha, the Little Kanawha, the Big Sandy and the Monongahela. The Potomac's South Branch drains the northeastern section of the State.

Climate. The climate has seasonable variations ranging from 30° below to 100° above zero, the mean average temperature of the state being 56° F. The average rainfall in the highest elevation is 35 inches, in the lowest 55 inches, and for the state 43 inches.

Mineral Resources. Coal, natural gas and petroleum are the most valuable mineral products of this richly-endowed commonwealth. Possessing 17,280 square miles of bituminous coal, West Virginia surpasses Pennsylvania in extent of deposits and in the annual yield of this mineral. The production in West Virginia steadily increased

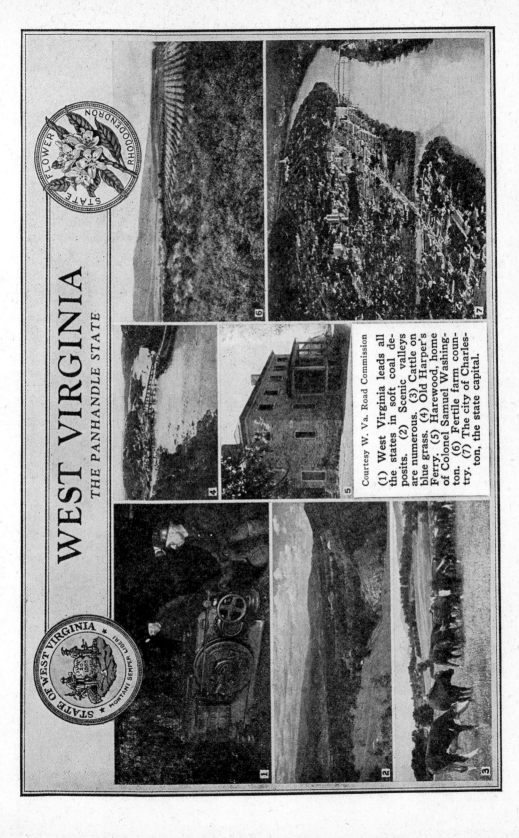

WEST VIRGINIA
THE PANHANDLE STATE

STATE FLOWER RHODODENDRON

STATE OF WEST VIRGINIA ★ MONTANI SEMPER LIBERI

Courtesy W. Va. Road Commission

(1) West Virginia leads all the states in soft coal deposits. (2) Scenic valleys are numerous. (3) Cattle on blue grass. (4) Old Harper's Ferry. (5) Harewood, home of Colonel Samuel Washington. (6) Fertile farm country. (7) The city of Charleston, the state capital.

for several years, but the output began to decline in the 1930's, because of the extensive use of other kinds of fuel and the development of hydroelectric power. The state produces no anthracite.

West Virginia has large deposits of natural gas, much of which is piped to cities of the state and to near-by industrial centers. Crude petroleum is another leading mineral. However, the development of the oil and gas fields of the Central West has reduced the rank of West Virginia in average production of these minerals.

Among other valuable products of the state are pig iron, sandstone, limestone, lime and salt. In average years West Virginia is the fifth state in mineral production.

Agriculture. Considering its mountainous surface, West Virginia ranks well as an agricultural state; about one-third of the whole land area is improved. The Ohio and the northeastern valleys are especially fertile. Corn is grown generally, and leads all other crops in production. Other profitable crops are wheat, oats, buckwheat, potatoes and tobacco. Sorghum cane is grown, and fruits thrive in various sections, especially in the panhandle regions. Apples, including the prized Grimes' Golden and Golden Delicious varieties, are the most important orchard crop, and peaches are second. Plums and grapes are also important fruits. Market gardening, stock raising and dairying are all carried on with profit.

Manufacturing. West Virginia has many natural advantages conducive to the development of manufacturing, such as an abundance of fuel, water power and good transportation facilities. It ranks high among the states in the manufacture of lumber and lumber products, one of its most important manufacturing industries. Wheeling, the principal manufacturing city, is the center of the iron and steel interests, one of the outstanding industries. West Virginia also ranks high in the production of lampblack, tanned leather articles, galvanized iron, coke, tin plate and terneplate. At Wheeling and other cities there are extensive glass factories, and at Charleston there is one of the largest ax factories in the world. Oil refining, pottery making, chemical production and the manufacture of tobacco products are also carried on.

Charities and Corrections. The charitable and correctional institutions include the Weston State Hospital, the Spencer State Hospital, the Huntington State Hospital, the State Tuberculosis Sanatorium, the Welch State Hospital, No. 1, McKendree Hospital, No. 2, the Fairmont Hospital, No. 3, the West Virginia Industrial School for Boys, the West Virginia Industrial Home for Girls, the West Virginia School for the Deaf and Blind, and the West Virginia Children's Home.

Transportation. The state secures water communication through the Ohio, the Monongahela and the Kanawha, which are navigable for large boats. Lumber was formerly floated down the Little Kanawha and the Big Sandy, as well as down the Ohio, which was used extensively to transport coal. Several trunk lines of railway traverse the state from east to west, one in the northern, another in the central and two in the southern section. Two lines extend north and south, connecting these in several places, and there are numerous cross lines and spurs, so that the northern and central parts of the state have good railway facilities.

Government. The legislature consists of a senate and a house of delegates, the former having thirty members, and the latter, ninety-four. One-half of the senators are elected every two years, for a four-year term, and the delegates are elected for two years. The legislature meets biennially, and the session is limited to forty-five days. The executive department consists of a governor, a secretary of state, a superintendent of free schools, a treasurer, an attorney-general and a commissioner of agriculture, each elected for four years. The courts consist of one supreme court of appeals, twenty-two circuit courts and thirty-eight courts of limited jurisdiction, together with courts of county commissioners, justices of the peace and municipal courts.

Education. Separate schools are maintained for white and colored pupils. The system of public instruction is in charge of a superintendent of free schools, and school attendance is compulsory for children between the ages of eight and fourteen. High school education is under the direction of a special supervisor. The higher institutions of learning include the West Virginia University, at Morgantown; the state teachers colleges at Athens, Fairmont, Glenville, Huntington, Shepherdstown and West Liberty; Bethany College; West Virginia

Wesleyan College, Buckhannon; Morris Harvey College, Barboursville; a normal school at Bluefield, for Negroes.

History. The state of West Virginia was, until 1863, a part of the state of Virginia. (For early history, see VIRGINIA, subhead *History*.) At the outbreak of the Civil War, many of the counties in the western part of that state had Union sympathies, while the remainder wished to secede and join the Confederacy. Therefore, in June, 1861, representatives of forty counties declared independence of the state of Virginia and organized a provisional government on a loyal basis under Francis H. Pierpont; representatives to Congress were elected and a constitution was adopted in April, 1862. Meantime, a "reorganized" provisional government of Virginia had given its consent to the formation of the state, and West Virginia was formally admitted June 20, 1863. It was the scene of some of the earliest fighting in the Civil War, and furnished far more than its quota to the Federal armies. After the war there was rapid development of the resources of the state and a great increase in population. It was Democratic in politics from 1872 to 1892, and although generally Republican since that time, it went Democratic in 1932, 1936 and 1940.

Related Articles. Consult the following titles for additional information:

CITIES

Bluefield	Huntington
Charleston	Martinsburg
Clarksburg	Morgantown
Fairmont	Parkersburg
Harper's Ferry	Wheeling

MOUNTAINS AND RIVERS

Alleghany	Monongahela
Blue Ridge	Ohio
Cumberland	Potomac
Kanawha	

WEST VIRGINIA UNIVERSITY, a co-educational state university, established at Morgantown in 1868, by the consolidation of the West Virginia Agricultural College, Woodburn Seminary and Monongahela Academy. It includes colleges of arts and sciences, engineering and mechanic arts, agriculture, medicine and law, schools of music, military science and tactics, and commerce. In 1928 a women's gymnasium was completed, also a field house for men, at a cost of $550,000. There are 300 instructors and about 3,000 students, including those in special departments and in the summer schools.

WEYLER Y. NICOLAU, *wa'lur e ne ko-lah'oo,* VALERIANO, Marquis of Tenerife (1838–1930), a Spanish general and administrator, born at Palma, Majorca. He received a military education in Spain, and was a military attaché of the Spanish legation in the United States at the time of the Civil War. He fought in Cuba under Balmaceda, from 1868 to 1878, and later in Spain against the Carlists. Afterwards he was successively governor of the Canary and the Balearic islands, and in 1889 he became captain-general of the Philippines. After later service as provincial governor of Catalonia, Spain, he became, in 1896, Spanish governor of Cuba. His administration there was marked by such harshness and cruelty that the United States protested, and in 1897 he was recalled. After the Spanish-American War he was for a time captain-general of Madrid.

WEYMAN, *wi'man,* or *way'man,* STANLEY JOHN (1855–1928), an English novelist, born at Ludlow, Shropshire, and educated at Oxford. He was admitted to the bar in 1881 and practiced for eight years. His first historical romance, *The House of the Wolf,* is a story of the French occupation of Quebec. *A Gentleman of France* established his reputation in the field of historical romance. Among other novels which brought him wide popularity are *Under the Red Robe, My Lady Rotha, The Man in Black* and *The Red Cockade.*

WHALE, a large marine animal, some species of which are the largest animals in existence. Even the prehistoric monsters of the Age of Reptiles did not equal the largest whales in length and weight. There is record of a specimen weighing eighty tons. The literature of the whaling industry is fascinating, and one story has become a classic—Herman Melville's *Moby Dick.* The scientific study of whales, including their life history, structural characteristics and classification, has greatly advanced since the advent of shore whaling and the erection of shore stations accessible to zoölogists. Though often classed as a fish, the whale bears only a superficial resemblance to the fishes. The tapering body terminating in a finlike tail and the fin-shaped paddle on each side of the body are the only points of similarity, but the dissimilarities are numerous.

The whale, first of all, is a mammal, bearing its young alive, and suckling it in infancy. It has well-developed brain and lungs, and warm blood, which circulates through veins and arteries. Its bones, joints and muscles are like those of the higher land mammals. The forelimbs contain the same bones as do those of other mammals. These are proportionately short, and, instead of toes, there is a paddle, about seven feet long, formed by a continuous skin; while in the rear part of the body are rudimentary bones which indicate the existence of hind legs in remote ancestors. The organ of locomotion is the fin-shaped tail, which is also used for purposes of defense. The whale is a timid creature and becomes combative only when attacked. When aroused it can capsize a large vessel with its tail, which is from five to six feet long and twenty to twenty-five feet broad, and destroy smaller craft by ramming it with its blunt nose.

Two distinguishing characteristics of whales are the proportionately large head, which is usually a third of the entire length of the body, and the thick layer of fat beneath the skin, which protects the animal from the cold. This fat, called blubber, is cut from the captured animal and reduced to oil. Before mineral oils came into general use, whale oil was burned in lamps in every part of the world.

The eyes of whales are small and there is usually only one nostril, frequently S-shaped, situated on top of the head. It is closed by a pluglike valve, opened only by pressure from inside. When the whale comes to the surface it expels the air from its lungs with great force through this nostril; and the hot, moisture-laden breath condensing in the cold air produces a column of vapor several yards high. The notion that a whale takes water into its mouth and blows it out through this hole is erroneous. The whale's mouth is large, but the throat is very small; however, a species known as the Greenland whale has a throat large enough to admit a man's body.

Whales usually are divided into two classes —the whalebone whales and those having teeth. The toothless whales are commercially the more important, and are hunted for both oil and whalebone, which latter is taken from the animal's mouth. The roof of the mouth is provided with vertical horny plates, called *baleen*, about 500 in number. These plates hang from the roof of the mouth in a fringe ten or twelve feet long. This equipment serves as a sieve for straining out the minute animals on which these whales

feed. The surface waters of the ocean teem with animal life, and whales in feeding swim with open mouth at high speed near the surface, traveling in this way until hunger is satisfied. The manufacture of cheap substitutes for whalebone has greatly decreased the commercial importance of whalebone whales.

The toothed whales are the larger, attaining a length of ninety feet and a weight of seventy tons. The young when born are from ten to fourteen feet long. Of these the sperm whale is the most valuable. The blubber produces sperm oil, while the oil of the head yields spermaceti, used in making candles and cosmetics. Another valuable product of this whale is *ambergris,* found in the intestines and used in making perfumes.

Before the middle of the eighteenth century whaling was an important industry, but since the discovery of petroleum it has rapidly declined. Modern whaling operations are conducted with swift vessels, and the whales are killed by harpoons shot from guns. On every coast where whale fishing is conducted there are stations along the shore to which the carcasses are towed and cut up and prepared for market.

Related Articles. Consult the following titles for additional information, as well as the article Mammal:

Ambergris	Cetacea	Sperm Whale
Blubber	Spermaceti	Whalebone

WHALEBONE, *hwale'bone,* or **BALEEN'**, a term applied to the horny plates attached to the palate of the toothless whale. They are arranged in a double row on the upper jaw and hang down parallel into the cavity of the mouth. The length of the plates varies from a few inches to twelve feet, and in number there are about 200 on each side of the mouth. The color varies according to the species, some kinds being black, some yellowish-white and others gray, striped with black or black and white.

This whale has no teeth, and this fringe of bony plates serves as a sieve or strainer of the animal's food which it takes in through wide jaws while traveling at high speed. From its strength, lightness and flexibility, whalebone has become an important article of commerce, being used for many purposes, as in the manufacture of corsets, ribs for umbrellas, whips and surgical instruments, though in some of these uses it has been largely superseded by steel.

WHARTON, Edith (1862-1937), whose maiden name was Edith Newbold Jones, was one of the most important contemporary novelists. She was born in New York City, was privately educated, and in 1885 married Edward Wharton of Boston. She early achieved distinction as a short-story writer and in 1899 published her first novel, *The Greater Inclination,* a study in human motives. *The Touchstone,* her second novel, showed a distinct advance in the author's power of psychological analysis, a quality for which she was chiefly distinguished. In *The House of Mirth,* in 1906, she reached the height of her artistic achievement. Also notable are *The Valley of Decision, The Fruit of the Trees, Tales of Men and Ghosts, In Morocco* and *The Age of Innocence.*

With the exception of *Ethan Frome* and one or two others, Mrs. Wharton's stories all are of the literary and artistic world and of the world of fashion. Important books not mentioned above are *The Reef, The Custom of the Country, Italian Villas and Their Gardens* and *Mother's Recompense.* During the Great War she engaged in Red Cross work in France and received two decorations. As a result of this experience she wrote *Fighting France,* and edited *The Book of the Homeless,* a book prepared and sold for the benefit of the Belgian refugees. Among later books are *Twilight Sleep, The Children, Certain People, A Backward Glance.*

WHEAT, one of the most valuable and widely-known cereal crops, has constituted the staple food of civilized nations for countless centuries. It grows readily in all climates, except the hottest parts of tropical regions and the extreme cold portions of the frigid zones. However, it is best adapted to the temperate regions, and within these regions the greater part of the world's crop is produced. It requires a rich clay soil or heavy loam, and clear, bright days while it is ripening.

Wheat is supposed to be a native of Western Asia, but it has been cultivated so many centuries that the place of its origin is not fully known. It was introduced into North America in the sixteenth century.

Varieties. In accordance with their method of growth wheats are divided into *bearded* wheat and *bald* wheat. The first has glumes attached to the seeds, while the second has none. In regard to the color of the kernel, the varieties are divided into *light-colored* and *dark-colored,* or *white* and *red* wheats. Classified according to the time of planting

all wheats are grouped under *winter* wheat and *spring* wheat. In each of these classes we find hard and soft wheats. The winter wheat is planted in the fall and is harvested early the following summer. It is well suited to warm temperate climates that have mild winters. The spring wheat is planted early in spring and matures the same season. It is adapted to the short season of the cool temperate regions. It is usually a hard wheat and of better quality than any of the varieties of winter wheat.

Production. The United States is the leading wheat-producing country in the world, and the raising of this grain is carried on in Minnesota, North Dakota, South Dakota, Kansas, Oklahoma and some other states on an extensive scale. The wheat farms or ranches are large, some of them embracing more than 25,000 acres. These are divided into sections, each of which has its stables for teams, sheds for storing machinery, and other buildings, and each is under the direction of a foreman. In the spring-wheat region the land is plowed in the fall, and the wheat is planted as early in the spring as the condition of the ground will admit. In the winter-wheat section the ground is plowed as soon as possible after the crop has been harvested. The time of planting depends upon the location. In the warmest regions it is later than in the cool portions of the winter wheat belt.

The work of planting and harvesting is done by machinery. The land is prepared by plows, sometimes by gang plows, which on the largest farms are drawn by tractors. The seed is planted by drills, or sowing machines, and the grain is harvested by self-binding harvesters and thrashed by machines operated by steam engines of such capacity as to thrash from 1,200 to 1,500 bushels in a day (see Thrashing Machine).

The wheat is hauled directly from the thrasher to the local elevators or to cars for shipment. From the local elevators it is transported to the great wheat centers, such as Minneapolis, Duluth, Chicago and Buffalo, where it is stored in large elevators, some of which have a capacity of 6,000,000 bushels; there it is kept until needed for use.

The average production in the United States is about 880,000,000 bushels a year, though in 1915 the crop was 1,025,801,000 bushels. The leading states in the production of winter wheat are Kansas, Ohio, Oklahoma,

Indiana and Illinois. The leading spring wheat states are Minnesota, North Dakota, South Dakota, Washington and Montana.

Spring Wheat

Saskatchewan
122

North Dakota
104

Winter Wheat

Kansas
123

Nebraska
66

Figures Represent Millions of Bushels

FOUR LEADERS
The figures represent the average of three years' crops.

Canada has become one of the great wheat countries of the world. In recent years its production of wheat has ranged from 300,-000,000 to over 550,000,000 bushels. Saskatchewan, Alberta, Manitoba and Ontario are the important wheat producing provinces. Winnipeg and Port Arthur are the great wheat centers of the Dominion.

United States
889

Russia
806

British India
353

France
326

Canada
243

Italy
185

Figures Represent Millions of Bushels

COUNTRIES LEADING IN PRODUCTION
The figures represent the average of three years' crops.

At the outbreak of the World War about one-half of the world's wheat crop was produced in Europe, and Russia was next to the United States in quantity of production. Germany, France and Italy were also important wheat countries. But Europe has not for many years been able to produce all the wheat consumed by the people, and large quantities have been imported from the United States and other countries.

When the production of European countries was almost stopped by the war, the

Outline on Wheat

I. GENERAL DESCRIPTION
   (a) Plant as a whole
   (b) Stalk
   (c) Leaves
   (d) Fruit
II. HISTORY
   (a) Where first cultivated
   (b) Early cultivation in general
   (c) Introduction into Europe and the United States
III. Species
   (a) Beardless
   (b) Polish
   (c) Spelt
IV. PROCESSES OF PRODUCTION
   (a) Planting
   (b) Harvesting
   (c) Threshing
   (d) Milling
V. USES
   (a) Food for Human Beings
      (1) Flour
      (2) Bran
      (3) Macaroni
      (4) Cereals
   (b) Other Products
      (1) Feed for animals
      (2) Straw
      (3) Straw-board
      (4) Paper
VI. MARKETS

Questions on Wheat

What is the average yearly production of wheat in the United States?

What are the other leading wheat producing countries in the world?

What proportion of the world's crop does the United States produce?

What machines are used in preparing the soil for wheat?

Who invented the harvester?

With what tool did our forefathers cut their grain?

Name the different varieties of bread that you know.

Which do you consider the best? Why?

Where are the great wheat regions of Canada?

How long has wheat been known?

Of what region is wheat probably a native plant?

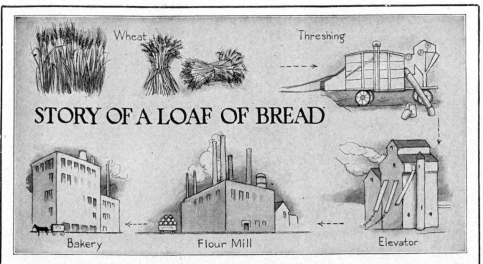

STORY OF A LOAF OF BREAD

Wheat

Threshing

Bakery

Flour Mill

Elevator

Tractor and gang plow preparing the soil for wheat. Wheat is the vital element in the world's food supply. In the first thirty years of the twentieth century the number of wheat eaters increased enormously. But the increased acreage devoted to wheat and the use of modern machinery have more than kept pace with the world's consumption needs. To restore the equilibrium measures have been taken to curtail production and to improve methods of distribution.

Courtesy International Harvester Co.

The latest type of header, a machine which reaps, threshes, and sacks the grain from forty acres in one day. The story of the development of the reaper is full of interest. Read about Cyrus McCormick and the Reaping Machine. The inventors of agricultural machinery have done more than all governments to stimulate the very rapid increase in the world's population which has taken place in the past one hundred years.

Courtesy International Harvester Co.

Great wheat elevators at Fort William, Ont. The faster wheat can be loaded and unloaded the more voyages a vessel can make in a year. How does this help to make bread cheaper? What is the capacity of the world's largest elevator? Read article, "Port Arthur, Ont." One hundred thousand bushels of wheat can be loaded automatically in four hours. The steamer can then go direct to Liverpool or Manchester and be unloaded by great suction pipes in about the same time.

In early times wheat was ground into flour by hand or by horse power, and this is still done in eastern countries. What a slow and laborious process it must be to get flour as this man is doing. Note the path made as the horse walks around and around. Try to imagine our waiting for bread from flour made this way!

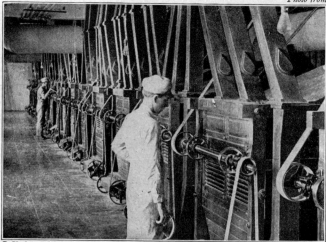

The purifying room in a big flour mill in Minneapolis, the flour capital of the world. From the time the wheat reaches the top of the mill on an endless conveyor, and passes down on belts and through tubes from floor to floor, until, as barreled flour, it is rolled out into freight cars at the bottom, every effort is made to have the flour absolutely clean, for it may travel into the tropics and be kept a year or more before being made into bread. It must have good "keeping" qualities.

A stand of breaks where the wheat grains are broken up into the first coarse flour, to be later refined and purified. The whole process of flour making represents the triumph of machinery over hands. Every step is automatic and carefully planned for the doing of the most work in the least time with the smallest use of power.

Sacking and weighing with automatic machines in a Minneapolis mill. The machines are set so that they let down into the container (sack or barrel) only the correct amount of flour, by weight. Endless belts move the tied sacks quickly to storage rooms or to freight cars. These men have no chance to go to sleep on the job. The machines don't wait for anyone.

© Underwood & Underwood

Now we come to the last, or the next to last, great stage of the journey from wheat farm to your table. In the modern bakery, also, machinery does the work. A dough-kneading machine. The dough is now being run into a trough to "rise." All the bread materials, flour, yeast, water, "cream," salt, are weighed carefully and put into the machine from the floor above.

When the dough has "risen" it is dumped down a chute to the shaping machine, which cuts the dough, puts it into the pans, and pats it into shape. In many cities there are laws to regulate the size of loaves of bread, so this machine cuts off just enough of the dough to give a loaf, when baked, of the correct weight.

A peep into an automat bakery. When the noon hour comes some millions of persons rush—and rush is the word—for food. About fifty-seven varieties of "quick lunch" must be ready on the dot, for the race, the second name of which is "Hustle," can't waste much time in eating. They demand quick action. They get it. To keep hungry America good-natured the baker must be on the job both day and night.

How many thousands of loaves of bread do you suppose the people of New York or Montreal eat every day? In hotels, restaurants, and homes wheat bread merits its title, "The Staff of Life." Without machinery the bakers never could keep up with the appetites of busy Americans. The boast of many bakeries, "No hands have touched your bread," is true. This machine wraps the loaves.

demand upon the United States for wheat exceeded its supply for exportation. The Food Administration restricted the sale of wheat flour in 1918 and ordered wheatless days in hotels, restaurants and homes. To encourage an increased production of wheat, the government guaranteed the farmers a price of $2.26 a bushel for the years 1918 and 1919. Canada, Argentina and other countries were also drawn upon for the wheat they could spare for export. White wheat bread contains more nourishment per pound than any other article of food, with the exception of beans, and the scarcity of wheat caused by the war gave every one a slight idea of what a calamity a failure of the wheat crop might bring upon the race.

Uses. The greatest part of the wheat crop is manufactured into flour (which see). By-products of this manufacture include *bran*, *shorts* and *middlings*. Middlings are used extensively in the manufacture of breakfast foods, and bran and shorts are used for feed for stock. Large quantities of starch are also made from wheat. The straw is used for fodder, for bedding in stables, and in the manufacture of straw board and the cheaper grades of wrapping paper.

Wheat Insects. Among the enemies of wheat, those most dreaded are the chinch bug, the Hessian fly and the wheat midge, a small, yellowish insect, with a dark back, related to the Hessian fly, but differing in habits. The wheat midge, which is now common in the Mississippi Valley, probably came from Europe and has occasioned a great deal of damage to wheat, especially in warm and moist seasons. The damage is done by the little orange-yellow larvae, which destroy the embryos of the grain and prevent the heads from filling. As the larvae can live for several months without either moisture or food, they are carried about in the wheat heads, and so the species is distributed. The chinch bug and Hessian fly are described under their titles.

WHEATSTONE, CHARLES, Sir (1802-1875), an English scientist and inventor. Early in life he began the business of making musical instruments, and in his study of the scientific principle involving their construction he made important discoveries in physics. In 1834 he was appointed professor of experimental physics in King's College, London, and there he made important experiments in electricity and, in collaboration with

an investigator named Cooke, devised an electric telegraph. From this apparatus developed the system of electric telegraphs used in England until 1870. Wheatstone was also the inventor of several other electric appliances, one of which enabled a system of clocks to be regulated from a central clock, by means of electro-magnets.

WHEEL, an instrument of torture, employed by the Greeks and Romans and later in Western Europe. "Breaking on the wheel" was instituted in France in 1534 and was abolished in 1789. Assassins, highwaymen, incendiaries and pillagers of churches were of the classes so punished. There were several modes of wheel torture. Sometimes the victim's bones were broken, and his body was then bent around a wheel, bound and left until death ensued, perhaps in twenty-four hours. To terminate sooner the victim's sufferings the executioner sometimes dealt him two or three heavy blows, called *coups de grace* (mercy strokes), on the chest or stomach.

WHEEL. See TRANSPORTATION.

WHEEL AND AX'LE, a continuous lever of the first class (see LEVER), consisting of a wheel and axle, fastened to the same axis. The radius of the wheel is the power arm, and the radius of the axle, the weight arm, of the lever. The law of equilibrium is that the power multiplied by the radius of the wheel is equal to the weight multiplied by the radius of the axle. In the figure, *A* represents the circumference of the wheel, *C* is the circumference of the axle, *R* the radius of the

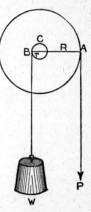

wheel, and *r* the radius of the axle. If the wheel has a diameter of three feet, and the axle has a radius of one foot, a power of one pound will balance a weight of three pounds. In making the computations, the same results are obtained, whether the radius of the wheel is compared with the radius of the axle, or the diameter of the wheel with the diameter of the axle. The most common use of the wheel and axle is in the windlass, for raising water. Here the crank often takes the place of the wheel, but the device operates on the same principle.

Combinations of the wheel and axle in which toothed wheels mesh into one another and are driven by a crank or an endless band, occur in machinery where great power is required. Derricks and the shears used for cutting iron bars and plates afford good illustrations of these combinations.

WHEELER, Benjamin Ide (1854-1927), an American educator, born at Randolph, Mass. He was educated at Colby Academy and Brown University and spent four years of study in the universities of Leipzig, Heidelberg, Jena and Berlin. He taught in the Providence High School, Brown University and Harvard and in 1886 became a professor in Cornell University, holding, successively, the chairs of comparative philology and Greek. From 1899 to 1919 he was president of the University of California. His written works include *Analogy and the Scope of its Application in Language, Introduction to the Study of the History of Language* and *Principles of Language Growth*.

WHEELER, Burton Kendall (1882–), an American Senator, prominently identified with the Liberal wing of the Democratic party. He was born in Hudson, Mass., and was educated for the law at the University of Michigan, beginning practice in Butte, Mont. As an appointee of President Wilson, Wheeler served as United States District Attorney from 1913 until his election to the United States Senate, in 1922. He was reelected in 1928, 1934 and 1940. In 1924 Senator Wheeler was the Vice-Presidential candidate on the Progressive ticket with Senator LaFollette. He led the opposition to President Roosevelt's foreign policies after the outbreak of war in Europe.

WHEELER, Joseph (1836–1906), an American soldier, born at Augusta, Ga. He was educated at the West Point Military academy, was appointed lieutenant of cavalry and served in New Mexico. When the Civil War broke out he joined the Confederate army. He was rapidly promoted, attaining the rank of lieutenant-general. He took part in the Battle of Shiloh, rendered distinguished service at Chickamauga and impeded Sherman on his march through Georgia and South Carolina. After the war he settled in Alabama, and in 1880 he was sent to Congress. He represented his district until 1898, when he reëntered the United States army as major-general of volunteers to the great delight of all America, with command of the

cavalry in the Army of Santiago. He rendered valiant service in the battles of Las Guasimas and San Juan Hill, and he was senior member of the commission which arranged for the surrender of Santiago. Later he served in the Philippines, until he was retired in 1900.

WHEELER, William Almon (1819-1887), an American statesman, born at Malone, Franklin County, N. Y. He studied for a time at the University of Vermont, studied law in his native town and was admitted to the bar. Later he engaged in banking. He was a member of the state legislature for two terms, and in 1860 he was sent to Congress, where he served continuously until 1877. He was nominated for the Vice-Presidency by the Republican party in 1876 and was elected with President Hayes. He returned to Malone at the expiration of his term in 1881. Wheeler rendered invaluable service to his country during reconstruction days by his conciliatory attitude as chairman of the committee on Southern affairs.

WHEELING, W. Va., county seat of Ohio County, sixty-three miles southwest of Pittsburgh, Pa., on the Ohio River and on the Pennsylvania, the Baltimore & Ohio and the Wheeling & Lake Erie railroads. Other transportation facilities include regular air service, river boats and bridges connecting with various points in Ohio and with Wheeling Island, a residential ward of the city built on an island in the Ohio River. The region is rich in coal, oil and lumber, and there is water commerce in iron ore, produce, fruit, cattle and poultry. The principal manufactures are steel, ceramics, glass, tobacco, textiles and metal products. The city has one of the largest electric power plants in the world and the Market-Auditorium, which combines an up-to-date market with a convention hall. A state teachers college and Bethany College are not far distant.

Wheeling was settled by Ebenezer Zane in 1769, and was the first town on the Ohio River. The town grew up about Fort Henry, built here in 1774; it was incorporated in 1806 and chartered as a city thirty years later. In 1818 Wheeling was made the western terminus of the National Road. The people of Virginia who were opposed to secession met here in 1861 and established "the restored government of Virginia." Two years later Wheeling was the scene of the convention which resulted in the separation from Virginia and the establishment of the new state, and the city was the state capital from 1863 to 1870 and from 1875 to 1885. The government is by city manager and a council elected by proportional representation. Population, 1940, 61,099.

WHIG, in English history, the name formerly applied to the political party advocating changes in the constitution in the direction of democracy. The term is of Scottish origin, but was early brought to England, where it was used as the name of the political party opposed to the *Tories,* or government party. The term *Liberals* is now generally applied to the representatives of the party formerly known as *Whigs.*

The Whig party in the United States opposed the Democratic party from about 1835 to 1856, when the Northern wing of the Whigs was merged in the new Republican party. See POLITICAL PARTIES IN THE UNITED STATES.

WHIP'POORWILL, a North American bird of the goatsucker family. The name is an imitation of the bird's peculiar call of three shrill notes ending in a rising inflection.

WHIP-POOR-WILL

This weird cry is repeated many times in close succession. The whippoorwill makes its home in the midst of thick woods, rarely visiting the haunts of men. It is active at night, feeding on night insects, which it catches on the wing. During the day it sits lengthwise on a limb, where, owing to its mottled plumage, it is not easily seen.

WHIRLPOOL, *whurl'pool,* a body of turbulent water with a spiral movement due to the shape of its channel, to meeting currents or to the conflict of winds and tides. Small whirlpools occur in rivers and are caused either by the forcing of the current into a circular core in the channel or by an opening in the bank of the stream which draws the water down to a lower level. Sometimes the position of rocks and the di-

rection of currents in the sea cause large and dangerous whirlpools. The most noted of these is the Maelstrom, off the coast of Norway, and the Charybdis, near Sicily. The most celebrated river whirlpool is that of the Niagara River, below the falls.

WHIRL'WIND, a sudden and swift spiral movement of the free air of the atmosphere, either the small eddy of the city street which whirls leaves and dust and other light objects about in it, or the more extensive whirls of the deserts and plains. Very powerful whirlwinds are called cyclones or tornadoes. Whirlwinds are caused by the meeting of currents of air, or the collision of currents moving in opposite directions, and except in the case of the small eddies, they all take the same direction—counter clockwise in the northern hemisphere, and clockwise in the southern hemisphere, being governed by the vast planetary movements of the atmosphere. See CYCLONE; TORNADO.

WHIS'KY, a spirituous liquor, distilled chiefly from the fermented mash of cereal grains. There are two main varieties of whisky, called malt whisky, in which malt predominates, and grain whisky, in which unmalted grains predominate. The latter was formerly manufactured almost exclusively in the United States, rye and Indian corn being chiefly employed.

In the making of whisky several processes are necessary to convert the starch of the grain into sugar and the sugar into alcohol. The grain is ground, and the starch is cooked in a steamer for several hours to render it soluble. It is then added to the malt, and the mixture is kept at a temperature of 145° F. for about four hours. This saccharine infusion, called *wort,* is then drawn off, yeast is added, and the wort is allowed to stand from three to nine days to ferment. The liquid thus prepared for distillation is technically known as *mash.* It is placed in a metal container called a *still,* subjected to high temperature, and the vapors pass off through a spiral tube known as a *worm* and are condensed. Whiskey requires a period of storage in wooden casks to bring about the changes which develop its aroma and make it palatable.

Related Articles. Consult the following titles for additional information:
Distillation   Prohibition
Malt

WHISKY INSURREC'TION, the name given to a revolt against the Federal government in Western Pennsylvania in 1794. It was the result of the excise law passed by Congress in 1791, imposing a tax on whisky. This tax was a peculiarly heavy burden to the people of Western Pennsylvania, most of whom were dependent for support largely upon the manufacture of whisky. They successfully resisted the attempts of the government to collect the tax and haughtily rejected the offer of amnesty in return for a promise of submission. Finally, in October, 1794, Washington sent 15,000 militia to the scene of the disturbance, and the insurrectionists promptly subsided. Two of the leaders were found guilty of treason, but President Washington pardoned them.

WHISKY RING, a term given in American history to a combination of distillers and Federal revenue collectors, who in Grant's administration conspired to defraud the government of the excise tax on whisky. This "ring" began operations in Saint Louis, where the revenue officers, having knowledge of technical violations of the law, blackmailed the distillers, under threats of prosecution. The decline in the revenue receipts was immediately noticeable, but all efforts at finding the conspirators failed, on account of the presence of their friends in the Treasury Department at Washington. It was only after the most thorough investigation by Benjamin H. Bristow, Secretary of the Treasury, that evidence sufficient to convict was found. The disclosures implicated the chief clerk of the Treasury Department and O. E. Babcock, President Grant's private secretary, but neither was convicted. About two hundred forty distillers and revenue officers pleaded guilty or were convicted in court, but most of the leading ones were pardoned. The total amount of which the government was defrauded was $1,650,000.

WHIST, a well-known game at cards, first clearly described by Edmond Hoyle, in his *Short Treatise on the Game of Whist* (1743). The game is played with the full pack of fifty-two cards, by four persons, two being partners against the other two, each player receiving thirteen cards, dealt out one by one in rotation. The last card dealt is turned face up and is called the trump card; it gives a special power to the suit to which it belongs. The cards rank ace (highest), king, queen, knave, and the others rank according to their number of spots. Play is commenced by the person on the left hand of the dealer, who lays down a card face up on the table; the other players follow in succession, with cards of the same suit, if they have them. When all have played, the player who has laid the highest card takes the four cards laid down, which constitute a trick. The winner of the trick then leads, as the first of a new trick, the winner of which becomes the leader, and so on. When a player cannot play a card of the same suit, he may play one of the trump suit and take the trick, or he may lay one of a different suit, which gives him no chance of winning the trick. When the hand is played out, the score is taken as follows: The partners who conjointly gain the majority of tricks score 1 point for every trick taken above six. The ace, king, queen and knave of the trump suit are called honors, in some systems of play, and count 1 each for the side who holds them; if one side hold three honors, they count 2 by honors, as the opposite side can have but one honor; if one side hold all the honors, 4 by honors is counted; should the honors be equally divided, neither side counts. In *long whist*, ten of these points make a game. In *short whist*, the number has been reduced to five, and in this form it is common to count by tricks alone. A rubber consists of a series of three games and is won by the side that secures two of them. In *duplicate whist* the game is played with as many sets of cards as desired. Each hand, as it is played, is laid aside, and at the close of the series of games the hands are exchanged, so that each game is played a second time, partners playing the hands of their opponents. The side that makes the greater number of points in the series wins.

Auction Whist, or **Auction**, as it is now commonly called, is a development of the game of whist, following a process of evolution, the first stage of which was known as Bridge Whist, or Bridge, now practically discarded. The game is played with a full pack of fifty-two cards, as in whist, by four persons, two being partners against the other two, and the cards having the same value as in whist. The trump suit is determined by bidding, the dealer having the first bid. Each player may bid or pass to the player on his left, as the strength of his hand warrants. The value of the suits, both for bidding and for counting in the score, is, Clubs, 6; Diamonds, 7; Hearts, 8; Spades, 9. A player may bid "No Trump," in which case and if so played, all suits have an equal value, and each trick over six counts 10. For example, if a player bids, "one heart" indicating he is prepared to play the hand with hearts as trumps, and to make seven or more tricks, the next bidder must bid "one spade," "one no trump," these bids indicating a higher value, or "two" or more of same suit, which means a larger prospective gain than "one heart," if successful. The player making the highest bid secures the privilege of playing the hand at his choice of trump, or "no trump." The player at the left of the successful bidder (the "declarer") leads the first card, and the declarer's partner places his hand face up on the table, in view of all the players. The declarer plays the exposed hand as well as his own.

Scoring. Each trick over six (a "book") counts, with clubs, six points; with diamonds, seven points; with hearts, eight points; with spades, nine points; with no trumps, ten points. The side first scoring 30 points wins the game. Two games won out of three constitute a rubber.

Honors	Clubs	Dia-monds	Hearts	Spades	No Trumps
Three honors, called "Simple".....	30	30	30	30	30
Four honors, in two hands............	40	40	40	40	40
Four honors, in one hand............	80	80	80	80	100
Four honors, in one hand and fifth in partner's.........	90	90	90	90	
Five honors, in one hand............	100	100	100	100	

Beside the point score, which determines games and rubbers, an "honor" score is kept, and is added in when the final score is reckoned up at the end of the rubber to determine the winner. The honor cards are the ace, king, queen, knave (or jack) and ten of the trump suit. If the declaration is "no trumps," the four aces are counted honors.

Contract Bridge, or Contract. This is a development of Auction, differing from the latter in two important respects: (1) in the bidding, the object is to contract, if possible, for game or slam, the successful declarer not being entitled to claim on his point score more than he bids, and suffering a penalty if he fails to make his contract; (2) the scoring is in much larger figures than in Auction, and the penalties for failure to make the bid are much more severe. In bidding, the value of the suits follows the same order as in Auction, but in counting points, clubs and diamonds are known as minor suits,

counting 20 each, hearts and spades as major suits, counting 30 each. 100 points constitute game. The method of play and the rules are set forth in convenient manuals prepared by leading exponents of the game.

WHISTLER, *whis'lur,* JAMES ABBOTT Mc-NEILL (1834-1903), an American painter and etcher. He was born at Lowell, Mass., of a prominent family, his father being a distinguished engineer in the United States army. The son was sent to West Point Military Academy, but after three years of uncongenial study he turned to art. He studied in France and England, and in time established a reputation as an etcher, taking rank with the greatest of etchers, Rembrandt. He became famous also for his paintings, pastels and lithograph drawings, which were marked by a unique originality. As a draughtsman Whistler was a consummate master, but in his pictures form was subordinated to color.

Whistler called his paintings nocturnes, symphonies, arrangements. They were executed in one color tone or two related tones, always in a subdued key. His London scenes, under cover of the night or fog, Venetian sketches and studies of the sea, are expressions of poetic moods rather than representations of actual scenes. Whistler's eccentricities brought him into continual conflict with artists and critics, who learned to fear his keen wit and incisive satire.

After 1859 Whistler lived chiefly in London and was for a time president of the Royal Society of British Artists. His best-known painting is a portrait of his mother, in the Luxembourg gallery, Paris. His etchings and paintings form a part of the permanent collections of all the greatest galleries. The best collection of his work is in the National Gallery, Washington, D. C. The artist possessed an unusual gift of literary expression and wrote, among other things, *Ten O'clock,* and *The Gentle Art of Making Enemies.*

WHITE, according to the theory of color, is that color which is a combination of all the colors of the solar spectrum—violet, indigo, blue, green, yellow, orange and red. The observer watching a beam of sunlight passing through a glass prism can see these colors, and they are also beautifully apparent in the rainbow. In practical usage a pure white pigment cannot be obtained by mixing together pigments corresponding to the seven spectrum colors, for pure pigments cannot be secured. Though white is called a color, in reality it is the presence of all colors. See COLOR; LIGHT.

WHITE, ANDREW DICKSON (1832–1918), an American educator, author and diplomat, born at Homer, N. Y. He was educated at Yale, the College of France and the University of Berlin. For a time he was professor of history and literature in the University of Michigan, and when Cornell University was founded he was chosen its first president. He retained the position for eighteen years, and when he resigned he bequeathed to the institution his historical library of 30,000 volumes. In recognition of this and other bequests, the departments of history and economics at Cornell were reorganized as the White School of History and Political Science.

In the course of his college presidency Dr. White rendered important service to the government. He obtained leave of absence and was United States minister to Germany from 1879 to 1881. After he severed his connection with the university, he served the government in several important diplomatic posts, as minister to Russia, as one of the commissioners to investigate the Venezuela boundary, for five years as ambassador to Germany and as president of the United States delegation to the Hague Peace Conference.

He was the author of numerous works on political and diplomatic subjects and of a large number of magazine articles. Among his most important works are *The Warfare of Science against Theology, Studies in General History, the New Germany, the European Schools of History, Chapters from My Diplomatic Life* and *Seven Great Statesmen.*

WHITE, EDWARD DOUGLASS (1845–1921), an American jurist, Chief Justice of the United States Supreme Court. He was born at Lafourche, La., educated at Mount Saint Mary's in Maryland, at the Jesuit College in New Orleans and at Georgetown (D. C.) College. He served during the Civil War in the Confederate army, after the war studied law, was admitted to the bar, entered politics and was state senator from 1874 to 1878. From the latter date until 1891 he was an associate justice of the Louisiana Supreme Court. After three years' service as United States Senator he was appointed Associate Justice of the United States Supreme Court, becoming Chief Justice in 1910, by appointment of President Taft.

WHITE, RICHARD GRANT (1821–1885), an American scholar and critic. He was educated for the law, but his literary tendencies drew him from a legal career, and his writings on Shakespeare soon made him recognized as one of the most prominent of Shakespearean scholars. Among his works are *Words and Their Uses, Everyday English, England Without and Within, Studies in Shakespeare.* His *Riverside Edition of Shakespeare* has had wide popularity.

WHITE, STEWART EDWARD (1873–), an American novelist, born in Grand Rapids, Mich., and educated at the University of Michigan. He spent his boyhood among the rivermen of Michigan and early acquired a liking for the forest, which he has so vividly described in *The Forest.* He has written short stories, as well as novels. Among his latest books are *Lions in the Path, Back of Beyond, Why Be a Mudturtle, The Long Rifle, Ranchero,* and *Dog Days.* His most famous books were *The Blazed Trail* and *The Leopard Woman.*

WHITE, WILLIAM ALLEN (1868–), an American journalist and writer, born at Emporia, Kans., and educated at Emporia College and the University of Kansas. In 1895 he became owner and editor of the Emporia *Gazette,* which became under his management noted for the excellence of its policies and editorials, one of which, "What's the Matter with Kansas," gained wide publicity. In 1912 White served as chairman of publicity of the Progressive National Committee. He is a member of the National Institute of Arts and Letters. As a penetrating observer and critic of the times White holds a foremost position. His books are not numerous, but are of the very highest quality. Most of them are stories and sketches of life in the Middle West, and include *The Real Issue, The Court of Boyville, Stratagems and Spoils, In Our Town, A Certain Rich Man, God's Puppets, In the Heart of a Fool* and *The Martial Adventures of Henry and Me,* and *The Old Order Changeth.* In 1925, he published a *Life of Woodrow Wilson,* which was well received.

WHITE ANT. See TERMITES.

WHITECAPS, in United States history, a name applied, because of the manner of their disguise, to a body of men who assumed the punishment of offenses against a community. In 1880 lawless bands in Southern Indiana undertook to control that section.

At an earlier date a band calling themselves the Knights of the Golden Circle was active in the same district. Whitecaps adopted all methods, from warning and intimidation to actual violence. The Whitecaps were not able long to continue their activities. The chief reason for the rise of such organizations is the slowness with which the law is often administered and the injustice arising therefrom.

WHITEFIELD, *whit'feeld,* GEORGE (1714–1770), an English evangelist, founder of the Calvinistic Methodists, born at Gloucester, England. At the age of eighteen he entered, as servitor, Pembroke College, Oxford. There he met the Wesleys, and became active in their organization, called derisively the "Holy Club." After his ordination as deacon he followed the Wesleys to America, but soon returned to England to raise money for an orphanage in Georgia. Subsequently he made six trips to America, preaching in Georgia, Pennsylvania, and New England. He preached in England, Scotland and Wales, and is said to have delivered 18,000 sermons. His Calvinistic doctrines separated him from the Episcopal Church and ultimately from the Wesleys, and in 1743 he founded the Calvinistic Methodist Society, which, owing to its loose organization, disintegrated after the founder's death, which occurred at Newburyport, Mass. The members joined the followers of Wesley, from which nucleus grew the denomination known as Methodists. See WESLEY.

WHITE FISH, a very important freshwater food fish of the salmon family, found in northern waters of both hemispheres. The common whitefish has an elongated body, with a hump back. The head is small and conical and the mouth toothless. Above, the color is bluish or olive, underneath, silvery. These fish live in deep water, feeding on mollusks, insects and larvae, but in the spawning season they migrate to shallow water in shoals. The common whitefish found in the Great Lakes is the most important freshwater fish in America. The yield of this fish for a single year in that country and Canada has been more than 30,000,000 pounds, valued at $1,500,000. So important is the industry that the United States Fish Commission has taken measures to promote the propagation of these fish.

WHITE HOUSE, called also the EXECUTIVE MANSION, the residence of the President of the United States, at Washington. It is on Pennsylvania Avenue, near several government administration buildings, and it is surrounded by a fine park. The first house on the site was occupied by President Adams in 1800. In 1814 the British army burned it, and the present building was completed in 1829. Extensive interior modifications have been made, and the building has been finished, practically according to the plans of the architect, James Hoban, who designed it in 1792. It faces toward the Potomac, though the entrance on Pennsylvania Avenue is the one in general use. The mansion is of freestone painted white, and is built in the colonial style, with long wings and an Ionic portico. On the second floor are the private apartments of the President and his family. Below are reception rooms, including the large East Room, in which public receptions are held, the Blue Room, in which diplomats making social calls are received, the Red Room, the Green Room, the State dining room and the conservatory. An important and needed addition to the building is a long wing containing the business offices of the President and his secretaries.

WHITE LEAD, a heavy white powder consisting of seventy-five per cent white lead and twenty-five per cent hydrated lead oxide. It is used extensively in the manufacture of white paint, and is prepared by several processes, that most generally employed being what is called the Dutch, or stack, process. Coils of lead are placed in the upper part of an earthen pot containing acetic acid. These pots are stacked, covered with fermenting tan bark or manure, and allowed to remain so for two or three months, in the course of which time the metal is changed to a white powder, known as white lead. In the French process a boric salt of lead is prepared, and from it boric carbonate is precipitated by means of carbon dioxide. There are several other processes, some of them electric. White lead is valuable as a pigment, because it has body and purity of color. It dries quickly and does not crack. Its poisonous quality should not be lost sight of.

WHITE MOUNTAINS, a short range of the Appalachian system, situated in the north-central part of New Hampshire, extending approximately northeast and southwest. Because of their lofty summits these mountains are called the "top of New England."

The mountains rest upon a plateau about forty-five miles long, thirty miles wide and 1,600 feet above sea level. Upon this elevation some twenty peaks rise to varying heights. Some of these are separated from one another by narrow valleys, called notches. The mountains are clustered in two groups, of which the eastern is generally known as the White Mountains, and the western, as the Franconia Mountains. These groups are separated by a tableland, varying in width from ten to twenty miles. The principal peaks in the White Mountains are in the Presidential range, so named from the names of the peaks. Of these, Mount Washington, 6,293 feet, is the highest and is also the second highest in the Appalachian system. The other important peaks are Adams, Jefferson, Clay, Monroe, Madison and Boot Spur, all of which exceed 5,000 feet, while Franklin, Pleasant, Clinton and Webster have altitudes of 4,000 feet or more. In the Franconia group the most prominent peaks are Lafayette, 5,269 feet, and Moosilaukee, Liberty and Profile, all exceeding 4,000 feet. Intermingled with these prominent peaks in each group are numerous other lower mountains.

The White Mountains are traversed by the famous Crawford Notch, a narrow defile, lined with walls 2,000 feet high, through which the Saco River wends its way toward the sea. The other objects of special interest in this group of mountains are Tuckerman's Ravine, a deep gorge on the south side of Mount Washington, which is always partially filled with snow, and the summit of Mount Washington, which is reached both by carriage road and by railway, the first cog wheel railway in the world. On the summit are a hotel and a station of the United States Weather Bureau.

The principal object of interest in the Franconia Mountains is the Profile, or Old Man of the Mountains. This is a representation of the human face, formed by the projection of three rocks from the face of a nearly perpendicular cliff on the east of Cannon or Profile Mountain. One rock forms the forehead; the second, the nose and mouth, and the third, the chin. The profile is about 1,500 feet above the road from which it is seen, and it is ninety feet in length. It looks down upon a beautiful little lake known as the "Old man's wash bowl." It was an object of worship by the Indians for centuries before it was known to white men, and it is supposed to have given Hawthorne the inspiration which enabled him to write his beautiful allegory, *The Great Stone Face.* Near by is Echo Lake, a beautiful sheet of water, so enclosed by hills that an ordinary tone of the voice is repeated five times.

The summits of the White Mountains are bare and are composed of a variety of rock known as mica schist. The reflection of the sunlight upon this rock, when seen at a distance, gives the mountains the appearance of being covered with snow; hence the name, White Mountains or White Hills. For a century these mountains have been the great playground of New England. Their bases and sides are clothed with forests, among which are many winding roads and enticing walks. Clear, rushing streams and sparkling cascades surprise the traveler at many a turn in the path, and summits easily reached afford enchanting views.

WHITE PLAINS, Battle of. When Washington evacuated Long Island he moved his main force to White Plains, N. Y., on October 23, 1776. An outpost of 1,400 men was stationed on Chatterton Hill. On this outpost a British force of 4,000 made attack on October 28, routing the Americans, who withdrew to the main camp. This engagement is known as the Battle of White Plains.

WHITE RIVER, the principal tributary of the Wabash in Indiana. It is formed by the union of the East and West branches, which rise near the eastern boundary of the state and flow in a general westerly direction. The two streams unite near Petersburg, and the main stream then flows southwest for fifty miles and joins the Wabash just above Mount Carmel, Ill. On the West Fork are situated Indianapolis, the state capital, Noblesville, Anderson and Martinsville, the latter at the head of navigation. The East Fork is navigable to Rockford.

WHITE RIVER, a river of Arkansas, which rises in the northwestern part of the state, in the Ozark Mountains, where it is formed by several small streams, and flows northeastward into Missouri, returns into Arkansas and, after a general southeasterly and southerly course, enters the Mississippi fourteen miles above the mouth of the Arkansas. Its length is about 800 miles. Locks and dams make it navigable for river steamers about 480 miles. The large towns on its banks are Clarendon, Batesville and Newport.

WHITE SEA, a large arm of the Arctic Ocean, which penetrates Northern Russia to a distance of about 500 miles. The width ranges from thirty-five to 150 miles. It is broad at the northern entrance, but near its middle it narrows to a strait. Below this it spreads out in three large branches— Kandalak Bay, in the northwest, and Onega and Dwina bays, in the southeast. The chief rivers flowing into it are the Onega, the Dwina and the Mezen. Onega and Archangel are the principal ports. This sea is ice-bound from September to June, but it has a brisk summer trade, being connected by canals with the Baltic and with the Black and Caspian seas.

WHITLOCK, B R A N D (1869–1934), an American diplomat, municipal reformer and writer. He was born at Urbana, Ohio, and was privately educated there. In his early years he had much experience as a newspaper reporter in Toledo, Ohio, and Chicago, Ill. He studied law, and in 1897 established a successful practice in Toledo. His books describing corruption in politics and injustice in business attracted much attention. In 1905 he was elected mayor of Toledo and three times thereafter, but declined a fifth nomination. In 1913 he was appointed by President Wilson United States minister to Belgium, and in that position gained the admiration of the world at the beginning of the World War through the tact, energy and efficiency shown in handling the difficult situation. In 1919 his post was raised to the rank of ambassador. His writings include *The Happy Average, Her Infinite Variety, The Fall Guy*, a volume of short stories, *On the Enforcement of Law in Cities, The Turn of the Balance, The Gold Brick, Abraham Lincoln*, a biography, *Forty Years of It*, an autobiography. In 1919 he published *Memories of Belgium, a Personal Narrative*, later issued in America under the title *Belgium*. His novels *Transplanted* and *Uprooted* are based on his observations in Europe. *LaFayette*, a biography, appeared in 1929.

WHITMAN, MARCUS (1802–1847), an American physician and missionary, born at Rushville, N. Y. He studied medicine at the Berkshire Medical Institution at Pittsfield, Mass., practiced four years in Canada, and in 1836 was sent by the American Board of Commissioners for Foreign Missions to explore the Oregon country and preach to the Indians. With his wife and two other missionaries he crossed the Rocky Mountains in 1836, taking the first wagon over the mountains. Other missionaries followed. Dissensions among them led the Board to withdraw its support; Whitman journeyed from the settlement, near the site of Walla Walla, to Boston, traveling much of the way on foot, and prevailed upon the Board to alter its decision. Whitman, his wife and twelve companions were murdered by Indians in 1847.

WHITMAN, WALT (1819 – 1892), an American poet, born at West Hills, Long Island, N. Y. He left the public schools of Brooklyn at the age of thirteen and applied himself to his father's trade, that of carpenter. Later he worked as a printer, school teacher and as general writer for the press. In these early years, as later, he sought with characteristic democracy the society of working men, and had many friends among them. During the Civil War he gave splendid service in the hospitals of Virginia and Washington, and permanently injured his health. At the close of the war he became a clerk in the Interior and Treasury departments at Washington, remaining until 1874, when a stroke of paralysis compelled him to resign.

In 1855 the first edition of his *Leaves of Grass* had been issued, and much of his later life was given up to the enlargement of this originally small volume. Whitman's avowed purpose was to be the prophet of democracy and of the common brotherhood of man. In his desire to free himself from all traditional trammels and to achieve naturalism, he often becomes tiresome. Though his work shocks many lovers of poetry by its lack of rhyme and rhythm, among discriminating critics it takes high rank, and it is becoming increasingly popular, not only among American readers, but also in Europe.

WHITNEY, ELI (1765–1825), an American inventor, famous as the originator of the cotton gin. He was born at Westborough, Mass., and was educated at Yale College. After graduation he went to Georgia as a teacher; later he took up the study of law. His leisure moments he often employed inventing useful devices, and, learning that the cotton industry was hampered by the difficult work of separating the cotton fiber from the seeds by hand, he set to work to invent a remedy. He labored under great disadvantage, for he had to make his own tools, but in time he produced a machine which would seed a thousand pounds in the same time that five could be seeded by hand.

At this juncture his workshop was broken into, and his apparatus was stolen before he could secure a patent. However, he and a man named Miller formed a partnership, and in 1793 they went to Connecticut to manufacture cotton gins; but the lawsuits in defense of Whitney's rights took all his profits, besides $50,000 voted him by the state of South Carolina. Finally, in 1798, Whitney turned his attention to the manufacture of firearms; he established a factory at Whitneyville, Conn., received large orders from the government and amassed a fortune. From his invention of the cotton gin, one of the most important of the whole series of inventions connected with the cotton industry, he reaped little financial reward. See COTTON GIN.

WHITNEY, GERTRUDE VANDERBILT (1878–1942), an American sculptress, the daughter of Cornelius Vanderbilt and the wife of Harry Payne Whitney, capitalist. Mrs. Whitney pursued her art studies in New York and Paris. Her most important sculptures include the *Aztec Fountain* in the Pan-American Building and the *Titanic Memorial*, both in Washington, D. C.; an equestrian statue in honor of "Buffalo Bill" Cody; the *El Dorado Fountain* in San Francisco; war memorials in New York, Arlington National Cemetery and Saint Nazaire, France. In 1931 she opened to the public the Whitney Art Museum, in New York, devoted to American art.

WHITNEY, JAMES PLINY, Sir (1843–1914), a Canadian statesman, born at Williamsburg, Ont., and educated at the Cornwall grammar school. He began the practice of law in 1876, and in 1890 was appointed queen's counsel. He was first elected to the legislature of Ontario in 1888, and was returned at each election up to and including that of 1908. In 1896 he was chosen leader of the opposition, and in 1905 was called upon to form a new government. In this he became the Prime Minister and assumed the office of Attorney-General. Later he relinquished the latter portfolio and became President of the Council. The honor of knighthood was conferred upon him by H. R. H. the Prince of Wales, in 1908, on the occasion of the celebration of the Quebec Tercentenary. He continued as Premier until his death.

WHITNEY, MOUNT, the highest peak in the United States proper, situated in the southern part of the California Sierra Nevadas. Its altitude is 14,502 feet, and its eastern slope rises steeply to a height of nearly 11,000 feet. Mount Whitney was named in honor of the noted geologist, Josiah Dwight Whitney.

WHITTIER, JOHN GREENLEAF (1807–1892), one of the foremost American poets. He was born near the town of Haverhill, Mass., Dec. 17, 1807. His parents were Quakers, who were always anxious to advance the interests of their children. The farm house was not far from the Merrimac River and near it was the brook whose "liquid lip" was companionship to them.

The young Whittier worked on his father's farm and learned the shoemaker's trade. He had little early education, except a few terms in the district school, and the wider training he received from his father and mother. Of books he had few and those not the best adapted to a child. The Bible, however, was thoroughly studied and its literary treasures fully appreciated. A volume of Burns fell into his hand and gave him the poetic inspiration. At the age of eighteen Whittier began writing for the press. One of his poems which appeared in the Newburyport *Free Press* attracted the attention of William Lloyd Garrison, its editor. Garrison visited the young poet at his home and induced him to give his pen and his life to the cause of freedom. This was the beginning of a life-long friendship. Garrison urged Whittier to obtain a better education, and assisted him in securing it.

Although Whittier had had comparatively little schooling, he had read widely and was well fitted to become, as he did, the chief poet of the abolition movement. In 1835 and 1836 he was a member of the legislature of Massachusetts, but ill health compelled him to resign and give up also the editorship of a paper which he was managing. In 1836 he moved to Amesbury, Mass. Later, Whittier went to Philadelphia; there he edited the *Pennsylvania Freeman*, anti-slavery paper. A mob burned the office after he had been at work on the journal barely four days. This did not compel Whittier, however, to give up the work, which he continued for two years. After his return to Amesbury, his poems on freedom continued to appear, and in 1843 a volume of ballads was published. Among his notable poems of these years, which appeared in *The National Era,* the *New England Magazine* and the *Atlantic Monthly,* were *Songs of Labor, Maud Muller* and *Barbara Frietchie. Snowbound,* published in 1865, brought great increase to Whittier's popularity and also an improvement in his worldly circumstances. He had no family, however, and most of his money was spent in charity. He died while on a visit to Hampton Falls, N. H.

Whittier's poems on slavery were too thoroughly inspired by the occasion for which they were written, too much given over to argument on this subject, to be permanently great poetry, but their energy and sincerity made them most effective aids toward the ends to which they were directed. Among his other poems, *The Barefoot Boy, Telling the Bees, Snowbound* and *Among the Hills* are most notable. They have a homely truth to life, a fineness of sentiment, a freshness and a quiet power which will make them live.

WHOOPING COUGH, *hoop'ing kof,* or pertussis, a contagious disease that frequently becomes epidemic. Half of those affected are less than 2 years old; adults rarely have it. It begins with the symptoms of a mild bronchitis. After a week or ten days the coughing is in paroxysms that end with a whoop, caused by a forcible indrawing of the breath. These paroxysms occur at rather short intervals, but between them the person feels reasonably well. After three to six weeks the attacks occur less frequently. Within two months they usually disappear entirely, although an ordinary cough persists for a few weeks longer. The disease is probably caused by a bacterium, the Bacillus Pertussis. It is sometimes fatal in infants because of complications, especially pneumonia. A child suspected of having whooping-cough should be kept from other children, for the disease is highly contagious. The patient should have nourishing food and live in the open air as much as possible. The sleeping room should be well ventilated, and whenever possible it is wise to sleep on a porch or in a tent.

WICHITA, *wich'i taw,* KAN., the county seat of Sedgwick County, 157 miles southwest of Topeka, at the junction of the Big and Little Arkansas rivers and on the Atchison, Topeka & Santa Fé, the Chicago, Rock Island & Pacific, the Saint Louis-San Francisco, the Missouri Pacific, the Midland Valley and the Arkansas Valley (electric) railroads. There are five airports and landing fields—one municipal field and one at each of the four aircraft factories in Wichita; three airlines serve the city.

Wichita is surrounded by a rich agricultural region with extensive trade in farm products. It is the largest broom-corn market in the world. Flour milling, livestock marketing, meat packing and oil refining are important industries. The four local airplane factories are widely known pioneers in aviation engineering. Important manufactures are aircraft, gasoline stoves and appliances, oil-field equipment, refrigerator cars, furnaces, building specialties and dairy products. Wichita is the center of the state's oil industry, and is one of the great wholesale centers of the Southwest.

The city is the seat of Friends University and the Municipal University of Wichita—the first municipal university in the state—and has also an art museum and a veterans hospital. Wichita was settled by Indian traders in 1869 and named after the Wichita tribe of Indians, who once roamed this region. It was chartered as a city in 1872, and since 1909 has been governed on the commission-manager plan. Population, 1940, 114,966.

WICHITA FALLS, TEX., the county seat of Wichita County, 114 miles northwest of Fort Worth, on the Wichita River near its junction with the Red River, and on the Fort Worth & Denver City, the Missouri-Kansas-Texas, the Wichita Falls & Southern and the Wichita Valley railroads. There is regular service from the municipal airport.

Wichita Falls is an important trading center for a rich agricultural and oil-and gas-producing region. The principal industries are oil refining and the manufacturing of oil-well equipment and supplies, glass products, clothing and flour. A state hospital for the insane is located here. The city was founded in 1874 and incorporated in 1876. Its settlement and growth date from 1882, when the Fort Worth & Denver Railroad reached the place. It has a city manager form of government. Lake Kemp in the Wichita River supplies its water. Population, 1940, 45,112.

WIDGEON, *wij'un,* a wild duck found in both Europe and America. The American widgeon, which is most abundant in the South, is often called the *bald pate,* from the white on the top of its head. It spends the winters in Central and South America and nests in Canada. The eggs, from seven to twelve in number, are buff-white. Widgeons are notorious for their trick of robbing canvasbacks and other diving ducks of the plant food picked from the beds of streams, by snatching it from their bills as they come out of the water.

WIESBADEN, *vees'bah den,* GERMANY, a celebrated watering place situated in the valley of the Salzbach, about two miles from the Rhine and six miles northwest of Mainz. The town has a beautiful location among densely-wooded hills, that protect it from cold winds. Mineral springs abound. It is purely a residence town, with no industries of importance. There are a number of churches of historic interest, a museum, a picture gallery, a public library, agricultural and industrial schools and an institution for the blind. Population, 1933, 159,755.

WIG'GIN, KATE DOUGLAS. See RIGGS, KATE DOUGLAS WIGGIN.

WIGHT, *wite,* ISLE OF. See ISLE OF WIGHT.

WIG'WAM, the conical tent of the American Indian. To make it he drives several saplings into the ground in a circle and fastens them together at the top. This framework he covers with grass matting or birch bark, leaving an opening at the top for the escape of smoke. A small opening in the side—always the side of the rising sun—serves as a door. This is ordinarily covered with a flapping deer-skin curtain.

WILBERFORCE, *wil'bur fohrs,* SAMUEL (1805–1873), an English clergyman, third son of William Wilberforce (see below), was born at Clapham. He was graduated from Oriel College in 1826 and two years later was ordained. He was successively curate of Checkendon church; rector of Brightstone, Isle of Wight; archdeacon of Surrey; rector of Alverstoke and canon of Winchester; chaplain to the prince, a position gained through an anti-slavery speech; dean of Westminster and bishop of Oxford, where he remained twenty-four years. Wilberforce, by his cleverness and persuasive power, was able to cope with the difficult situation in the Church at the culmination of the Oxford Movement, when many of the High Church party went over to the Roman Catholic Church. Among his writings are *Letters and Journals of Henry Martyn, Agathos, Rocky Island* and *History of the American Church.*

WILBERFORCE, WILLIAM (1759–1833), an English statesman and philanthropist, born at Hull, in Yorkshire. After completing his education at Saint John's College, Cambridge, in 1780 he was elected member of Parliament. In 1792 he succeeded in getting a bill for the gradual abolition of slavery through the House of Commons, but it was rejected by the House of Lords. Year after year he pressed this measure, and in 1807 it was passed, during the administration of Fox. His efforts finally resulted (1833) in a bill which abolished slavery in the British colonies. He was a man of remarkable versatility and personal attractiveness.

WIL'BUR, CURTIS DWIGHT (1867–   ), an American lawyer and jurist. He was born in Iowa, and graduated from the Naval Academy at Annapolis in 1888. He resigned from the navy soon afterwards and began the practice of law in Los Angeles, where he served the city and county as attorney and county judge for many years. In 1918 he was elected to the Bench of the Supreme Court of California, in time becoming Chief Justice, a position which he relinquished early in 1924 to accept the post of Secretary of Navy, tendered him by President Coolidge.

WIL'COX, ELLA WHEELER (1855–1919), an American poet and essayist. She was born in Wisconsin, was educated at the University of Wisconsin and was married in 1884 to Robert M. Wilcox. From her girlhood she contributed freely to newspapers and magazines, and some of her writings have acquired considerable popularity. Her volumes of verse include *Poems of Pleasure, Poems of Passion, Poems of Power and Maurine.*

WILD CAT, or **CAT'AMOUNT,** a wild animal belonging to the same family as the domestic cat, but of larger size than the latter.

WILD CAT

The European wild cat once common, but now seen only in the most isolated regions, has a very long body and legs and a short, thick tail. Its fur is yellowish-gray, with a dark marking down the back and other dark stripes on the sides and rings on the tail. In the United States the name is often applied to the lynx (which see).

WILDCAT BANKS, unstable banking institutions under loose state control, whose reckless issue of notes, followed by inability to redeem the same, were responsible for a series of financial panics in the United States in the generation preceding the Civil War. The most disastrous of these panics was that of 1837. President Jackson having removed the government deposits from the United States Bank and placed them in state banks, wildcat banks sprang up like mushrooms. Alarmed by the subsequent wild speculation, the President sought to correct the evil by ordering, through his famous "Specie Circular," that only gold and silver be received in payment for public lands. This precipitated a crash, and large numbers of wildcat banks failed. See JACKSON, ANDREW.

WILDE, OSCAR FINGAL O'FLAHERTIE WILLS (1856–1900), dramatist, essayist and novelist, was born at Dublin, Ireland, the son of a noted surgeon. After graduation from Oxford, where he won honors in literature, he went to live in London and became leader of a so-called aesthetic movement. His affectation of long hair, velvet knee breeches and a languishing air furnished a theme for much witty satire. He was lampooned by Du Maurier in *Punch* and by Gilbert in his opera *Patience.*

In 1881 Wilde published a volume of poems, and in 1888 a collection of fairy stories called *The Happy Prince and Other Tales.* These won high praise. Then appeared *The Picture of Dorian Gray,* a novel; *Intentions,* a volume of essays, and the plays *Lady Windermere's Fan, A Woman of No Importance, The Ideal Husband* and *The Importance of Being Earnest.* His drama *Salome* has been set to music by Richard Strauss. In 1895 Wilde was convicted of a serious offense against morality, and was condemned to two years' penal servitude. In prison he wrote *A Ballad of Reading Gaol,* a poem of much force, and *De Profundis.* His last years were spent in seclusion on the Continent.

WILDER, THORNTON NIVEN (1897–), an American author, born in Madison, Wis. He was educated at Oberlin, Yale and Princeton, and since 1930 has been on the faculty of the University of Chicago. Wilder's first novel, *The Cabala,* was published in 1925. His second, *The Bridge of San Luis Rey,* won the Pulitzer Prize in 1927 and was also a best seller. Later works include *The Woman of Andros, The Long Christmas Dinner* and *Heaven's My Destination.* His work has been greatly admired for its original material and finished style.

WIL'DERNESS, BATTLE OF THE, the first important battle of Grant's famous Virginia campaign in 1864, between a force of 120,-000 men under General Meade, supported by Warren, Sedgwick and Hancock, and with General Grant in supreme command, and the Army of Northern Virginia, under Lee, comprising about 62,000 men under Ewell, Hill and Longstreet. The Federals were encamped on the northern bank of the Rapidan, near Culpepper Court House. Grant began crossing the river on May 3, without a contest, Lee being confident that he could defeat the Federals when they had once become entangled in the Wilderness, a dense forest with thick underbrush. In the morning of May 5, General Warren was met by General Ewell, and an all-day battle resulted, with little advantage to either contestant. Grant at first believed that he was confronting only a part of Lee's army, but soon ordered Hancock to come up from Chancellorsville. Upon his arrival, he confronted General Hill, and another severe battle ensued, which paused at nightfall, only to recommence at dawn. It ended in a drawn battle; Grant had failed to make progress toward Richmond; Lee had failed to crush the opposing army. The losses of the Union forces were about 18,000; of the Confederates, from 10,000 to 12,000. See CIVIL WAR IN AMERICA.

WILHELMINA, *vil hel me'nah,* (1880–), queen of the Netherlands, born at The Hague. In 1890, on the death of her father, William III, she succeeded to the throne, but the Queen Mother, Princess Emma of Waldeck, acted as regent until 1898. Wilhelmina was married in 1901 to Henry Frederick, Duke of Mecklenburg-Schwerin (died 1934). Her daughter, Juliana, heiress to the throne, was born in 1909, and in January, 1937, was married to the German Prince Bernhard of Lippe-Biesterfeld. Holland maintained a position of neutrality in European affairs and prospered under the rule of Wilhelmina until 1940, when it was seized by Germany. The queen and her family fled to England.

WILKES, *wilks*, CHARLES (1798–1877), an American naval officer and explorer, born in New York City. He was educated in the common schools, entered the United States navy in 1818 and became a lieutenant in 1826. In 1838, in charge of an expedition authorized by Congress to explore the Southern Ocean, he visited many important places in the southern hemisphere, including the Philippine Islands, Hawaiian Islands, New Zealand, the Samoan and Fiji groups and many parts of South America. The mass of valuable scientific information collected on his voyages was published in several volumes. Wilkes was made a commander in 1843 and became a captain in 1855. Upon the outbreak of the Civil War he was given command of the frigate *San Jacinto*. On November 8, 1861, he overtook the English mail steamer *Trent* and arrested Mason and Slidell, the Confederate commissioners (see TRENT AFFAIR). He was retired in 1864, and became rear-admiral in 1866.

WILKES-BARRE, *wilks'bair re*, PA., the county seat of Luzerne County, 120 miles northwest of Philadelphia, on the north branch of the Susquehanna River, and on the Pennsylvania, the Lehigh Valley, the Central of New Jersey, the Delaware, Lackawanna & Western and the Delaware & Hudson railroads. There is regular air transport service. Thirty municipalities surround the city.

The city is in the heart of the anthracite region of the Wyoming Valley, the coal output of Luzerne County being greater in annual value than the entire gold production of the United States, exclusive of Alaska. Mining is the principal industry, but the abundance of fuel has made the city an important manufacturing center. The silk and lace mills are the oldest and among the largest in the United States, and there are besides manufactories of rayon, clothing, food products, metal products and tobacco products. Important manufactures are insulated copper wire, cutlery and airplanes and parts.

The Osterhaut Free Library has more than 40,000 volumes, and the Wyoming Historical and Geological Society has a reference library and a notable collection of Indian relics and geological specimens and fossils. Important structures are the Kirby Memorial Health Center, Fort Wilkes-Barre, built in 1776 as a protection against the Indians, and a monument marking the site of the Wyoming Massacre of the Revolutionary War.

The city was first settled in 1769 by families from Connecticut. It was named in honor of John Wilkes and Isaac Barré, members of the British Parliament who advocated the cause of the colonists before and during the Revolution. In 1784, during the controversy between Pennsylvania and Connecticut over the sovereignty of the Wyoming Valley, the settlement was burned. The Wyoming Monument marks the site of the conflict of the Americans with the loyalists and Indians, July 3, 1778. Wilkes-Barre was made the county seat in 1786 and was incorporated as a borough in 1806. After the Civil War it grew rapidly and was chartered as a city in 1871. Population, 1940, 86,236.

WILKIE, DAVID, Sir (1785–1841), a celebrated Scottish painter. He received his early art training at the Trustee's Academy, Edinburgh, and entered the schools of the Royal Academy, London, in 1805. His first works were scenes from every-day life, in which he showed the influence of the Dutch masters. In his later work, after his visits to Italy and Spain, he showed the influence of Titian and Velasquez and changed his theme to historical and portrait subjects. In 1811 he was made a member of the Royal Academy. Among his pictures are the *Blind Fiddler, Rent Day, The Village Festival, Penny Wedding, Cotter's Saturday Night, Duncan Gray, Blind Man's Buff, John Knox Preaching before the Lords of the Congregation* and *Wellington Writing a Dispatch.*

WILKINS, SIR GEORGE HUBERT (1888–   ), an English aeronaut, explorer, and scientist, born in South Australia and a member of the Australian Flying Corps in the World War. Before the war (1913), he was photographer for the Stefansson Arctic expedition, and became interested in the cold regions of the world. In 1919 he was navigator on an airplane flight from England to Australia; in 1921 he joined the Shackleton Arctic expedition; in 1928 he flew from Alaska to Spitsbergen, and in the next year headed an expedition into Antarctica, where he explored hitherto unknown lands. Wilkins attempted a hazardous submarine trip under Arctic seas in 1931, but it failed when he was 400 miles from the North Pole, because of mishaps to the unseaworthy vessel. It was his most dangerous exploit. In 1928 he was knighted by King George V.

WIL'KINS, MARY ELEANOR. See FREEMAN, MARY E. WILKINS.

WILL, that mental activity which gives a human being power of choice and action. Desire or feeling lies at the foundation of will, and the two are so interwoven that they cannot be separated.

J. B. Watson, the founder of behaviorism, once ventured the claim, "Give me a baby for three years and I will make any kind of a man of him you say." But so few babies receive perfect treatment that the psychologist finds many problems to solve. His professional counsel is often asked in guiding the growth of a young child's emotions and will, or in helping a painfully shy youth, or a law breaker, or a man who suffers a nervous breakdown, or a worker who cannot find the right job or perform his work safely, or a man and woman who will not live together happily as husband and wife. This wide field of service has attracted the psychologist, not because he is a jack of all trades but because most of the heartaches and failures in the world are due to the same cause: wrong mental and emotional adjustment—leading to a lack of will or to a will to do the wrong things.

This adjustment should properly take place in the first few years of life. Once this formative period has been past, it is hard to change a person's reactions to the world he lives in. It is, therefore, most important to know what the normal development of a baby is. During the first few years of life, the rate of growth of the brain and the amount of learning is much greater than it will ever be again. Even before birth, the nervous system controls the whole organism. A baby makes enormous advances both in controlling and in guiding his movements and in seeing the relationships in things and people around him. Recall that a new born baby has three instinctive emotions, love, fear, and anger; and that there are but a few certain causes which will produce any one of these emotions. A loud noise will make a baby shrink in fear. If every time he hears a loud noise, a rabbit is brought close to him, he will soon shrink from the rabbit even when there is no loud noise. His fear of rabbits was not inborn, as is his fear of noises. It has been acquired by association, or by what is called conditioning. This simple demonstration shows the way in which numerous fears, outbursts of temper and violent preferences that we find in older children and adults are built

up. It shows also that many of the actions of a person are not deliberately willed, but are reactions to circumstances.

The baby begins early to respond to the behavior of those around him. If the people who care for him are kind and intelligent in their care, he in his turn will smile and love. If they are cross and awkward, he soon learns to cry and kick and to be wilful.

Graded scales of tests have been standardized so that the behavior and abilities of a child can be compared with those of other children of the same age. For instance, a four months baby will push his hand against a block and perhaps be able to pick it up, but a typical twelve months old child will nicely grasp the block between his thumb and first finger. Since each individual develops at his own rate, a slight difference from the typical performance means little. A child should not be forced ahead faster than his natural rate. But when a child is found to be backward, far behind other children of his age, he should receive special help. This training is important not only so that he can take care of himself in the future, but also to protect him from unfortunate situations in which he is made to feel inferior, or perhaps is punished for being lazy. It should be carefully done, however, so that the child does not develop into a dependent person without a will of his own.

Soon, when the child can get about for himself in his small world, he finds innumerable fascinating objects to explore and to learn about. But with this wonderful new world before him, he also finds himself chained down by don'ts. At this point he must be taught to respect the property and rights of others. But if he is merely restricted, he will become rebellious and resentful. He may not always show this outwardly. In fact he sometimes becomes the most docile and obedient of children only later to flare out in ungovernable temper or really malicious revolt. On the other hand, he may begin to feel very inferior, and this is almost as bad. It is said that 75 per cent of lying is traceable to this feeling of inferiority. Irritability is frequent among adults who have been brought up in an atmosphere of repression and parental tyranny. The will of the child should be respected and developed—not thwarted.

At the other extreme is the child who is

always allowed to have his own way, never restrained, never punished. Although his parents may tolerate him, he soon finds that the outside world is a very different place where he cannot have his own way. The temper tantrums and crying which he found so convenient at home only react on himself. Some children brought up in such surroundings are never able to change, but grow up into men and women who are always getting into trouble. Such a person has never been taught that the wills of other people must be respected.

A child then should be brought up in surroundings as much as possible like those he will meet outside of his home. He should not be told arbitrarily not to do this or that, but be taught that other people have rights and that he cannot always do just as he pleases. When he comes to understand that his will is not supreme, he learns to fit very well into society.

When a child leaves home and starts to school he does not at once begin playing organized games. At about ten years he begins playing group games often competitive, and enters upon the "gang" age. He sometimes is the leader, sometimes follows. Although bad companions sometimes make this stage of development a dangerous one, the gang spirit when properly guided can be used to develop fair play and cooperation. This is really the best training ground for the will. The child meets his equals, and learns by trying to impose his will on others and by reacting against the imposition of their wills on him to develop a balanced character. In such situations the difficulties of superiority and inferiority are avoided. All these stages in a child's growth develop naturally at the proper time. They may be regarded as perfectly normal, not to be interfered with. Indeed, many times a child must be left alone—a lesson difficult for most parents and teachers.

If the child so far has been brought up sensibly and normally, he will find adolescence a happy and exciting experience.

Although the parent naturally wants his child to do as well as possible when he starts out to earn his own living, the parent should set tasks and goals which are within his capacity. In this way he becomes successful and happy, he gains confidence and poise, and retains the balance between dependence and independence which is typical of a properly developed will. Some of the most authoritative psychologists today say a nervous breakdown or social maladjustment is just prolonged childishness, the result of thwarted and under-developed will power.

WALTER VAN DYKE BINGHAM.

Related Articles. Consult the following titles for additional information:

Attention	Instinct
Feeling	Memory
Habit	Psychology

WILL, in law, the legal declaration of a person's wishes as to the distribution of property after his death. It is an individually-made law, which, if its intent is clear beyond doubt and it does not conflict with public policy, no court can set aside. Technically, a *will* can dispose only of real property, the document relating to the disposal of personal property being called a *testament.*

In most states no will or testament is valid unless it is in writing and signed at the end by the maker, or *testator,* or by some person in his presence and by his direction. This signature must be made and the document acknowledged by the testator, in the presence of two or more witnesses, not beneficiaries by the will, present at the same time, and such witnesses must attest and sign the will in the presence of the testator. The will usually names one or more persons, known as executors, to direct the execution of its provisions. If none such is named, or if no will is made, the court appoints an administrator to the estate. In the latter case the property goes to lineal descendants (For the rules for the disposal of the estate in the latter case, see DESCENT). Any alteration in the will must be duly signed by the testator and the witnesses. An addition to the will is known as a *codicil.* A will may be revoked by canceling, obliteration, tearing or burning, by a new will expressly revoking the former, or by one containing provisions inconsistent with it. The destruction of a later will revives a former will. At the death of the testator the will is recorded in the probate court, and that court directs settlements. See PROBATE.

WILLAMETTE, *wil lah'met,* a river of Oregon, 250 miles in length, formed by the junction of the McKenzie and the Middle Fork. It rises in the Cascade Mountains, flows northward through a fertile valley and into the Columbia River. It is navigable to

Portland, fifteen miles from its mouth. A lock canal enables small craft to go around Willamette Falls and ascend 150 miles to Eugene.

WIL'LARD, EMMA HART (1787–1870), one of the pioneers in the cause of women's higher education in America, and founder of the Emma Willard School. She was born at Berlin, Conn. She taught a number of years, became principal of a girls' academy at Middlebury, Vt., and in 1809 married Dr. John Willard. In 1814 she wrote and submitted to New York state officials *A Plan for Improving Female Education,* with the result that she was able to establish at Waterford, N. Y. a girls' seminary partly supported by the state. This institution was removed to Troy and the name afterward changed to Emma Willard School. Under Mrs. Willard's management, it gained a wide reputation and is still one of the leading schools for the higher education of women. Mrs. Willard wrote a number of text-books, and was also the author of the famous poem *Rocked in the Cradle of the Deep.*

WILLARD, FRANCES ELIZABETH (1839–1898), an American educator and reformer, born at Churchville, N. Y., and educated at Northwestern Female College, Evanston, Ill. She taught school for several years, traveled in Europe and the East and on her return became professor of æsthetics in Northwestern University and later its dean of women. She resigned in 1874, became secretary of the Woman's Christian Temperance Union and later its president, holding the latter office until her death.

FRANCES E. WILLARD

Miss Willard gave her entire time thereafter to the organization, traveling throughout the country from year to year, lecturing in prominent cities and writing extensively for the *Union Signal,* the organization's periodical, which she edited for six years. In 1883 she visited England and helped to form the World's Christian Temperance Union. Her former home, "Rest Cottage," in Evanston, is yet the headquarters of the national organization. In addition to articles in papers and periodicals, she was the author of *Nineteen Beautiful Years, Woman and Temperance, Glimpses of Fifty Years* and other books. See WOMAN'S CHRISTIAN TEMPERANCE UNION.

WILLIAM I, surnamed THE CONQUEROR (1027–1087), the first Norman king of England. He was the natural son of Robert II, Duke of Normandy, and as his father died without a legitimate heir, William became ruler and governed Normany with vigor and ability.

On the death of Edward the Confessor he claimed the crown of England as the nearest in line of succession. In 1066 he invaded England, overthrew Harold, the rival claimant, and then set about to subdue the people. The resistance of two powerful English nobles, Edwin and Morcar, who had formed an alliance with the kings of Scotland and Denmark and with the prince of North Wales, soon after drew William to the north, where he obliged Malcolm, king of Scotland, to swear allegiance. In 1069 an insurrection broke out in the north, and at the same time the English resumed arms in the eastern and southern counties, only, however, to be put down mercilessly.

William then established the administration of law and justice on a firm basis throughout England, conferred numerous grants of land on his own followers and introduced the feudal system of Normandy, in regard to land tenure and services. Toward the end of his reign he instituted that general survey of the landed property of the kingdom, the record of which still exists, under the title *Domesday Book.* Although the English had been completely subdued, William had to suppress several formidable revolts of his own vassals, and these he put down with an iron hand. Some of his measures were extremely severe, but they were in keeping with an age of brutality.

As a man William was not without a certain sense of equity and fair dealing, but was willing to sacrifice everything to make his kingdom stable. Viewed in the perspective of history, he is seen as one of the makers of modern England. See HASTINGS, BATTLE OF; DOMESDAY BOOK.

WILLIAM II (about 1056–1100), called RUFUS ("the Red"), son of William the Conqueror, was crowned king at his father's death. The Norman barons were discontented with this arrangement and sought to make his elder brother, Robert, who had received Normandy, king of England, but this project was defeated by William, with the aid of the English nobles. Having repressed the conspiracy, he forced the Norman barons to withdraw to Normandy and confiscated their English estates. On the death of Lanfranc, he also seized the estates connected with the vacant bishoprics and abbeys. In 1090 he sent an army into Normandy, to punish his brother Robert, while he himself crossed the Channel the following year. A reconciliation was effected between the two brothers, and in 1096 Robert mortgaged Normandy to his brother, for a sum sufficient to enable him to join a crusade to the Holy Land. William was shot while hunting in the New Forest, whether accidentally or otherwise is not known.

WILLIAM III (1650–1702), king of England, Scotland and Ireland. He was born at The Hague, the posthumous son of William II of Orange and Mary, daughter of Charles I of England. During his early life, all power in the Netherlands was in the hands of the grand pensionary DeWitt, but when France and England in 1672 declared war against the Netherlands, there was a popular revolt, in which DeWitt and his brother were murdered and William was declared captain-general, grand admiral and stadtholder of the United Provinces. In 1678 William concluded with France an honorable treaty at Nimeguen.

Meanwhile, William had married Mary, the daughter of James II of England. As she was heir presumptive to the English throne he kept close watch upon the policy of James II, and in 1688 issued a declaration recapitulating the unconstitutional acts of the English king and promising to secure a free Parliament to the people. Being invited over to England by the leaders of the English parties, he arrived suddenly at Torbay in November, 1688, with an army. A great part of the nobility declared themselves in his favor. In December James fled with his family to France.

The throne was then declared vacant, the Declaration of Rights was passed, and early in 1689 William and Mary were crowned. Scotland soon afterwards accepted the new sovereigns, but in Ireland, whither Louis XIV sent James with an army, the majority of the Catholics maintained the cause of the deposed king, until they were defeated at the Boyne (1690). In the war with France William was less successful; but in spite of

several defeats, he finally compelled Louis to acknowledge him king of England. In 1701 James II died and Louis XIV acknowledged his son as king of England. England, Holland and the Empire had already combined against Louis, and the War of the Spanish Succession was just on the point of beginning, when William died from the effects of a fall from his horse.

WILLIAM IV (1765–1837), king of Great Britain and Ireland, the third son of George III. He was educated for the navy, and although he had no real ability, he was promoted through successive ranks, until he became lord high admiral. In 1830 he succeeded his brother George IV on the throne. The great events which render his reign memorable are the passage of the Reform Act, the abolition of slavery in the colonies and the reform of the poor laws. William himself was mentally most unfit for ruling, but his ministers had matters almost entirely in their own control. He was succeeded by his niece, Victoria, whose reign was destined to be the longest and one of the most notable in English history.

WILLIAM I (1797–1888), king of Prussia and first emperor of Germany, crowned as such at Versailles in 1871. He was the son of Frederick William III of Prussia and Queen Louise. From his earliest years he received military training, and as early as 1814–'15 fought in the campaigns against Napoleon. He provoked the enmity of his people by his opposition to constitutional reform, to the extent of having to flee from the country at the beginning of the revolution of 1848. In 1849 he was in command of the army which crushed the uprisings in the Palatinate and Baden.

He became king of Prussia in 1861, and with the aid of his powerful minister, Bismarck, grew steadily in power. War against Denmark in 1864 was followed by war against Austria in 1866 and against France in 1870. The outcome of these conquests, in which William himself led the Prussian armies, was the consolidation of the German states into the empire whose aggressions forty years later involved the whole world in war (see GERMANY; WORLD WAR). It is an interesting fact that in 1919 German representatives signed a drastic peace treaty within one hundred feet of the spot where William I was crowned emperor. See VERSAILLES, TREATY OF.

WILLIAM II, in German, WILHELM II (1859-1941), the last king of Prussia and last German emperor before the founding of the republic in 1919. William II became emperor in 1888 at the age of twenty-nine, on the sudden death of his father, Frederick III, who had reigned only three months. A firm believer in the divine right of kings, as his grandfather, William I, had been, the young emperor early came into conflict with the strong-willed Chancellor, Prince Bismarck, forcing the latter's resignation in 1890, on March 18th.

WILLIAM II

Under the Kaiser, as he was commonly called, Germany became a great commercial and colonial power. Through his efforts the army was strengthened and the navy built to a strength second only to that of Great Britain. Although he was very popular with the people as a whole, he antagonized the Social Democrats by his hostility to electoral reform and his autocratic concept of kingship. The feud between him and the Socialists was bitter.

The outbreak of the World War in 1914 focused the attention of the world on the German emperor, who until recent years was held solely responsible for the conflict. In 1918 came Germany's defeat, the abdication of the emperor and the founding of the republic. William retired to the Castle of Doorn in neutral Holland, which, in 1920, refused to surrender him to the Allied powers to be tried for war offenses. The empress died in 1921; in 1922 William married Princess Hermine of Schonaich-Carolath. See GERMANY; WORLD WAR.

WILLIAM I, PRINCE OF ORANGE, COUNT OF NASSAU, called THE SILENT (1533-1584), founder of the Dutch Republic. He was brought up in the Catholic religion, although both his parents were Protestants. In 1544 he inherited from his cousin the Principality of Orange and large estates in the Netherlands. Under Charles V he served as commander of the army of the Netherlands and governor of Holland, Zeeland and Utrecht. Philip II employed him in various offices, without, however, really trusting him.

When the Duke of Alva entered the Netherlands, William withdrew to Germany. His first open resistance to Spain was an invasion of Brabant in 1568. This was unsuccessful, and a second attempt in 1572 met with no better fate. Before this time, William had been chosen stadtholder by Holland, Utrecht, Zeeland, Gelderland and Overyssel, and in 1576 he succeeded in bringing about the "pacification of Ghent," whereby the southern provinces united with the northern, to expel the Spaniards and secure religious liberty.

The southern provinces shortly broke away from their allegiance to William, but in 1579, by the Union of Utrecht, the seven northern provinces, Holland, Zeeland, Gelderland, Friesland, Utrecht, Groningen and Overyssel, were formed into a league. Two years later the league formally deposed Philip and declared itself a republic with William as hereditary stadtholder. A price had been set by the king of Spain on William's head, and several unsuccessful attempts were made to assassinate him; a few years later he was shot at Delft.

WILLIAM AND MARY, COLLEGE OF, a coeducational liberal arts college at Williamsburg, Va., chartered in 1693 by King William and Queen Mary of England, after whom it was named. It is, next to Harvard, the oldest college in the United States. The Christopher Wren Building, the central hall of the college, is the oldest academic building still in use in America. It dates from 1695 and has been three times seriously damaged by fire; it has been restored by John D. Rockefeller, Jr. Among the graduates of William and Mary are Chief Justice John Marshall and three presidents—Jefferson, Monroe and Tyler. The college offers pre-professional programs of study. The student body is limited by physical capacity to about 1,300, and the faculty numbers over 100. The library contains approximately 205,000 volumes and 300,000 manuscripts.

WILLIAMS, JOHN SHARP (1854-1932), an American statesman, born at Memphis, Tenn. He studied at the Kentucky Military Institute at Frankfort, the University of the South, the University of Virginia and the University of Heidelberg. He was admitted to the Tennessee bar in 1877, and in the following year removed to Yazoo City, Miss., where he practiced law and also became a planter. Taking an active part in Democratic politics, he was elected to Congress in 1893 and served continuously for sixteen years, becoming the leader of the Democratic party in the House. In 1911 he was elected United States Senator from Mississippi and was reëlected in 1917.

WILLIAMS, ROGER (1604–1683), a Puritan divine, founder of the colony of Rhode Island. He was born of Welsh or Cornish parents. Williams attended the Charter House School and the University of Cambridge. In 1631, because of his Puritan beliefs, he emigrated to New England. There he became pastor of a church at Salem, but his extreme views regarding the jurisdiction of the civil magistrate caused him to be banished from the colony of Massachusetts, and he went with a few companions to Rhode Island and founded a settlement, which he called Providence.

There he established the first Baptist church in America. He was twice in England, in connection with a charter for the colony, and on these visits he made the acquaintance of Milton and other prominent Puritans. He published *A Key into the Language of the Indians of America, The Bloudy Tenent of Persecution for the Cause of Conscience, The Bloudy Tenent Yet More Bloudy* and *George Foxe Digged out of His Burrowes.*

WILLIAMSBURG, VA., the county seat of James City County, about fifty miles southeast of Richmond on a peninsula between the James and York rivers, and on the Chesapeake & Ohio Railroad. The town was established in 1632 on a central section of Middle Plantation, so called because of its location between the two rivers; it was palisaded and for many years used as a refuge from Indian attacks. Originally called Middle Plantation, it was renamed in honor of William III in 1699, when by legislative act it became the capital of the colony of Virginia in place of Jamestown (which see). It was the first city of the colony to be chartered (1722). From 1699 until 1779, when the capital was moved to Richmond, Williamsburg was the chief metropolis of the colony. The Battle of Williamsburg took place here in 1862. Part of the city is included in the Colonial National Historical Park.

The College of William and Mary (see WILLIAM AND MARY, COLLEGE OF), established in Williamsburg in 1693 in a building following Christopher Wren designs, is one of the chief features of the city. Here also is the country's oldest publicly supported institution for the insane, which opened in 1773. Bruton Parish Church, erected in 1678 and completed in 1717, is the oldest church in America to be continuously in use; it was restored in 1905–1907 by Rev. Dr. W. A. R. Goodwin, who became its pastor in 1902. A courthouse dating from 1769 and numerous other colonial buildings still stand. The first newspaper in the South, the *Virginia Gazette,* was founded in Williamsburg in 1736.

The idea of restoring pre-Revolutionary Williamsburg originated with Dr. Goodwin. The actual restoration, begun in 1928, was made possible by the donation of over $12,-000,000 by John D. Rockefeller, Jr. The work is the result of thorough research and is authentic in every detail. More than 500 modern buildings on the site of colonial Williamsburg were torn down and about twenty were moved away. Nearly 300 colonial buildings have been restored or reconstructed, including the colonial capitol (destroyed by fire in 1832) and the Governor's Palace; the chief thoroughfare of the colonial capital, the Duke of Gloucester Street, has also been restored, so that Williamsburg has largely resumed its eighteenth-century appearance. Throughout the undertaking, its educational purpose has been emphasized.

The nation's interest in the restoration of Williamsburg was reflected in an increased use of the colonial style of architecture in home building. Population, 1940, 3,942.

WILLIAMS COLLEGE, a nonsectarian school for men at Williamstown, Mass., which developed from a free school established by Colonel Ephraim Williams. The funds donated by the colonel, who was killed in action in 1755, were invested and not used until 1793, when the school was chartered. The college has a faculty of over 100 members, an average enrollment of about 800 and a valuable library containing about 183,000 bound volumes, 40,000 pamphlets and 71,000 unbound government documents. The prosperity and high rank of the institution are largely due to the work and influence of Mark Hopkins, who was its president from 1836 to 1872. Among the well-known men who attended Williams are William Cullen Bryant, President Garfield and his son Harry A. Garfield; the latter was president of the college from 1908 to 1934, except during World War I, when he served as Fuel Administrator under President Wilson.

Williamstown is in Berkshire County, five

IN HISTORIC WILLIAMSBURG

The College of William and Mary, built in 1693. The Powder Horn, erected in 1732 for the storage of powder and ammunition for Virginia Colony. The oldest Episcopal church in America in continuous use; it dates from 1710-1715, and is on the site of two former churches, erected in 1674 and 1683.

miles west of North Adams. It had a population in 1940 of 4,294.

WILLIAMSPORT, PA., the county seat of Lycoming County, eighty-five miles north of Harrisburg on the West Branch of the Susquehanna River, and on the Pennsylvania, the Reading and the New York Central railroads. There is regular air service. Williamsport is on the Susquehanna Trail, midway between Washington, D. C., and Niagara Falls, N. Y. Once a lumbering town exclusively, the city now has over 100 diversified industries. The principal manufactures are aircraft engines and propellers, textiles, wire rope, sole leather, venetian blinds, paper and knit goods, steel and other metal products and furniture.

Settlers established themselves here in 1779. The city was founded in 1795 by Michael Ross, and was granted a city charter in 1866. It is governed by a mayor and council. Population, 1940, 44,355.

WILLINGDON, VISCOUNT (1866-1941), Governor-General of Canada, appointed in 1926 to succeed Lord Byng. Educated at Eton and Cambridge, he began his official life in Australia, and from 1905 to 1912 he was junior Lord of the British Treasury. In 1910, after ten years in the House of Commons, he was created First Baron of Ratton. In 1924 he was made Viscount Willingdon, and in 1935 a marquis. From 1931 to 1936 he held the post of Viceroy of India.

WILLIS, NATHANIEL PARKER (1806-1867), an American author, born at Portland, Me., educated at Andover and at Yale. During his college days he attracted some attention with his verse, and after graduation was employed by S. G. Goodrich to edit *The Legendary* and *The Token*. The *American Monthly Magazine,* from its establishment to its consolidation with the New York *Mirror,* was under his control. Willis traveled for some years as correspondent of the *Mirror* in France, Italy, Greece, Turkey, Asia Minor and England. After his return to America, he conducted several journals, most of which were short-lived. His works include poetry, travel articles and society sketches, in all of which he displays a facile style.

WILLKIE, WENDELL LEWIS (1892-   ), lawyer, public-utility executive and Republican nominee for President in 1940. He is descended from German stock, his four grandparents having fled to the United States as a result of the 1848 revolution in Germany. Both of his parents were lawyers, his mother being the first woman admitted to the Indiana bar. Willkie was born in Elwood, Ind., and studied at Indiana University. He taught school in Kansas, subsequently completing his law study, and was admitted to the bar in 1916. When America entered the war in 1917, he enlisted and saw service in France as captain in the United States army.

Willkie practiced law briefly in Elwood, Ind. In 1919 he went to Akron, Ohio, practicing there until 1929. In that year he became co-counsel for the Commonwealth and Southern Corporation, a utility holding company in New York. He became president of the company in 1933.

Willkie first came into national prominence as a result of six years of litigation with TVA over government competition with a Commonwealth and Southern subsidiary; the case ended, in 1939, in a compromise with the sale of the private-utility holdings to TVA for $78,600,000. This was $23,600,000 more than the government's first offer, which Willkie had contended was unfair to the stockholders.

In 1940 he was nominated at the Republican convention on a ticket that included Charles L. McNary, Senate minority leader from Oregon, as Vice-President. Willkie thereupon resigned his utility connections to devote his time to the Presidential campaign.

Willkie had never previously held or run for political office. His nomination represented a popular demand for a business type of nominee. Before 1938 he usually voted as a Democrat. In the campaign he showed himself in accord with the New Deal's social and defense programs, but not with their management. As his country's first duty in international affairs, he proposed the building of a strong, prosperous and united nation. While he was opposed to a policy of appeasing the dictators, he condemned President Roosevelt's management of foreign affairs as unwisely committing the United States, and at the same time he criticized the President for withholding essential information from the American people. He was, however, in agreement with the President's declared policy of giving material aid to Great Britain.

WILLOW, *wil'o,* a group of trees and shrubs common in the cold and temperate regions of the Northern Hemisphere, with a few representatives in Australia and some of the islands of the Southern Pacific. All thrive in moist ground, and are most common on the banks of streams and ponds and in marshes. The alternate leaves are long, slender and pinnate; these are preceded by flowers in the form of catkins. The catkins, which are clothed with long, glossy hairs, are popularly known as *pussy-willows*. On account of the flexible nature of the shoots of many species and the toughness of their wood and fibers, they have always been used as materials for weaving baskets, hoops and crates. Baseball bats, hoe handles and many similar articles are made from the wood of the white willow, and wooden shoes, pegs and other small objects are constructed from other species. The *weeping willow,* which is a native of China, is a fine ornamental tree that is often planted in parks.

WILMINGTON, DEL., the largest city in the state and the county seat of New Castle County, is twenty-seven miles southwest of Philadelphia, on the Delaware River at its junction with the Christina and the Brandywine rivers, and on the Baltimore & Ohio, the Reading and the Pennsylvania railways. Several airports are in the vicinity. Wilmington, containing almost half the population of Delaware, is the largest city and chief seaport and manufacturing center of the state. There are about 200 industries; of these the leading are the manufacturing of leather, cotton bleaching and dyeing, hard-fiber vulcanizing, shipbuilding and machinery manufacturing. The city is the headquarters for immense chemical and paper factories. A marine terminal on the Delaware River accommodates coastwise and ocean traffic; a sea-level canal connects Delaware and Chesapeake bays.

Eleuthère Irénée du Pont de Nemours in 1802 began the manufacture of powder on the Brandywine near Wilmington. His factory has become the largest chemical factory in the country. See DU PONT.

An interdenominational theological seminary is located in Wilmington; the state university is fourteen miles distant, at Newark. Holy Trinity Church, built by the Swedes in 1698 and popularly called Old Swedes Church, is one of the oldest churches in continuous use in the nation. Charitable institutions include an industrial school for girls, a home for friendless children, a home for orphan colored boys, two homes for the aged, the Florence Crittenton Home for unfortunate girls and the state hospital for the insane. One of the points of interest is Old Swede Rock, where the first white settlers

landed. These colonists formed the first permanent settlement of the state.

Wilmington was first settled by the Swedes under Peter Minuit in 1638. It was taken by the Dutch in 1655, and they in turn were succeeded by the English in 1664. It fell into decline until Thomas Willing laid out the streets in 1731. William Penn landed at a near-by point in 1682. The original First Presbyterian church was erected in 1741. General George Washington occupied headquarters in the city during the battle of the Brandywine. The charter for the borough was issued by William Penn in 1739. The city charter dates from 1832. The first iron steamship constructed in the United States was built here in 1836. The founder of the du Pont de Nemours family, manufacturers of powder, died near Wilmington in 1817. Population, 1940, 112,504.

WILMINGTON, N. C., the county seat of New Hanover County, 148 miles southeast of Raleigh, on the Cape Fear River about thirty miles from its mouth, and on the Seaboard Airline and the Atlantic Coast Line railroads, both of which maintain railroad shops here. The Bleuthenthal airport is near the city. Wilmington is the state's major deep-water port and is the center of a productive agricultural and trading area. The principal industries are fertilizer and lumber manufacturing, wood creosoting, the extracting of bromine from ocean water, petroleum product distributing and shipbuilding. Wilmington has a house of correction and a home for aged women. Camp Davis is thirty miles north, at Holly Ridge.

The city was founded by the English in 1730 as New Liverpool, receiving its present name in 1739. The Stamp Act resistance here in 1765 antedated the Boston Tea Party by eight years. Wilmington was Cornwallis' headquarters in the Revolutionary War (1781). In the Civil War the Confederates kept the port open until Fort Fisher fell on January 15, 1865. The city was incorporated in 1866; it has the commission form of government. Population, 1940, 33,407.

WIL'MOT PROVISO, *pro vi' zo*, an amendment presented in Congress in 1846 to a bill providing for the purchase of territory from Mexico. It was offered by David Wilmot, a Democrat from Pennsylvania, and provided that "neither slavery nor involuntary servitude shall ever exist in any part of such territory, except for crime whereof the party shall first be duly convicted." The amendment was adopted in the House, but did not come to a vote in the Senate, and in the next Congress the bill was finally passed without the amendment.

The debate in Congress over the question resulted in a breach between Northern and Southern Democrats, which led to the adoption by that party of the doctrine of popular sovereignty. This in turn resulted in the withdrawal of many Northerners, who joined the Free-Soilers and later became prominent in the Republican party.

David Wilmot (1814–1868), an American politician and jurist, born at Bethany, Pa. He was admitted to the bar in 1834 and began his practice at Towanda. He became a prominent Democrat and served in the House of Representatives from 1845 to 1851. There he opposed the extension of slavery into the territory acquired from Mexico and was the sponsor for the famous Wilmot Proviso. He later joined the Republican party, was an unsuccessful candidate for governor of Pennsylvania in 1857, served in the Senate for two years (1861–1863), and thereafter was judge of the United States court of claims.

WILSON, AUGUSTA EVANS (1835–1909), an American novelist, born at Columbus, Ga. In 1868 she married a Mr. Wilson and afterwards lived at Mobile, Ala. Her books are sentimental, but harmless, and make a wide appeal. They have retained a greater popularity over a longer period than the collected works of any other American novelist. The titles are *Inez, A Tale of the Alamo, Beulah, Macaria, Saint Elmo, Vashti, Infelice* and *At the Mercy of Tiberius.*

WILSON, HENRY (1812–1875), an American statesman, born in Farmington, N. H. His original name was Jeremiah Jones Colbraith, but he abandoned the name upon reaching manhood. He was first employed on a farm, later he learned the shoemaking trade, earned money to pay for an academic education and finally engaged in the manufacture of shoes at Natick, Mass. In 1840, as the "Natick cobbler," he addressed political meetings, winning wide fame, and in that year he was elected to the Massachusetts legislature. In 1848 he began to edit the Boston *Recorder,* as a Free-Soil organ. In 1855 he was chosen United States Senator, as a Free-Soiler or Know-Nothing, to succeed Edward Everett. His speeches against slavery are among the most important of the period. He served for a short time on the staff of General McClellan in the Civil War. In 1872 he was elected Vice-President, on the ticket with President Grant, but died before completing his term.

WILSON, JAMES (1742–1798), a native of Scotland, an emigrant to the American colonies in 1766, an eminent patriot and a signer of the Declaration of Independence. He became a member of the Colonial and Continental congresses, and also of the Constitutional Convention of 1787. His speech in the Pennsylvania convention later secured the ratification of the Constitution by that state.

WILSON, JAMES (1835–1920). an American statesman and administrator. He was born at Ayrshire, Scotland, and emigrated to America at the age of seventeen. He attended Iowa College, engaged in farming and later entered the state legislature, of which he became speaker. From 1873 to 1877, and from 1883 to 1885, he was a member of Congress. At different times he was regent of the University of Iowa, director of the Agricultural Experiment Station and Professor of Agriculture at the Iowa Agricultural College. In 1897 he became Secretary of Agriculture, remaining in that post sixteen years, a longer term than any other cabinet member has ever served.

WILSON, JOHN (1785–1854), a Scottish poet and essayist, better known as "Christopher North." He was born at Paisley, Scotland, educated at Glasgow University and at Oxford and on leaving college settled on an estate on Lake Windermere, where he gave himself up to literary work. Wordsworth, Southey and Coleridge were among his acquaintances. His first independent publication was a poem called *The Isle of Palms,* and this was followed by *The City of the Plague,* a second book of poems. When *Blackwood's Magazine* was established, in 1817, Wilson became one of its contributors, and for many years he wrote some of the most notable articles in that periodical. In 1820 he was appointed to the chair of moral philosophy in Edinburgh University, a position which he held for thirty-one years.

Most famous, perhaps, of the writings of Wilson are the *Noctes Ambrosianae,* which abound in graceful humor and sentiment. Among his other works are three novels, *The Lights and Shadows of Scottish Life, The Trials of Margaret Lyndsay* and *The Foresters.*

Woodrow Wilson

WILSON, [THOMAS] WOODROW (1856–1924), an American educator, writer and statesman, the twenty-eighth President of the United States, and the first Democrat after Andrew Jackson to serve two consecutive terms. His administrations are linked with stupendous changes in domestic and international history. He was a man of deep sympathy for the workers of all nations, and during his lifetime his writings were probably read and quoted more widely than those of any other public leader. In politics he was a liberal, and he sponsored much progressive legislation.

Early Life. Both of the grandfathers of Woodrow Wilson were born in the British Isles. Joseph Ruggles Wilson, the father of the future President, was a well-known educator and a distinguished clergyman of the Presbyterian Church, South. While Dr. Wilson was preaching in Staunton, Va., his third child and first son, Thomas Woodrow, was born, on December 28, 1856. The boy was taught at home until his ninth year, and in 1873, when a lad of seventeen, he entered Davidson College, N. C. Before the end of the first year he left school because of ill health, and when he again entered college, in 1875, he registered at Princeton.

Woodrow Wilson was graduated with the class of 1879, entered the law school of the University of Virginia, where he remained a year, and in 1882 began the practice of law in Atlanta, Ga. Within the course of a year he abandoned his practice to become a postgraduate student at Johns Hopkins University. Here he specialized in government and jurisprudence.

Career as Educator. In 1885 Wilson received his doctor's degree, having submitted as his thesis a book that is now a standard classic in its field—*Congressional Government: A Study in American Politics.* For a quarter of a century after leaving Johns Hopkins he rose steadily to distinction as an educator. From 1885 to 1888 he was associate professor of history and political economy at Bryn Mawr College, and from 1888 to 1890 held a similar position at Wesleyan University, Middletown, Conn.

Wilson was offered the professorship of jurisprudence and political economy at Princeton in 1890, and in that year began an association with his alma mater that was to last twenty years. In 1902 he succeeded Dr. Francis L. Patton as president. Among the several reforms inaugurated by Wilson as head of the university, the most radical was the introduction of the preceptorial system. On the whole, his record was sufficiently brilliant to make him a prospective nominee for governor in 1910.

In Politics. New Jersey was a Republican state, and the president of Princeton was a Democrat, but when the Democratic convention nominated Wilson, the liberal elements of all parties could approve the choice. The Democratic candidate presented a progressive platform and was elected by a plurality of 49,056.

As governor he showed exceptional qualities of leadership. When he met with "machine" opposition he did not hesitate to appeal to the people over the heads of the politicians. In the Democratic national convention of 1912, which met at Baltimore, Md., he was nominated after a somewhat protracted contest. His chief opponent, Champ Clark of Missouri, had the backing of the conservative elements, but the fight for Wilson's nomination was led by William Jennings Bryan, and his nomination was accepted with hearty approval by the rank and file of the party. Wilson's opponents were President Taft and Theodore Roosevelt. With Thomas R. Marshall of Indiana as his running mate, he carried forty states and received 435 electoral votes. A Democratic Congress was also elected by an overwhelming majority.

First Term. The Sixty-third Congress was called in special session on April 7, 1913, primarily for the purpose of framing a new tariff law. President Wilson excited much comment by appearing personally before the assembly and reading his message himself, a practice which had been abandoned after the administration of John Adams. The bill, which, after weeks of debate, was signed on October 3 by the President, brought about a general reduction of duties on a long list of commodities.

Meanwhile, preliminary work was being done on the revision of the banking laws, and the Federal Reserve Act received the President's signature in December.

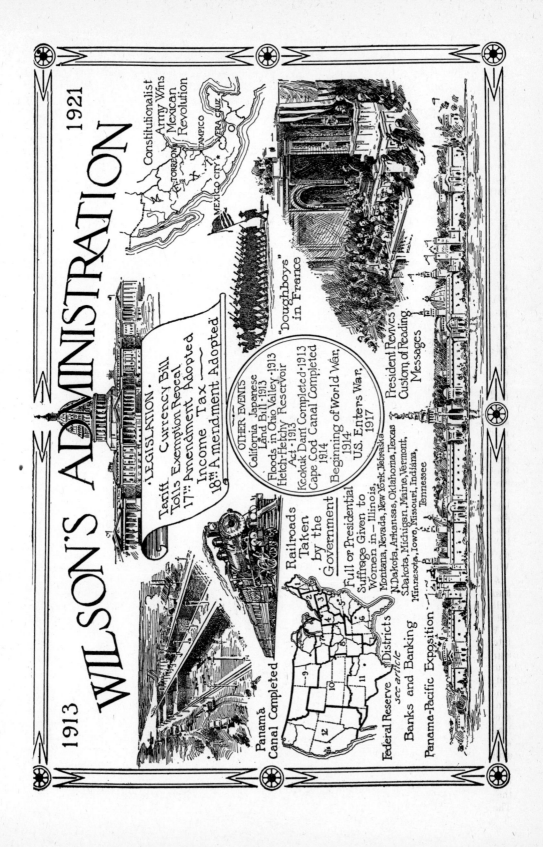

WILSON'S ADMINISTRATION

1913   1921

· LEGISLATION ·

Tariff Currency Bill
Tolls Exemption Repeal
17th Amendment Adopted
— Income Tax —
18th Amendment Adopted

OTHER EVENTS
California Japanese
Land Bill · 1913
Floods in Ohio Valley · 1913
Hetch-Hetchy Reservoir
Act · 1913
Keokuk Dam Completed · 1913
Cape Cod Canal Completed
1914
Beginning of World War,
1914
U.S. Enters War,
1917

Constitutionalist
Army Wins
Mexican
Revolution

TAMPICO
STRONGPOINT
MEXICO CITY ★ ★ VERA CRUZ

"Doughboys"
in France

President Revives
Custom of Reading
Messages

Panama
Canal Completed

Railroads
Taken
by the
Government

Full or Presidential
Suffrage Given to
Women — Illinois,
Montana, Nevada, New York, Nebraska
N.Dakota, Arkansas, Oklahoma, Texas
S.Dakota, Michigan, Maine, Vermont,
Minnesota, Iowa, Missouri, Indiana,
Tennessee

Federal Reserve Districts
see article

Banks and Banking

Panama-Pacific Exposition

After the midwinter recess Congress reassembled on January 20, 1914, and heard the President's message on anti-trust legislation. Two important laws followed—the Clayton Anti-Trust and the Trade Commission acts.

Complications with Mexico arose during President Wilson's administration, culminating in an expedition under General Pershing. War in Europe began in August, 1914.

The Campaign of 1916. In the summer of 1916 President Wilson and Vice-President Marshall were unanimously nominated to succeed themselves by the Democratic convention which met at Saint Louis. The Republicans nominated Charles Evans Hughes and Charles W. Fairbanks. The campaign lacked the dramatic elements of the campaign of 1912. The contest was close. Though Wilson increased his popular vote over that of 1912 by nearly 3,000,000, he won by an electoral vote of 277, only twenty-three more than Hughes received.

The Nation at War. In every way possible, President Wilson had tried to preserve neutrality. All hopes for peace were abandoned, however, when the German government announced, late in January, that unrestricted submarine warfare would be started on February 1.

Unhesitatingly the President broke off relations with Germany, and on April 6, 1917, signed the Congressional resolution that made the United States an associate with the Allies in the war. (Details will be found under the headings UNITED STATES and WORLD WAR.)

America and World Peace. The President announced that he would head the American delegation to the peace conference, and in December, 1918, he sailed for Europe.

With the exception of a brief interval late in February, when he returned home to sign bills passed by Congress, the President remained in Europe until the last of June. On his first trip he visited Italy and England, receiving there and in France extraordinary ovations from the people. He took a conspicuous part in the Paris discussions leading up to the treaty with Germany, signed it on June 28 in the Palace of Versailles, and reached home early in July, 1919.

During the President's absence formidable opposition in the Senate had developed to the provisions of the League of Nations. The Senate refused to ratify the treaty and the League Covenant. Wilson's health gave way under the strain, and when he gave up office in 1921 he was a sick man. He continued to reside in Washington as a private citizen, and exerted his influence constantly in the cause of international peace. In 1920 he had been awarded the Nobel Peace Prize. Wilson died in Washington on February 3, 1924. He was buried in the Cathedral of Saints Peter and Paul.

Other Events. Two amendments to the Constitution became effective, the XVIIth (1913), providing for the direct election of Senators, and the XVIIIth, making illegal the sale and manufacture of alcoholic liquor. The XIXth amendment, enfranchising women, was adopted by Congress in 1919. On July 1, 1919, the United States became temporarily a "dry" nation, in accordance with a war food-conservation measure.

The government took control of the railroads, the telephone and telegraph systems and the cables, and operated them for varying intervals. Another innovation was the establishment of daylight saving by having all clocks moved forward one hour on the last Saturday in March and moved back in October. The plan was in force one year.

Except for a few months after the outbreak of World War I, the United States enjoyed great prosperity during the Wilson administration. However, President Wilson was confronted by larger and more varied problems during his two terms than any other President since Lincoln.

The White House Family. President Wilson was twice married. He and his first wife, Ellen Louise Axsen, of Savannah, Ga., were married in June, 1885. She died on August 6, 1914. The second Mrs. Wilson, who had been Mrs. Edith Bolling Galt, became mistress of the White House on December 18, 1915. The three daughters of President Wilson created much quiet interest among Americans. The eldest, Margaret, was a singer of note, and active in social welfare work. Jessie and Eleanor Wilson were both White House brides, the former marrying Francis B. Sayre, and the latter William G. McAdoo, former Secretary of the Treasury.

Woodrow Wilson, Author. For distinction of scholarship and charm of style Wilson's writings have a high place. His *Congressional Government* has been mentioned. At Wesleyan he wrote *The State*. In 1893

Administration of Woodrow Wilson, 1913-1921

I. THE PRESIDENT
  (1) Ancestry
  (2) Birth
  (3) Education
  (4) Career as educator
  (5) Governor and President
  (6) Character
  (7) Writings

II. GOVERNMENT AFFAIRS
  (1) Domestic
    (a) Underwood Tariff Law
      (1) Revised tariff downward
      (2) Income tax provisions
    (b) Federal Reserve Act
      (1) Twelve Federal Reserve banks created
      (2) Stabilized financial conditions
    (c) Clayton Anti-Trust Act
    (d) Trade Commission Act
    (e) Repeal of Panama Tolls clause
    (f) Seventeenth Amendment
      (1) Direct election of Senators
      (2) In force, 1913
    (g) Eighteenth Amendment
      (1) Prohibition of liquor manufacture and sale
      (2) Effective January 16, 1920
    (h) Nineteenth Amendment
      (1) Women enfranchised
      (2) Adopted by Congress in 1919
    (i) Daylight saving adopted
  (2) Foreign
    (a) Mexico problem
      (1) Refusal to recognize Huerta
      (2) Tampico episode
        (a) Occupation of Vera Cruz
        (b) "ABC" mediators
      (3) Villa raid on Columbus, N. M.
        (a) Invasion by Pershing's troops
        (b) Withdrawal of troops
    (b) World War
      (1) Neutrality maintained until 1917
      (2) German aggressions against America
      (3) Diplomacy of President
      (4) Reëlection of Wilson in 1916
    (c) United States enters the war, April 6, 1917
      (1) Conscription
      (2) Army in France
      (3) Liberty Loans successfully floated
      (4) Government operation of railroads
      (5) Armistice, November 11, 1918
    (d) Peace Negotiations
      (1) President goes to Paris
      (2) Treaty presented to Senate
      (3) Controversy over league of nations

III. MISCELLANEOUS EVENTS
  (1) Completion of Panama Canal
  (2) Panama-Pacific Exposition
  (3) "War-time" prohibition effective July 1, 1919
  (4) Death of Theodore Roosevelt

Questions on Woodrow Wilson

Who were Woodrow Wilson's grandfathers?

Sketch his career as educator.

Why did he not continue the practice of law?

What was there unusual about his election as governor of New Jersey?

What precedents did Wilson ignore while President?

What amendments were proposed or became effective in his administrations?

In what ways was the Wilson era a period of change?

How long did he remain in Europe?

he published *Division and Reunion,* an account of American history from 1829 to 1889; the same year he brought out *An Old Master and Other Political Essays* and *Mere Literature and Other Essays.* His *History of the American People,* in five volumes, was published in 1902. Of later date were *The New Freedom, Guarantees of Peace* and *International Ideals.*

Bibliography. Ray Stannard Baker's *Woodrow Wilson, Life and Letters* (8 vols., 1927-1939), is the authorized biography. Sidelights on Wilson's career as President will be found in *The Intimate Papers of Colonel House* (4 vols.), covering the period 1912-1919. *Woodrow Wilson and His Work,* by William E. Dodd, is written from the standpoint of a friend; among others in personal touch with Wilson who contributed lives are Joseph P. Tumulty, Josephus Daniels and David F. Houston. R. S. Baker and W. E. Dodd edited his state papers and messages.

Related Articles. Consult the following titles for additional information:

Banks and Banking	Prohibition
Lusitania	Tariff
Mexico (history)	Woman Suffrage
Nations, League of	World War

WILSON, WILLIAM LYNE (1843-1900), an American statesman and educator, born in Jefferson County, Va. He was graduated from Columbian College, Washington, D. C., studied at the University of Virginia and served in the Confederate army. Later he became professor of Latin at Columbian College and practiced law from 1871 to 1882, when he was chosen president of the University of West Virginia. In 1883 he entered Congress as a Democrat and served twelve years. As chairman of the Ways and Means Committee, he led the opposition to the Sherman silver purchase law and was the author of the famous Wilson Tariff Bill (see TARIFF). In 1895 he was made Postmaster-General by President Cleveland, and at the close of his term became president of Washington and Lee University.

WINCHELL, ALEXANDER (1824-1891), one of America's greatest geologists, who produced more than twenty volumes on geological topics and who taught for many years. He was born in Dutchess County, N. Y., and was graduated in Wesleyan University in 1847. Immediately he was appointed to the chair of physics and civil engineering at the University of Michigan, but was soon transferred to the geological department. He was a founder of the Geological Society.

WIND, movements of the atmosphere caused by unequal heating and the resultant inequality of pressure on different parts of earth's surface. The temperature is highest and the atmospheric pressure is lightest at the equator, while at the poles the temperature is lowest and the air most dense.

The heating of the air at the equator produces an upward current, which continues until the rising air reaches layers of atmosphere of the same density, when the vertical motion is changed to a horizontal one, and currents set in toward the poles. As the warm air over the equator rises, the cool air on either side moves in to take its place, so that there are in the equatorial regions two sets of currents, blowing towards the equator, and an upper current blowing towards the poles. When the upper current reaches the temperate latitudes it becomes of the same density as the air near the surface and descends, mingling with the surface currents. For this reason there may exist areas where for many consecutive days there is no wind.

Were it not for the rotation of the earth, these currents would blow directly north and south. As it is, each is deflected from its course. The wind blowing toward the equator enters regions having a greater velocity of rotation than those from which it came. It is unable at once to acquire this velocity and, as it were, lags behind, producing easterly winds.

Winds blowing toward the poles are constantly entering regions having a lower velocity of rotation, and their eastward motion is greater than that of the land; hence they become westerly winds. In the northern hemisphere they blow from the southwest, and in the southern hemisphere, from the northwest.

In and near the tropics, these currents are quite regular, but as they approach the temperate latitudes and become nearer equal in temperature and pressure, they are subject to many local influences and become very irregular; hence no theory of wind which accounts for the general circulation of the atmosphere is sufficient to explain the prevailing winds in many localities, and the accounting for these is one of the most difficult problems with which the meteorologist has to contend.

A wind is named from the direction from which it blows; an easterly wind blows from the east, a westerly blows from the west. The

cylinder, several inches in diameter, with **a** square hole at each end, into which bars, called handspikes, can be inserted for turning it. As the roller is turned, it winds a rope or chain, which raises the weight. The windlass used for raising buckets of water from a well

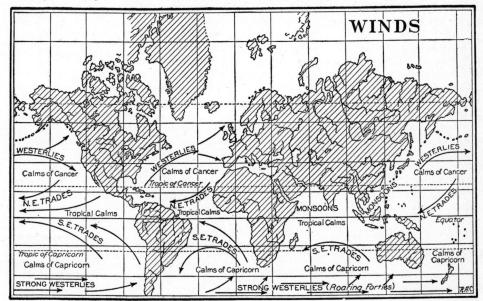

force of the wind depends upon its velocity, which is determined by the anemometer, an instrument constructed of four hemispherical cups at the ends of horizontal bars, mounted on a vertical axis and attached to a registering system of clock work.

Related Articles. Consult the following titles for additional information:

WINDERMERE, *win'dur meer,* the largest lake of England, situated in Westmoreland and Lancashire counties, in the northwestern part of the country. It is ten and one-half miles long and about a mile wide. It contains seven islands, and has steep and rugged shores. The beauty of its scenery inspired Southey, Wordsworth and Coleridge.

WINDHOVER, *wind' huv ur.* See KESTREL.

WIND'LASS, a mechanical device for raising weights with little power. The windlass is a modification of the wheel and axle, and in its simplest form it consists of a mounted

has a winch at one or both ends of the roller. The lifting power of a windlass may be greatly increased by fitting a cog wheel between the cylinder and the winch. See DERRICK.

WIND'MILL, a mechanical device which utilizes the energy of the wind for pumping water from wells, for grinding grain, cutting fodder for stock, for running churns, and many other purposes where a small amount of power is needed. The mill in general use on American farms has a wind wheel with radiating wooden or metal slats, placed close together and inclined, though not overlapping. This wheel rotates on a horizontal bar having at its opposite end a vane which keeps the wheel constantly facing the wind. The wheel is mounted on a frame twenty-five or more feet in height, to expose it to the wind's action. The speed of the mill is regulated by a gearing. The amount of power varies with the machine. There are mills which, under favorable conditions, furnish as high as four or five horse power. This type of mill is a distinct improvement upon the old-fashioned Dutch windmill, which has four radial arms covered with canvas. The latter is mounted on a tower on wheels and is turned by hand when a change in direction of the wind makes it necessary to set the sails to the breeze.

WIND'PIPE. See TRACHEA.

WINDSOR, HOUSE AND FAMILY OF, the name of the British royal family since July, 1917. When Victoria was crowned as queen in 1837, she was of the House of Hanover, the German line which gave Great Britain the four Georges and William IV. It will be remembered that George I knew no English and was not in sympathy with English ideals and traditions; he was more proud of his German title of Elector of Hanover. Victoria married into the House of Saxe-Coburg and Gotha when she took the German Prince Albert as her husband. The family name of Albert was Wettin; it was an illustrious family, coming into prominence in the tenth century. In time by conquest and marriage it controlled several duchies, among them Saxe-Coburg and Gotha.

In 1917, during the World War, the English royal family decided to substitute the name Windsor for that of Wettin, for out of the bitterness of the conflict there had developed a feeling of hostility toward all things German. Accordingly, by proclamation on July 17 of that year, the name was changed from the House of Saxe-Coburg and Gotha to the House and Family of Windsor. The name of George V became George Frederick Ernest Albert Windsor, and that of his son, the Prince of Wales, became Edward Albert Windsor, or, informally, David Windsor. When, in 1936, he abdicated as Edward VIII, his successor and brother, George VI, created him Duke of Windsor. See EDWARD VIII.

WINDSOR, win'zur, ONT., in Essex County, on the Detroit River, directly opposite Detroit, and on the Canadian Pacific, the Canadian National, the Michigan Central, the Wabash, and Pere Marquette railroads. It is connected with Detroit by ferry, by the new international bridge and by railway and vehicular tunnels under the Detroit River. It is one of the principal centers in Canada for the manufacture of automobiles and drugs, and also has large steel mills, machine shops, and a salt refinery that is one of the largest in the Dominion. Windsor was first settled in 1812. Population, 1921, 38,591; 1931, 63,108; 1941, 104,415.

WINDSOR CASTLE, one of the most magnificent royal palaces in the world, situated at Windsor on the Thames, about twenty miles from London. Windsor was the residence of the Saxon kings before the Conquest.

William the Conqueror first built a royal residence there, and succeeding rulers have added to, torn down and rebuilt it. The present structure was completed in the reign of George IV. The castle consists of buildings surrounding two great courts, between which is the round tower, or keep, the oldest part of the structure, built by Edward II. Saint George's chapel, an imposing part of the castle is a fine example of Gothic flamboyant architecture. It has a vault, in which are buried many members of the royal family, among whom are Henry VI, Edward IV, Henry VIII, Jane Seymour, Charles I, George IV, and George V. Adjoining this is Albert Chapel, one of the most beautiful of memorial buildings, built by Henry VII as a mausoleum. Under James II it was used as a Roman Catholic chapel, and after this it was neglected until George III rebuilt it as a royal tomb.

It was Queen Victoria who finished it in the most sumptuous manner, as a memorial to her husband, Prince Albert. Besides the private rooms of the royal family, there are in the castle richly furnished state apartments. See illustration, in the article ENGLAND.

WIND'WARD ISLANDS, a group of islands of the West Indies embracing Saint Lucia, Grenada, Saint Vincent and a chain of smaller islands, all under a British governor-in-chief. The islands are so called because of the fact that they are exposed on their eastern sides to the trade winds. See LEEWARD ISLANDS.

WINE, the fermented juice of fruits, particularly of grapes. The grape sugar contained in grape juice is readily changed through fermentation into alcohol. The process of manufacture is simple. To separate the juice the grapes are placed in a crushing machine having two corrugated cylinders which crush the grapes without crushing the seeds. The *must,* as the resulting mass of pulp is called, is then forced by pumps through hose to large wooden vats or tanks, where the fermentation takes place, usually slowly.

The fermentation is watched with the greatest care, for upon it depends the quality of the wine. It is hastened by raising the temperature or by placing in the must a small quantity of fermented pulp from another vat. When the fermentation is completed, the juice is strained from the pulp and placed in large reservoirs, called *tuns,* where it remains until the wine is ripe. It is then drawn into casks or bottles and is ready for market.

Wines are known as *dry* when complete fermentation takes place and all the sugar is converted into alcohol. When fermentation is arrested while there is yet some sugar, the result is a sweet or fruity wine. A sparkling wine is one which effervesces when the bottles are uncorked. Champagne is a good illustration. In such wines fermentation has been arrested before all the carbonic acid has escaped. In color, wines are known as *red* or *white.* Red wines are produced by allowing the skins of the grapes to remain in the vat during fermentation. The amount of alcohol in wine varies from 16 to 25 parts in 100. In light wines it may be from 7 to 12 parts in 100.

Wines are manufactured in almost endless variety, and many of them are named from the locality in which they are made, such as Port, Burgundy, Bordellais and Rhenish wines. The leading countries in the world in the manufacture of wine are France, Spain and Italy. In the United States wine has been extensively manufactured in California. Excellent wines are also produced in New York, Ohio, Virgina and other states.

Related Articles. Consult the following titles for additional information:

Champagne	Port Wine
Grape	Sherry

WINGED BULL, a type figure of ancient Assyrian sculpture. It was customary to place winged bulls with human heads before the entrances of royal palaces, as it was believed they guarded the buildings from enemies. Some of the larger bulls were seventeen feet high. The wings of the creatures were carved on huge plinths that covered the wall, while the body projected from the wall, the head and breast being outside the arch of the entrance.

Similar to the winged bull was the winged lion (see illustration). The bull typified strength; the lion symbolized courage.

WINGED LION, a famous piece of bronze sculpture representing a lion with wings. It is the emblem of St. Mark, and was cast in 1178 for the embellishment of one of the two large columns at the south end of the extension to Saint Mark's Square, Venice.

ASSYRIAN WINGED LION

WINGED VICTORY or **NI'KE OF SAM'OTHRACE,** a famous piece of antique sculpture, dug up in 1862 on the island of Samothrace, in the Aegean Sea, and placed in the Louvre, Paris. Nike, the Greek goddess of victory and winged messenger of Zeus and Athene, is here represented as standing on the prow of a ship, her transparent draperies whipped by the breeze. The statue, it is believed, was made to commemorate some military victory of the Greeks. It is badly mutilated, but what remains of it is treasured for its buoyant vitality, its sinuous grace and the noble dignity of its poise. In the Louvre the statue was placed at the head of a staircase. See SCULPTURE.

WINKELRIED, *vin'kel reet,* ARNOLD, a Swiss patriot, who, if legend be true, brought about the independence of Switzerland. According to the popular story, at the Battle of Sempach, when the Swiss were fighting for liberty against their Austrian oppressors, Winkelried, who was only a poor peasant, conceived the idea of leading his countrymen in close triangular formation. By deliberately sacrificing their lives they drove a wedge into the enemy and thus made a breach which opened the way for a successful attack and victory.

WINNEBA'GO, an important Siouan tribe, now numbering about 2,000, who live in Wisconsin and Northeastern Nebraska. When the Jesuits met the Winnebagos, they held a broad tract in Central Wisconsin, near Green Bay and Lake Winnebago. They were a tractable people, but many of them died from the ravages of smallpox, and their numbers greatly diminished.

WINNIPEG, LAKE, a lake situated in the south-central part of Manitoba. It has an area of 9,459 square miles, and is a little larger than the state of Vermont. The southern half is in the form of a narrow arm, which extends southward to within about thirty miles of the city of Winnipeg. Its entire length is 260 miles, its greatest width about sixty miles and its greatest depth 100 feet. It receives the Winnipeg, the Red River of the North and the Assiniboine on the south, and the Saskatchewan on the west. Its outlet is by the Nelson River, which, after flowing through several small lakes, reaches Hudson Bay. The fisheries are the most important in Manitoba, yielding $400,000 annually.

WIN'NIPEG, MANITOBA, the capital of the province, the county town of Selkirk County and the third largest city of the Dominion, is situated at the confluence of the Assiniboine and Red Rivers. It is about 66 miles north of the United States boundary and practically midway between Montreal and Vancouver. Its geographic position is unique; it lies in a great plain, midway between Lake Winnipeg and the international boundary, and is thus like a spout through which all the trade between eastern and western Canada must flow. It is entered by two great railway systems, the Canadian Pacific Railway and the Canadian National Railway, and their repair shops are among the largest industries of the city. The Great Northern and Northern Pacific lines give the city direct communication with Minneapolis and Saint Paul and other important commercial centers in the United States.

Winnipeg is a great wholesale center, and its manufactures are increasing in importance. It has over 400 factories, whose total annual output exceeds $75,000,000. The wholesale trade in normal times averages $250,000,000 a year. Over sixty buildings of the agricultural college were completed in 1920; there are a number of colleges, including the University of Manitoba, Saint John's College, Wesley College, Manitoba College and Manitoba Medical College. The city is well built, with wide, regular streets and many beautiful buildings, among which are the city hall, the post office, the parliament buildings, the courthouse, Carnegie Library, the new Fort Garry Hotel, Eaton's department store, two great railroad stations and the Hudson's Bay Company, McArthur, Sterling Bank and Ideal buildings.

The site of Winnipeg, in a rich river valley, early attracted settlers. The Hudson's Bay Company in 1812 erected Fort Douglas, which protected the colonists sent out by the Earl of Selkirk; these colonists were the first real settlers in Manitoba. Fort Garry, built in 1822 and rebuilt in 1835, was for years the seat of government in the Red River Valley. In 1873 the city of Winnipeg was incorporated. Its growth has been rapid, and it has enjoyed great prosperity.

In 1919 the most serious strike in its history occurred. Practically all of the union men stopped work, and for several weeks the situation was grave. The city government called for citizen volunteers to act as policemen, and they carried on public activities until the strike was broken. In 1870 the city had 215 inhabitants; by 1901 its population was 42,340; by 1941 it had increased fivefold, to 217,994.

WINNIPEGO'SIS, LAKE, a lake in the southwestern part of the Canadian province of Manitoba, lying west of Lake Winnipeg and northwest of Lake Manitoba. It has an area of 2,086 square miles, and is 122 miles long and twenty miles in width at the widest part. Small boats can safely ply the lake, but numerous shallow places prevent navigation of large vessels. Its waters are stocked with whitefish and pike, and it is much in favor with anglers. The lake discharges into Lake Manitoba through the Waterhen River.

WINO'NA, MINN., the county seat of Winona County, 103 miles southeast of Saint Paul, on the Mississippi River and on the Chicago, Burlington & Quincy, the Chicago & North Western, the Chicago Great Western, the Chicago, Milwaukee, Saint Paul & Pacific and the Green Bay & Western railroads. Winona conducts a large trade in grain, lumber and livestock. Its industrial plants include flour mills, railroad shops and manufactories of tire chains, drugs, medicines, extracts, toilet preparations, tinware, malt, furs, gloves, wood products, farm implements, food products and other articles.

There is a state teachers college here—the first teachers college to be established west of the Mississippi River. Other educational institutions are the College of Saint Teresa for women and Saint Mary's College for men. Winona is partially surrounded by bluffs of peculiar rock formation, Sugar Loaf and Trempeauleau mountains being particularly picturesque. The place was settled in 1851 on the site of an old Indian village; it was chartered as a city in 1857. Population, 1940, 22,490.

WINSLOW, John Ancrum (1811–1873), an American naval officer, commander of the *Kearsarge* in the battle between that vessel and the Confederate cruiser, *Alabama*, in 1864. The *Alabama* was sunk, and Captain Winslow, who had already won distinction in battle, was promoted to the rank of commodore. After the Civil War he commanded the Gulf squadron and later the Pacific squadron. He was made rear-admiral in 1870.

WIN'STON-SA'LEM, N. C., the county seat of Forsyth County, 110 miles west of Raleigh, on the Norfolk & Western, the Southern and the Winston-Salem Southbound railroads. There is regular air transportation. One of the leading industrial cities of the South, Winston-Salem has the world's largest tobacco-manufacturing plant; one of the largest leaf-tobacco markets in the world, where about 50,000,000 pounds of bright leaf tobacco are sold annually; extensive hosiery and underwear mills; and about seventy-five other plants, producing air conditioning machinery, textile products, furniture, metal products and other articles. Salem College and Academy for women, the medical school of Wake Forest College and Winston-Salem Teachers College for Negroes are here. Salem was founded in 1766 by the Moravians and was for a time governed as a Church community. Winston and Salem were consolidated to form the present city in 1913. Population, 1940, 79,815.

WIN'TER, the season of the year between autumn and spring, beginning with the winter solstice, about December 22, and ending with the vernal equinox, about March 21. In the United States, the months December, January and February are commonly regarded as the winter months, although winter does not begin until December 21 or 22.

WIN'TERGREEN, a small plant, several inches high, which grows in the woods of the northern hemisphere. Glossy, oval leaves, green all winter, grow on the ends of reddish stems. Small white or pink flowers spring from the base of the leaf stems and scarlet berries follow them. The leaves yield an oil which is much used for flavoring and for medicinal purposes.

WINTHROP, John (1588–1649), one of the early colonial governors in America, and one of the most admirable characters in early American history. He was born at Edwardston, Suffolk, England, of wealthy parents, and was educated at Trinity College, Cambridge. Puritan zeal prompted him to share the fortunes of the colonists, and in 1629 he sailed to America with 900 emigrants as governor of Massachusetts Bay colony. From then until the time of his death he worked for the spiritual and material interests of his people.

Winthrop helped to organize the New England Confederation, and was its first president. His *Journal* is a valuable record of New England events from 1630 to 1649.

WIRE, metal drawn into an even thread or slender rod, usually cylindrical in form. The metals most commonly employed in the making of wire are gold, silver, copper and iron. The finest wire is made from platinum. Wire was formerly produced by hammering metal into plates which were then cut into strips and rounded by beating. In modern wire manufacture, steel or iron billets are heated in a furnace to white heat and put through several trains of rolls, emerging from the last roll about a quarter of an inch in diameter. These rods are wound on reels while still hot, are coiled, boiled in sulphuric acid for cleaning, washed in water, coated in lime, baked for two hours at low temperature, and then turned over to the wire drawer.

In order to draw these prepared rods into wires of smaller diameter, the workman pulls them through a series of steel dies by means of a cast-iron reel. Very fine wires may be drawn as many as twenty times, each time through smaller holes. As the process of drawing causes brittleness in wire, it must be annealed as occasion demands by heating in cast-iron pots, this process always being followed by an acid bath for cleaning. Wire used for small springs or nails, when hardness is an essential, is not annealed. For drawing very fine wires of gold, silver or platinum, dies of diamonds, rubies or other hard stones are used. Wire for outdoor use is galvanized to prevent rusting.

The uses of wire are innumerable, from the forming of the gigantic steel cable, with a tensile strength of 130 tons to the square inch, to the delicate micrometer of the telescope, employing platinum wires as fine as $\frac{1}{50,000}$ of an inch in diameter. Telephone and telegraph wires, trolley wires, wire netting and wire fencing are some of the most common uses. In wartime immense quantities of barbed wire are used to form barriers to enemy advance.

WIRE GLASS, window glass made with an inside mat of open mesh wire. The wire is embedded in the molten glass at a temperature sufficiently high to insure adhesion of the glass to it. The surface of the pane can be finished in such style as to adapt the glass for different uses. It may be ribbed, polished or "rough rolled." Wire glass is strong, and is used for window panes where ordinary glass is apt to be broken. It is one of the most efficient safeguards against fire, since, if broken by heat, it does not fall. Two men claim the invention of wire glass, Frank Schuman of Philadelphia and Leon Appert of France.

WIRELESS TEL'EGRAPH. See TELEGRAPH, WIRELESS.

WIRELESS TELEPHONE. See TELEPHONE, WIRELESS.

WIRE'WORMS, a name commonly given to the larvae, or grubs, of several species of click beetles. The worms are hard, slender and cylindrical and of a brown or yellowish color. They bore into seeds that are in the germinating stage, and are especially destructive, to grain seed. They also attack roots of grains, vegetables, grass and cotton. The adults lay the eggs in sod and grassland, and the larvae are full-grown by mid-summer. Their life cycle is from three to five years. For the adult insect, see CLICK BEETLE.

WISCONSIN, a North Central state of the American Union, one of the foremost American commonwealths in educational and political matters, and industrially one of the most prosperous. Wisconsin is popularly called THE BADGER STATE, referring to the habits of the lead miners in early days, who lived in rude dugouts, after the fashion of the badger. The name *Wisconsin* is of Indian origin, and has been variously interpreted to mean *rushing river* and *great rocks*.

Location, Area, Population. Wisconsin lies north of Illinois and east of Minnesota and Iowa; nearly all of the western boundary is formed by the Saint Croix and the Mississippi rivers. A good portion of the eastern boundary line lies in Lake Michigan; the state adjoins the state of Michigan on the northeast, and at the extreme north it follows the shore line of Lake Superior. With a maximum length of 320 miles and a width of 295 miles, the state is irregularly oblong in shape and has an area of 56,154 square miles; of this total, 1,439 square miles are water. Twenty-four states surpass it in area and twelve in population, which was 3,137,587 in 1940, with a density of 57.3 persons to the square mile; it stands nineteenth among the states in the density of its population. According to the census of 1940, 53.5 per cent of the population live in incorporated places of 2,500 or more inhabitants.

Peoples and Cities. The founders of the state came largely from New England and New York State. The foreign-born at one time made up a third of the population, but their ratio to the total number has declined. Germans constitute one-third of the foreign-born; next in order are Poles, Norwegians, Czechoslovakians, Swedes, Russians, Canadians and Englishmen. There are thirty-three cities with populations of 10,000 or over. Milwaukee, with 587,472 inhabitants in 1940, is the largest city in Wisconsin and the thirteenth in size in the Union. The next seven cities, in order of size, are Madison (the capital), Racine, Kenosha, Green Bay, La Crosse, Sheboygan and Oshkosh.

The chief religious bodies are the Roman Catholics, Lutherans and Methodists. Nearly one-fourth of the people are Roman Catholics and about one-sixth are Lutherans.

Surface and Drainage. The surface of Wisconsin is generally a great rolling plain. A low height of land extends through the state north and south, a little east of the middle line, and at a point about 30 miles south of Lake Superior it meets another elevation extending east and west. The highest altitudes of this ridge are about 1,800 feet. These ridges form watersheds from which the land slopes in all directions. There are no high mountains in the state, but the rivers flow through well-worn valleys in some localities; and along the Mississippi and other streams there are bluffs. There is also a very conspicuous bluff along Green Bay. The lowest part of the state borders on Lake Michigan, which is slightly less than 600 feet above sea level.

Wisconsin is divided into three drainage areas. The northwestern part of the state is drained into Lake Superior by a few short rivers, chief of which are the Montreal and the Bois Brule. The area east of the watershed extending north and south is drained into Lake Michigan, and with the exception of the Fox, all of the rivers in this region are short. Some of the most important are the Menominee, forming a large part of the boundary between Wisconsin and the northern peninsula of Michigan, the Peshtigo and the Oconto.

Nearly three-fourths of the state is drained into the Mississippi River. The chief tributaries are the Saint Croix, forming a part of the western boundary, the Chippewa, the Black, and the Wisconsin, w h i c h flows through the central part of the state and is the largest river wholly within its boundaries. Each of these rivers has numerous tributaries, but none of them is navigable for large boats. Through a part of its course the Wisconsin has cut its way through sandstone bluffs, forming the Dells (or Dalles, which see), noted for their beautiful scenery. In the southeastern, north-central a n d northern parts of the state are numerous lakes which are the favorite resorts for summer residents and also for hunters and fishermen. The largest of these is Lake Winnebago, almost directly south of Green Bay. Lakes Geneva and Mendota are noted for their beautiful landscape setting. The former is a popular summer resort; on the latter is the city of Madison, seat of the state university.

Climate. The winters are long and severe, but of uniform temperature, with many dry, clear days; the summers are short and hot. But the cold of winter and the heat of summer in the eastern section are tempered by the waters of Lake Michigan. In northern Wisconsin, snow usually falls early in the winter and covers the ground until late in the

spring; in the south there is often little snow. The average rainfall is 30 inches.

Mineral Resources. Though the state derives much greater income from agriculture than from mining operations, it has valuable deposits of zinc, building stone, iron ore and clays. The total annual mineral output is valued at about $18,000,000. The most important building stones are granite, limestone and sandstone, with an annual value of over $5,000,000. Iron, zinc and lead are important products. Iron ore is found in the valley of the Menominee River and along the Penokee range in the northern part of the state. The deposits are a continuation of those in Michigan and Minnesota, and the ores are similar in quality. In quantity of output, however, Wisconsin is far behind Michigan and Minnesota. The products of each year often are valued at about $3,000,-000. Clay suitable for making brick and tiling is widely distributed, and the manufacture of cream-colored brick is one of the most important industries of the state. Other products of value include natural cement, graphite and mineral waters.

Agriculture. Originally a large part of the state was covered with forests; in the north the principal timber was pine. Regions between the forests consist of marsh or land covered with boulders. Hence this part of the state is not suited to general agriculture, but it is well adapted to dairying; this industry has been extensively developed. The middle and southern portions of the state consist of fertile prairie lands. They are supplied with an abundance of moisture, and the temperature is suitable for growing all crops produced in a medium or cool temperate climate.

Oats and corn are the most important grain crops; the annual harvest of oats at times exceeds 100,000,000 bushels. About 4,000,000 tons of hay are produced each year. Barley and rye are raised in large quantities; buckwheat is another important product. In the central region of the southern group of counties is a fertile tobacco belt by means of which Wisconsin holds seventh place among the states in the amount of tobacco raised. Sugar beets, potatoes, beans, peas, apples and small fruits are other flourishing products. The state is one of the few regions in America producing cranberries on a commercial scale; it is one of the first five states in the production of peas and beans.

Dairying is one of the most profitable lines of agriculture, and Wisconsin produces more cheese than any other state. Minnesota alone exceeds it in the output of creamery butter. Cows and heifers number more than 2,000,-000; to them must be added 1,000,000 other cattle.

Manufactures. Wisconsin ranks t e n t h among the states in manufactures. In 1880, when wheat was still a leading crop, flour and grist-mill products were first among her manufactures. Subsequently lumber and timber stood at the head of the list; still later butter, cheese and condensed milk stood first.

There is a great diversity of manufactures; among these motor vehicles stand first with a yearly value of about $219,000,000, while motor vehicle bodies and parts and rubber tires and tubes are worth an additional $136,-000,000. Butter, cheese and condensed milk are worth $203,000,000. Other industries are foundry and machine shop products, paper and wood pulp, engines, turbines, wholesale meat packing, boots and shoes, knit goods, electricial machinery and aluminum. Milwaukee holds a leading position in brewing.

Transportation and Commerce. The western part of the state has an outlet through the Saint Croix and the Mississippi rivers; the northwestern section sends freight through Lake Superior; while the eastern portion, bordering in its entire length upon Lake Michigan, has communication with the Great Lakes through Racine, Milwaukee, Sheboygan, Manitowoc, Sturgeon Bay and other points.

Wisconsin maintains about 7,300 miles of steam railways. The leading railroads are the Chicago, Milwaukee, Saint Paul & Pacific, the Chicago & North Western, and the Minneapolis, Saint Paul & Sault Ste. Marie, commonly called the "Soo." This line became a subsidiary of the Canadian Pacific and many years ago absorbed the old Wisconsin Central and thus gained connection with Chicago. The Green Bay & Western is the longest line extending wholly within the state. Several railroads developed to a great extent in other states have only a small mileage in Wisconsin; such are the Chicago, Burlington & Quincy, the Illinois Central and the Northern Pacific. Four strong bus companies have absorbed much of the traffic formerly carried by the interurban electric lines. Three interstate air lines serve Wisconsin.

The commerce of the state is extensive. Iron, dairy products, live stock, lumber and its manufactured products, flour and gristmill products, potatoes and other vegetables are exported in large quantities. The imports consist of manufactured goods and machinery.

Government. The legislature consists of a senate and a house of representatives, the senate having thirty-three members, and the house, 100. The members of the assembly are elected for two years; of the senate, for four years. The sessions are biennial and are unlimited as to time. The executive department consists of a governor, a lieutenant-governor, a secretary of state, a treasurer and an attorney-general, each elected for two years, and the superintendent of public instruction, chosen at a spring election for a four-year term. In the judicial system there are the supreme court of seven judges elected for ten years, and the circuit courts in the several judicial circuits established by the legislature, each circuit having one judge elected by the people.

Much of the work of government in Wisconsin is done by departments either established or put into present form within the twentieth century. Each of these greater departments is headed by a group of three persons, usually called commissioners. They are appointed by the governor, subject to confirmation by the senate, for six years; terms are arranged to overlap so that commissions may never lack experienced members.

The list of these commissions is as follows: public service, highway, industrial, commissions; board of control for state institutions; tax and banking commissions; and the department of agriculture.

Education. Wisconsin has a system of public education extending from the kindergarten through the graduate and professional schools of the state university. The elementary and secondary schools care for more than 800,000 pupils and cost about $22,000,-000 annually; and the total yearly expenditure of the state and its subdivisions for all types of education is about $70,000,000. The University of Wisconsin at Madison is at the head of the system, and is directly affiliated with the high schools throughout the state. There are nine institutions which began work as normal schools, but they are now called state teachers' colleges, and grant bachelors' degrees to graduates of their four-year courses. They are located at Milwaukee, Oshkosh, Platteville, River Falls, Stevens Point, Superior, Whitewater, La Crosse and Eau Claire; their aggregate enrollment is not far from 7,000. The state also supports Stout Institute at Menomonee in Dunn County, a nationally known training school for teachers of home economics, manual training and other vocational subjects. Wisconsin has a unique system of county training schools to prepare teachers for the rural schools. It has also been a great leader in vocational education. In connection with its educational department, Wisconsin maintains an excellent system of school libraries, which are so managed as to bring a large list of the best books within reach of every inhabitant of the state, at practically no expense. The traveling libraries have no connection with the educational department, being promoted by the state library commission. The library of the historical society at Madison is also one of great value. Another agency for extending popular education is the excellent extension system of the state university (see WISCONSIN, UNIVERSITY OF).

Important institutions of higher learning not under the control of the state include Beloit College at Beloit, Lawrence College at Appleton, Ripon College at Ripon, Milton College at Milton, Carroll College at Waukesha and Milwaukee-Downer College at Milwaukee. Of somewhat later foundation are Marquette University and Mount Mary College (for women), both of them Roman Catholic institutions located in Milwaukee.

Other Institutions. The school for the blind is at Janesville; the institution for the deaf and dumb is at Delavan; there are schools for the feeble-minded and epileptic at Chippewa Falls and at Union Grove in Racine County; the state public school for dependent children is situated at Sparta. There are hospitals for the insane at Mendota and Winnebago and a hospital for the criminal insane at Waupun; the incurable insane are cared for in county institutions which receive state aid. A state tuberculosis sanitorium was established at Wales in 1905 and later it was supplemented by a camp for male convalescents at Lake Tomahawk in Oneida County. There are also nearly twenty state-aided county tuberculosis sanitoria.

There is a state soldiers' home at Waupaca

Items of Interest on Wisconsin

Wisconsin was the last complete state made out of the Northwest Territory. There still remained as much of Minnesota as lay east of the Mississippi River, so that altogether the Northwest Territory became five and a half states.

Wisconsin's climate is marked by much sunshine and high temperature in summer and by clear sky with low temperature in winter; the climate is tempered to a limited degree by the large bodies of water east and north.

Many of the wild animals have been killed off, but deer are still plentiful in the northern part of the state, and wolves, black bears and foxes are occasionally seen; waterfowl of all kinds are abundant and fishing is both a great sport and an important business.

In Grant County there is a huge mound shaped like an elephant, with a trunk thirty-two feet long. This is a relic of the Mound Builders of prehistoric times.

Wisconsin's many lakes, waterfalls and rapids are the result of glacial action.

School attendance is compulsory for all children between the ages of 8 and 14, in cities for the entire school year, and in towns and villages for six months. Public schools are open to pupils aged 5 to 21.

The highest point in the state, Rib Hill, is in Marathon County. It has an altitude of 1,940 feet.

Questions on Wisconsin

Describe briefly the surface and drainage of Wisconsin.

Name five important agricultural products and four minerals.

What can you say about the importance of dairying in Wisconsin?

What is the most important manufacturing industry?

Name five other manufacturing industries.

Name five important agricultural institutions.

Explain, as fully as you can, Milwaukee's importance in commerce and manufactures.

and a national soldiers' home at Milwaukee. The penal and reformatory institutions consist of a state prison at Waupun, a state reformatory near Green Bay, an industrial school for boys at Waukesha, a house of correction and industrial school for girls at Milwaukee, and an industrial home for women in Fond du Lac County.

History. Probably the first white man to enter the territory of Wisconsin was Jean Nicolet, who was dispatched in 1634 by Champlain and who reached the shores of Green Bay. Other traders and missionaries followed, including Radisson and Groseilliers, Father Allouez and Marquette and Joliet. Meantime, several missions had been established, one at La Pointe on Lake Superior in 1665 and one at the site of De Pere in 1669. By the Treaty of Paris, in 1763, the territory, with all the northwest, was transferred to Great Britain and, after the Revolution, to the United States, where it formed a part of the Northwest Territory. However, the French and Indians in the region still remained hostile to the United States and fought against it during the War of 1812. The discovery of lead mines eventually brought on a rapid influx into the territory, and after the defeat of Black Hawk there was a large agricultural immigration.

Wisconsin was successfully joined to Indiana and Michigan; it was erected into a separate territory in 1836. In 1847, the population of the state having been vastly increased, a constitution was adopted, and Wisconsin was admitted to the Union in the following year. For a time the chief incident in the political history of the state was the scandal arising from the promiscuous granting and sale of public lands to railroads. One of the first movements leading to the organization of the Republican party was a convention at Ripon, Wis., in 1854. The state was consistently opposed to slavery, and its supreme court declared that the Fugitive Slave Law was unconstitutional in the state. During the Civil War, Wisconsin furnished more than her quota of troops. Since that period the state has been almost consistently Republican in politics. However, after 1901, when the elder La Follette became governor, the Republican party was divided into two factions, the Progressive and the Stalwarts; they have alternated in the political control of the state.

Since 1900, Wisconsin has passed many

progressive laws, including workmen's compensation, mothers' pension and child labor measures and a law regulating campaign contributions. In 1913 there was enacted a law requiring a physical examination for all men who applied for marriage licenses. This was subsequently upheld by the state supreme court. Wisconsin was the first state to enact a plan for unemployment insurance.

Related Articles. Consult the following titles for additional information:

CITIES

Appleton	Janesville	Oshkosh
Ashland	Kenosha	Racine
Beloit	La Crosse	Sheboygan
Chippewa Falls	Madison	Stevens Point
Eau Claire	Manitowoc	Superior
Fond du Lac	Marinette	Waukesha
Green Bay	Milwaukee	Wausaw

PHYSICAL FEATURES

Dalles	Mississippi River
Great Lakes	Wisconsin River

HISTORY

Black Hawk	Ordinance of 1787
Northwest Territory	

WISCONSIN, UNIVERSITY OF, one of the largest and most progressive of the American state universities; instruction began at Madison in 1849.

The university stands at the head of the educational system of the state and gives free tuition to students, who are residents in Wisconsin, in all departments except in the library school and the Wisconsin High School. Through an admirably equipped and organized extension department thousands of persons unable to attend regular university sessions are given exceptional advantages. The university maintains three colleges—letters and science, engineering, agriculture; six schools—law, medicine, nursing, education, library, graduate; two divisions—physical education and university extension.

The library building is one of the finest in the United States; it contains over 453,000 volumes. Adjacent is the library of the Wisconsin State Historical Society with 371,000 volumes and the library of the Academy of Sciences, Arts and Letters with 6,000 volumes.

During the regular session there are about 8,000 students in residence; the faculty numbers nearly 1,300. The report of the American Council of Education prepared by 2,000 educational experts placed the university second in the nation as qualified to give graduate instruction, that is, in 31 out of the specified 35 important fields of knowledge.

WISCONSIN RIVER, the principal river of the state whose name it bears. It rises near the boundary between Michigan and

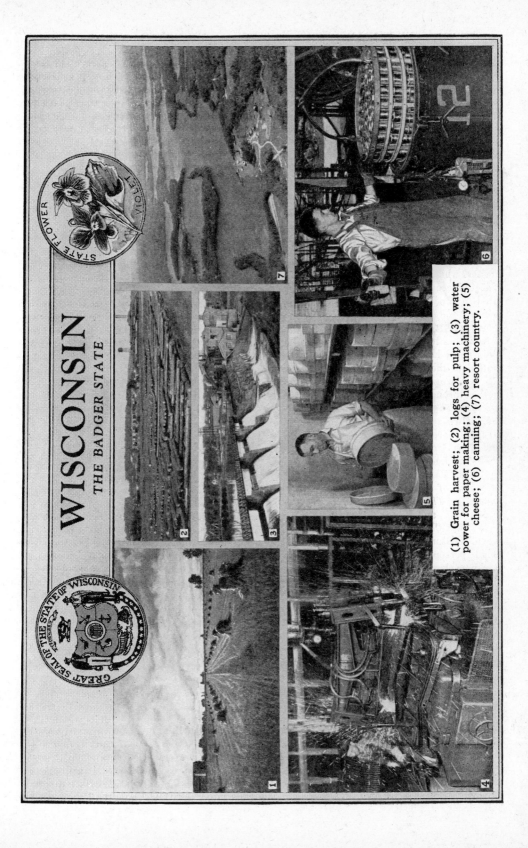

WISCONSIN

THE BADGER STATE

STATE FLOWER — VIOLET

GREAT SEAL OF THE STATE OF WISCONSIN

(1) Grain harvest; (2) logs for pulp; (3) water power for paper making; (4) heavy machinery; (5) cheese; (6) canning; (7) resort country.

Wisconsin, flows southward to Portage City, thence in a southwest direction, entering the Mississippi River four miles south of Prairie du Chien. Its length is about 600 miles, and it is navigable for steamboats to Portage City, about 200 miles. Here a canal connects it with the Fox River. Its passage through some deep gorges forms the celebrated Dalles, near Kilbourn City.

WISTA′RIA, a climbing shrub of the pea family, native to China and North America. Several varieties have been introduced into England. When in flower they are among the most ornamental of garden plants. The flowers, shaped like pea-blossoms, are of various tints and shades of lavender, and hang in clusters which sometimes are several feet long. The Chinese and American species are much used in the United States for garden ornament.

WIS′TER, Owen (1860-1938), an American novelist and story-writer, born in Philadelphia and educated at Harvard. He was admitted to the bar, but after two years gave up law work for literature and won wide notice through his stories of Western life. Of these *The Virginian* has been most popular. Owen Wister wrote biographies of *Grant, Oliver Wendell Holmes, Franklin,* and *Theodore Roosevelt.* Among his later books are *Lady Baltimore, The Simple Spelling Bee, The Seven Ages of Washington, Members of the Family, The Pentecost of Calamity, The Ancient Grudge, Neighbors Henceforth,* and *Watch Your Thirst.*

WITCH′CRAFT. At all times in the world's history there has existed a belief that some persons, in league with powers of darkness, had powers to cast "spells" or inflict injury at a distance by supernormal means. This belief became general in the fifteenth, sixteenth and seventeenth centuries, and in England and America the use of the supposed power to harm through coöperation of a demon was called *witchcraft,* meaning *craft or practice of a witch.*

Women were most often accused of witchcraft, though men and even children were suspected. Laws were passed to deal with them and persecutions were numerous. It is estimated that in England, Germany, France, Spain and Italy 100,000 innocent persons perished under the charge of witchcraft between the middle of the fifteenth and the middle of the sixteenth century. Various tests were applied to ascertain whether or not the person was a witch, such as pricking the body of the victim all over, to find the insensitive spots protected by the devil, and throwing witches into deep water, under the presumption that they would float if possessed.

The witchcraft frenzy broke out among the Puritans of New England in 1648. In Salem, Mass., Cotton Mather, a clergyman of wide influence and great power as a pulpit orator, wrote a work entitled *Memorable Providences Relating to Witchcraft and Possessions* and another entitled *Wonders of the Invisible World.* By the distribution of his writings and his utterances in the pulpit, he succeeded in arousing the superstition to the highest pitch, at a time when it was beginning to abate in Europe.

Many of the teaching men of the province were influenced by his writings and sermons, and, as clergymen in those days constituted a part of the magisterial authority, he succeeded in procuring the execution of nineteen persons. The good sense of the Puritans at last revolted against these atrocities, and a reaction set in. Samuel Parris, a clergyman, who was one of the chief persecutors, made a confession; others also relented, and there were no more persecutions for witchcraft in the American colonies. In England the last trial for witchcraft was in 1722, and it resulted in acquittal.

WITCH HA′ZEL, a North American shrub which is of economic importance as the source of a healing lotion obtained by distilling the leaves in alcohol. The plant has branches of a very peculiar appearance, for they twist and curve in all directions. In olden times the witch hazel was believed to have supernatural power, and the forked twigs were used as divining rods. The plant does not bloom until late in the fall, and the fruits ripen the following year. The yellow flowers grow in showy clusters. A small, woody capsule encloses the seeds.

WITENAGEMOT, *wit e nah ge mote′,* in English history, the name given to the old Anglo-Saxon assembly, which consisted of the king, the ealdormen, the higher ecclesiastics and the thanes. This body had power to elect the king, when a succession was in dispute, or to depose a king if it saw fit, to make treaties, to collect revenue and to enact laws. Under a weak king it was able to exercise all of these functions, but a strong king might easily make most of them merely nominal. The Norman Conquest put an end to this assembly, and the Parliament which grew up later in England was a separate institution, though it had its roots in this early body.

WIT'NESS, in law, (1) one who signs his name as affirmation of the genuineness of another's signature; (2) a person who gives testimony under oath in a judicial proceeding. Any person can be summoned before a court to give evidence. If he fails to appear he is liable to punishment for contempt (see CONTEMPT). The summons by which he is ordered to appear is called a *subpoena;* if he is ordered to bring a document or other thing in his possession, he is summoned by a *subpoena duces tecum,* meaning *bring with you under penalty.*

WITTE, *vit'te,* SERGEI YULIEVITCH (1840-1915), a Russian statesman and diplomat, born at Tiflis. After his graduation from the New Russian University at Odessa, he took up journalism; later he was engaged by the government in railway service. In the Russo-Turkish War Witte had charge of the transportation of troops on the Odessa railway and so distinguished himself that at the close of the war he was made manager of the Southwestern Railway of Russia. Two years later he became chief of the Imperial Railway department and president of the tariff commission. His next promotion was to the office of Minister of Finance, in 1893. His policy in this office led to the rapid development of manufacturing industries in Russia. He introduced the gold standard, made the sale of alcohol a government monopoly, concluded several important commercial treaties, especially with Germany, and made large foreign loans, whereby the Trans-Siberian Railway could be built. In 1903 a strong opposition arose and Witte was removed from power and made president of the Committee of Ministers. At the Treaty of Portsmouth, N. H., at the close of the Russo-Japanese War, Witte was especially prominent. When he returned to Russia, the czar conferred upon him the title of count. In 1905 he was appointed Prime Minister of Russia, but in 1906 he resigned this position.

WITTENBERG, *vit' ten berK,* GERMANY, a town in the province of Saxony, Prussia, situated on the Elbe, fifty-nine miles southwest of Berlin, of special historical interest because of its association with Luther and Melanchthon. It was to the door of the Schlosskirche at Wittenberg that Luther nailed his celebrated theses, and within this church both Luther and Melanchthon are buried. (See LUTHER, MARTIN; REFORMATION). The town contains a number of educational institutions, in one of which, the University of Wittenberg, Luther for a time was instructor. The industries include the manufacture of woolen and linen goods, hosiery, machinery, pottery, etc. Population, about 20,000.

WOAD, *wode,* a group of plants of the mustard family, chiefly natives of the Mediterranean region. *Dyer's woad,* a species yielding a blue dye, was formerly much cultivated. This has been superseded by indigo; but a fine blue is still obtained by mixing the two. The leaves when gathered are reduced to a paste, fermented for two weeks, made into balls, sun-dried, and subjected to further fermentation.

WODEN, *vo'den.* See ODIN.

WOLF, a carnivorous animal, allied to the dog. The common European wolf, found almost everywhere in North America, also, is yellowish-gray, with a blackish band, or

WOLF

streak, on the fore legs. The ears are erect and pointed. The hair is harsh and strong, the tail straight, bushy and drooping. The height at the shoulder is about two and a half feet. The wolf is swift of foot and crafty, an enemy to animal life. It usually runs in packs to hunt the larger quadrupeds, such as deer and elk. When hard pressed with hunger, these packs have been known to attack isolated travelers and even to enter villages and carry off children. In general, however, wolves are cowardly and stealthy. They are still plentiful in many parts of Europe and North America. They probably ceased to exist in England about the end of the fifteenth century. The small *prairie wolf* or *coyote*, a member of the wolf family, living on the western plains of the United States, is a burrowing animal.

WOLFE, JAMES (1727–1759), a British general, whose victory in the Battle of Quebec, September 13, 1759, won Canada for Great Britain. Wolfe was born at Westerham, Kent, England. He entered the army early and served in Scotland and in Flanders. When it was decided, in 1758, to send an expedition to Cape Breton, Wolfe was appointed by Pitt brigadier-general. He advised an attack on Quebec and was selected to lead the enterprise, in which capacity he showed wonderful courage and genius. After having been driven back from the fortress, he led his men, by night, up a steep, narrow path, to the Heights of Abraham, above the city, and here he met the French under Montcalm. While leading a charge, he had one of his wrists shattered by a shot, but he did not stop. Another shot struck him, and he still advanced, but a third lodged in his breast and proved fatal. His last words, when he was told that the French were retreating, were, "Now God be praised; I die in peace." A monument on the battlefield bears a simple inscription in honor of the conqueror. Since 1773 another monument has graced Westminster Abbey in London, and one is in Governor's Garden, Quebec.

WOLF FISH, a savage fish, that has a mouth armed with sharp, strong teeth. When captured, the fish is said to bite the nets and even to attack the fishermen. Around the coasts of Great Britain it attains a length of six or seven feet, but in more southern seas it grows to a still larger size. In Iceland the natives eat the flesh and make the tough skin into a sort of leather suitable for purses, bookcovers and the like.

WOLSELEY, *wool'ly,* GARNET JOSEPH, Sir, Viscount (1833–1913), a British general, born in Ireland. He entered the army as ensign in 1852, took part in the second Burmese War, where he was severely wounded, and served with distinction in the Crimean War. He engaged in the siege and capture of Lucknow during the Sepoy Rebellion, and was in command in 1860 in the Chinese War. In the following year he was dispatched to Canada, and in 1870 he carried the Red

River expedition to a successful issue. Three years afterward he was appointed to the command of an expedition to punish the king of Ashanti, and after a brief campaign he entered Kumassi and subdued the king. He was publicly honored and given a grant by the government of $125,000.

He was placed in command in Egypt, in 1882, where his forces successfully stormed the lines of Tel-el-Kebir and captured Arabi Pasha. For this he received the thanks of Parliament, was created a baron and was promoted to the rank of general. In 1882 he was sent to Egypt to rescue General Gordon at Khartum, but arrived two days after Gordon had been killed and Khartum had fallen. On his return to England he was created a viscount. In 1890 he was made commander of the troops in Ireland, and in 1895 he was raised to the supreme command of the British army.

WOLSEY, *wool'zy,* THOMAS, Cardinal (1475?–1530), an English statesman, for many years the most powerful man in England, below the king. He was born at Ipswich, the son of a butcher, and was educated at Magdalen College, Oxford, where he took his degree as a scholar of distinction. When Henry VIII became king, the advancement of Wolsey was rapid. Successively he was appointed canon of Windsor, dean of York, bishop of Lincoln, archbishop of York, lord chancellor of the kingdom, cardinal and Pope's legate.

His power and his revenues were equaled only by those of the Crown. Part of his immense revenues he expended in display, and part for the advancement of learning. He endowed the College of Christ's Church, Oxford, founded several lectures and built the palace at Hampton Court, which he presented to the king. His preferment by the king was largely the result of a remarkable series of diplomatic victories, in which Wolsey had been the means of enabling Henry to hold the balance between Francis I and Emperor Charles V.

In his ambitious career the cardinal had made many enemies, who were held in check so long as he retained the favor of his royal master. This favor Wolsey lost when he failed to obtain from Pope Clement a decision granting the king's divorce from Catharine of Aragon. The enemies of the fallen prelate now succeeded in banishing him from court and stripping him of his dignities.

Finally, after a brief respite, during which he was restored to some of his offices and had returned to his see of York, he was arrested on a charge of high treason. On his way to London, as a prisoner, he died at Leicester Abbey.

WOLVERINE, *wool vur een'.* See GLUTTON.

WOMAN'S CHRISTIAN TEMPERANCE UNION, THE NATIONAL, a woman's organization, founded in Cleveland, Ohio, in 1874, for the purpose of unifying the work of women in temperance and social reform. It now has state, district, county and local societies in every state and territory, and it contains a membership of over 300,000. It is the largest organization exclusively of women that has ever been effected and has over forty distinct lines of work, each under the management of national, state, district, county and local superintendents. The society has been instrumental in securing in nearly every state the enactment of laws requiring the public schools to give instruction in the effects of stimulants and narcotics on the human system; through their influence many laws for the better protection of girls and women have also been passed, and industrial homes for girls and houses of refuge for fallen women have been established. The official organ is the *Union Signal,* published at Chicago. Headquarters of the society are at Evanston, Ill., in "Rest Cottage," the former home of Miss Frances E. Willard.

The World's Christian Temperance Union was formed in 1883, through the influence of Miss Willard. It now has local organizations in most Christian countries. The badge of members everywhere is the white ribbon.

WOMAN'S RELIEF CORPS, a patriotic organization founded in Denver, Colo., in 1883, by a group of women desirous of acting in coöperation with the G. A. R. The specific objects of the society may be stated as follows:

To aid and assist the G. A. R. and perpetuate the memory of their heroic dead; to find homes for the Union Veterans, their widows and orphans, and to emulate the deeds of our army nurses; to maintain true allegiance to the United States of America; to inculcate lessons of patriotism and love of country among our children and in the communities in which we live; to encourage the spread of universal liberty and equal rights to all.

Though few members of the G. A. R. survive, the Relief Corps maintains its organization in most Northern states.

WOMAN SUF'FRAGE, the right of women to vote on an equality with men. The agitation to give women a political status equal to that of men is merely one phase of the great movement to recognize woman in every possible way—legally, socially, intellectually, morally, politically—the equal of man. The outbreak of the World War enabled women to demonstrate their abilities in the business world, where the agitation for a fair and equal opportunity made most progress.

The woman-suffrage movement is distinctly a product of the nineteenth century, although many authors and statesmen since Plato have discussed the position of women and have urged equal rights. One of the first American suffragists was Abigail Adams, the wife of John Adams; she wanted the Constitution to recognize women as voters. While the movement in England began as early as 1838 with Chartism (which see), women did not receive the vote there until 1918. Women were enfranchised in New Zealand as early as 1893; now, in all the British Dominions and in a number of the colonies, some form of woman suffrage is found.

The World War gave new impetus, in nearly all civilized countries, to the recognition of woman's right to vote; and in most of the countries liberated from autocracy as an outcome of the war, women were given political rights when the new governments were set up. In Europe, the first country to grant woman suffrage was Norway (1906). The movement suffered reverses, however, with the rise of totalitarian nations. In Asia, women vote in Turkey, Thailand (Siam) and some provinces of India. The movement had gained ground in China before the war with Japan. Women also vote in several of the South American countries.

In the United States. In the United States the movement for woman suffrage really dates from 1848, when the first woman suffrage convention was held, in Seneca Falls, N. Y. Among its leaders were Elizabeth Cady Stanton and Lucretia Mott. In 1869, through the efforts of Mrs. Stanton and Susan B. Anthony, the National Woman's Suffrage Association was formed. In 1890 this organization united with one founded the same year by Henry Ward Beecher, and the name National American

Woman's Suffrage Association was adopted. The organization in coöperation with numerous state societies worked tirelessly for the extension of women's political rights, and in

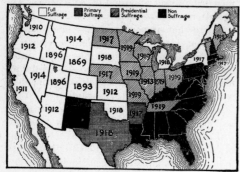

BEFORE THE AMENDMENT

The map shows the status of women suffrage on August 1, 1920. The white areas were full-suffrage states; slanting lines indicated Presidential suffrage; squares, primary suffrage; black, no suffrage. A Constitutional amendment to grant suffrage to all women of the United States passed the House of Representatives on May 21, 1919; the Senate, June 4. It was ratified in 1920.

1919 a woman suffrage amendment to the Constitution passed both Houses of Congress. It was sent to the states for ratification, and in August, 1920, this was accomplished. By referring to the map the reader may see the progress of the movement.

WOM'BAT, a burrowing mammal belonging to the same order as the kangaroo, having the characteristic pouch for carrying the young (see MARSUPIALS). Wombats are found only in Australia and Tasmania. They look somewhat like small bears, are two to three feet in length and have a coat of long, coarse fur, yellowish-black or grayish-brown in color. The head is broad and flat, the eyes and ears are small, and the tail is short. The creatures feed on leaves, roots and vegetables, coming out of their burrows at night in search of food. Their flesh tastes somewhat like pork; the fur is used in making rugs and mats.

WOMEN'S CLUBS. With the increase in facilities for the education of women and with their growing share in public life, came the feeling of the necessity for coöperation along lines in which they were interested. The first societies of women were religious, charitable and social organizations. As educational advantages were extended to women, study clubs sprang up among them, and from these have developed the highly efficient women's organizations of to-day.

At present there exist in the United States a great number of clubs for women. A great many of these clubs are *departmental*, that is, are divided into groups interested respectively in literature, household economics, municipal improvements, politics, and so on, each group coöperating with the others and the interests and activities often overlapping. Others are devoted exclusively to politics, art, travel, domestic science, or are made up of members of some profession.

Within recent years women's clubs have brought about many reforms in school administration and municipal management. They have turned their attention systematically to promoting child welfare, improving the condition of working women and awakening the public conscience generally to a realization of the need of reform. In many cities, owing to their influence, vacant property has been converted into playgrounds or into kitchen gardens for the poor. Prisons, asylums, charitable organizations, dance halls and innumerable other institutions have felt their influence.

The General Federation of Women's Clubs is the largest women's organization in the world. It includes about 14,000 clubs, and these are found in every state of the Union, in Alaska and other territories, and in many foreign countries. It is a federation of clubs representing great diversity of interest, but it excludes sectarian, political and secret organizations. The General Federation was first planned in 1889 and formally organized in 1890, when a constitution was adopted. In 1901 it received a charter from Congress. In the United States, the local clubs are organized into state federations. The national convention is held biennially and there is a council which meets in the alternate years.

WOOD, LEONARD (1860–1927), an American soldier and administrator who was the originator of military camps for college students and citizens' training camps, such as that at Plattsburg, N. Y. He was born at Winchester, N. H., and educated at Pierce Academy, Middleboro, and Harvard University, where he was graduated in medicine in 1884. He joined the medical staff of the army, and in 1886, as assistant surgeon, he was the medical line officer in Captain (afterwards Major-General) Lawton's campaign against the Apache Indians. In 1908 he received the Congressional Medal of Honor for distinguished services in that campaign. He was appointed assistant surgeon of the army in 1888, and in twelve years rose to the rank of major-general of volunteers.

At the outbreak of the Spanish-American War, General Wood (then Colonel) and Theodore Roosevelt organized the First Cavalry, known as the "Rough Riders." Wood was first and Roosevelt second in command of the regiment which is famous for its gallant charge at San Juan Hill.

General Wood was appointed governor-general of Cuba in 1899 and continued in the position until the United States retired from the island in 1902. He displayed rare tact and administrative ability, especially in improving the sanitary conditions of Santiago and Havana. Yellow fever, a former scourge of the island, has been practically unknown in Cuba since General Wood's administration. In 1903 he was placed in charge of a division of the army in the Philippines and in the same year was made a major-general in the regular army. In 1908 he was made chief of the Department of the East, with headquarters at New York. Iu 1910 he was special ambassador to Argentina, and the same year was appointed chief of staff, retaining the position until 1914, when he returned to the command of the Department of the East.

While he was chief of staff, General Wood inaugurated military training camps for college students and the citizens' training camps, which later were important agencies in training officers for the army. He has always been a strong advocate of military preparedness. When the United States entered the World War, General Wood was transferred to the Department of the South, with headquarters at Charleston, S. C. In April, 1918, he was assigned to the command of the 89th Division at Camp Funston, Kansas. The Washington administration did not permit him to take a command in France. From Camp Funston he was transferred to the Central Department, with headquarters at Chicago, in 1919. In 1920 he sought the Republican Presidential nomination, and in 1921 was appointed governor-general of the Philippine Islands by President Harding.

WOOD AL'COHOL, or METHYLATED ALCOHOL, a liquid having the appearance and many of the properties of pure alcohol. It is obtained from the destructive distillation of wood, and is used as a solvent for resin and varnishes and as a fuel in the same way as ordinary alcohol. It mixes with water in all proportions. A mixture of seventy-five per cent water and twenty-five per cent alcohol in an automobile radiator will prevent freezing at a temperature of five degrees above zero; a mixture of fifty per cent each will prevent freezing at twenty degrees below zero. Wood alcohol should never be used medicinally, either externally as a liniment or internally, as it is very poisonous, producing vertigo, coma, blindness and death.

WOOD'BINE. See HONEYSUCKLE.

WOOD CARVING, the art of producing sculpture in wood. Wood carving was probably the earliest form of sculpture. As far as known, the Egyptians were the first wood carvers. Specimens of their work, made more than 4000 B. C., are still in existence, and it is quite probable that the Greeks obtained their first ideas of sculpture from the wood carving of these people. The Romans also carved many of their early statues from wood. In the first century of the Christian era wood carving was used in the decoration of churches, and many pieces still in existence show the remarkable skill of the artists and workmen of that time. From the early centuries of the Christian Era wood carving fell into disuse, until about the eleventh century, when it was again revived, and used, as before, in the decoration of churches.

Wood carving as practiced to-day is confined to the ornamentation of altars, pulpits and choir stalls for churches; to a few articles of the most expensive furniture; to the decoration of expensive interiors of dwellings and public halls, and to ornaments. Among European nations the art is practiced with the greatest skill in Tyrol, Switzerland, and some of the provinces of Italy and Germany. Among the Eastern nations the Persians are remarkably skilful in carving wood. The work is finely executed, but shows a tendency to overcrowding, which mars the general effect. The Chinese and Japanese also produce wood carvings of decided merit.

All the finest work is done by hand, with small chisels, shaped for the purpose. Oak, mahogany, ebony and many of the softer woods are used. Before carving, the wood should be thoroughly seasoned. The completed work is usually finished by rubbing down in oil. In the United States but little hand carving is done, though in some manual training schools it is now a part of the course.

WOOD′CHUCK, the popular name of an animal of the squirrel family, common in the United States and Canada. The woodchuck is the American marmot and is often called the *ground hog.* It is of a heavy form, from fifteen to eighteen inches long, blackish or grizzled above and chestnut red below. It feeds on vegetables and is very destructive to crops of red clover and alfalfa. In the winter it hibernates in burrows. There is a popular superstition that the woodchuck first comes out on Candlemas Day (February 2); if it sees its shadow it returns to sleep, because it knows that six weeks of cold weather will follow.

WOOD′COCK, a bird belonging to the same family as the snipe, differing from the latter in having a more bulky body and shorter legs. It is widely distributed over North America, Europe, Northern Asia and Japan. It spends the summers in pine forests and the winters in southern swamps and moist woodlands, where worms, snails and slugs are plentiful. It is active by night but quiet during the day. The bird is about twelve inches long. The upper plumage is an intermingling of ruddy, yellowish, and ash, and is marked with black spots. Underneath, it is yellowish red with zigzag markings. The eyes are large and are set far back. The bill, nearly half the length of the body, is used with great skill in digging worms.

WOOD DISTILLATION, conversion of the volatile substances in wood to obtain charcoal, wood alcohol, acetic acid, acetone, creosote and wood turpentine. Coniferous as well as deciduous trees lend themselves to distillation. Wood turpentine is a by-product of the former, but the yield of acid is less than with hard woods. The still or retort into which the liquid is heated, the condenser which cools the vapors and the receiver which collects the distillate constitute the simplest distillation apparatus.

WOOD ENGRAVING. See ENGRAVING, subhead *Wood Engraving.*

WOODEN HORSE. See MYTHOLOGY, *The Trojan War.*

WOODMEN OF AMERICA, MODERN, a fraternal and insurance society founded in 1883 at Lyons, Iowa, and the following year chartered under the laws of Illinois. It is one of the largest fraternal benefit organizations in America, having a membership of more than a million. The head officer is known as head consul, and the various geographical divisions, of which there are more than 14,000, are called camps. Since its founding the order has paid out in death and benefit claims more than $500,000,000. One of the beneficial features of the society is a large and well-equipped tuberculosis sanatorium at Woodman, Colo.

WOODMEN OF THE WORLD, a fraternal and insurance order founded in 1890 at Omaha, Neb. The organization is divided geographically into three main camps, one of which is the Sovereign Camp of the World, whose executive committee is also the governing body of the entire order. The Woodman's Circle, an affiliated organization, of which Woodmen may become members, is controlled by a body called the Supreme Forest. Woodmen pay old-age benefits and erect monuments to deceased members. By levying a special assessment they were able to pay benefits in all cases of members killed in World War I. Since its founding the order has paid out in benefits more than $100,000,000. It has thousands of subordinate camps and a membership of approximately half a million.

WOOD′PECKER, the name of a large group of climbing birds, of which there are

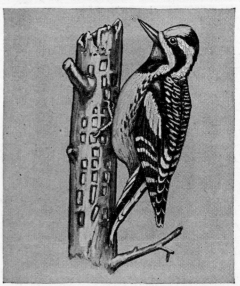

YELLOW-BELLIED SAP SUCKER

a number of different species. They have long, straight, angular beaks, adapted to perforating the bark of trees. Their tongues are long, slender and armed with a barbed, horny tip. They can thrust their tongues far out of their mouths and so spear insects in the depths of their burrows. Their tongues are also covered with a sticky, slimy substance, that helps to hold their prey. When feeding, they usually ascend the tree spirally, aided by the spiny points which terminate their tail feathers. They tap here and there on the tree-trunk, searching for the holes in which insects are hidden, and often tear away large parts of rotten trees, for the larvae concealed in them.

The *sap sucker* is a species that is fond of the sap of trees and bores round holes, which it arranges with geometrical exactness in broad bands around the trunk of a tree. It especially favors the pines, and in feeding it moves about over the checkerboard of holes, taking the sap from them regularly, as it accumulates. The *ivory-billed woodpecker* of the southern United States is a large bird, about twenty-one inches long, bright black and white in color, the male having a large bright scarlet crest. Like most of the other woodpeckers, this one excavates its nest in suitable dead trees. The *red-headed woodpecker*, the *black and white woodpecker*, the *hairy woodpecker* and the *downy woodpecker* are well known in the Northern states. The redheaded woodpecker often lights on the shingles of houses or on a hollow branch and strikes his bill in a noisy clatter, stopping now and then to call out his hoarse, rough note. The woodpeckers are found in almost every temperate part of the globe, except that none ever existed in Australia and Egypt. See FLICKER.

WOOD PE'WEE, a little bird of the fly-catcher family, related to the phoebe. It is brown on the back and yellowish-white underneath; the quills are brown, with light edges. The spread of the wings is about twelve inches. The bird has a rapid flight and catches insects with skill. Its low, plaintive little note, *pee-a-wee*, may be heard in the woods, all through the long summer, at early dawn and during the twilight hours. The birds spend the summer in the United States and Canada, and in winter they migrate to South America. The nest is a wonderful structure of mud, grass and moss lined with down and other soft materials, and hangs bracketlike against a beam or tree. Two broods are raised annually in spring and autumn. See PHOEBE.

WOOD SPIRIT. See METHYLATED SPIRIT.

WOODSTOCK, ONT., the county town of Oxford County, is situated about midway between Detroit and Niagara Falls, on the Canadian Pacific and the Canadian National railways, and on a line of the latter which runs from Port Dover on Lake Erie to Owen Sound and other Georgian Bay ports. It is also connected with the Michigan Central and Wabash systems by a branch of the Canadian Pacific. The city is beautifully situated at the confluence of the Thames River and Cedar Creek. Its famous avenues of trees, general attractiveness and healthfulness make the city a favorite summer resort. Many American tourists visit the city in summer.

Woodstock is an important manufacturing and commercial center. The leading manufactures include furniture, pianos and organs, textiles, wagons and sleighs, harness, cereals, flour, agricultural implements, automobiles, stoves and furnaces and numerous other products. The city has excellent hotels, a collegiate institute and a Y. W. C. A. It is also the seat of Woodstock College. Population in 1941, 12,339.

WOOL AND WOOL'EN MANUFAC'TURE. Wool, the modified hair of sheep and several species of goats, is, with the exception of cotton, the fiber most extensively used in the manufacture of cloth and clothing. Woolens afford warmth without great weight, and are a protection against extreme heat as well as against cold. They are soft and flexible, and of them the most healthful clothing is made.

Structure and Grades. If we draw a fiber of wool through the fingers from tip to base it feels rough; if we draw it from base to tip, however, it is smooth and soft. An examination of wool through the microscope shows the cause of this difference. Wool fiber consists of minute scales or plates, which overlap like the scales on a fish. The difference in quality of the fiber is due to the difference of these scales in size and shape.

Wool is graded as coarse, medium and fine, according to the length and size of the fiber. The finest sheep's wool is obtained from the Merino sheep and varieties that have been developed from this breed. The wool from which alpaca and mohair are made is that of the Cashmere goat, from which the soft, silken Persian shawls and rugs are made. Some wool resembles fur in fineness.

For purposes of manufacture, wool is divided into *carding wool*, which includes that of short, curly fibers, and *combing wool,* which includes the long fibers. The coarsest of the long fiber wools are known as *carpet* and *blanket wools.* The quality of wool varies in the same fleece, that on the shoulders and sides being the best and that on the back the poorest.

Production. The demand for wool has not decreased by reason of the introduction of substitutes. The cotton market has to meet the competition of rayon products; though some rayon has a cotton base, much of it has a wood foundation. Though no competing textile challenges woolen cloth, in the manufacture of woolen goods there is frequently considerable adulteration; "all-wool" fabrics incline to be increasingly expensive, for not always is the supply in keeping with the demand.

The principal wool-producing countries are Argentina, Australia, the United States, British India, China, Italy, Russia, South Africa, Spain, and New Zealand. Canada is not a large world factor, for the Dominion has only about 3,500,000 sheep. The number of sheep in the United States averages somewhat more than 50,000,000 from year to year, and the fleeces secured from them exceed 350,000,000 pounds. The entire wool production of the world is about 3,500 million pounds.

Manufacture. The following are the chief processes employed in making woolen cloth:

When the wool is brought to the factory, it is carefully sorted, and that having the same grade of fiber is placed together. It is then thoroughly cleaned by being dusted, scoured with soap or lye and hot water, and then rinsed. After this, if colored cloth is to be made, the wool is dyed. It is then dried and is ready for the second important step in the process, that of preparing it for the loom.

The dried wool is first run through a machine, which removes any burs that may have adhered to the fiber. It is then run through the *picker,* which pulls all of the little tufts of wool apart and also enables the manufacturer to mix wools of different colors in any proportion desired. By mixing white and brown or blue and black or blue and gray, many very pleasing effects are obtained. After picking, the wool passes through the carding machines, of which there are usually three. Each of these draws out the fiber and straightens it and places the wool in the form of a loose band, or roll. Each successive machine straightens the fiber and reduces the size of this band, making it each time proportionately stronger. When the wool leaves the third card, it is in the form of a *sliver,* an untwisted yarn a little larger than the heavy crocheting yarn. As it comes from this machine it is wound upon large spools, or bobbins, and is ready for spinning.

The spinning is done on the mule jenny, and a large number of threads are spun at a time. The size of the thread and the hardness of the twist depend upon the way in which the machine is gauged. For a fine thread that is hard twisted, a machine which revolves very rapidly and also draws the thread out rapidly, is necessary. The spun yarn is wound upon spools ready for being placed in the loom. The arrangement for this consists of frames upon which these spools are placed in such a position that the thread unwinds from them directly, to make the warp of a width and number of threads desired. The woven cloth is finished in the style desired, possibly re-dyed, pressed and wound into bundles containing about fifty yards each, in which form it is placed upon the market.

The manufacture of worsted is much like the production of woolens. Threads for woolen goods are carded, but the fibers are left mixed and matted so that the thread is irregular. Worsted thread is not only carded but it is combed as well. The fibers lie parallel to each other and the thread is regular with the short fibers removed. The thread also presents a brighter appearance, a distinct pattern and a smooth weave.

The principal styles in worsteds are cashmeres, voiles, merinos, crepe-de-chines, delaines and materials for coats and trousers.

Related Articles. Consult the following titles for additional information:

Alpaca	Sheep
Cashmere Goat	Shoddy
Dyeing	Spinning
Felt	Teasel
Fiber	Tweeds
Flannel	Weaving
Mohair	Worsted

WOOLLCOTT, ALEXANDER (1887-), an American author and critic, born in New Jersey and educated at Hamilton College and Columbia University. He spent two years in France as an enlisted man and was one of the editors of *The Stars and Stripes.* Woollcott wrote several books, the most successful being *While Rome Burns.* Other volumes of note are *Going to Pieces* and *Two Gentlemen and a Lady.*

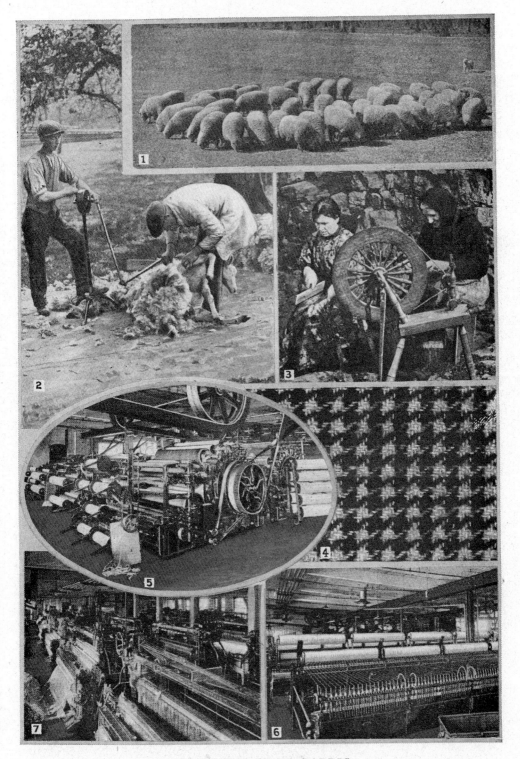

FROM FLEECE TO FABRIC

(1) Sheep before shearing; (2) power-driven clippers removing the soft, heavy fleece;
(3) carding wool, and spinning yarn to use in weaving homespun tweed (4); modern power
machines for carding (5); (6) spinning machines; (7) power looms.

THREE MARKET GRADES OF LAMBS

Wool buyers do not trust appearances; they handle animals to discover their qualities. In the illustrations, A and B represent choice lambs, wooled and after shearing. C and D are examples of medium lambs, wooled and shorn. E and F exhibit the lowest grade, cull lambs, before and after shearing.

WOONSOCKET, R. I., in Providence County, fifteen miles northwest of Providence, on the Blackstone River and on the New York, New Haven & Hartford Railroad. With abundant water power from the Blackstone and its two tributaries, Woonsocket is a prominent textile community, ranking high in the production of fine woolens and worsteds. Machine tools and gauges, rubber goods and rayon yarns are also manufactured here. The place was settled about 1866 and was a part of Cumberland until 1867, when it was separately incorporated as a town. Several factory villages joined Woonsocket to form the present city, which was incorporated in 1888. Population, 1940, 49,303.

WORCESTER, *woos' tur*, MASS., the second city in size in the state and one of the county seats of Worcester County, Fitchburg being the other. It is on Lake Quinsigamond, forty-four miles west of Boston, and on the New York Central, the Boston & Maine and the New York, New Haven & Hartford railroads. Worcester is one of the most important manufacturing centers of New England, producing abrasives, shoes and leather, chains, clothing, paper goods, food products, foundry and machine-shop products, machinery, tools, wire and textiles. The city is one of the largest producers of machine tools in the world. Six insurance companies have their home offices in Worcester.

In Worcester are a state teachers college for women and four colleges for men—Clark University, Worcester Polytechnic Institute, Holy Cross College and Assumption College. Other cultural centers are the art museum, the library of the American Antiquarian Society, the library and museum of the Historical Society and the museum of the Natural History Society. A music festival is held here annually. There is a state hospital for the insane in Worcester.

Worcester was first settled in 1673, but was abandoned on the outbreak of King Philip's War, two years later. A second attempt in 1684 was also given up because of Indian depredations, and the first permanent settlement was not made until 1713. In 1722 Worcester was incorporated as a town, and in 1848 was chartered as a city. Its development was stimulated by the completion in 1828 of the Blackstone Canal connecting it with Providence, R. I. Worcester is the birthplace of the historian George Bancroft, who was also Secretary of the Navy in President Polk's Cabinet. Many famous people have lived here; among these were Elias Howe, Eli Whitney, General Rufus Putnam, Dorothea Dix, Clara Barton and Edward Everett Hale. Population, 1940, 193,694.

WORDSWORTH, *wurdz'wurth*, WILLIAM (1770–1850), an English poet, a leader in the Romantic movement which transformed English poetry early in the nineteenth century. Wordsworth, Coleridge and Southey were the founders of the so-called Lake School of poetry. Of these representative poets, Wordsworth had the most enduring influence (see LAKE SCHOOL). He was born at Cockermouth, Cumberland. After the death of his father, he was sent, at the age of eight, to Hawkshead grammar school. The natural surroundings of this place made a deep impression on young Wordsworth, and implanted in him that ardent love of nature which was so vital a part of his poetic genius. In 1787 he entered Cambridge University, graduating in 1791. Later in the same year he went to France. At first he felt the most ardent sympathy with the Revolution, but the excesses which developed out of it shocked him greatly, and as time went on he settled down to a staid conservatism. Shortly after his return from France, Wordsworth published his first poems, *An Evening Walk* and *Descriptive Sketches Taken during a Pedestrian Tour among the Alps.*

In 1795, Wordsworth, with his sister Dorothy, settled first at Racedown in Dorset, and then at Alfoxden, near Coleridge. Here the two poets held daily intercourse, and after a twelvemonth they published *Lyrical Ballads.* This volume contained as Wordsworth's contribution, among others, *We are Seven* and *Lines on Tintern Abbey.* Although the poems were received with almost complete public indifference, yet Wordsworth felt that he had found his mission, and after a winter spent in Germany, he and his sister settled at Grasmere. Incidents in his later life include his marriage, in 1802, with Mary Hutchison; his appointment, in 1813, to an inspectorship of stamps and his removal to Rydal Mount; several journeys into Scotland and to the continent; his acceptance of a D. C. L. degree from the University of Oxford in 1839, and his accession, in 1843, to the laureateship, on the death of Southey.

The public and the critics were slow to recognize Wordsworth's ability, refusing to accept his idea that poetry may deal with simple and natural subjects, presented in simple and natural language. Coleridge, Lamb, De Quincey, Southey, Keats and others were his admirers, however. His intended great philosophic poem received only a fragmentary accomplishment in *The Prelude, The Excursion* and *The Recluse*. Yet enough was achieved in his smaller poems to set him apart among the greatest of England's poets. His sympathy with nature and his belief in the brotherhood of man find expression in all of his poems. Among the most beautiful are *Tintern Abbey,* the *Ode on the Intimations of Immortality, Ode to Duty, The Solitary Reaper, To a Highland Girl, I Wandered Lonely as a Cloud* and *Yarrow Revisited.* His sonnets are among the finest produced in English.

WORK, a general term for effort expended toward a given end. It also implies motion against a resisting force, that certain results may be obtained. A man who lifts a weight, in labor or in play, performs work; the resisting force he encounters is the force of gravitation. The impulse which sends the electric current along a copper wire to light a room or run a motor performs work. The falling water which wears away solid rock performs work as surely as does that which falls over a water-wheel and turns machinery. Work is accomplished whenever one body transfers its energy to another body.

WORKMEN'S COMPENSATION LAWS. See EMPLOYER'S LIABILITY.

WORLD COURT. See PERMANENT COURT OF INTERNATIONAL JUSTICE.

WORLD'S COLUMBIAN EXPOSITION, an international exposition of arts and industries, in commemoration of the four hundredth anniversary of the discovery of America by Columbus. It was built in Jackson Park, Chicago, on the shore of Lake Michigan, and was open from May 1 till November 1, 1893. The exhibition comprised over 400 buildings, covering fully 200 acres of ground.

The architectural beauty of the whole exposition was one of its greatest triumphs. The center of the main group of buildings was the Court of Honor, consisting of a wide plaza, with a lagoon in its center, having at one end a beautiful electric fountain, sculptured by McMonnies, and at the other a graceful semicircular peristyle.

The attendance from the opening to the closing day was 27,539,041.

WORLD WAR, the name applied to each of two great wars, both of which involved nearly all the world. These wars, beginning in 1914 and in 1939, were not two separate conflicts, however, but divisions of the same war. The causes which created trouble in 1914 were still the underlying causes in 1939, and the unsolved problems of the first war aided in precipitating the second. The very treaty of peace which ended the First World War had in it the germs of dissension which demanded another (see VERSAILLES, TREATY OF). The First World War had no parallel in wars to that time, in number of nations involved, cost in men and money, and changes resulting from it, but the Second World War surpassed it.

Basic Causes. These wars had their origin in Central Europe, with its complex problems. Small nations set down in the midst of larger ones were confronted with the need for expansion and survival. Lack of raw materials, of trade routes and of foodstuffs produced friction. The small nations were subject to the control, direct or indirect, of the large ones. In almost all the nations there were minorities, small groups of people allied closely to their own native country and alien to the one where they lived. They wished to preserve their nationality and the country of their homes wished to absorb them. Thus, economic, racial and political problems led to the First World War.

WORLD WAR I

Immediate Causes. Although a war had long been prophesied, and the eyes of the world had been turned particularly on Austria-Hungary and on the Balkans, "powder-keg of Europe," the actual beginning of the conflict came as a surprise. On June 28, 1914, Archduke Francis Ferdinand, heir apparent to the Austrian throne, and his wife were assassinated while visiting Sarajevo, capital of Bosnia. The assassin was Gavrilo Princip, a young man who was one of the principals in a scheme to incorporate Bosnia in a Greater Serbia. The Austrian government believed the assassination had been plotted in Belgrade, capital of Serbia, instead of among the Serbians of Bosnia. Austria presented heavy demands to Serbia, and expressed dissatisfaction with the reply. Consequently, Austria declared war on Serbia on July 28. That was the beginning.

OVER THERE IN WARTIME

Scene in the center of a forest in France, during the tumultuous days of 1917-1918. An American division is shown on the move to the battle front. The battered buildings in the upper left indicate that the area had already been exposed to enemy fire. Scenes such as this were common throughout the period of American participation in the war.

ON THE FIGHTING FRONT

(1) Somewhere in France, winter of 1915. Standing in ice-cold water, the men developed trench foot. (2) A raiding party going through their own wire entanglements after a climb over the top into No Man's Land. (3) Scenes in Ypres at the close of the war. (4) An American battalion of infantry leaving for the front. (5) Victory Liberty Loan poster drawn by Howard Chandler Christy.

AMERICANS ALL!

HONOR ROLL

Du Bois
Smith
O'Brien
Cejka
Haucke
Pappanikopolous
Andrassi
Villotto
Levy
Turovich
Kowalski
Chriczanewicz
Knutson
Gonzales

Victory Liberty Loan

Germany supported Austria; Russia joined Serbia; France naturally supported Serbia, as France and Russia were allied. Great Britain entered the war because Germany refused to respect the neutrality of Belgium.

The list of war declarations for 1914 is as follows:

Austria-Hungary, on Serbia.........July 28
Germany, on Russia.................Aug. 1
Germany, on France................Aug. 3
Germany, on Belgium...............Aug. 4
Great Britain, on Germany.........Aug. 4
France, on Germany................Aug. 4
Austria-Hungary, on Russia........Aug. 6
Montenegro, on Austria-Hungary....Aug. 7
Montenegro, on Germany............Aug. 9
Serbia, on Germany................Aug. 9
France, on Austria-Hungary........Aug. 10
Great Britain, on Austria-Hungary..Aug. 12
Japan, on Germany.................Aug. 23
Austria-Hungary, on Japan.........Aug. 27
Austria-Hungary, on Belgium.......Aug. 28
Russia, on Turkey.................Nov. 3
France, on Turkey.................Nov. 5
Great Britain, on Turkey..........Nov. 5

Italy joined the Allies in 1915. War declarations for that year:

Italy, on Austria-Hungary..........May 23
San Marino, on Austria-Hungary......June 2
Bulgaria, on Serbia................Oct. 13
Great Britain, on Bulgaria..........Oct. 15
France, on Bulgaria................Oct. 16
Russia, on Bulgaria................Oct. 19
Italy, on Bulgaria.................Oct. 19

In 1916, the following nations were added:

Germany, on Portugal...............Mar. 8
Austria-Hungary, on Portugal.......Mar. 15
Italy, on Germany.................Aug. 27
Rumania, on Austria...............Aug. 27
Germany, on Rumania...............Aug. 28

And in 1917, headed by the Allied triumph of the entrance of the United States, the list was as follows:

United States, on Germany..........Apr. 6
Cuba, on Germany...................Apr. 8
Panama, on Germany.................Apr. 9
Greece, on Germany.................July 22
Siam, on Germany...................July 22
Liberia, on Germany................Aug. 7
China, on Germany..................Aug. 14
Brazil, on Germany.................Oct. 26
United States, on Austria-Hungary....Dec. 7
Panama, on Austria-Hungary.........Dec. 10

The following nations severed diplomatic relations with Germany:

Bolivia	Honduras
Costa Rica	Nicaragua
Ecuador	Peru
Guatemala	Santo Domingo
Haiti	Uruguay

Events of 1915. The war during this year was fought on two fronts: the western and the eastern. In 1914, during the early weeks of the conflict, Germany had violated the neutrality of Belgium, shelled its towns, and marched across it to France, succeeding in reaching within forty miles of Paris before being forced to retreat, after the first Battle of the Marne. The German troops entrenched themselves at the Aisne River. A deadlock of over two years resulted.

In the winter of 1914–15 there was little fighting and France and Britain were frantically trying to assemble war materials and machines. In April, the Germans used gas for the first time in the war, while endeavoring to reach Calais. The summer was a time of heavy fighting, always from trenches, which were dug in all across the northeast of France and western Belgium; trench warfare characterized World War I. On the eastern front, the Russians successfully held back Germany and Austria until lack of munitions brought disaster and they were forced to retreat. They did, however, clear the Turks from the Caucasus. An appeal to Britain resulted in the unsuccessful Dardanelles campaign, where Allied troops held a position on Gallipoli from April until the end of the year.

Events of 1916. The great event of 1916 on the western front was the Battle of Verdun, which was fought from February to September, with many bitter attacks and counterattacks. The Germans advanced only four miles in six months, and finally stopped attacking when within three miles of the main fortress. Meanwhile, the Allies began another conflict, the Battle of the Somme, which raged from July to the end of the year. Supplied with proper artillery, and with great guns capable of smashing trenchworks and outposts, the Allies used tanks for the first time and slowly but steadily pushed the Germans back in a disastrous campaign.

Russia, having reorganized and acquired more munitions during the winter, in June began a heavy offensive against the Austrians, driving them into the Carpathian Mountains, and occupying the Bukowina crownland. Italy, having joined the Allies, made a number of small attacks, aimed at Austria. After brief successes, Rumania was overrun by German and Bulgarian troops, and half the country, including the oil and wheat territories, fell into German hands. In Asia, the Russian victories in Armenia were about the only successes of the Allies. By the end of the year, however, the Allies had control of almost all German colonial territory.

British naval supremacy had early driven German commerce from the seas, and for the most part the main German fleets remained at their bases at Kiel and Wilhelmshaven, protected by mines and fortifications. However, several German cruisers, including the *Emden* and the *Königsberg,* did great damage to Allied shipping before they were destroyed. Important engagements were the defeat of the German Far East Squadron off the Falkland Islands in December; the sinking of three German cruisers and two destroyers off Helgoland in August; and the only battle of the war in which the main fleets of Germany and England participated. This was the Battle of Jutland, on May 31. It was apparently without decisive results, but the German fleet was actually near overwhelming defeat, being saved only by fog and skillful seamanship, and did not venture out again during the war.

Events of 1917. In this year, the collapse of Russia was offset by the entrance of the United States into the war. The Verdun campaign resulted in the withdrawal of the German forces early in the year to a strong defensive position which came to be known as the Hindenburg Line. In April, the Allies began a new offensive. Its spectacular feats included the capture of Vimy Ridge by the Canadians, and, in June, the taking of Ypres and the ending of the threat to Calais. A French drive on the Aisne, and fighting by the British in Flanders, in an attempt to drive the Germans from the Belgian coast, were other outstanding efforts.

In Russia, political upheaval reached a climax in March with the long-threatening revolution which broke out in Petrograd. The czar was forced to abdicate, a democratic provisional government was set up, and loyalty to the Allies declared. But the revolutionists could not hold the armies together as a fighting machine, and German propaganda further weakened morale. A reorganization of the government under Lenin and Trotsky resulted in a treaty with the Central Powers whereby Russia made a separate peace and withdrew from the war.

Rumania was forced to give up the struggle and make peace, because of Russia's collapse. These withdrawals gave the Central Powers valuable territory and economic and political concessions. Italy, after heartening advancement, was driven out of the territory occupied, and German armies entered and occupied some 1,000 square miles of Italian territory.

In Asia, there were Allied victories in Mesopotamia and Palestine. Greece entered the war in July, but it was the entrance of the United States that was important to Allied morale and military strength. This step was precipitated by the refusal of Germany to respect the rights of all nations on the high seas and the announcement of the intention to sink neutral and enemy vessels anywhere on the seas, without warning.

After severing diplomatic rights, arming merchant vessels and endeavoring peaceably to combat this menace, the United States declared war. Major-General John J. Pershing was put in command of the American Expeditionary Force, the first contingent of which reached French soil on June 27. Sixteen German and Austrian passenger ships, interned in American waters, were commandeered to add to the transport service. Training camps were set up and conscription was employed. The American Navy was sent to European waters.

Events of 1918. In March, the Germans began an offensive on a fifty-mile front in northeastern France. The British, pushed back twenty-five miles in places, made a stand and were the victims of a second offensive in late May, this time toward Paris. On June 1 the Germans were within forty-six miles of Paris, but their drive was slowed. United States forces proved effective in a notable battle at Belleau Wood. American Marines, in the second Battle of the Marne on July 21, threw back the Germans at Chateau Thierry. With the French they pushed their advantage until the Germans withdrew from the Marne. General Foch had been made supreme commander of the Allies in the critical month of March.

Slowly the defense became an offensive against the Germans, who were forced to withdraw steadily. Soissons, Cambrai, Saint Quentin and Lille again became French, and the Hindenburg Line was broken. The American First Army Corps, asked to drive the Germans from the southern end of the battle line, cleared the Saint Mihiel salient and began to drive the enemy from the hilly Argonne Forest. In Belgium, meanwhile, the Germans were being driven out.

In the Balkans, Bulgaria was forced to surrender to the Allies, clearing the way for freeing Serbia, Montenegro and Rumania. Turkey was forced to yield. In October, Italy began a major offensive against Austria, which asked for an armistice on October 31. A political upheaval in Germany followed the capitulation of Bulgaria, and President Woodrow Wilson was asked to take steps toward peace. On November 11th the Armistice was signed, calling for German evacuation of occupied territory, release of Allied prisoners and various other demands.

Some Interesting Figures. America's part in World War I is summarized in the following statement, given out by the chief of the statistical branch of the General Staff:

Total armed force, including army,
   navy and marine corps............ 4,800,000
Total men in the army............. 4,000,000
Men who went overseas............ 2,086,000
Men who fought in France......... 1,390,000
Total registered in draft.........24,234,021
Total draft inductions............. 2,810,296
Cost of war to April 30, 1919, $21,850,000,000.
Battles fought by Americans, 13.
American deaths from battle wounds, 50,327.
Americans wounded, 205,690.
Deaths from disease, 58,073.
Total casualties in army, 322,182.

During the war 7,450,000 men were killed, the various belligerents suffering as follows:

Russia 1,700,000
Germany 1,600,000
France 1,385,000
Great Britain 900,000
Austria 800,000
Italy 300,000
Turkey 250,000
Serbia and Montenegro............. 125,000
Belgium 102,000
Rumania 100,000
Bulgaria 100,000
United States 48,900
Greece 7,000
Portugal 2,000

Related Articles. In addition to topics listed below, the reader is referred to articles on the various countries involved in the war.

STATESMEN AND RULERS

Albert I	George, David Lloyd
Balfour, Arthur J.	Grey, Edward, Sir
Bernstorff, Count	Nicholas II
Charles I	Poincaré, Raymond
Clemenceau, Georges	Venizelos, Eleutherios
Constantine I	Victor Emmanuel III
Francis Joseph I	William II
George V	Wilson, Woodrow

MILITARY AND NAVAL COMMANDERS

Beatty, David, Sir	Joffre, Joseph J.
Bullard, Robert L.	Kitchener, Horatio H.
Foch, Ferdinand	Liggett, Hunter
French, John, Sir	Moltke, Count von
Haig, Douglas, Sir	Pétain, Henri
Hindenburg, Paul von	Pershing, John J.
Jellicoe, John, Sir	Sims, William S.

WORLD WAR II

Immediate Causes. In addition to the causes listed at the beginning of this article, there were some which led directly to the opening of World War II. The treaty provisions had led to wide unrest in Germany, to the growth of the National Socialist party and the dictatorship of Adolf Hitler. The terrible destruction of World War I had resulted in world-wide depression and unemployment, lowering of currency value, heavy taxation and consequent economic upheaval and conflict. The dictator countries in particular began heavy censorship of the press, radio and public meetings, and by means of propaganda inculcated beliefs of racial and political superiority in the minds of the masses.

Germany was rearming. The League of Nations failed to protect Ethiopia when Mussolini seized it in 1935, just as it failed to stop Japanese aggression in China, the Italian conquest of Albania, and aid by Germany and Italy to General Franco in Spain.

Hitler's aggressions were opposed only with an appeasement policy, and there were many of them before an actual world war was under way. Briefly they include:

1936—remilitarization of the Rhineland
1938—annexation of Austria
1938—Sudetenland given Hitler by the Munich settlement
1939—dismemberment of Czechoslovakia
1939—annexation of Memel
1939—conquest of Poland, September 1 to 28; division between Germany and Russia

These years had been marked by the signing of various treaties of friendship and alliance among the European nations, all of which proved mere "scraps of paper" when their governments wished to ignore or repudiate them. Great Britain and France, having tried to stop Hitler from attacking Poland, declared war on Germany on September 3, two days after his armies crossed the border.

Events of 1939. The conquest of Poland, with the heroic resistance and downfall of Warsaw, culminated in utter defeat of the Poles. The territory acquired by Russia proved incentive to further gain, and on November 30 the U.S.S.R. attacked Finland. The excuse was Finland's refusal to sign, with other Baltic states, "mutual assistance" pacts which gave Russia strong bases within Baltic territory. The Finns fought effectively but were forced to surrender in March, 1940.

Events of 1940. Early in April, Hitler invaded the Low Countries. Denmark offered no resistance, and was occupied immediately by German forces, which used it as a springboard to reach Norway. By June, the desperate resistance of the Norwegians had been crushed, the British had withdrawn, and Hitler had set up a government under Major Vidkun Quisling.

From the beginning of war with France and Great Britain, there was little fighting until in the summer of 1940. The German and French armies massed behind their great defensive lines, the Westwall and the Maginot Line. However, in May, Hitler suddenly sent his armies through the Netherlands, Belgium and Luxemburg, to reach France. The Dutch defenses by water, and the munitions proved inadequate and the country was soon captured. As a lesson to the Allies, Hitler bombed Rotterdam, systematically destroying the heart of the city. Queen Wilhelmina barely escaped to England.

Luxemburg was overrun in one day. The Germans won the Battle of the Meuse, and drove toward the Somme River and the English Channel. The French and British troops in France were cut off from the Belgians and the Allied soldiers with them, who were trapped in a pocket. King Leopold of Belgium, with no further hope of aid or supplies, surrendered and was taken prisoner. The remaining French and British in Belgium fought frantically, retreating toward Dunkirk, from which hundreds of thousands were rescued across the Channel by a motley fleet of small boats and yachts.

Then, within four days, the Germans in a great offensive in France won victory. Paris was occupied on June 14, and on June 22 France signed an armistice with Germany. A section including the Channel ports was occupied by Germany, and a government of unoccupied France was set up in Vichy under Marshal Henri Philippe Pétain.

Meanwhile, Prime Minister Chamberlain of Great Britain had retired. Winston Churchill took over his office. Hitler had promised to crush Britain by the middle of August, but he could not carry out his threat. Through this year, however, he massed boats and men on the continental side of the Channel, strengthened occupied ports and systematically bombed the great English cities and ports, destroying many historic and irreplaceable treasures and buildings. He also employed submarine attack against shipping to England.

Italy had joined the war on the side of Germany a few days before France fell. Italian forces pushed toward the Allies in Egypt and Libya, and the great African seesaw was under way. For two years, Allied and Axis forces fought back and forth in North Africa, now one side gaining, now the other. High points in 1940 were the siege of Bardia by the British and the encirclement of Tobruk and Bengasi.

Events in 1941. Early in March, the government of Jugo-Slavia was overthrown, and Hitler sent forces through the country toward Greece, where an Italian attack through Albania had been bravely withstood. Jugo-Slav soldiers, escaping to the hills, organized in Chetnik guerrilla divisions and continued formidable resistance.

Gradually, the Greeks were forced to retreat before the Nazis, who looted the country and put it on a starvation basis. On April 27, with Athens occupied, Greece capitulated. The government and soldiers had fled to the island of Crete, which was bombed and occupied by Nazi parachute troops. The British evacuated the island on June 1. Attempts at German infiltration and control in Iraq and Iran were defeated, not without fighting in Iraq. The British occupied southern Syria and the Vichy government signed an armistice on July 8.

A German attempt at regaining territory lost in Africa resulted in a strong attack on the British and the winning back of captured Libyan territory. Late in the year, however, the British began a campaign to release the British besieged for seven months in Tobruk, and regain the land. In May, Haile Selassie, through the aid of the British, had been returned to his empire in Ethiopia, and in November the land stronghold in the country surrendered.

Suddenly, however, on June 22, German armies, which had been massing for weeks on the Russian border, marched into Russia. They regained territory the Russians had occupied in Poland, met strong resistance at the Stalin Line, and slowly advanced, aided by the Finns, who were trying to regain what they had ceded to Russia the year preceding. Soldiers from occupied countries were taken into battle, and by

November the Germans had advanced a considerable distance. Leningrad was partly encircled, troops were within forty miles of Moscow, the Crimean Peninsula was held except for the fortress of Sevastopol, and Rostov, on the Don River, was occupied.

In the following month, the Russians began strong resistance, greatly aided by their knowledge of Russian winter weather, which the Germans found overwhelming. The Donetz Basin, with its valuable minerals, was recaptured, and Rostov released.

The United States, which had acquired by lease eight Atlantic bases from England in 1940, during the year set up several new outposts, including those at Greenland and Iceland. G e r m a n submarines torpedoed American merchant and naval vessels. The United States had put into practice Lend-Lease aid for the Allies; had voted huge sums for civilian defense; and in 1941 extended the time of peacetime service under the conscription law by eighteen months.

The United States Enters the War. On December 7, while Japanese representatives were negotiating for peace at Washington, D.C., Pearl Harbor, United States base in Hawaii, was attacked from the air by Japanese planes. Many planes were destroyed at their hangars; and the United States fleet, caught in the harbor, suffered heavily. The battleship *Arizona,* three destroyers, a target ship and a mine-layer were sent to the bottom, and a number of others were damaged.

On the day following, the Japanese bombed the Philippines, concentrating on three airfields and destroying the greater part of the airplane force which defended the islands. Soon after, the little outpost at Guam island was overwhelmed and captured. Wake Island was held by only 378 Marines, who had a dozen planes, but they took heavy toll of Japanese planes and warships before surrendering on the day before Christmas. Three days later, General MacArthur, in command in the Philippines, who had withdrawn his forces from Manila, declared it an open city. It was nevertheless bombed by the Japanese.

Events in 1942. Japan struck also all along the route in Asia to the Philippines. Hong Kong had surrendered on Christmas Day, 1941. By early February, 1942, the Japanese were occupying the entire Malay Peninsula, and on February 15, Singapore,

Britain's "invincible" naval base, was in their hands. By skillful landings in the Netherlands Indies, the Japanese established bases on the chief islands and largely occupied them. They also drove the British out of Burma, cut the Burma Road and made new inroads in China. There they encountered resistance from American air forces.

General MacArthur, who had withdrawn his troops to Bataan Peninsula, put up a strong fight until ordered by President Roosevelt to proceed to Australia and take command of forces in that area. Under General Jonathan Wainwright, the American and Filipino troops fought heroically against disease, lack of food and merciless bombing, first on Bataan and then in the rocky fortress of Corregidor, until forced to surrender on May 7.

The United States Pacific Fleet raided Japanese forces on the Gilbert and Marshall islands on January 31, on Wake Island on February 24 and on Marcus Island on March 4, with considerable damage to Japanese ships, planes and supplies. A surprise raid on Tokyo under General James Doolittle on April 18 greatly lowered the morale of the Japanese and bolstered that of China. In June the Japanese occupied three islands in the western Aleutians. The Americans and Australians launched an offensive in the Solomon Islands in August.

In Africa, the Germans again gained victories and again the British rallied, and sought to win back lost territory. In Russia, the Crimea was lost with the fall of Sevastopol to the Germans. A renewed German attack in the summer brought Axis armies sweeping north into Russia. They crossed the Don and reached the oil fields of the northern Caucasus. Russia faced the loss of valuable oil and food supplies.

After the United States was attacked, Costa Rica, Cuba, the Dominican Republic, El Salvador, Guatemala, Haiti, Honduras, Mexico, Nicaragua and Panama declared war on the Axis; Brazil declared war on Germany and Italy in August, 1942. The other South American republics, except Argentina and Chile, broke off diplomatic relations. Besides Italy and Japan, the allies of Germany were Albania, Bulgaria, Croatia, Finland, Hungary, Manchukuo, Rumania, Slovakia and Thailand.

Related Articles. The reader is referred to the topics listed below, in addition to the articles on countries involved in World War II:

Army	Hitler, Adolf
Chamberlain, Neville	Leopold III
Churchill, Winston	Mussolini, Benito
Conscription	Navy
Franco, Francisco	Roosevelt, Franklin D.
George VI	Stalin, Joseph
Haakon VII	Wilhelmina

WORMS, *wur'mz,* a term loosely applied to many small, rather long, creeping animals, lacking feet entirely, or having very short ones, including such various forms as the earthworm, the grubs of certain insects and intestinal parasites. The zoölogist, however, confines the term to animals belonging to the branch known as Vermes, and excludes the larvae of insects. See VERMES.

WORMS, *vormz,* GERMANY, an historic city located on the Rhine, twenty-six miles southeast of Mainz and twenty miles northwest of Heidelberg. Worms was founded in antiquity and retains parts of its original walls and towers. The fine Romanesque Cathedral of Saints Peter and Paul and the Gothic Church of our Lady are notable edifices. In this city, in 1521, Martin Luther appeared before the famous Diet convened by Charles V, and in the presence of the emperor, he refused to retract his religious beliefs (see LUTHER, MARTIN). Worms is a manufacturing and trading center of some importance. Population, 1933, 51,346.

WORSTED, *woos'ted,* or *wur'sted,* a tightly-twisted woolen thread made from long-fibered wool. The name comes from Worsted, the English village where it was first made. The thread is used for knitting and for weaving cloth. See WOOL AND WOOLEN MANUFACTURE.

WOUNDS, *woonds,* injuries to any of the soft parts of the body, occasioned by external violence and attended by a greater or less amount of bleeding.

Wounds are of four kinds: (1) *contusions,* or *bruises,* chiefly under the skin, caused by a fall, a blow from some blunt object, or squeezing; (2) *incised* wounds or *cuts,* where the skin or tissues are cut sharply and bleed freely; (3) *lacerated* wounds, torn irregularly by a blunt instrument, bleeding less severely but more likely to become infected; and (4) *punctured* wounds or *stabs,* made by sharp-pointed instruments such as nails or bullets, usually bleeding little, difficult to clean and often infected.

A sterile pad of gauze on the wound, and a pressure bandage or adhesive strap, will usually control bleeding. In severe cases, a tourniquet may be used. Iodine may be painted on to prevent germs from entering the wound. All wounds should be covered promptly with a sterile bandage or pad. Punctured wounds must be watched, as tetanus (lockjaw) frequently follows. Infection in such a wound should be brought to the attention of a doctor.

In World War I, French surgeons used *Dakin's solution* to irrigate wounds. The sulfa drugs were of exceptional value in World War II; powdered sulfanilamide sprinkled directly on wounds prevented infection, even though treatment was long delayed. See HEMORRHAGE; SURGERY; TOURNIQUET.

WREN, a very active little bird, common in America, Europe and Asia. The wrens are distinguished by their small size, slender beaks, short rounded wings, brown or gray mottled plumage and erect tails. The common *house wren* of the United States builds its nest in boxes or crevices, seeming to have no fear of human beings and never hesitating to attack cats, dogs, swallows and other trespassers. The eggs, three to nine in number are white, dotted with salmon. The song of the wren is melodious and flute-like. The bird destroys large numbers of noxious insects. The largest wren in the United States is the *cactus wren* of the Southwest; the smallest is the *winter wren,* only four inches long.

WREN

WREN, CHRISTOPHER, Sir (1632–1723), one of the greatest of English architects, born in Knowle, Wiltshire. He was educated at Waldham College, Oxford, became a fellow of All Saints in 1653, and was professor of astronomy at Gresham College and Savilian professor of astronomy at Oxford.

As a scientist, he was appointed one of the commissioners to restore Saint Paul's Cathedral. Wren was gradually drawn by consultations deeper and deeper into the problems of construction. Thus prepared, the labor of building Saint Paul's devolved largely on him, and he was occupied with the work from 1675 to 1710. At the same time he made many designs for other public buildings, and in the forty years following the great fire of 1666 there was not an important public building in London that he did not design.

Among the notable buildings he designed are the modern part of the palace at Hampton Court; the library of Trinity College, Cambridge; the Church of Saint Stephen's,

Walbrook; those of Saint Mary-le-bow and Saint Michael, Cornhill; that of Saint Bride, Fleet Street, and the campanile of Christ Church, Oxford. In 1680 he was chosen president of the royal works, and from 1685 to 1700 he represented various boroughs in Parliament. Over the north doorway of Saint Paul's is a memorial tablet with the words, *Si monumentum requiris, circumspice* (If thou seek his monument, look about thee).

WRESTLING, *wres'ling*, a competitive sport engaged in by two persons, each of whom tries to throw the other prone upon the ground. Wrestling brings into play every muscle of the body, and when under the proper restraining rules is one of the most beneficial of sports. The winner is usually the more skillful and alert.

In all Greek athletic contests, wrestling had a prominent part. The Greek wrestlers oiled their bodies. Grace was insisted upon, and the most stringent rules were enforced. Roman wrestling was of a rougher sort, in which participants were not infrequently killed. In the Graeco-Roman wrestling of modern France, the contestants are stripped to the waist. Most of the struggle takes place after both men are on the mat, and a fall is scored when one of them forces both shoulders of his opponent to the ground.

The Irish method of wrestling is known as the *collar and elbow*. The wrestlers wear short jackets with stout collars and sleeves, to afford a good grip. Each man seizes the collar of the other with his right hand and the sleeves near the elbow with his left hand. If his grip loosens, he loses. A man is thrown when two shoulders and a hip or a shoulder and two hips touch the ground.

In England a good method of wrestling is known as the *black-hold catch*. Each contestant stands with his chin on the shoulder of the other, grasping the other about the body, the right arm of each under the left arm of the other. If a contestant loses his grip or if his shoulders touch the floor, he loses.

A freer method of wrestling, common in both England and America, is the *catch-as-catch-can* method, in which holds are taken at random. Two shoulders on the floor constitute a fall. Recognized "holds," which give a wrestler great advantage, are the *grape-vine lock*, the *chancery*, the *half-Nelson* and the *hammer-lock*.

The Japanese have a system of wrestling known as *jujutsu*, a method of self-defense without weapons. A master of jujutsu can, by a slight, swift movement, benumb an opponent's brain, dislocate his hip or shoulder, or burst or twist a tendon. See JUJUTSU.

WRIGHT, FRANK LLOYD (1869–   ), an American architect, born at Richland Center, Wis. He studied civil engineering at the University of Wisconsin, but architecture became his life work. Wright began practice in Chicago in 1903; his designs at once attracted attention for their individuality and departure from conventional forms. His work was characterized by his use of projecting eaves and low, horizontal planes. He was the architect of the Imperial Hotel in Tokyo, Japan, and of many homes and public buildings in America, and the author of numerous books on architecture and essays on the relation of art to life.

WRIGHT, HAROLD BELL (1872–   ), a popular American novelist, born in Rome, N. Y., and educated in the preparatory department of Hiram College, Ohio. He was at various times a painter and decorator, a landscape painter and a minister in the Disciples of Christ Church, and his first novel, *That Printer of Udell's* (1903), was written while he was preaching in Missouri. It was followed by *The Shepherd of the Hills,* a great popular success. In 1908 he retired from the ministry to devote himself entirely to writing. His later works include *The Calling of Dan Matthews, The Uncrowned King, The Winning of Barbara Worth, Their Yesterdays, The Re-Creation of Brian Kent, The Mine with the Iron Door, A Son of His Father* and *God and the Groceryman.*

WRIGHT, ORVILLE (1871-   ), and WILBUR (1867-1912), two brothers who won undying fame as inventors of a practical airplane. Orville was born in Dayton, Ohio, and Wilbur in Millville, Ind. Both were educated in the public schools. They began to study aeronautics in 1896. At this time they had a bicycle shop in Dayton.

In 1900 they began experimenting in aviation with machines of their own invention and manufacture, and three years later they had produced a machine which would remain in the air over a minute. Kitty Hawk, N. C., was the scene of early tests. In 1905 they made the first long-distance flight, near

Dayton; and in 1908 Wilbur made his first public flight in France. After the brothers had won gold medals and homage in Europe they were recognized at home, and their machine was accepted by the United States government for use in the army. The Wright machines paved the way for the improved planes of today. See FLYING, STORY OF.

WRIT, in law, a formal order issued by a court enjoining the person mentioned therein to perform some specified act. It is issued under seal, attested by the proper officer and addressed to the sheriff or some other legally authorized officer.

The following are the writs in most common use:

A writ of summons commands an authorized officer to notify a person to appear in court to answer to a complaint.

A writ of replevin is an order permitting the recovery of goods illegally seized.

A writ of mandamus is a command to a person or corporation to something pertaining to his, or its, office or duty.

A writ of quo warranto is a command to show by what right an act is performed or an office held.

A writ of error is issued to remove an action to a higher court, by reason of error in the proceedings of the inferior court.

A writ of certiorari is issued by a court of review, requiring the record of a case to be sent up from an inferior court for examination.

For writ of subpoena see Witness. See, also, Habeas Corpus; Injunction; Capias.

WRITING, signs or characters inscribed on a surface for the purpose of recording and communicating thought. The earliest form of writing, practiced by all primitive peoples, was picture writing, or the copying of objects direct from nature. After this came symbolical writing, developed in its highest form in the cuneiform system of Western Asia and the hieroglyphics of Egypt. The latter were abbreviated pictures used as arbitrary symbols, first of things and later of sounds and words. These systems marked the transition from ideographic to phonetic writing, in which signs represent sounds.

Of systems of writing in which signs represent syllables, the most notable is the Chinese. As the same sound may have several meanings, it is often necessary to add to a syllable some sign to indicate which meaning is intended. The Phoenicians, basing their system on the Egyptian, are said to have invented the first phonetic alphabet, which is reputed to have been introduced into Greece by Cadmus of Boeotia, about the seventeenth century, B. C. The Greek forms, modified, spread to Sicily and Italy.

Various systems of writing differ in the arrangement of their symbols. Chinese characters are read in columns from top to bottom. Mexican picture writing is read from bottom to top. Hebrew writing, a modification of one form of the ancient Egyptian, is read from right to left. Sanskrit, Greek, Latin and all modern European languages are read from left to right.

Whole medieval manuscripts were written in large or small capitals. Uncial letters, which prevailed from the seventh to the tenth century, were rounded capitals, with few hair strokes. Gothic characters, fanciful deviations from the Roman types, became common from the thirteenth to the fifteenth century. In England, in the early Middle Ages a variety of styles called Saxon prevailed. A mixed style was formed of a combination of Roman, Lombardic and Saxon characters; the Norman style came in with William the Conqueror; and the English court hand, an adaptation of Saxon, prevailed from the sixteenth century to the reign of George II.

There have been various unsuccessful attempts to introduce phonetic writing. Systems of shorthand are generally phonetic. Thus, shorthand users write *enough* as if it were spelled *enuf*, and *tough* as *tuf*.

See ALPHABET; HANDWRITING; HIEROGLYPHICS; SHORTHAND.

WRITS OF ASSISTANCE. In American colonial days the British customs officials were provided with general search warrants to aid them in collecting import duties. These warrants were called *writs of assistance*. These writs differed from ordinary search warrants in that they did not limit the officer's search to a specified time or place, or to specified goods, but authorized him to seize any suspected goods.

The first writ of this kind was issued in 1761 and aroused much opposition. James Otis, advocate-general of the colony of Massachusetts, resigned his office and became leading attorney in a case in opposition to the issuance of the writs. The writ was declared legal, but it was rarely, if ever, used.

WRY'NECK, a European bird related to the woodpeckers, but, unlike the latter, unable to climb. It makes its nest in the natural cavities of trees, and lays from seven to

WRYNECK

twelve shiny, white eggs. It eats ants and other ground insects, which it captures with its bill or with its wormlike tongue. When disturbed, the bird thrusts its head out over its nest with an undulating movement, which has given it its name. Its habit of hissing has earned for it the sobriquet *snake bird*.

WUPPERTAL, GERMANY. See ELBERFELD.

WURTTEMBERG, *vürt'em berK*, GERMANY, formerly a kingdom and one of the divisions of the German Empire prior to 1918, became a division of the Third German Reich in 1934. It joins Bavaria and Baden. It has an area of 7,528 square miles, and a population of nearly 3,000,000. In the Middle Ages, Württemberg was a county. In 1495 it was erected into a duchy and in 1806 became a kingdom.

WYANDOTTE, *wi' an dot*. See HURON.

WYANDOTTE CAVE, remarkable natural cavern in Crawford County, Ind., five miles northwest of Leavenworth. It is next to Mammoth Cave in size and has been explored for about twenty-three miles. It is noted for its large chambers, some of which are 200 feet high and 300 feet broad. The stalactite formations in this cave are of unusual magnitude and beauty. Those in the room called Pillared Palace are of especial interest. Monument Mountain is a group of stalagmite columns 175 feet high.

WYCLIFFE, or **WICLIF**, *wik'lif*, JOHN (about 1320–1384), an English reformer, born at Hipswell, in Yorkshire, England. At sixteen he entered Oxford, became a fellow of Merton College, and later master of Balliol College.

In disputes between Edward III and the Papal court, concerning tribute, the English Parliament had resolved to support the sovereign. Because Wycliffe took a promi-

nent part in this affair, Pope Gregory XI wrote letters to the king, the Archbishop of Canterbury and the University of Oxford, to have him tried for heresy. In subsequent sermons, Wycliffe attacked the higher clergy, accusing them of having assumed undue power and unbecoming arrogance.

In 1380 he opposed the doctrine of transubstantiation at Oxford, and two years later he was summoned to appear before a commission of bishops and doctors at London. He refused to attend the trial. Ten out of twenty-four articles culled from his writings were condemned as heretical, and fourteen were declared erroneous. He was deprived of his professorship and expelled from the university. Wycliffe returned to Lutterworth, in Leicestershire, where Edward had given him a rectory. Part of his time was spent in translating the Bible from the Vulgate. This first systematic attempt to translate the whole Bible into English was an important contribution to English prose. Wycliffe continued to uphold the Scripture itself as the highest explanation of the divine law. Young men sent out by him to preach the plain, straightforward word of God were known as *poor priests*. Wycliffe's followers were active in spreading his teachings, which for about a generation after his death were a powerful religious and political factor. See LOLLARDS; BIBLE; LITERATURE; REFORMATION, THE.

WYOMING, a Rocky Mountain state in Northwestern United States, located on the Rocky Mountain Plateau. It is rectangular in form, its boundaries being formed by meridians of longitude and parallels of latitude. It lies between Montana on the north and Colorado on the south, with South Dakota and Nebraska on the east and Idaho and Utah on the west. The name, meaning *large plains,* was taken from that of the Wyoming Valley in Pennsylvania. The word

Wyoming is from the Delaware Indian name *Maughwauwama*. Yellowstone National Park, which with its adjoining forest reserve has an area of 5,000 square miles, occupies the northwestern corner, extending over the boundary into Idaho and Montana. Grand Teton National Park, of 150 square miles, was established in 1929. (See illustration in the article PARKS, NATIONAL.) Wyoming from east to west extends 355 miles; the width is 276 miles. The area is 97,914 square miles, of which 408 square miles are water. Wyoming is eighth in size among the states.

The People. In 1940 the population was 250,742, with a density of 2.6 persons per square mile. Nevada is the only state having a smaller and a more sparsely settled population. Less than ten per cent of the inhabitants are foreign-born; of these the English, Swedes, Germans, Italians, Scotch, Russians, Jugoslavs and Canadians are the most numerous. The Shoshone and Arapaho Indian reservations—west of the central section and near the Continental Divide—cover an area of about 3,000 square miles; the Indian population is over 2,000. In 1940 the population was 37.3 urban.

Surface and Drainage. The surface of the state, for the most part, is composed of mountains and plateaus. The great plains of the Mississippi valley slope away from the foothills in the east. The elevation varies from 3,500 to 13,785 feet, the highest point being Mt. Gannet. The main axis of the Rocky Mountains, which forms the Continental Divide, extends from north to south. The northern group of these mountains finds here its greatest development and is noted for its wild character and its picturesque scenery. Yellowstone National Park, 3,348 square miles in area, occupies the northwestern corner of the state. In the west central part are the Wind River Mountains; in the north central part, the Big Horn Mountains, and in the extreme northeast, the Black Hills, extending into South Dakota; in the southeast is the Laramie range; in the south, the Medicine Bow Mountains, and in the west the Teton, Gros Ventre and Shoshone ranges. The southwestern portion of the state slopes towards the Pacific Ocean and forms a part of the Grand River Valley. From the eastern and western slopes of the Rocky Mountains, several rivers take their rise, among them the North Platte, the Green, the Snake, the Laramie and the Shoshone.

Climate. Wyoming has the typical climate of the mountainous region of the northwest. The air is pure and dry, clear weather prevails and the high altitude is for many healthful. The average annual temperature is 45.5°; the mean annual rainfall, 12.98 inches.

Mineral Resources. In every mountain range of Wyoming, gold, silver, lead and copper ores are to be found, but as yet the resources have not been largely developed. Coal mining is most important, the annual output being about 8,000,000 tons, and there are over 20,000 square miles of coal lands, from which a steadily-increasing tonnage is being mined. Valuable iron deposits are found in various localities in the state. Petroleum occurs in Fremont and Natrona counties, and its production is next to that of coal in importance; in 1922 this amounted to 26,200,000 barrels. Extensive phosphate beds are found in Uinta County. The state also possesses extensive deposits of soda and an abundance of valuable building stone. Gold, silver and copper are mined in paying quantities.

Agriculture. Below the timber line, the mountains are covered with forests of coniferous trees. Between the mountain ranges are broad plateaus, with arable soils, which by means of proper irrigation yield prolific crops. On account of the slight rainfall it has been supposed that only a small part of the state was capable of cultivation. However, modern methods of moisture conservation have brought vast areas under cultivation. Irrigation ditches also have been carried long distances from the source of water supply. The result has been an immense increase in the tillable area. The raising of livestock is the most important agricultural industry. The nutritive grasses which so abundantly cover the great ranges of the pasturage support many thousands of cattle and sheep. Oats, potatoes, wheat and hay are the principal crops.

Irrigation is being largely extended. The Shoshone project, the greatest in the state, includes a remarkable dam, 328 feet high, across a narrow canyon. The dam is only 85 feet long at the bottom and 200 feet at the top. A smaller dam diverts the waters of the Shoshone River, through a tunnel 3¼ miles long, into a canal which for 40 miles passes only the upper edge of a broad and fertile valley containing 150,000 acres. Near

WYOMING
THE EQUALITY STATE

Chicago, Burlington & Quincy R. R.

(1) Grand Canyon and Great Falls of the Yellowstone, in Yellowstone National Park. (2) Roundup of beef cattle, important in Wyoming's livestock industry. (3) Devils Tower National Monument, consisting of five-sided columns of volcanic rock; the oldest national monument in the United States. (4) Old Faithful, in Yellowstone National Park. (5) Sugar beets.

Douglas, in Converse County, and in Natrona, Johnson and Sheridan counties there are large irrigated areas.

Manufactures. As Wyoming is an agricultural and mineral state and still in the first steps of material development, it has no distinctive manufacturing interests. The most important manufacturing industry is car construction and railway repair, and next in importance is the manufacture of lumber and timber products.

Transportation. The principal railroads are the Union Pacific, the Chicago, Burlington & Quincy and the Chicago & North Western. The total operative mileage is over 2,000.

Government. The legislature has a senate of 27 members, elected for four years, and a lower house of 62 members, elected for two years. The sessions are biennial, and are limited to forty days. The executive department consists of a governor, a secretary of state, an auditor, a treasurer and a superintendent of public instruction, each elected for four years. The courts consist of a supreme court, consisting of a chief justice and two associates, and such inferior courts as the legislature may establish.

Educuation. The University of Wyoming, chartered in 1886, is situated at Laramie and is the leading educational institution. The expenses of the public school system are provided for in part by the rental of government lands which are set aside for school purposes. The total extent of lands which may be so used is 3,600,000 acres.

The state school system is in charge of a State Board of Education, with a commissioner, elected by the board, as the executive officer. There is a state superintendent of public instruction, who is a member of this board, but his relation is chiefly advisory.

Institutions. There is a soldiers' home at Buffalo, a hospital for the insane at Evanston, a school for defectives at Lander, an industrial institute at Worland and a state hospital at Rock Springs. The penitentiary is at Rawlins. At Thermopolis there is the Big Horn Hot Springs Reserve.

Cities. The chief cities are Cheyenne, the capital, Casper, Laramie, Sheridan and Rock Springs.

History. Wyoming was a part of the territory included in the Louisiana Purchase of 1803, with the exception of the southwest corner, which was a part of the territory acquired from Mexico in 1848. The first white man supposed to have visited the region was Sieur de la Verendrye, in 1734. He was seeking sites for fur-trading posts. White hunters visited the Yellowstone region in 1807, and from that time hunters began to traverse the territory.

The first permanent settlement was made at Fort Laramie in 1834. Most of the immigration to California and Oregon passed through the territory, but not until the completion of the Union Pacific Railroad in 1869 were settlers attracted to the country. The Indians were hostile, and long before the construction of the railroad the government had built a chain of forts for the protection of immigrants. The discovery of gold in 1867 increased the number of settlers, and in 1869 Wyoming became an organized territory. Yellowstone National Park (which see) was created in 1872. Wyoming was admitted into the Union as the forty-fourth state on July 10, 1890. From the organization of its first government the state has given women equal suffrage with men. From this practice it received its popular name, THE EQUALITY STATE.

Related Articles. Consult the following titles for additional information:

Bighorn River
Black Hills
Cheyenne
Laramie
Rocky Mountains
Shoshonean Indians
Snake River
Yellowstone National Park
Yellowstone River

WYOMING, UNIVERSITY OF, a coeducational state institution, founded at Laramie in 1886. It comprises colleges of liberal arts, agriculture, engineering, education and law; divisions of music, home economics, commerce and university extension; and a summer school. The agricultural experiment station and the co-operative agricultural extension service are operated in connection with the agricultural departments. There is a staff, including instructors, administrators and others, of over 200 and a student enrollment of more than 3,500. The library contains 97,000 volumes.

WYOMING VALLEY MAS'SACRE, a fearful massacre in Wyoming Valley, Pa., on July 3 and 4, 1778, perpetrated by an English and Indian force against the American settlers of the valley. A vast majority of the inhabitants, including women and children, were slain in the course of two days' slaughter, and the rest fled eastward to the nearest settlements. The valley was not settled again for several years.

1300-1000 B.C. PHOENICIAN

Circa 500 B.C. GREEK

50 B.C. ROMAN

7th Century ANGLO-SAXON

POST X

8th Century IRISH

7th Century ROMAN UNCIAL

14th Century LOMBARDIC

16th Century GERMAN GOTHIC

X, the twenty-fourth letter of the alphabet and the representative of what might as well be denoted by *ks* or *gs*. The letter *x* was originally Phoenician, and until a late date the last in the Roman alphabet, but *y* and *z* were finally added from the Greek. As an initial letter, it is pronounced like *z*.

In algebra, *x* is the usual symbol for the unknown quantity. In Roman numerals X signifies ten, perhaps from the fact that it represents a V standing upon a second V inverted.

XANTHIPPE, *zan thip'pe*, the scolding wife of the philosopher Socrates, whose forbearance with her quarrelsome temper was a salient trait in his character. The name has become proverbial as that of a scolding shrew.

XAVIER, *zav'e er*, FRANCISCO DE (1506–1552), better known as SAINT FRANCIS XAVIER, was a Jesuit missionary in Asiatic countries, earning the title "Apostle of the Indies." He was a native of Northern Spain, the son of a nobleman whose family seat was Xavier. He was sent to Paris to be educated, and with Loyola he founded the Society of Jesus. In the early part of 1540, he was chosen for the mission to India. From Goa, where he arrived in May, 1542, he extended his labors southward to Ceylon, Malacca and Celebes. He spent two years in Japan and returned to Goa to organize a mission to China, but before he could overcome the difficulties in his way, he died. Xavier was canonized in 1622.

XENIA, *ze'ne ah*, OHIO, the county seat of Greene County, fifty-five miles southwest of Columbus, on the Little Miami River and on the Baltimore & Ohio and the Pennsylvania railroads. The city is in a productive farming region. There are extensive cordage works, shoe factories, machine shops and rubber and candy factories. The Xenia Theological Seminary and the Ohio soldiers' and sailors' orphans' home are located here. A courthouse, a Carnegie Library and a Federal building are prominent features of the city. Wilberforce University for colored students is located three miles north. There are interesting Indian mounds and relics in the vicinity, as well as in other near-by sections of the state. Xenia was settled in 1803, and was incorporated five years later. Population, 1920, 9,110; in 1930, 10,507; and in 1940, 10,633.

XENOPHON, *zen'o fon* (about 434–about 355 B. C.), an Athenian historian and general, a pupil of Socrates. When about forty years of age, he joined the expedition of Cyrus against Artaxerxes. Cyrus was killed in the Battle of Cunaxa, and the Greek generals were put to death. The ten thousand mercenaries then chose Xenophon as their leader, and he brought them out of the strange country to the Black Sea. On his return to Greece he fought with Sparta against Athens.

Xenophon wrote numerous works, and all of these, it would seem, have come down to us. His leading works include the famous *Anabasis,* which describes the expedition of Cyrus already referred to, especially the retreat of the Ten Thousand; the *Memorabilia,* a record of the life and teachings of Socrates; the *Hellenica,* which gives a somewhat dull account of forty-eight years of Greek history and is a continuation of the history of Thucydides, and several minor works. Xenophon's writings are clear and accurate, and are among the best sources of information regarding some of the most important events of past history; but his style is often commonplace and monotonous.

XERXES, *zurk'zeez*, the name borne by three kings of Persia, the most celebrated of whom was Xerxes I (see next page).

Xerxes I, the son of Darius I, succeeded to the throne of Persia on his father's death, in 485 B. C. After suppressing a revolt in Egypt, he began to make plans for the invasion of Greece, the preparations for which had been begun by his father. These preparations were on the most enormous scale. Provisions were stored up on the intended route for three years, a transport fleet was collected, the engineering skill of the day was exerted to remove land obstacles and the resources of the vast Persian Empire were taxed to the utmost to produce an armament sufficient to crush Greece. According to ancient computation, the invading army numbered over two million, and although this, possibly, is an exaggeration, it must have been numerically the greatest army on record.

At the head of his enormous host, Xerxes advanced unopposed till he came to Thermopylae, but here his fleet was seriously damaged by a storm, while the narrow pass was effectually held by Leonidas, at the head of a determined, though small, band of Spartans. At last the passage was effected through treachery, and Xerxes marched on through Phocis and Boeotia to Athens, which he entered without opposition. In the meantime the Persian fleet had met with several mishaps. In two engagements with the Greek ships at Artemisium, it had suffered considerable damage, and a storm which occurred between the two conflicts was the cause of still greater loss. Finally, at Salamis (480 B. C.) a naval battle was fought, one of the most decisive in the history of the world, in which the Persians were defeated with terrible loss. Xerxes, who from a lofty eminence had watched the destruction of his fleet, fled panic-stricken to Sardis, leaving in command of his army, Mardonius, who was defeated the following year at Plataea. He spent the rest of his life in obscurity and was murdered by Artabanus, the commander of his bodyguard, who was plotting to make himself king of Persia. He was succeeded by his son Artaxerxes I.

Xerxes II was the son of Artaxerxes I. He was born about 450 B. C. and lived twenty-five years. On the assassination of his parents he ascended the throne but was murdered about a month later.

The third Persian ruler of this name, who was also called OARSES, ruled about 337 B. C.

X-RAY. See ROENTGEN RAYS.

XYLOPHONE, *zi'lo fone,* a musical instrument. Small bars of wood, selected for

XYLOPHONE

their sounding quality, or pieces of metal of graduated length are fastened upon a horizontal frame in such a manner as to form the chromatic scale. The performer plays with two small mallets, one in each hand.

X Y Z CORRESPONDENCE, the name given to the dispatches sent in 1797–1798 to the United States government by its commissioners, Charles Pinckney, John Marshall and Elbridge Gerry, in Paris. These men were sent to France to settle certain difficulties with that government. On their arrival they were not received officially, but were compelled to communicate with the government through three agents, who informed them that the first step toward negotiation would be the payment of a large sum of money to the Directory, which was then in control of French affairs. The American commissioners, with the exception of Gerry, promptly withdrew and transmitted the correspondence to President Adams, who, in turn, laid it before Congress, substituting for the names of the French commissioners the letters X Y Z. The correspondence aroused the bitterest feeling in the United States, and a naval war with France was actually begun, but the French government receded from its position and thus averted a struggle. See ADAMS JOHN.

Y, the twenty-fifth letter of the English alphabet, resembling in its form the Greek upsilon. It is, like *w*, both a consonant and a vowel, but it differs from *w* in that it is often used by itself as a vowel, as in *by, deny, pony*. In this use it is superfluous, as it might be replaced by *i*.

In algebra, *y* stands for the second of the unknown quantities.

YABLONOI, *yah blo noi'*, **MOUNTAINS,** a Siberian range extending from Northern Mongolia in a northeasterly direction about 1,000 miles and merging with the Stanovoi. The highest peaks, at the southern end of the range, attain an altitude of more than 8,000 feet. Many other peaks are 6,000 feet high.

YACHT, *yot*, **AND YACHTING,** *yot' ing*. A sailing boat, used for pleasure, for traveling or for racing, is known as a yacht. There are three principal rigs for sailing yachts— cutter, schooner and yawl. A *cutter* has one mast and a running bowsprit and usually carries four sails, namely, mainsail, gaff-topsail, foresail and jib. A square sail is also frequently set by the larger vessels of this class. A *schooner* has two masts, mainmast and foremast, a standing bowsprit and jib-boom, or not infrequently, instead of these, a running bowsprit, like that of a cutter. A *yawl* is rigged exactly like a cutter, with the addition of a small mizzenmast. It is a very convenient cruising rig and is becoming common for yachts of over 50 tons. Steam yachts are common, and in many localities they are put to practical uses by their owners. The speed attained by some is remarkable.

The history of yachting is the history of yacht racing, inasmuch as competition improved yachts, just as horse racing improved the breed of horses. Very arbitrary rules obtain with reference to the building of yachts for racing purposes. The first international contest between the United States and England took place in 1851, when the *America* defeated fifteen English yachts in their own waters, and won the $500 cup offered by the Royal Yacht Squadron. The trophy has remained ever since in the possession of the New York Yacht Club, though several English yachts have tried to win it back. In 1870 the *Cambria* was defeated. In 1885 the *Genesta* was defeated by the *Puritan*, and a year later the *Galatea* by the *Mayflower*. The *Volunteer*, the *Defender*, the *Reliance*, the *Resolute* and the *Enterprise* are American yachts that have more recently maintained supremacy over the English challengers.

The principal English competitors since 1899 have been vessels constructed for the purpose by Sir Thomas Lipton and named respectively the *Shamrock* I, II, III, IV and V. The races are usually sailed off Sandy Hook, a few miles south of New York harbor. In 1920, the *Resolute* defeated *Shamrock* IV, and in 1930, *Shamrock* V, Lipton's last challenger, was defeated by the *Enterprise*. See SAILBOAT AND SAILING.

YAK, an animal of the ox tribe, found only in Tibet, Asia. It is found wild and is the ordinary domestic animal of the inhabitants of that region, supplying milk, food and raiment, as well as serving as a beast of burden. The size is that of a small ox. The horns are long, nearly cylindrical, smooth and pointed at the ends, and they have a peculiar and characteristic curve. Some of the domestic yaks are hornless. Their most remarkable external characteristic is the excessive growth and peculiar distribution of the hair.

The upper parts of the body and sides are clothed with thick, soft, woolly hair, more fully developed along the middle of the back, especially on the shoulders, where it forms a great bunch. From the upper parts of the limbs and the whole of the lower surface of the body hangs a thick growth of long, straight hair, in old animals sweeping the ground and almost concealing the somewhat short legs. The tail is profusely covered with a thick mass of such hairs. The wild animals are nearly uniformly black; the domestic yaks are often quite white. The silky and tough hair and the skins are often used in the manufacture of caps, coats, blankets and ropes.

YAKIMA, *yak'he mah,* an Indian tribe, formerly living on both sides of the Columbia River and on the northerly branches of the Yakima in Washington. They were mentioned by Lewis and Clark in 1806. In 1855 the United States made a treaty with the Yakima and thirteen other tribes whereby they were required to cede valuable lands to the government and confine themselves to the Yakima reservation. The Indians resorted to war, and it was not till 1859 that the provisions of the treaty could be carried out.

YAKIMA, WASH., the county seat of Yakima County, is on the Yakima River and the Northern Pacific and Union Pacific railroads, and an interurban road, and is about 200 miles southwest of Spokane. There is a county airport. It is a distributing center for a large surrounding territory. It has extensive fruit canneries, flour mills, sawmills, other wood-working factories and warehouses. There is a fine Federal building, a Carnegie Library, a state armory, and a hospital. The state fair is held here. The commission form of government is in operation. The name was changed from North Yakima in 1917. Population, 1940, 27,221.

YALE UNIVERSITY, a foremost American institution of higher learning. It began in Branford, Conn., in 1701, when ten Congregational clergymen met for the "founding of a college in this Colony." Instruction in the college was first given in Killingworth; later the school moved to Saybrook, and in 1716 it was permanently established in New Haven. Two years later it took the name of Yale College to honor Elihu Yale, who had made a large gift for its support. Yale is the third oldest college in the United States, as its establishment followed that of Harvard and William and Mary.

The transition from college to university began under the elder Timothy Dwight, president from 1795 to 1817. Permanent professorships were established then, and the medi-

cal school was founded; schools of divinity and law soon followed. Yale had the first college art gallery in America in 1832. The work of the university is now carried on in twelve schools. The Freshman Year provides the first year of instruction in the four-year course of the other undergraduate schools—Yale College (liberal arts), the Sheffield Scientific School and the School of Engineering. There are the following graduate and professional schools: a graduate school, a medical school, a divinity school (undenominational) and schools of law, the fine arts, music, forestry and nursing. Women are not admitted to the undergraduate schools or to the school of forestry.

The faculty has about 500 full-time teaching members and about 500 others in research or administration. The enrollment of candidates for degrees remains constant at about 5,200, as the numbers are limited in all schools. There are about 2,200,000 volumes in the Yale library. The endowment exceeds $110,500,000. Among notable structures are the Memorial Quadrangle, the Harkness Tower, the Sterling Memorial Library, the Payne Whitney Gymnasium and Yale Bowl.

Yale is especially famous as the mother of colleges. Jonathan Dickinson was the first president of Princeton; Samuel Johnson was the first president of King's College, later Columbia University; Eleazar Wheelock founded Dartmouth College. Among other eminent Yale alumni were Nathan Hale, Jonathan Edwards, Lyman Beecher, John C. Calhoun, Eli Whitney, Samuel F. B. Morse, Noah Webster and William Howard Taft.

Elihu Yale (1648–1721), an English merchant and philanthropist, was born near Boston. His father was one of the original settlers of New Haven, Conn. The son was educated in England and began his career as a merchant, engaging in trade in India. From 1687 to 1692 he was governor of the East India Company's fort at Madras. He then returned to England. Mr. Yale became interested in the schools founded at Saybrook and afterwards located at New Haven, Connecticut. During his life he made several bequests to this institution, and in 1718 he announced a large gift. The trustees then honored him by naming the school Yale College.

YALU, *yah loo',* **RIVER,** a river of Eastern Asia, which rises on the eastern borders of China and flows southwestward and southward, forming during its entire course a part of the boundary between China and Chosen (Korea). Its length is about 300 miles, and it is navigable for about thirty miles. At the mouth of this river a famous naval battle was fought in 1894, during which the Japanese destroyed the Chinese fleet. The forcing of the passage of this river at its mouth by the Japanese in 1904 was the first movement in the land operations of the Russo-Japanese War. Since the Japanese annexed Chosen they have called the river ORYOKU (*o ri o'ku*). See RUSSO-JAPANESE WAR.

YAM, a plant having edible roots much like the sweet potato. It is found in the temperate and subtropical parts of America, in China

YAM

and in the islands of the Southern Pacific. In Australia and China a species known as *winged yam* produces edible tubers from one and a half to three feet long which sometimes weigh thirty pounds. The skin is dark brown and the reddish flesh is sweet and juicy and very palatable when baked. A large yam is also found in India, though there the small white yam is more in demand for food.

The yam has become an important vegetable in the United States. While it contains less starch than the Irish potato, it contains more nitrogen and a high percentage of sugar.

YANCEY, *yan'sy,* WILLIAM LOWNDES (1814-1863), an American publicist and orator, born in Georgia. He began practicing law in 1834, at the same time editing a Unionist paper. Moving to Alabama in 1836, he entered the legislature and gained prominence as a Whig orator. When he entered Congress in 1844, he supported the Southern cause. Upon his retirement in 1846 he became influential as a leader and orator, doing perhaps more than any other man to strengthen secession sentiment in the South. He was a member of the mission seeking European recognition of the independence of the Confederacy. Later he served in the Confederate Senate.

YANGTZE, *yahng'tze,* one of the largest and most important rivers of Asia, and China's chief waterway. It rises in the south-central part of the continent, in the plateau of Tibet; the upper part of its course is between mountains, where the channel is narrow and the stream rapid, with frequent falls. It flows irregularly northeastward to the Yellow Sea, which it enters through an estuary about thirty miles wide—a total distance of 3,000 miles.

The Yangtze is navigable to ocean steamers as far as Hankow, 680 miles inland. Smaller steamers can travel some 500 miles farther, to Ichang; beyond Ichang navigation is difficult, although flat-bottomed steamers negotiate the gorges westward. Chinkiang, the first important town on the Yangtze, is on the north bank at the entrance of the Grand Canal, which connects the Yangtze with the Hwang. Nanking, the seat of Japan's Central government in China, is on the south bank, 235 miles inland. Where the Kialing flows into the Yangtze is Chungking, trading center for West China and provisional capital of the Nationalist government.

The chief tributaries, some of which are navigable, are the Han, from the north, and the Wu, the Heng and the Kan, from the south. The river bears much sediment. It is estimated that the amount of sediment deposited by the Yangtze at its mouth each year equals about five-sixths of that deposited by the Mississippi.

YANK'EE, in America, the popular name for a New Englander; in Great Britain it is often applied indiscriminately to the whole population of the United States, and during the World War it was the common designation of the American soldier, regardless of his state. In its origin it was a corruption of the word *English* as pronounced by the Indians. It seems to have been first applied about 1775 by the British soldiers as a term of reproach to the New Englanders, who themselves afterward adopted it. Since the Civil War the Southern people have applied it to all people of the North.

YANKEE DOODLE, a national song of the United States, sung to a very old tune, which dates from the tenth century. The words, which are mere doggerel, were probably written at the time of the French and Indian War by an English army surgeon, Dr. Richard Schuckburgh, in derision of the ill-trained continental troops. Notwithstanding its mockery, it was taken up by the "Yankee" soldiers and became widely popular.

YANKTON, S. D., the county seat of Yankton County, sixty-five miles southwest of Sioux Falls, on the Missouri River and on the Great Northern, the Chicago & North Western and the Chicago, Milwaukee, Saint Paul & Pacific railroads. The city is the center of a large agricultural and stock-raising district, and has one of the largest seed and nursery companies in the Middle West. Other industries include poultry packing and the manufacture of dairy products, fireworks, egg cases and fillers and other articles. Yankton is the seat of a state hospital for the insane and of Yankton College (Congregational).

Yankton is the oldest settled community in the Dakotas. It was settled in 1858 and was the capital of Dakota Territory from 1861 to 1883. It has the commission form of government. Population, 1940, 6,798.

YAQUI, *yah'ke*, **INDIANS,** a native tribe of the Mexican state of Sonora, numbering about 20,000 and representing a well-developed type of civilization. They are said to be the only Indian tribe that has never been fully subdued by the white man. They made a treaty with the Spaniards in 1610, but their history from 1740 down to the present has been a series of revolts. In 1906 the Mexican government took the extreme measure of attempting to subdue them by deportation to Yucatan. The industries of the Yaquis are agriculture, cattle raising and the manufacture of cotton and woolen stuffs. They also make hats of palm leaves and baskets of reed. Many are employed as laborers in fields and mines.

YARKAND, *yahr kahnd'*, a city situated in the chief oasis of Sin Kiang (Western China), southeast of Kashgar. It is at an elevation of over 3,800 feet, is enclosed by a wall and surrounded by a moat. The buildings are constructed of stone and clay, and most of them are of one story. The city has numerous bazaars, mosques and caravansaries. It is also the seat of some Mohammedan colleges. It is surrounded by an agricultural and stock-raising region and carries on a trade in silk, dyes, leather, wool, tea and sugar. Yarkand is not so important a commercial center as formerly, owing to the fact that railway lines elsewhere have diverted much of its caravan trade. Population, about 70,000.

YARMOUTH, *yahr'muth*, Nova Scotia, the county seat of Yarmouth County and an important seaport, situated on a small bay of the Atlantic Ocean, 205 miles southwest of Halifax. It is served by the Canadian National and Dominion Atlantic railways. It has regular steamship connection with Boston, Halifax and Saint John. Its commercial prestige is due largely to its fisheries and fish preserving industries and its lumber trade. Strawberry growing and fur farming are carried on. Excellent roads make this a popular center for tourists, and also for sportsmen. Fish and game are plentiful.

Yarmouth was founded in 1861, and was incorporated as a town in 1890. It is a city of beautiful homes, fine streets and attractive surroundings. Population, 1921, 7,073; in 1931, 7,055; in 1941, 7,699.

YARMOUTH, or GREAT YARMOUTH, England, a seaport and watering place situated on the east coast, nineteen miles east of Norwich. The town occupies a narrow peninsula between the Yare River and the North Sea, and is connected by bridges with Suffolk and other places on the right bank of the Yare. The river is lined with extensive piers. Yarmouth is an important commercial port, and is the chief center of the herring fisheries of England. Other industries include shipbuilding and the manufacture of ropes, nets and sails. Dickens has described the salty, fishy air of Yarmouth and the charm of its seafaring folk in his novel, *David Copperfield.* Population, 1931, 56,769.

YARN, thread made by twisting the fiber of wool, cotton, flax, silk, hemp or other materials. The yarns are woven into fabrics, or used in knitting, embroidering and sewing. For the process of making yarn, see Spinning.

YATES, Richard (1818–1873), an American political leader, born in Warsaw, Ky., but taken in childhood to Springfield, Ill. He graduated at Illinois College, Jacksonville, and began the practice of law at Springfield, where he became a prominent Whig. He was elected to the state legislature, serving from 1842 to 1849, and he was a member of Congress from 1851 to 1855. He became a Republican at the organization of the party and was elected governor of Illinois in 1860. During five years' service, he gained fame as one of the greatest of the war governors and was a close friend and adviser of President Lincoln. In 1865 he was elected to the United States Senate, where he served one term. His son, Richard Yates (1860–1936), was governor of Illinois from 1901 to 1905, and in 1918 was elected a member of Congress from Illinois.

YAZ′OO, a river of Mississippi, formed by the junction of the Tallahatchie and the Yalabusha. It has a winding course to the south and southwest and enters the Mississippi about five miles above Vicksburg. Its length is 300 miles, and it is navigable for steamboats throughout its course. The name is an Indian word meaning *river of death.*

YEAR, the period of time during which the earth makes one complete revolution in its orbit, or the period which elapses between the sun's leaving either equinoctial point, or either tropic, and its return to the same. This is the *tropical,* or *solar,* year, which is the year in the strict and proper sense of the word. This period comprehends what are called the twelve calendar months, and it is usually considered to commence on January 1, and to end on December 31. It is not quite uniform, but its mean length is 365 days, 5 hours, 48 minutes and 46 seconds. In popular usage, however, the year consists of 365 days, and every fourth year of 366. The extra day is always added to February, and the fourth year is called *leap year.* The *sidereal* year consisting of 365 days, 6 hours, 9 minutes and 9 seconds, is that used in astronomical calculations.

Related Articles. Consult the following titles for additional information:

Calendar	Precession of
Equinox	the Equinoxes
Leap Year	Seasons

YEAST, *yeest,* the ferment used in bread-making and in brewing, composed of a mass of small one-celled yeast plants. These cells are so small that 3,000 of them, laid end to end, would scarcely measure an inch. Under favorable conditions they multiply very rapidly, breaking up the sugar in the substance upon which they feed, setting free carbonic acid gas and forming alcohol. Yeast manufactured for commercial purposes may be liquid, dry or compressed in form.

Related Articles. Consult the following titles for additional information:

Bread	Fermentation
Brewing	

YEATS, *yates,* William Butler (1865–1939), an Irish poet and dramatist, born in Dublin, the son of a distinguished artist. At an early age he turned his attention to literature, and became a leading figure in the Irish literary revival. With Lady Gregory he helped to establish the Irish Literary Theater, from which the Irish National Theater Society developed. He made lecture tours in the United States and Canada in 1903 and 1914. Yeats' peculiar gifts as a dramatist are conspicuous in *Cathleen ni Hoolihan, The Pot of Broth, The Hour Glass, Deirdre* and *The Land of Heart's Desire.* His verse is of the highest lyrical quality, and possesses the same sort of elusive charm that is found in his essays and plays.

YED′DO, Japan. See Tokyo.

YELLOW, one of the three primary colors. Lemon and canary yellow may be taken as pure yellows. Chrome yellow has a slight orange tint. A peculiarity of yellow is that an increase of light seems to strengthen the color; and that the color is also greatly intensified when placed beside its complementary color, blue. Moreover, it reciprocally intensifies the blue. Yellow is the national color of China.

YEL′LOWBIRD. See American Goldfinch.

YELLOW FEVER, an infectious and highly fatal disease of the warm regions of America and Africa, communicated to the human system by the bite of a species of house mosquito. The disease was first recognized in 1647 in the West Indies. In 1691 there was a disastrous epidemic of it in Barbados. In 1878 a severe visitation of the disease in the lower Mississippi valley killed about five thousand persons in New Orleans and Memphis alone. Since the liberation of Cuba and the occupation of the Canal Zone, the disease has been practically stamped out in those regions. Proper sewerage, disposal of garbage, isolation of patients and their protection by screens from mosquito bites, disinfection of buildings in which cases occur and the destruction of the breeding places of the mosquitoes themselves have proved effective methods of combating the disease.

Yellow fever is so called because the skin of its victims takes on a yellow hue owing to jaundice which spreads over the whole of the body. The disease actually sets in about three or four days after infection, and is usually characterized by severe chills or rigors. Temperature rises rapidly, and may reach 105° or even higher. In favorable cases the fever abates at the end of the fourth day, and with rest and careful feeding recovery may be complete in two or three weeks. In severe cases blood may be discharged from the bowels and there may be bleeding of the nose or gums. Delirium sets in, and the patient lapses into unconsciousness. Death is due to hemorrhage, heart depression, suppression of the urine or the direct action of poisons upon the vital centers. See MOSQUITO.

YEL'LOW-HAMMER, one of the numerous names of the American golden-winged woodpecker, or flicker. In England the name is applied to the yellow bunting. This bird is bright yellow, with patches of brown. The wings are black, bordered with gold. The bird builds in hedge-rows; the eggs are spotted with red. See FLICKER.

YELLOW JACKET, the common name for any wasp whose body is marked with yellow. See WASP.

YEL'LOWLEGS, an American snipe found in marshes and along shores. It is black and white on head, breast and back, and light underneath. It nests in Canada as far north as the Arctic Circle, laying three or four buff-colored eggs in a depression of the ground. In winter the birds migrate as far south as Argentina, traveling a distance of 8,000 miles twice yearly—one of the longest flights made by a migrating bird.

YELLOW RACE. See MONGOLIAN RACE.

YELLOW SEA, an arm of the Pacific Ocean, invading the continent of Asia 600 miles, between China and Chosen (Korea). It is connected with the Japan Sea on the north by Korea Strait, and its northern projections form the gulfs of Liaotung and Pechili and Korea Bay. The Yellow Sea is over 300 miles wide in its broadest part, on the south, but is nowhere over 300 feet deep. The chief inflowing rivers are the Hwang, the Yangtse and the Yalu, or Oryoku. The

Yellow Sea (Hwang-hai in Chinese) receives its name from the large quantities of yellow mud deposited by the Hwang and Yangtse rivers. See maps under ASIA.

YELLOWSTONE NATIONAL PARK, oldest and largest of national parks, is America's most celebrated wonderland. Chiefly in northwestern Wyoming, it was created in 1872. It has an area of about 3,472 square miles. It is unique, and marvelous; it has the greatest geyser region in the world, deep canyons, beautiful waterfalls, rushing rivers, lovely lakes, mountains, forests, colorful rocks, hot springs and wild animals. Seldom can such great diversity of picturesque scenery and wonders of nature be found within so small a space.

Surface. The park consists of a broad plateau, 7,000 to 8,000 feet high, bordered by mountain ranges with tall peaks. Electric Peak, highest in the park, is 11,155 feet above sea level. Great valleys, including beautiful Hayden Valley along the Yellowstone River, separate the mountains.

Rivers, Waterfalls and Lakes. The Yellowstone, the Missouri and the Snake river systems drain the park, the first two to the Atlantic slope, and the third into the Pacific. The Continental Divide, entering the park at the southeast corner and leaving near the center of the western boundary, divides the rivers between east and west. On Two Ocean Plateau, in the southeast, during high water, streams flowing toward both oceans are fed from the same source.

Waterfalls and cascades are numerous. The greatest are the Falls of the Yellowstone, actually two waterfalls. The Upper Falls, 109 feet high, plunge over a precipice in a narrow channel; and the Lower Falls, 308 feet high (twice the height of Niagara Falls), drop like a veil of lace, with mist and spray rising from the bottom of the gorge. Tower Falls, 132 feet high, is the spectacular rush of Tower Creek into Yellowstone Canyon, in a region of natural basalt columns, spires and towers. Firehole Falls and Firehole Cascades make froth of Firehole River, flowing over volcanic boulders in a gorge.

Of the many lakes, Yellowstone is by far the most important. With an area of 138 square miles and a hundred-mile shore line, it is the largest body of fresh water in the world at that elevation (7,731 feet)

THE GIANT GEYSER. EACH ERUPTION THROWS A STREAM OF WATER
250 FEET HIGH FOR NINETY MINUTES.

Travel Magazine

WONDERS OF THE YELLOWSTONE

The Falls of the Yellowstone River, in a region of surpassing beauty. Below, richly colored formations of Mammoth Hot Springs terraces.

except Lake Titicaca in Peru, which is about 12,500 feet above sea level and more than 2,600 square miles in area. The basin of Yellowstone Lake is irregularly shaped, projecting into a bay at the west called West Thumb, which is in itself larger than any other body of water within the park. There are several islands within the lake. A hot-water area parallels the lake; fountain geysers erupt on its surface, and muddy paint pots boil on shore; Fishing Cone at West Thumb can be seen above the surface. Large trout in the lake make this a haven for fishermen, who need no license within the boundaries of the park. Next largest lakes are Heart, Lewis and Shoshone, dotted to the south and west of the Yellowstone. Water in the lakes, as in the rivers, is usually clear and cold.

Grand Canyon of the Yellowstone. Startling in its beauty and grandeur, the Grand Canyon of the Yellowstone extends for nearly twenty miles above the foam-edged blue ribbon of the Yellowstone River. The canyon is 1,200 feet deep, at places as deep as 1,400 feet; and 2,000 feet wide at its greatest extent. Its walls are richly colored in shades of yellow, brown, orange, red and purple. A forest so dark as to be almost black extends to the edge of the canyon drop.

Geysers and Hot Springs. Yellowstone National Park is famous for its geysers and hot springs, of which there are more than 3,000. The largest geyser area is called the Lower Geyser Basin, and covers an area of ten square miles. In addition to the geysers in this basin there are hot pools, paint pots and mud volcanoes. The best-known and largest geysers, however, are found in the Upper Geyser Basin. Here Old Faithful, king of all the geysers and unique in the world, for four minutes flings a misty plume of hot water into the air.

Regularly, every seventy minutes, it shoots 10,000 gallons of water from 120 to 170 feet high, and the foamy white of this uprush of steaming water has become the symbol of Yellowstone to all the world. The Giant and Giantess, in contrast, erupt but once in several months, but for several hours then they throw water 200 feet into the air. Grand Geyser makes a showy display; the Grotto reveals unique architecture; the Jewel is rich with crystals. See GEYSER.

Mammoth Hot Springs is the most noted area of hot springs in the park. Through the years, minerals in the water have raised up a hill, with steps and terraces, white when dry, but colored by the algae in the water where it is flowing over them. Here is the Devils Kitchen, a circular pit, interior of an extinct hot spring; conelike Liberty Cap; the Devils Thumb; Angel Terrace; and delicately colored Jupiter Terrace, largest travertine terrace in the world. Between this hot-springs region and Norris Geyser Region, the hottest area in the park, are such attractions as Obsidian Cliff of black volcanic glass, and Roaring Mountain, so named because of the sound it makes from the outrush of gas escaping from it in a hundred places.

Other Attractions. The park is the greatest wild game and bird refuge in America. In the forests and valleys can be found elk, antelope, moose, deer, buffalo, bison, mountain sheep, beaver and many other animals. Bears are tame and friendly; black and grizzly bears are fed at special grounds each evening during summer for the benefit of tourists. Eagles circle the mountain crags; wild geese, ducks and pelican frequent the waters of Yellowstone Lake. There are altogether more than 200 species of birds.

Of the fossil forests in the northern section, one is accessible near Tower Junction, and in places observers can discern a succession of twelve such forests, formed one upon the other. A scenic mountain drive from Old Faithful to West Thumb is rich in attractive views. It crosses the Continental Divide twice within a few miles. Park highways extend in a figure eight in the center of the park, covering all points of interest, and connecting with the five gateway entrances. Hotels, lodges, cabins and camping grounds provide accommodations.

YELLOWSTONE RIVER, a river of the United States, the largest tributary of the Missouri. It rises in Northwestern Wyoming, in the Continental Divide, flows northeast through Montana and into the Missouri a short distance beyond the boundary of North Dakota. Its length is about 1,100 miles. Throughout most of its course the river is followed by the Northern Pacific Railroad.

YE'MEN, a territory of Southwestern Arabia, bordering on the Red Sea. It embraces an area of about 73,800 square miles, and is a region of mountains and plateaus, from 8,000 to 10,000 feet in altitude. The coast lands are arid, but the valleys are gardens of tropical vegetation. Excellent coffee is grown. The people, numbering about 2,500,000, are engaged chiefly in stock raising. There are no railroads, but there are several caravan routes from the interior to the coast. Hodeida is the principal port. At the close of the World War there was under way a movement to have Yemen included in a united Arabian state free from Turkish control. See ARABIA; TURKEY.

YEN, the monetary unit of Japan, equivalent to about fifty cents of United States money. The yen was formerly coined in both gold and silver, but in 1897 Japan adopted a gold standard, and since that time no single gold yens have been coined, but two-yen, five-yen, ten-yen and twenty-yen pieces are in common use. The smaller denomination in Japanese money is the sen, equivalent to a half cent. The 5-sen is coined in nickel; 10-sen, 20-sen and 50-sen pieces, in silver.

YENISEI, *yen e say'e*, a river of Asia, one of the longest in the world. From its sources in the Sayansky Mountains, in Northwestern Mongolia, it flows in a general northwesterly direction and enters the Arctic Ocean near the Gulf of Ob, through an estuary about 500 miles long. Above the estuary its length is 2,500 miles. An area of 1,000,000 square miles is drained by it. South of Krasnoyarsk, near which it is crossed by the Trans-Siberian Railway, it is ice-free half the year, and it is navigable to Minusinsk, at the mouth of the Angara River. With its navigable tributaries and canal connections the Yenisei is of the greatest commercial importance to Western Siberia.

YER'KES OBSER'VATORY, an astronomical observatory situated at Williams Bay, an arm of Lake Geneva, Wisconsin. It is owned by the University of Chicago, and was named in honor of Charles Tyson Yerkes, who donated the money for buildings and instruments. The refracting telescope of this observatory is the largest of its kind in the world, having a diameter of forty inches. See TELESCOPE.

YEW, *yu*, an evergreen tree of the pine family, with dense, spreading branches, thickly covered with very dark green linear leaves. The common yew of Europe is very long-lived, and in England it is planted in cemeteries and is considered an emblem of immortality. The leaves and seeds are poisonous, but the red berries are not. The tough, elastic wood was used for making bows in the days before firearms were invented. The American yew is commonly known as *ground hemlock*, and is a low shrub, with straggling branches, common in dense forests.

YGGDRASIL, *ig'dra sil*, in Norse mythology, the enormous ash-tree which binds together heaven, earth and the underworld. It was the tree of life, fate, time and space.

YID'DISH, the dialect spoken by the Jews of Eastern Europe, used by more people than any other Hebrew form of speech. It represents a combination of various languages, notably Hebrew, German, Aramaic and Slavic, and has been carried to all parts of the world. In the United States Yiddish is widely used as a newspaper language, and has been the vehicle of many noted Jewish writers.

YOKOHAMA, *yo ko hah'mah*, JAPAN, the chief commercial center of the empire, is situated on the east coast of Hondo, on the Bay of Tokyo, seven miles southwest of the latter city, with which it is connected by railway. It is on a large harbor, which is protected by breakwaters. The city is well planned and has a number of excellent public buildings. Most important of these are the customhouse, the postoffice, the courthouse and the railway station. The city has a number of modern churches and in most respects resembles a European town. The harbor is lined with massive docks, and the surrounding heights are occupied by fine residences. It is the port through which most visitors enter Japan. On September 1, 1923, a violent earthquake followed by tidal waves and destructive fires brought ruin to this and other Bay cities, with loss of thousands of lives. Population, 1930, 620,306.

YONGE, *yung*, CHARLOTTE MARY (1823–1901), a novelist and essayist, born at Otterbourne, England. She was an exceedingly prolific writer, and produced in all about 125 volumes, including novels, short stories, essays, biographies, histories and school books. Her best-known novels are *The Heir of Redclyffe, The Daisy Chain, The Dove in the Eagle's Nest*, and a life of Hannah More. Her historical works include *Cameos of English History, English Church History* and *Landmarks of History*. She gave large sums to schools and to church and missionary work throughout the world.

YON'KERS, N. Y., in Westchester County, on the east bank of the Hudson River and on the New York Central Railroad, fifteen miles from the New York City terminal. It is beautifully located on gradually-rising ground, opposite the Palisades, with several fine residential sections. Yonkers has four and one-half miles of deep waterfront for ocean-going vessels, administered by the Port of New York Authority. It is an important industrial and commercial center. Hats have been manufactured here since 1840 and elevators since 1854; other products are chemicals, machinery, sugar products and carpets. Important buildings include the Boyce Thompson Institute for Plant Research, founded here in 1924, and Hollywood Inn, a pioneer club for workingmen, built in 1894. Of historic interest is the Philipse Manor House, dating from 1682; the original home of the Philipse family, it now houses the Hudson River Museum.

Yonkers was settled by the Dutch about 1650. From 1672 to 1788, when the township of Yonkers was organized, it was part of Philipse Manor. During the Revolution Washington's forces occupied it for a time. The settlement was called Philipsburg until its incorporation in 1855 as the village of Yonkers. In 1872 the northern part of the township was chartered as the city of Yonkers; the southern part was later annexed to New York City. Population, 1940, 142,598.

YORK, ENGLAND, county town of Yorkshire, situated on the River Ouse at its confluence with the Foss, 175 miles northwest of London. It is the seat of the York Cathedral, one of the finest Gothic structures in the world, and has many relics and reminders of early and medieval English history. The old city is surrounded by massive stone walls, and has narrow, irregular streets. A beautiful modern suburb has been built on the opposite bank of the Foss. The city's industries include flax spinning and the weaving of linen, iron founding, construction of railway cars, and the manufacture of gloves, combs, glass, etc. There is a thriving river trade. The railway station is one of the finest in Great Britain. Population, 1911, 82,282; in 1921, 84,052.

YORK, PA., the county seat of York County, ninety-six miles west of Philadelphia, on Codorus Creek and on the Pennsylvania, the Western Maryland and the Maryland & Pennsylvania railroads. It is situated in a rich and beautiful agricultural valley, of which it is the commercial center. Its diversified industries include printing and the manufacture of machinery of various types, bank safes and vaults, paper products, pianos, furniture, pottery products, stained glass windows, fertilizer, lime, cement and cigars. York County Academy, now combined with the York Collegiate Institute, a private college preparatory school, was founded at York in 1787; Thaddeus Stevens (which see) once taught here.

York was settled by Germans in 1734; in 1641 the town was laid out. At the approach of Gen. Howe's forces, the Continental Congress withdrew from Philadelphia to York, where it met from September 28, 1776, to June 27, 1777. York was incorporated as a borough in 1787 and chartered as a city in 1887. It adopted the commission form of government. Population, 1940, 56,712.

YORK, HOUSE OF, a royal family of England, which attempted in the Wars of the Roses to wrest the crown from the Lancastrian House, as represented by the king, Henry VI (see ROSES, WARS OF THE). The Yorkists had, indeed, the superior claim, as Richard, Duke of York, was descended from a third son of Edward III, while Henry VI was descended from a fourth son. Richard died in 1460, and his son continued the struggle; after a short time he was crowned king as Edward IV. With the exception of a short interval, Edward was king until 1483, and after his death his son was crowned king as Edward V. Richard, Duke of Gloucester, the brother of Edward IV, killed his royal nephew and was made king, but was overthrown by Henry Tudor (Henry VII), Earl of Richmond, the head of the Lancastrian House, who united the claims of the two families by marrying Elizabeth, the daughter of Edward IV.

YORKTOWN, VA., the county seat of York County, seventy miles southeast of Richmond. It has filled large space in American history on two occasions. In 1781, in the Revolutionary War, it was fortified by Cornwallis and was captured by American arms only after a siege lasting from August to October. On April 5, 1862, in the Civil War, McClellan, in command of 95,000 Federal soldiers, began a siege of the place, then strongly held by 55,000 Confederates. It capitulated on May 4. The population is now only about 500.

YOSEMITE, *yo sem' e te,* **NATIONAL PARK AND VALLEY,** one of the most magnificent scenic areas of the American Continent.

Yosemite National Park, a section of the world's "enchanted lands," lies in the central part of California, just west of the Sierra Nevada Mountains. It has an area of a little over 1,100 square miles, and includes the famous Yosemite Valley, the Tuolumne Valley and three groves of sequoias, or California Big Trees.

Yosemite Valley. This valley, which has been aptly described as a "mere crack in the rocks," is one of the most famous of the world's regions. The valley was formed by the Merced River and by glacial action. It is seven miles long, and from one-fourth of a mile to a mile wide. The floor of the valley is a flat meadow carpeted with flowers, and from its sides rise vertical cliffs to heights varying from 3,000 to 6,000 feet. The most widely-known of the great summits guarding the valley are Cathedral Rocks, 2,500 feet; El Capitan, 3,600 feet; Sentinel Dome, 4,100 feet; Half Dome, 4,900 feet, and Cloud's Rest, 6,000 feet.

Over the sides of these cliffs numerous rivers rush headlong to the valley below, forming some of the highest and most beautiful waterfalls in the world. Among them are Yosemite Falls, which drop 1,430 feet in a single fall; Lower Yosemite, immediately below, with a fall of 320 feet; Vernal, 320 feet; Nevada Falls, 600 feet; the celebrated Bridal Veil, 620 feet, and the Ribbon Falls, 1,612 feet. This is one of the highest single falls in the world. These falls are at their best in May and June, when the winter snows are melting. Mirror Lake, in whose waters a remarkable reflection of the surrounding mountains may be seen, is another attractive feature of the valley.

Yosemite Valley is about 150 miles nearly east of San Francisco, and may be reached from Merced on the Santa Fé and Southern Pacific railroads, and by the Yosemite Valley Railroad, which extends to the western border of the park. From the railway terminus stages take tourists through the valley. The roads are good, and during the tourist season, from May 1 to November 1, hotel and camp accommodations are ample. The park is free to all, and anyone is at liberty to provide his own transportation and to travel at his pleasure, subject to such rules as are necessary for the protection of the scenery. From Yosemite Valley roads lead to Mariposa and other groves of Big Trees and to Tuolumne Valley.

Yosemite Valley was discovered in 1851 by a party in pursuit of a band of Indians, who made it their hiding place, supposing it to be inaccessible to white men. In 1864, by act of Congress, it was granted to California for a state park, upon condition that it should be kept for the use of the public and that its scenery should never be injured. The Mariposa grove of big trees, adjoining the valley, was also granted the state at the same time. Since 1890 it has been known as the Yosemite National Park. The most desirable months in which to visit the valley are June, July and the early part of August. Later in the season a number of the streams become dry, and their falls disappear.

YOSHIHITO, *yosh i he'toh,* HARUNOMIA (1879-1926), emperor of Japan, succeeded to the throne on the death of his father, Mutsuhito, July 29, 1912. He was educated at Tokyo, and spoke fluently French, English and German. He was simple and direct in his manner and speech, and his policy was progressive. Much tact and discretion have been shown by him as a harmonizing influence between the traditions and ideals of old Japan and the up-to-date ideas of the Western world, with which Japan must keep abreast to maintain its position as a world power. The emperor's personal taste inclined toward outdoor sports, and he was a lover of dogs and horses. In 1900 he married his cousin, Princess Sada-Ko, and had three children, the oldest, Hirohito, succeeding him on his death in December, 1926.

YOUNG, *yung,* BRIGHAM (1801–1877), the sucessor of Joseph Smith as president of the Church of Jesus Christ of Latter-Day Saints. His father was a Vermont farmer, and he himself learned the trades of painter and glazier. Early in life he joined the Baptists, but was converted to Mormonism and joined the sect at Kirtland, Ohio, in 1832. In 1835 he was ordained one of the Council of Twelve Apostles. When the sect began to be persecuted Young and Smith selected Nauvoo, Ill., as the site for a new colony. On the death of Joseph Smith, in 1844, Young was unanimously chosen president.

When the Mormons were expelled from Nauvoo he led them through toils and dangers over the plains and tablelands to the splendid valley where, between the Wasatches and the Great Salt Lake, he founded, in July, 1847, the settlement which became Salt Lake City. The Mormons organized their territory into a state, and Young became governor. Later, difficulties arose with the Federal government and President Buchanan appointed a territorial governor to succeed Young. He continued ruler of his sect until his death in 1877. He was a man of strong character, remarkable foresight and unusual executive ability.

YOUNG, CHARLES AUGUSTUS (1834–1907), an American astronomer, who graduated at Dartmouth in 1853 and after teaching at Phillips Academy, Andover, in 1856 became professor of natural philosophy and mathematics in the Western Reserve College, Ohio. In 1877 he was appointed professor of astronomy and natural philosophy at Princeton, after serving in the same capacity at Dartmouth. Young made the first observation of the spectrum of the solar corona (the luminous envelopes of the sun) in August, 1869, and later he made many other important observations. He gave his assistance to the eclipse observations in Iowa in 1869, in Spain in 1870, in Denver in 1878, and was one of the party who studied the transit of Venus at Peking in 1874. He was one of the foremost authorities on the subject of spectra. *The Sun, General Astronomy, Elements in Astronomy* and *Lessons in Astronomy* are among his publications, which include also textbooks and papers on miscellaneous scientific subjects.

YOUNG, EDWARD (1683–1765), an English poet, born at Upham, Hampshire. His earliest large work was *Busiris,* a tragedy written in 1719. This was followed by *Revenge* and a group of satires entitled *The Love of Fame, the Universal Passion.* He took holy orders, and in 1730 became rector of a church at Welwyn in Hertfordshire. Young is chiefly remembered for his *Night Thoughts of Life, Death and Immortality,* a religious poem containing numerous pointed verses which have become axiomatic.

YOUNG, OWEN D. (1874–   ) an American lawyer and financier. He was born at

Van Hornesville, N. Y. His education was gained at Saint Lawrence University and Boston University law school. In 1896 he began the practice of law in Boston. He was a law partner of Charles H. Tyler, but in 1912 he broke the connection to become chief legal adviser for the General Electric Company; later he became vice-president and in 1922 he was chosen as president of the board of directors.

He served at later dates in several important posts: head of the Radio Corporation of America, director of the Federal Reserve Bank of New York, of the General Motors Corporation, of the International General Electric Company, chairman of the American section of the International Chamber of Commerce, a member of the second industrial conference appointed by President Wilson, and chairman of the committee on business cycles appointed by President Harding.

Probably his most distinguished service was given to the matter of reparations that were to be paid by Germany to the victorious allies. He was a member of the "Dawes Committee" appointed in 1923, and was summoned as agent-general to supervise the execution of the plan contained in the report of the commission. Later he resigned this position, but was chosen chairman of a new commission charged to fix the amount of payment that should be demanded of Germany. By June 1929 the new plan was completed; it involved laying aside several important features of the Dawes plan to make way for the Bank of International Settlements.

YOUNG MEN'S CHRISTIAN ASSOCIATION, or the "Y. M. C. A." an international alliance of organizations in thirty-three countries; each organization is made up of local societies.

The object is to promote character education through informal activities based upon the voluntary interest of the member. Associations seek the physical, intellectual, social and religious development of youth so that they may embody Christian ideals and seek for the realization of Christian principles in society.

George Williams organized the first association in London in 1844. In 1851 groups of young men in Boston and Montreal took up the movement and immediately it began to spread throughout the country. The cen tral committee supervised these activities beginning with 1866.

Buildings with dormitory facilities, gymnasiums and other social and educational equipment are characteristic of the city associations; but s m a l l town and country associations, high school and college associations and certain others carry on non-equipment activities.

Individual services include personal counseling, part-time educational activities, job placements, dormitory residence and other needed assistance.

The association movement has had its largest development in North America where are to be found more than one-half of the total members, two-fifths of the buildings and two-thirds of the employed secretaries.

In the entire United States there are about 1,200 associations with nearly 1,000,-000 members. Among the members 65 per cent are over 18 years of age. More than half of the activities of the associations are carried on in the cities. The headquarters of both the national and international work is in New York City.

During the World War at government request the associations sent out 20,000 special workers among the nation's armed forces at home and abroad.

The "Y" has become a fixed part of American culture and a prominent institution among the organizations operating for the public welfare. It renders a service that has inspired similar organizations among non-Protestants.

Extension work in foreign lands at one time required the labors of about 250 secretaries sent out by the international committee; four-fifths of the foreign associations have now become self-supporting with but 8 per cent of their leadership supplied from the United States.

YOUNGSTOWN, OHIO, the county seat of Mahoning County, sixty-seven miles southeast of Cleveland, on both sides of the Mahoning River, and on the Erie, the Baltimore & Ohio, the Pennsylvania and the New York Central railroads. There is regular service from the fine municipal airport eleven miles north of the city. Iron, coal and limestone are found in the vicinity. Youngstown is one of the great steel centers of the United States, manufacturing a variety of iron and steel products. The gates of the Panama Canal were made here.

Youngstown College was founded in 1927. Other important institutions include Stambaugh Auditorium and the Butler Art Gallery. Mill Creek Park, nearly 2,000 acres in extent, is regarded as the most beautiful natural park in the state of Ohio. The first settlement was made in 1796 on a tract of land purchased by John Young in that year from the Connecticut Land Company (see WESTERN RESERVE). It was incorporated as a city in 1848 and became the county seat in 1876. David Tod, the "war governor" of Ohio, was a pioneer at Youngstown in coal-mining, canal and railway enterprises. Population, 1940, 167,720.

YOUNG WOMEN'S CHRISTIAN ASSOCIATION, a voluntary organization of women and girls who are convinced of the supreme importance of the Christian way of living. It was organized in London in 1855; three years later the first association was organized in the United States. Fifty different countries are represented in the international organization; headquarters is in Geneva, Switzerland.

In the United States there are over 1,000 local organizations; more than half of them are found in the colleges and universities; 168 organizations serve foreign communities, Indians and Negroes. Members number about 400,000. American headquarters is in New York City.

YOUTH MOVEMENTS, a term applied to group activities of persons usually aged fourteen to twenty-five who in many countries are seeking readjustment to present-day conditions. The phrase does not denote a planned campaign managed from international headquarters, but refers to outbreaks of youthful enthusiasm and eagerness to take part in the affairs of society.

German Movements. In Germany about 1908 there occurred a revolt against social trends that seemed fruitless and antiquated. Young people discovered that the schools stood apart from practical life; that parents were dominating and very conservative; that judgments passed on young people by adults were trivial and beside the mark. Consequently there arose a cry for release and liberty. Hence sprang up the wandering bands of young persons, and lodging-places were opened for these travelers. Finally came the recognition of the youths of Germany as a powerful and insistent social group.

The earlier period of the movement was largely an emotional outburst; later on an intellectual trend set in. Organized groups of youths met in a great conference at Cassel in 1913, but war reduced their numbers from 12,000 to 7,000.

The consequences may be summed up as follows: an increased simplicity in living that touched dress, food and the like; wide acquaintance through travel and culture, through study and recreation; the union of the younger, the older and the matured young people in one organization; an increased comradeship between the sexes; education conducted by comrade-leaders; a strong sense of the moral value in the search for truth and a religious faith in the good in life.

Swiss and Russian Movements. In Switzerland the demand for greater freedom was very urgent, but the young people took their parents along with them instead of revolting against domestic influence. They scorned the philosophies of antiquity and bent their gaze on the things of today; there was some indifference to the churches but not to religion.

In both Switzerland and Germany the movement changed in the course of its growth, and yet it forced readjustments in the old educational and social programs.

In Russia 5,000,000 boys and girls, and young men and women, belong to the *Consomol,* the official, organized movement. The Soviets dominate the whole policy and use the institution as a means of training in politics and economics. New importance has been attached to cleanliness, neatness, stability of the family, education and a general attitude such as prevails in Western Europe; in fact the youth movement of Russia is changing certain aspects of Russian policy in a remarkable degree.

American Movements. In the U n i t e d States, when 3,000,000 persons aged 16-25 are neither in school nor at work a development of the youth movement is to be expected. Not content with a cynical and defeated state of mind young leaders have sprung up with a call to action. "The National Youth Movement" began at a fireside conference of three persons and finally enrolled thousands after applying fusion methods in an attack on the politicans of Kansas City. The Seattle Movement seemed at one time about to seize the political power of the state. (The "Young Republicans" of New York State formed political study clubs.)

The "National Conference of Students in Politics" is composed of eleven liberal, radical, pacifist and religious college organizations; it opposes the training of reserve officers, race discrimination and cutting of educational privileges. The "National Student League" is communistic; The "League for Industrial Democracy" follows Norman Thomas. The "National Student Federation" is made up of campus politicians with a middle-of-the-road viewpoint, but critics discern a fascist leaning.

"The First American Youth Congress" assembled in August, 1934. Communists were denied leadership and the following proposals were indorsed: Federal expenditures for education, unification of school curricula, sex-education, reform of divorce laws, opposition to war, social insurance, a system of youth lodging-places, a Federal apprentice plan and assistance in establishing homes.

YPRES, *é pr',* BELGIUM, a partly ruined city around which were waged three sanguinary battles of the World War. Although left almost wholly unrestored, as a war memorial, some of the historic buildings have been repaired or reconstructed. The beautiful cathedral of Saint Martin, dating from the thirteenth century, has been repaired. The famous Belfry of Ypres was reconstructed in 1934 and restored to its former sculptural beauty. Before the war Ypres had a population of 19,000.

YSAYE, *e zah'ye,* EUGENE (1858-1931), a Belgian violinist, born at Liége. He was taught by his father, an able violinist, who in time sent him to the Liége conservatory. Subsequently he studied under great masters of the violin. He showed such promise that the state helped him to complete his studies at Paris. In 1881 he began the concert tours which were to reveal him to the world as one of its foremost violinists. Five years later he became director of the violin department of the Brussels conservatory, where he organized the famous Ysaye quartet. He retired in 1898 to devote all his time to concert work. Ysaye's playing was characterized by a sound and brilliant technique and a rich, full tone having an infinite variety of shading. He wrote a number of compositions for the violin; among them are the well known six concertos and his "Suite Wallone." He was for a time conductor of the Cincinnati orchestra, beginning in 1918.

YUAN SHI KAI (1858–1916), Chinese statesman, first president of China. Li Hung Chang observed his powers as a military leader and placed him in civil office. He rose rapidly, became a reformer and yet supported the monarchy. He was the chief executive in the republic that displaced the empire; but his ambition to become emperor was defeated by mutinies, revolts and the intervention of the powers. He died in 1916 from poisoning, as reported. See CHINA, subhead *History*.

YUCATAN, *yoo kah tahn'*, a peninsula constituting the extreme southeastern part of Mexico and embracing the territory of Quintana Roo, the states of Campeche and Yucatan, and small parts of British Honduras and Guatemala. It projects northward between the Gulf of Mexico and the Caribbean Sea; it is smaller than West Virginia, with an area of 23,926 square miles.

Physical Features. The coast on the west and north is sandy and flanked with low sand dunes. On the east there are bluffs, and several islands off shore. Beneath the surface soil is a vast bed of coraline limestone; from this the thin and now infertile soil has been developed through weathering processes. The climate is hot and dry, with an annual rainfall insufficient for extensive agriculture on the uplands. Cool sea-winds and the "northers" modify the intense heat throughout its entire area.

Products. On the coast lands valuable forests provide mahogany, vanilla, logwood and other dye-woods. Field products are maize, sugar cane, cotton, coffee, tobacco and the principal crop of henequen from which sisal hemp is manufactured. Here is the world's chief source of sisal hemp, of which as much as 200,000,000 pounds have been exported in one year.

History. It appears that Yucatan had one of the oldest civilizations in the Western world. The Mayas, driven by hostile forces, discovered and entered the peninsula between A. D. 471 and A. D. 530 in a series of invasions, but their civilization had been developing for at least a thousand years. The great exodus from their empire in central Mexico resulted in the forming of city-states in Yucatan; three of these larger ones established an alliance that led to great prosperity. Huge stone buildings with extensive sculptured decorations were built everywhere. Pyramid temples appeared in towns and even villages. In 1201 the alliance broke down from internal rivalry and with the aid of Toltec-Aztec allies. These newcomers assumed leadership and introduced rites and customs which required building of temples for the new gods. The Kukulcan temple for example was erected for this purpose; it covers an acre of ground and reaches to the height of 100 feet. Ceremonies attracted worshippers who lived hundreds of miles away.

The Mayan buildings, which extensive excavations have brought to light, have become world-famous; they include pyramids, temples, altars, palaces and dwellings. No mortar was used; the corners were not bonded; hence vegetation easily entered the cracks and wrecked such structures.

These early Mayans used maize as the principal food. They engaged in hunting, trapping, fishing, bee-keeping and poultry-raising. They carried on also quarrying, weaving and pottery. Little use was made of metals, but copper was employed to some extent. Gold came into use in later centuries.

The first Europeans to reach Yucatan were twenty shipwrecked Spaniards who were captured in 1511 or 1512. Slave hunters arrived in 1517. Cortez passed through in 1524. By 1552 the Spaniards were in full control of the country, and even resisting some of the avaricious conquerors among their own number who sought to exploit the natives. The population reported in 1700 was 300,000; wars, famines and disease did not for a long time diminish this native population.

Mexico became independent of Spain in 1821. Yucatan joined immediately in the movement to set up a republic, but her relations to the central government were fast and loose until 1854. Under Diaz misery fell upon the masses and Yucatan suffered with other districts. Leaders have arisen and the two states of Campeche and Yucatan have shared in Mexico's political agitations and later development. Conditions have vastly improved since the Revolution beginning in 1910. Population nearly 400,000. See MAYA and MEXICO.

YUC'CA, a genus of plants belonging to the lily family, native of southern United States. A species known as *Bayonet plant*, or *Adam's needle*, bears beautiful bell-shaped flowers and long stiff evergreen leaves.

It is a popular plant for a shrub border. The *Yucca gloriosa* has a two-foot stem, on the end of which grows a cluster of leaves, from which springs a flower stalk bearing numerous drooping bells, striped with purple. The bough fiber of the *Yucca glauca* is used by southwestern Indians in making baskets.

YUGOSLAVIA. See JUGO-SLAVIA.

YUKON RIVER, one of the largest rivers of North America and fifth in capacity in the world. It rises in the west central part of Yukon Territory, Canada, flows northward and northwestward into Alaska, then westward and southwestward, entering Bering Sea 60 miles southwest of Michael. Its total length is about 2,300 miles. It is fed by numerous streams which are the outlets of marshes and lakes. In some places the current is swift and the river is obstructed by rapids. Small steamers have descended these rapids, but those at White Horse form an impassable barrier to up-river steamers, so that the river is divided into two navigable sections, which are now connected by railway. However, the river is navigable for the whole course of 1,200 miles within Alaska and for 800 miles in Canada. During the open season steamers make regular trips as far as White Horse, and small boats go to Dawson, in the Canadian Yukon Territory.

YUKON TERRITORY, a political division of the Dominion of Canada, popularly called The Yukon. It is located in the extreme northwest between the North West Territories on the east and Alaska on the west. British Columbia bounds the territory on the south, and the Arctic Ocean is on the north. The sixtieth parallel forms the dividing line between the Yukon and British Columbia, and the 141st meridian (W.) the line between the territory and Alaska. The North West Territories and the Yukon are separated by the Rocky Mountains.

Having an area of 207,076 square miles, The Yukon is about one-half the size of Ontario, one-sixth the size of the North West Territories, and lacks about 59,000 square miles of being as large as Texas. Of the total area 1,730 square miles are water. The territory is irregularly triangular in shape, the broadest portion being the southern boundary, and the narrowest the Arctic shore line. In 1901 during the gold-mining boom the population was 27,219; this declined to 4,687 by 1941. Dawson is the capital and chief town; population, about 820.

Physical Features. In general the surface of the territory is a rolling plain diversified by mountains and river valleys. The average elevation is from 2,000 to 3,000 feet, but in the extreme southwest, near the Alaska border, Mount Logan towers 19,539 feet above the sea. It is the highest peak in Canada, and next to Mount McKinley is the highest in North America. There are several other peaks in this region which are from 15,000 to 18,000 feet in altitude. Branches of the Yukon River traverse the territory over most of its area, but the southeastern corner is drained by the Liard River, which belongs to the Mackenzie River system. The line of perpetual snow is at 4,000 feet altitude. Vegetation flourishes during a short season.

Resources and Industries. Gold is by far the most valuable resource of the Yukon. In 1896 rich deposits were discovered in the Klondike, near the Alaska boundary, and when the fact became known thousands of prospectors flocked to the district to make their fortunes. In 1900, when the boom was at its height, gold to the value of $22,275,000 was taken from the mines. After the exhaustion of the placer deposits, more expensive methods of mining were introduced, which caused a marked decline in yield and in the population of the region. The yearly output is now valued at about $5,000,000. As much as 2,839,633 ounces of silver have been produced in a year. The lignite and anthracite coal deposits have been developed for local use. Home requirements are partially met in farming, gardening and manufacturing. The chief grains are barley and rye. The summers are very short and frosts occur throughout the year, but these disadvantages are somewhat offset by the long summer days; at Dawson the longest days have about twenty hours of daylight.

Government. Before the discovery of gold in the Yukon, the territory was inhabited only by a few Indians, but the sensational finds in the Klondike brought in as many as 30,000 settlers in one year. Parliament organized a government to meet the requirements of the population. The Territory is now governed by a comptroller responsible to the Canadian Department of the Interior, and sends one representative to the Dominion House of Commons.

Related Articles. Consult the following titles for additional information:

Alaska
Dawson
Klondike
Yukon River

Z, the twenty-sixth and last letter of the English alphabet, occupying the same position as in Latin. It is derived, through the Greek and Latin, from the Phoenician alphabet, in which, however, it was the seventh character. In English *z* was little used before the fifteenth century. It is properly a double consonant, compounded of *d* and *s*, but it has acquired the pronunciation of the hard terminal *s*. *S* or *ss* is, indeed, frequently used in place of *z*, as in *choose, dissolve.*

ZAMBE′ZI, a river of Southern Africa, which rises in the eastern part of Angola, where it is formed by the union of several smaller streams, generally known as the Seven Springs. It flows southward, eastward, northeastward and then southeastward, finally entering the Mozambique Channel through a number of delta arms. For a part of its course it forms the boundary between Northern Rhodesia and Southwest Africa. Its upper course is through an expanse of country clothed with grass and forest. After entering Rhodesia it plunges over a precipice nearly 400 feet high, forming the celebrated Victoria Falls (see VICTORIA FALLS). Below the falls the river has a winding course of about eighty miles through a deep canyon, with almost perpendicular banks. In its lower course it flows through a low, open country.

Its entire length is about 1,650 miles. It is navigable for large steamers to the first series of rapids, 400 miles from the sea. Above this point another section is navigable to Zumbo, on the western border of Portuguese East Africa. Several lines of steamers ply regularly upon the river, and the Cape-to-Cairo railway crosses it on a magnificent steel bridge erected just below Victoria Falls. The Zambezi is the fourth river in Africa in size and, together with its tributaries, exceeds 4,000 miles in length. The first European to see the river was Livingstone, who reached it in 1854.

ZANESVILLE, *zaynz′vil,* OHIO, the county seat of Muskingum County, sixty miles east of Columbus, on the Muskingum River, at the mouth of the Licking, and on the Baltimore & Ohio, the Pennsylvania, the New York Central and the Wheeling & Lake Erie railroads. The surrounding country contains deposits of limestone, clay and coal. The rivers furnish good water power; and there are potteries, sheet mill plants, railroad shops, flour mills and factories producing glass products, tile, cement, radiators, boxes and barrels, shoes and other articles. The tile plant is one of the largest in the world.

A concrete Y-shaped bridge crosses the two rivers on which the city is built. Other important structures are the Art Institute, a home for aged women and the birthplace of Zane Grey, the novelist. The town was founded by Jonathan Zane and John McIntire in 1799, and was named for Ebenezer Zane, who laid out Zane's Trace, a mile-square tract from which the present city has developed. Zanesville was the capital of the state from 1810 to 1812; it was incorporated in 1814. Population, 1940, 37,500.

ZANG′WILL, ISRAEL (1864-1926), a British miscellaneous writer, born in London, of Jewish parentage. He was educated at the Jews' Free School, Spitalfields, London. His lectures in England, Ireland and the United States brought him prominently before the public, and he became a leader in the Zionist Movement (which see). His writings include essays, dramas, novels and humorous sketches; he is particularly clever in depicting Jewish life and character. Early Jewish studies are *Children of the Ghetto* and *Ghetto Tragedies. Dreamers of the Ghetto* contains sketches of great Jewish thinkers. *The Mantle of Elijah, They That*

Walk in Darkness and *Ghetto Comedies* are among his other writings. His most successful plays are *Merely Mary Ann* and *The Melting Pot*.

ZANZIBAR, *zahn ze bahr'*, an island off the eastern coast of Africa, forming a part of the British protectorate of Zanzibar. Its area is 640 square miles, and it is mostly low, the highest point being only 1,000 feet above the sea. The island is fertile and well cultivated. Cloves, copra, tobacco, vanilla, cocoa-nuts and other crops are grown. Fishing and cattle raising are important industries. The population of the protectorate, 236,000, includes Arabs, Persians and representatives of most of the native tribes of Eastern Africa. There are only a few Europeans. Mohammedanism is the chief religion.

Zanzibar, the capital and chief town of the island, contains the palaces of the sultan, the barracks, the fort, hospitals and a number of mission stations. It is an important port in the Eastern trade and has some manufactories. Population, 1931, 45,276.

The nominal head of the government is a native sultan, under British protection. The island is administered by British officials.

ZEALAND, *ze'land*, the largest and most easterly island belonging to Denmark, containing Copenhagen, the capital and largest city of the kingdom. It is situated between the peninsula of Jutland and Sweden, and its outline is very irregular. The greatest length from north to south is eighty miles, its greatest breadth is sixty-five miles, and the area is 2,680 square miles. Most of the island is low, the greatest elevation not exceeding 400 feet. The land is covered with forests or fertile fields.

ZE'BRA, a wild animal of South Africa, closely related to the wild ass and the horse, and having habits similar to those of the latter. It is gray- ish or cream-white in color, and is con- spicuously marked with dark stripes on head, legs and body. In Africa zebra-hunting is a popular sport. The natives eat the flesh and use the hides for leather and as

ZEBRA

rugs. Until comparatively recent times great herds of zebras were common in Southern

Africa; to-day the animals are rare, for they are victims of white and native hunters. They may be domesticated and made to accept the harness, but training is difficult.

ZE'BU, a species of ox, a native of India, whence it has spread into Persia, Arabia and Eastern Africa. It is used as a beast of burden, for plowing and hauling. The animal is remarkable for a convex forehead, short horns, large drooping ears and a fatty hump on the back. It is very gentle and docile.

ZEBU

Zebus vary greatly in size, the smallest being no larger than a large dog, while others are the size of a large ox. The colors vary. The white zebu bulls are regarded as sacred among the Hindus (who call them *brahmany*) and are allowed a free range. Zebus have been imported to Jamaica and Central America for use on farms.

ZEB'ULUN, one of the twelve tribes of Israel, named, according to Genesis XXX, 20, after the sixth son of Jacob and Leah. The name was also given to a country in Northern Palestine.

ZECHARIAH, *zek a ri'ah*, son of Berechiah, son of Iddo, appeared as a prophet in Jerusalem, along with Haggai, in the second year of Darius Hystaspes (520 B. C.), encouraging the Jews to commence the restoration of the Temple.

ZEDEKI'AH, last king of Judah, the son of Josiah, and successor of Jehoiachim. He broke his oath of allegiance to Nebuchadnezzar and united with Egypt against him. He was made captive when Nebuchadnezzar conquered Jerusalem in 586 B. C., his sons were killed in his presence, and he was taken a prisoner to Babylon, where he died. The name was borne also by two false prophets.

ZEISLER, FANNY BLOOMFIELD. See BLOOMFIELD-ZEISLER, FANNY.

ZEMST'VO, the governing body of a province or district in Russia before the revolution

ZENANA 3940 ZEUXIS

of 1917. It was composed of representatives chosen by the peasants, the householders of the towns and the landed proprietors. This body was presided over by the president of the nobility of the district or province, and it was charged with the administration of economic affairs. The executive power of the zemstvo was entrusted to an *upraba,* elected by the assembly. See RUSSIA.

ZENANA, *ze nah'nah,* among the Hindus that part of the house set apart for women. In Bengal the women occupy a separate building behind that of the men; the rooms open upon an inner court, and the inmates are entirely separated from the outside world. In 1855 Protestant missionaries organized the Zenana Mission for the purpose of alleviating the conditions of zenana inmates.

ZEND-AVES'TA, the sacred book of the Parsees, a religious sect of India, followers of Zoroaster. It contains songs of praise, prayers, the liturgy and a priestly code. It was first translated in 1771 by Anquetil-Duperron, a French scientist.

ZE'NITH, a term used in astronomy to indicate the point in the heavens directly overhead. It is opposite of nadir (which see).

ZE'NO, the founder of the Stoic school of philosophy, was born of a merchant family of Citium, in Cyprus, about the middle of the fourth century B. C., and is said to have lived about eighty years. According to tradition, he was shipwrecked and went to Athens, where he first read the works of Socrates' disciples. He studied Cynic doctrine, then turned to Stilpo, later to the teachings of Xenocrates and of Polemo. He then founded at Athens a school of philosophy in what was called the "Painted Porch," where he is said to have taught fifty-eight years. He practiced and taught temperance and virtue and was much esteemed by his fellow citizens, who erected a bronze monument to his memory after his death. See STOICISM.

ZENO'BIA, queen of Palmyra, Arabia, who succeeded to the throne as regent for her son, on the murder of her husband, Odenathus, in A. D. 267. She aimed at a dominion which should include Egypt, Syria and Asia Minor, and should make good her title of "Queen of the East." Her ambitions clashed with Rome, and in 272 her armies were defeated by those of Aurelian. She was taken captive to Rome, but the emperor was so impressed with her beauty and elevation of character that he gave her a villa on the Tiber, and Zenobia's daughters were married into noble Roman families.

ZEPHANIAH, *zef a ni'ah,* a Hebrew prophet, who flourished in the reign of Josiah, 600 B. C. His book of three chapters, the ninth of the Minor Prophets, predicts the desolation of Judea, as a punishment for idolatry and worldliness.

ZEPPELIN, *tsep e leen',* COUNT FERDINAND (1838–1917), a celebrated aeronaut, born in Constance, Germany. He was educated at the Polytechnical School in Stuttgart and at the military school at Ludwigsburg. In the Franco-German War he was promoted to the rank of lieutenant-general. After many experiments with dirigible balloons, of which he was the inventor, he made his first flight from Berne to Lucerne in 1892. After this he made numerous models and improvements and in 1913 constructed a passenger airship which traveled from Baden-Baden to Vienna in eight hours, half the time required for the trip by train. A Zeppelin designed for trans-oceanic travel exploded in mid-air in 1913, destroying all on board. Zeppelins were much used in the World War, but did not fulfill the expectations of their makers as vehicles for bombing or scouting expeditions, being outstripped for war purposes by the lighter and swifter aeroplane. See FLYING, STORY OF.

ZE'RO, in mathematics, a symbol (0) denoting the absence of quantity or value; also, the symbol of an infinitesimal quantity. The same term is used to represent the point from which measurement is recorded on a scale. It is also used on thermometers. In this connection, however, zero does not denote temperature. On centigrade thermometers it indicates the freezing point of water; on the Fahrenheit scale it indicates 32° below the freezing point. Entire absence of heat, scientists agree, is represented by a temperature of 273 degrees (C.) below zero. See THERMOMETER.

ZEUS, *zuse.* See JUPITER.

ZEUXIS, *zuke'sis,* a famous Greek painter, probably born at Heraclea, on the Euxine, about 450 B. C. Time has effaced his masterpieces—*Hercules Strangling the Serpent, Jupiter among the Gods, Marsyas Bound, Pan and Helen*—which were the admiration of ancient critics. Zeuxis was a contemporary of the celebrated painter Parrhasius. See PAINTING.

ZINC, *zink,* or **SPEL'TER,** a metallic element, in appearance resembling lead but much harder than the latter metal and about one-third as heavy. At 212° it becomes malleable, at 302° it can be drawn out into fine wire. It is obtained from ores, and is one of the most useful metals known. The principal zinc ores are the carbonate, or *Smithsonite;* the oxide, or *zincite;* the hydrated silicate, or *calamine;* and the sulphide, or *sphalerite,* commonly called *zinc blende.* From the last most of the zinc of commerce is obtained. Deposits of zinc ore occur in most of the countries of Europe; in the United States the ores are found chiefly in Missouri, Kansas, New Jersey, Pennsylvania, Wisconsin, Tennessee and Arkansas. British Columbia is a source of supply. The Missouri and Kansas mines are the most important in America, producing about sixty per cent of the country's total annual output of 400,000 tons. Zinc is known in the trade as spelter.

Commercial zinc is produced chiefly by a smelting process. The ore is roasted; the oxide thus set free is heated with charcoal in earthen pipes, and the powder is reduced to a liquid in iron crucibles. Zinc is marketed in the form of sheets and small bars. It is employed in the arts, especially in the manufacture of brass, German silver and other alloys, and in making printing plates for etchings. It is also used in making the positive plates for electric batteries, in galvanizing iron sheets for roofing and iron wire for telegraphs; in lining tanks and in protecting woodwork from the heat of stoves.

Among the most important commercially of the compounds of zinc are *zinc chloride,* a compound of zinc and chlorine, used in medicine as a caustic, a disinfectant and a deodorizer. It is a preservative of timber, the chloride solution being forced under pressure into the pores of the wood. Railway ties are treated in this way. The same compound is also used to add weight to cotton goods. *Zinc sulphate,* formerly known as *white vitriol,* is a white powder used in dyeing and calico printing, in the manufacture of varnishes and drying oils, and in the preparation of zinc white (used in making white paint for interiors) and other zinc compounds.

ZINC ETCHING, a plate for the reproduction in printing of drawings or lettering in ink; also the process by which it is made, sometimes called the line-cut process. A photograph on glass is made of the drawing, and the negative, reversed, is clamped to a highly-polished plate of zinc which has been coated with wax or some other substance to protect it from the action of acid. The zinc plate is then subjected to electric light or to sunlight till the drawing is transferred to the sensitized surface, the lines are etched by means of a corrosive acid, and the plate is nailed to a block to make it the same height as type. Zinc etchings are quickly and inexpensively made, and for this reason are commonly used in the illustration of newspapers and many books. For the reproduction of photographs and other pictures, in which it is necessary to preserve the shading, the more complex halftone process must be used. See HALFTONE; PHOTOGRAPHY.

ZIN'NIA, a genus of plants belonging to the family Compositae. There are sixteen species, native to Mexico and the Southwestern United States. Zinnias bloom freely all summer, and thrive best in a rich loam with sunny exposure. The garden zinnia, with single and double flowers of many shades of red and yellow, is the best-known species. The stem is stiff and hairy, and grows to a height of one to two feet. Each of the several branches is topped by a single flower head made up of many florets. When successfully cultivated, the zinnia is a showy plant with vivid scarlet, crimson, yellow and other hues. It does not always turn out well, however, as the colors sometimes are muddy. The flowers lack pleasing fragrance.

ZI'ON. See JERUSALEM.

ZI'ONIST MOVEMENT, or **ZI'ONISM,** the most recent world movement among the Jews arising largely from persecutions of them in various countries and having as its object the reëstablishment of a Jewish state in Palestine. Ever since Jerusalem was wrested from the Jews by Rome (see JERUSALEM), the Hebrew people have hoped to recover this land of their early fathers, and at various times Zionist agitations have been set on foot.

By far the most significant of these was started in the last years of the nineteenth century. Unlike earlier Zionist movements which sought primarily to gain possession of the Holy City, the idea behind this one was practical and political, as well as religious, and was an attempt to solve the problem of persecuted Jews in many lands by finding a home for them where they might enjoy some form of self-government. This idea found expression in a pamphlet written in 1896 by Dr. Theodore Herzl, a Vienna journalist. Interest in the movement led to an international Zionist congress at Basel, Switzerland, in the following year.

The congress discussed means for obtaining governmental grants as a necessary preliminary to establishing settlements of Jews in Palestine. Subsequent congresses provided for the establishment of a national fund, and about $2,000,000 was collected from Jews throughout the world to promote the project. Negotiations were started with a view to making Palestine a tribute-paying state under the suzerainty of Turkey, and when the plan failed an attempt was made to secure a grant of territory from Great Britain in the vicinity of the Holy Land. This also was without fruition, and the offer by Great Britain in 1913, of the East Africa Protectorate as a site for a Jewish colony, was wrathfully rejected by the Jews, who refused to accept any nationalist plan which did not embrace the traditional idea of Palestine regained.

Within recent years the Zionist leaders have been chiefly interested in developing the physical resources of Palestine and in ameliorating the condition of Jews already there, as well as encouraging mass immigration. This has resulted in the emigration of many Russian and Rumanian Jews to Palestine and the establishment of self-governing colonies there. The way has been opened to promote agriculture and the trades. Schools began to flourish, and a banking system was inaugurated. The Hebrew language was revived. The World War stopped further immediate development; at that time Palestine contained about forty colonies, with a total population of about 55,000.

The outcome of the World War made the establishment of a Jewish state in Palestine a near possibility. In December, 1917, the British captured Jerusalem, and before the close of the war all Palestine had been freed from Turkish rule.

Early in 1918 a Zionist commission was sent from England to Palestine, the American Zionist organization providing most of the funds for its activities. A legion of Jewish young men from various countries was formed to aid the movement, all being volunteers.

Palestine remained under British military control until 1920, and was then placed under mandate to Great Britain, and a civil government was established. Under British protection, Jewish immigration has been fostered. The hostile Arab majority presents a grave problem, and is retarding progress. A Jewish city, Tel-Aviv, has grown to considerable size and importance (population, 46,116 in 1931).

ZIRCO'NIUM, a metallic element occurring either in the form of a black powder or as gray crystals. It was discovered in 1789 by Klaproth, in combination with silica, in the mineral known as zircon. Its use is very limited. The powder combined with oxygen forms the dioxide known as zirconia, used in making mantles of Welsbach lights and Nerst lamps.

ZITH'ER, a common, stringed musical instrument, especially popular in Germany and the Tyrol. About thirty gut and wirebound silk strings are arranged horizontally on a frame over a wooden sounding board. The instrument is placed on a table or on the knees. The strings are

ZITHER

plucked by the fingers of the right hand and with the thumb the latter capped with a metallic plectrum.

ZO'DIAC, the zone or belt of the celestial sphere extending eight degrees on each side of the ecliptic, or plane of the sun's center containing the earth's orbit. It was divided by early astronomers into twelve sections of thirty degrees each, and the constellations within the respective sections came to be designated, for brevity's sake, by certain signs.

The twelve signs of the zodiac are Aries (♈), the Ram; Taurus (♉), the Bull; Gemini (♊), the Twins; Cancer (♋), the Crab; Leo (♌), the Lion; Virgo (♍), the Virgin; Libra (♎), the Balance; Scorpio (♏), the Scorpion; Sagittarius (♐), the Archer; Capricornus (♑), the Goat; Aquarius (♒), the Waterman; Pisces (♓), the Fishes.

ZODI'ACAL LIGHT, a nebulous light which appears in the west after sunset and in the east before sunrise. It is triangular in shape, with base resting on the horizon and apex at varying heights. In the tropics it is visible the year round and is as distinct as the Milky Way. In middle latitudes it is seen in the winter and spring in the evening, and at dawn from September to spring. It is believed by some astronomers to be the reflection from a multitude of meteorites revolving about the sun.

ZOLA, *zo lah'*, EMILE (1840–1902), a noted French author. He had published several novels and won considerable notice before beginning, in 1869, his great series in twenty volumes, recounting the complete story of an imaginary French family under the Second Empire. The entire work is known as *The Chronicle of the Rougon-Macquart Family*. These books, like so many of Zola's other works, deal largely with the dark side of life, with crime and vice, and picture vividly and accurately certain phases of Parisian society. Some of the titles in the series are *The Fortune of Rougon, the Curée, The Conquest of Plassans, The Fault of Abbé Mouret* and *His Excellency Eugène Rougon*. Of his later works the most important were two series: *Lourdes, Rome, Paris* and *Fruitfulness, Labor, Truth* and *Justice*. The last was unfinished at his death.

Zola championed the cause of Captain Dreyfus, an officer in the French army unjustly accused of selling military secrets to Germany. In 1898, in the newspaper *Aurore,* he published a devastating exposé of the conspiracy which had ruined Dreyfus, in the form of a letter beginning *J'accuse*. A libel suit followed, and Zola found it expedient to leave the country. In 1899, after President Loubet had pardoned Dreyfus, Zola returned to Paris. His death occurred in 1902, four years before the complete vindication of the man who owed so much to him (see DREYFUS, ALFRED).

ZOLLVEREIN, *tsole'fe rine,* a German word meaning *customs-union,* is the name of a German commercial union formed under the leadership of Prussia, in 1818. At the beginning of the last century, Germany was made up of numerous small independent states, each with its own tariff regulations. This complicated system restricted commerce, and in 1818 an agreement was reached whereby internal customs were abolished. All import duties were collected on a common frontier, and the revenue thus received was divided among the several states according to population. Three unions were formed: the North German, the Middle German and the South German unions. In 1834 these were merged in a single union, or Zollverein. In 1871, when the German Empire was formed, the constitution provided that the Zollverein was to include the entire empire, with the exception of the free cities of Bremen and Hamburg. Later, these cities, too, with the exception of a part of Hamburg, were represented in the Zollverein.

ZONE, in geography, one of the five great divisions of the earth, bounded by imaginary circles, which are parallel to the equator. The zones are named according to the prevailing temperature in each. The torrid zone extends 23° 30′ north and 23° 30′ south of the equator, thus being 47° wide. It is bounded on the north by the Tropic of Cancer and on the south by the Tropic of Capricorn. The north temperate zone extends from the Tropic of Cancer to the Arctic Circle and is 43° wide. The south temperate zone extends from the Tropic of Capricorn to the Antarctic Circle and is of the same width as the north temperate zone. The north frigid zone extends from the Arctic Circle to the North Pole, and the south frigid zone from the Antarctic Circle to the South Pole. Although the parallels named mark the arbitrary boundaries of these zones, the climate of each merges so gradually into that of the zones adjoining upon either side, that no distinct climatic boundary exists between them.

Related Articles. Consult the following titles for additional information:

Antarctic Circle	Equator
Arctic Circle	Geography
Climate	Tropics

ZOOLOGICAL, *zo o loj'i cal,* **GARDEN,** or **ZOO,** a park or enclosure where living animals are kept for exhibition. The Jardin des Plantes, in Paris, founded in 1804, was the first of such establishments, and the number has increased steadily, until at present many of the large cities in Europe and the United States maintain zoölogical collections of some sort. The gardens at London, Antwerp, Berlin, Vienna and Amsterdam are among the best in Europe. Most of the European collections are maintained by societies or corporations, the city merely furnishing the land. In the United States many cities have municipal zoos, that at Bronx Park, New York City, being the largest and finest in the world. The zoos of Lincoln Park and Brookfield, Chicago, and Highland Park, Pittsburgh, are also important, and Philadelphia, Cincinnati and Washington have zoölogical gardens. The National Zoölogical Park at Washington is under the control of the Smithsonian Institution and is supported by the government.

ZOOLOGY, *zo ol'o jy.* We are all interested in animals, and like to watch them and to learn about their habits; but it does not often occur to us that such an interest has any connection with a science with so forbidding a name as zoölogy. And indeed zoölogy is much more than a knowledge of the looks and the habits of animals; in its various branches it considers the form and structure of organisms, their activities and their relations to one another and to their surroundings.

To be sure, one may be happy and prosperous and fairly well equipped mentally if zoölogy be never studied, but certain facts relating to this science should be known by everyone. An elementary knowledge of the subject will save one from frequent embarrassment. For instance, if the statement be made that a whale and a man belong to the same class of animals, the uninformed person may be tempted to deny the fact. The household cat and the lion, king of beasts, are related, and only a little study is required to trace the relationship and to learn why scientists so classify them.

The fact of these relationships has not always been known even to scientists; indeed, it is only in comparatively recent times that exact classifications of animal life have been made. Far back in ancient times, Aristotle made studies of animal life, dissected specimens, and made a certain classification, and his work stood for the most part unquestioned until after the Middle Ages. Some of it is accepted to-day, modern scientific investigation having confirmed the theories of the old Greek scholar.

Plants and Animals. The word *biology* means *science of life,* and the science of biology treats of all forms of life, plant and animal. The fact that this one science of life is composed of two distinct sciences, one of which—botany—treats of plants, while the other—zoölogy—treats of animals, indicates that the two forms of life are distinct. Indeed, it seems to be a very simple matter to distinguish members of the plant world from animals. Usually it is easy; a bee on a flower, an ox grazing in a field of grass, a moth fluttering on a blossom are instantly classified. But there are among plants some with very simple organisms and among the lowest species of animals some whose organisms are not in the least complex; to tell which is plant and which is animal is difficult indeed. One may say that the animal is alive and can move, while the plant, though alive, has no power of motion. This is an error, as witness the sudden closing of the Venus's fly-trap (which see), when it entraps its food, the turning of some flowers so they will continually face the sun, and the twining of tendrils around sticks and strings. Most green plants live on inorganic matter—on carbon and carbonic acid gas—and this is what gives them their greenness. But some plants, the fungi, live on organic matter and are not green, and exist because they are able in a wonderful manner to change the organic matter they select for food into inorganic substance. When a plant substance is single-celled and has cell walls in many respects like those of single-celled animals, it is impossible for the wisest scientist to tell them apart.

What All Animals Need. A fish that has been taken from the water and left high and dry on the shore will not live long; a cat or a bird or a man will die in even shorter time if held under water. This does not mean, however, that a fish and a land animal breathe different substances—that one breathes water and the other breathes air. They both require the same substance, and cannot live without it; that substance is air. But a fish is so formed that it draws the air it needs from the water, which a land animal cannot do. No animal, from the lowest to the highest, can live without air, or rather without that element of air which is called oxygen.

Relationships. Earlier in this discussion brief reference was made to some of the odd relationships that exist in the animal world. This is one of the most interesting topics with which zoölogy deals. The word *cat* ordinarily

THE DOG FAMILY
1. Saint Bernard. 2. Fox terrier. 3. Fox. 4. Coyote. 5. Wolf.

means to us the little animal, gray or white or black, which plays about our homes; but after we have made the acquaintance of this science, the word *cat* gains a new meaning. It means the powerful lion, the lithe tiger, the graceful leopard, the sharp-eyed lynx—all wild, ferocious beasts that seem as different as possible from the household pet which we are used to thinking of as the most domestic of the animals. (See illustration in the article CAT.)

The dog family is not so surprising. The wolf, the dog, the fox and the coyote look much alike, despite their numerous points of difference. If we can imagine ourselves as never having seen any of the animals before and then as being shown a wolf, a collie and a little black-and-tan, we will admit that we

should be likely to assume that the wolf and the collie were more closely related than the collie and the little terrier. We have all watched cattle and sheep grazing in a field, but it has probably never occurred to any of us to think of them as belonging to the same family. And yet a study of the picture of the ox family, shown in this article, reveals that goats, the African buffalo, the bison and the antelope belong with cattle and sheep to the same family.

The bobwhite is a plain little bird, dressed in quiet colors. Who would ever suspect for a moment that he belongs to the same family as the great bronze turkey or the gorgeous peacock? He may, however, claim such a relationship; and the guinea fowl, the partridge and our barnyard hens and roosters are members of the same family, together with the bird which has given its name to the whole group—the pheasant.

Resemblance. Among the most interesting of the many wonderful facts about the animal world with which zoölogy acquaints us is what is known as resemblance or mimicry. We have perhaps looked, in a zoölogical garden, at the bears—the grizzly bear, the cinnamon bear, the polar bear; and he ever be able to come close to his prey unobserved? But the polar bear harmonizes with his surroundings, and is almost unnoticeable against the white background. In the forest regions or mountain regions a white bear could be seen a long way off, while the darker-haired animals are much less conspicuous. The foxes and hares of the polar regions are pure white also, while a certain kind of weasel which lives in a region where

THE OX FAMILY

1. Cow. **2. Head of antelope.** **3. Rocky Mountain Goat.** **4. Sheep.** **5. African buffalo.** **6. Bison, or American buffalo.**

we have known that the polar bear came from the arctic regions where snow covers the ground during most of the year, while the other bears come from more temperate regions—regions of forest and rock and mountain. But probably it never occurred to us that there was any particular reason for the differences in color.

Let us imagine, in the region of perpetual snow, a bear creeping upon his prey. He is a huge bear, and stands out with startling distinctness against the white ground. Would snow covers the ground during only a part of the year changes from its summer coat of reddish brown to a winter coat of white. See FUR AND FUR TRADE.

There is one example of this changing of colors with which we are all familiar; that is in the little lizard which we call the chameleon. Its ability to make its color match that of its surroundings is commonly overestimated—it cannot change to any or every color; but it does grade through various shades of brown and green.

Questions on Zoölogy

NOTE—For additional questions on animal life refer to *Nature Study*. In that department will also be found interesting outlines on animals, birds, fish, insects, etc.

What is zoölogy?

What is the derivation of the term zoölogy?

What does "cold-blooded" signify when applied to animals?

What are the difficulties of classification in the case of the lowest forms of animal life?

What are the causes of the migratory habit of animals?

Which are the more abundant, the higher or lower forms of life? Why?

What animal is born without a covering? Why?

What are the most useful animals to man for domestic purposes?

What animals are known as ruminants?

What parts of the deer are of commercial value?

How are flesh-eating animals equipped to eat their food? To obtain it? They are satisfied with one meal at a time, eaten rapidly; why?

Why does live stock have to graze so continuously?

What is the difference between an animal and a plant?

Name some of the many ways in which nature has provided for the safety and preservation of wild animals?

What animals produce the most expensive furs?

What do you mean by vertebrates?

In general, what one part of wild animals is of commercial value?

Name the domestic animals in what you think to be the order of their usefulness.

Perhaps the most wonderful of these resemblances are shown among the insects. There is the insect known as the walking-stick, which, with its long, slender wingless body and its dull color looks so like a dead twig that when at rest it cannot be distinguished from the twigs to which it attaches itself; there is the greenleaf insect, which has broad, leaf-green wings, which show the veins, the markings and even the discolorations of leaves; and most wonderful of all, there is the huge dead-leaf butterfly. The upper side of this remarkable butterfly's wings are dark, with orange and purple markings; but when it settles on a branch to rest it folds its wings close over its back, hides its head, and looks so exactly like a withered leaf that even close scrutiny cannot always distinguish it. The dead-leaf color is there, the short tail which looks exactly like a leaf stalk, the midrib, the veins, and even the two colorless spots which resemble holes eaten out by insects.

There is one other type of resemblance or mimicry. This is seen in the case of the harmless, non-poisonous insects which imitate exactly in their color and markings certain poisonous insects which really differ from them widely. By this mimicry the harmless insects are saved from the birds which would otherwise devour them.

Protective Coloration and Mimicry. When we use the words mimicry and resemblance, we must constantly bear in mind one fact: that is, that there is no consciousness, no intention on the part of the mimic. The insect or animal does not voluntarily imitate.

The Struggle for Existence. If all the animals that are born were to live, in a very short time the earth would be crowded to suffocation. For instance, it is stated that if all the eggs laid by the conger-eel were hatched, and every little eel grew and reproduced itself, it would take less than ten years for the sea to become solidly full of conger-eels. It is clear that only a small proportion of the animals born survive. So fierce, indeed, is the struggle, that it is usually only by means of superior strength, cunning or agility or by means of some special protective device, such as the mimicry spoken of in the last paragraph or poisonous secretions, that animals can live and thrive. First there is the struggle within the species—fox fights against fox, and the stronger wins. Then there is the struggle with animals of other species, and finally with the conditions of life, or forces of nature. If in any given locality, only enough food exists for a certain number of animals, all above that number must starve or migrate. Innumerable birds, insects, fish, animals of all species die of starvation; many die from climatic condi-

THE PHEASANT FAMILY

1. Peacock.   2. Turkey.   3. Domestic hen and rooster.   4. Partridge.   5. Guinea fowl.
6. Bob white.   7. Golden pheasant.

tions; in settled parts of the country many are killed by man. By all of these means the animal population of the world is kept down. In most districts which are uninhabited, the number of a certain species of animals remains nearly constant; where man joins his destructive forces with those of Nature, the forms of wild life diminish rapidly.

Related Articles. Consult the following titles for additional information:

Amphibians (with list)	Invertebrates
Animal	Lamarck, Jean
Animal Intelligence	Baptiste
Arachnida	Linné, or Linnaeus
Arthropoda	Larva
Birds (with list)	Mammals (with list)
Carnivora	Marsupials
Cell	(with list)
Cephalopoda	Metamorphosis
(with list)	Mollusca (with list)
Cetacea (with list)	Molting
Chiroptera	Myriapoda
Coelenterata	Neuroptera
Crustacea (with list)	Orthoptera
Cuvier, George L.	Primates (with list)
Darwin, Charles	Protective Coloration
Echinoderms	and Mimicry
Edentata (with list)	Protoplasm
Egg	Protozoa
Evolution	Radiolaria
Feathers	Reptiles (with list)
Fish and Fisheries	Rodents
(with list)	Ruminants
Hemiptera	Scales
Hibernation	Ungulates
Horn	Vertebrata
Infusoria	Vorticella
Insectivora	Worms
Insects (with list)	Zoölogical Garden

Outline on Zoölogy. The following outline contains the classification of animals generally accepted by the leading authorities. This is a natural classification, based on similar structure and probable kinship. The large divisions are called *phyla.* Each phylum is divided into *classes;* and each class into *orders;* each order into *families;* each family into *genera;* and each genera into *species.* The eleven phyla generally recognized today are given; lower divisions are given only as examples, for identification.

I.   **Protozoa** (15,000 species; single-celled)
   (1) Sarcodina (moving by false feet)
      (a) Amoeba
   (2) Mastigophora (moving by means of flagella)
   (3) Sporozoa (having a spore stage)
   (4) Infusoria (moving by means of cilia)
      (a) Paramoecium

II. **Porifera** (3,000 species; the sponges)

III. **Coelenterata** (5,000 species; usually marine; radially symmetrical)
   (1) Hydrozoa (polyps)
      (a) Stinging coral
      (b) Portuguese man-of-war
   (2) Scyphozoa (large jellyfishes)
   (3) Anthozoa (polyp stage but no medusae)

(a) Sea anemone
(b) Stony coral
(c) Red coral; sea fan
(d) Sea feather

IV. **Ctenophora** (100 species; free-swimming marine animals; biradially symmetrical)
  (1) Sea walnuts or comb jellies

V. **Platyhelminthes** (6,500 species; flatworms)
  (1) Turbellaria (body covered with cilia)
  (2) Trematoda (parasites)
    (a) Liver fluke
  (3) Cestoda (parasites; no intestine)
    (a) Common tapeworm
  (4) Nemertinea (chiefly free-living; marine)

VI. **Nemathelminthes** (3,500 species; thread or round worms; chiefly free-living)
  (1) Nematoda (intestine; no proboscis)
    (a) Hookworm
    (b) Trichina
    (c) Pinworm
  (2) Acanthocephala (no intestine; proboscis)
    (a) Spineheaded worms (parasitic)

VII. **Echinodermata** (5,000 species; spiny-skinned; radially symmetrical marine animals)
  (1) Asteroidea (starfishes)
  (2) Ophiuroidea (brittle-stars)
  (3) Echinoidea (sea-urchins)
  (4) Holothurioidea (sea-cucumbers)
  (5) Crinoidea (sea-lilies)

VIII. **Annelida** (5,000 species; segmented worms)
  (1) Chaetopoda (marine, fresh-water, or terrestrial)
  (2) Archiannelida (small, marine)
  (3) Hirudinea (leeches)
  (4) Gephyrea (no segmentation; marine)

IX. **Mollusca** (78,000 species; usually bilaterally symmetrical; often with calcium carbonate shell)
  (1) Amphineura (chitons)
  (2) Gastropoda (flat foot for creeping; aquatic)
    (a) Snail
    (b) Slug
  (3) Scaphopoda (toothshell; marine)
  (4) Cephalopoda (marine)
    (a) Squid
    (b) Devilfish
    (c) Cuttlefish
    (d) Octopod
    (e) Nautilus
  (5) Pelecypoda (bivalves)
    (a) Clam
    (b) Mussel
    (c) Oyster
    (d) Scallop
    (e) Cockle

X. **Arthropoda** (675,000 species; joint-footed)
  (1) Crustacea (aquatic; breathe with gills)

(a) Water flea
(b) Goose barnacle; rock barnacle
(c) Lobster
(d) Crayfish
(e) Crab
(f) Shrimp

(2) Onychophora (characteristics of both Anthropods and Annelids)
(3) Chilopoda (contipedes)
(4) Diplopoda (millipedes)
(5) Insecta (air-breathing; bodies divided into head, thorax, abdomen)
  (a) Thysanura (bristletails)
    (1) Silver-fish or fish-moth
  (b) Collembola (springtails)
  (c) Orthoptera (grasshoppers)
    (1) Cursoria (walking or running)
      (a) Walking sticks
      (b) Mantis
      (c) Cockroaches
    (2) Saltatoria (leaping)
      (a) Crickets
      (b) Grasshoppers
  (d) Isoptera (termites or white ants)
  (e) Neuroptera (aphis-lions; ant-lions)
  (f) Ephemeroptera (Mayflies)
  (g) Odonata (dragon-flies; damselflies)
  (h) Plecoptera (stone-flies)
  (i) Psocoptera (bark and book lice)
  (j) Mallophaga (chicken and turkey lice)
  (k) Emioptera (Embiids)
  (l) Thysanoptera (thrips)
  (m) Anoplura (sucking lice)
    (1) Head louse
    (2) Crab louse
    (3) Body louse or cootie
    (4) Dog louse
  (n) Hemiptera (true bugs)
    (1) Aquatic
      (a) Water boatmen
      (b) Back swimmers
      (c) Water bugs
    (2) Terrestrial
      (a) Leaf bugs
      (b) Bed bugs
      (c) Chinch bugs
      (d) Squash bugs
      (e) Stink bugs
  (o) Homoptera (many economically important)
    (1) Cicadas
    (2) Hoppers
    (3) Plant lice
    (4) Scale insects
  (p) Dermaptera (earwigs)
  (q) Coleoptera (beetles)
  (r) Strepsiptera (stylopids; parasites)
  (s) Mecoptera (scorpion flies)
  (t) Trichoptera (caddice flies)
  (u) Lepidoptera
    (1) Moths
    (2) Skippers and butterflies

    (v) Diptera (flies; midges; mos-
        quitoes)
    (w) Siphonaptera (fleas)
    (x) Hymenoptera
        (1) Gall flies
        (2) Ants
        (3) Wasps
        (4) Leaf-cutters
        (5) Bees (bumble; honey)
  (6) Arachnoidea (mainly spiders)
    (a) Merostomata (king or horse
        crab)
    (b) Arachnida (spiders; scorpions;
        ticks and mitea)
    (c) Pynogonida (sea spiders)
    (d) Tardigrada (water bears)
    (e) Penlastomida (wormlike para-
        sites)

XI. **Chordata** (40,000 species; chiefly verte-
    brates. This phylum consists of all
    the animals that possess a support-
    ing axis.)
  (1) Cyclostomata (hagfish and lam-
      preys)
  (2) Elasmobranchii (s h a r k s; rays or
      skates)
  (3) Pisces (fishes)
  (4) Amphibia (frogs; toads; salaman-
      ders)
  (5) Reptilia (all reptiles)
  (6) Aves (birds)
  (7) Mammalia
    (a) Duckbill and spiny ant-eater
    (b) Marsupials
        (1) Opossum
        (2) Kangaroo
    (c) Insectivora (hedgehog; mole)
    (d) Dermoptera (flying lemur)
    (e) Chiroptera (bats; flying fox)
    (f) Primates
        (1) Lemur
        (2) Monkeys
        (3) Man
    (g) Edentata
        (1) Ant-eater
        (2) Sloth
        (3) Armadillo
    (h) Pholidota (scaly ant-eater)
    (i) Rodentia (gnawing animals)
        (1) Squirrel
        (2) Beaver
        (3) Mice
    (j) Lagomorpha (hares; rabbits)
    (k) Carnivora (flesh-eating)
        (1) Dog
        (2) Wolf
        (3) Cat
        (4) Lion
        (5) Walrus
    (l) Odontoceti (toothed whales)
        (1) Dolphin
        (2) Porpoise
    (m) Mystacoceti (w h a l e b o n e
        whale)
    (n) Tubulidentata (Aardvarks)
    (o) Proboscidea (elephants)
    (p) Hyracoidea (coneys)
    (q) Sirenia (sea-cows)
    (r) Perisodactyla (odd-toed)

        (1) Horse
        (2) Zebra
        (3) Tapir
        (4) Rhinoceros
    (s) Artiodactyla (even-toed)
        (1) Pig
        (2) Hippopotamus
        (3) Giraffe
        (4) Deer
        (5) Bison
        (6) Domestic cow

ZORN, *tsorn*, ANDERS LEONHARD (1860–1920), a Swedish artist, famed as a landscape and portrait painter, etcher and sculptor. He was born at Mora, of peasant parents. Zorn expected at first to devote himself wholly to sculpture, and to that end studied in Stockholm for six years; subsequently he took up etching and water color painting in London. His first oil painting, *Fisherman from Saint Ives*, was purchased for the Luxembourg Museum in 1888. Zorn's fame steadily increased with time, as he showed genius in all phases of art which he undertook. He became a foremost portraitist, showed a mastery of the technique of sculpture, and won equal fame as an etcher. His portraits include *King Charles of Sweden*, a study of himself (in the Uffizi), *Maja* and *The Toast*. Among his etchings is a remarkable series of portraits, including studies of Renan, Strindberg, Anatole France, Rodin and other celebrities. Notable pieces of sculpture include a statue of Gustavus Vasa, *Faun and Nymph* and *Grandmother*.

ZOROASTER, *zo ro as'ter*, a teacher and reformer of ancient Persia, who formulated one of the chief religious systems of the world. It is not definitely known when he lived, but it was probably between 660 and 583 B. C. Legend associates with his life such supernormal phenomena as miracles, symbolic dreams, visions and temptations by an evil spirit. His teachings are embodied in the Zend-Avesta, the sacred book of the Parsees and Ghebers, his followers at the present time. They embrace the idea of conflicting forces of good and evil in the world, and man's power to choose between them. Good thoughts, good words and good deeds form the watchword of the faith. See GHEBERS; PARSEES; ZEND-AVESTA.

ZOUAVES, *zwahvz*, or *zoo ahvz'*, originally a body of troops in the French army. It derived its name from a tribe of Kabyles inhabiting the mountain of Jurjura, in the

Algerian province of Constantine. General Clausel, of the French army in Algiers, created, in 1830, two battalions of Zouaves, in which each company consisted of French and Zouaves in certain proportions, officers, subalterns and soldiers being selected from both. The Zouaves, though retaining their Moorish dress, were armed and disciplined after the European fashion, and the battalions were recruited by voluntary enlistment.

The mixing of soldiers proved unsatisfactory, and after 1839 no more natives were recruited, though regiments of Algerian sharpshooters were formed of men of exceptional physique and courage. These regiments became an integral part of the French army, and won distinction not only in Africa, but also in the Crimea, Italy, Mexico, Tunis and Tongking. A large force of these *Turcos,* as they were called, fought in World War I. As later organized in the French army, the Zouaves consisted of six regiments of three battalions each, and were stationed in North Africa.

In the United States during the Civil War, some Northern regiments adopted the Zouave uniforms and were known as Zouaves. Most famous of these was a New York regiment, under the command of Colonel Ellsworth.

ZUIDER ZEE, *zi'dur ze',* a large, shallow arm of the North Sea, extending into the northwestern part of the Netherlands. The reclamation of the land under the Zuider Zee and its transformation into a fertile area was one of the successful projects of the Netherlands (see NETHERLANDS, pages 2512-2513). The inlet consists of an oval inner portion, a horn-shaped outer portion and a narrow strait connecting the two. The area is about 2,000 square miles. Originally the inner portion was a lake, situated in a region of fens and marshes. In the thirteenth century severe storms caused an inundation of the North Sea and the submergence of large sections of land.

ZULUS, *zoo'looz,* a warlike people of Bantu stock, inhabiting parts of South Africa. They support themselves chiefly by raising millet and breeding cattle. They live in thatched and plastered houses, supported by poles, which are beehive in form and arranged in large circles, enclosing the cattle pens. These communities, or villages, are called *kraals.* Pottery making, basket weaving, iron smelting and hide tanning are en-

gaged in to a certain extent. The principal weapons are the assegai and the knobkirri. Polygamy and wife purchase are customary. Chaka, the chief ruler during the first quarter of the nineteenth century, dominated South Africa from the Zambezi to Cape Colony. Cetewayo reigned from 1874 to 1878, and by his depredations he embroiled his people in war with England. Dinizulu, his son, was crushed in 1879, but, as he continued to incite the natives to fighting, he was banished. The Zulus are gradually becoming civilized.

Zululand, *zoo'loo land,* a region of Southeastern Africa, forming a part of the British province of Natal, to which it was annexed in 1897. Its area is about 10,450 square miles, and its population is about 230,000, the most of whom are natives. See NATAL.

ZUNI, *zoo'nyee,* the popular name of a Pueblo Indian tribe which inhabits four pueblos, or villages, in New Mexico. The most important of these villages is also called Zuñi. The Zuñi, or Ashiwi, as they call themselves, have lived in the same locality for centuries; the Spanish explorers discovered them there in 1539, and missions were established later among them.

Zuñi is built about a central court, surrounded by a continuous high wall which is scaled by ladders on both sides, intended originally for defense. The entrances to the houses are on the roofs; and these also are reached by ladders inside and out. The people number about 2,000. They support themselves by cultivating the soil and raising stock. See PUEBLO.

ZURICH, *zoo'riK,* SWITZERLAND, capital of the canton of Zurich and the largest city of the republic. It is on the Limmat, at the northern end of Lake Zurich, sixty miles northeast of Bern. The city is divided by the Limmat into two parts, known respectively as the Little City and the Great City. The old historical quarter of Zurich is picturesque, with its steep, narrow streets and quaint, dark houses, but the newer part of the city has handsome buildings and wide, attractive streets. Among the more noteworthy buildings are the old Wasserkirche, which now houses the municipal library; the old church known as the Grossmünster, of which Zwingli was pastor; the townhall, the university buildings and the Swiss national museum, the largest museum in Switzerland.

The educational institutions of the town include the university, with about 800 students, and the Federal Polytechnic, which has about 1,100 regular students, besides special students who attend lectures. Commercially and industrially, Zurich is of considerable importance. It is the banking center of Switzerland. The silk industry is large, and cotton, paper and machinery are also manufactured. During the Middle Ages the town of Zurich was prosperous and important. It was the scene of the beginning of Zwingli's reformation. Population, 1930, 249,820.

ZURICH, Lake, a lake of Switzerland, lying mostly within the canton of Zurich, but extending for a short distance into Schwyz and Saint Gall. It is about twenty-five miles in length and from one-half to two and one-half miles in width, and is somewhat in the shape of a crescent. Its scenery is picturesque and charming, although not so imposing as that of some of the other lakes of Switzerland.

ZUYDER ZEE, *zi'dur ze'*. See ZUIDER ZEE.

ZWINGLI, *tsving'lee*, ULRICH or HULDREICH (1484–1531), an illustrious Swiss reformer. In 1506 he was ordained by the bishop of Constance, becoming in the same year pastor of the large parish of Glarus.

His studies in the New Testament gradually led him to question many of the doctrines in which he had been trained, and by degrees he became known as an ardent reformer, as well as a prominent patriot. He had no communication with Luther, but by 1516 he had begun a work in Switzerland very similar to that which had been started by the great German reformer. In 1522 he demanded of the bishop of Constance and all the governments of the confederation the abolition of the law imposing celibacy upon the priests, and his suggestions for one reform after another widened his breach with the Church.

In 1529 he went to Marburg, to confer with Luther and the other German reformers upon the possibility of uniting the reform movements, that a stronger resistance might be made to their opponents. Zwingli was willing to make concessions, but Luther objected to the fact that the religious movement in Switzerland was allied with a movement for civil reform, and this, together with their differing views on the Lord's Supper, prevented coöperation. In 1531, when open war broke out between the Catholic and the Protestant cantons of Switzerland, Zwingli accompanied the Zurich regiment as chaplain and was killed at Kappel.

Foreword to the
TOPICAL INDEX

MODERN encyclopedias are arranged alphabetically, with the accumulated information of the world divided into smaller sections. This arrangement enables the reader to find any desired information quickly, and relieves him of the necessity of reading a great deal of extraneous material. For instance, a student may wish to look up the story of the compass for any one of a number of reasons. He may be interested in aviation, sailing, the history of exploration, the break-up of feudalism or in magnetism. In using an alphabetical reference work, he turns to the "C" department of the set and finds the story of the compass under its own heading. On the other hand, he may be interested in following a course of study of which the story of the compass becomes an integral part.

In the making of an encyclopedic index, two basic plans confront the editor, and a choice must be made. The first type may consist of titles alphabetically arranged. Such an index is said to be analytical because it breaks down a mass of material, thus enabling the reader to find particular items of information. It is of especial value in a complete book on a subject. An analytical index has heretofore been supplied in this set of books, but because the articles are intentionally broken into small areas for quick reference, the index was not much used. Therefore the second type has been substituted. It is organized as a topical index.

Such an index draws together the articles on small areas and thus supplies a completed picture for the reader who wishes broad vistas of information. This series of volumes can now be used in two ways. Specific details can be found through the alphabetical arrangement; and completed courses of reading are made available through the cross references in the text and, more elaborately, through the index. Each item of knowledge may be combined or recombined with other items to answer questions, solve problems and promote understanding. Our topical index assists in this combining.

After a topical form of index was chosen, the problem arose as to what topics or combinations should be considered. Modern school courses of study were followed—courses that break down the old formal lines of history, geography, chemistry, etc., and give cross sections of life in units of human experience. Numerous educators assisted in this planning and in the writing.

In all countries and at all times, man's activities and interests may be considered from the standpoint of five areas of human experience: Health, Human Relationships, Vocations, Science and Recreation. Our presentation of these areas demonstrates the great advantages to the common man of the democratic way of life.

It is hoped that the use of this index will contribute to a more complete understanding of the duties of citizenship, as well as demonstrate the advantages of living under our form of government.

In this index, therefore, the thousands of facts that together form a picture of the modern age are assembled, evaluated and interpreted. This interpretive text material comprises more than half of the space allotted to the entire index. It is broken at logical points by carefully chosen lists of pertinent articles appearing in the encyclopedia, and by bibliographies of standard literature, compiled by an experienced librarian and designed to enrich the reading of the student.

In the next three pages is a table of contents. A perusal of the areas, subdivisions and minor divisions will disclose the wide fields covered.

Contents of the TOPICAL INDEX
Covering the Five Areas of Human Experience

Above: Vaccinating for smallpox, as it was introduced by Edward Jenner in May, 1796.
Below: William Harvey demonstrating his theory of the circulation of blood.

HEALTH

Overview for Health

Our familiar greeting—"How are you?" —has its counterpart in the languages of many other peoples. Implied in this greeting is a general recognition of the importance of good health. When we write to our friends, when we welcome them to our homes and when we bid them farewell, we express, more often than any other sentiment, our best wishes for their health.

The question is often asked, "Is the human race growing healthier?" Statistics show that there are more middle-aged people alive today than there were at the beginning of this century. In fact, there has been a ten-year increase in life expectation since 1900. This lengthening of the life span is due chiefly to the lowered death rate for babies and a decrease in number of deaths caused by infectious diseases. Progress in medical and sanitary science and improved care of infants, together with directed training of mothers, are responsible for the results mentioned above.

Heart disease and mental ailments, however, are increasing. Authorities attribute this condition to the growing tension of modern living, with its speed, noise and worries. For all of us, in this Machine Age, deaths from accidents are a growing hazard.

Medical science is constantly working in our behalf; its goal is the conquest of disease, the elimination of mental ills and the improvement of health habits. No one need be ignorant of the basic principles of healthful living. Everyone should be vigilant in applying them.

We must not forget that the completely healthy person is one who not only rejoices in a strong body but who radiates good cheer. We can do much to develop good mental hygiene. Good books and music, a fire on the hearth, laughter and the clasp of a friend's hand—these make life worth living. Appreciation of values such as these will help us to harmonize our mental with our physical well-being and so achieve the ideal of the sound mind in the sound body.

The foregoing material is introductory to the study of health and health habits. It suggests such basic reading material as may be found in the following articles:

Biology	Hygiene
Child Study	Longevity
Fatigue	Mortality, Law of
Games and Plays	Sanitary Science
Health, Boards of	Sleep

Bibliography

AARON, HAROLD. *Good Health and Bad Medicine.* R. M. McBride and Co.
CRAMPTON, C. W. *Boy's Book of Strength.* McGraw-Hill Book Co.
DEIHL, H. S. *Healthful Living.* McGraw-Hill Book Co.
HEISER, V. G. *Toughen Up, America!* McGraw-Hill Book Co.
HOLWAY, H. K. *Story of Health.* Harper & Bros.
HUNT, TERRY. *Exercise and Keep Fit.* Prentice-Hall.
LANE, JANET. *Your Carriage, Madam! A Guide to Good Posture.* John Wiley & Sons.

The Key to Efficiency and Happiness

THE BODY MECHANISM

The human body is an intricate machine, and to keep it in good running order we need to understand its structure and how it works. In the human skeleton, bones and cartilage are fashioned into a strong, basic framework. There are over 200 bones, of different shapes and sizes, all of which have special functions. Cartilage is an elastic white tissue which is attached to the ends of bones to form joints.

The bony framework protects and supports vital organs, including the heart, lungs, stomach, liver and kidneys. The brain, seat of man's reasoning powers, is enclosed in a rounded, bony skull. Twenty-six vertebrae are fastened together to form the spinal column. Enclosed by this spine is the spinal cord, from which important nerve systems branch. In addition, the bony framework has the long, straight bones of the arms and legs, the short bones of the wrists and ankles, curving ribs and many other parts, all necessary for the functioning of the body.

One would not think of trying to change the shape or size of his bones, but the hygiene one follows has an important part in the growth and health of the bones. Diet, sunshine and exercise are all important in the development of healthy bone structure. Children whose food lacks Vitamin D and who are deprived of sunshine are liable to rickets, a bone disease that causes bowlegs and other deformities. The bones contain cells that are supplied with nutrient by means of blood vessels. Healthy blood is necessary for well-nourished bones.

Muscles are joined to the bones by cords of strong tissue called tendons. Most of our bodily movements are produced by contractions of the muscles. It is through muscular action that we walk, run, lie down, breathe, and perform a multitude of other movements. Certain muscles are essential in such vital functions as digestion and circulation.

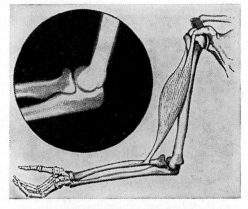

BONE AND MUSCLE

Biceps muscle moves arm, which is held rigid by bone. Inset shows socket at elbow.

For health and growth, our muscles require alternating periods of exercise and rest. The pre-school child, playing actively so many hours of the day, requires regular sleep periods. School children need regular periods of play or other physical activity during school hours. While at their desks they should be taught correct posture. Badly trained muscles result in round shoulders and hollow chests.

For adults, exercise tones up flabby muscles, improves one's carriage, stimulates vital functions and helps the morale.

For more detailed information concerning the structure and functions of the human body, the reader is referred, first, to the basic article, PHYSIOLOGY, and then to the following titles:

Abdomen	Chest
Adenoids	Cilia
Alimentary Canal	Circulation
Anatomy	Connective Tissue
Aorta	Diaphragm
Arm	Ear
Arteries	Eye
Biceps	Face
Bile	Fibrin
Blood	Foot
Bone	Gall Bladder
Brain	Ganglion
Breathing	Glands
Capillaries	Haemoglobin
Cartilage	Hair
Cell	Hand
Cerebellum	Heart
Cerebrum	Hiccough

Intestine	Reflex Action
Joints	Saliva
Jugular Vein	Scalp
Kidneys	Secretion
Lachrymal Glands	Senses
Lacteals	Serous Membranes
Larynx	Skeleton
Ligament	Skin
Liver	Smell
Lungs	Snoring
Lymph	Spinal Cord
Lymphatics	Spleen
Membranes	Stomach
Mucus	Taste
Muscle	Teeth
Muscle Sense	Tendons
Nails	Thirst
Nerves	Thoracic Duct
Nervous System	Tissues
Nose	Tongue
Palate	Tonsils
Pancreas	Touch
Pelvis	Trachea
Pericardium	Urine
Perspiration	Veins
Pharynx	Villi
Pleura	Vision
Pulse	Voice

Bibliography

CARLSON, A. J. *Machinery of the Body.* University of Chicago Press.

CLENDENING, LOGAN. *The Human Body.* Alfred A. Knopf.

GRENFELL, SIR W. T. *Yourself and Your Body.* Charles Scribner's Sons.

MARTIN, H. N. *Human Body.* Henry Holt & Co.

STILES, P. G. *Human Physiology.* W. B. Saunders Co.

TODD, M. E. *The Thinking Body.* Harper & Bros.

HEALTH AND THE DIET

The best diet for a person in normal health is one containing, in right proportions, all the different classes of food—meat (including the flesh of fish and poultry), eggs, dairy products, fresh vegetables and fruits. From these foods are obtained the six basic elements of man's diet: proteins, carbohydrates, fats, minerals, vitamins and water. All of these elements are found in a balanced diet, one made up of the proper variety of foods. It is no longer difficult to obtain a variety of foods throughout the year. Because of fast trains and motor vehicles and the development of cold storage and refrigeration, fresh fruits, green vegetables and fresh meats are available in all markets.

It is important to know how the various kinds of food materials nourish the body. The special function of protein is to build and repair body tissues. The fats and carbohydrates are important fuel-making elements, providing heat and energy. Minerals help to regulate vital functions of the body and provide essential nutrients, such as iron and calcium.

Vitamins protect the body against disease and are necessary for normal health and growth. We obtain an adequate supply of

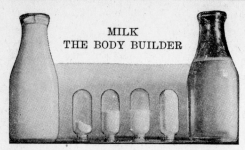

MILK
THE BODY BUILDER

Commercial Milk	7% Minerals	32% Protein	37% Fat	5% Sugar	87.4% Moisture

vitamins in a well-balanced diet, and as a rule do not need to buy special vitamin preparations. For the cure of certain diseases, vitamins in concentrated form are valuable, but such concentrations should be taken only upon the advice of a reliable physician.

Water is not in itself a food, but it is an important constituent of foods and of the blood that carries food materials to nourish the body tissues. It also is essential in the chemical changes that take place in the body. Seventy per cent of the weight of the body is made up of water.

The fuel value of food is measured in calories, units of heat production of energy. The United States Department of Agriculture has compiled tables showing the average heat values of common foods. These tables are available to the public. They are useful as a guide to the proper selection of a diet suited to one's age and habits. It is wise to consult a specialist before undertaking any drastic course of dieting.

No one should rely on dietary information obtained from inexperienced persons or unauthorized sources. Health fads with no scientific basis should be shunned. Taboos against certain combinations, such as proteins and carbohydrates, usually have no validity. Some people go to extremes in the use of roughage in the diet. Bulky foods, generally speaking, are helpful in overcoming constipation, but they are harmful in certain forms of colitis. In eating for health we need to use intelligent discrimination.

The basic principles underlying a healthful diet are contained in such articles as DIET, FOOD, NUTRITION and DOMESTIC SCIENCE. Supplementing these topics are the following:

Absorption	Bread
Albumen	Butter
Assimilation	Cacao
Bacon	Caffeine
Baking Powder	Calorie
Beef	Candy and Candy
Benzoate of Soda	Making

Canning	Macaroni
Carbohydrate	Meat
Casein	Meat Packing
Caviar	Milk
Cheese	Mutton
Chocolate	Nut
Chyle	Oils
Chyme	Oleomargarine
Cod-Liver Oil	Olive Oil
Coffee	Peptones
Cold Storage	Pickles
Cookery	Pork
Digestion	Preservatives, Food
Egg	Proteins
Fat	Pure Food Laws
Fish and Fisheries (with list)	Saccharin
	Sago
Fruits (with list)	Saliva
Gastric Juice	Salt
Glucose	Sausage
Gluten	Spice (with list)
Grains (with list)	Starch
Ham	Stomach
Herbs	Tea
Honey	Vegetables (with list)
Intestine	Vinegar
Ketchup	Vitamins
Lard	

Bibliography

BOGERT, L. J. *Nutrition and Physical Fitness*. W. B. Saunders Co.

COOPER, L. F. *Nutrition in Health and Disease*. J. B. Lippincott Co.

FISHBEIN, MORRIS. *Your Diet and Your Health*. McGraw-Hill Book Co.

FURNAS, C. C. *Man, Bread and Destiny*. Reynal & Hitchcock.

SENSE, ELEANORA. *America's Nutrition Primer: What To Eat and Why*. M. Barrows & Co.

SHERMAN, H. C. *Food and Health*. The Macmillan Co.

FIRST AID IN EMERGENCIES

Cuts, burns, broken bones, suffocation and many other accidental injuries are among the hazards of civilian life. Such injuries often need a physician's care, but there are times when professional aid is not available. Sometimes, too, the injured person must have immediate help if he is to survive. Ability to apply first-aid measures in emergencies is so useful and important that instruction in first aid is being given in many schools, in industrial plants, in community classes, and in boys' and girls' clubs. Wise mothers, too, will have emergency supplies, with directions for use, on hand in the home.

The largest American volunteer organization to develop courses of instruction in first aid is the Red Cross. Local chapters of this organization conduct classes and issue printed material available to anyone interested in learning the fundamental first-aid measures.

There are four important rules that everyone should memorize: (1) A person who has stopped breathing because of asphyxiation, drowning, suffocation or electrocution must be given artificial respiration at once. (2) Serious bleeding or hemorrhage must be stopped to prevent the victim from bleeding to death. (3) In cases of severe accident, watch out for shock. (4) Persons with broken bones must be kept from moving until splints can be applied to the fractures.

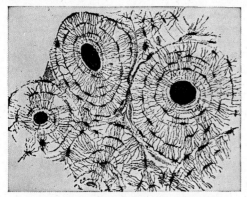

BONES ARE MADE OF CELLS
The cells shown here have been magnified 150 times.

Red Cross instructions for stopping severe bleeding identify six pressure points. To forestall fatal hemorrhage, the first-aid worker exerts pressure upon one or more of these points, according to the location of the wounds, and stops the blood flow until a tourniquet or other device can be applied. The Red Cross warns against the use of rope or cord for a tourniquet. A strip of cloth at least two inches wide is necessary.

Shock following injuries needs special treatment. The face of the victim will be pale, the skin cold and clammy, and there will be weakness or perhaps unconsciousness. Chills and nausea may be present. If conscious, the patient should be given warm, non-alcoholic stimulants. He must be kept warm and must lie down.

Poisons taken internally may be forced from the stomach by induced vomiting. A spoonful of ground mustard in a glass of warm water is a simple but effective emetic. There are antidotes for many poisons, and it is a wise precaution for the housewife to secure a list of such preparations from the family physician, as well as specific directions for treatment of poisoning. All receptacles should be plainly marked.

Suggestions for applying emergency first aid in various types of injury may be found in the articles listed below:

Antidote	Hemorrhage
Arteries	Poison
Asphyxiation	Sprain
Burns and Scalds	Sunstroke
Drowning	Veins
Fainting	Wounds

Bibliography

BAARSLAG, KARL. *Coast Guard to the Rescue.* Farrar & Rinehart.

CANNON, F. V. *Rehearsal for Safety, a Book of Safety Plays.* E. J. McLaughlin.

COBB, W. F. *Everyday First Aid.* D. Appleton-Century Co.

CRUMP, IRVING. *Boy's Book of Firemen.* Dodd, Mead & Co.

DULL, C. E. *Safety First—and Last.* Henry Holt & Co.

ELIASON, E. L. *First Aid in Emergencies.* J. B. Lippincott Co.

EVANS, W. A. *Safety; Your Problem and Mine.* Lyons & Carnahan.

GARTNER, P. W. *First Aid Afield.* The Macmillan Co.

RED CROSS, U. S. *American Red Cross First Aid Textbook.* P. Blakiston's Son & Co.

STACK, H. J. *Safety in the World of Today.* Beckley-Cardy Co.

MAN'S WAR AGAINST DISEASE

The struggle to rid the world of disease has called forth the best of man's intellectual and spiritual forces. The enemy forces have included filth, insects, parasites, rodents and mankind's ignorance and superstition. The victims of disease throughout the centuries cannot be counted. During the Middle Ages, unnumbered millions perished in Europe and Asia in the epidemics that swept those continents periodically. In 1665 the Black Death (bubonic plague) killed 70,000 persons in London alone. In the eighteenth century almost the entire population of the city bore the scars of smallpox.

Yellow fever occurred in epidemic form in the American South until late in the nineteenth century, and in the Spanish-American War there was one case of typhoid for each seven men enlisted. When the United States Army undertook to build the Panama Canal, its medical and sanitary divisions had to wipe out malaria and yellow fever in the Canal Zone before the project could be completed.

In communities where modern hygiene and sanitation prevail, control of infectious diseases is the rule. Enlightened methods of prevention and scientific knowledge of the cause of such diseases make the former devastating epidemics a rarity. The world owes much to the pioneers in this crusade. Edward Jenner, an Englishman, did more than anyone else to introduce vaccination as a preventive of smallpox. Napoleon had his army vaccinated in 1805, and during that century the disease was brought under control. For much of the progress made in the fight against tuberculosis, we honor Robert Koch, discoverer of the causative bacillus.

There have been two lines of attack against typhoid fever—inoculation with a prepared vaccine, which confers immunity for about three years; and sanitary precautions. The typhoid bacillus contaminates milk, water and food, and in communities

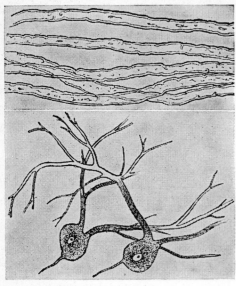

NERVES OF THE HUMAN BODY
Top, white nerve fibers. *Bottom*, nerve cells from gray matter of brain. Greatly magnified.

where strict sanitary regulations are enforced, typhoid is almost unknown.

Diphtheria mortality has decreased since the discovery of the Schick test. By means of this test, physicians determine whether a person is susceptible to diphtheria. If the reaction is positive, the person tested may secure immunity by injections of toxin-antitoxin.

The conquest of yellow fever was made possible by the discovery of the carrier of the germ. An American mission headed by Dr. Walter Reed was sent to Cuba in 1898, to carry out experiments. At the risk of their lives, the doctors found that the stegomyia mosquito is the carrier and infects men through its bite. Elimination of the mosquito in Cuba and, later, in the Canal Zone wiped out yellow fever in those areas.

Hospital practice and technique have advanced greatly since the beginning of the nineteenth century. The great French scientist, Louis Pasteur, was the first to offer conclusive proof that specific germs cause in-

fections. His work was the basis for the antiseptic methods of Dr. Joseph Lister, of Edinburgh, who showed physicians how to avoid post-operative infection. The use of anesthetics was also developed in the nineteenth century.

Among later healing agents, X-rays, radium, the iron lung and blood transfusion take high rank. Some types of cancer are now being cured by X-rays and radium, and the X-ray has been found helpful in the treatment of acne, a stubborn skin disease. These are but a few of the medical uses of the two remarkable healing agents.

The iron lung is an ingenious piece of apparatus for supplying artificial breathing in cases where the respiratory muscles have been paralyzed. The older type, the body-size Drinker respirator, has been supplemented by a jacket type which permits greater freedom. In some cases of infantile paralysis, patients who have recovered partial use of the legs are able to walk for limited periods by using the smaller form of respirator.

The perfected technique of blood transfusion is saving countless lives among civilians and soldiers wounded in battle. To be effective, the new blood given a patient must be of the same chemical type as his own blood. There are four types, and precise tests are necessary to determine the character of the blood of any donor. Blood banks are kept in hospitals. Dried plasma (blood minus red and white corpuscles) is now being used for emergency treatment. Red Cross first-aid kits containing plasma are supplied to medical corps in the battle zones. Among civilians, transfusions are applied in cases of severe bleeding, exhaustion following major operations, streptococcic infection and other ailments.

Another modern procedure is the feeding of patients unable to absorb food in the normal manner. Such patients are given glucose by intravenous injections.

Advanced experimentation has also produced valuable preparations from the ductless glands. Among these medicines are adrenalin, insulin and thyroxin, used respectively to revive heart action, to counteract diabetes and to treat goiter. Since 1933, many remarkable cures have resulted from the use of sulfanilamide, a dyestuff obtained from coal tar. It is the most effective agent known for the cure of streptococcic infections and for the prevention of gangrene in wounds. The drug also has several valuable derivatives, including a remedy for pneumonia.

The story of man's fight against disease covers centuries of heroic endeavor. The articles GERM THEORY OF DISEASE and MEDICINE may be read as an introduction to the subject. Then read the articles listed below for interesting details:

Bibliography

CLAPESATTLE, H. B. *The Doctors Mayo*. University of Minnesota.
CURIE, EVE. *Madame Curie, a Biography*. Doubleday, Doran & Co.
DE KRUIF, PAUL. *Men Against Death*. Harcourt, Brace & Co.
HALLOCK, G. T. *Edward Jenner*. D. C. Heath & Co.
FLEXNER, J. T. *Doctors on Horseback*. The Viking Press.
GORGAS, M. C. *William Crawford Gorgas, His Life and Work*. Doubleday, Doran & Co.
LEESON, J. R. *Lister as I Knew Him*. Grosset & Dunlop.
SCHULZ, C. L. *Your Career in Nursing*. McGraw-Hill Book Co.
VALLERY-RADOT, RENÉ. *Life of Pasteur*. Doubleday Doran & Co.
ZINSSER, HANS. *Rats, Lice and History*. Little, Brown & Co.

PUBLIC HEALTH AND WELFARE

The maintenance of public health cannot be left to individuals. Organized health service is the responsibility of local, state and national governments, all working together for the public good. In the United States, foods and drugs produced and marketed in the country must meet certain standards set forth in the Federal Food, Drug and Cosmetic Act, which is enforced by the Food and Drug Administration, a division of the Federal Security Agency. Impure and misbranded products may be confiscated by government officials. Advertisements of foods and drugs are examined by the Federal Trade Commission, which is authorized to order the discontinuance of false statements.

The United States Health Service, another unit of the Federal Security Agency, co-operates with state and local health agencies on such matters as sanitation and public education. It conducts quarantine activities at ports of entry, inspects passengers on ships and planes arriving from foreign ports, and acts to prevent the spread of communicable diseases between states by means of interstate traffic.

State and local bodies co-operate with Federal agencies by passing laws designed

GOVERNMENT TESTING OF FOOD
Scientists protect our health by testing the purity of our food.

to protect public health and control disease within their jurisdictions. Garbage and sewage disposal, purity of water supply, the handling of foods in public markets, compulsory vaccination, community quarantine, physical examination of school children and the maintenance of clinics, visiting nurses and infant-welfare stations fall within the jurisdiction of state or local bodies.

The Social Security Act provides for assistance to the blind, the handicapped and impoverished aged persons, with the Federal government co-operating with the states. Such measures are a direct benefit to public health, as are child labor laws and legislation compelling health and safety precautions in stores and factories. Many large industries maintain hospitals for their employes and have systems of accident and sickness insurance.

The protection of public health and concern for the general welfare by private and governmental agencies covers a broad field. It includes the work of individuals and youth groups, as well as official agencies. Many phases of this program are treated in the following articles:

Addams, Jane
Blindness
Boys' and Girls'
  4-H Clubs
Boy Scouts
Building Laws
Camp-Fire Girls
Camps and Camping
Charity and Charities
Child Labor
City
Cold Storage
Community Center
Drainage
Employer's Liability
Epidemic
Factory and Factory
  Legislation
Fly
Food
Garbage
Girl Scouts
Health, Boards of

Heating and
  Ventilation
Housing Problem
Hygiene
Insurance
Labor Legislation
Labor Organizations
Lip Reading
Meat Packing
Medicine
Mosquito
Old Age Pensions
Pure Food Laws
Quarantine
Red Cross Societies
Sanitary Science
Sewage and Sewerage
Social Security
Social Settlements
Sweatshop System
Water Purification
Waterworks

Bibliography

CHAMBERS, M. M. *The Community and Its Young People*. American Council on Education.
EHLERS, V. M. *Municipal and Rural Sanitation*. McGraw-Hill Book Co.
ENGELHARDT, N. L. *Planning the Community School*. American Book Co.
HOLWAY, HOPE. *Story of Water Supply*. Harper & Bros.
LAMB, R. DE F. *American Chamber of Horrors*. Farrar & Rinehart.
PHILLIPS, W. C. *Adventuring for Democracy*. Social Unit Press.
RYAN, W. J. *Water Treatment and Purification*. McGraw-Hill Book Co.
SMILLIE, W. G. *Public Health Administration in the U. S.* The Macmillan Co.
SOULE, E. S. *Community Hygiene*. The Macmillan Co.
TURNER, C. E. *Community Health*. D. C. Heath & Co.

SOCIALIZED MEDICINE

In spite of the progress made in the control and prevention of disease, too many families and individuals lack adequate medical care because of their inability to pay for it. Many surveys have been made in America which bear out this statement. In the low-income groups, acute and chronic illnesses are far more prevalent than among the groups in comfortable circumstances, and the mortality of babies is much higher in families that lack the means to care for their children properly. In one survey the investigators found that the number of school children needing medical and dental service was as high as seventy-five per cent in many schools. Such conditions have strengthened the agitation for a government program of socialized medicine. This is a system whereby free medical aid is extended to the needy, physicians being paid from funds provided by governmental bodies or by benevolent groups.

In 1935, after the passage of the Social Security Act, President Roosevelt appointed a committee to co-ordinate health and welfare activities authorized by the act. A national health program was prepared by this committee, and the report was transmitted to Congress by the President in January, 1939. In February of that year, Senator Wagner of New York introduced in the Senate a bill authorizing Federal appropriations to match state funds for extending public-health services. The bill was offered as a series of amendments to the Social Security Act. It provided for grants to states for maternal and child welfare, medical services for crippled and otherwise handicapped children, public-health work and investigations, hospitals and health centers, and temporary disability payments. The proposed law met with powerful opposition from the American Medical Association and its adoption was deferred pending further study.

Although the Federal government has not established a nation-wide system of socialized medicine as such, it has encouraged various group movements employing the principle of socialized medicine. By the payment of small fees at regular intervals, individuals or families are entitled to receive medical care at hospitals or clinics for specified periods. These group plans have been adopted in all parts of the country.

The trend is toward further extension of health services through health insurance, mutual benefit associations, group plans or direct government assistance. The program of national socialized medicine is attacked on the ground that it would encourage political abuses, increase government costs, lower professional standards and decrease the earning ability of thousands of physicians whose education and practice have been acquired at great sacrifice. Defenders of socialized medicine point to the injustices of a system that permits large numbers of the population to suffer from inadequate medical care in a country of scientific progress and great resources and believe that proper organization will prevent injustice to established medical groups.

Bibliography

BRYAN, E. S. *Art of Public Health Nursing*. W. B. Saunders Co.
BURNS, C. D. *Challenge to Democracy*. W. W. Norton & Co.
CLARKE, JAMES, *Picture of Health*. The Macmillan Co.
COYLE, D. C. *Roads to a New America*. Little, Brown & Co.
DE KRUIF, P. H. *Fight for Life*. Harcourt, Brace & Co.
MUNRO, W. B. *Municipal Administration*. The Macmillan Co.
RAINEY, H. P. *How Fare American Youth?* D. Appleton-Century Co.

HUMAN RELATIONSHIPS

Overview for Human Relationships

Our modern social order is based on human relationships. The instinct that impels individuals to live and work together—the urge to share with others the responsibilities of community life—has been a driving force from earliest times. Society as organized today is the outgrowth of man's contacts with his fellow men through the centuries of human progress.

As man advanced through the different stages of social organization—family, tribal and national—he found himself in a world that steadily became more complex. Step by step he gained greater control over his environment, learning how to use raw materials and how to make tools, and discovering new ways of improving his shelter, food and clothing. The crude modes of transportation and communication of primitive folk gave way to faster means of travel and to the arts of speech and writing. When men were able to venture forth from their limited areas of habitation they became explorers and traders. Eventually they crossed unknown oceans and opened vast regions to settlement.

While man was improving his economic condition, he was also developing the arts, establishing churches and schools and testing new theories of science and government. The development of science was accompanied by inventions and discoveries that transformed living conditions and gave man almost complete mastery of time and space.

The changes that have chiefly affected our own age occurred after the opening of the nineteenth century. The period since 1800 has seen, among other things, the development of the Industrial Revolution, the establishment of the factory system, the rapid growth of the trades-union movement, the introduction of mass production in industry, and the invention of the reaping machine, the telegraph and telephone, vulcanization of rubber, the phonograph, incandescent lighting, the automobile, the airplane, radio communication, talking motion pictures and television.

These developments have been too rapid for man to adjust himself to them. The discoveries that have made life richer and easier have created problems that are sorely in need of a solution. As long as they remain unsolved, the modern social order will fall short of its highest possibilities.

The Area on Human Relationships covers man's activities in eight basic fields. The problems arising in these fields are set forth and analyzed from the standpoint of social values. It is important for us to seek a scientific solution of these problems, for they will not solve themselves.

Man's Search for New Horizons

EARLY MILESTONES

The history of man's progress from lowest savagery is a fascinating story. In the beginning his sole aim was self-preservation, but there came a time when he made conscious, though uncertain, efforts to improve his condition. Thereafter, each forward step prepared the way for new discoveries. Civilized man is a thinking, reasoning being who has wonderful achievements to his credit. Yet he still seeks to learn and to advance.

Our earliest ancestors lived in trees. They lacked fire, permanent shelter and the most elementary conveniences. Their methods of finding food were haphazard; they lived on wild plants and on raw meat—the carcasses of animals they found dead and the flesh of such other animals as they could kill with their bare hands. In the dawn of human history, man had no weapons, no tools and no clothing. His aim in life was to keep from starving and to avoid being attacked by wild beasts.

But savage man had a divine spark that saved him from being forever a prey to natural forces. He was capable of making use of his discoveries. The first great milestone in his slow, upward climb was the creation of fire by friction. It is believed that, long before this remarkable event, primitive men kept hot embers, obtained from burning forest trees, in their caves or rock shelters. Fire gave them warmth and light, cooked their food and kept wild beasts away.

In time, men discovered that certain ingredients of the soil could be baked or melted by means of fire, and they learned to make

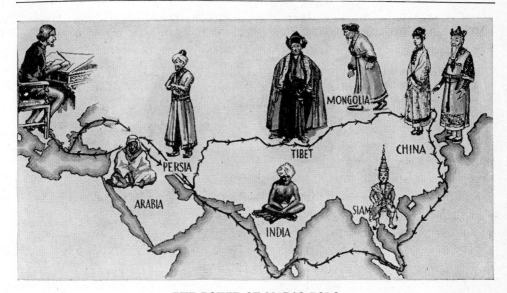

THE ROUTE OF MARCO POLO
This Venetian was the first traveler to cross the whole of Asia.

fire-resistant dishes of clay and to fashion tools and weapons from molten metal. Another important invention was the bow and arrow. With improved weapons, man could kill large, powerful animals, whose skins were used for clothing and whose flesh served for food. Man thus began to have control of his food supply.

From hunting, man advanced to the status of a herder, for he found that he could domesticate certain animals. Cattle and sheep provided hides, wool and meat. The horse and ox could be trained to work. Man learned, too, that many wild plants could be grown in fields to provide a regular source of food, and he then became a farmer. Agriculture had its beginnings when the first crude plow—a forked stick—was used to scratch the soil to prepare it for the seed.

By exploration and discovery, early man achieved in some degree control of his environment. Many interesting facts about this search for comfort and security may be found in the following articles:

Agriculture	Cave Dwellers
(Primitive)	Evolution
Anthropology	Fire
Archaeology	Illumination
Architecture (First	Iron Age
Builders)	Lake Dwellings
Bronze Age	Stone Age

Bibliography

CRUMP, IRVING. Og, Son of Fire. Dodd, Mead & Co.
ERLEIGH, EVA. In the Beginning. Doubleday, Doran.
GILBERT, MARION. Jade Brings Luck. Longmans, Green & Co.
HIBBEN, THOMAS. Carpenter's Tool Chest. J. B. Lippincott Co.
LANSING, M. F. Man's Long Climb. Little, Brown & Co.
QUENNELL, M. C. Everyday Life in the Old Stone Age. G. P. Putnam's Sons.
REASON, JOYCE. Bran the Bronze Smith. E. P. Dutton & Co.
ROBINSON, W. W. Ancient Animals. The Macmillan Co.
VAN LOON, W. H. Story of Mankind. Garden City Publishing Co.

High-School List

BAIKIE, J. Ancient Crete. The Macmillan Co.
BUCHAN, JOHN. Last Secrets. Houghton, Mifflin Co.
LEAKEY, L. S. B. Adam's Ancestors; an Up-to-date Outline of What Is Known about the Origin of Man. Methuen & Co.
LUCAS, M. Man's First Million Years. Harcourt, Brace & Co.
MILLS, DOROTHY. Book of the Ancient World. G. P. Putnam's Sons.
NIDA, R. H. Man, the Nature Tamer: from Caveman to American Citizen. Henry Holt & Co.
THOMAS, LOWELL. The Untold Story of Exploration. Dodd, Mead & Co.

DISCOVERING NEW LANDS

The first abodes of mankind were the warmer regions of the globe. After men had won partial control of their environment they began to spread out into colder regions and thus became traders and explorers. Travel on land and on water developed from the most primitive methods. On land there was first the footpath, over which man walked with his goods on his back. Later, he loaded his merchandise on beasts of burden. The first vehicle was a two-wheeled cart. Water travel began when the first adventurer paddled a log on a stream. Out of these crude beginnings have come the swift modern carriers of land, sea and air.

By the fourteenth century, land routes connected all the trading centers of Europe and Asia, but the vast stretches of North and South America were unknown to Europeans until after the voyages of Columbus, late in the fifteenth century. In the early days of navigation, fear of the unknown

PREHISTORIC PICTURE WRITING

seas and general ignorance of geographical facts kept seamen from going very far from home.

In the rivalry for world trade that followed the discovery of America, the rounding of Africa and the circumnavigation of the globe, the ships of Spain, Portugal, England, France and Holland sailed the seas in quest of riches, and the two American continents were explored and colonized by Europeans. In a favored section of North America, thirteen English colonies broke away from the Mother Country and, under their own flag, marched westward, developing a rich, powerful and democratic nation in the great expanse between the Atlantic and Pacific oceans.

The northern part of the continent became a Dominion of the British Empire.

The history of man's exploration of the globe is told in part in the following articles:

Bibliography

CARUS, HELEN. *Metten of Tyre.* Doubleday, Doran & Co.
COLUM, PADRAIC. *The Voyagers: Legends and History of Atlantic Discovery.* The Macmillan Co.
FINGER, C. J. *Heroes from Hakluyt.* Henry Holt & Co.
HANSON, L. S. *Eric the Red.* Doubleday, Doran & Co.
HEWES, A. D. *Spice and the Devil's Cave.* Alfred A. Knopf.
KENT, L. A. *He Went with Marco Polo.* Houghton, Mifflin Co.
OUTHWAITE, LEONARD. *Unrolling the Map.* Reynal & Hitchcock.
SHERWOOD, MERRIAM. *Road to Cathay.* The Macmillan Co.
SYNGE, M. B. *Book of Discovery.* G. P. Putnam's Sons.

High-School List

BELLOC, HILAIRE. *The Crusades, the World's Debate.* Bruce Publishing Co.
GAITHER, MRS. F. O. *The Fatal River, the Life and Death of La Salle.* Henry Holt & Co.
LAMB, HAROLD. *Crusades.* Doubleday, Doran & Co.
LAUT, A. C. *Pathfinders of the West.* The Macmillan Co.
SKINNER, C. L. *Adventures of Oregon; a Chronicle of the Fur Trade.* Yale University Press.
REPPLIER, AGNES. *Pere Marquette.* Doubleday, Doran & Co.
REPPLIER, AGNES. *Mere Marie of the Ursulines.* Doubleday, Doran & Co.
REPPLIER, AGNES. *Fra Junipero Serra.* Doubleday, Doran & Co.
VAN LOON, H. W. *The Story of the Pacific.* Harcourt, Brace & Co.

EXPLORING THE WORLD OF KNOWLEDGE

Man's first achievement not connected with his physical needs was the development of speech. In the beginning, speech may have been no more than exclamations or cries coupled with gestures. Yet the languages of today grew out of some such crude efforts of early man to communicate with his fellows. The next major step in the intellectual field was the invention of writing. It is interesting to know that men painted or carved pictures of the hunt on the walls of their caves before they learned to write, and that elaborate forms of picture writing preceded the kind of writing we use today—writing based on the alphabet. Centuries after the invention of the alphabet came printing from movable type, which greatly advanced the spread of learning and the growth of popular education.

Far back in human history men were studying the heavens and forming theories about the movements of the sun, stars and planets. These studies became the science of astronomy. Men also pondered the nature of the world and their relation to it. Philosophy and the natural sciences took form and religions were founded. There was progress along social and political lines. Small groups of families became tribes; nations were formed; governments were organized. Man also developed his cultural and artistic talents.

Further information on man's progress in the various fields mentioned above may be found under such headings as:

Alphabet	Languages of the
Arithmetic	World
Astronomy	Monasticism
Book	Music
Crusades	Painting
Cuneiform	Paper
Inscriptions	Papyrus
Feudal System	Printing
Government	Religion
Hieroglyphics	Renaissance
Language and	Sculpture
Grammar	Writing

Bibliography

BANKS, E. J. *Seven Wonders of the Ancient World.* G. P. Putnam's Sons.
HARTMAN, GERTRUDE. *Medieval Days and Ways.* The Macmillan Co.
HODGDON, J. R. *The Enchanted Past.* Ginn & Co.
KUMMER, F. A. *First Days of Knowledge.* Doubleday, Doran & Co.
LANSING, MARION F. *Magic Gold: A Story of the Time of Roger Bacon.* Little, Brown & Co.
LANSING, M. F. *Great Moments in Science.* Doubleday, Doran & Co.
MAXWELL, MARJORIE. *Story of Books.* Harper & Bros.
MORRISON, L. P. *Last Queen of Egypt.* Frederick A. Stokes Co.

High-School List

BAUER, MARION. *How Music Grew from Prehistoric Times to the Present Day.* G. P. Putnam's Sons.
CHALLIS, GEORGE. *The Golden Knight.* Greystone Press.
KING, G. C. *Rise of Rome.* Doubleday, Doran & Co.
LOWNSBERY, ELOISE. *Out of the Flame.* Longmans, Green & Co.
MAYER, JOSEPHINE. *Never to Die; the Egyptians in Their Own Words.* The Viking Press.
STRATTON, CLARENCE. *Swords and Statues; a Tale of 16th-Century Italy.* John G. Winston Co.
VAN LOON, H. W. *The Arts.* Simon & Schuster.

MODERN ADVENTURES

What is there left for man to discover or explore? He has visited most of the land surface of the globe and settled much of it. Antarctica, the ice-bound continent about the South Pole, has been partially explored and mapped, but this great continental mass offers great opportunities for further study. Portions of the jungle areas of the world, in Africa and elsewhere, have been opened to man because of his increasing control of tropical diseases; yet this field of exploration has by no means been exhausted. The study of earth's composition and the nature of the prehistoric world still offer unlimited opportunities to the geologist and the archaeologist.

With the airplane, flights are being made into the stratosphere and across all lands and seas. In the future there will be an even greater development of flying, in air-

EXPLORERS AND DISCOVERERS ALL

planes larger and more powerful than those of today.

Notwithstanding brilliant discoveries regarding the atom, cosmic rays, vitamins and many other subjects, scientists are on the threshhold of more profound revelations. Control of atomic energy, the cure for cancer, the development of television—these and many other problems engage the efforts of the modern thinker.

The need of substitutes for our decreasing supplies of natural fuels will engage other research workers. The creation of synthetic foods and clothing is also a promising field of research.

In the field of human relations the opportunities for improvement are beyond estimate. Can nations ever remain at peace, one with another? What is the solution for such ills as unemployment, poverty and crime? Man's happiness depends upon the answers to these questions and a host of others.

Interesting facts regarding man's achievements and opportunities as an explorer in new fields may be found in the following articles:

Abruzzi, Prince Luigi	Invention
Amadeo, Duke of the	Kane, Elisha Kent
Airplane	Lindbergh, Charles A.
Amundsen, Roald	Nansen, Fridtjof
Andrews, Roy	North Polar
Chapman	Exploration
Archaeology	Peary, Robert E.
Beebe [Charles]	Radio
William	Scott, Robert F.
Byrd, Richard Evelyn	South Polar
Chemistry	Exploration
Cosmic Rays	Stefansson,
Flying, Story of	Vilhjalmur
Franklin, John	Stratosphere
Geology	Unemployment
Greely, Adolphus W.	Wilkins, George
Housing Problem	Hubert

Bibliography

BYRD, R. E. *Little America.* G. P. Putnam's Sons.
COLLINS, F. A. *Mountain Climbing.* D. Appleton-Century Co.
COTTLER, JOSEPH. *Map Makers.* Little, Brown & Co.
CRUMP, IRVING. *Our Airmen.* Dodd, Mead & Co.
ELLSBERG, EDWARD. *On the Bottom.* Dodd, Mead & Co.
PEARY, R. E. *The North Pole: Its Discovery in 1909.* Frederick A. Stokes Co.
PHILP, C. G. *Conquest of the Stratosphere.* Sir I. Pitman & Sons.
TURLEY, CHARLES. *Voyages of Captain Scott.* Dodd, Mead & Co.

High-School List

EXPLORERS CLUB, N. Y. *Explorers Club Tales; True Stories of Exploration, Research and Adventure.* Dodd, Mead & Co.
FINDLAY, ALEXANDER. *Chemistry in the Service of Man.* Longmans, Green & Co.
HANSON, E. P. *High Road to Adventure; an Anthology.* Robert M. McBride & Co.
HATHAWAY, E. V. *Partners in Progress.* McGraw-Hill Book Co.
JOHNSTON, S. P. *Horizons Unlimited; a Graphic History of Aviation.* Duell, Pearce & Co.
YOST, EDNA. *Modern Americans in Science and Invention.* Frederick A. Stokes Co.

AS MAN LEFT IT   AS HE FOUND IT

Control and Use of Natural Resources

Wise management, thought for the future and thrift are constructive terms in connection with national and individual economy. Opposed to them are waste, irresponsibility and extravagance. The wealth of a nation is represented by its soil and forests, its water and wildlife, its mines and factories, and by its citizens. Poor management of any of these resources weakens a people and if carried too far can bring about a national disaster. Eroded or worn-out soil endangers a nation's food supplies. When forests disappear, soil, climate and human health are affected. Human resources are wasted by poverty, crime, disease and illiteracy.

The answer to waste and mismanagement is conservation. This implies the coöperation of the people as a whole and the integrity of their government in protecting its natural and human resources. The government practices conservation when it sets aside large forest and mineral areas to protect them from private exploitation; or when it preserves for the enjoyment and education of the people regions of natural beauty or of great historic interest. Laws to prevent the extinction of wild animals, birds and fish are based on the same principle. Very often such conservation policies restrict the individual, but the good citizen will place the nation's welfare above selfish interests.

Shortsighted policies in the use of natural resources affect a people economically, politically and morally. Such policies cause agricultural depressions and widespread unemployment. Relief for thousands of unemployed men and impoverished families places a severe drain on the taxpayers, who in time become cynical and resentful. On the other hand, relief dispensed over a long period often affects the character and morale of the persons receiving it, in that self-reliance ceases to be a virtue.

The expenditure of public funds for relief carries with it the obligation to expend the funds honestly and without political bias. The temptation to reap political advantage, to misuse funds and to seek personal gain is very real. How the problem is met is a test of a nation's integrity.

Conservation touches nearly all phases of national life. Upon it depends national welfare and prosperity.

SOIL CONSERVATION

In the early years of American history, the farmers adopted a policy of moving westward to new lands when the soil they were cultivating began to wear out. This policy was responsible for the extension of the cotton empire westward to Texas and for the occupation of vast fertile areas in the Mississippi Valley. Because the land seemed inexhaustible, farmers harvested the same crops year after year, until the fertility of the soil was so depleted that production sharply declined.

As time went on, grasslands of the Great Plains were converted into croplands, although in this region the grass was needed to hold the soil and conserve moisture. During the 1930's, in a series of drought years the unprotected land became a veritable Dust Bowl. Entire farms reverted to desert conditions and large numbers of families lost everything they owned.

Another foe of productivity is erosion, causing disappearance of soil from the fields. The United States Department of Agriculture has stated that, considering all types of land, soil erosion has ruined or seriously impoverished about 282,000,000 acres, an area exceeding the acreage of Texas and

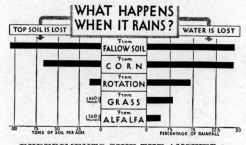

EXPERIMENTS GIVE THE ANSWER

California combined. The direct cost of erosion to American farmers is estimated to be $400,000,000 a year.

The problems arising from unwise management of the soil are being met in a variety of ways. The United States Farm Security Administration makes loans to

destitute and low-income farm families for the purchase of equipment and livestock and for family subsistence. A program of resettlement projects serves to help needy rural families make a new start on land capable of producing a decent living for them.

In addition to the aid to distressed rural populations, the government carries on a diversified program of soil reclamation and

EROSION CAN BE PREVENTED
Water washes away soil on cutover land.

rebuilding. Under the provisions of the Agricultural Adjustment Act and its amendments, the Department of Agriculture encourages farm practices that protect and improve the soil. Producers who adopt special soil-building methods, or who increase the proportion of land devoted to crops that conserve the soil, benefit by special grants of money appropriated by Congress.

State agricultural colleges, experiment stations and farmer coöperatives encourage such constructive measures as crop rotation, fertilization, soil analysis and weed control. These methods are all helping to restore and save the agricultural lands of America.

For a general background of the subject, read the article SOIL. Further information on soil conservation and allied subjects may be found in the articles listed below:

Agriculture	Geology
Arid Region	Humus
Clay	Lime
Conservation	Loess
Drainage	Manures
Dry Farming	Marl
Erosion	Nitrate
Fertilizers	Phosphates
Geography, subhead	Rotation of Crops
The Geography of	Weeds
Soils	

Bibliography

FAIRBANKS, H. W. *Conservation Reader.* World Book Co.
HILL, H. C. *Life and Work of the Citizen.* Ginn & Co.
MCNEELY, M. H. *Jumping-off Place.* Longmans, Green & Co.
PRICE, O. W. *Land We Live In.* Dodd, Mead & Co.
SCARBOROUGH, DOROTHY. *Story of Cotton.* Harper & Bros.
SCHMIDT, S. L. *New Land.* Robert M. McBride & Co.
SIMON, C. M. *Robin on the Mountain.* E. P. Dutton & Co.

SAVING THE FORESTS

The forests of a nation are among its priceless assets. From forest trees come food and raiment, materials for shelter, cellulose, tar and turpentine, medicines and a host of other products. Trees are important for shade and windbreaks; they provide shelter for forest creatures; and they serve as watersheds, reducing flood danger and soil erosion and protecting sources of water supply.

Yet man has often been careless about his forests, unmindful of the future. The magnificent timber lands of the United States were mismanaged and depleted for years before a national policy of conservation was adopted. The first national forestry division, established in 1880, was hardly more than a statistical bureau. Fortunately, wise men such as Grover Cleveland, John Muir, Gifford Pinchot and Theodore Roosevelt awakened the nation to the necessity of saving the nation's forests, and today the Forest Service is promoting the conservation and use of forest lands whose area is at least one-fourth the total area of the United States.

Directly under the supervision of the Forest Service are about 160 national forests. The Service is engaged in improving these forest lands, protecting them from fire, insects and disease and in managing their resources. Technical methods are applied to the planting of trees and the harvesting of timber. Livestock grazing is regulated in the interest of range conservation. Watersheds are managed scientifically. Forest areas are also maintained as recreation and camping grounds for the people, who are urged to remember that, while it takes years to grow one forest tree, hun-

dreds of trees may be destroyed in a few hours by a lighted match carelessly thrown on the ground. Forest rangers are con-

CARELESSNESS (SMOKERS - CAMPERS)		33%
MALICIOUSNESS (INCENDIARIES)		25%
NEGLIGENCE (BRUSH BURNING, RAILROAD, LOGGING)		18%
OTHER MAN-CAUSED (LARGELY PREVENTABLE)		17%
LIGHTNING (NOT PREVENTABLE)		7%

Each tree represents 2,000 forest fires annually

CAUSES OF AMERICAN FOREST FIRES

stantly on guard in these areas and other sections of the national forests.

Blackened trunks, barren hillsides, eroded slopes and ruined farms bear witness to past years of neglect. Present conservation methods give hope for a brighter picture in the years ahead.

For further information on the conservation of forests, the reader is referred to the following articles:

Forests and Forestry Pinchot, Gifford
Lumber Roosevelt, Theodore
Muir, John Tree (Planting Trees)

Bibliography

CHAPMAN, MARISTAN. *Timber Trail.* D. Appleton-Century Co.

CRUMP, IRVING. *Boys' Book of Forest Rangers.* Dodd, Mead & Co.

MEADER, S. W. *Lumberjack.* Harcourt, Brace & Co.

MEIGS, CORNELIA. *Swift Rivers.* Little, Brown & Co.

PACK, C. L. *Forest Facts for Schools.* The Macmillan Co.

YEAGER, D. G. *Bob Flame, Ranger.* Dodd, Mead & Co.

High-School List

DU PUY, W. A. *The Nation's Forests.* The Macmillan Co.

GAER, JOSEPH. *Men and Trees; the Problems of Forest Conservation.* Harcourt, Brace & Co.

HOLBROOK, S. H. *Tall Timber.* The Macmillan Co.

PERRY, JOSEPHINE. *Forestry and Lumbering.* Longmans, Green & Co.

PINCHOT, GIFFORD. *The Training of a Forester.* J. B. Lippincott Co.

VAN NAME, W. G. *Vanishing Forest Reserves; Problems of the National Forests and National Parks.* R. G. Badger Co.

WHITE, S. E. *Blazed Trail.* Doubleday, Doran & Co.

USE AND CONTROL OF WATER

When we consider the useful and beneficent aspects of water, we think of it as giving life to the soil, filling irrigation ditches and beds of navigable rivers, and furnishing power to operate machines. But another picture comes to mind when we think of the enormous destructive force of floods—water out of control.

The Ohio and Mississippi valleys and many other areas with river systems are menaced periodically by the swift rise of water following sudden thaws or abnormally heavy rainfall. Back of the flood there is often a story of man's destruction of forests, those natural sponges that soak up excess moisture. On land denuded of trees the soil becomes washed and furrowed. Surplus water, gathering force as it flows through furrows and gullies, and thence into small streams, finally rushes into the main artery in such volume that the river spills over its banks, destroying homes and carrying away valuable topsoil. In some parts of the West, where forest fires have laid bare the slopes of mountains and foothills, rich valley lands have been devastated by flood waters following cloudbursts.

The United States is alert to the need of checking losses of life and property through recurring floods. Among the government agencies whose activities include flood control are the Army Engineer Corps, the Soil Conservation Service and the Federal Power Commission. The technical staff of the Federal Power Commission has a special bureau that handles flood-control projects.

There are various methods of controlling floods. One that attacks the underlying cause is the replanting of areas where the run-off water can be absorbed by trees. Floods due to erosion in cutover areas near

Erosion
Flood
Flood Plain
Irrigation
Jetty
Levee

Mississippi River
Rain
Reclamation,
  Bureau of
Reservoir
Water Power

Bibliography

BOND, A. R. *Pick, Shovel and Pluck*. Scientific American Publishing Co.
HODGINS, ERIC. *Behemoth, the Story of Power*. Doubleday, Doran & Co.
LORENZ, PARE. *The River*. Stackpole Sons.
ROGERS, FRANCES. *Fresh and Briny*. Frederick A. Stokes Co.
SIMON, C. M. *Teeny Gay*. E. P. Dutton & Co.
WILLIAMSON, THAMES. *Flood Fighters*. Houghton, Mifflin Co.

High-School List

BURMAN, BEN. *Big River to Cross*. John Day Co.
CRONEIS, C. G. *Down to Earth; an Introduction to Geology*. University of Chicago Press.
DALY, R. A. *Architecture of the Earth*. D. Appleton-Century Co.
MARSHAK, I. I. *Men and Mountains*. J. B. Lippincott Co.
MITCHELL, MRS. L. S. *My Country 'Tis of Thee; the Use and Abuse of Natural Resources*. The Macmillan Co.
Rivers of America Series; ed. by CARL CARMER. Farrar & Rinehart, Inc.

WILDLIFE CONSERVATION

The pioneers who settled the regions now included in the United States found such an abundance of wild animals, birds and fish that they slaughtered them without thought of the future. In the early days of America, as in later times, there was waste-

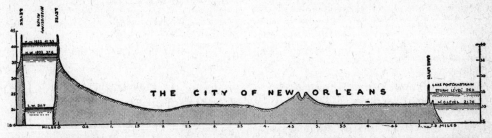

A CITY BELOW WATER LEVEL LEARNS THAT IT MUST PLAN OR PERISH

the headwaters of rivers often can be prevented by strip cropping and terracing. Check dams on tributaries and large dams on the main streams are effective in keeping swollen currents under control. Other flood-control projects include dikes, levees, debris basins, flood-water reservoirs and artificial river channels.

Conservation of a nation's water resources includes, besides flood control, the production of hydro-electric power, the construction of irrigation canals and the improvement of navigable waterways. For the various phases of this subject, see:

Alluvium   Dam
Canal   Delta

ful depletion of one of the country's most important resources.

Millions of buffalo, or bison, once roamed the woodlands and plains between the Alleghenies and the Sierra and Coast ranges. The Indians fiercely resisted the white man's slaughter of these useful animals, for it deprived them of skins for tepees and clothing and of flesh for food. If the United States and Canadian governments had not protected the last remaining herds, there would be no specimens of the American bison alive today. The elk, moose and other types of deer, grizzly bears, wild sheep and goats and a host of smaller animals have also been victims of the white man's march westward.

The development of the fur industry in North America was marked by the reckless slaughter of such animals as the beaver, seal, fox, mink, otter, marten, muskrat and raccoon. Today, most of the American fur-bearers are found in numbers only in the wilds of Canada and in Alaska.

Wild birds have been decimated by the hunter's gun and by the destruction of the

BANDING A MALLARD DUCK
Bird bands help in studying migratory habits.

feeding places of migratory birds. The classic example of bird destruction is the extinction of the beautiful passenger pigeon, the last specimen having died in 1914. At one time, these birds were so numerous that it took hours for a flock to pass a given point. Many waterfowl, too, have become rare, and are in danger of extinction.

Certain food fishes have decreased because of wasteful methods of capture, pollution of streams and the practice of building dams across rivers used by fish for spawning.

The conservation of our wildlife is the concern of Federal and state governments and of individuals and organizations. State game laws specify seasons for hunting and fishing and stipulate the number, size, age and sex of animals taken. The Federal Fish and Wildlife Service coöperates with the states in the establishment of refuges for birds and other creatures, and for this purpose it acquires lands by reservation of the public domain and by gift and purchase. The fishery conservation policies of the Service include the development of hatcheries, the elimination of water pollution and the maintenance of fish ladders on dams.

All the national parks are wildlife sanctuaries, for hunting is prohibited within their boundaries. Olympic National Park, in Washington, has over 3,000 specimens of the Roosevelt elk, now nearly extinct in other areas. Isle Royale, in Lake Superior, is noted for its moose herd. There are buffalo herds in Wind Cave Park, South Dakota, and a buffalo range is maintained in Yellowstone Park. These are typical examples.

To preserve North American birds, the United States coöperates with Canada and Mexico. Treaties providing for the protection of migratory birds are observed by the three countries. In force, too, are the Whaling Treaty Act and laws for the protection, under international agreements, of sea otters, fur seals, walruses and sea lions.

A famous bird sanctuary, the gift of Edward W. Bok, is a fifty-acre park near Mountain Lake, Fla. Its most notable feature is the beautiful Singing Tower, 205 feet high.

Supplementary information on wildlife conservation, together with interesting reading material, may be found under such titles as:

Audubon Society	Game (Laws; Preserves and Reservations)
Biological Survey (Fish and Wildlife Service)	
	Hunting
Bird (Protection of Birds; Bird Reservations)	Isle Royale
	Parks, National
	Pigeon (Passenger Pigeon)
Buffalo (Bison)	Reindeer
Deer	Seal
Elk (American Elk)	Sea Lion
Fish and Fisheries (Fish Culture)	Yellowstone National Park
Fur and Fur Trade (Fur Farming)	

Bibliography

BAKER, OLAF. *Buffalo Barty.* Dodd, Mead & Co.
CRUMP, IRVING. *Boys' Book of Fisheries.* Dodd, Mead & Co.
DANIEL, HAWTHORNE. *Bare Hands.* Grosset & Dunlop.
MEADER, S. W. *King of the Hills.* Harcourt, Brace & Co.
———. *Trap Lines North.* Dodd, Mead & Co.
ROURKE, CONSTANCE. *Audubon.* Harcourt, Brace & Co.
WILLIAMSON, THAMES. *Lobster War.* Lothrop, Lee & Shepard Co.
———. *North After Seals.* Houghton, Mifflin Co.

High-School List

AUDUBON, J. J. *Birds of America.* The Macmillan Co.
BENCHLEY, MRS. B. J. *My Life in a Man-Made Jungle.* Little, Brown & Co.
CHAPMAN, WENDELL. *Wilderness Wanderers; Adventures Among Wild Animals in Rocky Mountain Solitudes.* Charles Scribner's Sons.
GABRIELSON, I. N. *Wildlife Conservation.* The Macmillan Co.
MUIR, JOHN. *John of the Mountains; the Unpublished Journals of John Muir.* Houghton, Mifflin Co.
PEATTIE, D. C. *Singing in the Wilderness.* G. P. Putnam's Sons.
ROSS, M. I. *Morgan's Fourth Son.* Harper & Bros.
WILLIAMSON, HENRY. *Salar, the Salmon.* Little, Brown & Co.

MINERAL RESOURCES

Man's cultural progress is divided into periods based upon his use of minerals. The most ancient of these periods was the Stone Age. It was followed by a transition period when copper was used for tools and weapons. When man learned to make the first alloy, a mixture of tin and copper, he began living in the Bronze Age. The Age of Iron and its outgrowth, the modern Steel Age, cover the period of the world's greatest industrial development—the period of inventions that have transformed man's ways of living.

History shows that minerals are the basic resources that determine a nation's world-position in industry and commerce. Plentiful supplies of coal and iron made possible England's rise to world supremacy. The development of vast mineral resources enabled the United States to become a great exporting nation and to develop an economy based on both industry and agriculture.

Soil can be used for crops year after year, and forest land can be reclaimed, but minerals, once they are mined, can never be replaced. A nation that regards its mineral resources as inexhaustible and exploits them wastefully is inviting disaster.

Although petroleum, coal, and some other minerals have been exploited with too little regard for the future, the United States is taking steps to conserve its mineral resources. For instance, the Federal government will not sell public lands containing mineral deposits, and any private companies permitted to mine such lands under leases must abide by recommendations of the surveyors who have examined and classified the deposits.

The Bureau of Mines in the Department of the Interior carries on field and laboratory tests with a view to improving methods of mining. It conducts investigations on the utilization of lower-grade ores and makes suggestions regarding the creation of substitutes for essential mineral products. Private industry, too, carries on similar studies on methods of preventing overproduction and waste.

For basic information on minerals and their use, the articles METALS and MINING may be read to advantage. See, also, titles below:

Coal   Geological Survey
Gasoline   Iron
Geography, subhead   Iron Age
   Minerals   Petroleum

Bibliography

GREENE, HOMER. *Coal and the Coal Mines.* Houghton, Mifflin Co.
GRUENING, MARTHA. *Story of Mining.* Harper & Bros.
HEYLIGER, WILLIAM. *Wild Cat.* D. Appleton-Century Co.
MERSEREAU, S. F. *Materials of Industry: Their Distribution and Production.* McGraw-Hill Book Co.
PETERSHAM, M. F. *Story Book of Earth's Treasures.* John C. Winston Co.
RUGG, H. O. *Man at Work: His Industries.* Ginn & Co.
WILHELM, DONALD. *Story of Iron and Steel.* Harper & Bros.

High-School List

DAVIS, WATSON. *Story of Copper.* D. Appleton-Century Co.
DOBIE, J. F. *Apache Gold and Yaqui Silver.* Little, Brown & Co.
FENTON, C. L. *The Rock Book.* Doubleday, Doran & Co.
GLASSCOCK, C. B. *Then Came Oil, the Story of the Last Frontier.* The Bobbs-Merrill Co.
HOLBROOK, S. H. *Iron Brew, a Century of American Ore and Steel.* The Macmillan Co.
MARSHAK, I. I. *Men and Mountains; Man's Victory Over Nature.* J. B. Lippincott Co.
STRACK, L. H. *Asbestos—Nickel—Radium; The Magic Minerals.* Harper & Bros.
VERRILL, A. H. *Minerals, Metals and Gems;* also, *All Rocks and Stones.* L. C. Page & Co.

USING OUR BY-PRODUCTS

Smoke and soot are undesirable by-products formed in the combustion of soft coal, and much ingenuity is expended to lessen or eliminate them. But when soft coal is heated to produce coke and illuminating gas, a by-product is yielded that is one of our most useful substances.

This is a black, gummy liquid called coal tar. From coal tar and its derivatives we get perfumes, drugs, fertilizers, explosives, preservatives, saccharine, disinfectants, plastics, and a host of other things that make the world more livable.

The utilization of valuable by-products is an essential factor of modern economics. In agriculture and industry, materials formerly considered waste are more and more being converted to useful purposes. In the packing house it is an axiom that every part of the pig is used but the squeal. Animals slaughtered principally for their meat also yield hides, bones, hoofs, hair, and blood, all of which are processed.

In the lumber industry, waste from the sawmills has been found practicable for laths and other wood products, and even the sawdust is useful, since it contains cellulose and also is suitable for wood pulp used in making some grades of paper.

Corn and cotton are among the farm plants that yield valuable by-products. There is scarcely any waste in the utilization of these plants.

Scrap metal of all kinds, scrap paper, rags, bones, tin cans, bottles, rubber oddments and many other articles once discarded as waste are being converted into useful products. The sale of scrap iron has itself become an important industry, for the scraps of metal are melted down and used again by steel manufacturers.

The following articles indicate the value and uses of many products and by-products of agriculture and industry:

Bakelite	Glycerine
Bone	Kerosene
Carbolic Acid	Leather
Carbon	Linseed
Casein	Lumber
Cellophane	Naphtha
Celluloid	Oils
Cellulose	Paint
Charcoal	Palm
Clay	Paper
Coal Tar	Paraffin
Coconut	Pepsin
Cod-Liver Oil	Perfumes
Coir	Petroleum
Coke	Resins
Copra	Rosin
Corn	Rubber
Cotton	Soap
Cottonseed Products	Steel
Creosote	Sugar
Dextrin	Tree
Fermentation	Tung Oil
Gasoline	Turpentine
Glucose	Whale
Glue	Wood Distillation

Bibliography

ABBOT, C. G. *Everyday Mysteries.* The Macmillan Co.

DARROW, F. L. *Boys' Own Book of Great Inventions.* The Macmillan Co.

EHRENFELD, LOUIS. *Story of Common Things.* G. P. Putnam's Sons.

PACKARD, L. O. *Nations at Work.* The Macmillan Co.

PRYOR, W. C. *Paper Book.* Harcourt, Brace & Co.

SLOSSON, E. E. *Creative Chemistry.* D. Appleton-Century Co.

TAPPAN, E. M. *Makers of Many Things.* Houghton, Mifflin Co.

WORTHINGTON, JOSEPHINE. *Our Clothing.* F. A. Owen Publishing Co.

High-School List

BURLINGAME, ROGER. *Engines of Democracy; Inventions and Society in Mature America.* Charles Scribner's Sons.

FINDLAY, ALEXANDER. *Chemistry in the Service of Man.* Longmans, Green & Co.

GILES, DOROTHY. *Singing Valleys; the Story of Corn.* Random House.

HOLMES, H. N. *Out of the Test Tube.* Emerson Co.

LOCKREY, A. J. *Plastics in the School and Home Workshop.* D. Van Nostrand Co.

MANSPERGER, D. E. *Plastics; Problems and Processes.* International Textbook Co.

VERRILL, A. H. *Perfumes and Spices; Including an Account of Soaps and Cosmetics.* L. C. Page & Co.

WASTE THROUGH ACCIDENTS

Another phase of the conservation movement is the campaign to reduce the number of casualties resulting from accidents. Soil may be reclaimed, forests replanted and factories rebuilt. A human life snuffed out is lost forever.

In a single year in the United States, as many as 100,000 persons have been killed by accidents, many of which were preventable. Millions of other persons are disabled in such accidents, some of them permanently. One can hardly estimate the drain on the

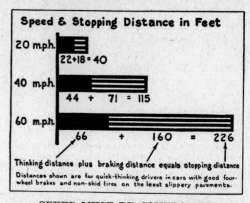

SPEED MUST BE CONTROLLED

The greater the speed the less control. Clear minds are needed for safe automobile driving.

manpower of the nation through this waste of human talent, knowledge and energy, year after year.

During an extended period in which statistics have been compiled, motor vehicles have been the chief cause of death and injury among the civilian population of the United States. Accidents in homes are responsible for the next largest number of deaths. Occupational accidents rank third. A fourth category includes public accidents not caused by motor cars, such as those occurring in train wrecks, fires, storms, floods, and airplane crashes. Although plane wrecks are spectacular, they cause fewer deaths in civilian accidents than do automobiles.

The campaign to educate the public for greater safety has grown to nation-wide proportions. Leaders in this movement include the National Safety Council, the American Red Cross, life-insurance companies, Federal, state, and local governing bodies, public schools and colleges and private industry. Education for safety is aided by pamphlets, magazines and newspapers, posters and slogans, radio talks and training classes conducted by public and private agencies.

States and municipalities are more and more recognizing the importance of uniform regulations governing motor traffic. A

Model Municipal Traffic Ordinance drafted by the National Conference on Street and Highway Safety has been adopted by many cities, and the list is growing.

Industrial accidents are declining because of more stringent laws governing safety appliances in mines and factories. In a modern factory where labor is exposed to many hazards, the workers wear helmets, face shields, eye protectors, asbestos clothing and other protective devices. Mechanical appliances making use of the electric eye have saved numerous workers from injury or death.

Supplementary information may be found under the following headings:

Airplane
Automobile
Building Laws
Coast Guard
Employer's Liability
Factory and Factory Legislation
Fire
Fire Department
Insurance
Red Cross Societies
Rules of the Road
Safety Lamp

Bibliography

ARNOLD, J. O. Coöperative Citizenship. Row, Peterson & Co.
COLLINS, F. A. Sentinels Along Our Coast. D. Appleton-Century Co.
DULL, C. E. Safety First—and Last. Henry Holt & Co.
FLOHERTY, J. J. Fire Fighters! Doubleday, Doran & Co.
FLOHERTY, J. J. Youth at the Wheel. J. B. Lippincott Co.
GENTLES, H. W. Habits for Safety. The Bobbs-Merrill Co.
NORRIS, MARGARET. Heroes and Hazards. The Macmillan Co.
WHITING, J. D. Storm Fighters: True Stories of the Coast Guards. The Bobbs-Merrill Co.

High-School List

DUNSHEE, K. H. Engine! Engine! A Story of Fire Protection. Harold V. Smith.
EATON, E. L. Weather Guide for Air Pilots. Ronald Press Co.
GEDDES, N. B. Magic Motorways. Random House.
NATIONAL FIRE PROTECTION ASSOCIATION. Fire Defense. The N. F. P. Association.
NOLAN, J. C. The Story of Clara Barton of the Red Cross. Julian Messner, Inc.
WALES, MARGUERITE. Public Health Nurse in Action. The Macmillan Co.
WILLIAMS, S. J. Safety. The Macmillan Co.

WASTE THROUGH CRIME

A person who turns to crime harms not only himself but the social structure that depends on good citizens for its well-being. Another tragic effect of crime is the loss to society of men and women who are victims of the criminal. Property lost by theft and destruction represents a waste of money that could have been devoted to constructive purposes. The tracking down and punishment of criminals causes a further drain on the financial resources of society, since the maintenance of police departments, criminal courts and jails and penitentiaries requires the continuous expenditure of funds. An awakened public conscience has improved conditions in many cities where the local government was too corrupt or too indifferent to end such practices as racketeering and extortion. The national government, through the Federal Bureau of Investigation, has done much to wipe out kidnapping and other crimes in which offenders cross from one state to another.

Sociologists recognize the importance of checking criminal tendencies in the young. Many gangsters come from slum areas where conditions breed delinquency in young children. This phase of the war on crime is engaging the attention of numerous social workers and reform groups.

For other information concerning the crime problem, see the following articles:

Crime, subhead
Criminology
Juvenile Court
Police
Prison
Reform Schools

THE HOUSING PROBLEM

We have pointed out that the poor environment of slum districts encourages the formation of criminal habits. It is likewise true that sickness is more common in such areas, and the death rate of infants born in impoverished slum dwellings is abnormally high. Fire hazards are greater because the homes lack fireproof construction, and facilities for lighting and heating are out of date. Overcrowding and the attendant lack of elementary privacy have a bad effect on the moral standards of the people.

Conditions such as these are not limited to the poorer districts of large cities. There are too many inadequate houses in the towns and in rural areas, as well.

The Federal government has attempted to improve conditions through a program of slum clearance and low-cost housing. Enormous housing projects for families in the lower-income groups have been built in a number of cities. These projects rent for less than comparable homes built by private industry because they are financed by public funds.

Another form of government aid is the system of home-owner loans to be repaid over a period of years. Programs of this nature have helped a great many families, but only a beginning has been made in the effort to improve housing conditions.

The great war-production program of the 1940's stimulated so-called defense housing in the sections employing large numbers of factory workers. The numerous agencies dealing with housing were consolidated into a single National Housing Agency after the United States entered World War II.

Additional information on the subject of housing may be found under the following headings:

Architecture, subhead   City Planning
     Housing Projects   Federal Housing
Building   Administration
Building Laws   Housing Problem

Bibliography

BAARSLAG, KARL. *Robbery by Mail: the Story of the U. S. Postal Inspectors.* Farrar & Rinehart, Inc.
CRUMP, IRVING. *Our G-Men.* Dodd, Mead & Co.
HARTMAN, GERTRUDE. *These United States.* The Macmillan Co.

HUBERMAN, LEO. *"We, the People."* Harper & Bros.
LINDLEY, E. K. *A New Deal for Youth; the Story of NYA.* The Viking Press.
WHEELER, F. R. *Boy with the U. S. Secret Service.* Lothrop, Lee & Shepard Co.

High-School List

ADAMIC, LOUIS, *Dynamite; the Story of Class Violence in America, 1826–1934.* The Viking Press.
BEARD, MRS. M. R. *The American Labor Movement; a Short History.* The Macmillan Co.
CANTOR, N. F. *Crime.* University of Chicago Press.
DOUGLAS, P. H. *Social Security in the U. S.; an Analysis and Appraisal of the Federal Social Security Act.* McGraw-Hill Book Co.
FURNAS, J. C. *How America Lives.* Henry Holt & Co.
———. *Housing America*, by the editors of "Fortune." Harcourt, Brace & Co.
MANES, ALFRED. *Insurance; Facts and Problems.* Harper & Bros.
MUMFORD, LEWIS. *Culture of Cities.* Harcourt, Brace.

Living in the Machine Age

Should you ever visit the department of a modern canning factory where tin cans are receiving their labels, you would be fascinated by the inspection service. From the wrapping machine the cans pass by on a continuously-moving conveyor. Most of them will be properly wrapped, but occasionally there will be one without its covering. At some point, probably, the wrapping machine ran out of paper. But an accurate, tireless inspector is keeping watch. Whenever a defective can goes by, a lever pushes out and jerks it to one side. Although the operation seems to be directed by human intelligence, the heart of the mechanism performing the service is a vacuum tube that responds electrically to light. We often speak of it as the electric eye.

It is one of the thousands of mechanical servants that do much of the work of the modern world. Because of machines we are better fed, clothed and sheltered, more widely traveled and more highly entertained than people have ever been.

The changes that have transformed living conditions since American pioneer days may be better appreciated if we visualize the frontier home of the seventeenth century. The pioneer family lived in a log cabin with a thatch or dirt roof and a dirt floor. The one door hung on bark or leather hinges. That home and its furnishings were made with simple hand tools. For food, vegetables were grown in the clearing and game was killed in the forest. All meals were cooked in the fireplace. Natural products, processed at home, served the pioneer family for clothing, dyes, soap, ink and candles.

In the chapters that follow, we shall see how machines have made a new world.

Bibliography

BAILEY, C. S. *Children of the Handicrafts.* The Macmillan Co.
FIELD, RACHEL. *Calico Bush.* The Macmillan Co.
GARDINER, A. C. *Good Wind and Good Water.* The Viking Press.
MEIGS, CORNELIA. *Wind in the Chimney.* The Macmillan Co.
PRESCOTT, D. R. *Day in a Colonial Home.* Marshall Jones Co.
ROBINSON, E. F. *Houses in America.* The Viking Press.
SKINNER, C. L. *Debby Barnes, Trader.* The Macmillan Co.
SNEDEKER, C. D. *Beckoning Road.* Doubleday, Doran & Co.

High-School List

BECKER, M. L. *Growing Up with America; an Anthology.* Frederick A. Stokes Co.
CHASE, M. E. *A Goodly Heritage.* Henry Holt & Co.
EATON, JEANETTE. *Narcissa Whitman, Pioneer of Oregon.* Harcourt, Brace & Co.
KENT, L. A. *In Good Old Colony Times.* Houghton, Mifflin Co.
LANSING, MARION. *Nicholas Arnold, Toolmaker.* Doubleday, Doran & Co.
ROBERTS, E. M. *The Great Meadow.* The Viking Press.
UPDEGRAFF, F. M. *Coat for a Soldier.* Harcourt, Brace & Co.

THE COMING OF THE INDUSTRIAL AGE

Men had been using cotton as a textile for thousands of years before they perfected efficient machines for spinning and weaving it. It was the invention of these machines, late in the eighteenth century, that helped to inaugurate the Industrial Revolution and bring about the decline of hand labor and the establishment of the factory system.

Cotton manufacture in England was originally a cottage industry, performed with simple wheels and hand looms. In 1733 a "flying shuttle" was perfected that enabled the weavers to work faster, but the weavers

HARGREAVES' SPINNING JENNY
This was one of the inventions that made mass
production possible.

were so fearful that the device would reduce
the number of jobs available they destroyed
the machinery of the inventor and drove
him out of the country. They were later
to find that the shuttle created a demand
for more yarn and more workers.

Hostility of the cotton workers to new
inventions could not stop the march of
progress, and machines such as the spinning
jenny of James Hargreaves, the spinning
frame of Richard Arkwright and the power
loom of Edmund Cartwright revolutionized
the entire industry within half a century.

Meanwhile, English colonists had been
building settlements along the Atlantic coast
of America. A brisk trade in cotton had
developed between the colonies and the
Mother Country; raw cotton was shipped
from the South and cotton fabrics were sent
back from England. To protect her growing
industry England refused to permit the export of machines or their designs.

It took the ingenuity of a young mechanic,
Samuel Slater, to circumvent the ban. As

an apprentice of Richard Arkwright's partner, he had become familiar with the cotton-
spinning machines. In 1789 he went to
America, and the following year he set up
a cotton-spinning mill at Pawtucket, Rhode
Island, working from plans drawn from
memory. The mill was run by water power.
Slater's Pawtucket factory housed the first
power-operated cotton-spinning machine in
America. Steam-driven machines were introduced in the textile mills somewhat later.

The only drawback to increased production was the difficulty of separating the
small seeds from the cotton fiber. Working
by hand, one picker could separate the seed
from only one pound of cotton in a day.
This problem was met in 1793 by Eli Whitney's invention of the cotton gin, a device
that vastly increased the volume of work
done. The year before the cotton gin was
introduced, only 4,000 bales of raw cotton
were marketed in America.

It is difficult to overstate the effect of
this epoch-making invention. Production of
raw cotton reached millions of bales a year,
Negro slavery became an established institution in the South and cotton manufacture
developed as an industry of first importance
in Old and New England. Both England
and the United States became great industrial nations in the nineteenth century.

The social effects of the Industrial Revolution were far-reaching. Two social groups,

WHITNEY'S COTTON GIN
This invention directly affected the course of
American history.

the capitalists and the workers, came into
being along with the factory system. The
rapid development of manufacture stimulated transportation and the growth of cities.
As the expansion of industry created a de-

mand for more workers, the United States opened its doors to a great tide of immigration. This tide was not checked until sharp competition for jobs gave rise to laws restricting immigration. A downward trend in rate of population increase followed.

Even the most intricate machines that do our bidding are based on six primary machines—the lever, the wheel and axle, the pulley, the inclined plane, the wedge and the screw. These machines are analyzed in the SCIENCE section.

Further information about the machine and its effect on society, together with a discussion of the industrial era, will be found under the following titles:

Factory and Factory Invention
  Legislation   Labor Organizations
Industrial Revolution Machine

Bibliography

ALLEN, N. B. *Cotton and Other Fibers.* Ginn & Co.
COLLINS, A. F. *Bird's Eye View of Invention.* Thomas Y. Crowell Co.
HOLLAND, R. S. *Historic Inventions.* Macrae Smith Co.
LARCOM, LUCY. *New England Girlhood.* Houghton, Mifflin Co.
McFEE, I. N. C. *Stories of American Inventions.* Thomas Y. Crowell Co.
QUENNELL, M. C. *History of Everyday Things in England.* Charles Scribner's Sons.

High-School List

HOLLAND, MAURICE. *Industrial Explorers.* Harper & Bros.
MOTT-SMITH, M. C. *The Story of Energy.* D. Appleton-Century Co.
THOMPSON, HOLLAND. *The Age of Invention; a Chronicle of Mechanical Conquest.* 1921. Yale University Press.
USHER, A. P. *A History of Mechanical Inventions.* McGraw-Hill Book Co.
WESTWAY, F. W. *The Endless Quest; Three Thousand Years of Science.* Blackie & Son.

The automobile is one of the machines that has affected the lives of nearly everyone. Articles dealing with the automobile industry include:

Automobile   Induction Coil
Carburetor   Petroleum
Ford, Henry   Pneumatic Tires
Gas Engine   Rubber

Bibliography

BUNN, H. F. *Trailer Tracks.* The Macmillan Co.
GIBSON, C. R. *Great Inventions and How They Were Invented.* J. B. Lippincott Co.
RECK, F. M. *Automobiles from Start to Finish.* Thomas Y. Crowell Co.
SALT, HARRIET. *Automobiles.* G. P. Putnam's Sons.
SIMONDS, W. A. *Henry Ford, Motor Genius.* Doubleday, Doran & Co.

High-School List

GUMPERT, MARTIN. *Trail-blazers of Science.* Funk & Wagnalls Co.
HAMILTON, J. R. *Safe Driving; Human Limitations in Automobile Driving.* Doubleday, Doran & Co.
HATHAWAY, E. V. *Partners in Progress.* McGraw-Hill Book Co.
MAXIM, H. P. *Horseless Carriage Days.* Harper & Bros.
WILKINS, H. T. *Marvels of Modern Mechanics; the Mastery of Land, Sea, and Air.* E. P. Dutton & Co.

The invention of devices depending upon applied electricity has been an outstanding development of the Machine Age. Many phases of the story are told under such headings as:

Dynamo   Electro-Motive Force
Edison, Thomas A.   Electroplating
Electric Battery   Electrotyping
Electricity   Faraday, Michael
Electric Light   Galvanometer
Electric Meter   Franklin, Benjamin
Electric Motor   Magneto-Electric
Electric Railway   Machine
Electro-Chemistry   Marconi, Guglielmo
Electrode   Steinmetz, Charles P.
Electrolysis   Tesla, Nikola
Electro-Magnet   Transformer
Electro-Magnetism

Bibliography

COTTLER JOSEPH. *Heroes of Civilization.* Little, Brown & Co.
FRANKLIN, BENJAMIN. *Autobiography.* Houghton, Mifflin Co.
HAMMOND, J. W. *Magician of Science.* D. Appleton-Century Co.
MEADOWCROFT, W. H. *Boys' Life of Edison.* Harper & Bros.
MORGAN, A. P. *First Electrical Book.* Charles Scribner's Sons.
WILLIAMS-ELLIS, AMABEL. *Men Who Found Out.* Coward-McCann, Inc.

High-School List

APPLEYARD, ROLLO. *Pioneers of Electrical Communication.* The Macmillan Co.
CROWTHER, J. G. *Famous American Men of Science.* W. W. Norton & Co.
GIBSON, C. R. *Heroes of the Scientific World.* Seeley, Service & Co.
MILLER, D. C. *Sparks, Lightning, Cosmic Rays; an Anecdotal History of Electricity.* The Macmillan Co.
MORGAN, A. P. *The Pageant of Electricity.* D. Appleton-Century Co.

Man learned to handle and work the various metals in very early times. The metal industry has developed through many hundreds of years. For interesting details about this industry, see the following articles:

Acetylene   Iron
Alloy   Metallurgy
Annealing   Mining
Bessemer, Henry   Pneumatic Tools
Die   Steel
Die-Sinking   Welding
Founding   (And articles on im-
Galvanized Iron   portant metals)

Bibliography

BACHMAN, F. P. *Great Inventors and Their Inventions.* The American Book Co.
DARROW, F. L. *Thinkers and Doers.* Silver, Burdett & Co.
HYLANDER, C. J. *American Inventors.* The Macmillan Co.
KAEMPFFERT, W. B. *Popular History of American Invention.* Charles Scribner's Sons.

High-School List

BRIDGES, T. C. *Master Minds of Modern Science.* L. MacVeagh.
LENARD, P. E. A. *Great Men of Science; a History of Scientific Progress.* The Macmillan Co.
THOMAS, L. J. *Men of Danger.* Frederick A. Stokes Co.
U. S. STEEL CORP. *A Pictorial Presentation of a Basic American Industry.* U. S. Steel Corp.

The invention of printing with movable type was one of the great milestones of human progress. Later inventions increased the speed of printing and attractiveness of the printed page. The following references deal with this interesting subject:

Book   Lithography
Bookbinding   Monotype
Caxton, William   Newspaper
Electrotyping   Paper
Engraving   Photography
Faust, Johann   Photogravure
Gutenberg, Johannes Printing
Linotype   Printing Press
Literature   Stereotyping
  (page 2118)   Type

Bibliography

COFFMAN, RAMON. *Child's History of the Human Race.* Dodd, Mead & Co.
HAAREN, J. H. *Famous Men of the Middle Ages.* American Book Co.
KELLY, E. P. *At the Sign of the Golden Compass.* The Macmillan Co.
LOWNSBERY, ELOISE. *Lighting the Torch.* Longmans, Green & Co.
MARSHAK, I. I. *Black on White.* J. B. Lippincott Co.
MAXWELL, MARJORIE. *Story of Books Up Through the Ages.* Harper & Bros.

High-School List

FENTON, A. H. *Dana of the Sun.* Farrar & Rinehart, Inc.
MCMURTRIE, D. C. *The Book; the Story of Printing and Bookmaking.* Covici-Friede.
ORCOTT, W. D. *The Kingdom of Books.* Little, Brown & Co.
POTTINGER, D. T. *Printers and Printing.* Harvard University Press.
VAN LOON, H. W. *Observations of the Mystery of Print and the Work of Johann Gutenberg.* Book Manufacturers Institute.

Transportation has been profoundly affected by the invention of machines that have brought speed and comfort to the traveling public and efficiency to the distribution of goods. Interesting information about the development of the railroad will be found under the titles listed below:

Air Brake	Railroad
Diesel Engine	Steam Engine
Elevated Railway	Stephenson, George
Locomotive	Westinghouse, George

Bibliography

BINGER, W. D. *What Engineers Do.* W. W. Norton & Co.
FERNALD, H. C. *Smoke Blows West.* Longmans, Green & Co.
MCSPADDEN, J. W. *How They Carried the Mail.* Dodd, Mead & Co.
MEIGS, CORNELIA. *Railroad West.* Little, Brown & Co.
VAN METER, T. W. *Trains, Tracks and Travel.* Simmons-Boardman Pub. Co.
WEBSTER, H. H. *Travel by Air, Land and Sea.* Houghton, Mifflin Co.

High-School List

BURLINGAME, ROGER. *March of the Iron Men.* Charles Scribner's Sons.
CRESSY, EDWARD. *Discoveries and Inventions of the 20th Century.* G. Routledge & Sons.
HUNGERFORD, EDWARD. *Locomotives on Parade.* Thomas Y. Crowell Co.
JUDSON, C. I. *Railway Engineer; the Story of George Stephenson.* Charles Scribner's Sons.
QUIETT, G. C. *They Built the West; an Epic of Rails and Cities.* D. Appleton-Century Co.
STEVERS, M. D. *Steel Trails; the Epic of the Railroads.* Minton, Balch & Co.

For interesting information on the history of textile manufacture, and for biographies of inventors of machines connected with the industry, the reader is referred to the following articles:

Arkwright, Richard	Linen
Cartwright, Edmund	Sewing Machine
Cotton	Silk
Cotton Gin	Spinning
Flax	Textile
Hargreaves, James	Weaving
Howe, Elias	Whitney, Eli

Bibliography

EATON, JEANETTE. *Behind the Show Windows.* Harcourt, Brace & Co.
MCGOWAN, E. A. B. *Textiles and Clothing.* The Macmillan Co.
MORRIS, CHARLES. *Heroes of Progress in America.* J. B. Lippincott Co.
PARKMAN, M. R. *Conquests of Invention.* D. Appleton-Century Co.
STUART, D. M. *Boy Through the Ages.* J. B. Lippincott Co.

THE MACHINE AND POWER

The steam that drives the engine of a locomotive, the force that turns the blades of an electric fan and the gas that moves the motor of an automobile are all sources of power as applied to machines.

Before there were power machines, natural power was at work everywhere. It was in the muscles of the human worker; in the flow of the swift-moving current, in the

Westinghouse

A POWER TRANSFORMER STATION

movement of the wind. It is because a few men, more alert than the majority of their fellows, saw the possibilities of mechanical power that we have air conditioning, streamliners, radio and television and the thousand other conveniences and luxuries of our age.

The raw materials upon which modern power is based are water, coal and petroleum. The production of steam, electricity and gas depends upon these materials and their developments. Thus the story of the transformation of power into goods and services is to be found in the history of the essential raw materials.

Consider the effect on daily living, industry and government through the failure of one or more of the basic power machines. If the electric facilities of our community and homes were completely shut off, telephones and radio sets would be silenced, street lights would go out, streetcars would stop, and dozens of home comforts would be affected.

Before steam or electricity was employed, the power created by running water was used for turning machines. There is interesting information on the use of water power in the following articles:

Barker's Mill	Irrigation, subhead
Hydraulic Engine	American Dams
Hydraulic Ram	Turbine
Hydraulics	Water Power
Hydrostatic Press	Water Wheel

The applications of steam and electricity are endless, for these forms of power have much wider scope than water power. The references on pages 3980 and 3981 in the preceding section may be reviewed at this point. See, also, the following:

Boiler	Steam
Fitch, John	Steam Engine
Fulton, Robert	Turbine, subhead
Ship, subhead	Steam Turbine
Sail and Steam	Watt, James

The power of gases of various types has been utilized for a great many purposes. The following references will be of interest:

Acetylene	Gas, Natural
Diesel Engine	Gas Engine
Gas	Gasoline
Gas, Illuminating	Petroleum

Bibliography

BOND, A. R. *On the Battle Front of Engineering.* D. Appleton-Century Co.

DARROW, F. L. *Masters of Science and Invention.* The Macmillan Co.

EATON, JEANETTE. *Story of Light.* Harper Bros.

HAWKS, ELLISON. *Engineering for Boys.* Thomas Nelson & Sons.

HODGINS, ERIC. *Behemoth, the Story of Power.* Doubleday, Doran & Co.

MORGAN, A. P. *Story of Skyscrapers.* Farrar and Rinehart, Inc.

High-School List

ABRAMS, E. R. *Power in Transition.* Charles Scribner's Sons.

ADAMS, ORVILLE. *Elements of Diesel Engineering.* Henley Co.

BLACK, ARCHIBALD. *The Story of Tunnels.* Whittlesey House.

HARTMAN, GERTRUDE. *Machines and the Men Who Made the World of Industry.* The Macmillan Co.

MILLER, J. A. *Master Builders of Sixty Centuries.* D. Appleton-Century Co.

THE MACHINE AND THE MODERN HOME

The home of today is a product of the Machine Age to the same degree that the home of the American pioneer was the product of manual labor. In modern building, an architect, one or more contractors and a labor force are required, all of whom depend on labor-saving devices. In building the pioneer home, the settler was his own designer and his house was the work of his own hands.

From the excavation of the basement to the installation of the last fixtures, machine and machine-made products are essential in modern construction. A power shovel digs out the earth, a mechanical device mixes the concrete for the foundation. Materials are transported to the site in motor trucks.

Back of the finished materials is a story of mechanical operations in mine and

WHEN NAILS WERE MADE BY HAND
Making nails in colonial times was a home industry.

quarry, forest and factory. These materials may be some or all of the following: lumber, stone, brick, steel, concrete, glass, metals, plaster, paint, varnish, wall paper, screening, insulating material, lacquers and tile.

Many crafts are represented by the workmen who build and embellish the house. Carpenters, roofers, masons, painters, plasterers, plumbers, electricians, and men trained to install air-conditioning systems and insulation are among the workers. The tools they use and the materials they handle are products of the machine. So, too, are the fixtures—light switches and floor plugs, door knobs, sinks, faucets, drains, stall showers, bath and laundry equipment and heating equipment.

A few references describing materials, processes and equipment will be of value:

Architecture, sub- head Modern Trends	Furnace Glass
Asbestos	Heating and
Brick and Brick-	Ventilation
laying	Illumination
Building	Lock
Building Stone	Lumber
Cements	Plastering
Concrete	Plumbing
Electric Heating	Tiles
Electric Light	Varnish
Fuel	Wall Paper

Bibliography

ALLEE, M. H. *House of Her Own.* Houghton, Mifflin Co.

BUTTERFIELD, E. H. *Young People's Story of Architecture.* Dodd, Mead & Co.

CARPENTER, F. G. *How the World Is Housed.* American Book Co.

COATSWORTH, ELIZABETH. *Here I Stay.* Coward-McCann, Inc.

EARLE, A. M. *Home Life in Colonial Days.* The Macmillan Co.

LAMPREY, LOUISE. *Days of the Colonists.* Frederick A. Stokes Co.

LAMPREY, LOUISE. *All the Ways of Building.* The Macmillan Co.
MORGAN, A. P. *Story of Skyscrapers.* Farrar and Rinehart, Inc.
ROBINSON, L. F. *Jack's House.* The Viking Press.
SEREDY, KATE. *Listening.* The Viking Press.

High-School List

ABERCROMBIE, R. K. *How to Buy or Build Your Home Wisely.* The Macmillan Co.
ARCHITECTURAL FORUM. *The House for Modern Living.* Harcourt, Brace & Co.
COON, HORACE. *Small Homes of Distinction.* R. N. McBride & Co.
DANIEL, HAWTHORNE. The *Householder's Complete Handbook.* Little, Brown & Co.
PEET, MRS. L. J. *Household Equipment.* John Wiley & Sons.
WAUGH, ALICE. *Planning the Little House.* McGraw-Hill Book Co.

In selecting the furnishings for our new home, we may decide on furniture made of wood. If so, the stores will show us pieces in maple, walnut, mahogany or oak. We do not have to buy solid wood, for choice veneers have both elegance and wearing quality. Furniture made of plastics also is available. If we admire the modernistic style, we may consider buying metal furniture in the streamlined mode, with chromium finish.

As our home becomes more familiar to us, we can add new touches to give its furnishings more warmth and color. Curtains, draperies, upholstery and tapestries, made perhaps of glass cloth or rayon, will serve very well. The interesting material called cellophane is excellent for shower curtains and may be bought in various bright colors. Cellophane bags to hold odorous vegetables or fruits are useful when these foods are placed in the refrigerator. Dishes made of an unbreakable plastic, bakelite, surely belong in the modern kitchen, along with stainless steel knives.

For further information on home furnishings, consult the following:

Carpet	Porcelain
Chippendale, Thomas	Pottery
Clock	Rugs
Electric Clock	Sheraton, Thomas
Furniture	Vase

Bibliography

BRUCE, MARJORIE. *Book of Craftsmen.* Dodd, Mead & Co.
FRIEND, M. R. *First Book in Home Economics.* D. Appleton-Century Co.
SMITH, S. C. G. *Made in America.* Alfred A. Knopf.
———. *Made in England.* Thomas Nelson & Sons.
———. *Made in France.* Alfred A. Knopf.

High-School List

HESS, MRS. K. P. *Textile Fibers and Their Use.* J. B. Lippincott Co.
PICKEN, MRS. M. B. *Sewing for the Home; How to Make Fabric Furnishings in a Professional Way.* Harper & Bros.
RAMSAY, JOHN. *American Potters and Pottery.* Hale, Cushman & Flint.
WIER, A. E. *The Piano; Its History, Makers, Players and Music.* Longmans, Green & Co.
WILLIAMSON, S. G. *American Craftsman.* Crown Publishing Co.

The servant problem will not vex us in this modern home, for our house is to be equipped with mechanical servants. On wash day we shall wash and wring the clothes with an electrical machine. Hot water from an automatic heater will be always on tap. An electric ironer will finish the job of the weekly laundry.

The old-time drudgery of preparing meals will be absent from our modern kitchen, equipped as it is with vegetable peelers, automatically controlled cookers, electric food mixers, beaters and juicers, and a refrigerator that keeps food from spoiling. Another machine will automatically wash and dry the dishes. Electric devices will also help us keep the house spotless. Many cleaning operations will be done mechanically.

As befits a modern home, we shall have among its furnishings a radio-phonograph with short-wave, frequency modulation and television bands. When television is fully perfected, we shall be able to see as well as hear the orators, actors and musicians who entertain us over the air waves.

EVOLUTION OF THE KITCHEN

Above: A colonial kitchen. *Below:* Kitchen of a modern home.

The living room of our home will not be like the old-fashioned parlor that was opened to sunlight only when the family had company. Our living room will be spacious, airy and attractive and will really be lived in. In addition, we may decide to have a sun room with a special kind of glass that admits the healing ultra-violet rays of the sun.

Our automobile garage will be connected with the house. When our car approaches the garage, the doors will open automatically; the mechanical servant performing this service will be the electric eye. Looking to the future, we shall have a flat-roofed garage to provide a landing place for an autogiro.

For further reading on conveniences of the modern age, consult the following titles:

Domestic Science	Telephone
Electric Bell	Television
Radio	Thermostat
Talking Machine	Vacuum Cleaner

HOW THE MODERN FAMILY IS FED

Science has increased food supplies, improved their quality and brought about greater variety for the modern family. On today's dinner table we find fresh fruits and vegetables throughout the year. This improvement in dietary conditions is the result of mechanical refrigeration and a quick-freezing process that keeps perishable foods from losing flavor or nutritive value over long periods.

The development of mechanized farming has enormously increased food production. Every one of the processes that early man performed by laborious hand labor is accomplished today by machinery. The soil is prepared, the seed is planted and the crops are harvested by ingenious and efficient machines. Both time and labor are saved. One tractor, drawing several machines, will plow, harrow and seed a given area in a small fraction of the time required by old methods of cultivation.

One of the most efficient farm machines is the combine, a harvester that reaps and thrashes the grain in one continuous operation. These enormous reapers are especially adapted to harvesting the crops of the great wheat ranches of the West.

In some localities, the owner of a combine takes his crew to different farms and harvests the crops under contract.

Further information regarding the development of farm instruments may be found under the following headings:

Agriculture, subhead	Reaping Machine
Modern Tools	Silo and Silage
Cream Separator	Sowing Machine
McCormick, Cyrus H.	Thrashing Machine
Plow	Traction Engine

Bibliography

HAWKS, ELLISON. *Boy's Book of Remarkable Machinery*. Dodd, Mead & Co.
HINE, L. W. *Men at Work*. The Macmillan Co.
MEISTER, MORRIS. *Heat and Health*. Charles Scribner's Sons.
PRYOR, W. C. *Cotton Book*. Harcourt, Brace & Co.
WILDMAN, EDWIN. *Famous Leaders of Industry*. L. C. Page & Co.

High-School List

CROWTHER, J. G. *Men of Science*. W. W. Norton & Co.
GREENO, F. L. *Obed Hussey, Who, of All Inventors, Made Bread Cheap*. Published by author.
HUTCHINSON, W. T. *Cyrus Hall McCormick*. Century Co.
McCORMICK, C. H. *The Century of the Reaper*. Houghton, Mifflin Co.

The control of animal and plant diseases and pests has been another factor in increasing farm production. The farmer has been greatly helped in such control by the United States Department of Agriculture and by the state agricultural experimental stations.

A MECHANIZED FARM PRODUCES MORE FOOD PER WORKER

The development of plant strains that are resistant to diseases and pests is also important. A good example of such a strain is a hybrid corn that is resistant to the chinch bug and the corn borer. A wheat resistant to rust has also been developed.

The regular inspection of farm animals, to determine whether they are free from disease, is now standard practice. Quarantine of infected animals and use of vaccines and serums for curative or preventive purposes have proved very beneficial.

The following references will provide detailed information about the natural enemies of the farmer's crops:

Army Worm	Galls
Boll Weevil	Gypsy Moth
Brown-Tail Moth	Insecticides
Chinch Bug	and Fungicides
Codling Moth	Locust
Curculio	Mildews
Diseases of Plants	Rusts
Ergot	Smuts

Information regarding enemies of farm animals may be found under the following titles:

Anthrax	Heaves
Foot and Mouth	Lumpy Jaw
Disease	Mange
Gapes	Mites
Glanders	Spavin

Bibliography

CALDWELL, O. W. *Open Doors to Science.* Ginn & Co.

DUNCAN, F. M. *Plant Friends and Foes.* Oxford University Press.

DuPUY, W. A. *Our Insect Friends and Foes.* John C. Winston Co.

McINTOSH, D. C. *First Problems in Agriculture.* American Book Co.

STEPHENSON, M. B. *World of Invisible Life.* Follett Publishing Co.

The modern agriculturist is on the alert for new varieties of plants for special purposes. A particular kind of grass that grows in dust-blown soils and special grains adapted to arid regions are examples of such plants.

The soybean, one of the basic food plants of the Orient, has become an important farm crop in America because it yields, besides food, a large number of industrial products and by-products.

The reader will find further information on plant improvement and allied topics under the following headings:

Agriculture, sub-	Corn, subhead
head Agronomy	Hybrid Corn
Breeding	Fertilizers
Burbank, Luther	Rotation of Crops

Bibliography

CLEMENS, NANCY. *Under Glass.* Longmans, Green & Co.

KNOX, R. B. *Marty and Company.* Doubleday, Doran & Co.

MALLETTE, GERTRUDE. *For Keeps.* Doubleday, Doran & Co.

MEISTER, MORRIS. *Living in a World of Science.* Charles Scribner's Sons.

SLUSSER, E. Y. *Stories of Luther Burbank and His Plant School.* Charles Scribner's Sons.

The scientific study of the care and feeding of farm animals is a part of the movement to raise the quality of animal food

TRANSPORTING FOOD PRODUCTS
Refrigerator cars carry perishable foods. Such foods may be shipped thousands of miles and arrive at the market in good condition.

products. At experimental stations, numerous tests have been made to establish standards for food rations, with particular emphasis on a balanced diet and vitamin content.

By regulating the diet of his cattle the farmer is able to increase milk production in dairy cows and meat production in beef cattle and to improve the products of these animals.

Foods that are distributed in interstate commerce must conform to high standards. There is regular inspection of animal quarters by government agents, for the purpose of checking on the methods used in handling milk and other foods. On large farms the cows are milked by machines. Farmers are required to observe official sanitary regulations, whatever the method of milking.

Scientific poultry raising has produced some interesting results. Eggs are hatched in a mechanical incubator and the chicks are kept warm in a mechanical brooder. They are fed a carefully controlled diet, and when they are of the proper size they are separated into two groups. The egg-laying chickens are fed a diet that produces yolk and white and a sturdy egg shell. Even the color of the yolk can be regulated. The other chickens are fed a flesh-producing ration. Egg-laying periods are prolonged by means of artificial light, so that more eggs may be produced.

For further information, see the following articles:

Cattle	Hog
Dairying	Poultry

Much attention is now given to the arrangement and packaging of food products for display in the markets. Usually, in the better stores, the eggs in every carton are of the same size and color because they were graded and sorted before being packed. Vegetables and fruits are also carefully arranged and sorted. By special treatment with wax, foods that readily dry up are kept from withering.

Food poisoning due to improper canning occurs much less frequently than once was the case. The canneries that supply the modern market have perfected airtight cans that preserve the food from spoilage.

Modern methods of milk treatment, including pasteurizing, together with the prevalence of good home refrigeration, assure the modern family milk of the best quality. Canned condensed milk, which is now a staple product, is particularly valuable in situations where liquid milk is not available. Powdered milk is likewise on the market. It has the advantage of taking up comparatively small space when shipped.

Throughout this story of food for the family runs the theme of the machine constantly at work to give us food in greater variety and of better quality.

The raw materials produced on the mechanized farm are processed in mills, packing plants, canneries, bakeries and dairy plants, all by means of ingenious machinery.

Raw products are transported to the industrial plants by railroad, steamship or motor truck, and the finished products likewise reach the markets by mechanical transportation. In the home, mechanical servants aid in the preparation of food for the table.

The following references will be of value in the study of better methods of preparing foods and distributing them to the consumer:

Agriculture, subhead	Meat Packing
Marketing	Milk
Canning	Pure Food Laws
Cold Storage	Wheat (series
Creamery	of illustrations)

Bibliography

BRIGHAM, A. P. *How the World Lives and Works.* American Book Co.
CAMP, R. O. *Story of Markets.* Harper & Bros.
DuPUY, W. A. *Our Animal Friends and Foes.* John C. Winston Co.
NIDA, W. L. *Farm Animals and Farm Crops.* A. Flanagan Co.
PENNOYER, SARA. *Polly Tucker, Merchant.* Dodd, Mead & Co.
TAPPAN, E. M. *Farmer and His Friends.* Houghton, Mifflin Co.

One other element enters into this picture of food and machines—the scientific forecast of weather conditions. The United States Weather Bureau operates an organized system of weather observation and (except when restricted by war regulations) sends out forecasts and warnings.

The agriculturist who grows oranges or grapefruit, for example, may save a valuable crop if he knows in advance that a severe frost is on the way. Citrus fruit orchards are equipped with heating appliances that protect the trees from the effects of temperatures that are below freezing. A weather forecast also may enable a farmer to cut and cure his hay before a rainy period.

Back of the compilation of weather information are many mechanical devices used to measure and record temperature, air pressure, rainfall, wind velocity, etc. In the relaying of information, use is made of radio, facsimile transmission of weather maps, the telegraph and the telephone.

What will science do for mankind in the years to come? Already, men are attempting to create synthetic foods having the same combination of chemical elements as do natural foods. Tray farming has had some success. Plants are grown in water containing the particular combination of food materials needed by those plants. No soil enters into the process. Experiments such as the foregoing are interesting examples of man's desire to seek out new sources of food.

The following references may be profitably read in connection with weather forecasting:

Barometer	Thermometer
Rain Gauge	Weather Bureau

Bibliography

CARPENTER, F. G. *How the World Is Fed.* American Book Co.
CRISSEY, FORREST. *Story of Foods.* Rand McNally & Co.
PICKWELL, G. B. *Weather.* Hugh F. Newman & Co.
WHEELER, F. R. *Boy with the U. S. Weathermen.* Lothrop, Lee & Shepard.
WORTHINGTON, JOSEPHINE. *Our Food.* F. A. Owen Publishing Co.

High-School List

BROWN, MRS. R. J. *Look Before You Cook; a Consumers' Kitchen Guide; with the Assistance of Consumers' Union.* Robert M. McBride & Co.
CHENOWETH, W. W. *Food Preservation.* John Wiley & Sons.
DOBIE, J. F. *Longhorns.* Little, Brown & Co.
HARRIS, F. L. *Foods, Their Nutritive, Economic and Social Values.* Little, Brown & Co.
MONROE, DAY. *Food Buying and Our Markets.* Barrows Publishing Co.
SHERMAN, H. C. *Food Products.* The Macmillan Co.
SMITH, GRACE. *Through the Kitchen Door; a Cook's Tour to the Best Kitchens of America.* Stackpole Sons.
SPENCER, E. R. *Just Weeds.* Charles Scribner's Sons.
WESTCOTT, CYNTHIA. *Plant Doctor; the How, Why and When of Disease and Insect Control in Your Garden.* Frederick A. Stokes Co.

HOW THE MODERN FAMILY IS CLOTHED

In the days of the early American settlers, the father, mother and children all helped to prepare the family clothing. Shirts, trousers and leggings for the male members of the household were made of deerskin sewed with leather thongs. The mother wove a crude kind of cloth for the garments worn by herself and her daughters. For yarn she used nettle fibers or shreds of hickory bark. When, later, flax and wool were available, the pioneer women and girls had woolen dresses for winter and linen ones for summer, or garments made from a mixture called linsey-woolsey. These home-woven fabrics were dyed with coloring material obtained from berries and bark.

At the close of the eighteenth century, cloth making moved from the home to the factory, and as new inventions were perfected, fabrics of varied designs and colors were placed on the market.

In 1845 a new chapter in the story of clothing began. In that year Elias Howe invented the sewing machine. The original model and the improved machines that followed had a wide sale, for with them the family sewing could be done much more quickly and with less effort.

The adoption of machines by clothing manufacturers led to an industry that today employs hundreds of thousands of workers. As new machines were developed and mass-production methods were adopted, the consumer found in the markets ready-made apparel of endless variety as to fabric, color, style and size, priced to suit every purse.

Spinning and weaving with hand machines continue to be taught as industrial arts, but the masses do not depend on these crafts for today's clothing.

Clothes for the changing seasons, for sports and for different occupations are available because of machine methods of manufacture. For the athletic woman there is specialized apparel for riding, tennis, golf and hiking. For the lady of fashion there are garments for every social occasion, including the hostess gown for home entertaining. Tailored clothes for the business woman and house dresses for the matron are available in attractive designs. The cost of such varied clothing would be prohibitive if garments were not made by modern processes.

Men's clothing, too, has followed a similar development through the adoption of machinery and mass production.

Complete layettes for the new baby, rompers and sunsuits for the toddlers, and

HOME INDUSTRIES IN COLONIAL DAYS

home, school and "dress-up" garments in sizes ranging from kindergarten to college age may be purchased ready-made because machines have replaced hand labor.

The various phases of the story of clothing, including processes of manufacture, are covered more fully under the titles listed below:

Bleaching	Glove
Boots and Shoes	Hat
Calico and Calico	Knitting Machine
Printing	Lace
Cloth	Leather
Dress	Sewing Machine
Dyeing	Spinning
Embroidery	Spinning Wheel
Felt	Weaving
Fur and Fur	Wool and
Trade	Woolen Manufacture

From ancient times, the principal textiles used for clothing have been silk, cotton, wool and linen (from flax). Because the raw materials for these textiles are produced in different parts of the world and no country has a monopoly on them, there has been an intensive search for substitute materials.

Since 1920, the commercial manufacture of rayon has been an outstanding development of the textile industry. This silklike fiber is made from cellulose. Nylon, another fiber resembling silk, is produced from coal, air and water. It has had enormous popularity as a material for hosiery. Aralac and Lanital, produced from casein, a skim-milk by-product, have also been introduced. Experiments have been made in the use of paper, rubber, glass cloth and cellophane as materials for clothing.

The search for new materials is a fascinating field of applied chemistry. The success already attending this research points to new discoveries and new additions to the list of synthetic textiles.

More about the world's textiles, old and new, will be found in the following articles:

Cotton	Linen
Fiber	Nylon
Flax	Rayon
Hemp	Silk
Jute	Textile

Bibliography

ALLEE, M. H. *Judith Lankester.* Houghton, Mifflin Co.
———. *Off to Philadelphia.* Houghton, Mifflin Co.
BRINK, C. R. *Caddie Woodlawn.* The Macmillan Co.
FOX, G. M. *Lona of Hollybush Creek.* Little, Brown & Co.
STUART, D. M. *Girl Through the Ages.* Doubleday, Doran & Co.

High-School List
CONSALUS, F. H. *Distinctive Clothes, How to Select and Make Them.* Ronald Press.
DANA, MARGARET. *Behind the Label; a Guide to Intelligent Buying.* Little, Brown & Co.
DOOLEY, W. H. *Economics of Clothing and Textiles; the Science of the Clothing and Textile Business.* D. C. Heath and Co.
HAWES, ELIZABETH. *Men Can Take It.* Random House.
ROGERS, FRANCES. *5000 Years of Glass.* Frederick A. Stokes & Co.
STALEY, EUGENE. *Raw Materials in Peace and War.* Council on Foreign Relations.
SADTLER, S. S. *Chemistry of Familiar Things.* J. B. Lippincott Co.

Before leaving the subject, let us consider why mass production reduces the cost of ready-made clothing or any other commodity that is widely distributed.

Suppose a skilled mechanic decided to assemble the machines necessary to make an automobile. The cost of machinery and materials would be quite heavy for one car, but if the mechanic decided to make a second car he could produce it more cheaply, since the cost of equipment would be divided between the two automobiles. Carrying the example further, we readily see that a thousand automobiles can be manufactured for less money per car than a hundred automobiles. Multiple use of machines, whereby many items are produced at a lower cost per item, is the basic principle of mass production.

Analyzing still further, we note that in mass production there is a special machine for each step in the process, with each machine operated by a workman trained for a particular job. Shifts of workmen can keep the machines operating continuously if needed, and there is a minimum of lost motion.

Another factor in mass production is the principle of interchangeable parts. When a machine breaks down it is not necessary for the manufacturer to install a new machine. He can repair the old one by inserting a new part that fits, even to a small fraction of an inch.

Materials are bought and shipped to the factories in large quantities. Marketing is also on a large-scale basis. Many large corporations produce their own raw materials and own their shipping facilities. These methods are typical of mass production. The savings effected are passed on to the consumer.

PROBLEMS CREATED BY THE MACHINE

It is usually impossible to foresee how a new invention will affect the habits of a people using it. Experience shows, however, that mechanical devices do have profound social effects.

A good example is the American automobile. In the heyday of its popularity it created a new kind of tourist trade, brought prosperity to resorts in sections off the beaten track, created the modern auto camp as a competitor of hotels, replaced the corner blacksmith shop with filling stations and garages, made Americans acquainted with their national parks, and seriously affected the revenues of the nation's railroads.

When, however, the Japanese occupation of the chief rubber-producing regions made it difficult for Americans to replace their wornout tires, another set of effects became apparent.

Because there were fewer automobiles to carry people to their jobs or for social driving, trolley cars, which had been declining for a long time, were once more in demand for transportation. In many towns, trolley buses or gasoline buses had replaced the old street cars and the tracks had been torn up. The added strain on the already curtailed bus services created a problem difficult to solve. Many people who had moved into the suburbs began to seek dwellings nearer the offices or factories where they worked, and city rentals were affected.

The trend toward suburban expansion was checked, at least in real estate developments without convenient transportation. Stores in small communities began to get back the trade lost when people could drive to towns with better shopping facilities. Small-town movie houses likewise profited, as did the neighborhood theaters of the cities.

Curtailment of store deliveries by trucks revived personal shopping and brought back the market basket carried on the arm of the shopper who walked to her neighborhood store.

Both the moving picture and radio created new lines of employment while curtailing opportunities in older established occupations. The introduction of new mechanical devices usually causes temporary unemployment for many workers. Some of these workers may be forced to learn new skills in order to earn a living. Older workers who find their jobs gone and few employers willing to hire them are at a special disadvantage in getting readjusted.

The machine, then, has not only brought comforts and luxuries to mankind but it has created problems that are still unsolved.

The question of employment is complicated by the necessity of making adjustments between the different groups of the modern social organization. Farmers, laborers, manufacturers, stockholders, retailers and bankers all have a special slant on the problem.

The farmer rightly asks a fair price for his hogs and cattle, his wheat and corn. High farm prices, however, mean that people in the towns and cities must pay more for their food. Because of the rise in food costs, workers demand higher wages and the wage increases are reflected in higher cost of manufactured products. Thus the farmer has to pay more for his tractor and harvester and for household necessities.

The manufacturer and the retailer are in business to make a living. Each has certain obligations to meet before he can realize a profit. These items include rent, taxes, wages and salaries, advertising and, in case of large corporations, dividends to stockholders and interest on bonds. Prices of wholesale and retail goods must be high enough to cover such expenditures and leave a margin for profit. If prices are too high, customers may refuse to buy and business will fall off. Bankers will be slow to make loans under such conditions.

In a country where business operates on the principle of free enterprise, there are periods when it is impossible to maintain the right balance among the different economic groups. In such periods there may be strikes, lockouts and widespread unemployment.

WHAT ONE INDUSTRY CAN MEAN

The opposite extreme is a dictator government which maintains stability by exercising complete control over production and distribution, labor, prices and wages.

The ideal solution would seem to be the coöperative effort of free men determined to solve the problem in the democratic way.

Below, the reader will find a list of articles dealing with various phases of the subject:

Bibliography

ARNOLD, J. I. *Cooperative Citizenship*. Row, Peterson & Co.

BRIGHAM, A. P. *How the World Lives and Works*. American Book Co.

Building America: Illustrated Studies of Modern Problems. Society for Curriculum Study.

BUNN, H. F. *Cooperative Life and Business*. E. M. Hale & Co.

GIBSON, C. R. *Great Inventions and How They Were Invented*. J. B. Lippincott Co.

HUBERMAN, LEO. *Man's Worldly Goods*. Harper & Bros.

LANGDON-DAVIES, JOHN. *Radio*. Dodd, Mead & Co.

RUGG, H. O. *Changing Governments and Changing Cultures*. Ginn & Co.

WOODBURN, J. A. *Active Citizenship*. Longmans, Green & Co.

High-School List

CROWTHER, J. G. *The Social Relations of Science*. The Macmillan Co.

DILTS, M. M. *Telephone in a Changing World*. Longmans, Green & Co.

KAEMPFFERT, WALDEMAR. *Science Today and Tomorrow*. The Viking Press.

LANGDON-DAVIES, JOHN. *Radio; the Story of the Capture and Use of Radio Waves*. Dodd, Mead & Co.

MORGAN, A. P. *Getting Acquainted with Radio*. D. Appleton-Century Co.

ROST, O. F. *Distribution Today*. McGraw-Hill Book Co.

SHERWOOD, M. H. *From Forest to Furniture; the Romance of Wood*. W. W. Norton.

Using the Products of Labor

Buying and selling are the heart of modern business. Goods are produced to be sold and used. In the science of economics, use of goods is called consumption. Buying for consumption is the basis of the industrial life of every community. When demand for goods slackens and buyers are few, there follows a downward business trend that leads to unemployment and financial distress.

Men who seek to sell merchandise apply certain principles based on sales psychology. There are many avenues of approach, both direct and indirect. The buyer should exercise judgment in weighing the arguments presented. Such consideration will be more intelligent if the buyer has authentic information upon which to base his decision in making a purchase.

Consideration of materials, workmanship and prices is made difficult by the great variety of goods offered for sale. Very few people are specialists in more than one field. The woman who has been a professional buyer in the linen department of a city department store will know how to select her own tablecloths and bed linen wisely, but she may not know values when she considers purchasing Oriental rugs. The intelligent buyer will not be slow to seek information or to ask advice.

In the sections that follow, the various problems involved in the sale and purchase of merchandise are considered from the viewpoint of the seller and the consumer.

Bibliography

BALDERSTON, L. R. *Housewifery; a Textbook of Practical Housekeeping*. J. B. Lippincott Co.

FURNAS, C. C. *Man, Bread and Destiny*. Reynal & Hitchcock.

HARMES, EARL. *Furniture of Yesterday and Today*. Bruce Publishing Co.

MONROE, DAY. *Food Buying and Our Markets*. Barrows Publishing Co.

APPEALS TO THE CUSTOMER

Wherever there is competition for mass buying, producers and retailers have to make special efforts to attract interest in their products. Such appeals are forms of advertising.

In a retail store the arrangement and packaging of the goods, as well as the appearance of the store itself, may have great customer appeal. It is human nature for people to want to patronize a store in which goods are displayed artistically and the place is neat and orderly. Another way for the owner to attract customers is to train his helpers to be pleasant, courteous and interested in the buyer's needs.

Window dressing has developed as a highly paid vocation requiring specialized training. In the larger city department stores, the outlay for window displays represents a considerable percentage of the budget for advertising. Even the small shop in a residential district can attract buyers by interesting and artistic display of its goods.

In the effort to sell merchandise, producers and retailers go far afield to advertise their wares. The billboard placed conspicuously near the automobile highway, with its colorful picture and slogan, is known to everyone. A nationally advertised product is sometimes publicized in this manner from one end of the country to the other. Electric and neon signs make a similar appeal to the eye.

Newspapers and magazines, unless they are subsidized, depend on advertising for much of their revenue. Hence it is to their advantage to solicit well-presented advertisements. Department stores, especially, use the pages of their local papers to tell the public the merits of their merchandise. Expert copy writers are employed to give these advertisements distinction and effectiveness.

Competing briskly with printed advertising is the commercial sales talk presented by radio. Immense sums are spent for radio programs by sponsors of nationally known products. The audiences for these programs are very large but it is also true that the listeners may be irritated when the program is interrupted by a sales talk. However, the repeated mention of a firm name and its product over a long period does increase sales.

Testimonial advertising, too, has had a remarkable development. It is no longer confined to the country newspaper, almanac or booklet carrying letters praising patent medicines. Full-page testimonials in the best magazines, signed by leaders in the fields of entertainment, sports and fashion, are accepted as first-class advertising. There is good psychology in presenting to the public the opinion of its favorite movie star or baseball hero.

Manufacturers regard slogans, brand names and trade-marks so highly that they protect their rights to these devices by registering them. Used repeatedly in advertising, a striking name, timely slogan or ingenious trade-mark is worth thousands of dollars to its owner.

In the articles listed below, the reader will find further information on the methods used to create customer interest in goods offered for sale:

Advertising   Photography
Moving Pictures   Photogravure
Newspaper   Radio

Bibliography

CHARLES, DAVID. *The Camera in Commerce.* Pitman Publishing Corp.
GRUMBINE, E. E. *Reaching Juvenile Markets.* McGraw-Hill Book Co.
MAYER, R. C. *How to Do Publicity.* Harper & Bros.
NIXON, H. K. *Principles of Advertising.* McGraw-Hill Book Co.
RORTY, JAMES. *Our Master's Voice: Advertising.* John Day Co.
TRAFTON, G. H. *Science in Daily Life.* J. B. Lippincott Co.

DEVICES FOR SELLING

During a period of depression in the moving-picture industry, it was customary for certain movie theaters to offer prizes to people who would patronize their shows. Other houses held bank nights and "Screeno" nights to lure patrons into the theaters. In some cases, the buyer of an admission at the box office would be handed a lottery ticket which gave him a chance on an automobile.

Devices such as these are typical of special favors competing merchants offer pros-

Swift & Co.

A MEDIEVAL COUNTRY FAIR
Trading was done largely by barter.

pective customers. Downtown stores in cities have been known to offer suburban customers transportation tickets or permits for parking automobiles. Another sales device is the plan of selling a purchaser two articles instead of one, at the cost of a small extra sum.

Bargain sales, dollar-day sales and week-end and seasonal events are familiar selling devices in communities where sales pressure is strong. The instinct to hunt a bargain is lacking in few people. Besides attracting large numbers of buyers who are eager to see the bargains offered, these "specials" may result in sales of other merchandise. Often a customer decides to buy something a little better than the article that is marked down, or she may be attracted by an article in another section. Thus the sale helps to sell unadvertised goods.

Periodic sales tend to build up a group of regular customers who watch the papers for announcements of such events. This result in itself makes the special sale a profitable venture for the tradesman.

Prizes, coupons and give-away devices are regarded by the merchant as advertising, and they are charged to that account. The customer who thinks that he is getting something for nothing often pays for the favor by buying another article at an advanced price.

EVOLUTION OF THE STORE

Top: Restoration of Lincoln's store. *Middle:* A country store of not so long ago. *Bottom:* A modern city store.

Although special sales do offer good values, as when a store is getting rid of overstocked items, bargains are not always what they seem. No one should buy hastily, even in the excitement of a sale, and inferior goods are not worth even the reduced price one pays for them.

Deferred payments, installment purchasing and charge accounts are forms of credit that have made buying attractive for millions of Americans. At one time, a person with a regular income could pay for a trip

to Europe on the installment plan. It is significant that when the United States found it necessary to curtail spending as an anti-inflation measure, restrictions were placed on these forms of credit.

To finance installment buying, the seller asks an additional payment which is called interest or a service charge. In effect, the installment buyer pays more for the goods in return for the privilege of spreading the payment. A charge account is more flexible, as the buyer uses it at his pleasure and pays the bills as they are rendered, either fully or in part.

There is no doubt that credit buying has led to an enormous exchange of goods in the United States. It has probably justified itself in periods of prosperity. In depression periods, however, great losses to merchants have resulted, and many bankruptcies may be traced to the inability of businessmen to collect the bills incurred by credit buyers.

For additional information the reader is referred to the following articles:

Chain Stores   Debt
Credit   Supply and Demand

Bibliography

AMERICAN MANAGEMENT ASSOCIATION. *Packaging, Packing and Shipping.* Elliot Publishing Co.
BABSON, R. W. *Folly of Instalment Buying.* Frederick A. Stokes Co.
BECKMAN, T. N. *The Chain Store Problem.* McGraw-Hill Book Co.
LAIRD, D. A. *What Makes People Buy.* McGraw-Hill Book Co.
REICH, EDWARD. *Consumer Goods; How to Know and Use Them.* American Book Co.

SEASONAL AND STYLE SALES

Why do furriers offer sealskin coats in August and why do milliners display fall hats in July? The answers to these questions are based on the effect of seasonal changes on merchandising.

Clothing manufacturers have always distributed to their customers goods adapted to the four seasons. Keen competition influenced the more alert merchants to advertise their goods ahead of season, and to hold early sales in order to interest the public in their new stock. The plan worked so well that advance seasonal sales are now the rule in the retail trade.

Changes of style also are reflected in special sales. Advance and clearance styles at the first and last of the month are the merchants' response to the desire of the public to keep abreast of style changes. Sometimes a new style fails to "take" and over-optimistic retailers are left with a stock of goods no one wants.

Style changes also affect the turnover of furniture, household wares, toys and a great many other lines of merchandise. A good example is the popularity of the spinet type of piano, which replaced the upright style because it is better adapted to the apartment living room, is more easily moved and has more attractive lines.

Bibliography

ALLEN, J. R. *Heating and Air Conditioning.* McGraw-Hill Book Co.
BAXTER, LAURA. *Modern Clothing.* J. B. Lippincott Co.
JAFFE, BERNARD. *Outposts of Science.* Simon & Schuster.
PHILLIPS, M. C. *Skin Deep.* Vanguard Press.
RYAN, M. G. *Your Clothes and Personality.* D. Appleton-Century Co.

EDUCATION OF THE BUYER

In choosing an automobile, a prospective buyer must consider the type of car best suited to his purposes and also the price that he can afford to pay. How does he go about choosing the car? What questions should he ask the salesman? The same principles apply when a householder desires to purchase food for the family table, clothes for the children or new furniture. Ill-considered buying is never economical.

One of the progressive movements of recent years is the program designed to train the consumer to buy intelligently. Work along this line has been done by private corporations desiring to protect their own products from the competition of inferior goods. The American Medical Association has been a pioneer in exposing the claims of dishonest purveyors of foods and drugs. An organization of businessmen, the National Better Business Bureau, carries on a program aimed at maintaining high standards of production for the benefit of the consumer.

The interests of the buying public are also protected by consumer organizations which have laboratory facilities for testing and comparing goods that are nationally advertised. Printed matter containing reports on price and quality is sent regularly to members of these consumer unions, and the members are given instructions on judging various kinds of goods. Similar educational work is done by the Consumers' Coöperative Movement.

Several consumer advisory services are maintained by the United States government. The Consumers' Counsel Division, under the direction of the Agricultural Marketing Administrator, publishes the *Consumers' Guide*. The National Bureau of Standards aids business and user groups in the voluntary establishment of grades, quality and other standards as a basis for purchasing and testing manufactured goods other than foods and drugs. The Food and Drug Administration is authorized to enforce laws safeguarding the purity of foods, drugs and cosmetics.

Information on family budgets and suggestions for economical purchasing of food, clothing and household furnishings are contained in bulletins of the Home Economics Bureau. These bulletins are supplemented by press releases and radio talks.

Available to consumers are the reports of local health departments on standards maintained by dairy companies and other food purveyors in any community.

The following articles contain information relative to the protection and education of the consumer:

Blue-Sky Laws	Pure Food Laws
Budget	Securities and Ex-
Consumption	change Commission
Domestic Science	Standards, United
Federal Trade	States National
Commission	Bureau of

Bibliography

CHERINGTON, P. T. *People's Wants, and How to Satisfy Them.* Harper & Bros.
FOWLER, B. B. *Consumer Cooperation in America.* Vanguard Press.
KALLEN, H. M. *Decline and Rise of the Consumer.* D. Appleton-Century Co.
MUNRO, W. B. *Municipal Administration.* The Macmillan Co.
REID, M. G. *Consumers and the Market.* F. S. Crofts & Co.

High-School List

BRINDZE, RUTH. *How to Spend Money; Everybody's Practical Guide to Buying.* Vanguard Press.
CLEMEN, R. A. *By-Products in the Packing Industry.* University of Chicago Press.
GAER, JOS. *Consumers All; the Problem of Consumer Protection.* Harcourt, Brace & Co.
GAMBLE, MRS. M. T. *To Market, to Market.* The Bobbs-Merrill Co.
JACKMAN, D. N. *Chemistry of Laundry Materials.* Longmans, Green & Co.
JORALEMON, I. B. *Romantic Copper; Its Lure and Lore.* D. Appleton-Century Co.
LAZO, HECTOR. *Who Gets Your Food Dollar?* Harper & Bros.
MADDOX, H. A. *Paper, Its History, Sources and Manufacture.* Pitman Publishing Corp.
MORRISON, A. C. *Man in a Chemical World: the Service of Chemical Industry.* Chas. Scribner's Sons.
RADELL, N. H. *Accounting for the Individual and Family.* Prentice-Hall, Inc.
TODOROFF, ALEXANDER. *Food Buying Today.* Grocery Trade Publishing House.
VERRILL, A. H. *Foods America Gave the World.* L. C. Page & Co.
WOLF, HOWARD. *Rubber; a Story of Glory and Greed.* Covici, Friede, Inc.
WOODWARD, MRS. H. R. *It's an Art.* Harcourt, Brace & Co.

Man Conquers Space and Time

Prior to the adoption of the Twentieth Amendment to the Constitution, in 1933, the legal date for the inauguration of the President of the United States was March 4, four months after the national election. Why was there such a lapse of time before a new Administration could take over the reins of office? The answer lies in the slow methods of communication and travel that prevailed in the early days of the American republic.

Congress set the inaugural date in March in order to allow time for all sections of the young republic to learn the results of the election, and time for the newly elected officers to reach the capital for the ceremonies. Because governments are slow to change established customs, the United States continued to hold the ceremonies on March 4 for nearly a century and a half. The President is now inaugurated in January.

Today, radio stations report the election returns as the votes are counted, and voters in California, three hours behind New York in time, sometimes know who has been elected President before the California polls are closed. An elected official living on the Pacific coast could reach the capital by airplane in a matter of hours.

These changes are typical of what has happened to world communications. Space and time have been mastered by great inventions, and, measured in these terms, our globe has shrunk to a fraction of its size since the first ships sailed upon its waters.

The article TRANSPORTATION provides a general background for further reading about man's modes of travel from early to modern times. For supplementary articles, the following may be read:

Automobile	Gyro-Compass
Balloon	Lindbergh, Charles A.
Bicycle	Locomotive
Boat	Magellan, Ferdinand
Camel	Motor Boat
Canoe and	Motorcycle
Canoeing	Sailboat and
Caravan	Sailing
Caravel	Ship
Compass	Steam Engine
Dirigible Balloon	Wright, Orville
Flying, Story of	and Wilbur

Bibliography

BROWN, C. L. M. *Conquest of the Air: An Historical Survey.* Osgood Press.
CHARNLEY, M. V. *Boy's Life of the Wright Brothers.* Harper & Bros.
DENISON, MERRILL. *Advancing America: The Drama of Transportation.* Dodd, Mead & Co.
FINGER, C. F. *Courageous Companions.* Longmans, Green & Co.
GILCHRIST, M. E. *Rolling Along Through the Centuries.* Longmans, Green & Co.
WILLIAMS, ARCHIBALD. *Engineering Feats.* Thomas Nelson & Sons.

High-School List

DOGLIESH, ALICE. *America Travels; the Story of a Hundred Years of Travel in America.* The Macmillan Company.
HAWTHORNE, HILDEGARDE. *Rising Thunder; the Story of Jack Jouett of Virginia.* Longmans, Green & Co.
MEADER, S. W. *Boy with a Pack.* Harcourt, Brace & Co.
MEIGS, CORNELIA. *Covered Bridge.* The Macmillan Co.

ROAD BUILDING THROUGH THE YEARS

From the footpath in the forest to the high-speed motor road carrying many lanes of traffic there is a gap of many centuries. One of the surprising things about the story of road building is that man put up with so much inconvenience in his travel over land before he became a builder of first-class highways.

The Romans, who were the greatest road builders of the ancient world, constructed a magnificent system of stone-paved highways linking all parts of the empire with Rome. Portions of the system remain to this day because the Roman *via* was built for durability and not for speed. Judged by modern standards, it was far from smooth, but it served the Romans admirably.

After the fall of Rome, Europeans neglected the highways built by the Caesars, and road building languished for centuries. Throughout the Middle Ages and into the modern period, travelers struggled on foot, horseback and coach through mud and mire. Such city pavements as were laid were crude and rough.

When the first English settlers arrived in America, the only roads were the Indian trails. During the colonial period the people traveled over dirt, plank and corduroy roads, the last named consisting of logs laid lengthwise and crosswise on the trail. The larger towns had streets paved with cobblestones. During the Revolutionary War, communications were so difficult because of a lack of good roads that the patriot leaders found it almost impossible to keep the people informed about the progress of the war.

150 YEARS OF PROGRESS—FASTER AND FASTER AND FASTER

In the period following the establishment of the United States government under the Constitution, trade and manufacture developed rapidly and thousands of energetic pioneers traveled across the Appalachians in quest of new frontiers. The restless spirit of the times demanded better roads for travel and interchange of products. At the close of the eighteenth century, numerous companies were organized to raise capital for the building of turnpikes, and several thousand miles of these private roads were constructed in New England, New York and Pennsylvania. To meet costs of construction and operation, the owners of the turnpikes collected tolls from the users. These highways were America's first improved roads. Some of them were merely improved dirt roads, but others were surfaced with gravel.

The first of these private roads, connecting Lancaster and Philadelphia, was begun in 1791 and completed in 1797. The Lancaster Pike, as it was called, was bought by Pennsylvania in 1917.

With the opening of the West, the United States government saw the need of closer contacts between the commercial East and the new settlements, and in 1806 Congress appropriated funds for the construction and marking of a paved highway between Cumberland, Md., and the Ohio River. Over a period of years and at a cost of $7,000,000, the historic Cumberland Road, or National Pike, was extended 800 miles west of Cumberland. Its influence on the development of the Ohio and Upper Mississippi valleys is almost beyond estimate, but it was a long time before the Federal government again invested national funds in roads.

After the Civil War, the government centered its interest on the rapidly expanding railroads, not foreseeing the need of a national highway system. It was the vogue of the bicycle, late in the nineteenth century,

that created a demand for better roads. A road built of crushed stone, compacted to make a smooth surface, was popular during the bicycle era. It was called *macadam* from its inventor, John L. McAdam. Although it was ideal for a light vehicle, the macadamized road was not strong enough for the automobiles and trucks that revolutionized America's highway system after the turn of the century.

Widespread use of motor vehicles made good roads a necessity. The so-called Good Roads Movement swept the country, and in 1916 Congress passed the first Federal-Aid Road Act. In 1921 Congress authorized

ROADS OF YESTERDAY AND TODAY

Top: The Oregon Trail in Wyoming, gouged five feet deep in solid limestone by the prairie schooners. *Bottom:* A modern high-speed motor roadway.

financial aid to the states through the Federal Bureau of Public Roads. Within the next two decades, funds granted the states

A 1905 AUTOMOBILE
This twelve-horsepower, four-cylinder car could go forty miles an hour. It sold for $1,400.

for road construction and improvement reached a total of more than a billion dollars. In 1939 the Bureau of Public Roads became the Public Roads Administration, a division of the independent Federal Works Agency.

For many years the United States government, in coöperation with the states, has been building roads at the rate of 50,000 miles a year. In the whole country there are over 306,000 miles of surfaced primary roads in the rural state systems, and over a million miles of surfaced feeder roads. The Second World War program stimulated the construction of roads leading to military camps and other war establishments.

Elimination of railroad grade crossings and the building of super-highways without cross traffic are interesting developments of the good-roads program. Typical of the super-highway is the 160-mile Pennsylvania Turnpike, a toll motor highway connecting Pittsburgh and Harrisburg. It was completed in 1940 at a cost of $70,000,000, just ten times the cost of the old Cumberland Road. The new Turnpike was partly financed by a loan from the RFC. Tolls were assessed to pay off the RFC bonds.

In 1942 the last link was completed in a motor highway across Canada, traversing the towering Canadian Rockies. Work was also begun on a highway extending northward from the United States to Alaska by way of Alberta and British Columbia. A highway linking North and South America has been under construction for several years. Even now we can visualize a motor

road of the future, extending from Alaska through North and South America, to the southern end of the continental mass.

The social effects of the Good Roads Movement in the United States are known to us all. When all parts of the Americas are connected by surfaced highways, the English-, Spanish- and Portuguese-speaking nations of the New World will truly be Good Neighbors.

Under the titles listed below, the reader will find information on the construction of roads and streets and descriptions of some of America's great highways:

Asphalt	Lincoln Highway
Concrete	Pavement
Cumberland Road	Roads and Streets
Dixie Highway	Toll

Bibliography

ABRAHAM, HERBERT. *Asphalts and Allied Substances.* D. Van Nostrand Co.
BENNETT, J. M. *Roadsides; the Front Yard of the Nation.* Strafford.
BLACK, ARCHIBALD. *Story of Tunnels.* McGraw-Hill Book Co.
BORMAN, H. H. *Bridges.* The Macmillan Co.
SALT, HARRIET. *Mighty Engineering Feats.* Penn Publishing Co.

THE CANAL AND THE RAILROAD

During the first half-century following the adoption of the Constitution, there was

AN ERIE CANAL PACKET BOAT

great activity in canal building in the United States. Lack of adequate roads and the persistent desire of settlers to push westward were the main factors that inspired the building of these waterways.

Between 1789 and 1802, a few canals were built by private companies to by-pass the unnavigable rapids on rivers flowing into the Atlantic, but the first really important American canal was the Erie, completed in 1825 and built by New York state. It connected Buffalo, on Lake Erie, with Albany, on the Hudson, thus providing a continuous water route from the new West to the Atlantic Ocean. For years it was crowded with barges and boats carrying freight and passengers back and forth, and it contributed greatly to the development of the region that it served. To the Erie Canal, New York City owed its rapid rise to a position of commercial and financial supremacy in the second quarter of the nineteenth century.

In the earlier period of operation, the Erie, like other canals, used horses and mules to tow the boats. Robert Fulton's steamboat, the *Clermont,* successfully navigated the Hudson River in 1807, but it was years before the canals were deepened sufficiently to accommodate boats powered by steam. Nineteenth-century fiction includes several interesting stories of the towpath.

The importance of canals in the water transportation of America is treated more fully in the following articles:

Canal
Cape Cod Canal
Erie Canal
Lock (in canals)
New York State Barge Canal

Panama Canal
Sault Sainte Marie Canal
United States, sub-head Waterways

Bibliography

BEARD, C. A. *Making of American Civilization.* The Macmillan Co.
BRITT, H. A. *Boys' Own Book of Frontiersmen.* The Macmillan Co.
COOPER, J. F. *The Pathfinder.* G. P. Putnam's Sons.
KRAPP, G. P. *America; the Great Adventure.* Alfred A. Knopf.
MEIGS, CORNELIA. *New Moon.* The Macmillan Co.

High-School List

BERRY, ERICK. *Lock Her Through.* Oxford University Press.
MEADOWCROFT, E. L. *Along the Erie Towpath.* Thomas Y. Crowell Co.

Ohio, Maryland, Pennsylvania and other states, influenced by the success of New York, built many miles of canals between 1825 and 1840. There was a good deal of unwise speculation in canal bonds; many of these waterways were financial failures. Yet they had their share in the development of the new West, and they might have remained the principal highways to the frontier settlements had they not met powerful competition in the railroads.

Only six years after the completion of the Erie Canal, steam locomotives were hauling cars on the Baltimore & Ohio tracks between Baltimore and the Ohio River. The day of the railroad had arrived, although few realized that it would spread over the country in a vast network. The early railroads were crude affairs. Charles Dickens, after

RAILROADS HELPED OPEN THE WEST
Advertisement of the first transcontinental steam railroad.

a trip on the Boston & Lowell Railway, described the road as consisting of "a great deal of jolting, a great deal of noise, a great deal of wall, not much window, a locomotive engine, a shriek and a bell." He wrote of the trip in *American Notes.*

In 1853 Cornelius Vanderbilt merged a number of local Eastern lines into a new system that eventually became the present New York Central Railroad. It is significant that his purpose was to create a railway approach to New York City that would divert business from the prospering Erie Canal. The American railroad of today owes much to his foresight.

The Civil War proved the value of the railroad as a means of transporting troops, supplies and munitions, and stimulated pop-

A HORSE CAR OF THE LATE 1800'S

ular demand for a rail system connecting the East and the Pacific coast. California and Oregon, already members of the Union, were potential markets for Eastern products.

In 1864 Congress passed legislation offering public lands and a cash subsidy as liens on a transcontinental railroad, and capital was raised for the construction of the road. Begun in 1864 and completed in 1869, the Union Pacific, America's first transcontinental line, was influential in the development of the great commercial empire beyond the Mississippi. The road was built in two sections. The Central Pacific Railroad, which had tracks from San Francisco to the California-Nevada border, built eastward. The newly incorporated Union Pacific built westward from Council Bluffs, Iowa, and the two lines met at Promontory Point, Utah, on May 10, 1869. The last spike, of California gold, was driven with appropriate ceremonies amid great rejoicing. [See illustration, page 3997.]

During the period of railroad expansion that followed, canal building was almost at a standstill, but there was a revival of interest in artificial waterways after the opening of the twentieth century. The New York State Barge Canal, comprising the Erie and three other canals, was completed in 1917 at an initial cost of $150,000,000. It was believed that grain shipments from the Northwest would be diverted from the railroads and Canadian waterways, but the

Barge Canal did not fulfill expectations. Nearly all inland waterway improvements are now financed by the government.

Outstanding developments in railroad transportation since 1930 include the general use of air conditioning for passenger coaches, the improvement of second-class trains, greater speed through the use of the Diesel engine and aluminum construction for streamliners, and additional luxury items for first-class Pullmans.

The Western roads obtained increased business by introducing a tourist sleeper that compares favorably with the older standard Pullmans. Streamlined coach trains with reclining chairs and modern equipment have been introduced on practically all railroad systems. Clean, speedy and inexpensive, they are a far cry from the old-fashioned day trains. The streamlin-

TRAVEL TODAY IN COMFORT
A deluxe dining car on a modern railroad.

ers travel at speeds ranging from sixty to ninety miles an hour. Using one of these trains, a person can cross the United States from coast to coast in less than sixty hours.

Further information about the railroad may be found under the following headings:

Air Brake	Railroad
Diesel Engine	Subway
Electric Railway	Tunnel

Bibliography

KIMBALL, W. A. *Trailer for Pleasure and Business.* McGraw-Hill Book Co.
MILWAUKEE MECHANICS INSTITUTE. *Elementary Principles of Diesel-Engine Construction.* Bruce Publishing Co.
QUIETT, G. C. *They Built the West.* D. Appleton-Century Co.
RAYMOND, W. G. *Elements of Railroad Engineering.* John Wiley & Sons.
REED, BRIAN. *Railway Engines of the World.* Oxford University Press.
VAN METRE, T. W. *Trains, Tracks and Travel.* Simmons-Boardman.

TRUCKS CARRY A GREAT PART OF THE NATION'S COMMERCE

SPECIAL PROBLEMS

Competition between the railroads and the canals influenced transportation in the nineteenth century, and in the twentieth the railroads met stiff competition from motor vehicles. The interurban electric cars of an earlier day disappeared in many sections when motor-bus lines introduced interstate and coast-to-coast service. In the 1930's, railroad revenues were so reduced that many systems were forced into receiverships. The public benefited by getting better service and lower rates from the railroads.

Although duplication of service is sometimes wasteful, the country in normal times cannot dispense with the services of any of its public or private carriers. The proper balance between them is an economic problem that needs further study.

The railroad freight train is probably the best carrier for heavy goods transported over long distances. It is frequently the best carrier for conveying large cargoes of livestock from local markets to distant city packing houses. Generally speaking, trucks are more efficient than railroads for small loads, for short-haul cargoes and for goods shipped to railroad terminals from surrounding markets.

Trains, buses, private automobiles and trailers all have their special points as carriers of passengers. It has been said that the faster one travels the less he sees, and, conversely, the slower the pace the more one sees. When walking, an observant person misses little. In the automobile he sees more of the countryside than he can observe from a train window. In the train he is conscious of detail that he could not possibly discern from an airplane.

The modern traveler has a variety of conveyances from which to choose. Determining factors would include expense, distance, the time available, weather conditions, personal preferences, purpose of the journey and the state of the nation (whether at war or not).

In a country the size of the United States, there comes a time when the various transportation systems need regulation. Motor, rail and water carriers engaged in interstate commerce are under the jurisdiction of the Interstate Commerce Commis-

LAYING A PIPE LINE

Oil, petroleum and natural gas are transported by pipe lines.

sion. The original act creating the Commission, which was passed in 1887, has been broadened by amendments for the greater protection of the public. The Commission is authorized to adjust rates, regulate routes, pass upon mergers and otherwise serve the interests of the people. It is no longer possible for a strong railroad to create a monopoly by lowering its rates at the expense of smaller systems.

The following references on regulation of public services will be of value:

Common Carrier	Justice, Depart-
Federal Trade	ment of
Commission	Monopoly
Interstate Commerce	Public Utilities
Act	Trusts

The development of rapid transportation created a new factor in the business of supplying the public with common necessities. That factor was speed. The frontiersman, separated by miles of bad roads from the nearest trading post, carried home sufficient supplies to last him for months, on his infrequent trips to the post. As the wilderness gave way to farms, villages and towns, there was less and less need to accumulate large stocks of food and other necessities. Finally, settled communities were brought by fast trains and trucks within daily reach of needed supplies. Improved transportation thus completely changed methods of commercial buying and selling.

Modern transportation has also stimulated interchange of products between different countries. Except when the world is disrupted by war, cargoes of raw materials and manufactured goods are constantly being shipped across the seas from one

A FREIGHTER FOR COMMERCE

country to another, in carriers powered by steam or electricity. When nations are preparing for war, they buy up huge stocks of essential goods in preparation for the time when sources of supply will be endangered or cut off. No nation is wholly self-sufficient in essential raw materials and manufactured products.

Further information on the commercial relations between nations and on allied subjects may be found under the following headings:

Commerce	Tariff
Free Trade	Treaty
International Law	War
Reciprocity	War, Declaration of

Bibliography

BUTLER, N. M. *The Family of Nations.* Charles Scribner's Sons.

CARR, E. H. *International Relations Since the Peace Treaties.* The Macmillan Co.

DUNN, F. S. *Peaceful Change: A Study of International Procedures.* Council on Foreign Relations.

DUPUY, R. E. *If War Comes.* The Macmillan Co.

MADARIAGA, S. DE. *Theory and Practice in International Relations.* University of Pennsylvania Press.

A MODERN OCEAN LINER

WHAT OF THE FUTURE?

Within the span of a lifetime, men have crossed the United States in a covered wagon, an automobile and an airplane. The first journey took months; the second, less than two weeks; the third, less than a day. We may visualize a person near the end of his life, watching the landscape from a swift airplane and thinking of that long, hard journey of his boyhood. What would he see if the curtain of the future were drawn aside?

We ourselves may speculate on air travel of the years ahead. It is quite probable that passenger planes with accommodations for hundreds of persons will be flying not only across the United States but from continent to continent. Traveling at speeds of 300 to 400 miles per hour, these ships of the air will enable one to eat breakfast in New York and enjoy afternoon tea in London, all in the same day. Cargo planes of comparable size will be plying the trade routes of the air over all seas and continents.

Problems of intense cold, oxygen supply and air pressure will have been mastered, and in especially designed planes passengers may be traveling far above bad-weather altitudes in the clear realm of the higher stratosphere.

It is reasonable to expect that the autogiro, a plane that requires only a small landing field, will be used in cities to supplement surface transportation. Flat roofs, designed to serve as landing areas, would then be a structural feature of office buildings. Business men using the autogiro could commute daily from suburban homes a hundred miles away.

There is no doubt that there will be fewer accidents in the air travel of the future. Man is steadily perfecting devices that will eliminate crashes due to ice, fog and other hazards. Thus man may look forward to safe, comfortable and swift travel above and around the world.

CARRIERS FOR IDEAS

The beckoning hand, the smile and the frown, the nod of approval and the look of disdain are understood by men of every language and race. In the world of long ago, before the time of the spoken word, men had to communicate with one another by just such means—facial expression and gestures. The sign language used by deaf-mutes today is an organized system of communication based on the same principles.

Man continued to be handicapped in communicating his ideas because rapid transportation came long after the invention of speech. Fire and smoke signals, drum beats and running couriers were used to convey messages even by highly civilized peoples of the ancient world.

The invention of printing, in the fifteenth century, was a great event because it made

CARRYING THE MAIL
Top: The Pony Express. *Middle:* A modern city post office. *Bottom:* Rural free delivery.

possible the spread and duplication of ideas through books and periodicals. Yet it did not lessen the time gap between widely separated countries or between communities in the same country. As late as the second quarter of the nineteenth century, the arrival of a letter in San Francisco nearly eight days after it left Missouri by Pony Express was considered a wonderful feat.

The steam railroad was then in its early development. But soon to appear was a device to convey messages through the agency of electricity. This invention was the electro-magnetic telegraph.

For a more complete story of man's progress in communicating his ideas, during the period covered in the foregoing section, the reader is referred to the following articles:

Alphabet	Printing
Carrier Pigeon	Rosetta Stone
Cuneiform Inscrip-	Semaphore
tions	Shorthand
Heliograph	Signaling
Hieroglyphics	Sign Language
Philology	Writing
Postage Stamps	

Bibliography

CLODD, EDWARD. *Story of the Alphabet.* D. Appleton-Century Co.
DAVIS, WATSON. *Advance of Science.* Doubleday, Doran & Co.
DRIGG, H. R. *Pony Express Goes Through.* Frederick A. Stokes Co.
ELLSWORTH, LINCOLN. *Exploring Today.* Dodd, Mead & Co.
JORDANOFF, ASSEN. *Through the Overcast; the Art of Instrument Flying.* Funk & Wagnalls Co.
McMURTRIE, D. C. *The Book; the Story of Printing and Book Making.* Covici, Friede, Inc.
McSPADDEN, J. W. *How They Carried the Mail.* Dodd, Mead & Co.
WATSON, H. O. *Chanco; a U. S. Army Homing Pigeon.* Harper & Bros.

THE TELEGRAPH AND THE TELEPHONE

No one reading these pages remembers the advent of the electro-magnetic telegraph, but all of us can imagine the amazement of

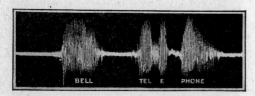

SENDING WORDS BY ELECTRICITY

Photograph of an electric current when "Bell Telephone" is said into the transmitter.

those Americans who first learned, in the spring of 1844, that messages had been carried over wire between two widely separated points. In that year, Congress granted the inventor, Samuel F. B. Morse, $30,000 to construct a telegraph line for public use. It was strung between Washington and Baltimore, and had reached Annapolis Junction

on May first. The first bit of political news transmitted over the line—the nomination of Henry Clay for President—was telegraphed to Washington on that day, and the completed line was opened officially on May 24 with the message, "What hath God wrought!"

The telegram brought to our door by uniformed messenger is one of several messages sent over the same wire. The first Morse lines could carry but one message at a time. In modern telegraphy, automatic machines have greatly increased the speed of delivery, and the operators of these machines do not have to learn the Morse code. Social telegrams—messages of congratulation, anniversary and holiday greetings and announcements of family events—are as common today as the regulation business and emergency wires. The practice of varying the rates according to speed of delivery has greatly encouraged the use of the telegraph by the general public.

In 1876, in Boston, Alexander Graham Bell made the first successful demonstration of the telephone, telegraphy's companion form of swift communication. "Writing far off" and "speaking far off," as their names are defined, together make nations, and communities within the same nation, close neighbors.

If the transmission of sound over wire seemed miraculous in 1844, how much more wonderful is communication without benefit of wire. Within our own time we have witnessed the extension of wireless telegraphy and telephony (radio) throughout the whole world.

Radio waves were discovered in 1887 by Heinrich Hertz while he was conducting an experiment in a laboratory. After scientists proved that the waves were electro-magnetic, they sought to find a way to use them as carriers of sound. Many physicists worked on the problem, but special honor is due Guglielmo Marconi, who in 1896 succeeded in using wireless telegraphy to send a message between stations two miles apart.

The electro-magnetic carriers that bring words and music to our homes travel with the speed of light, over 186,000 miles a second. A radio wave travels around the world in about one-seventh of a second. The words of a speaker in an auditorium, when they are broadcast, may be heard by listeners thousands of miles distant before they are perceived by the audience in the hall, since the immediate listeners receive the words by the slower sound waves.

The first ship to sail around the world completed the historic voyage in three years, from 1519 to 1522. Three and three-quarters of a century later, instantaneous communication was accomplished by Marconi. Thus has man conquered space and time by the agency of machines.

The world has found a multitude of uses for radio telegraphy and telephony. Radio is indispensable for safety in marine navigation and flying. It helps men to carry on the work of the world. Businessmen talk to each other by radio telephone across oceans. Correspondents communicate by radio with their home newspaper offices from remote lands. Governments know well the value of radio as a medium for propaganda.

The rapid improvement in radio apparatus has helped to make the public radio-conscious. Radio sets with short-wave bands are becoming more and more common, and a voice from one country may be heard at the same time by millions of people in various parts of the world.

The articles listed below give further information about man's conquest of distance through the invention of the various forms of telegraphy and telephony:

Bell, Alexander G.	Radio
Cable, Submarine	Signaling
Edison, Thomas A.	Telegraph
Field, Cyrus W.	Telegraph, Wireless
Marconi, Guglielmo	Telephone
Morse, Samuel F. B.	

Bibliography

BAARSLAG, KARL. *S O S to the Rescue.* Oxford University Press.
DUNLAP, O. E. *Marconi, the Man and His Wireless.* The Macmillan Co.
HYLANDER, C. J. *American Inventors.* The Macmillan Co.
ROGERS, FRANCES. *Heels, Wheels and Wires.* Frederick A. Stokes Co.
YATES, R. F. *These Amazing Electrons.* The Macmillan Co.

High-School List

NICOLAY, HELEN. *Wizard of the Wires; a Boy's Life of Samuel F. B. Morse.* D. Appleton-Century Co.
WADE, MRS. M. H. B. *Master Builders.* Little, Brown & Co.
———— *Wonder Workers.* Little Brown & Co.

THE NEWSPAPER

The production of a modern newspaper depends upon many of the industrial products we have dealt with in the preceding sections. These products include a paper used for printing, metals utilized for engravings and type, typesetting machines and the presses that print the completed editions. In the gathering of the news and the dis-

tribution of the newspaper, the telephone, telegraph and radio, motor trucks, railroads, airplanes and ships all have a part.

What kind of newspapers circulated when there were no machines and no means of rapid communication? It is interesting

National Life Insurance Co.

AMERICA'S FIRST PRESS, 1638

to know that the metropolitan daily of our great cities developed from humble beginnings in ancient Rome. In that city, daily news bulletins (*Acta Diurna*), written by hand, were posted in the public market place and later handed around by messenger. Scribes made copies for distribution in the provinces. Handwritten news sheets were the only form of newspaper available to the people of Europe until the invention of printing. People who lived far away from the source of news learned of important events long after they were actually "news."

The earlier printed newspapers were produced by slow, laborious processes. Type was set by hand and printing was done with flat or horizontal presses. The invention of the rotary press, in the nineteenth century, greatly increased the speed of duplication. Printing from curved plates clamped on cylinders, a rotary press can turn out a thirty-two-page edition at a rate of over 50,000 copies an hour. Equally important in technical advancement was the invention of the linotype machine, a typesetting device which stepped up the rate of composition tremendously.

Men who get and write news stories range from local reporters to correspondents in remote places thousands of miles away. Stories are received at newspaper offices by telephone and telegram, radio, cable, mail and personal delivery. A story transmitted

Chicago Daily News

THE NEWSPAPER INFORMS THE WORLD

by wire is received on the teletype, a machine which transforms telegraphic messages into printed form.

In modern journalism, newspaper correspondents often report battles on land and sea while they themselves are under fire. The stories they send to the home office are often obtained at great personal risk and under very difficult conditions.

After the story has been revised in the copy room, it is set in type in the composing room. From there it goes to the casting room, where it is made into plates to be clamped onto the press. Stories of world-wide significance may be read on the streets of our cities within a short time after the events actually occurred.

Photographs, transmitted by wire and radio, make these news stories doubly vivid. In fact, the increased use of photography is one of the outstanding developments of modern journalism. Some newspapers are really picture journals, with illustrations and captions occupying more space than regular type matter. Color photography is being used with telling effect in metropolitan dailies. The rotogravure section is also a standard feature of many Saturday or Sunday editions. Supplements consisting almost wholly of pictures are put out by syndicates and supplied to newspapers.

An established feature of moving-picture programs is the newsreel, covering sports,

domestic and foreign news and personalities of the day. There are successful moving-picture theaters devoted entirely to news-reel presentation.

We may expect further developments in newspaper making. It is possible, through use of the photo-electric cell, to transmit by radio a newspaper page for reception on a zinc plate ready for printing. With this device, it would be possible to broadcast an entire edition to a number of outlying plants. Thus the distribution of newspapers could be immensely speeded up over a large area.

Facsimile transmission, which has been used successfully to a limited extent, has great possibilities. With this process, news bulletins may be broadcast from radio stations and received in printed form on a home or school receiving set. Television, the transmission of both pictures and sound by radio, may be a competitor of the newspaper when it is further developed.

Other interesting material on the newspaper and related subjects may be found in the following articles:

Halftone	Printing
Linotype	Printing Press
Monotype	Stereotyping
Newspaper	Television
Photo-Engraving	Type

Bibliography

ALLEN, J. E. *Newspaper Make-up.* Harper & Bros.
CRUMP, IRVING. *Boy's Book of Newsreel Hunters.* Dodd, Mead & Co.
HAYWARD, W. R. *Story of Man's Work.* Minton, Balch & Co.
JACKSON, J. H. *Extra! Extra!* The Macmillan Co.
KELIHER, A. V. *News Workers.* Harper & Bros.
LEE, J. M. *History of American Journalism.* Garden City Publishing Co.
McSPADDEN, J. W. *How They Sent the News.* Dodd, Mead & Co.

High-School List

CONKLIN, IRVING. *Guideposts of the Sea; The Modern Aids to Navigation and How They Are Cared For.* The Macmillan Co.
COON, HORACE. *American Tel. and Tel.; The Story of a Great Monopoly.* Longmans, Green & Co.
DUNBAR, SEYMOUR. *History of Travel in America.* Tudor Publishing Co.
HARLOW, A. F. *Old Towpaths; The Story of the American Canal Era.* D. Appleton-Century Co.
HOWE, QUINCY. *The News and How to Understand It in Spite of the Newspapers, in Spite of the Magazines, in Spite of the Radio.* Simon & Schuster.
LAZARSFELD, P. F. *Radio and the Printed Page: An Introduction to the Study of Radio and Its Role in the Communication of Ideas.* Duell, Sloan & Pearce.
MILLER, J. A. *Fares, Please! From Horse-Cars to Streamliners.* D. Appleton-Century Co.
MOTT, F. L. *American Journalism; A History of Newspapers in the U. S. Through 250 Years.* The Macmillan Co.
OSWALD, J. C. *History of Printing, Its Development Through Five Hundred Years.* D. Appleton-Century Co.
PRATT, FLETCHER. *Secret and Urgent; The Story of Codes and Ciphers.* The Bobbs-Merrill Co.
RECK, F. M. *Romance of American Transportation.* J. T. Crowell Co.
VAN CLEEF, EUGENE. *Trade Centers and Trade Routes.* D. Appleton-Century Co.

PROBLEMS CREATED BY MODERNIZED COMMUNICATION

As a conveyor of news and opinion, the newspaper wields great influence, both for good and for evil. Centralized news services, such as the Associated Press, release identical versions of news events to the newspapers belonging to the respective associations, and these versions are printed exactly as received. Thus, millions of persons may read exactly the same account of an event about which they have no personal information. Another feature of modern journalism which undoubtedly helps to mold public opinion is the syndicated column, appearing, perhaps, in hundreds of newspapers of enormous circulation.

Any newspaper which prints centralized news dispatches or a syndicated column may express other points of view in its editorials and feature articles written by special correspondents. Thus the effect of an avalanche of identical material is counterbalanced, and the open-minded reader will weigh and compare before he makes up his mind about controversial subjects.

If any group, political or otherwise, should gain complete control of radio and of centralized news agencies, millions of listeners and readers would hear and read only such facts or interpretations as the group desired them to receive. In totalitarian countries, such control of news and ideas prevails to a degree little understood by democratic nations. In the United States, freedom of the press is guaranteed by the Constitution.

Except in time of war or grave national emergency, American newspapers are not subject to censorship. Only the power of public opinion can restrain such papers as abuse freedom of the press by distorting news, playing upon the emotions of minority groups, preaching intolerance or serving as spokesmen for special interests. Persons slandered may sue for damages.

Other agencies of communication are more directly controlled. The government itself operates the postal service. Telephone and telegraph companies are subject to regulation by the Federal Communications Commission. The Commission is authorized to issue licenses to radio stations and may cancel or withhold such licenses for cause.

Worship and Faith in a Changing World

As the term is commonly understood, religion is the expression of belief in a supernatural being or power entitled to worship and obedience. Religious faith of this nature is found in every tribe, nation and race. The great world religions having supernatural elements number among their adherents more than a billion and a half persons (see the article RELIGION).

In another sense, religion may be thought of as a personal conviction which determines a man's attitude toward moral and ethical questions. There are persons religious in this sense who devote themselves to good works or great causes and at the same time remain apart from organized churches. Meditation in the quiet of one's home is an expression of religious conviction satisfying to many persons. Participation in a Church service with music and ceremonial rites may inspire a great many more. However one worships, he is seeking strength and guidance from spiritual forces.

The trend of modern thought has been to permit the individual to express his own religious beliefs and to worship in his own way. Such freedom encourages the breaking up of organized groups and the formation of smaller bodies, as, for example, the divisions among Protestant Churches since the Reformation. On the other hand, the same freedom has fostered the reunion of Church groups by encouraging them to overlook minor points at issue and to emphasize the fundamental truths that draw them together.

ORIGIN AND DEVELOPMENT OF RELIGION

There are two explanations for the origin of religion. One theory holds that the religious sense was implanted in the human soul by God, directly. The other theory is based on evolution of the religious idea through man's development.

Those supporting the second theory believe that, in the beginning, men lived in terror of nature, without religion and without understanding. Light and darkness, sun and stars, storm and wind were mysterious or fearsome to primitive man. He did believe, however, that rocks, trees, streams and mountains were endowed with personality. From this idea came animism, the belief that natural objects are the abode of spirits. Therein is the beginning of religion, for out of animism came the practice of magic, ceremony and sacrifice.

In his superstitious attempts to placate unfriendly spirits, man became a worshiper of idols, and the idols became his gods. These he endowed with traits which he himself knew about. His gods and goddesses

THE FRENCH EXPLORERS CARRIED THE CROSS TO THE NEW WORLD

became the heroes and heroines of wonderful tales in which they performed miraculous deeds and exhibited such contradictory qualities as kindness and cruelty, courage and weakness. Hundreds of such stories survive as myths.

In the course of time a formal worship developed, characterized by rites and ceremonies. From the educated classes came priests, men who were trained to conduct the rites and to act as intercessors between the gods and the people.

In the tribal organization of society, regulations for the conduct of individuals and families came to have the force of religion. These rules were thought to have divine sanction. Those who refused to obey them courted severe punishment. It was unlawful to touch certain objects; hence the rise of taboos. Exacting rules about food, dress, marriage and burial were formulated and strictly enforced.

A rigid moral system was instrumental in holding the Jewish tribes together in their early history. The laws formulated by Moses and other leaders are contained in the Old Testament. Instead of worshiping a number of lesser deities, the Hebrews practiced monotheism, the worship of one God. This doctrine was their outstanding contribution to the religious thought of their time.

Also rooted in antiquity was the idea of the prophet, a great leader who was qualified to communicate with a deity and interpret his commands. In the three great monotheistic religions—Judaism, Christianity and Mohammedanism—the concept of the prophet is a fundamental idea.

Christianity, based on fulfillment of the Jewish prophecy that God would send a Messiah to save His people, is a revealed religion. To the oppressed and poor it brought new hope in its doctrines of peace and love, the brotherhood of man and the Fatherhood of God. The teachings of Christ, its founder, gave dignity to the common man and exalted the personality of the individual in an age of tyranny and oppression.

Other founders of world religions include Zoroaster, a teacher of ancient Persia (Iran); Buddha, the sage of India who antedated Christ; Confucius, a great Chinese moralist whose followers gave his teachings the force of a religion, and Mohammed, the prophet of Islam. Brahmanism, the dominant faith of the Hindus, is based on the ancient Vedas and is controlled by a priestly caste, the Brahmans.

GROWTH OF CHRISTIANITY

The immediate followers of Christ faithfully spread his teachings after the Crucifixion, but the greatest missionary of the period was Paul of Tarsus, author of. some of the finest literature of the New Testament. He also founded Churches, and before his death Christianity had become established in many parts of the Roman Empire. It was over three centuries, however, before Christianity became the state religion of Rome. The early Christians suffered cruel persecutions, but their faith never faltered.

After the fall of the Western Roman Empire, in 476, Christianity wielded a strong influence over the lives of the common people, who were poor and ignorant but devoted to their religion. The age produced splendid cathedrals that symbolized the self-sacrifice and faith of the masses.

As the Church grew in power, some of its leaders became critical of certain practices and asked that reforms be adopted. The movement culminated in the Reformation and the establishment of Protestant sects in various parts of Europe in the sixteenth century.

Religious wars brought years of unrest and turmoil to Europe, and both sides were guilty of persecution. The Church surmounted its difficulties, however, and out of the bitterness there developed a spirit of tolerance and understanding.

For additional reading concerning the development of religion during primitive times, consult the following headings:

Druids	Image Worship
Fetish	Nature Worship
Fire Worship	Stonehenge
Idol	

Interesting information on the pagan religions of the Greeks and Romans may be found in the article MYTHOLOGY. For typical stories about the gods and goddesses, consult the following:

Apollo	Neptune
Bacchus	Oracles
Ceres	Orion
Cupid	Pan
Deucalion	Pandora
Diana	Perseus
Fauns	Phaethon
Furies	Pluto
Graces	Prometheus
Hades	Psyche
Juno	Rhea
Jupiter	Saturn
Mars	Styx
Mercury	Venus
Muses	Vulcan

The religion of the ancient Egyptians is discussed under the headings listed below:

Ammon	Isis
Anubis	Osiris
Apis	Re
Architecture	Serapis

In the story of religion, the mythology of the Norsemen plays an important part. Consult the following articles:

Balder	Mythology
Frey	Odin
Freya	Sigurd
Frigga	Thor
Heimdall	Valhalla
Lok	Valkyries
Niflheim	Yggdrasil

Articles and stories concerning the history and religion of the Jews may be found under these headings:

Abraham	Jews
Babel, Tower of	Job
Bible	Joshua
Bible Stories	Judea
Cain	Judges, Book of
Canaanites	Leviticus
Chronicles, Books of	Messiah
Cities of Refuge	Moses
David	Nehemiah
Deborah	Noah
Decalogue	Numbers, Book of
Delilah	Palestine
Deluge	Passover
Eden	Pentecost
Elijah	Pharisees
Esau	Philistines
Esther	Proverbs
Ezekiel	Psalms
Ezra	Ruth
Gabriel	Sadducees
God	Samson
Goliath	Samuel
Hebrew Language	Sanhedrin
and Literature	Saul
Herod	Semites
Hosea	Semitic Languages
Isaac	Sinai
Jacob	Solomon
Jehovah	Tabernacle
Jeremiah	Tabernacles, Feast of
Jerusalem	Talmud, The

For the origin and early history of Christianity, consult the following articles:

Abbey	Jesus Christ
Apostles	John, Saint
Augustine, Saint	John the Baptist
Bethlehem	Joseph
Calvary	Judas
Catacombs	Luke, Saint
Constantine	Magdalene, Mary
Corinthians,	Mark, Saint
Epistle to the	Mary, The Virgin
Cross	Matthew, Saint
Crucifixion	Monasticism
Galilee	Paul, Saint
Gethsemane	Peter
Gospels	Philip
Herod	Revelation,
James, Saint	Book of
(The Greater)	Thessalonians,
James, Saint	Epistles to the
(The Less)	Timothy
Jerusalem	Titus

For information on the history, organization and practices of the Roman Catholic Church, see the following articles:

Ash Wednesday	Lateran
Ave Maria	Litany
Canonization	Mass
Canon Law	Papal States
Cardinal	Pope
Catholic Church	Roman Catholic
Conclave	Church
Eucharist	Rosary
Heretic	Shrove Tuesday
Holy Family	Unction
Indulgence	Vatican City
Inquisition	Vulgate

The story of the Reformation is told under many headings. For information on its fore-runners and leaders, its causes and its history, and other related material, consult the articles listed below:

Augsburg	Luther, Martin
Confession	Nantes, Edict of
Calvin and	Protestants
Calvinism	Reformation, The
Counter-Reformation	Savonarola, Girolamo
Cromwell, Oliver	Thirty Years' War
England, Church of	Wolsey, Thomas
Huguenots	Worms
Huss, John	Wycliffe, John
Hussites	Zwingli, Ulric
Knox, John	

There are many topics dealing with Christian practice and doctrine that are too general in their application to be included in the foregoing lists. They include such articles as:

Apostolic Succession	Church
Archangel	Greek Church
Archbishop	Holy Ghost
Baptism	Holy Week
Bishop	Lent
Catechism	Missions and
Cathedral	Missionaries
Christianity	Priest

Details concerning other Oriental faiths may be found under these headings:

Allah	Minaret
Ancestor Worship	Mohammed
Brahma	Mohammedanism
Brahmanism	Mosque
Buddha	Nirvana
Buddhism	Parsees
Caste	Sanskrit Language and
Confucius	Literature
Fakir	Shintoism
Hegira	Sikhs
Islam	Siva
Koran	Towers of Silence
Mecca	Vedas
Medina	Vishnu

Bibliography

BAIKIE, JAMES. *Lands and People of the Bible.* The Macmillan Co.

BONSER, EDNA. *How the Early Hebrews Lived and Learned.* The Macmillan Co.

BULFINCH, THOMAS. *The Age of Fable.* Frederick A. Stokes Co.

GAER, JOSEPH. *How the Great Religions Began.* Robert M. McBride & Co.

HODGES, GEORGE. *When the King Came.* Houghton, Mifflin Co.

MALKUS, A. S. *Dark Star of Itza.* Harcourt, Brace & Co.

MARTIN, A. W. *Seven Great Bibles.* Frederick A. Stokes Co.

MORRISON, LUCILE. *Lost Queen of Egypt.* Frederick A. Stokes Co.

SNEDEKER, C. D. *Perilous Seat—The Story of a Girl of Delphi.* Doubleday, Doran & Co.

STEELE, F. A. *Adventures of Akbar.* Frederick A. Stokes Co.

WILMOT-BUXTON, E. M. *Stories of Norse Heroes from the Eddas and Sagas.* Thomas Y. Crowell Co.

RELIGION IN AMERICA

The desire for religious freedom was an important reason for the settlement of the first English colony in Massachusetts, in 1620. The men and women who established Plymouth Colony were Separatists—dissenters from the Established Church. They crossed the ocean and braved the hardships of colonial life in order to worship according to their own convictions.

Ten years later a company of English Puritans established themselves at Boston, becoming founders of Massachusetts Bay

JOHN ELIOT OF MASSACHUSETTS
PREACHING TO THE INDIANS

Colony. In 1634, Maryland became a refuge for oppressed Catholics. Lord Baltimore, the proprietor, promised religious freedom to all Christian settlers, Catholics and non-Catholics alike. Rhode Island was founded by Roger Williams and Anne Hutchinson, dissenters from the political and religious codes of the Puritans. William Penn opened Pennsylvania to all persecuted Europeans, regardless of their creed.

When the Constitution of the United States was submitted to the states for ratification, there was a popular demand for amendments safeguarding individual liberties. Among the ten amendments adopted was one guaranteeing freedom of religion. No other clause of the Constitution is more deeply cherished by the American people.

The settlers in Massachusetts were punctilious about their observance of religious rules. A blessing was asked at every meal, family worship was conducted daily and all children were given instruction in religious matters. Sunday was literally a day of rest and worship. The Sunday services were held in austere, unheated buildings, and everyone was obliged to attend. Levity in dress, speech and conduct was severely frowned upon. Religion truly pervaded the lives of the New England pioneers.

Although this absorption in religion was not characteristic of the frontier settlers of the new West, as the country was developed and settlements were transformed into cities, America became a land of churches, with every Christian denomination represented.

The adherents of Judaism and other Oriental religions have also been free to establish their places of worship. The influence of religion on the education and moral progress of America has been outstanding.

Information on denominations and leaders of religion who have figured in the history of the United States, together with other information dealing with religion in America, may be found in the following articles:

Amana Society	Moravian Brethren
Baptists	Mormons
Christian Endeavor	Penn, William
Society	Pilgrims
Christian Science	Plymouth Colony
Congregationalists	Presbyterians
Disciples of Christ	Puritans
Eddy, Mary Baker	Quakers
Episcopal Church	Reformed Church
Epworth League	Religious Liberty
Evangelical Church	Rhode Island, sub-
Free Methodists	head History
Hutchinson, Anne	Shakers
Jesuits	Smith, Joseph
Latter-Day Saints	Universalists
Marquette, Jacques	Unitarians
Maryland, subhead	Wesley
History	Williams, Roger
Mennonites, The	Young, Brigham
Methodists	

Bibliography

BEARD, C. A. *Making of American Civilization*. The Macmillan Co.
CLARK, E. T. *Small Sects in America*. Cokesbury Press.
EARLE, A. M. *Home Life in Colonial Days*. The Macmillan Co.
HALL, M. E. *Roger Williams*. The Pilgrim Press.
HOLLAND, R. S. *William Penn*. The Macmillan Co.
MARTIN, H. R. *Tillie, a Mennonite Maid*. Grosset & Dunlop.
SNEDEKER, C. D. *Uncharted Ways*. Doubleday, Doran & Co.
SWEET, W. W. *Makers of Christianity*. Henry Holt & Co.

RELIGION AND SCIENCE

In ancient times, man associated the processes of nature with the deities of his religion. The mythologies of the Greeks and Romans and the Norse peoples are full of stories that give a supernatural explanation to natural phenomena. Elements of this view of the physical world have persisted to modern times. The direct intervention of God in the creation of the earth and of all living things, as expressed in the Old Testament, is believed today by a large body of Christians.

In the light of modern science, many others have felt it necessary to harmonize their religious beliefs with the new discoveries. Such persons have met the problem by giving the Bible accounts a symbolical meaning.

A solution acceptable to many is this: Religion and science occupy different spheres. One deals with worship, belief in God and moral principles. The other has to do with observations, research and experi-

CHRIST'S CHURCH, ALEXANDRIA, VA.
Washington and Lee worshiped here.

mentation in the realm of nature. The one is spiritual; the other is concerned with material things. The truly religious man has a personal experience and a faith that defy scientific analysis. Even an advanced scientist would say that there are experiences above and beyond the world of reality.

Thus science continues to advance and to improve the material condition of man, and religion remains his spiritual hope and comfort, sustaining him through life's trials.

CHURCH AND STATE

The concept of the union of Church and state has played an important part in history. After the fall of Rome, in the period when monarchies were being established in Europe, the king was head of the Church in his nation and also head of the government.

Complete separation of Church and state has always been a fundamental policy of the United States government. The Constitution forbids the enactment of laws establishing a government-supported Church.

In such strong Catholic countries as France, Spain and Mexico, revolutionary movements overthrew the established Church, but a counter-revolution in Spain brought about a restoration. Anti-religious laws in

France and Mexico have been greatly modified. The Russian revolution of the First World War period not only disestablished the Russian Church but attempted to discourage all forms of worship. The Soviet Union today does not molest those who desire to worship, but the government exercises control over all religious bodies.

In totalitarian countries generally, the tendency is for the ruling political party to assume control of the education of youth and to restrict the Church in various ways.

Further information concerning the relationship of Church and state may be found in the following articles:

Constitution of the   Mexico
    United States, sub-   Naziism
    head The Twenty-   Religious **Liberty**
    one Amendments   Spain
Divine Right of Kings   Russia
Henry VIII

Bibliography

BARR, JAMES. *Religious Liberty in the Totalitarian States.* Allenson & Co.
DICKENS, CHARLES. *Child's History of England.* Houghton, Mifflin Co.
HARMAN, N. B. *Science and Religion.* The Macmillan Co.
HARKNESS, G. E. *Recovery of Ideals.* Charles Scribner's Sons.
ROBERTS, S. H. *House That Hitler Built.* Harper & Bros.
TAPPAN, E. M. *Story of Our Constitution.* Lothrop, Lee & Shepard Co.

THE CHURCH IN A CHANGING WORLD

One of the outstanding developments of the modern Church is its interest in social questions. In addition to strictly religious matters, Church groups today give their attention to such problems as labor relations, housing, unemployment, poverty and the improvement of moral standards. International peace and the attitude of the Church toward war are matters of vital interest to all religious bodies. Both the Vatican and responsible Protestant organizations have adopted a liberal social creed.

The Church in medieval times took the lead in caring for the poor, the sick and orphaned children. The monasteries were centers of such charitable aid, and members of various religious orders devoted themselves to the poor. Thus the charitable work of the modern Churches has been a natural development. So, too, has been their interest in problems resulting from the Industrial Revolution and the factory system.

Education has been another matter of deep concern to religious organizations. The Roman Catholic educational system extends from parochial schools to colleges and universities. Convent and monastery schools prepare students for religious work. Many colleges and universities have also been endowed by Protestant groups.

The Churches have sought in various ways to improve or maintain standards of literature, the drama, moving pictures and radio. A trend toward objectionable motion pictures was checked by the firm stand of Catholic, Protestant and Jewish leaders.

The interest of the Churches in the welfare of youth has led to the founding of organizations combining educational, social and religious activities. Examples are the Y.M.C.A., Y.W.C.A. and similar Catholic and Hebrew organizations. The Salvation Army is known the world over for its evangelistic and welfare activities and for its success in reaching those who have reached the depths of poverty and despair.

Additional information concerning the activities of religious groups and the new trends may be found under such articles as:

Charity and Charities   Volunteers of America
Salvation Army   Young Men's Christian
Social Settlements   Association
Sunday Schools   Young Women's Chris-
United Church of   tian Association
    Canada

Bibliography

CARRIER, BLANCHE. *How Shall I Learn to Teach Religion?* Harper & Bros.
CHAMBERS, M. M. *Youth Serving Organizations.* American Council on Education.
ERVINE, ST. JOHN. *God's Soldier: General William Booth.* Heinemann & Co.
HAYWARD, P. R. *Young People's Method in the Church.* Abingdon Press.
SIMS, M. S. S. *Natural History of a Social Institution.* Woman's Press.
SPERRY, W. L. *What You Owe Your Child.* Harper & Bros.

PROBLEMS OF THE MODERN CHURCH

How to keep religion a vital force is a major problem of the modern Church, faced as it is with the new interests and discoveries of our age. Neglect of church-going is just one phase of the problem. The automobile, moving pictures, radio, golf and other means of recreation fill the Sunday leisure hours of many who were brought up to attend Sunday school and other religious services regularly.

Many city organizations attempt to meet the problem by constructing attractive Church buildings and providing good music and sermons that touch on the vital religious interests of today. Modern Church buildings often include parish houses containing rooms designed for social and athletic activities. In many towns, several denominations have combined to form the Community Church, with the wise slogan in mind—"In unity there is strength."

The practice of broadcasting sermons and sacred music has brought religious services to the chair or bedside of the invalid shut-in. Whether the same service keeps able-bodied people at home is a question difficult to answer. Probably the net result of such broadcasting is favorable to the Church, and it may arouse a renewed interest in those who have lost their church-going habits.

The effect of war on missions and missionary enterprises is especially deplorable. Christianity also has to face the hostility of paganist and atheistic trends in certain countries, and of intolerance and racial prejudice contrary to the spirit of religion. More than ever the Church needs courage, vision and great spiritual leaders in this modern age.

Bibliography

DAVIS, JEROME. *Contemporary Social Movements*. D. Appleton-Century Co.
EMBREE, E. R. *Prospecting for Heaven*. The Viking Press.
LINK, H. C. *Return to Religion*. The Macmillan Co.
WIEMAN, R. W. *Modern Family and the Church*. Harper & Bros.

High-School List

BENNETT, J. C. and others. *The Church Through Half a Century*. Charles Scribner's Sons.
BRADEN, C. S. *The World's Religions; A Short History*. Cokesbury Press.
BROWN, W. A. *A Creed for Free Men, A Study of Loyalties*. Charles Scribner's Sons.
COMPTON, A. H. *The Human Meaning of Science*. University of North Carolina Press
GAGGIN, E. R. *Down Ryton Water*. The Viking Press.
HIGH, STANLEY, and others. *Faith for Today*. Town Hall Press.
MEAD, F. S. *The March of Eleven Men*. The Bobbs-Merrill Co.
MORTON, H. V. *Through Lands of the Bible*. Dodd, Mead & Co.
PARKHURST, H. H. *Cathedral, a Gothic Pilgrimage*. Houghton, Mifflin Co.
WIEMAN, MRS. R. H. W. *The Modern Family and the Church*. Harper & Bros.

Going to School in the Modern World

Man has always been learning in life's school, but ages passed before he received formal instruction in schools. The modern American school is the result of the changes that have taken place since 1900 in equipment, curriculum and teaching methods. To appreciate this development, let us consider what schools were like in early America.

COLONIAL SCHOOLS

A few colonial children were tutored at home and others attended pay schools. Not all children, however, attended school or even learned how to read and write.

In the Massachusetts Bay Colony, some officials believed that too many children were growing up in ignorance, especially in regard to the Bible. Accordingly they passed, in 1647, a law requiring every township of fifty families to provide a common school.

These schools consisted usually of a one-room log building, lighted by oiled-paper windows and heated by an open fireplace. The children were ranged on rude benches facing the schoolmaster, who sat on a stool before a high desk. Ever mindful of the much-used birch rod hanging on the wall near by, the pupils frequently droned out their lessons in unison. From time to time, however, each pupil was called before the master to recite, receiving his praise for knowing the lesson or a scolding or a touch of the dreaded birch rod for being negligent.

One of the most popular textbooks of the time was the *New England Primer,* through the study of which the children learned moral and religious maxims as they learned to read. The children's prayer, "Now I lay me down to sleep," first appeared in the *New England Primer.*

A child strove for good handwriting by copying over and over the sample letters in his copy book. His sums he worked on a slate; older pupils sometimes learned to solve difficult problems by mental arithmetic. For many years the three R's—"reading, 'riting and 'rithmetic"—constituted the entire education of the child. The pupils fortunate enough to be sent to the schools beyond the ones that taught the three R's were by all odds in the minority.

HIGHER EDUCATION

The grammar schools prepared students for college, offering Greek, Latin and the classics. The colleges, in turn, prepared most of their students for the ministry. The grammar schools and colleges were for men only; until some courageous women established female seminaries, girls could receive more than a common-school education only by private tutoring. Later, some men's colleges admitted women, and new colleges were established on a coeducational basis.

THE FIRST PUBLIC SCHOOLS

The Massachusetts law establishing the common school provided also that families should contribute to its support. Childless families did not at first contribute willingly to these schools, arguing that they did not

National Life Insurance Co.

A COLONIAL HORNBOOK
The "lesson," fastened to a paddle-shaped piece of wood, is protected by a transparent piece of horn. Children were taught to be neat.

benefit from the money so invested. They were finally convinced, however, that children must be educated to be good citizens and good workers. Out of this idea has come our system of free, public education for all children.

Some of the other colonies were much slower in adopting the public-school system. Children there were educated in either private religious schools or charity schools. When the idea of charity schools became distasteful to the parents of children attending them, they joined the movement to establish tax-supported schools such as we have today.

See the article on EDUCATION for a general survey of the subject. Further information on the subject of education and schools in the earlier and later periods in America is found under the following titles:

Coeducation	High School
College	Kindergarten
Common Schools	Mann, Horace
Compulsory Education	Montessori, Maria
Corporal Punishment	Montessori Method
Education, Office of	Normal Schools and
Froebel, Friedrich	Teachers Colleges
Wilhelm	University

Bibliography

ALLEE, M. H. *House of Her Own.* Houghton, Mifflin Co.
CURTI, M. E. *Social Ideas of American Educators.* Charles Scribner's Sons.
EARLE, A. M. *Child Life in Colonial Days.* The Macmillan Co.
EGGLESTON, EDWARD. *Hoosier School Boy.* Charles Scribner's Sons.
GRAVES, F. P. *Students' History of Education.* The Macmillan Co.
MEDARY, MARJORIE. *College in Crinoline.* Longmans, Green & Co.
SMITH, M. P. W. *Jolly Good Times at Hackmatack.* Little, Brown & Co.

THE RURAL-SCHOOL PROBLEM

In many parts of the United States, the one-room school provides all the elementary instruction that many rural children receive. One teacher, not always properly trained, teaches all eight grades. With such a crowded schedule, the class periods must be very short. Library facilities are lacking, and such cultural subjects as art and music are often omitted entirely from the curriculum. The cost of education in these one-room rural schools is high, since a school must be maintained even if there is only one child of school age in the district.

Conditions have been particularly serious in certain mountain and impoverished rural districts such as those serving the Southern sharecropper. Civic, educational and social-welfare leaders have given much thought to this problem, to the extent that one sees constant progress in the housing and equipping of rural schools in these areas.

RURAL-SCHOOL PROGRESS—FROM ONE ROOM TO THE CONSOLIDATED SCHOOL

The consolidated school offers one solution to the rural-school problem. With several districts pooling their resources, such a school is better equipped and is staffed by better-trained teachers. Since it has two or more classrooms, each teacher has fewer classes; consequently, class periods are longer. However, schools can be consolidated only in areas where the roads are graded and surfaced. Usually, pupils are taken to and from school by bus, and good roads are necessary to make this transportation of pupils possible.

Bibliography

FOX, GENEVIEVE. *Mountain Girl.* Little, Brown & Co.
GROUT, R. E. *Handbook of Health Education for Rural Schools.* Doubleday, Doran & Co.
HALL, E. G. *Here-to-Yonder Girl.* The Macmillan Co.
KNOX, R. B. *Marty & Co.* Doubleday, Doran & Co.
MULLER, H. M. *Federal Aid for the Equalization of Educational Opportunities.* H. W. Wilson & Co.
RAINEY, H. P. *How Fare American Youth?* D. Appleton-Century Co.

EQUIPPING THE MODERN SCHOOL

In many ways has mechanical progress contributed to the modern American school, not the least of which are the provisions made for the health and safety of the pupils in constructing the building. Fresh air at uniform temperatures is sent to all parts of the structure from central heating and ventilating systems. Plenty of light and sunshine is admitted through the large window area, and on dark days there is electric lighting.

Modern desks are comfortable and permit freedom of movement; they are adjusted to the proper position for reading and writing, and are placed so that light reaches the pupils' work at the proper angle. Mechanical sweepers and proper cleaning materials keep the rooms clean and free from dust. The application of acoustical principles eliminates undue noise, and steel construction makes modern schools practically fireproof.

Careful attention, too, is paid to the care of the child's vision in the selection of books, chalk, blackboards, wall maps and charts; and children with visual and hearing defects are given special materials and mechanical aids. Many cities maintain special schools for handicapped children.

Modern schools are equipped with many mechanical devices that enrich teaching. Copying devices such as the mimeograph enable the teacher to prepare teaching materials quickly and easily. The phonograph is useful in teaching music appreciation and foreign language. The moving picture is invaluable in visual education; government and industrial sources have prepared and distribute for school use—either free or at small cost—moving pictures on industrial processes, sports, travel and many other subjects of an educational nature.

Radio has an acknowledged place in the modern schools. Besides regular broadcasts of news, music, speeches and other programs helpful to students, there are educational broadcasts during school hours; provision is also made for re-broadcasting, from transcriptions, programs given in out-of-school hours or at times inconvenient for class use. Many schools have installed public-address systems; these aid hearing in a large auditorium, permit announcements to be made from the school offices and enable a principal to listen to a discussion in any classroom or to address the pupils in several rooms at once.

Schools also have rooms equipped to teach the varied courses of the modern curriculum —manual training, machine-shop practice, science, cooking, sewing, printing, art, stagecraft, music, the commercial subjects and journalism.

For further information on subjects relating to the construction and equipment of the modern school, consult the following titles:

Acoustics	Radio, subhead Social
Building	Implications of Radio
Copying Devices	Talking Machine
Electric Light	Thermostat
Heating and	Typewriter
Ventilation	Vision
Moving Pictures	

Bibliography

HARRISON, MARGARET. *Radio in the Classroom.* Prentice-Hall, Inc.
HOLMES, R. E. *Air Conditioning in Summer and Winter.* McGraw-Hill Book Co.
KOON, C. M. *Motion Pictures in Education in the U. S.* University of Chicago Press.
MARSHAK, I. J. *Turning Night into Day.* J. B. Lippincott Co.
ROEMER, JOSEPH. *Basic Student Activities.* Silver, Burdett Co.

THE WIDER CURRICULUM

As the American school developed, its curriculum was expanded to include—besides the original three R's—such subjects as geography, history and grammar. At a later period, in spite of opposition, such "unnecessary" subjects as music, art, public speaking and physical education were added. A still later development was the introduction of vocational subjects, for their practical value in training students to earn a living.

Today, vocational training, including vocational counseling, is a permanent feature of the public-school system. Some boards of

Knox College

AN INFORMAL STUDY GROUP
A geology class examines the tooth of a prehistoric mammoth.

education maintain separate vocational high schools; in some schools, vocational courses are a regular part of the curriculum.

The modern American school also offers its students a wide variety of extra-curricular activities—debating, dramatics, parliamentary drill, music and various hobbies. These are usually elective, non-credit activities carried on after school; some schools, however, have included them in the regular course of study.

The articles listed below are suggestive of the content of the modern course of study in American grade and high schools:

Agriculture	Literature
Algebra	Manual Training
Archaeology	Mathematics
Arithmetic	Music
Astronomy	Mythology
Biography	Nature Study
Biology	Orthography
Botany	Phonetics
Chemistry	Physical Geography
Civil Government	Physical Culture
Domestic Science	Physics
Drawing	Physiology
Economics	Reading
Elective Studies	Rhetoric
Geography	Sanitary Science
Geology	Shorthand
Geometry	Singing
Handwriting	Spelling
History	Themes
Language and	Trigonometry
Grammar	Zoölogy

Bibliography

BLAIR, HERBERT. *Physical Education Facilities for the Modern Junior and Senior High School.* A. S. Barnes & Co.
DOUGLASS, H. R. *Secondary Education for Youth in Modern America.* American Council on Education.
HOVIOUS, CAROL. *Flying the Printways: Experience Through Reading.* D. C. Heath & Co.
LOCKHART, E. G. *My Vocation, by Eminent Americans.* H. W. Wilson Co.
NORTON, J. K. *Foundations of Curriculum Building.* Ginn & Co.
YOAKUM, G. A. *Reading to Learn.* The Macmillan Co.

METHODS OF INSTRUCTION

New teaching methods and a new attitude toward the pupils characterize the modern school. Student self-government and training in self-control have replaced formal discipline; and the teacher, no longer a stern taskmaster, works with the pupils, guiding them in working out the activities which they themselves have planned.

Much of today's teaching is accomplished through activities rather than through formal drill. Children may learn arithmetic, for instance, by keeping personal accounts or organizing and carrying on various school enterprises. The pupils today get as much information as possible first-hand, rather than from books. They therefore make frequent excursions to such places as industrial plants, libraries and farms.

Placing less emphasis on imitation and rote learning than did the colonial school, the modern school, through such subjects as art, music, dramatics, handwork and composition, gives children many opportunities for creative expression. The satisfaction realized in these activities makes better students of the pupils, trains them to be good citizens and gives them a basis for worthwhile activities in leisure time.

Memorizing of facts has given way in the modern school to understanding of facts; and the modern child is taught to use these facts in working out opinions of his own, rather than always accepting the opinions of others—important training in a period when propaganda is particularly rife. He is taught to be open-minded and not to be influenced by prejudice and self-interest in forming his judgments. In short, the modern school aims to teach him not *what* to think, but *how* to think.

The following articles give further information on teaching methods and teacher training:

Adolescence	History, Methods of
Child Study	Teaching
Child Training	Inductive Method
Corporal Punishment	Kindergarten
Correlation	Methods of Teaching
Deaf and Dumb, sub-	Montessori Method
head Education of	Normal Schools and
the Deaf and Dumb	Teachers Colleges
Feeble-Minded, Edu-	Number, Methods of
cation of the	Teaching
Games and Plays	Pedagogy
Gymnasium	Vocational Education

Bibliography

BAIN, W. E. *Parents Look at Modern Education.* D. Appleton-Century Co.
JUDD, C. H. *Education and Social Progress.* Harcourt, Brace & Co.
NATIONAL CONGRESS OF PARENTS AND TEACHERS. *Our Public Schools.* National Congress of Parents and Teachers.
SKINNER, C. E. *An Introduction to Modern Education.* D. C. Heath & Co.
TIPPETT, J. S. *Schools for a Growing Democracy.* Ginn & Co.
WILLIAMS, J. F. *Methods and Materials of Health Education.* Thomas Nelson Sons.

HEALTH AND RECREATION

The modern school, recognizing the relationship between a child's physical wellbeing and his success in school, supervises his health through regular physical examinations, arranging for treatment of physical defects, checking for contagious diseases and teaching health habits. Minor defects are often cured by early diagnosis.

The school also takes an important part in the child's recreational program, which became an important problem with the removal of children from industry. Many school subjects provide for a variety of profitable hobby interests in out-of-school hours. The school also coöperates with the community in providing for leisure-time activities, and opens its building to evening programs put on by the pupils or by outside talent.

Another function of the modern school, particularly important in rural or city communities where the home cannot provide for the child's social life, is its attempt to develop the child socially, through parties, dances, athletic contests and clubs.

Games and sports play a large part in the health program of American schools. The following articles discuss some of the more popular of these, as well as other subjects related to the school's part in the child's health and recreation:

Athletics	Gymnasium
Baseball	Lawn Tennis
Basket Ball	Open-Air Schools
Football	Physical Culture
Games and Plays	School Garden
Gardening	Swimming

Bibliography

ALLEE, M. H. *Great Tradition.* Houghton, Mifflin Co.
ARNOLD, N. H. *Tinker of Stone Bluff.* Doubleday, Doran & Co.
BARBOUR, R. H. *School That Didn't Care.* D. Appleton-Century Co.
KINLOCH, LUCY. *World Within a School.* Random House.
ROBINSON, M. L. *Bright Island.* Random House.
TUNIS, J. R. *Iron Duke.* Harcourt, Brace & Co.

ADULT EDUCATION

Nearly sixty per cent of the young people in America of elementary, high-school and college age are in school. But what about the other forty per cent, or the many people who have passed the normal school age but whose formal education is far from complete?

Many of these adults are taking academic, vocational and professional courses by correspondence. Through the aid of state agricultural colleges and the United States Extension Service, rural men and women are being instructed in agriculture and home economics. Foreigners learn English and citizenship in Americanization schools. And many people are attending night school to learn new trades, to become more proficient in their own vocations, or to secure their elementary or high-school diplomas.

GRADUATION FROM COLLEGE IS COMMENCEMENT TO LIFE

So rapidly do technical theories and methods change that many professional groups have organized conferences and institutes to keep abreast of the latest developments. University extension and summer courses accommodate students who cannot avail themselves of the regular classes. They are very popular with teachers.

In the 1930's the Federal government established adult-education projects that offered academic, cultural and vocational courses, and trained many unemployed for new lines of work.

By consulting the following articles, one may secure additional information on the subject of adult education:

Adult Education
Evening Schools
Illiteracy
Schools, subhead Correspondence Schools
University Extension

OTHER PATHWAYS IN EDUCATION

In no other age have there been so many channels, other than the schoolroom and the opportunities for adult education, through which one might come to a fuller understanding of the world he lives in. Of the many avenues of instruction, perhaps none reaches a wider public than the radio and the motion picture, which offer informative programs of music, literature, travel, sports, current problems and other subjects.

The printed word is reaching more people than ever before. The illiteracy rate is constantly decreasing, with a corresponding increase in the reading public. More books and magazines are being published and sold than at any previous time. Libraries make books available to almost everyone, and librarians help patrons to select books intelligently.

Hobbies, too, provide a means of acquiring useful and interesting information. Stamp collecting, for example, may develop into a study of geography and history. Travel—in normal times a hobby for many people—is an enjoyable way of learning about the modern world and its ways.

The following articles give interesting information on many of the agencies that contribute to man's fund of knowledge, other than formal education:

American Association for the Advancement of Science
American Library Association
Audubon Society
Book
Carnegie Foundation for the Advancement of Teaching
Chautauqua Institution
Corcoran Art Gallery
Education Association, National
Encyclopedia
Library
Metropolitan Museum of Art
Moving Pictures, subhead Entertainment and Instruction
Museum
National Museum of the United States
Newspaper
Radio, subhead Social Implications
Rockefeller Institute for Medical Research
Russell Sage Foundation
Smithsonian Institution

Ewing Galloway

TWO GREAT DEMOCRATIC DOCUMENTS
Original copies of the Declaration of Independence and the Constitution are preserved in the Library of Congress.

Bibliography

ADAM, T. R. *The Museum and Popular Culture.* American Association for Adult Education.
BOND, F. F. *Give Yourself Background.* McGraw-Hill Book Co.
JOHNSON, ALVIN. *The Public Library—A People's University.* American Association for Adult Education.
VAN DE WALL. *The Music of the People.* American Association for Adult Education.
NEILSON, W. A. *Roads to Knowledge.* W. W. Norton & Co.
STUDEBAKER, J. W. *The American Way.* McGraw-Hill Book Co.
ROLFE, M. A. *Our National Parks.* Benjamin H. Sanborn & Co.

High-School List

ALSOP, G. F. *She's Off to College; a Girl's Guide to College Life.* Vanguard Press.
AMIDON, BEULAH. *Democracy's Challenge to Education.* Farrar & Rinehart, Inc.
COLBY, MERLE. *Handbook for Youth.* Duell, Sloan & Pearce.
EDWARDS, NEWTON. *Equal Educational Opportunity for Youth; a National Responsibility.* American Council on Education.
FACULTY OF SWARTHMORE COLLEGE. *An Adventure in Education.* The Macmillan Co.
EDUCATIONAL POLICIES COMMISSION (N. E. A.). *Education and Economic Well-Being in American Democracy.* National Education Association.

Man and His Government

Modern civilization is the outcome of man's eternal quest for freedom. At first he desired freedom from the restrictions placed upon him by Nature. After he had conquered his environment, his concept of liberty changed. First it meant freedom from the oppression of one group by another; then, freedom of worship; and, more recently, political freedom.

FREEDOM AND RESTRAINT

While man has sacrificed his life for freedom of one kind or another, he has also, for the protection of society, imposed restraints on this freedom in the form of laws. What these laws should be, how far government should go in enforcing them and how large a part government should play in men's lives—these questions, debated for centuries, have never been more pertinent than they are today.

When the United States was established, it was commonly held that men were freest when their governments imposed the fewest restrictions upon them, or, as Thomas Jefferson expressed it, "That government is best which governs least." But such a concept of liberty does not work in the more complex society of today. Economic freedom has become man's chief goal; and, instead of a government that governs least, men are now supporting a centralized government, believing that they must accept less individual liberty in order to have greater liberty for all. Twentieth-century applications of this theory range from moderate demands that the government grant workers the right of collective bargaining to agitation for a world revolution of the working classes.

What has brought about this change? For one thing, the eighteenth-century philosophy of political freedom did not take into account the effects of the Industrial Revolution. Men like Jefferson believed that democracy could flourish because farmers predominated in the population and that democracy would educate people to meet changing conditions. But a democracy founded on the principle of the equality of men could not keep pace with an economic system based on *laissez-faire* (let the people do as they please).

As the United States changed from an agricultural to an industrial nation, workers found it necessary to form unions to secure the improvement of working conditions brought about by the growth of big business. They looked to government to give them economic freedom; and the government, yielding to constant pressure, gradually came to have more authority over big business. The depression of the 1930's greatly stimulated the struggle for economic freedom.

A number of theories have been advanced as to how this freedom might be achieved. Two—communism and socialism—hold that goods should be produced for the use of all the people, rather than for a single individual or group; they believe that in this way all the people will share the wealth of a nation and thus achieve equality, on the basis of which economic freedom is won.

Liberalism would secure economic unity gradually by educating the people to that end. Conservatism, on the other hand, upholds the *status quo* and in its extreme form resists any movement or law that would attempt to take power away from those that have it. Between these two extremes are many gradations of political thought.

Individualism, in modern political science, is economic conservatism, and endorses the right of an employer to conduct his business without restriction. Reaction is the tendency, as in Fascist countries, to check any measures that tend toward political or economic freedom and to revert to regulations that halt such movements.

FREEDOM IN PRACTICE

The restraints that society has imposed on absolute freedom are evident in every aspect of modern life, but especially where people live in close contact with one another. In cities, for instance, zoning and building laws usually restrain a man who wishes to build a house. Laws also make it a misdemeanor to create undue noise or disturbance, to leave garbage or other refuse uncovered or to allow it to accumulate in an exposed place. Trees and shrubs must not be placed at intersections where they will obstruct the view of motorists; and quarantine laws impose restrictions where contagious diseases break out. In just such ways, laws protect the greater number by restraining the liberty of the individual.

Criminal laws are good examples of the restrictions placed upon individual conduct for the protection of society as a whole. The history of criminal laws reveals that as people become educated to the value of certain laws and are willing to abide by them, they feel less restricted by them. For that reason, education is important in promoting good citizenship and a consequent increase in individual happiness. Illiterate peoples are usually the most backward.

The evolution of modern society and the adjustment between individual freedom and the interests of the group are discussed under many headings. The article GOVERNMENT describes the leading forms in the world today. Such articles as the following give additional interesting information on these and related subjects:

Building Laws	Liberal
City Planning	Liberty of the Press
Civilization	Naziism
Civil Law	Prohibition
Communism	Public Utilities
Conservative	Pure Food Laws
Declaration of	Quarantine
Independence	Religious Liberty
Factory and Factory	Roosevelt, Franklin
Legislation	Delano
Fascisti	Rules of the Road
Laissez Faire	Russia
Law	Socialism

Bibliography

LEIGHTON, J. A. *Social Philosophies in Conflict.* D. Appleton-Century Co.
LUDWIG, EMIL. *Roosevelt; A Study in Fortune and Power.* The Viking Press.
RUGG, H. O. *Changing Governments and Changing Cultures.* Ginn & Co.
SAYRE, W. S. *Your Government.* Barnes & Noble.
STEARNS, H. E. *America Now; An Inquiry Into Civilization in the United States.* Charles Scribner's Sons.
WOODBURN, J. A. *Active Citizenship.* Longmans, Green & Co.

THE GROWTH OF FREEDOM

Man's struggle for self-government began early in history. For centuries absolute authority was vested in one man, advised by a few close friends. This man was the king or emperor, who ruled on the theory that his authority was God-given—that everything he did was right because God had willed it. His friends were made nobles and given special property and personal rights; the common people, however, who constituted by far the largest part of the population, had no rights as men, but only such as the king or his nobles cared to grant them.

During the twelfth century great walled cities were growing up in Europe. Trade flourished and the cities so prospered that the kings turned to the wealthy and powerful merchants of these cities for financial aid and advice in carrying on their wars. The meetings of the rulers and the representatives of the city, called Great Councils, developed into the parliaments of Europe, which eventually became more powerful than the king himself. In constitutional monarchies, kings have limited authority.

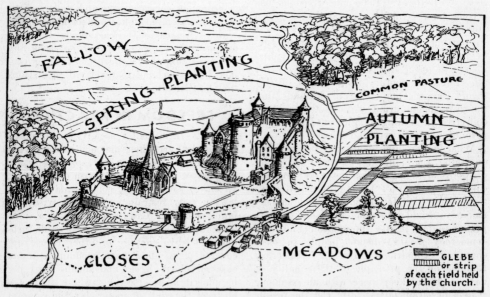

THE ESTATE OF A FEUDAL LORD—WHEN MIGHT WAS RIGHT

The power of the king was definitely limited in 1215, when certain English feudal barons compelled King John of England to sign the Magna Charta, which asserted that the king was responsible to the law and could not change it at will. The barons pledged to pass on to the common people the rights granted to them by the Charter.

Between the middle of the seventeenth and the end of the eighteenth centuries a number of rulers were replaced by popular governments. The Dutch began by overthrowing the rule of King Philip of Spain; revolutions in England increased the power of Parliament; the American colonies revolted from England.

The French Revolution followed shortly after that in America, and the American Declaration of Independence, which affirmed the equality of men and the privilege of men to alter or abolish a government which violated the people's rights, was the model for the French Declaration of the Rights of Men. Several South American countries, also, revolted from Spain and Portugal and set up republics of their own.

The first ten amendments to the American Constitution, called the Bill of Rights, guarantees certain rights to the people. The right of free speech, perhaps the chief of these rights, protects the press and the radio from government censorship. In actual practice, however, this freedom is not absolute; it is curbed by slander laws, wartime restrictions, government supervision of the radio and pressure groups such as advertisers. Freedom of worship and the right of assembly are also guaranteed. However, meetings of people who hold views that diverge from the conventional are sometimes broken up, usually on the strength of a technicality in a local law.

These and other fundamental rights guaranteed by the Bill of Rights are considered the basis of democratic government and are jealously guarded by the American people.

Bibliography

COTTLER, JOSEPH. *Champions of Democracy.* Little, Brown & Co.
HARTMAN, GERTRUDE. *Medieval Days and Ways.* The Macmillan Co.
LANSING, M. F. *Great Moments in Freedom.* Doubleday, Doran & Co.
MILLS, DOROTHY. *Book of the Ancient Greeks.* G. P. Putnam's Sons.
ROBINSON, J. H. *History of Civilization.* Ginn & Co.
WARREN, CHARLES. *Making of the Constitution.* Little, Brown & Co.
WILLIAMS-ELLIS, AMABEL. *Story of English Life.* Coward, McCann, Inc.

GOVERNMENT IN THE UNITED STATES

The Federal government is made up of the legislative, executive and judicial branches. The legislative department, or Congress,

International

A JOINT SESSION OF CONGRESS
Gathered in the House of Representatives, Congressmen hear Roosevelt's 1941 war message on December 8, after Pearl Harbor.

makes the laws. The executive department, made up of the President and his administrative officers, including the Cabinet, carries out the acts of Congress. The judicial branch, composed of the courts and their judges, see that all laws are correctly interpreted and administered. Federal courts protect the legal rights of the people.

At the time the Constitution was written, men feared government as being a power of oppression, more than they respected it. Therefore some of the framers of the Constitution wished to protect the people from being oppressed by giving them more power through their representatives. Others, however, believed that people were still too ignorant for political responsibility and advocated that power be centralized in the President and a few men of property. The American Constitution is a compromise between these two views; a system of checks and balances gives each branch of the government powers that check powers of the others, and prevents any branch from getting too powerful.

For example, the President can veto a bill passed by Congress, but Congress can pass it over his veto. The President can appoint officers and make treaties, but Congress can reject either. The Supreme Court, the highest judicial body, may declare laws passed by Congress unconstitutional; but appointment of the Supreme Court Justices is made by the President and approved by the Senate. Congress in turn may impeach the President and the Justices.

Time has brought about an overlapping of powers and duties in the operation of the three branches of government. For instance, the President may now indicate to Congress legislation which he desires passed; and administrative officers in a sense make laws by the liberty they exercise in putting laws into effect.

Courts influence legislation by establishing precedents in passing on the constitutionality of laws and by interpreting laws in hearing lawsuits. The legislature performs executive powers when it writes into laws conditions of their enforcement or administration, and controls the courts by controlling appointments to the judiciary.

There are also a number of bureaus and commissions with executive, legislative and judicial functions. For instance, the Interstate Commerce Commission exercises these three powers in regulating commerce between the states. Much of the confusion and duplication caused by overlapping bureaus has been dispelled by government reorganization.

The states are made up of legislative, executive and judicial departments. Within the states are many local governments, some of which overlap; these include counties, townships, cities, towns and school districts. United States citizens are subject to the laws and regulations made by the governmental units within whose jurisdiction they live, vote for their officials and pay taxes for their support.

Before the adoption of the Constitution placed a central government over all the states, each colony was an independent unit. It was only the common struggle for independence from England that united the

colonies into a loose confederation. After the Revolutionary War, the Articles of Confederation were inadequate to develop a

FEDERAL HOUSING CLEARS SLUMS
Above: A typical slum playground. *Below:* A wholesome environment through low-cost housing built by public funds.

strong nation, and from their weaknesses developed the present Constitution.

·The states then had more power than they do today. But the industrialization of the nation brought new problems. Factories multiplied, commerce developed and the Federal government was called on to supervise interstate trade and to regulate business and industry.

The development of rapid transportation created problems in crime control. The Federal government has jurisdiction where stolen goods are carried across state borders, and the extension of this power under present laws permits Federal officers to apprehend kidnapers, automobile thieves and other criminals who have escaped into another state to avoid capture.

Because the natural resources of the country belong to the people, the Federal government is responsible for their conservation. The national government also establishes and maintains the national parks, sponsors soil erosion projects (with state and local cooperation) and has launched huge projects for flood control, irrigation and the development of hydroelectric power.

Federal and state governments coöperate in public improvements, as, for instance, the construction of transcontinental highways; this is done through the joint action of state highway departments and the Federal Public Roads Administration. This principle of Federal aid was extended greatly during the depression of the 1930's to include the construction, through the Public Works Administration, of buildings, playgrounds and other public works.

In times of war, financial panics or other national emergency, the Federal government may assume powers which the Constitution does not specifically grant it. Washington, Lincoln, Wilson and the two Roosevelts were all accused of being dictators and of having exceeded their constitutional authority. Generally speaking, the people will support this exercise of powers in an emergency, but are quick to defend their democratic rights when the national government is slow in giving up these powers.

A trend in recent years toward forming regions having the same economic interest throughout the area, regardless of political boundaries, is termed *regional development*. Since these agricultural, mining, manufacturing or trade regions may cover parts of several states, the ultimate effect of their development on a wide scale would be to weaken the influence of state government and in some cases even to wipe out state boundaries entirely.

The term *metropolitan areas* also indicates a shift in the relations of governments. Several American cities grew so large that their governments and problems could no longer be controlled by the state legislatures. This condition has led in some instances to a constant struggle between the city and the rest of the state, in others to arrangements giving a city area practically complete home rule and, occasionally, to agitation for a status of city state, with complete freedom from state control.

Just as the national government has taken control from the states, the states tend to take control from local governments. The state, for example, through its power to tax local communities, somewhat regulates their affairs. State governments are giving greater financial aid to local schools. There are also state-wide taxation systems, such as the sales tax, which support local activities; and the gasoline tax, which every motorist pays for the maintenance of state highways.

Additional information on the United States government, its three branches, powers and activities of the government and various aspects of the government's relations with the smaller units will be found by consulting the following articles:

Agriculture, Department of
Army, subhead United States
Cabinet
Census
Charter
Citizen
City
City Manager
Civil Government
Civil Service
Commerce, Department of
Commission Form of Government
Confederation, Articles of
Congressional Record
Congressman-at-Large
Congress of the United States
Conservation
Constitution of the United States
Contract Labor Law
Copyright
County
Court
Customs Duties
Dead-Letter Office
District Attorney
Election
Electoral College
Eminent Domain
Excise Tax
Executive Department Law
Extradition
Farm Relief
Federal Communications Commission
Federal Housing Administration
Federal Trade Commission
Game, subhead Game Preserves and Reservations
Government
Impeachment
Income Tax
Inheritance Tax
Interior, Department of
Internal Revenue
Interstate Commerce Act
Judge

Justice, Department of
Justice of the Peace
Juvenile Court
Labor, Department of
Labor Legislation
Lands, Public
Legislature
Lobby and Lobbying
Mayor
Mint
Money
Municipal Government
National Guard
Naturalization
Navy, subhead The United States Navy
Navy, Department of the
Neutrality
Parks, National
Police
Postoffice Department
President of the United States
Public Utilities
Reclamation, Bureau of
Representatives, House of
School District
Securities and Exchange Commission
Senate of the United States
Social Security
Speaker
State
State, Department of
States' Rights
Suffrage
Supreme Court of the United States
Tariff
Tax
Territory
Town Meeting
Township
Treasury Department
Treaty
United States, subhead Government
Veto
Vice-President
War, Department of
Weather Bureau
Woman Suffrage

Bibliography

BANNING, KENDALL. *West Point Today.* Funk & Wagnalls Co.
CUNNINGHAM, A. S. *Everything You Want to Know About the Presidents.* A. C. McClurg & Co.
FINGER, C. J. *Our Navy; an Outline History.* Houghton, Mifflin Co.
FORMAN, S. E. *American Democracy; the Spirit, Form, and the Functions of Government.* D. Appleton-Century Co.
KNAPP, G. L. *Uncle Sam's Government at Washington.* Dodd, Mead & Co.
MUNRO, W. B. *Government of the United States; National, State and Local.* The Macmillan Co.
WHITE, L. D. *Government Career Service.* University of Chicago Press.

HOW THE POLITICAL PARTY GOVERNS

George Washington was elected by the unanimous vote of the people. Almost before his term was up, however, the party system of government began. Today we are largely governed by the political party receiving a majority of votes cast at an election.

The organization of a political party extends from the national committee down to the individual voter. The national committee, composed of one man and one woman from each state, plans the organization of the party convention where the candidates for President and Vice-President are nominated.

When the convention opens, many of the state delegations are pledged to men from their own states. The final nomination may come easily because of the popular appeal of some one candidate or because one of the rival party factions has secured the support of a majority of the delegations early in the convention. Or it may come only after a long and bitter struggle has narrowed the choice to about two outstanding nominees.

Sometimes a "dark horse"—a candidate either comparatively unknown or so obscure as to have made few enemies in the party—may be nominated to break a deadlock in the convention. Often the Vice-Presidential nomination may be given the candidate of a state whose votes are needed to nominate someone else for President. Thus the final party choice for President and Vice-President may not always be the persons most suitable for the offices.

The state committee of a political party—the connecting link between the national committee and the local organization—holds a convention where the party slate is endorsed for the state primary election. Its main duty, however, is to carry on the campaign for President and Vice-President, for Congressmen and for governors, legislators and other state officers.

The typical city is divided into wards, which are political divisions of the party organization headed by ward leaders, or bosses. Each ward is divided into precincts headed by precinct captains. The precinct captain is the key man in the whole party organization, for it is his job to deliver the votes in his area.

Several illegal forms of pressure have been used to get votes. Precinct workers have been given cash to hire people to vote for the party candidates; and these paid voters sometimes cast their ballots at a number of polling places, being paid for each time they vote. These repeaters are usually men who have no established residence except for a short time before elections. A more vicious type of pressure is by intimidation of voters by threats of violence or loss of jobs. Party organizations have also on occasion taken control of the ballots after an election and falsified the returns. These methods are punishable by law and are only resorted to by extremely corrupt party organizations and when election results are doubtful.

Nearly every large city has its political machine, which controls elections and governs the city. Generally there are two machine organizations, each bearing the name of a political party. The machine in power is, of course, the prosperous one, controlling the many jobs in the city government and such political favors as contracts for construction, materials and services demanded by the city government—favors which are handed out in return for political support.

The two party machines may have a working agreement whereby the machine out of office is to have a small number of positions, the favor to be returned if the voters change parties. Party workers, seeing a change in party control, may change party allegiance in the middle of a campaign on the promise of favors under the new administration. One of the most vital problems in city government is to free the city from machine politics and corrupt practices.

Political campaigns are costly. Candidates have been known to have received and distributed funds amounting to many times the salary they hoped to receive. The more flagrant of these practices are now prevented by laws against the raising and spending of huge sums to carry on a political campaign. Federal laws, for instance, prohibit corporations from contributing to a campaign fund, limit the amount which a candidate may spend and prohibit candidates and parties from soliciting money from civil-service employees. Some states require publication of the names of all contributors, and many also require an itemized account of campaign expenditures.

FOR BETTER GOVERNMENT

The merit system, commonly known as the civil service, has proved to be a most effective means of improving government. Doubtless changes in administration are made more easily and smoothly with this great body of civil-service workers carrying on the work of government secure in their positions, regardless of political change. The extension of this system tends to weaken political control of elections, for there are fewer jobs to promise in return for political support.

Reforms in voting have been made to lessen political corruption. One means is the literacy test for voters, in effect in several states. Some states have adopted permanent registration of voters to prevent repeaters from voting more than once.

The referendum and the recall have been found effective in encouraging official responsibility in government. The referendum provides a means of referring any government action to the voters for their approval or disapproval; the recall allows citizens to determine whether an official should be dismissed before his term is up. Many states have adopted the short ballot, referendum and recall as a means of giving citizens a more direct control over government officials.

The city-manager plan is designed to replace political control with a business-like administration. Under this plan the mayor and his counsel members are still elected, and make plans and form policies. But the business administration of the city is in the hands of a city manager and his assistants, who are chosen on the strength of their ability and hold office as long as their service is satisfactory. Under the city-manager plan there is less emphasis on political organization than formerly, and less opportunity for graft and corruption.

Probably the greatest improvements in government, however, have resulted from the demands of the people for better services from their government. Even the most corrupt political machine will heed the demands of outraged citizens for reform, even though it may use public improvement to hide corruption in other directions. As citizens take a more intelligent interest in government, better government will result.

The following articles discuss the mechanics of voting and various subjects dealing with politics and good government:

Alderman
Anti-Trust Laws
Australian Ballot
Ballot
Blue-Sky Laws
Caucus
Citizen
City Manager
Civil Service
Civil Service in Canada
Commission Form of Government
Election
Electoral College
Initiative
Labor Legislation
Lobby and Lobbying
Municipal Government
Municipal Ownership
Political Parties in the United States
Poll Tax
Primary Election
Public Utilities
Pure Food Laws
Recall, The
Referendum
Short Ballot
Suffrage
Tammany
Voting Machine
Woman Suffrage

A CIVIC INVESTMENT FOR FUTURE CITIZENS
Boys' clubs help to produce strong bodies and clean minds.

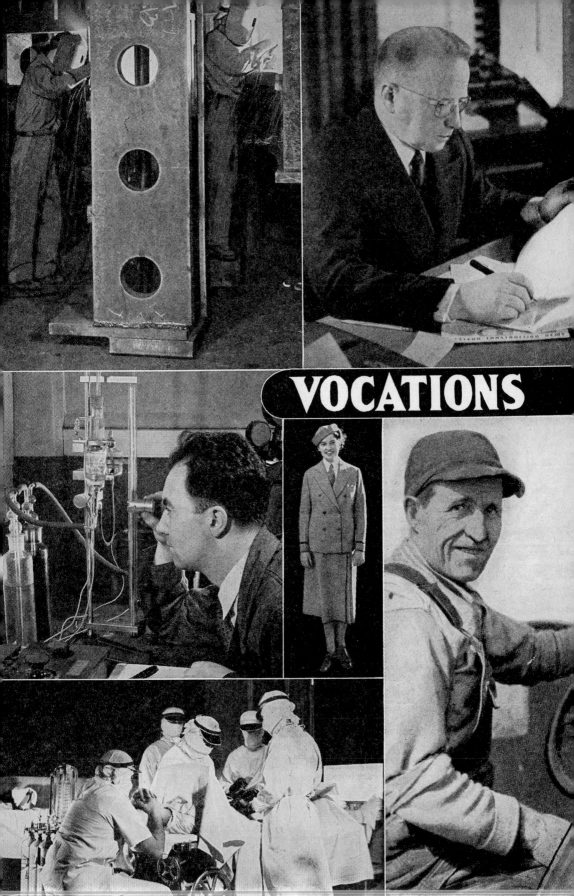

VOCATIONS

Overview for Vocations

There was a time when the pressure of newcomers to the New World sent wave after wave of immigrant trains westward to new land and fresh opportunities. Before 1900, however, the United States was settled from coast to coast; there were no further frontiers to conquer, and people had to make their livings where they were—in the face of competition from an ever-increasing number of settlers.

Further competition arose when in the first half of the nineteenth century the machine began to replace man in industry, and the factory system supplanted home industry. Machines that did the work of many men nullified the skills of many a craftsman, and made unemployment a great social problem in the United States. It remains a problem even today—a century after the effects of the Industrial Revolution were first felt in the United States, and about a half century after the closing of the frontier made it impossible to escape the economic pressure caused by the influx of new workers from the Old World.

Perhaps those who most keenly feel this pressure are those who lack training in the specific skills needed in modern industrial life. This group includes those who, for one reason or another, fill the ranks of unskilled labor; those whose skills, because of shifts in industry and new inventions, are no longer needed; and those whose education did not train them for their place in the working world.

We also find large numbers of others who are not satisfied with the work they are doing. The satisfaction of the skilled artisan of an earlier day is denied the modern factory worker, for instance, who is responsible only for one small task in the whole manufacturing operation. Therefore it is a great challenge to the men and women of today to find jobs that are congenial to their tastes and abilities, and to learn to do their jobs well. It is a well-known fact that one enjoys what he can do well—that failure to succeed in a vocation often causes him to dislike it. Therefore it is necessary to choose a vocation carefully, in order to experience the full satisfaction in it to which one is entitled.

The challenge to the modern industrial world, then, is to train workers for their proper place in it and to supply jobs for all job-seekers. How is modern society meeting this challenge?

In the following pages the problems indicated above are discussed more fully, as to their origins, their implications and the steps being taken to combat them and to enlarge man's sphere of usefulness.

How the Modern World Works

As modern society is organized, the problem of making a living is a serious matter for the majority of the population. It is no longer true that anyone with a strong back and a willingness to work can always find employment.

When the country was new, there were always trees to be cut, land to be cleared and fields to be farmed. The expanding frontiers and the growth of towns and cities required tradespeople, printers, doctors, blacksmiths and others. More workers were needed as factories were established. Indeed, until the frontier had disappeared and with it the ever-increasing need for laborers and craftsmen, and until machines had taken over much of the work formerly done by men, unemployment was not a problem in the United States.

TIMES HAVE CHANGED

To appreciate what has happened, let us consider working conditions when America was young. In colonial times, youths found their places in the working world with little or no difficulty. So great was the demand for workers that young boys were sometimes kidnaped in England and sold into bondage in the American colonies to supply the demand. There was a great need for sailors on the whaling and trading vessels, and many young boys were attracted to a life on the sea by the often exaggerated tales of the opportunities offered the seaman. Adulthood came early to colonial youth, so great was the need for workers in that period. Boys were men at eighteen, and girls even younger were trained housekeepers.

Westinghouse

GIRLS DO SKILLED WORK IN FACTORIES
These girls are inserting copper wire in the cores of electric motors.

It was common for the colonial boy to follow his father's trade, which he learned at a very early age. Or he might be apprenticed while still very young to a tradesman, who taught him a trade and gave him, in return for his services, board and lodging and, perhaps, a small sum of money. When he had completed his apprenticeship, he either succeeded to his master's business or went into business for himself. Girls, also, began in early childhood to learn how to cook, spin, weave, sew and perform the many tasks of a colonial housekeeper, so that when they married they were fully prepared to manage a home.

Men and women migrated from England to the colonies in great numbers. Many who had no money became "indentured servants"; that is, they signed a bond offering to work for an American who would pay their passage. At the close of the period of their indenture, they were free to get other jobs in shops or homes, or to secure farms of their own.

The increased need for workers as the young nation expanded attracted an ever-growing number of immigrants. With the Industrial Revolution came the factories and the greater demand for workers—a demand largely met by the employment of women and children because they would work for less than would men.

The spread of the Industrial Revolution over the United States brought with it many undesirable conditions. Factory workers often labored fourteen hours a day, with only a half hour off for breakfast and another half hour for lunch. Money was scarce and the number of workers was increasing; so the workers had to accept the long hours and small pay in order to hold their jobs. They had little leisure for recreation or education.

The effects of these unsatisfactory working conditions were readily apparent. Both the physical and the mental well-being of the workers suffered.

So long as new lands beckoned to the West, workers could always find employment. With the passing of the American frontier, however, workers who could not make a living in one place could not hope to make a fresh start in a new community. Furthermore, labor-saving machinery was constantly replacing human power. It is true that the work day was shortened finally to eight hours and that the pitifully low wages of factory workers were increased. In many states, too, the drudgery of women and children was lessened. But the labor supply was great and jobs were scarce, with the result that children were frequently put to work in factories to supplement their father's all too meager income.

Child labor reached its peak in the period between 1890 and 1910. So great were the abuses that civic-minded people sought to correct conditions by legislation. Unsuccessful attempts were made to amend the Constitution so as to give Congress the power to pass legislation regulating child labor. In 1941, however, the Supreme Court upheld provisions of the Fair Labor Standards Act regulating hours of work for children, thus establishing the right of Congress to regulate child labor in all cases involving interstate commerce. All other cases are still left to state regulation.

An example of the effect of machines on labor may be seen by an examination of the statistics of the textile industry. Where one person could tend only one spindle in 1784, he could by 1831 tend twenty; by 1850 he could tend sixty and today he can tend eighty spindles. This same thing has happened in other industries. For instance, where gangs of hundreds of men once dug ditches or excavated for new buildings by hand, a power shovel operated by one or two men now does the work. In mines, also, machinery has replaced men who worked with pick and shovel.

This replacement of human workers by machinery has been felt most by unskilled laborers; today, only about one-fifth of the nation's work is done by unskilled labor; about one-half is done by the semi-skilled workers who have replaced them.

The very machines that have replaced man power in some fields have opened up new avenues of employment in others. Machine power has produced goods for man's use and enjoyment in greater quantities, so that more workers have been needed to distribute them; therefore, the number of people working in the transportation industry, in advertising and selling and in the "white collar" fields generally has increased as the number of manual laborers has been lessened by the machine. Another trend has been the shift of workers from agriculture to industry—a trend usually reversed in depression periods.

For further information on the subject, including the effects of invention and the use of machines, consult the following titles:

Child Labor	Labor Legislation
Commerce	Machine
Factory and Factory Legislation	Slavery: Modern Revival of the Slave Trade
Guild	
Immigration and Emigration	Sweatshop System Unemployment
Industrial Revolution	United States: The People
Invention	
Labor, Department of	Wages
Labor, Division of	

Bibliography

BRAINARD, D. S. *Problems of Our Times*. McGraw-Hill Book Co.
COCHRAN, R. C. and MILLER, WM. *Age of Enterprise: A Social History of Industrial America*. The Macmillan Co.
EBERLE, IRMENGARDE. *Famous Inventions for Boys and Girls*. A. S. Barnes & Co.
HUBERMAN, LEO. *We the People*. Harper & Bros.

UNEMPLOYMENT CONDITIONS

Except for certain specialized fields, the records over a period of years show more job-seekers in the United States than there are jobs to be had. Even in prosperous times there are many persons who are employable

THE LABORER WORKS WITH TOOLS

but unable to find work, and this number may rise tremendously in periods of depression. The number of those able to work but unemployed, compared with the number of workers with jobs, is a fair index of the economic conditions in the country.

The problem of finding work is hardest for unskilled workers; they are most likely to find employment in boom periods, when such fields as the building trades show increased activity. Skilled and semi-skilled workers in mass-production industries face a keen competition for jobs when declining prosperity causes a drop in consumer purchasing power; wage-cuts, lay-offs, part-time work, or, at last, unemployment, may be their lot. Office workers share this financial insecurity; however, not usually being organized, they cannot exert pressure by mass action. "White collar" unions are greatly in the minority.

The depression of the 1930's was the most prolonged period of "hard times" the country has ever known. Every wave of bank failures, factory closings and reduction of office personnel brought with it another drop in purchasing power and a further rise in unemployment—a downward trend that was stopped only when the Federal government expended large sums on a variety of projects to meet the emergency.

In this period, youth was especially affected by the employment problem; the Federal census takers discovered that at the close of this period about two million youths were totally unemployed and seeking work and another million were working at government relief jobs. Young people as they left high school or college found no place for themselves in industry, and had to compete for jobs with older and more experienced workers. Many had no mechanical skill because they had taken academic courses.

Here the Federal government intervened with the National Youth Administration, which helped some of these young people in school to earn money in order to continue

LABOR LEADERS IN SHOP MEETING
All walks of life provide opportunities for service. These men have great responsibilities.

their education, and provided work projects for others not in school; however, although this program did much good, it did not provide a solution for the problem.

In professional and semi-professional vocations, too, youth was handicapped. Isolated surveys showed that from thirty to forty-two per cent of the young people questioned wanted to enter these occupations at a time when only about sixty-seven per cent of all American workers were engaged in them. Seventy-one per cent of those questioned in one survey were dissatisfied with the work they were doing—a sad commentary on the plight of youth in the working world in the depression era.

Youth was not the only group affected by the depressed business conditions. Men and women of mature years and better than average qualifications found themselves replaced

by younger workers. Indeed, many employers refused to hire men over forty-five.

One of the effects of this trend was to stimulate the movement for pensions for older people. One of the most widely discussed proposals was the Townsend Plan of revolving pensions, introduced into Congress in 1935; according to this plan, unemployed people over sixty years of age were to receive $200 monthly, which they would be required to spend within the month. The movement culminated with the passage in 1935 of the Social Security Act; this provides regular Federal payments to retired workers of sixty-five and older and, in cooperation with state systems of old-age benefits, gives old-age assistance to the needy. Many large business and industrial organizations have established pension plans for their own retired workers. Retirement plans for teachers and civil-service employes are also in operation.

A general survey of the problems will be found in the articles OLD AGE PENSIONS and UNEMPLOYMENT. Read the following articles for further information on employment problems and the attempts to correct conditions:

Chain Stores	Pension
Child Labor	Profit Sharing
Contract Labor Laws	Socialism
Convict Labor	Social Security
Employer's Liability	Strike
Labor Organizations	Syndicalism
Lockout	Vocational Education
Minimum Wage	Wages
Open Shop	

Bibliography

BAKKE, E. W. *Insurance or Dole?* Yale University Press.
CHASE, STUART. *The Road We Are Traveling, 1914-1942; Guide Lines to America's Future as Reported to the Twentieth Century Fund.* Twentieth Century Fund.
DAVIS, KINGSLEY. *Youth in the Depression.* University of Chicago Press.
DAVIS, MAXINE. *They Shall Not Want.* The Macmillan Co.
HUGHES, R. O. *Today's Problems.* Allyn & Bacon.
LINDLEY, BETTY. *A New Deal for Youth; the Story of the NYA.* The Viking Press.
LORWIN, L. L. *Labor Relations Board.* Brookings Institution.
McWILLIAMS, CAREY. *Ill Fares the Land: Migrants and Migratory Labor in the U. S.* Little, Brown & Co.

LATER TRENDS

The defense program of 1940, launched to meet the challenge of the war that had broken out in Europe the preceding year, gave a strong impetus to employment in the United States. The aircraft, munitions and allied industries drew hundreds of workers; and engineers and others with technical skill were greatly in demand. The induction into service of large numbers of men stimulated the food, clothing and building trades that equipped and sheltered them, and left their jobs to be filled by people in need of employment.

Then came the entrance of the United States into the war in December, 1941. The automobile industry and other manufacturers using essential war materials—especially metals—converted their factories to the making of planes, tanks, guns, ammunition and other military supplies.

These changes took their inevitable toll of workers, causing a widespread displacement of labor in industries affected by the transition to wartime production. Among the workers affected were those employed by the metal-using industries in sales, financing, advertising, servicing and similar capacities. Also affected were travel bureaus, vacation resorts, suburban real-estate developments, gasoline service stations and other enterprises dependent upon the automobile trade, as well as workers in civilian industries affected by the diversion of essential materials to government use and the inability to secure goods from foreign sources. Thus, while the general trend was toward increasing employment, many found themselves out of work during the period of adjustment to wartime production; some, indeed, had to make a completely fresh start in a new line of work. However, some industries of waning importance were stimulated by these conditions; such, for instance, as the manufacture of wagon parts and other products for which the shortage of motor vehicles and rubber for tires brought a new demand.

CHOOSING A VOCATION

Will labor-saving devices affect this industry? What is the policy of this industry toward older workers? Is this industry affected by seasonal or fluctuating demands? No one should choose a career before he has tried to answer these questions about it.

It is important for young people to study industrial trends. They should know which industries are growing and which declining, and how these trends influence the number and kinds of jobs available. The industries that supply us with public services, for instance, demand many workers, for they supply light, fuel and power for business and domestic use, and are the essential industries in communication and transportation.

SKILLED WORKERS NEEDED
Electricity has brought many advantages to mankind, but must be controlled to be useful.

Our governments are demanding more and more trained workers to carry on their many functions. Since 1870, the number of employes of the Federal government alone has increased from 73,000 to over a million. These are supplied through the national Civil Service, which provides a growing number of positions that offer permanent tenure and opportunities for advancement.

The National Resources Committee of the Federal government reports a number of inventions, which, it is believed, may influence the future production of goods. Since this influence may also affect the number and kinds of workers then needed, it is well for young people to consider them in choosing a vocation.

One of these inventions is the cotton picker, which, as a labor-saving device, may deprive many men of their jobs. Air-conditioning equipment, on the other hand, has initiated a new industry and employs many workers. The same is true of the photoelectric cell, which is constantly finding new uses and will undoubtedly provide many new jobs in the future. This device is a vacuum tube that responds electrically to light and performs automatic operations.

Plastics, used as a substitute for wood and metal, and cellulose, employed in the manufacture of the synthetic fabric rayon, demand many new workers for the new processes involved, but at the same time displace workers in other industries affected by their development.

The making of prefabricated houses, by which the parts are constructed in a factory and assembled at the spot where the building is to stand, will create new lines of work, but may cause a loss of work in the building trades.

Gasoline from coal will replace gasoline from petroleum as the supply of the latter dwindles; the shift of employment from the one to the other will therefore be somewhat equalized. The increased demand for the autogiro, helicopter and other steep-flight aircraft in areas where landing space is limited will call for more workers, but may limit employment in other transportation industries.

The development of soilless agriculture on a large scale would stimulate employment in such fields as the chemical industry, which supplies the materials necessary for plant growth, but may cause a drop in the number of agricultural workers.

Within established industries, too, recent developments will require new and trained workers. There is an increasing use for the Diesel engine, for instance, and technical schools give special courses in Diesel engineering. In metal work, such as in stream-lined structures, tanks, etc., welding is now replacing riveting. Indeed, many major industries maintain research staffs that are constantly seeking new and improved methods and processes, and each development will have its effect on employment.

Some occupations are seasonal, providing employment for just a part of each year. Certain crops, for instance, require extra workers during the harvest season only; construction work, largely dependent on the weather, is not a year-around occupation, and employment in canneries and lumber camps is likewise seasonal.

To earn a living wage for the whole year, seasonal workers must eke out their incomes as best they can. Some follow the harvest periods from south to north; for many years, men followed the wheat harvest from Texas to Canada. Others pursue several different seasonal occupations during the year. Not all, however, find other work to supplement their incomes, and these persons must turn to Federal agencies for assistance.

Changing styles and fashions cause a type of seasonal employment in the clothing industry, and fads, which enjoy a fleeting popularity, provide at best only a temporary employment for workers. People entering these occupations should realize these facts before deciding to make them their principal lines of employment.

Consult the following articles for information on various occupations or their products:

Accounting	Homeopathy
Advertising	Kindergarten
Agriculture	Landscape Gardening
Airplane	Leather
Architecture	Library
Art and the Arts	Lumber
Automobile	Machine Tools
Bookkeeping	Masonry, Stone
Brick and Bricklaying	Meat Packing
Building	Medicine
Cabinet Making	Mining
Calculating Machines	Moving Pictures
Cash Register	Newspaper
Chiropractic Healing	Osteopathy
Civil Service	Paper
Copying Devices	Petroleum
Dairying, or Dairy Husbandry	Pharmacy
Dentistry	Photography
Dredging	Plumbing
Engineering	Printing
Fur and Fur Trade, subhead Fur Farming	Proof and Proofreading
Geology, subhead Practical Applications	Quarrying
	Radio
	Rubber
Glass	Steel
Gold Beating	Surgery
Heating and Ventilation	Veterinary Medicine
	Wheat
	Wool and Woolen Manufacture

Bibliography

Youth in the World Today. Public Affairs Pamphlet No. 22.

ANDERSON, H. P. *Your Career in Agriculture.* E. P. Dutton & Co.

BENNETT, G. V. *Exploring the World of Work.* Society for Occupational Research.

BERNAYS, E. L. *An Outline of Careers; A Practical Guide to Achievement by Thirty-Eight Americans.* George H. Doran.

BROOKE, E. E. *Career Clinic; The Answer to Your Job Problem.* Farrar & Rinehart, Inc.

BROWN, E. L. *Physicians and Medical Care.* Russell Sage Foundation.

BROWN, E. L. *Professional Engineer.* Russell Sage Foundation.

CARLISLE, N. V. *Civil Service Careers for Boys.* E. P. Dutton & Co.

FLOHERTY, J. J. *Aviation from Shop to Sky.* J. B. Lippincott Co.

FLOHERTY, J. J. *Your Daily Paper.* J. B. Lippincott Co.

HORNUNG, J. L. *Radio as a Career.* Funk & Wagnalls Co.

KLINEFELTER, L. M. *Electrical Occupations. Covering the Entire Field of Electrical Occupations Available to Boys When They Grow Up.* E. P. Dutton & Co.

KLINEFELTER, L. M. *Medical Occupations Available to Boys When They Grow Up.* E. P. Dutton & Co.

LEYSON, BURR. *Photographic Occupations.* E. P. Dutton & Co.

LOCKHART, E. G. *My Vocation, by Eminent Americans.* H. W. Wilson & Co.

LOGIE, I. M. R. *Careers in the Making; Modern Americans When They Were Young and on Their Way.* Harper & Bros.

McCLINTOCK, MARSHALL. *Millions of Books; the Story of Your Library.* Vanguard Press.

MATTOON, C. S. *Your Career in Aviation; the How, When, Why and Where of Finding Your Place in Aviation.* Foster & Stewart.

PICTURE FACT ASSOCIATES:
  Air Workers.   News Workers.
  Farm Workers.   Nurses at Work.
  Household Workers.   Office Workers.
  Library Workers.   Radio Workers.
  Movie Workers.   Railroad Workers.
WALTZ, G. H. What Do You Want to Be? Henry
  Holt & Co.
WOODHOUSE, C. G. Dental Careers. Funk & Wagnalls
  Co.
YATES, R. F. Science Calls to Youth; a Guide to
  Career Planning in the Sciences. D. Appleton-
  Century Co.

WOMEN IN THE WORKING WORLD

It was formerly considered improper for women to work outside their own homes, and those who found employment in factories, offices or other homes did so at the expense of their social standing. Even those women who attended colleges and universities met the disapproval of society. Today, however, this traditional attitude has largely disappeared, and women are now found in practically all types of work, and hold positions of responsibility and distinction in the business and professional world.

Domestic and personal service accounts for the largest group of working women; these range from servants and laundresses to seamstresses and hairdressers. However, an ever-fewer number of women are engaged in these occupations. Furthermore, the shift of labor from the home to factory and shop is causing a marked change in this type of work. For example, because more and more housewives are either washing their own clothes with improved devices or sending them to commercial laundries, the number of independent laundresses is declining; the laundress is now a wage earner in industry instead of a domestic servant. Personal service, too, has been affected by this shift. Women who were formerly housemaids are now maids or waitresses in hotels and restaurants, filling the demand caused by the growing number of people who live in hotels and have their meals away from home.

Clerical workers—stenographers, typists, file clerks, bookkeepers, receptionists and cashiers—account for a large group of working women. A smaller group has become successful as decorators, window dressers, real-estate agents, insurance agents and bankers.

Although women have worked in factories since the beginning of the Industrial Revolution, the percentage of increase in this field has never kept pace with that of men, because machinery replaced women in the

finishing processes and demanded more men to operate and repair them. However, the defense program in World War II caused an unprecedented demand for women to work in factories devoted to war production.

Women comprise over a third of all people in the professions. The greater part of these are teachers and nurses; others are

WOMEN PLAY AN IMPORTANT PART IN INDUSTRY

musicians, artists, authors, editors, copy writers, research workers, photographers, doctors, chemists, laboratory technicians, lawyers, dentists and architects. A smaller percentage are social-service workers, pastors' assistants, missionaries and other workers trained for religious service.

The number of women in the trade, communication and transportation industries is increasing at a faster rate than that of men. More women than men, for example, are telephone operators. As automatic telegraph apparatus, or teletype, is introduced, more women are finding employment in telegraph offices. Women far outnumber men as sales clerks in shops and stores.

Women are at the very start of their importance in government service. With the granting of suffrage to women in 1919, much of the opposition to their participating in public life vanished. Today they are entering government service in ever-growing numbers. Many have been appointed or elected to positions in local or state government; several have been elected to the Senate and the House of Representatives of the United States; still others have become judges and state governors. One, indeed, was appointed to the President's Cabinet. In 1942, women took their place in the military service of the United States as members of the Women's Army Auxiliary Corps and in the Navy as the Women's Naval Reserve (WAVES), where formerly they were admitted only as nurses.

Dress designing and interior decorating are fields in which women have in recent years proved themselves to be especially adapted. Women also handle a number of personal services established by large department stores for the convenience of their customers. Personal shoppers, for instance, either select articles for a customer who may telephone or write her instructions, or aid the customer to make a selection in the store. Special advisers help a bride select her trousseau; aid in the selection of clothing or home furnishings; or advise in the selection of books and toys for children.

Women are also employed as demonstration experts, sent out by companies to acquaint people with the character and use of special goods or products; as dieticians in hospitals, restaurants and the like; as social directors in hotels and on ocean liners, for the entertainment of guests and passengers; and as hostesses on trains and airliners. Women of executive ability are finding their place in hotel, club and apartment-house management, and are being employed as vocational counselors and in psychological clinics for mental behavior.

The increase in leisure time has provided avenues of employment for women as storytellers, private-entertainment directors and instructors in bridge and dancing. Radio and the moving picture have likewise expanded the opportunities for the woman, in such capacities as actress, scenario writer, story editor, research director and critic.

Unquestionably, the opportunities for women in the working world will continue to increase; in some occupations they may replace men. In a few occupations, as that of medicine, women have met considerable opposition; women, too, are seldom paid as much as men doing the same work. Nevertheless, there is a definite trend toward a more favorable treatment of women.

Additional information on women's work may be found in the following articles:

Cookery	Shorthand
Domestic Science	Typewriting
Nurse	Woman Suffrage

Bibliography

ALLEE, M. H. *Great Tradition.* Houghton, Mifflin Co.

AMERICAN YOUTH ASSOCIATION OF SCHOOL ADMINISTRATORS. *Youth Education Today.*

BAKER, J. C. *On Going into Business.* McGraw-Hill Book Co.

BROWN, E. L. *Nursing as a Profession.* Russell Sage Foundation.

BROWN, E. L. *Social Work as a Profession.* Russell Sage Foundation.

BUGBEE, EMMA. *Peggy Covers the News.* Dodd, Mead & Co.

CARLISLE, N. V. *Civil Service Careers for Girls.* E. P. Dutton & Co.

COLBY, MERLE. *Handbook for Youth.* Duell, Sloan & Pearce.

KLINEFELTER, L. M. *Medical Occupations for Girls; Women in White.* E. P. Dutton & Co.

LEUCK, M. S. *Fields of Work for Women.* D. Appleton-Century Co.

MAULE, FRANCES. *The Road to Anywhere; Opportunities in Secretarial Work.* Funk & Wagnalls Co.

PECKHAM, BETTY, *Sky Hostess.* Thomas Nelson & Sons.

PENNOYER, SARA. *Polly Tucker, Merchant.* Dodd, Mead & Co.

SCHULTZ, GLADYS. *How to Be a Fashion Designer.* Robert M. McBride & Co.

TRAINING FOR A JOB

Unfortunately, young people do not always receive training for their life work in their homes, and the apprentice system as it was once known is a thing of the past. The average youth of today, then, goes to work with inadequate guidance and training, either taking what is offered him, or accepting what promises the highest pay or best future, rather than what is best suited to his abilities. Too large a number, also, are fitted only for unskilled labor.

The vocational-guidance movement is attempting to solve this problem. In schools, social-service agencies and private organizations, vocational counselors offer expert advice to prospective workers.

Schools, however, are the most suitable agency in vocational guidance. Not only do they offer counseling service, but through specially planned courses they offer training directly useful in a vocation, and also foundational training for further vocational education.

Once all high schools aimed only at preparing their graduates for college, and this, unfortunately, is still the case in many instances. Many pupils, however, do not continue their education after high school; others, unsuccessful and disinterested in the rigid college-entrance courses, become discouraged and drop out of school before graduating. Neither of these groups are prepared for earning their livings; for the youths in the latter group, indeed, only the lowest-paid jobs are available, for they have neither the general background nor the training for the better jobs.

Modern high schools, on the other hand, have adapted or are adapting their curriculums to meet present conditions. Courses in machine work, woodworking, business training and homemaking now enable high-school students to enter a vocation or to enroll in a technical or other special school to complete their vocational training after leaving high school.

These students do not confine their high-school work to these vocational courses, but are always encouraged to study English, foreign languages, science, mathematics and other subjects designed to broaden their outlook, to train them in oral expression or in writing and to prepare them for assimilating general culture.

Guidance in selecting a vocation and preparing for it are as important as the training itself. Young people failing in their school work too often drop out of school to take the first job offered. Wise and sympathetic guidance might have led them to choose subjects which would have prepared them for suitable vocations or to take a technical course in a vocational school. It could at least have steered them away from jobs that have no future or are only temporary.

Many high schools now offer courses designed to aid a student in selecting vocations intelligently. These courses begin with a general survey of the occupational field, where a student can analyze his own interests and abilities in the light of one or more vocations and proceed to an intensive study of the working conditions, wages, opportunities for advancement and other aspects of the vocations selected.

The student then makes a detailed job analysis that would reveal the qualifications for success in the vocation studied. This job analysis would later be checked against the student's own abilities as revealed by tests and self-analysis devices.

This complete inquiry into a student's interests and abilities is an important part of vocational guidance. A mental test informs the counselor of the student's general intelligence level and helps him to estimate how much training he needs. This may be followed by tests to determine special abilities.

A more accurate picture of an individual may be derived from the personal-analysis chart. On this chart is a list of qualities and characteristics and a space for indicating the student's rating in each quality; these ratings are *below average, average, above average* or *superior*. If the student marks his own chart, and several people who know him well rate him on similar charts, the vocational counselor is able to

INTELLIGENCE—GREAT PATIENCE
Scientists use their delicate instruments and trained minds for the good of the human race.

make a fairly accurate estimate of the student's abilities and personality.

Young people who have no special vocational interest in mind may be asked to check, from a long list of interests, those they enjoy the most. These interests may include reading, doing mechanical or mental puzzles, writing, etc.; from them the counselor might obtain a clue as to an individual's possible vocational interest.

The vocational counselor assembles this information—the record of the student's mental ability, special aptitudes, personality and interests. He then analyzes it in the light of the requirements of the vocation which the student has selected, as they are shown by the job analysis and other information, taking into consideration the student's limitations and their possible effect on his chances for success. He then lays this information before the student in a

Occupational Distribution of Job-Seekers Registered at Public Employment Offices by the United States Employment Service in a Typical Month

OCCUPATION	MEN		WOMEN	
	UNDER 21 YEARS OF AGE	45 AND OVER	UNDER 21 YEARS OF AGE	45 AND OVER
Total....................	288,762	1,130,784	206,570	236,707
Professional and managerial.....	5,160	42,494	1,872	10,205
Professional	1,732	16,264	828	6,998
Semi-professional	3,140	5,832	1,005	813
Managerial and official........	288	20,398	39	2,394
Clerical and sales..............	39,727	66,720	73,056	30,556
Clerical and kindred..........	26,451	29,775	50,989	16,763
Sales and kindred............	13,276	36,945	22,067	13,793
Service	20,550	97,665	53,324	92,352
Domestic service.............	3,154	6,681	40,799	61,344
Personal service..............	13,380	35,008	12,143	26,526
Protective service............	217	30,599	10	816
Building service workers and porters	3,799	25,377	372	3,666
Agricultural, fishery, forestry and kindred.................	40,364	111,424	1,122	3,282
Agricultural, horticultural and kindred	40,184	110,017	1,089	3,240
Fishery	146	1,058	31	42
Forestry (except logging) and hunting and trapping.......	34	349	2	0
Skilled	30,165	369,407	4,416	32,738
Manufacturing	11,027	112,808	4,008	31,800
Non-manufacturing	6,512	193,737	29	154
Miscellaneous	12,580	44,947	373	226
Foremen	46	17,915	6	558
Semi-skilled	44,384	178,049	20,027	44,259
Manufacturing	8,329	79,525	11,817	38,911
Non-manufacturing	23,817	71,497	930	4,584
Miscellaneous	12,168	26,486	7,280	757
Apprentices	70	541	0	7
Unskilled	68,885	257,771	17,536	15,104
Manufacturing	21,092	55,195	12,330	11,735
Non-manufacturing	24,405	177,246	677	1,446
Miscellaneous	23,388	25,330	4,529	1,923
No recent work experience.......	39,527	7,254	35,217	8,211
Unemployables	49	2,154	40	948
Recent students..............	38,599	115	33,986	190
Persons without work experience	298	1,869	455	5,488
Unspecified	581	3,116	736	1,585

Courtesy Reports and Analysis Division, Bureau of Employment Security, Social Security Board.

personal interview, advising him how he may proceed and acquainting him with the difficulties, if any, that he might encounter.

The personnel record is an important tool of the vocational counselor. It should be started for a student in school, and should record his educational achievements, scholastic records, regularity in attendance and general behavior; by the time the student leaves school, it should contain also the information from tests and analysis charts, interest records, recommendations by those who know his qualifications and records of counseling interviews.

The plan of vocational tryouts, adopted in some schools, permits students periods in which they may actually work in vocations that interest them, and so to determine whether they have made a good choice and whether their chances of success in it are sound.

Colleges and universities offer training in the professions, engineering, commerce and other highly specialized fields. Proper guidance in high school starts students in courses that will prepare them for this higher training; and personnel directors, student advisers and deans continue this guidance in college. The aim in all cases is to avoid poorly planned and poorly coördinated courses of study.

Sometimes school courses and vocational guidance are not enough to fit youths for their place in the working world. For these, there are the technical and vocational schools, where the courses range from short, intensive courses to courses a year or more in length. While these schools are usually private, there are a few technical high schools in the public-school system which offer full-length vocational courses and good opportunities for postgraduate work.

Private vocational schools usually guarantee complete training and sometimes even guarantee placement in a job on completion of the course. Because a few of these schools have been dishonest in their claims, it is well for anyone to check with vocational counselors, school officials or chambers of commerce in cities where the schools are located in order to be sure that the school selected is a good one.

Of modern development is the activity of the Federal government in training youth for their place in industry. Apprentice systems are sponsored by the Federal Committee on Apprenticeship, which is made up of representatives of employers, labor and Federal agencies. These train high-school youth in a variety of trades, combining "on-the-job" work assignments with technical classroom instruction. Another plan, designed to meet the demand for skilled workers in the national defense program, is the program of vocational training sponsored by the National Defense Advisory Commission, acting through the United States Office of Education and state and local vocational education authorities.

Vocational guidance is carried on to some degree by public employment bureaus. The unemployment problems of the 1930's caused an expansion of the Federal employment service and prompted the establishment of such government agencies as the Civilian Conservation Corps, which provided vocational training courses and vocational tryouts in its work activities.

Private employment bureaus also carry on a form of guidance through their system of credentials and records and through the advice given applicants for placement. Another helpful agency is the Adult Education Council, composed of retired teachers, which offers free guidance service to those who desire it. Young people's organizations, such as the Scouts, guide indirectly by encouraging the development of special interests.

Additional information on the problems of vocational training and placement may be secured by consulting the following articles:

Adult Education
Agricultural College
Business College
Dental Schools
Education (also Related Articles)
Employment Bureau
Evening Schools
Journalism, Schools of
Manual Training
Medical Schools
Military Schools
Normal Schools and Teachers Colleges
University Extension
Unemployment
Vocational Education

Bibliography

BLEECKER, KATHARINE. *Business Etiquette; the ABC of Making Good.* G. P. Putnam's Sons.
CHALFANT, A. B. *What's Holding You Back?* McGraw-Hill Book Co.
FEDDER, RUTH. *The Girl Grows Up.* Whittlesey House.
GARDINER, G. L. *How You Can Get a Job.* Harper & Bros.
MCKOWN, H. C. *The Boy Grows Up.* Whittlesey House.
MCLEAN, DONALD. *Knowing Yourself and Others.* Henry Holt & Co.
PRICE, WILLODEEN. *Index to Vocations.* H. W. Wilson Co.
REILLY, W. J. *How to Find and Follow Your Career.* Harper & Bros.
ROSENGARTEN, WM. *Choosing Your Life Work.* McGraw-Hill Book Co.
SEABURY, DAVID. *Build Your Own Future.* Frederick A. Stokes Co.
VITELES, M. S. *Science of Work.* W. W. Norton & Co.

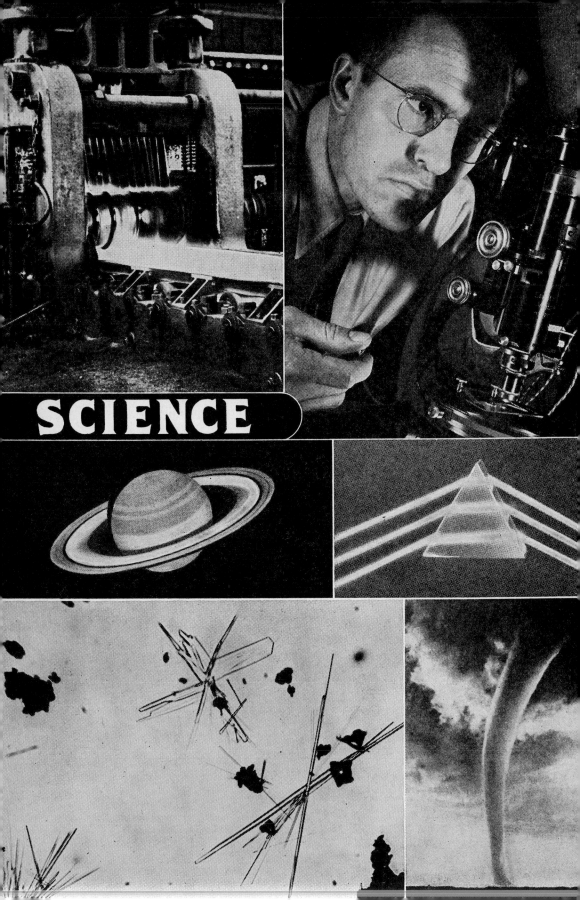

SCIENCE

Overview for Science

The steady gain which the social order has made in the control of our environment has come about through scientific discoveries, inventions and advances in technology. Progress has been especially rapid in production, transportation and communication. When we consider the length of time that man has inhabited the earth, we realize that the more recent changes have come with breath-taking speed. The majority of the people living about 1890 had never ridden in an automobile, never seen a motion picture and never heard of radio. Air conditioning, electric refrigeration, streamlined trains, passenger planes and television were all in the future.

These developments and others like them were not accidental. They represented the efforts of scientific thinkers to get definite results. The scientist works for the betterment of society, although society has not made the best possible use of scientific discoveries. For example, machines were made that liberated millions of men for creative work in other fields. Yet, because men did not plan for the future, they brought upon themselves the problem of unemployment and the economic ills that go with it. Scientific achievements speeded up the wheels of production, but the unemployed could not purchase the goods.

In spite of past mistakes, however, we must look to science for the improvement of our social and economic conditions. We, in turn, bear a responsibility to the scientist. The only hope for the progress of true science is in a democratic society. The scientist follows a trail in search of truth, regardless of where it may lead. He cannot be dictated to. Einstein did not formulate the theory of relativity because he was ordered to do so by an autocratic ruler, but because he had a free and inquiring mind. Such thinkers seek the truth, to add to the world's knowledge.

Because some knowledge of science is necessary to the understanding of human problems, we should all have a broad, general conception of basic scientific principles. In the following sections the author discusses these topics: man's use of science to understand himself and his environment; how science aids man to understand and improve plants and animals; how science aids man to utilize physics and chemistry; the meaning and scope of science, and the outlook for science.

Man Uses Science to Understand Himself and His Environment

ASTRONOMY

According to his earlier beliefs, man and his small settled areas were the centers around which the heavenly bodies moved solely for his convenience. Because modern science has pushed back our mental and physical horizons, we now have a different conception of the universe and our relation to it. Astronomy is the science that has given us this broader view. It has taught us that we cannot explain things in their relation to man alone.

Men have been observing the heavens from ancient times. During those centuries, the telescope was perfected and other astronomical instruments were developed. Many of the facts revealed by scientific study of the skies are discussed in this section.

The earth on which we live belongs to a group of heavenly bodies of which the sun is the center. This group is called the solar system. The earth is one of at least nine planets that revolve about the sun as it travels on its endless journey through space. The sun is a star with a circumference of 2,723,000 miles. When we compare that figure with the 25,000 miles of the earth's circumference, the sun seems enormous. However, as compared with other stars it is merely of average size. In the heavens it looks large to us because it is so much nearer than any other star.

Among all celestial objects, the sun is of greatest importance to us, because we depend upon it for heat and light. Primitive people worshiped the sun as the giver of all life and energy, and we realize now

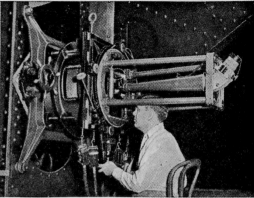

Westinghouse

BRINGING THE STARS NEARER
Left: The 200-inch reflecting telescope for Mt.
Palomar. *Right:* Photographing faint nebulae
at Mt. Wilson Observatory.

that they were justified in their idea. There is no significant source of energy for the earth except the sun. It has been estimated that as much energy falls on the surface of the earth in one minute as can be utilized in one year.

The earth is one of the smaller planets, being exceeded in size by Jupiter, Saturn, Uranus and Neptune. It is larger than Mercury, Venus and Mars and possibly larger than Pluto, discovered in 1930. The planets all move around the sun in the same direction in orbits that are slightly flattened circles, or ellipses. The names of the planets, their relative sizes and their distances from the sun may be found in the article PLANET, in these volumes.

Revolving between Mars and Jupiter are thousands of small bodies called asteroids or planetoids. The largest, Ceres, is 480 miles in diameter. It is believed that there are 50,000 of these midget planets visible through the largest telescopes.

What holds the planets in their courses? What is the underlying force which keeps

such a group of spheres moving in complete harmony, never colliding, never withdrawing from the sun and never ceasing to move in the same path? Also, we might ask why the planets are not drawn to the sun to be instantly vaporized.

Sir Isaac Newton (1642–1727) was the first scientist to formulate laws satisfactorily explaining the secret of the planetary movements. They are known as the laws of gravitation.

Newton said that all bodies of matter attract all other bodies in proportion to their weight and inversely proportional to the square of the distance between them, and for that reason the huge sun would maintain control over the planets even though they were at great distances. He added another law which states that bodies at rest tend to remain at rest and bodies in motion tend to remain in motion until acted upon by an outside force. In accordance with this law, the revolving planets continue to move around the sun with no apparent decrease in speed, held in their places by gravity.

WE ARE VERY SMALL
The planets and moon compared in size with a segment of the sun.

SATELLITES OF THE PLANETS

In 1610, when Galileo studied the skies with his first crude telescope, he saw four of the small bodies that travel around Jupiter, just as our moon revolves around the earth. Since then, several other moons have been discovered. Saturn has nine, Jupiter eleven, Uranus four, Neptune one and Mars two.

There are five moons larger than our own but none so large in proportion to the planet it accompanies. Our earth and moon form a combination that is called a double planet. Because of the size of the moon and its closeness to the earth, gravitational forces are strong between the two bodies. These forces are the cause of the tides. Our moon rotates on its axis at the same speed with which it revolves around the earth, and for that reason it always has the same face turned toward us.

Naturally, as all these bodies in the solar system are revolving around one another, and all of them are traveling around the sun, they interfere with the light from the sun at various times. This phenomenon is known as an eclipse. When the moon gets between the earth and the sun we have a solar eclipse; then the sun is partially or completely darkened by the shadow of the moon. When the earth gets between the sun and the moon, a dark shadow is cast on the moon.

COMETS AND METEORS

There are a few other travelers through space which rightly can be considered members of the solar system. Some of these bodies are comets. A comet is composed of a swarm of small particles which swing around the sun and then disappear for years, only to return on schedule time, just as do all heavenly bodies that follow regular orbits. Halley's comet, one of the best known, made its last appearence in 1910 and will not be back until 1985. Comets travel in immense elongated paths shaped like a flattened circle.

Another thrilling spectacle is the flash of a "shooting star." We know that the stars are too far away to show movements that we can quickly discern. Instead of being stars, these flashes result from the instan-

MOUNTAINS OF THE MOON
These volcanic peaks, as shown by the artist, are at least 36,000 feet high.

taneous combustion of small fragments of matter that have plunged into the earth's atmosphere from outer space. Some estimates indicate that as many as 100,000,000 fragments, large and small, fall toward the earth every day. Most of them are burned completely as friction, caused by their rapid motion through the atmosphere, quickly raises their temperature to incandescence. Sometimes a fragment will get through the earth's protective air layer and reach our globe as a meteorite. Many of these meteoric stones have been placed in museums.

Left: Planetary orbits, moons and relative distances from the sun. Right: The average temperatures indicate that only the earth may sustain life as we know it.

BEYOND THE SOLAR SYSTEM

Where is the sun taking us? That question occurs to all of us when we are told that our sun is moving through space at the rate of twelve miles per second toward a star group called Hercules. Planets, moons and comets are going with the sun. The movements around the sun are not being influenced by this other motion; all parts of the solar system are traveling as a unit.

The stars we see are other suns moving through space, possibly with planets and satellites following them. These stars are so far away that their distance is measured in light years. A light year is the distance light travels in one year, or about six million million miles. The nearest star is 4.3 light years from us. Since the speed of the sun is twelve miles per second, it would have to travel 70,000 years to get to the nearest star.

The larger masses of stars are grouped into swarms, each having a denser part. Each of these swarms is an independent stellar universe in the infinite reaches of space, endless and eternal. Our swarm or Galaxy, of which the Milky Way is the central plane, contains about one billion counted stars with billions uncounted. Our Galaxy is only one of millions. No one knows what lies beyond the remote galaxies, but man is constantly learning new secrets about this stupendous universe.

THE LORE OF THE STARS

Curiosity is natural to all of us, as it was with the earliest human beings. This curiosity led to an attempt by primitive man to explain the earth and the sky and how man fits into the whole scheme of things.

When the ancients looked at the heavens they built up mental pictures in which the brighter stars outlined favorite animals and heroes. They thought they saw the Great Bear (Ursa Major) and Little Bear (Ursa Minor) playing tag across the northern heavens. Orion, the great hunter, is represented by his belt and sword. These star groups are constellations. About a hundred of such groups have been named.

Man tried to read into the movement of the heavenly bodies some relationship to his destiny, and many superstitious ideas were developed. The appearance of a comet or an eclipse was a divine message or warning.

There is an historical instance of an army on the point of victory, which retreated because of the appearance of an eclipse.

Before the knowledge of the heavens was placed on a scientific basis, it was known as astrology. Since the astrologers could predict the appearance of an eclipse it was thought they were in direct communication with the gods and could foretell the future of an individual by the position of the stars at the time of his birth.

Although the attempt of early man to explain his surroundings resulted in many superstitious ideas, it led to the acquisition of much that was worth while and laid the basis for a true science—astronomy.

The history of astronomy may be traced back to about 2500 B. C., in records of Chinese scientists. The study was carried on by the Greeks and other ancient peoples.

The foregoing material gives a general picture of the universe and describes in some detail various types of heavenly bodies. After reading the article ASTRONOMY, the student will find the references below of value for further reading:

Apsides	Milky Way
Asteroids	Moon
Astrology	Nebula
Aurora Borealis	Nebular Hypothesis
Bear, Great	Neptune
Cassiopeia	Newton, Isaac
Comet	Observatory
Constellations	Orion
Copernicus	Planet
Earth	Satellite
Eclipse	Saturn
Ecliptic	Solar System
Einstein, Albert	Solstice
Equinox	Southern Cross
Fixed Stars	Spectroscope
Galileo	Star (with list)
Gravitation	Telescope
Jupiter	Tides
Light	Transit
Mars	Uranus
Mercury	Venus
Meteor	Zodiac

Bibliography

ABBOTT, C. G. *Earth and the Stars*. D. Van Nostrand Co.

BAKER, R. H. *When the Stars Came Out*. The Viking Press.

BARTKY, WALTER. *Highlights of Astronomy*. University of Chicago Press.

BERNHARD, H. J. *Handbook of the Heavens*. McGraw-Hill Book Co.

DOBISON, C. H. *Earth and Sky*. The Macmillan Co.

EDDINGTON, A. S. *Expanding Universe*. The Macmillan Co.

FROST, E. B. *Let's Look at the Stars*. Houghton, Mifflin Co.

HALE, G. E. *Beyond the Milky Way*. Charles Scribner's Sons.

HARDING, A. M. *Astronomy: the Splendor of the Heavens*. Garden City Publishing Co.

JEANS, J. H. *Universe Around Us*. The Macmillan Co.

LEMON, H. B. *From Galileo to Cosmic Rays*. University of Chicago Press.

MITCHELL, S. A. *Eclipses of the Sun*. Columbia University Press.

REED, W. M. *Stars for Sam*. Harcourt, Brace & Co.

SLOSSON, E. E. *Easy Lessons in Einstein*. Harcourt, Brace & Co.

WOODBURY, D. C. *The Glass Giant of Palomar*. Dodd, Mead & Co.

GEOLOGY: THE EARTH, OUR HOME

Our planet has not always been the abode of the human race. For millions of years before man appeared, plant life and animals were developing, and in the still more distant past the earth was probably a part of the sun. The generally accepted theory as to the origin of the earth and the other planets is called the planetesimal hypothesis.

According to this theory, our sun was originally a body of gaseous matter, without planets, traveling through space. By chance a large star, perhaps a billion years old, passed close enough to the sun to raise tremendous tides on its surface by the force of gravitation. As the visiting star continued to move past, great masses of material were pulled from the sun. Part of the material was carried away as the star passed on into space, but several masses remained under the attraction of the sun and began revolving about it. The larger masses attracted to themselves smaller planetesimals and became the nine planets of the solar system. The earth acquired its hard crust through gradual cooling and solidification over a very long period.

Because of the rotation of the earth, it is slightly flattened at the Poles. Since the equator moves at a speed of 1,000 miles per hour, centrifugal force has a tendency to pull that section of the earth slightly away from the center. It is therefore several miles less from the Poles to the center of the earth than from a point on the equator to the center. The rotation of the earth is so steady and varies so little from century to century that we make use of this regularity for measuring time.

The earth's surface is divided into twenty-four belts, each being 15° of longitude in width. The prime meridian, which passes through Greenwich, England, is used as a basis for time as well as position on the earth's surface. When it is high noon at Greenwich the sun will be low in the western sky at a point far east of Greenwich, and will be just rising at points in the United States. In fact, for every 15° of longitude, we have a difference of one hour in the sun's position.

Volcanoes, geysers and hot springs indicate internal heat below the surface. Descent into a deep mine shows a gradual rise of temperature with depth. If this increase of heat continued we would not have to go many miles before the temperature would be sufficient to account for molten rocks. Careful checking of tidal forces and earthquake data lead to the conclusion that the inside of the earth is as rigid as steel, in spite of the high temperature.

Meteorites which hit the earth show a large proportion of iron. We have reason to believe that our earth and the meteors originally were derived from the same source and, therefore, that the earth should contain a large percentage of iron. The average density of the earth is about seven-tenths that of iron. The outer crust of the earth is only one-third as heavy as iron. We are led to conclude, therefore, that the inner core of the earth is composed of iron and possibly other heavy metals, with lighter materials toward the outside.

By a study of the seismograph record of earth tremors, the conclusion reached by scientists is that the earth is a series of shells. If we were able to examine the inside of the earth from the center out, we

POWER AND BEAUTY IN A WATERFALL

should probably find a core of iron about 2,000 miles thick, then 1,000 miles or more of sulphides, oxides and similar compounds, and then another zone of rock extending to a point about fifty miles from the surface. At this point we have a level below which some authorities believe that there are no changes taking place; and they think that no changes have ever taken place below this level. The last fifty miles form the changing crust of the earth, the part that attracts our chief interest.

A study of the upper crust of the earth shows three distinct types of rock—igneous, sedimentary and metamorphic. Igneous rocks, formed by the agency of fire, include lava, basalt and pumice. Sedimentary (water-formed) rocks include sandstone, shale, slate and limestone deposits. Metamorphic rocks are those formed through the agencies of heat, pressure or chemical action. A typical metamorphic rock is marble, which has changed from limestone by crystallization. Among these three types of rock we find the minerals and ores which are of commercial value to man.

EARTH'S STORY TOLD IN THE ROCKS

The age of the earth has presented a riddle which man has partially solved. Mother Earth has written her autobiography in the rocks, and it is for us to read it. Geologists have known for many years that certain rock layers contain fossils of plant and animal remains deposited there when the rocks were formed. Considering only the upper fifty miles of the earth's crust, we find that many distinct layers of rock can be counted.

In the very deepest layers of sedimentary rock there are no traces of fossils, because the earliest forms of life were bits of protoplasm which left no hard skeletons to form fossils. These rocks, called the Archean, are the oldest which show any change from the original cooling mass that formed the planet. The era in which they were formed is called the Archeozoic.

If we go back further in the earth's history, we find that geologists have given the name Azoic to all those hundreds of millions of years when our planet was in the formative state.

Following the Archeozoic Era in geological history is the Proterozoic, which lasted about 600 million years. This era marks the appearance of primitive forms of plants and animals. The following era, the Paleozoic, lasted about 250 million years. During this era the sea was teeming with invertebrate animals, including worms, shellfish and coral. The first land animals appeared, and there was an abundant growth of plant life. Later in the era the first insects made their appearance and the first reptiles developed. Sharks and other fish marked the appearance of marine vertebrates. Coal deposits were formed when the heavy vegetation accumulated to depths of hundreds of feet and was later covered with sediment when the land sank below the ocean. Thus coal is of plant origin.

Los Angeles Museum

THE PLEISTOCENE ERA IN CALIFORNIA
The scientist's conception of animal life in this age shows saber-toothed tigers stalking great bears, with mastodons and bison grazing in the background.

The Mesozoic Era comes next in our reading of the earth's history. The rocks show fossils of the dinosaurs, flying reptiles, early forms of mammals and flowering plants. The last great age before modern times is called the Cenozoic Era. During this period mammals developed and great ice sheets swept down from the north for the last time.

For further information about the origin of the earth and its movements and structure, the articles EARTH and GEOLOGY may first be read. Then continue by referring to the topics listed below:

Day	Meridian
Earthquake	Metamorphism
Fossil	Minerals and
Geyser	Mineralogy
Igneous Rocks	Pole
International Date	Rock
Line	Standard Time
Latitude	Soil
Longitude	Volcano
Longitude and Time	Year

Bibliography

ALLEN, V. T. *This Earth of Ours.* Bruce Publishing Co.
COLEMAN, A. P. *The Last Million Years; a History of the Pleistocene in North America.* University of Toronto Press.
MORREL, M. M. *When the World Was Young.* Houghton, Mifflin Co.
WHITE, A. T. *Lost Worlds: Adventures in Archaeology.* Random House.

THE EVER-CHANGING SURFACE

We can truthfully say that the earth is always changing, that the surface is not the same today as it was yesterday. What are the forces which cause these changes? How fast do they act and how do they affect human life?

The forces that are ceaselessly at work are of two kinds—those that wear down the surface and those that build it up. Important among the wearing-down processes is erosion, or weathering. Moving air, moving water and glaciers are forces which work relatively fast; chemical changes and temperature changes, although they act more slowly, are just as important.

There are sections of our own continent where an arid climate prevails and where wind laden with sand and dust acts like a sand blast, cutting away the solid rock. In the Garden of the Gods in Colorado and in the Bad Lands of South Dakota are formations that reveal the tremendous cutting effect of wind-driven sand. In the Great Plains section of the United States, excessive use of the land for crops and a cycle of

Union Pacific

ERODED ROCK
Ostler's Castle, Bryce Canyon National Park.

drought years removed the protective covering of vegetation and laid bare the soil, creating the "Dust Bowl."

Moving water is so common that we often overlook its ability to wear away rock and transport valuable material to the sea. It has been estimated that the silt annually carried by the Mississippi River has twice the weight of all freight arriving at Chicago during the same period.

Rain water has a tendency to sink into the soil as long as there is a covering of vegetable matter. The roots of the growing plants make the soil porous and the rain is

WATER CUTS THROUGH ROCK
Big Thompson River, paralleled by a manmade road, in its spectacular gorge.

absorbed. Later, the water finds its way slowly to springs, much of it evaporating. The first step toward making a country barren is to cut down the timber and plow the soil. Rains and running water soon cut deep gullies in the hills and gentler slopes. The rich soil layer is rapidly washed away and clay and bare rock result.

And what becomes of the silt? An old river like the Mississippi meanders through its wide valley, depositing soil here and digging out new beds there. Much of the dirt carried finally reaches the ocean. There the speed of the water is slowed down so much that the dirt is dropped, filling up a triangular piece of new land called a delta.

Glaciers are examples of moving water in its solid form, ice. At different periods in the earth's history, large portions of the surface have been covered with ice.

In recent geological history, northern North America was covered with an ice sheet extending as far south as the Ohio River. This sheet may have been as much as one mile thick. Any irregularities were smoothed down by this great ice sheet. Huge basins were carved out, forming the Great Lakes. When the front of the glacier melted, it deposited the material it had collected, forming moraines. The path of the ice sheet can be traced by the granite boulders that were brought from great distances and dropped.

Weathering as a result of temperature change is common where there are extremes of temperature. When water freezes it expands. When water, seeping into depressions, freezes, its expansion causes pieces of the rock to break off. Gradually, a great boulder will split into a number of smaller parts which are further acted upon by ice and other forms of erosion.

Volcanoes are the best proof that the interior of the earth is very hot. Pressure is relieved at intervals by the extrusion, or seeping out, of a mass of liquid stone. This release of internal pressure may be a disastrous explosion which blows up the entire mountain, covers the country with boulders and lava for miles around, and causes tidal waves in the near-by ocean which destroy cities. Such catastrophes have appeared a number of times in history.

The most violent eruptions, however, are insignificant compared with the great upheavals that formed our mountain systems.

Mountain ranges are the result of the buckling and folding of the earth's crust. The formation of a mountain range is probably a long-term movement consisting of a series of tremendous earthquakes. All our present mountain ranges show great age, and it is probable that man was not on earth when even the youngest mountain was formed.

Diastrophic (continent-forming) changes in the earth's crust show themselves in various ways. One interesting example is the slow but tremendous tipping of the continent. We picture the continent as a large body of granite floating on a slightly plastic lower stratum of basalt. That the continents do dip, there can be no doubt; caves carved out by water are visible high up on cliffs at points which the ocean never reaches today. That circumstance would indicate a rising coast line. On the other side of the continent, the ocean would be creeping up valleys. Both the Hudson and St. Lawrence have definite river beds far out from the present coast line. The fact that rivers once flowed into the sea miles to the east of the present shore is proof of a sinking coast line.

A second movement of the earth is the one which places sidewise pressure on the surface layers and folds them into mountain

FOLDED ROCK STRATA
Mountains carved by weathering and erosion.

ranges. It is a peculiar fact that most of the mountain ranges of the earth are near the ocean. Such uniformity of position leads us to believe that heavy materials, accumulating at the ocean edge by erosion, build up a pressure on the rocks beneath, which ultimately push up the lighter materials close by to form new mountain ranges. The forces of erosion, motivated by gravity, are therefore continually trying to tear down the high places and make the entire earth's surface level, while the forces of vulcanism (volcanic action) and diastrophism are just as tirelessly building up the lower places.

Let us examine one other effect of diastrophism. Cracks which develop in the earth's crust often cause rocks to slip. These cracks are known as faults. During the great earthquake at San Francisco, in 1906, the surface along the San Andreas fault was displaced as much as twenty feet in some places. The ends of a road at the break were out of line entirely. Water pipes were broken and stream beds altered. This fault had been known before the quake occurred, and geologists realized that movement along the fracture of the earth's crust would take place at some future time.

Yellowstone National Park in Wyoming and the Grand Canyon in Arizona are spectacular examples of the changes that are ceaselessly altering the surface of the earth.

For additional reading, the following references may be consulted:

Arid Region	Flood
Atmosphere	Geyser
Canyon	Glacial Period
Cave	Glaciers
Coal	Lava
Delta	Mountain
Dune	Rivers
Dust, Atmospheric	Seismograph
Erosion	Stalactite
Fault	Volcano

Bibliography

CRONEIS, C. G. *Down to Earth; An Introduction to Geology.* University of Chicago Press.

DANA, E. S. *Minerals and How to Study Them.* John Wiley & Sons.

ENGLISH, G. L. *Getting Acquainted with Minerals.* McGraw-Hill Book Co.

FABRE, J. H. *This Earth of Ours.* D. Appleton-Century Co.

FENTON, C. L. *Along the Hills.* Reynal & Hitchcock.

FITZHUGH, E. F. *Treasures in the Earth.* Caxton Printers.

GAMOW, GEORGE. *Biography of the Earth; Its Past, Present and Future.* The Viking Press.

LOOMIS, F. B. *Field Book of Common Rocks and Minerals.* G. P. Putnam's Sons.

LYNCH, JOSEPH. *Our Trembling Earth; a Popular Account.* Dodd, Mead & Co.

SHAND, S. J. *Earth-Lore; Geology Without Jargon.* E. P. Dutton & Co.

VERRILL, A. H. *Minerals, Metals and Gems.* L. C. Page & Co.

SEASONS AND CLIMATE

In those parts of North America where most of us live there is a regular succession of seasons through the year—spring, summer, fall and winter. The earth revolves about the sun in a year of 365¼ days, and rotates on the axis once in approximately every twenty-four hours. This rotation gives us our alternate periods of day and night. Our seasons are due to the fact that the earth's axis, which always points toward the North Star, is not perpendicular to its orbit around the sun, but tips about $23\frac{1}{2}°$ from that perpendicular. Also, the earth does not make a perfectly circular path around the sun; it is about 3.4 per cent closer to the sun in January than it is in July, for its orbit is slightly elliptical.

In January the axis of the earth is inclined away from the sun in the Northern Hemisphere and the sun is not visible at the North Pole. There the sun does not rise for six months, traveling entirely around the horizon each twenty-four-hour day.

In July the earth has covered half of its orbit in the intervening six months, and its axis is inclined toward the sun at the North Pole. The Polar day is now six months long and there is a night of six months in Antarctica. At just one moment in the spring and one in the fall does the sun shine directly on the equator. Those points of time, when day and night are of equal length, are called the vernal (spring) and autumnal equinoxes. They occur each year about March 21 and September 23. The accumulated cold of winter makes March the colder month.

During our summer the sun has apparently moved north and the days are longer than the nights. The longest day is June 21 or thereabouts, when the sun's direct rays reach a point $23\frac{1}{2}°$ north of the equator. In the winter, about December 21, the earth is exactly opposite in its position relative to the sun, and we have our longest night on that date.

For all practical purposes we can ignore the difference in distance to the sun and say that our seasons vary with the angle at which the sun's rays strike the earth's surface. When the sun shines directly down, a square foot of radiant energy will strike one square foot of the earth's surface. When the rays strike at an angle the surface covered is greater, and consequently the energy is less per unit area.

In considering factors that affect climate, we first think of latitude. From the equator to each Pole there is, generally speaking, a gradual lowering of temperature. On this basis the surface of the earth is divided into five climatic zones—the north and south frigid, the north and south temperate and the torrid zones.

Various factors other than latitude determine climate, and to say that there is a progressive change of temperature from equator to Pole is to speak only in general terms. High in the Andes Mountains of South America are villages near the equator where snow remains on the ground all the year. A few miles to the east is the torrid jungle of the Amazon Valley. These different climates are due to altitude or distance above sea level. The air blanket that surrounds the earth is densest at sea level, where the atmospheric pressure is nearly fifteen pounds to the square inch. At sea level there is more heat energy retained than at higher points, for the air grows progressively rarer as the earth's elevation increases. As the air becomes thinner, it is less able to retain the sun's heat.

Large bodies of water tend to moderate the climate of neighboring territory. Because water absorbs heat rather slowly, lands

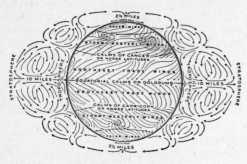

PLANETARY WINDS
Shaded areas indicate rainy sections.

that border the oceans are cooled by breezes from these adjoining bodies of water. The water also gives up its heat slowly, and when the land cools off, the water is comparatively warm, thus moderating the severity of winter weather.

Another factor governing climate is an irregularity of the earth's surface, such as a mountain range which cuts off cooling or rain-carrying winds.

METEOROLOGY

The study of the weather and causes of weather changes is called meteorology. Climate is the average of weather conditions over a period of time. Hence the study of weather is really the basis for the study of climate. Among the most important factors

affecting weather are temperature, humidity, or amount of water vapor in the air, and winds.

The scientist's study of weather has resulted in a well-organized system of forecasting. One of the important divisions of the Federal Department of Agriculture is the Weather Bureau.

There is a great deal of weather lore that passes for fact, but which is largely fancy. Such superstitions as the ability of the groundhog to foresee the weather for six weeks ahead are no longer given credence by well-informed persons. And the old-fashioned almanac that predicted the weather for a year in advance has been superseded by scientific reports based on exact observation and precise instruments. One of the more recent instruments is the radiosonde, a device that is attached to a balloon. From a height of ten miles it sends back radio signals telling of pressure, temperature and humidity. It returns to earth by means of a small parachute.

Weather forecasts of the government are nearly ninety per cent correct. There is always a chance that some condition which cannot be foreseen may make a prediction inaccurate. The future will probably see the development of long-range predictions, which will affect many phases of modern living.

The aviation industry depends upon weather forecasts for the safety of its passengers. Airlines get information directly from the Weather Bureau and are thus in a position to decide whether a passenger liner should be allowed to start on a scheduled trip. They also know the probable air condition over the territory of the contemplated trip. If conditions are unfavorable the pilot is directed to avoid the storm area or the plane is grounded until the weather improves. Today, many planes are flying in the stratosphere above the storm area.

The articles CLIMATE and METEOROLOGY provide a general background for detailed study of the material in the foregoing sections. Supplementary topics are listed below:

Antarctic Ocean
  and Lands
Arctic Ocean and
  Lands
Barometer
Calms, Regions of
Condensation
Equinox
Evaporation
Gulf Stream
Humidity

Ocean Currents
Prevailing
  Westerlies
Rain
Seasons
Solstice
Temperature
Thermometer
Trade Winds
Weather Bureau
Wind

Man Uses Science to Understand and Improve Plants and Animals

BIOLOGY

Biology is the study of life. The study of plant life is known as botany, and the study of animal life as zoölogy.

What is life? No simple answer can be given to that question. Chemically, living

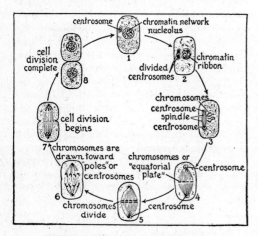

DIVISION OF AN ANIMAL CELL

material is the same as non-living. If the living and the non-living contain the same chemical elements, in what way do they differ? We know that the basis of life is protoplasm, a complex jelly-like, colorless material that possesses the property of life because of its peculiar structure. We do not know when life originated or how. It is enough for us to know that when this planet became habitable, life in a very simple form appeared. The primitive organisms that then existed produced their kind, and from that time there has been a continuous flow of the stream of life.

Biologists agree that the earliest form of life was neither plant nor animal, but at a very early period the distinction between plant and animal life occurred.

We are interested chiefly in learning how man has used biology to improve plants and animals by applying the laws of heredity.

The fundamental concept of heredity is that like begets like. Many characteristics may be transmitted from generation to gen-

eration, while others are not transmitted. The tendency of insanity may be passed down from parent to children, but the loss of a leg is not passed on to the next generation. Thus, as each form of life transmits certain peculiarities to the next generation, we find that, irregularly, there are biological variations which may be a step forward in the evolution of a new living form. These variations may be the result of man-controlled breeding or may take place in nature.

The new organism starts from the union of a female egg cell and a male sperm cell. Each body cell has in its nucleus varying numbers of minute bodies known as chromosomes. There is a variation in the number of chromosomes in different animals; for example, there are forty-eight in man and sixty in the horse. Similarly, there is a wide variation in the number of chromosomes in a plant; the number varies from fourteen in the pea to sixty-four in the brake fern. The chromosomes carry the heritable peculiarities of the organism.

An Austrian monk named Mendel deserves the greatest praise for his research on the subject of heredity. In his garden he con-

MENDEL'S LAW OF HEREDITY
Black indicates dominant traits; white, recessive. Hybrids are in center (3 and 4).

ducted a series of experiments with two varieties of peas, one a dwarf and the other a tall variety. Starting with pure stock of each kind, he allowed cross pollination to occur between the two varieties. His laws explain the dominant and recessive traits which govern the reproduction of new organisms. Certain tendencies or characteristics are stronger in their effect on the new descendants than others; the dominant therefore stands out in the next generation. The recessive characteristics are there, however, and in twenty-five per cent of the third generation they again assert themselves to the exclusion of the dominant.

DIVISIONS OF THE PLANT WORLD

As stated earlier, the first forms of life were neither plant nor animal. Some organisms eventually developed a green coloring matter, chlorophyll, which enabled them to manufacture their own food with the aid of sunlight, air and water. From the chlorophyll-producing organisms, plant life has developed to present specialized forms.

The plant world today is divided into four great branches or phyla. In the first phylum are the thallophytes, plants producing neither leaves, stems nor roots. Each is made up of a simple plant body, or thallus. The lowest of the thallophytes are the blue-green algae. They are followed in order of complexity by the green, brown and red algae. In the next group are the fungi, including molds, yeast, lichens, mushrooms and similar organisms.

The first plants to show the development of organs for the performance of special functions are included in the second phyllum, the bryophytes. Liverworts and mosses make up this group. They possess primitive forms of roots, stems and leaves.

The next phylum consists of ferns, horsetails and club moss. These plants, the pteridophytes, have true roots, stems and leaves.

The spermatophytes, constituting the fourth phylum, are plants in which special organs have been developed for the production of seed. These are the plants that man has chiefly utilized for food, clothing and shelter. The seeds may lack a seed case or they may be enclosed. Plants bearing naked seeds are gymnosperms, such as the pines; those with enclosed seeds are angiosperms, as typified by our common trees and garden flowers.

Angiosperms are divided into two main groups—monocotyledons and dicotyledons.

FUNCTIONS OF PLANTS

The processes by which plants live, grow and reproduce are best explained through a study of the specialized organs of the higher plants. Water and plant foods are obtained from the soil by roots, which may also serve to store food. There may be one main root (the taproot) extending downward with practically no side branches, or fibrous roots branching out in all directions. Fine root hairs on the smaller divisions of the roots are in contact with soil water, and obtain water and mineral matter in solution by the process of osmosis.

This process consists of the mixing of two liquids of different density, separated by a thin membrane. Osmotic pressure causes the lighter liquid to flow toward the heavier. In plants, water and material held in solution pass through the membranes of the root hairs to the denser protoplasm, which has the power of selecting substances needed to nourish the plant.

The stem of the plant is provided with a conducting system for the conveyance of water and dissolved minerals to the leaves, which are the plant organs that manufacture

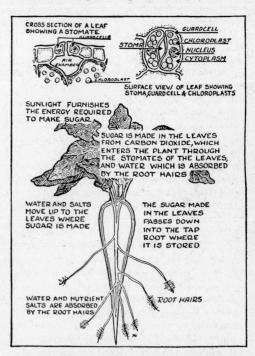

THE STORY OF THE SUGAR BEET

food. There are two sets of conducting cells—the xylem, or water-bearing tubes, and the phloem, or food-conducting tubes. The phloem conveys manufactured food from the leaves to other parts of the plant. The xylem conveys water to the leaves.

Plant food is elaborated by the leaves from water and carbon dioxide. Water, as noted above, is taken from the soil. Carbon dioxide is obtained from the atmosphere by tiny breathing pores, or stomata, which are openings through the surfaces of the leaves. The elaboration of usable plant food from the raw materials is known as photosynthesis; that is, synthesis with the assistance of light. This marvelous process, which man can describe but not duplicate, takes place only in the presence of sunlight, for the sun provides the energy needed.

Utilizing this energy, the green leaf manufactures sugar and starch (carbohydrate material) and liberates oxygen, which is returned to the air. The carbohydrate food in liquid form (sap) is carried by the phloem to parts which need food. Part of the food is employed as building material, part may be stored for future use and part may be used as fuel. Thus the higher plants absorb and assimilate foods, release waste, create energy by oxidizing food, and build new tissue. The process constitutes plant metabolism.

Reference was made above to the breathing pores of the leaves. Respiration of plants, like that of animals, involves an interchange of oxygen and carbon dioxide. The leaves absorb oxygen through their stomata and set free carbon dioxide. In the process complex substances are broken down and there is a corresponding release of energy. Similar openings, called lenticels, are the breathing pores of the stem. Roots, too, require air, and land plants will die if the soil is flooded to such an extent that the roots cannot obtain it.

Another function of the leaf is transpiration, or the release of excess water carried from the roots. Some trees liberate several gallons of water each summer day.

The most common type of reproduction is best studied in connection with flowering plants. The flower itself has one particular purpose—perpetuation of the species. To carry on this function, it is provided with specialized organs, which we call the floral parts. In a typical flower there are four of these parts—sepals, petals, stamens and pistil. The first three of these are arranged in rings around the pistil, which is in the center. The sepals, usually green and leaflike, surround the petals, the showy part of the flower. Inside the petals is the ring of club-shaped stamens, which contain the pollen grains. The pistil has an enlargement at the top called the stigma; and a bulbous arrangement at the bottom called the ovary. This latter contains ovules or egg cells. In botanical language we speak of the pistil as the female part of the plant, the stamens as the male part.

Within each pollen grain are produced two germ cells or sperms. Essential to the reproductive process is the combining of sperms and ovules. Pollen is carried to the pistil by the wind or on the bodies of insects seeking nectar. When the grains come into contact with the stigma of the pistil, each grain produces a tube which is sent down through the stem of that organ. When the tip of the tube reaches the ovary, the sperms are discharged into it, and here is accomplished the union of sperm and egg.

The fertilized ovule produces an embryo plant, the growth of which is soon checked by the hardening of the body walls. As a result, a seed is formed. The seed carries within it nourishment for the young plant. Under favorable conditions of moisture and warmth, it starts growing; that is, it germinates. The reproductive process in flowering plants is thus a cycle consisting of pollination, fertilization and germination.

In order to insure cross pollination, the pollen and the ovules in the same plant may mature at different times; thus the plants cannot pollinate themselves. Some species of plants have the pollen and egg cells on two entirely separate plants as a further protection against self-pollination.

Various devices have been adopted by different types of plants to disperse their seeds. In early summer the air may be filled by the downy fluffs from the seed balls of the poplar trees. In fact, the seeds are scattered in such abundance that they become a nuisance around dwellings. The seeds of maples and box-elders have wings around them. They may spin and sail for some distance through the air. Russian thistles form tumbleweeds, which may be blown across the prairie for miles, scattering the seeds as they roll.

Wind is not the only means of dispersal. Round fruits roll a considerable distance when they fall from the trees. Birds scatter the seeds of many edible fruits.

Some seeds are distributed because of other mechanical devices. The sand bur and cockle bur stick to the fur of animals or the clothing of man and may be carried long distances. The wild geranium, or crane's-bill, has a mechanical device on the seed pod. When the ripened pod is touched, this spring-like device is released, throwing the seeds in all directions.

The study of plants gives real enjoyment to those who are interested in their environment. A trip to the woods and walks along a woodside may be very instructive to anyone with observant eyes and an inquiring mind. The study of nature is a fascinating hobby and it will pay dividends to all who follow it.

The articles BIOLOGY and BOTANY provide a basis for further study of the subjects covered in the preceding sections. Supplementary information may be found in the following articles: [See lists with general articles.]

ORGANIZATION AND FUNCTIONS OF ANIMALS

The simplest type of animal, the amoeba, is capable of thrusting out small sections of the cell body. When one of these "fingers" touches an object that will serve as food, the amoeba flows around it and absorbs it. Waste matter passes out through the general surface of the body. There is an interchange of gases that is the counterpart of breathing in higher animals. Lastly, the amoeba reproduces by cell division. Thus it carries on, in the simplest manner possible, the essential functions of a living animal.

Next in the scale of animal development are the pore-bearing sponges, creatures that live as fixed objects on the bottom of the sea. They are the lowest of the many-celled animals. The ordinary sponge of commerce is the internal skeleton of one of these animals. In living sponges, water enters through tiny pores and circulates through a system of canals. The sponge secures its food and oxygen from the water, which is kept in motion by tiny processes that act as beaters. Special cells carry on the work of digestion and assimilation and waste is excreted through an opening.

A further specialization is seen in animals of the next group, including sea anemones, jellyfish and the fresh-water hydra. For example, the hydra has a tubular body which is attached to twigs and weeds in the water. The anterior end of the body has a fringe of waving arms, or tentacles, equipped with stinging cells. The tentacles paralyze the water insects on which the hydra feeds, and draw the food into the body cavity, where it is digested. The power of movement is further developed, for the hydra can extend its body sixteen times the measure of its diameter, or contract the body into a ball-shaped mass.

As specialization continues, the vital functions are performed by organs of increasing complexity. Rudimentary nervous and circulatory systems develop, as well as special organs for sight and hearing, taste and touch. Mouth parts become differentiated. Legs and wings give increased power of movement, enabling the animals to go from place to place. The nervous system reaches its final development in animals with a spinal column, the vertebrates. The highest class of this group consists of the mammals; the highest species of mammal is man.

In the human body, the digestive, circulatory, respiratory, and nervous systems are highly specialized. The human digestive tract is called the alimentary canal. Food entering the mouth is moistened by saliva, chewed into a pulp, and swallowed. It is conveyed through the esophagus to the stomach, which is a pear-shaped sac, and from the stomach it passes into the small intestine. The usable portions are absorbed through the walls of the small intestine and carried to the blood stream by the aid of the lymphatics. Gastric juice, secreted by glands in the mucous lining of the stomach, the intestinal juices, the pancreatic juice and bile all aid in the digestive process.

The blood circulates through the heart, arteries, veins and capillaries. The fluid contains dissolved food material, mineral salts, water and waste material. The red corpuscles contain a substance known as hemoglobin, which combines with oxygen to form the red color characteristic of human blood. Since the red corpuscles can take up oxygen or release it, they are oxygen carriers. The white blood corpuscles are much larger and less numerous, and are sometimes called the scavengers of the blood stream. They are also found in the lymph, and, in fact, appear to go where needed to combat disease or injury.

The heart is the pump of the circulatory system. The human heart is a muscular, four-chambered organ. The two upper chambers are the auricles, and the two lower the ventricles. Impure blood from the veins enters the right auricle, and passes through a valve into the right ventricle, where it is pumped to the lungs to receive its supply of oxygen and give up its carbon dioxide.

The food that nourishes the body cells is really fuel for the organism, just as coal is fuel for a steam engine. In either case, the fuel must be burned before it can release its energy. The food in the cell combines with the oxygen that has been brought there and is literally burned. This combination produces heat and waste. Some of the cell material is worn down, and there is also a conversion of food material into a new protoplasm. This combined building-up and tearing-down process is called metabolism. Since oxygen is necessary for metabolism, the rate at which metabolism occurs in the body can be determined by measuring the intake of oxygen and the outflow of carbon dioxide. This metabolism test is a common hospital procedure.

Respiration, or breathing, is a fundamental part of metabolism. Essentially, it is the taking in of oxygen and the liberation of carbon dioxide. Man and other higher vertebrates breathe with lungs. Air is inhaled through the nose. The warmed and cleansed air passes through the larynx, or voice box, to the trachea, or windpipe, which divides into the right and left bronchial tubes after entering the chest cavity. Minute subdivisions of these tubes convey air to the countless tiny sacs that make up the lung tissue. Across the chest cavity below the lungs is a muscular membrane called the dia-

phragm. As the diaphragm contracts, it flattens out and makes more room in the chest cavity. Incoming air expands the lungs to fill this extra space. When the diaphragm relaxes and takes its original position, it forces the air out of the lungs. While the air is in the lungs the blood picks up the oxygen and replaces it with carbon dioxide.

When the food is burned, certain waste products are formed. One of the wastes, carbon dioxide, is expelled by the lungs. When the complex, nitrogen-containing foods are oxidized in the process of metabolism, urea, uric acid, salts and water are formed. These products are eliminated by the kidneys and the skin. The blood filters through the kidneys, which remove urea, uric acid and salts; these wastes are then carried to the bladder for expulsion from the body.

Waste products similar to those removed by the kidneys are eliminated by the skin through the sweat glands. When perspira-

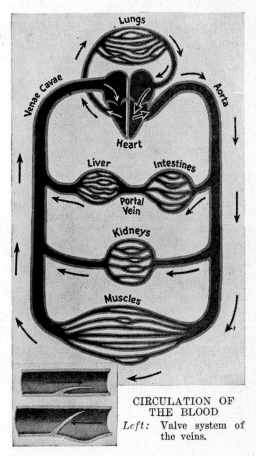

CIRCULATION OF
THE BLOOD
Left: Valve system of
the veins.

tion evaporates, the waste products are left upon the surface of the skin; hence the importance of regular bathing. The skin also nelps regulate the body temperature. Evaporation always has a cooling effect. If the perspiration of the body evaporates properly, we feel cool. If it evaporates slowly, we are warm.

To co-ordinate the sensations and the functions of the body, man has a marvelously organized nervous system. The nervous system consists of the brain, the spinal cord and a network of nerves. Functions are carried on by both the cerebro-spinal and the sympathetic nerves.

The foregoing activities serve only to keep the organism alive and ensure its growth. The stream of life is perpetuated by reproduction, a function of all plants and animals. There are two kinds—asexual and sexual. In the former, one part of the organism forms a new individual, as in the simple cell division. In sexual reproduction there is a union of two different cells. Asexual reproduction produces organisms like the original. No new characteristics are developed. The union of two different cells, on the other hand, introduces new qualities. The result is a new organism, not merely duplication of the original plant or animal.

Sexual reproduction is accomplished by the union of male and female germ cells, or gametes. In some of the lower animals, such as the hydra and earthworm, both cells are produced by the same individual. In the higher animals, the sperms, or male eggs, are produced by one individual and the female eggs by another. In the more simply organized vertebrates, such as fishes, eggs are produced in the body of the female and are deposited in a favorable location for fertilization by the sperms. Such a method fertilizes only a small fraction of the eggs, but these are produced in sufficiently large numbers to ensure perpetuation of the species. Reptiles and birds reproduce by means of eggs fertilized in the body of the female.

Mammals, the highest class of animals, usually bear their young alive. The young are nourished by the mother's milk. The egg cell is fertilized inside the body of the mother, and the embryo develops in her body until it has reached a stage of development where it can be born alive.

For additional information in regard to the structure and functions of animal life, the following articles may be consulted:

Absorption	Lacteals
Assimilation	Larva
Amoeba	Lymph
Anatomy	Lymphatics
Animal	Man
Arteries	Metamorphosis
Blood	Nerves
Breathing	Nervous System
Capillaries	Perspiration
Caterpillar	Skeleton
Circulation	Skin, The
Digestion	Spinal Cord
Heart	Veins

For the names and descriptions of the major branches, or phyla, into which animals are divided, consult the article ZOÖLOGY. See, also, the following headings for detailed accounts of various zoölogical groups and for lists of specific animals:

Amphibians	Invertebrates
Arachnida	Mammals
Arthropoda	Marsupials
Birds	Mollusca
Cephalopoda	Myriapoda
Cetacea	Primates
Coelenterata	Protozoa
Crustacea	Radiolaria
Echinoderms	Reptiles
Edentata	Rodents
Fish and Fisheries	Ruminants
Insectivora	Ungulates
Insects	Vertebrates

CULTIVATION OF PLANTS FOR USE

The cultivation of plants is one of the basic divisions of agriculture. It was the first agricultural pursuit of primitive man, and is carried on today in nearly every part of the inhabited world. Plants are grown for food, clothing, shelter, medicine and decorative purposes.

Essential to the growth of plants are certain chemicals and a sufficient supply of soil moisture. A soil containing these materials will produce good crops if the chemical elements present meet the requirements of the plants grown. All plants need ten elements—carbon, hydrogen, oxygen, phosphorus, potassium, nitrogen, sulphur, calcium, iron and magnesium. Nature has been fairly generous with these minerals, but many soils become depleted through excessive planting. Heavy rains also may wash out valuable minerals from the soil.

Devitalized soil can be restored to fertility if the proper chemicals are added to it. The minerals most often needed are nitrates, phosphates and lime. The addition of manure, the nitrogenous wastes of farm animals, will provide nitrates, the most common deficiency.

Rotation of crops will aid in preventing soil depletion. Some crops remove more of one plant food than do others. If a plot of ground is planted to a different crop each year, the danger of wearing out the soil is greatly lessened.

Leguminous plants, such as alfalfa and clover, add to soil fertility through bacteria found in tiny nodules on their roots. These bacteria have the power to take nitrogen from the air and to change it into nitrates.

Besides maintaining the fertility of the soil, the farmer, by means of proper cultivation, has learned how to get a maximum yield from his farm. The seed bed must be prepared properly to hold moisture and give the seeds a chance to germinate. The top soil must be stirred after rains to kill weeds and to conserve moisture. In regions of insufficient rainfall for plant growth, dry farming is practiced. Instead of planting a crop the first year, the farmer cultivates the soil frequently, to save all moisture possible. The second year a crop is planted and cultivation continued. By keeping a dust mulch on top, the farmer is able to prevent evaporation and thus conserve whatever moisture the soil contains.

Experimentation has developed strains and

MAN GETS FOOD FROM THE EARTH

Sugar-beet roots go down six or seven feet. Left in the earth at harvest, they decompose and help fertilize the soil.

hybrids that result in greatly increased yields. Also, by crossing different forms of the same or closely related plants, many plant breeders have produced new varieties of commercial value. All such improvements are based on scientific principles.

The cultivation of plants for ornamental purposes is an industry of great importance. The landscape is made beautiful by the natural growth of green trees and other vegetation. Man grows trees, shrubs, flowers and grass to beautify homes, city parks and gardens and other sites. Many new trees and shrubs have been developed in greenhouses, nurseries and botanical gardens.

For further reading on the subject of plant cultivation and improvement, the following references will be of value:

Agriculture	Floriculture
Botanical Garden	Flowers
Botany	Gardening
Breeding	Grafting
Burbank, Luther	Landscape Gardening
Dry Farming	Soil
Fertilizers	Tree

IMPROVEMENT OF ANIMAL LIFE

Man has used his knowledge of animal life and the laws of heredity to utilize and improve animals. By careful selection and breeding, he has developed animals possessing the qualities he desires.

Because of the selective process of evolution, nature evolved the three-toed horse, which was about the size of a rabbit, into a fairly large animal. Then man selected and improved the animals to the point where he had types of horses for his particular needs.

On the farm, where horses are needed for heavy work, the draft horses have been carefully selected and bred. Several breeds have been developed, such as the Percherons, Shires, Clydesdale and the Belgian. These horses have large feet to give traction in pulling and are heavily muscled. Some of them weigh a ton or more and are capable of doing very heavy work for long periods of time.

Race horses have been bred for their stamina and speed. Horses in between these types have been developed for special purposes. Man merely hastened the process of evolution that had been slowly carried on by nature.

In the case of cattle there is much the same story. There are two general types of cattle, beef and dairy. Milk cows have been carefully selected and the animals possessing the qualities of good health and abundant milk production have been allowed to produce their kind. In turn, the offspring possessing the desired qualities have been used to produce more milk cattle. This process has gone on for generations until now the cows produce many times the quantity of milk that was produced by cows one hundred years ago. Of course, part of the credit for the increased milk production should be given to the scientific feeding that was not known at that time.

Several breeds of cattle have been developed into milk cows. Some are desirable because of the quantity of milk produced and some because of the cream content of the milk. The Holstein is one of the heaviest milk producers; the Jerseys and Guernseys produce the highest percentage of cream in their milk.

Beef cattle have been developed that are far superior to the native cattle. Hereford and Shorthorn cattle are two of the leading breeds that are raised for beef. They produce only enough milk to supply their calves, but they are capable of turning their food into fat until they bring a much better price on the market than ordinary cattle.

Shorthorn breeders, especially, have developed a dual-purpose cow—one that is capable of becoming fat enough to bring a good price for meat, but also capable of producing paying quantities of milk.

The old saying that "like begets like" is demonstrated quite clearly on the farm. The farmer who has "scrub" cattle and crossbreeds them always has an inferior herd of cattle, profitable neither for milk nor for beef production. If he keeps the same herd, but crosses them with cattle of superior type, he can eventually build up his herd into one of much higher quality.

Man has domesticated wild fowls and then carefully selected and bred them until they are far superior to their ancestors. Chickens are the most common of the domesticated fowls. Here again he has developed them with two purposes in mind—eggs and meat. Some breeds, as the Leghorns, are very small but are prolific layers. Other breeds are more valuable as meat producers.

The study of animals for cultural reasons is encouraged by the establishment of public zoölogical gardens.

RELATIONSHIPS AND ADAPTATIONS

In the scheme of nature, life is a system of checks and balances. Note what takes place, for example, in a glass bowl containing goldfish. The fish liberate carbon dioxide in respiration and absorb oxygen from the water. The green plants in the bowl use the carbon dioxide released by the fish and manufacture food, at the same time releasing more oxygen to be used by the fish. Snails are placed in the bowl to keep it clean by devouring refuse. So the cycle is completed.

The same cycle takes place on a large scale in the world of nature. Besides the carbon-dioxide cycle, there is a nitrogen cycle. Plants require nitrogen in the form of nitrates. Animals use the plants for food

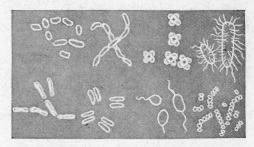

MICROSCOPIC VIEWS OF BACTERIA
The rod-shaped ones are *bacilli;* the spherical, *cocci;* and the spiral, *spirilla*. Bacilli and cocci are the commonest forms.

and eliminate wastes. Bacteria cause the waste matter to decay and form ammonia. Nitrifying bacteria change the ammonia to nitrites and finally to nitrates, which the plants take from the soil. Thus plants deplete the soil by using nitrates and animals make up for the loss. If this balance is upset the soil loses its fertility. It has been said that "all flesh is grass," because animals depend directly or indirectly upon plants for food.

These cycles are general and apply to the whole plant and animal kingdom. There are also individual relationships between plants and animals, between one plant and another plant, and between one animal and another animal.

An interesting relationship is that between insects and flowers. Many flowers are brightly colored and have markings that lead to the base of the flower, where nectar is formed. An insect, attracted by the color and the presence of the nectar, crawls into the flower. Its body becomes dusted with pollen. Then the insect flies to another flower and crawls into it to secure nectar. As the insect enters the second flower, the stigma of the pistil comes in contact with the pollen on the back of the insect and the flower is pollinated. The repetition of this process causes numerous flowers to be pollinated and ensures the production of countless seeds. The process is known as cross pollination.

Ants and plant lice have a peculiar relationship. The ants carefully protect the eggs of plant lice, and when the young lice hatch, the ants place them on the roots of the corn plant. The lice feed on this plant and secrete a sweet substance which is food for the ants.

Birds and insects illustrate the check and balance system in nature. Insects are the most prolific form of life. If they had no natural enemies they would overrun the earth in a short time. The offspring of a common house fly would number millions in a single season if nothing happened to any of the generations produced. Birds are natural enemies of insects and help to keep them in check. For that reason, wild bird life should be protected. It has been estimated that life on the earth could not exist more than ten years if all birds were destroyed. Insects would have destroyed all forms of vegetation. Birds are also useful in carrying seeds from one location to another.

Each form of life appears to have a natural enemy that keeps it in check. Man sometimes upsets the balance of nature. For instance, he imports fruit trees subject to insect pests. In the country of their origin, these trees are protected by natural enemies of the fruit-eating pests. In the country to which the trees are brought there are no natural enemies to prey on the insects, and the latter, brought in with the trees, become a menace to other species.

The United States Department of Agriculture has made a study of this problem and will give information on request.

Plants and animals have been engaged in an intense struggle for existence since the era of primitive life. If an organism appeared that was particularly well adapted for life in its environment, it survived. Organisms less well adapted became extinct. During the geological past, when the earth's surface underwent great alterations, many forms of life were unable to adapt themselves to changed conditions and perished. Others became modified in various ways. The struggle for existence is going on today, and very interesting are some of the adaptations by which plants and animals obtain food and protection and ensure the perpetuation of their kind.

The hermit crab and the sea anemone typify adaptation for protection. The hermit crab protects itself by living in an abandoned shell. As a further protection it carries upon the back of this shell one or more sea anemones. Sea anemones are animals that look like flowers because of the tentacles grouped around the open end of the tubular body. The sea anemone shoots out stinging darts at animals upon which it preys or which it wishes to avoid. This mode of attack also helps to protect the crab. The crab, by moving about, gives the anemone a means of transportation.

Deep-sea fish must adapt themselves to the absence of light and great pressure. How do they meet these conditions? The eyes project from the head like a flashlight and have a phosphorescent glow that enables the fish to see their prey. They have also developed great internal pressure to counteract the pressure of the water.

The long neck of the giraffe enables it to get food from the higher trees. The wolf can run swiftly to catch his prey and has sharp teeth to tear the flesh. The horse has flat teeth for grinding his food. The cow, which is a cud-chewing animal, has a stomach compartment for storing the grass which it swallows as it grazes and enjoys later when resting.

Plants that are unable to secure necessary nitrogen capture insects and devour them. Typical examples of these carnivorous plants are the pitcher plant and Venus's flytrap. The name of the pitcher plant refers to the shape of the leaves. It is easy for the insect to follow the bright markings on the lip of the pitcher and crawl downward, but its return path is blocked by sharp bristles. The insect falls into water at the bottom of the pitcher and is drowned. The plant is nourished by the decayed body of the insect. In the case of Venus's flytrap, each leaf has a broadened tip hinged in the center. The leaf margins are prolonged to form hairs. When the insect touches the hairs the two halves of the leaf close upon it.

Some plants in order to survive have formed a willing and sometimes an unwilling partnership with other plants. Among them are such parasites as the mistletoe and dodder. The mistletoe has seeds which are carried by birds to a tree, where they lodge in the bark. The seeds germinate and produce roots that penetrate into the vascular system of the tree. The mistletoe then is almost a part of the tree. It has green leaves and can manufacture some of its food, but it depends upon the tree in large part. Dodder, a yellow tangle of slender vine, is a parasite common to a number of plants.

In the tropics and semitropical regions, plants have adaptations that enable them to live without roots. There are air plants, such as Spanish moss, that hang from branches of trees. Air plants absorb the required moisture from the air.

There are several interesting devices used by animals for eluding enemies. The squid, a sea animal, when too closely pursued, ejects an inky fluid into the water that bewilders its enemy or its prey. The puff fish starts to swell when touched, and reaches a size sufficient to startle an enemy and accomplish its own escape.

The opossum, when hopelessly cornered, feigns death, hoping to deceive its enemy. Many birds pretend to be crippled and let an observer pursue them for a considerable distance before they fly away. Such birds merely lead intruders away from their nests.

The turtle lives in an armor or shell that is effective protection. When seriously threatened it withdraws its head and feet into its shell, and it is very difficult for an enemy to reach any vital spot in the turtle's body. The oyster also has a protective shell. The porcupine is covered with quills that are easily loosened and cause painful wounds when they penetrate flesh. It would be a foolhardy animal that attacked a porcupine.

A different type of adaptation is shown in the seasonal migration of birds. A few stay in one locality the year round, but most birds spend the winter in one region and the summer in another. The wild Canada geese lay their eggs and raise their young in the far north, and on the approach of winter fly to the South Atlantic and Gulf states, where food is plentiful. The golden plover breeds above the Arctic Circle, and then migrates to the southeastern part of South America. The homes of these birds during the two seasons are thousands of miles apart. Some birds travel steadily during migration until they reach their destination. They sometimes fly fifty miles per hour, even crossing large stretches of ocean.

In warfare, measures are taken to alter airdromes, planes and ships by means of camouflage. They are painted or disguised in such manner that their color blends with their surroundings. Nature accomplishes the same result by protective coloration. It is difficult to see a tiger in a woods where there are alternate patches of sunlight and shadow. A woodcock sitting on her nest may be overlooked, even though an observer is almost upon her. The white polar bear can hardly be seen against the white background of snow and ice. The chameleon, a lizard, changes its color to blend with those of its surroundings, although this is not a voluntary act. There are some animals, particularly birds, that are brightly colored to attract their mates during the breeding season.

Animals sometimes imitate other objects or animals. The monarch butterfly is very distasteful to birds. The viceroy butterfly looks much like the monarch, but does not have its disagreeable odor and taste. This similarity keeps it from being eaten by birds. Certain leaf insects have their wings shaped and colored like foliage. When one of them alights upon a twig and closes its wings, it requires very careful scrutiny for an observer to tell the insect from the tree.

These are only a few of the methods adopted by plants and animals to protect themselves in the struggle for existence. Plants and animals also have various ways of preventing their extinction as a race. Fish ensure perpetuation of the species by producing thousands upon thousands of eggs. Large numbers are eaten by sea animals and many others are never fertilized, but enough eggs are hatched to keep the various kinds of fish from extinction. It has been estimated that a female cod of average size will produce 2,700,000 eggs in one spawning season.

The articles listed below contain interesting material on various phases of the subjects covered in the foregoing paragraphs:

Bibliography

BARROWS, W. M. *Science of Animal Life.* World Book Co.

BEEBE, W. *Arcturus Adventure.* G. P. Putnam's Sons.

BOULENGER, E. G. *Natural History of the Seas.* D. Appleton-Century Co.

BURBANK, LUTHER. *Harvest of the Year.* Comstock Publishing Co.

CHAPMAN, F. M. *Bird Life.* D. Appleton-Century Co.

COMSTOCK, A. B. *Handbook of Nature Study.* Comstock Publishing Co.

COMSTOCK, J. H. *Insect Life.* D. Appleton-Century Co.

CURTIS, F. D. *Everyday Biology.* Ginn & Co.

DE KRUIF, PAUL. *Microbe Hunters.* Harcourt, Brace & Co.

DITMARS, R. L. *Reptiles.* The Macmillan Co.

HALDANE, J. B. S. *Animal Biology.* Oxford University Press.

HEGNER, R. W. *Parade of the Animal Kingdom.* The Macmillan Co.

HOGBEN, LANCELOT. *Principles of Animal Biology.* W. W. Norton & Co.

HORNADAY, W. T. *Mind and Manners of Wild Animals.* Charles Scribner's Sons.

KENLY, J. C. *Green Magic.* D. Appleton-Century Co.

MILLS, ENOS. *Adventures of a Nature Guide.* Doubleday, Doran & Co.

NATIONAL GEOGRAPHIC SOCIETY. *Book of Birds.*

——. *Book of Animals.*

QUINN, VERNON. *Seeds: Their Place in Life and Legend.* Frederick A. Stokes Co.

SETON, E. T. *Lives of Game Animals.* Doubleday, Doran & Co.

THOMPSON, SIR J. A. *Biology for Everyman.* E. P. Dutton & Co.

WEED, C. M. *Our Trees: How to Know Them.* J. B. Lippincott Co.

YATES, R. F. *Exploring with the Microscope.* D. Appleton-Century Co.

Man's Use of Physics and Chemistry to Improve His Condition

Man's present mastery of natural forces is the result of his superior intelligence, his capacity for reasoning and certain physical advantages, such as his upright posture and flexible hand with an apposable thumb. Through his understanding and applications of energy, machines and chemical reactions, he has made great strides in the conquest of time and space, in the mastery of disease and in economic and social improvement.

The physical sciences, probably more than any other branch of knowledge, have been used by man to improve his economic and social condition. Of these sciences, physics and chemistry are among the most important. Both are concerned with matter, energy and the laws governing changes of matter.

Physics is essentially a study of the properties of matter and the use of energy to create power. Chemistry deals with the changes in matter that result in the production of new materials. The two sciences are so closely related that it is impossible to separate them completely. The chemist cannot carry out reactions without considering energy. In the research laboratories of our great universities the physicist and the chemist are frequently at work on similar problems.

By applying the principles of physics and chemistry man has done much to make his lot easier. The following sections present examples of such application of scientific laws.

UTILIZATION OF AIR AND WATER

One of man's great achievements is his utilization of air and water in connection with machines. A typical example of the use of air may be seen daily in an automobile garage. In the pneumatic tires of the cars are myriads of air molecules striking ceaselessly against the walls of the inner tubes. According to the kinetic theory of matter, the molecules of all material bodies are in constant motion, but because the molecules of gases possess small power of cohesion, such a substance as air (a gas) tends to expand indefinitely. When it is compressed in a container such as a pneumatic tube, the movement of the molecules produces great pressure on the walls of the tube. For this reason the inflated tire provides an elastic cushion that prevents excessive jarring on rough surfaces.

Travel on swift trains has been made safe by brakes operated by compressed air. The

AVIATORS DEPEND UPON THE AIR

top speed of any conveyance should be judged more by its ability to stop than by the power of the motor that starts it and keeps it moving, in spite of friction between the machinery and the air. The air brake was invented by George Westinghouse shortly after the close of the Civil War. Up to the time of his history-making invention, all trains were stopped by application of hand brakes on the individual cars. A crew of men was needed to keep the train under control, even at low speeds common at that time.

Molecules of water may also be put to work, both in liquid form and in the gaseous state called steam. The motive power of water is utilized today through the construction of dams which form artificial lakes containing many cubic miles of water. In falling, every cubic foot of water gives out as much energy by that fall as would be required to raise it to its original position. When one cubic foot of water, weighing 62.4 pounds, falls over the face of a cliff or a dam and drops 100 feet, the amount of work done is equal to 6,240 foot pounds, friction being disregarded. When work is being done at the rate of 550 foot pounds each second, we say that work accomplished has the value of one horse power.

Horse power does not actually measure the rate at which a horse can do the work. Years ago the arbitrary rate of 550 foot pounds per second was set up as the standard unit of power. If one pound is lifted 550 foot pounds in one second, or fifty-five pounds are lifted ten feet in one second, or 550 pounds are lifted one foot in one second, the rate of doing work is the same, namely, 550 foot pounds per second, or one horse power.

In the production of electric power, the kinetic (moving) energy of water is used

to move a turbine, which in turn drives the generator of a hydroelectric plant, transforming mechanical into electrical energy.

For further reading on the use of air and water as sources of power, and for related topics, consult the following articles:

Air Brake	Hydraulics
Atmosphere	Hydrostatic Press
Compressed Air	Hydrostatics
Dam	Pneumatic Tires
Energy	Pneumatic Tools
Expansion	Pneumatic Tubes
Foot Pound	Turbine
Force	Water
Gas	Water Power
Horse Power	Water Wheel
Hydraulic Ram	Work

APPLIED ENERGY OF FUELS

The energy of falling water is described as kinetic energy. Energy of position, or stored energy, is potential energy. Such is the energy of fuel before it is subjected to heat. When fuels are heated or burned, potential energy is transformed into kinetic energy and useful work may be done or useful products evolved.

When coal is heated in a closed container without a supply of oxygen, several products are given off. The process is known as destructive distillation and results finally in the solid product, coke. For many years coke ovens were operated wastefully, since the valuable gaseous products of soft coal were permitted to escape. Now the gases are conserved and utilized. Coal gas is evolved in large quantities and stored in steel tanks. Ammonia gas, a second product of the destructive distillation, is removed from the gas by treatment with sulphuric acid, which combines with the ammonia to form ammonium sulphate. Tar is also removed from the gas by being condensed on tubes carrying cold water.

The product remaining in the ovens at the end of the heating process is coke. From one ton of coal the following products are obtained: 1,200 pounds of coke, a fuel used in smelting iron and other metals; 200 pounds of ammonium sulphate, used for fertilizer; 100 pounds of tar, and 8,000 cubic feet of gas. These figures are approximate, as the quantities vary with the kind of coal. Hard coal, or anthracite, gives off very little gaseous product when heated, and it burns with a short, blue flame. The flames from burning soft coal are long and yellow.

When wood is heated in a closed vessel it also decomposes into a variety of products. The residue will be charcoal; the gases driven off contain acetone, wood alcohol and acetic acid, or wood vinegar. Charcoal has great power to absorb odors and colors from organic compounds. Charcoal from very dense woods, such as fruit stones, is used in gas-mask canisters, since it has the power of ensnaring the comparatively large molecules of poisonous gases as they pass through with the air. The purified air passes to the facepiece, and chemicals mixed with the charcoal slowly destroy the poisonous compounds.

Acetic acid from wood has wide use in the preparation of artificial fibers, film for photographic purposes and vinegar. Acetone finds use as a solvent in various industries, and wood alcohol is used as an anti-freeze preparation for automobile radiators. It is also employed as a solvent in the manufacture of varnishes. Wood alcohol is a poisonous compound which causes blindness or death when taken internally.

In certain sections of the world, rich stores of petroleum and natural gas are found. Until late in the nineteenth century, not more than a few barrels of petroleum were used each year, but the development of the kerosene lamp built up a demand for what was then called coal oil. With the invention and rapid improvement of the automobile, the demand for petroleum products increased tremendously. In fact, our machine age is dependent on liquid fuels and the petroleum lubricants which grease the wheels of industry. Some of our largest corporations have developed in connection with the petroleum industry. Modern streamlined trains, airplanes, battleships and the automobile owe their energy of motion to the combustion of oil fuels derived from petroleum. Probably petroleum has had a greater

effect on modern industrial progress than any other natural product.

Natural gas is now being piped to all parts of the United States. Chicago burns gas which left the ground in Texas. Natural-gas wells on farms provide a seemingly inexhaustible supply of fuel for light, cooking and heating. How long will this supply of oil and gas last? Some experts predict a fast-dwindling supply of easily obtained oil. But, as the demand for petroleum products increases, oil wells go deeper into the ground and produce new supplies of the precious fluid. A few wells have been drilled to a depth of over three miles.

Although man should not be wasteful of the fuels now being exploited, he has other sources upon which to draw. There are limitless supplies of oil-bearing shale from which oil can be extracted. The cost of this process is as yet too high for commercial use; however, as the supply of underground petroleum nears exhaustion, new and more efficient methods will be devised to recover the petroleum found in oil-bearing rock. Another possibility is the development of liquid fuels from certain plant materials grown on the farm.

Where a fuel is to be burned to give mechanical or electrical energy, a special type of apparatus is needed. Such a mechanism is an engine. There are two general types of this heat-using machine—the internal-combustion and the expansion type— represented by the gas engine of an automobile and the steam engine of a railroad locomotive.

In the former, fuel combines with oxygen to form gases that expand under the heat of the burning and push on the piston of the engine. Another type of internal-combustion engine was invented in 1892 by Rudolph Diesel, a German engineer. In the Diesel engine, use is made of the principle that gases develop heat by compression. Hence a spark is not needed to ignite the mixture of fuel and air. Diesel engines weigh more per unit of power developed than other types of internal-combustion engines, and are finding use in trains, boats and stationary powerhouses rather than in pleasure automobiles and airplanes. Future developments, of course, may change the picture entirely.

In the steam engine the fuel is burned under a boiler and the heat energy is passed to the water in the boiler, which is converted into steam. The water molecules in the form of steam possess great kinetic en-

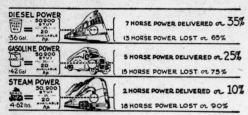

THE EFFICIENCY OF PRIME MOVERS

ergy, which is passed on to the piston. As the gas expands it cools, and the heat energy of the steam is converted into mechanical energy of the piston. In the turbine the expansion takes place against a series of blades which drive the rotating section of the turbine at high speed, developing power very efficiently.

In the operation of a heating plant in the modern home, the latent energy of coal, gas or other fuel is converted into kinetic energy. Heat energy is distributed through the building from a furnace or other central plant. There are several ways by which this distribution is accomplished. The heat may be carried through pipes to the rooms in the form of heated air which circulates throughout the house, losing its heat energy and finally returning through a cold-air duct to be reheated and recirculated.

A second method depends on the fact that heated water will rise. Pipes convey the rising hot water to radiators in the various rooms. There the water transfers its heat energy to the air in the room and, having cooled off, sinks through return pipes to the boiler to be reheated. Both the hot-water and hot-air systems depend on convection, which is the upward movement of masses of liquids or gases, caused by the expansion of these substances when heated. This expansion results in a decrease of density. The lighter air or water is pushed up by heavier particles, and the result is the formation of convection currents.

Steam heating finds favor in many large buildings. When water at 212° F. changes to steam at 212° F., a large quantity of heat energy is absorbed. The steam passes through pipes to the rooms of the building. In the radiator, the steam returns to the liquid state, but does so only by releasing

the same heat energy as was required to make steam from water. Air-conditioned buildings are equipped with air-heating and air-cooling machinery.

For additional information on the subject of energy, use of fuels and kindred topics, see the following headings:

Automobile	Heating and
Boiler	Ventilation
Boiling Point	Humidity
Calorie	Melting Point
Carbon Dioxide	Oils
Carburetor	Oxidation
Charcoal	Oxygen
Coal	Petroleum
Coke	Steam
Combustion	Steam Engine
Diesel Engine	Tar
Distillation	Temperature
Evaporation	Thermometer
Gas, Natural	Thermostat
Gasoline	Vapor
Heat	Wood Alcohol

Bibliography

ANDRADE, E. N. *Engines.* Harcourt, Brace & Co.
DIGGLE, E. G. *Romance of the Modern Liner.* Oxford University Press.
DORRANCE, J. G. *Story of a Forest.* American Book Co.
EHRENFELD, L. *Story of Common Things.* Minton, Balch & Co.
ELLSBERG, E. *On the Bottom.* Dodd, Mead & Co.
FRASER, C. *Story of Aircraft.* Thomas Y. Crowell Co.
GOLDSMITH, M. *Zeppelin: A Biography.* Wm. Morrow & Co.
HARNEY, L. B. *Skycraft.* D. C. Heath & Co.
HAWKS, E. *Romance of Transport.* Thomas Y. Crowell Co.
HUSBAND, J. *A Year in a Coal Mine.* Houghton, Mifflin Co.
INNIS, H. A. *Fur Trade in Canada.* Oxford University Press.
KOHLER, K. *A History of Costume.* Harper & Bros.
LARGE, L. A. *Air Travelers.* Lothrop, Lee & Shepard Co.
MARSON, P. *Glass and Glass Manufacture.* Sir I. Pitman & Sons.
MILLS, E. *Story of 1000 Year Pine.* Doubleday, Doran & Co.
MOTT-SMITH, M. *Story of Energy.* D. Appleton-Century Co.
MURPHY, C. J. W. *Parachute.* G. P. Putnam's Sons.
NORMAN, O. E. *The Romance of the Gas Industry.* A. C. McClurg & Co.
RICHARDSON, J. M. *Man's Wings.* Reilly & Lee Co.
ROSENDAHL, C. E. *Up Ship!* Dodd, Mead & Co.
SHEARD, C. *Life-Giving Light.* Williams & Wilkins Co.
TALMAN, C. F. *The Realm of the Air.* The Bobbs-Merrill Co.
TEALE, E. W. *Book of Gliders.* E. P. Dutton & Co.
UNDERHILL, C. R. *Electrons at Work.* McGraw-Hill Book Co.

PRINCIPLES AND APPLICATIONS OF THE MACHINE

Man controls natural forces through the use of machines. An analysis of the mechanical details of all known machines shows that they are based on six primary machines. These six machines can be grouped into two general classes—machines embodying the principle of the lever and those based on the inclined plane. To the former group belong the lever itself, the wheel and axle and the pulley. To the latter class belong the inclined plane itself, the wedge and the screw. In using machines we increase force, gain speed or change the direction of an applied force. The advantage thus gained is known as the mechanical advantage.

In its simplest form, the lever is a bar free to turn about a fixed point called the fulcrum. Mathematically stated, the weight multiplied by the weight arm (the distance the weight moves) is equal to the force multiplied by the force arm (the distance the force moves). The arrangement of weight, force and fulcrum varies, but the mathematical statement holds for all cases. It should be remembered, however, that the law stated above disregards friction, and is only theoretically true; that is, it is mathematically correct only when applied to frictionless machines.

The wheel and axle is used as such in mine hoists operated manually. Here the weight is attached to a rope which winds up on the axle of the machine, while the force acts on the rim of the wheel. The radius of the axle is really the lever arm of the weight, while the radius of the wheel is the lever arm of the force. Two geared wheels on the same shaft constitute a similar machine.

Different-sized pulleys are also examples of levers, although the balance of forces requires a somewhat different mathematical treatment.

The fundamental principle of the inclined plane is that a small force acting through a long distance will equal a large force operating over a small distance. For instance, if a workman wishes to hoist a 600-pound barrel into a truck which is five feet high, he must do 3,000 foot pounds of work to place it there. Whether the barrel is lifted directly up to the truck or is moved along an inclined plane such as a plank, the work done is the same (friction being ignored). If he places one end of a twenty-foot plank on the ground and the other end on the floor of the truck, by rolling the barrel the length of the plank he will have raised the object the necessary five feet and will have done the 3,000 foot pounds of work required. (Work is always force times distance.)

The force which he must apply for the twenty-foot push will not be the entire weight of the barrel, but must be more than enough to counterbalance its tendency to roll down the incline. Most of the weight of the barrel will rest on the plank. To do the needed 3,000 foot pounds of work, a force of 150 pounds must act on the barrel for the entire length of the plank.

The common jackscrew works on the same principle, but in this case friction plays a large part. This machine is raised by means of a force applied to a bar or handle which moves in a circle around the screw.

Man uses the principles of simple machines to gain a mechanical advantage over gravity or cohesive forces. We may calculate a mechanical advantage by noting how many times larger the weight moved is than the force that acts upon it. If a steel bar (lever) is used to move a stone weighing 1,000 pounds and the force applied is 100 pounds, the mechanical advantage is 1,000 ÷ 100, or 10. When a 600-pound barrel is hoisted into the truck by a 150-pound force, the mechanical advantage is 600 ÷ 150, or 4.

Although the simple machine seems to be an ideal arrangement, we must remember that friction partially defeats the purpose of the machine by deducting some of the usable mechanical advantage. To eliminate as much friction as possible, almost all fast-moving machines now run on ball bearings or roller bearings. These smooth, round surfaces cause the least possible friction, especially when all surfaces are bathed in lubricating oil or grease. Graphite, one of the forms of carbon, makes an excellent lubricating agent for chains and slow-moving gears. Certain alloys are on the market which contain the lubricating agents in the metal and hence need no additional lubrication.

The applications and principles of the machine are further considered under the following titles:

Friction	Pulley
Gearing	Screw
Inclined Plane	Wedge
Lever	Wheel and Axle
Machine	

Bibliography

BOCK, G. E. *What Makes the Wheels Go Round.* The Macmillan Co.

BUSH, M. G. *How We Have Conquered Distance.* The Macmillan Co.

HIBBEN, THOMAS. *Carpenter's Tool Chest.* J. B. Lippincott Co.

LANSING, M. F. *Man's Long Climb.* Little, Brown & Co.

MARSHALL, L. C. *Story of Human Progress.* The Macmillan Co.

MEISTER, MORRIS. *Energy and Power.* Charles Scribner's Sons.

High-School List

FRASER, CHELSEA. *Story of Engineering in America.* Thomas Y. Crowell Co.

HUBERMAN, LEO. *Man's Worldly Goods: The Story of the Wealth of Nations.* Harper & Bros.

MILLER, J. A. *Master Builders of Sixty Centuries*. D. Appleton-Century Co.

PEET, CREIGHTON. *How Things Work*. Henry Holt & Co.

ROGERS, AGNES. *From Man to Machine*. Little, Brown & Co.

SCHMUCKER, S. C. *Man's Life on Earth*. The Macmillan Co.

MAN'S UTILIZATION OF ELECTRIC ENERGY

Most of our present-day machines use electricity in some form. The practical application of electricity is dependent on the mutual relationship between electricity and magnetism. Electrical generators and transmission of electric energy for light and power are of comparatively recent date. But certain fundamental facts about electricity and magnetism have been known for many centuries.

Before the time of Columbus, the mariner's compass had been invented. It was a magnetized needle which was free to adjust itself in the magnetic field of the earth, which is itself a huge magnet. One end of the compass will always point toward the magnetic pole of the earth. Since the magnetic north pole is not located at the corresponding geographical pole, but about 20° south of it, the compass will read incorrectly for various points on the earth's surface. Maps have been prepared which show the amount of magnetic deviation for all localities. By use of this correction, the true north can be determined without difficulty.

Early investigators found that a piece of soft iron could be given a temporary magnetic condition if an insulated wire was wrapped around it many times and electric current passed through the wire. This type of magnet, by far the most important kind, is called an electro-magnet. It is the basis of all our electric power and of electric motors, the telegraph, the electric bell and other electro-magnetic devices.

We picture a magnet of either the permanent or electro-magnet type as being surrounded by a field of force. The field of magnetic force may be thought of as made up of imaginary curved lines running between the north and south poles of the magnet. The important fact about the magnetic field is that, if the lines are cut by a wire, an electrical current is set in motion in the wire. As long as the lines are being cut the current flows; the amount of current depends on the rate at which the lines are cut and on the number of wires doing the cutting.

It is upon this principle that our largest electrical generators operate. Very powerful electro-magnets are rotated on a shaft so that the lines of force which surround them cut through many turns of wire on the stationary frame of the machine. Since no energy can be produced except at the expense of some other energy, we are correct in assuming that the turbines which turn the electric generator are delivering enor-

Westinghouse

ELECTRICAL ENERGY MAKES LIGHT

Left: Fluorescent lights for industry. *Right:* Rotating beacons to guide night flyers; the beams can be seen for twenty miles.

Westinghouse

GENERATORS OF GREAT RESERVOIRS OF ELECTRIC POWER
Left: A closeup of a 500-ton generator. *Right:* An 1100-ton steam turbo-generator.

mous quantities of energy which they have received from the steam or water power which turns them.

After electricity has been generated, it must be distributed before it can be put to useful work. A remarkable system of distribution has been developed in America. Power-generating stations are linked up in such a way that electric power produced at Boston might conceivably be used in Kansas City, or the reverse might be true. High-voltage power lines are found in all sections of the country. Mounted on high steel towers, these wires in some cases carry electrical energy at a pressure of 200,000 volts. The ordinary electric light uses current at 110 volts. For the economic transmission of current, it has been found best to generate it at about 12,000 volts and then raise the voltage, by use of a step-up transformer, to such pressures as 200,000 or more volts. When the current is used, a step-down transformer lowers the voltage to any pressure required.

In our homes we have many devices which use electrical energy to lighten the daily work of the housewife. All require more or less energy that must be paid for. Two factors determine the amount of current used—voltage, or pressure, and amperage, or strength. These two factors, when multiplied, give watts of energy. An electric meter, located on the premises of each customer, automatically measures both amperage and voltage, multiplies them and determines how long the current has been used. The final reading shows how many watts of energy were used and for how

many hours. As a convenience, we use the kilowatt hour, a kilowatt being 1,000 watts.

To protect the wiring of our homes from dangerous overloads or short circuits, we place a fuse in the line. The fuse is composed of a short piece of metal which will melt if too much current flows, and thereby break the circuit until a new fuse is installed. Because of the increase in home appliances, wiring systems of today are carefully engineered, so that no part of the circuit is overloaded. All wires are carried through iron-pipe conduits as a precaution against any chance loss of insulation and short circuits which might cause fire.

Benjamin Franklin was the first prominent American to carry on experiments in connection with electricity. His greatest discovery was that lightning and electricity are identical. History does not tell us of any practical use for Franklin's discovery except the lightning rod. That piece of equipment may be seen projecting from the roofs of farm buildings in certain localities.

Another American, S. F. B. Morse, used electricity to carry messages over a wire. By means of a key, he passed an interrupted current through a wire to the receiving instrument, where the current created an intermittent electro-magnet by passing through a coil of wire wound around a piece of soft iron. Whenever the current flowed, the electro-magnet attracted a piece of soft iron, causing a clicking sound. This series of audible clicks, arranged as a code of dots and dashes for the letters and figures, soon made it possible for code messages to be sent with considerable speed.

Naturally, the next step in the progress of communication was to send the human voice. That great achievement was accomplished by Alexander Graham Bell in 1876. Bell's first telephone used a small box containing granules of carbon which could be closely packed or loosely packed by vibrations from a diaphragm. A variable current passed through the wires because the pressure on the carbon granules changed the conductivity of the circuit with each vibration caused by the air waves of the speaker's voice. This fluctuating current went to the receiver at the other end of the circuit, where it set up vibrations in another diaphragm by means of electro-magnetic action that varied with the current flowing in the line. The result was an exact duplication of the vibrations of the speaker's voice in the receiver at the other end of the circuit.

Such simple machines would be neither convenient nor efficient now, but they were the forerunners of the highly developed communication system that now serves all parts of the United States. Today it is as easy to call San Francisco from New York as it was to get a station ten miles away in 1900. And with the advent of radio, all parts of the world were brought into close communication with one another.

Transoceanic telephone calls are first transmitted by wire to short-wave broadcasting stations, whence they are sent to Europe by radio. Messages may then be relayed by wire as far as Australia. The submarine cable also may play its part in transmitting messages to be continued by radio telephony. When the message is transmitted by radio, it is customary to "scramble" the sounds; thus no listener hears anything during the transit except a noise which has faintly familiar characteristics, but no meaning.

Seeing by radio waves is now possible by means of television. A variable light source causes electric currents of varying intensity. These can be transmitted by wire or radio and reconverted into light beams duplicating the original source, thereby reproducing a picture of everything seen at the sending station.

The story of electricity and magnetism, including the applications of these forces to the industrial progress of the modern world, is told at length under the headings listed below. Other details may be found in this index on pages 4002 and 4003.

Armature	Electro-Motive
Cable, Submarine	Force
Chemistry	Electroplating
Compass	Electrotyping
Dynamo	Fuse
Electric Battery	Lightning
Electric Bell	Lightning Rod
Electric Heating	Magnetism
Electricity	Magneto-Electric
Electric Light	Machine
Electric Meter	Pole
Electric Motor	Radio
Electro-Chemistry	Telephone
Electrode	Telegraph
Electrolysis	Telegraph, Wireless
Electro-Magnet	Television
Electro-Magnetism	Volt
Electrometer	Watt

ENERGY OF SOUND

Sounds are caused by vibration of matter. The vibrating body—tuning fork, string, column of air in a whistle, etc.—causes a train of air waves which spread out from the source and move in all directions, gradually decreasing in intensity until we say that the noise is out of "hearing distance." The series of compressions and intervening rarefactions carry the sound through the air at a speed of about 1,100 feet per second. Yet this velocity is insignificant when compared to the speed of light, about 186,300 miles per second.

When sound waves are regular in frequency, they have a musical sound. The pitch of the musical note is determined by the number of waves per second. Middle C on the piano represents 256 vibrations per second; each octave ends in a C which has twice the vibration rate of the C below it.

From the standpoint of sound, a noise differs from a musical tone in the irregularity of the waves. The vibrations from a passing train have no musical qualities unless the bell rings or the whistle is blown.

For additional information, refer to the following titles:

Acoustics	Harmony
Chord	Music
Chromatic	Physics
Ear	Tone
Echo	Scale
Harmonics	Sound

ENERGY OF LIGHT

We live in a world near the middle of the scale of things large and things small. We use a telescope to look at stars that dwarf our sun; we use a microscope to see living organisms which are too small to be seen with the unaided eye, but which are complete entities. Beyond the microscope lies a field of study as complex as the world of stars and just as important to mankind.

Man has developed optical instruments which will permit him to put light to his own use. The ultra-microscope shows molecular motion; the X-ray photographs of crystals show the arrangement of the molecules and atoms in the crystal; the Wilson cloud chamber makes visible the paths, collisions and transmutation of atoms far beyond the vision of man. The operations of all these machines depend upon the properties of light.

Light is propagated as a wave motion, the motion being at right angles to the direction in which the light is traveling. The rays which produce the different colors vary in wave length and frequency, or number of vibrations per second, but all of them travel at the same speed, nearly 186,300 miles per second. The short waves with high frequency make up the violet end of the rainbow of colors known as the spectrum. The long red rays, with lower frequency, are found at the other end of the spectrum. In between lie the other colors—orange, yellow, green, blue and indigo.

Beyond the visible spectrum in both directions lie rays of varying wave lengths. Waves longer than those at the red end of the spectrum include the infra-red rays, which affect certain photographic films and produce heat, and radio waves of lengths up to several miles. Beyond the violet end of the spectrum we find ultra-violet rays, X-rays and gamma rays, of very short wave length and very high frequency. All the rays mentioned above are electro-magnetic in character. Gamma rays are emitted from radium atoms.

The similarity between the human eye and a camera is striking. The eye has a lens which is adjustable in thickness by the action of involuntary muscles. The variable thickness of the lens gives the necessary compensation for viewing close objects and distant objects. The image that enters the eye passes through the lens and is thrown on the retina at the back of the eyeball. There, nerve endings take the light impulses to the brain, where they are interpreted.

For further information, the following articles may be consulted:

Camera	Mirror
Color	Photography
Electro-magnetic	Prism
Theory of Light	Roentgen Rays
Eye	Spectacles
Lens	Spectroscope
Light	Spectrum Analysis
Microscope	Telescope

STRUCTURE OF MATTER

Even though man has improved the microscope greatly, we are far from seeing the ultimate particles of which matter is composed. If one cannot see these particles, how do we know that they exist? The chemist and physicist have amassed great evidence to support our modern idea of the structure of matter.

If a powerful beam of light is passed through a vessel containing smoke, and a microscope is focused on the smoke itself, small points of light can be seen dancing rapidly across the field of the microscope. This zigzag movement of particles is called the Brownian movement. We explain this motion, which never ceases no matter how long we wait, as being caused by collisions of molecules of air with the particles of smoke floating in the air.

The smoke particles are too small to be seen with the microscope, but the reflection of light from the minute surfaces of the particles can be seen. The many collisions keep the smoke particles in never-ending motion. We are able to see the result of the collision of molecules even though we cannot see the molecules themselves.

Matter is found in three states—as a gas, a liquid and a solid. Ice is water in the solid state. An ice crystal has a regular arrangement of the water molecules, in which the individuals are free to vibrate very rapidly around some more or less fixed point. In liquids the molecules are free to move among themselves, but they are held loosely together by cohesive forces. Gravity causes the liquid to have a horizontal surface; if we could see that surface in great enlargement, we would see molecules rising out of the surface and dropping back constantly.

When fast-moving molecules escape from the surface and join the air molecules above, the liquid is said to undergo evaporation. Heat applied to a liquid increases the average kinetic energy of the molecules, and some are speedy enough to escape the attractive forces which tend to keep the material in liquid form.

Gases are quite different in their physical state. A gas is free to move throughout the container, subject to the numerous collisions of its molecules with one another. A gas, therefore, will occupy the entire container, no matter how large it may be. If a colored substance like liquid bromine is placed at the bottom of a closed cylinder and allowed to vaporize, the red fumes will slowly spread through the entire cylinder, taking an hour or more to reach the top. Collisions with air molecules retard the free motion of the bromine molecules. But if an apparatus is so arranged that the cylinder can be evacuated by means of a good vacuum pump, and then a small vial of bromine is broken inside the evacuated cylinder, the entire vessel will fill with red fumes almost instantly. This experiment shows that gases spread throughout and very rapidly, too, if unhindered by the presence of other gases.

Molecules are divisible into smaller particles called atoms. Water is a compound

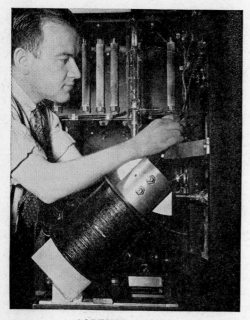

SORTING ATOMS
The mass spectrometer sorts atoms by weight.

because its molecules are composed of atoms not all of the same kind. That is, the individual atoms are not identical with water. The smallest particle of water is the molecule. The smallest particle of each of its elements—hydrogen and oxygen—is the atom. All known substances in the stars, sun and planets are composed of only ninety-two elements. The chemist uses his ninety-two elements somewhat as we use the twenty-six letters of the alphabet. We combine our letters to make different words; the chemist

combines his ninety-two elements to form compounds.

Before we can understand how the elements combine to form compounds, we must examine a single atom. The hydrogen atom is pictured as a system of two electrical charges. One positive charge, or proton, is in the center, and one negative charge, or electron, whirls around the central proton at high speed. The proton forms the nucleus of this simplest of atoms. The encircling electron weighs only 1/1850 as much as the proton. The oxygen atom is more complex. We believe it has a central core or nucleus in which there are eight protons and eight neutrons. Eight more electrons constituting an extra-nuclear negative charge are whirling around the nucleus in what must certainly be a complicated system.

Further information on the organization of matter is contained in the following articles:

Atom   Electricity
Atomic Theory   Gas
Atomic Weights   Liquid
Chemistry   Molecule
Cohesion   Radium

Bibliography

BEERY, P. G. *Chemistry Applied to Home and Community.* J. B. Lippincott Co.
BRAGG, W. *Concerning the Nature of Things.* Harper & Bros.
———. *The World of Sound.* E. P. Dutton & Co.
BURLINGAME, ROGER. *Engines of Democracy; Inventions and Society in Mature America.* Charles Scribner's Sons.
COX, R. T. *Time, Space and Atoms.* Williams & Wilkins Co.
DARROW, F. L. *Story of Chemistry.* The Bobbs-Merrill Co.
FOSTER, W. *Romance of Chemistry.* D. Appleton-Century Co.
GIBSON, C. R. *Our Good Slave, Electricity.* J. B. Lippincott Co.
HAAS, A. *The World of Atoms.* D. Van Nostrand Co.
HARROW, B. *The Romance of the Atom.* Boni & Liveright.
HOWE, H. E. *Chemistry in the World's Work.* D. Van Nostrand Co.
———. *Chemistry in Industry.* Chemical Foundation.
KENDALL, J. *At Home Among the Atoms.* Century Co.
LAMBERT, C. B. *Talking Wires.* The Macmillan Co.
LANGDON-DAVIES, J. *Inside the Atom.* Harper & Bros.
MOYER, J. A., & FITTZ, R. V. *Refrigeration.* McGraw-Hill Book Co.
SCHLESINGER, H. I. *General Chemistry.* Longmans, Green & Co.
WARD, HAROLD. *New Worlds in Science.* Robert M. McBride & Co.

CHEMICAL REACTIONS AND PROCESSES

A large body of evidence supports our imaginary picture of the structure of the elements. A better idea will doubtless be obtained when man learns to put the elements together or tear them apart at his will. Let us study the cloud of electrons that swarm about the nucleus. Most of the ninety-two elements have a tendency to either gain a few more electrons or give up a few, depending on the orientation of the electrons in the neutral atom. For instance, hydrogen likes to give up its one electron, thereby acquiring a positive charge. Oxygen, on the other hand, likes to gain two electrons or two units of negative charge.

Here, then, is the secret of why the elements combine in varying numbers of atoms. Water, as stated above, is a compound of hydrogen and oxygen. Because unlike charges attract, two hydrogen atoms attach themselves to the one oxygen atom to form one molecule of HOH or H_2O. The letters used to indicate the elements are symbols. When combined to show the composition of the molecule, they constitute the chemical formula of the substance. The formula for a molecule of carbon joined to chlorine atoms is CCl_4.

The measure of the ability of an element to take up electrons or give off electrons is known as its valence. When we know the valence of an element we can write the formula for any of its compounds by getting the elements arranged so that there are as many positive charges as negative charges in the molecule. If we know that aluminum has a valence of three positive charges and sulphur has two negative charges, it is apparent that to have a balance we must combine two aluminum atoms with three sulphur atoms to give aluminum sulphide (Al_2S_3). The chemist has catalogued and studied hundreds of thousands of compounds. New ones are being made synthetically as the chemist improves on natural materials and adapts them to new uses.

If elements combine with other elements because they gain or lose electrons, then the chemist is immediately interested in controlling this function of the elements. If the positive charge of some metallic element like aluminum is neutralized, it no longer has the ability to combine with other elements and the result is a free and uncombined metal. The metals are most important to man when they are in the free state. Usually, we find them in nature in the combined state; for example, aluminum oxide (Al_2O_3) and iron oxide (Fe_2O_3).

To free the metal from its compounds we reduce the positive charge to zero by adding electrons to the element. This process bears the special name of reduction. The opposite action, in which an element is made more positive, is known as oxidation. A large majority of chemical reactions depend on the reduction and oxidation of various elements dealt with.

The rusting of iron is an example of oxidation. The prevention of unwanted oxidation becomes a problem of prime importance in a world where metals are used so extensively. They are essential in the construction of large buildings, bridges, transportation machinery and manufacturing equipment. Fortunately, some metals are not subject to the action of oxygen under ordinary conditions and we may use them to plate iron for protection.

Acids, bases and salts make up the majority of our common chemicals. Acids have a sour taste and usually react with metals. All contain hydrogen. Examples of acids include the hydrochloric acid found in the human stomach; citric acid, found in lemons; boric acid, used as a weak antiseptic; acetic acid, a constituent of vinegar; nitric acid, and many others.

Bases are bitter and they may have a caustic action in contact with the skin; all contain some kind of mineral. A few examples of bases are limewater, milk of magnesia and potassium hydroxide. They have the power to neutralize acids. Naturally, the reverse is true: acids neutralize bases. The result of such neutralization is a salt and water. The chemical term *salt* refers to several different substances, one of which is common table salt, sodium chloride (Na Cl). Other familiar salts are epsom salts (magnesium sulphate, Mg SO_4) and baking soda, or sodium bicarbonate ($NaHCO_3$). Many salts are poisonous in a more or less violent manner. Bichloride of mercury ($HgCl_2$) has caused many fatalities because of its very poisonous properties; but it has valuable uses as a disinfectant when used externally by those who understand it.

Acids, bases and salts have an interesting property exhibited when they are dissolved in water. All acids contain hydrogen, and when the acid is put into water the molecule breaks into positive hydrogen ions and a negative ion of another sort, depending on what acid is under investigation. Sulphuric acid (H_2SO_4) gives two ions of hydrogen and one ion of sulphate. An ion is an atom or group of atoms carrying an electrical charge.

Bases ionize when placed in water, to give negative hydroxide ions in every case, and a positive ion depending on the base in question. Limewater is a solution of calcium hydroxide which ionizes to give two negative hydroxide ions and one positive calcium ion.

Salts behave in a similar manner, breaking down to form ions when dissolved in water. Aluminum chloride would give one ion of aluminum and three ions of chloride.

Some chemical reactions take place with much heat and light. Hydrogen gas will combine with oxygen in an explosive mixture if the proper proportions are used. Some chemical reactions like fire are often too rapid for man to control, and result in great loss of property and life. Other chemical reactions such as decay and corrosion take place slowly.

Certain small organisms such as yeast cause a chemical change to take place in sugar. This action is called fermentation, alcohol and carbon dioxide being formed. Pasteur made a study of yeasts early in his remarkable career. The wine industry of France called on him to save its product from ruin. He discovered that unwanted types of yeast were getting into the wine from the air and producing chemical changes and products that affected the taste of the wine. After careful study, Pasteur recommended that the wine be heated to kill all micro-organisms, then seeded with the desired strain of yeast to cause the required fermentation. This process, called pasteurization, was used in connection with wines long before being applied to milk.

Probably the most spectacular chemical reactions are to be seen in the steel industry. Except for small samples of pure iron in meteorites, iron is found in nature only in the combined state. The ore may be mined by sinking a shaft to the ore beds and then hoisting it to the surface, or it may be scooped up by large shovels from open pits.

When ore arrives at the steel mills it must first be reduced by chemical action to free iron. In large blast furnaces, the oxygen is taken from the iron ore (Fe_2O_3) by the action of carbon at high temperature. The molten iron is either formed into pigs of cast iron or is converted into steel immediately. To make steel, the cast iron is purified of excess carbon, sulphur, phosphorus and other impurities. Then a controlled amount of carbon and other elements is

THE EARTH GIVES MAN SHELTER
Steel, brick and wood come from the earth.

added in order to prepare a steel possessing certain properties. The finished steel is usually poured into ingot molds, and after solidifying is processed in the rolling mills, where it is formed into rails, beams or sheets, as needed.

The method used to recover iron from its compounds is used, in principle at least, for the metallurgy of copper, tin and zinc. In each case the problem is to reduce the metal chemically by taking away its positive charge so that it is incapable of attaching itself to the oxygen or sulphur found with it in nature. All metals except the noble metals—gold, platinum and silver—are found in a combined state in nature. In some sections pieces of free copper are found, but most of our copper is reduced from its ores.

The noble metals—gold, silver and platinum—have been mentioned as those which occur uncombined in the earth's crust. In recovering these metals, it is customary to eliminate the waste rock by washing away the lighter rock, leaving the heavy metal. Early gold-mining operations depended largely on the fact that the heavier gold remained behind in pans or troughs and the lighter gravel was washed away.

A metallic element thousands of times more valuable than platinum or gold is radium. It is one of the intermediate products in a long series of internal explosions of heavy atoms. In this process, called radioactivity, the heavy atoms shoot off

4069 MAN'S USE OF PHYSICS AND CHEMISTRY

electrons and positively charged helium nuclei with terrific speed, leaving a nucleus of another element. Radium is one of the elements evolved in the breaking down of uranium, the most complex element known. Chemists and physicists are constantly studying the radioactive elements in the hope of discovering a method of controlling the immense energy locked in their atoms.

The articles listed below are suggested for further reading:

PRACTICAL USES OF CHEMISTRY

Man has used his knowledge of chemical processes to increase and improve his food supply, to create new industrial and agricultural products, to combat disease and to lessen pain. Some of the products he has created are now employed for destructive purposes, but the general effect of chemical research has been to improve living conditions.

The chemist must be given credit for creating numerous new substances. He has ninety-two different kinds of atoms with which to work, and there are endless possibilities in the arrangements of these building stones. Especially noteworthy are the chemist's achievements in the field of dyes. For instance, coal-tar dyes have been made as substitutes for natural coloring matters. Indigo was prepared from the plant of that name until a young British chemist, William H. Perkin, discovered that dyes could be prepared from the by-product of the coke oven. Investigation showed that the tar was as valuable as the coke when distilled and separated into the naphtha, carbolic acid, creosote, anthracene and pitch which it contained. The chemist can duplicate almost any organic product by analyzing its molecular structure.

Cellulose is the basis for a number of substances which have been developed by the chemist. Cellulose occurs in nature as the cell wall of plants. In the manufacture of paper, cellulose fibers of wood are separated by beating and grinding machines. The fiber is bleached and refined before going through the paper-making machines.

When cellulose is dissolved in a suitable solvent and forced through fine openings into a hardening bath, it makes a thread which is used in place of silk for many purposes. The synthetic fabric is widely sold under the name rayon. A similar solution forced through a narrow slit into a hardening bath results in cellophane, the uses of which are known to all. Celluloid is another product of cellulose. The photographic industry is the largest user of celluloid, although this transparent, flexible substance is the basis of other plastics used to make toilet articles, buttons and other small non-metallic objects.

The chemist is responsible for great improvements in the art of soap making. In colonial days, the housewife made her own soap by boiling animal fat with lye or the water from soaked wood ashes.

Soap does its work of dirt and grease removal because of the peculiar structure of its molecule. The molecule has a first name, sodium; and sodium seems to have an affinity for water. The last name, representing the negative part of the molecule, is stearate. Stearate has a natural affinity for greases and other organic substances. The soap therefore forms a connecting link between the water and the substances to be removed, and makes possible their separation from fabrics. Hard water causes some difficulty with soap because the calcium, magnesium and iron in the water form a curdy insoluble material when they react with the soap. To combat this condition, some homes have water softeners which remove the metals named, before the water is used for household purposes.

A prominent soap company has attacked the hard-water problem from an entirely different angle by making a material in which the grease-attracting part of the molecule is the positive part, rather than the negative, as it is in ordinary soap. This product cleans like soap, but forms no insoluble curd with hard water. Again the chemist meets a problem and improves on an old time-honored product. Soap may well be considered as an index to the degree of civilization.

The chemist furnishes the air forces with smoke-screening material, white-phosphorus bombs and thermite bombs. These are in addition to the high-explosive bombs used by all modern armies in action. It is to be hoped that man may find ways of settling difficulties so that he will use the force of high explosives only to blast out wide roads through mountains, construct better harbors, clear waste land and bring about a cleaner and better world.

The combination of nitrogen from the air with other elements is known as fixation. Certain plants, such as alfalfa, are able to absorb nitrogen from the air and convert it into combined nitrogen that becomes part of the plant. Fixation of nitrogen is an important chemical process, since fertilizer for purposes of peaceful agriculture, and explosives for peaceful pursuits as well as war, can be prepared independently of natural deposits of nitrogen compounds. Several different methods have been perfected to combine nitrogen with other elements. Nitrogen is an inactive element, not easily induced to form a compound, and when it is once in a compound, it escapes with violence at the first opportunity. For that reason, nitrogen compounds are used in all explosives.

Let us look briefly at one other field in which chemical progress has led the way. Without drugs whose purity and strength can be relied upon, the doctor cannot hope to cure disease. Pasteur and Lister were pioneers in the field of sanitation. Lister was the first to advocate aseptic conditions in surgery. Before his time, operations were conducted with no adequate precautions against infection. The chance of living after an operation was the long chance every patient took. Today, every precaution is taken to exclude germs from operating rooms; instruments are sterilized by steam, and chemicals and drugs used for post-operative treatments are the most efficient that can be procured.

Anesthetics are a development of the nineteenth century. Opium and related drugs have been produced in India and China for years. Morphine and other alkaloid poisons are prepared from opium and are valuable drugs when properly used under the direction of a physician. Nitrous oxide is used today by dentists for anesthesia during extractions, and the gas has proved successful for use in major surgical operations.

Before the Civil War, ether, known to the chemist as ethyl oxide, was found to have anesthetic properties. Ether has become the most widely used chemical for major operations because of the ease of administering the anesthetic and the complete relaxation of the body muscles while the patient is under its influence. The perfect anesthetic has yet to be discovered; such a one would have a pleasant odor, would produce quick insensibility, be completely relaxing and lack the usual nauseating after-effects. In his attempts to find such an anesthetic, the chemist serves humanity.

Local anesthetics are many in number, and some are a direct product of the chemist's laboratory. Various natural drugs, with their complicated molecules, have pain-killing properties but also have a poisonous or habit-forming effect. Opium is such a drug. The chemist has studied the structural picture of these compounds, and determined which part is responsible for the good properties, and which causes the poisonous effects. He has then taken the molecule apart, eliminated the bad, retained the good and thereby constructed a new compound, never found in nature and also an improvement on nature. There is no doubt but that the future holds further discoveries.

For additional reading in connection with the practical uses of chemistry, consult the following:

Anesthetic	Fertilizers
Aniline	Gunpowder
Blasting	Helium
Canning	Indigo
Cellophane	Milk, Condensed
Celluloid	Nitric Acid
Cellulose	Nitrogen
Coal Tar	Nitroglycerine
Cold Storage	Paper
Cordite	Perfumes
Dyeing	Poison Gas
Dynamite	Pure Food Laws
Explosives	Refrigeration

Bibliography

BLUM, W. Electroplating and Electroforming. McGraw-Hill Book Co.

CHENOWETH, W. W. Food Preservation. Wiley Agricultural Service.

CHAMBERLAIN, J. S. Chemistry in Agriculture. Chemical Foundation.

CLARKE, B. L. Marvels of Modern Chemistry. Harper & Bros.

CLEMEN, R. A. By-Products of the Packing Industry. University of Chicago Press.

FREEMAN, B., & HOPPE, F. G. Electroplating with Chromium, Copper and Nickel. Prentiss-Hall.

HOLMES, H. N. Out of the Test Tube. Long & Smith.

MUNDY, N. H. Short Story of Sugar. W. A. Havemeyer & Co.

SPRING, LAV. W. Non-Technical Chats on Iron and Steel. Frederick A. Stokes Co.

WILEY. H. W. Foods and Their Adulteration. P. Blakiston's Son & Co.

The Nature and Scope of Science

The growth of science has been a gradual one. It had its beginning in man's curiosity concerning natural phenomena, especially those that were difficult to understand. Curiosity is a laudable reaction of the mind of man. Gradually, through this reaction of man to his environment, much information was collected. At first a portion of it consisted of an accumulation of unrelated facts.

This acquisition of facts about man's surroundings eliminated a good many of his superstitious ideas, but it still did not develop into a scientific course of action. That stage was to come later.

The second stage in the evolution of science was the sorting and classifying of the information man had acquired. This classification divided knowledge into appropriate groups, established the different sciences and marked the beginning of experiments. Even if these experiments were conducted merely to confirm suspected facts, they placed science on a firm foundation as a means of solving problems.

Thus the first two steps—observation and experimentation—established the scientific attitude. Man is now in the third stage of scientific endeavor, the deliberate conquest of nature. We are now striving for the accomplishment of definite goals instead of merely confirming facts about our environment.

SCIENTIFIC THINKING

In reality, science is a method of thinking and acting. The scientific method has been applied to most fields of activity as a means of solving problems.

What is the scientific method of approach to a problem? First, we must know where we are going; even decide what problem we intend to solve. We should limit the problem so as not to consider too many factors at one time. After we have set up a definite goal for our scientific investigation, we begin to collect data and facts bearing on the problem.

Experimental facts are those we can prove. It is not an experimental fact that thunder makes milk sour. Such a belief is purely superstition; no one has carried on an experiment to prove the connection between thunder and the souring of milk. Scientists would tell us that the same weather conditions that cause thunder are favorable to the growth of bacteria that cause milk to sour. The scientists would exclude all folklore, gossip and unproved rumors and consider facts.

After all possible data have been obtained and the proved facts have been catalogued, the scientist studies the entire matter, trying to see some system in the whole picture and attempting to assemble a mental concept of the problem. If these data and related facts are sufficient, a tentative conclusion is reached which fits all known facts. But the scientific method does not stop until the tentative conclusion of the theory stage is tested by new experimentation. Every new fact has a bearing on the problem. We do not try to fit the facts to the theory, but we extend, alter or reject our old theories until they fit the known facts. When all facts have been assembled and conclusive

Westinghouse

CHEMISTRY ON A SMALL SCALE

The chemist has just dropped acid in his miniature crucible. *Inset:* Scientists' models of atomic structure.

experimental evidence has been accumulated, the scientist comes to a decision on his problem and announces his findings.

The scientific method has been used in working out practically all our great scientific discoveries. It is true that a few important discoveries have been made accidentally, but they were based upon some principles that had been worked out scientifically. After the accidental discovery was made, some scientific thinking had to be done or the value of the discovery would not have been recognized. The work in all the great scientific laboratories is based upon a logical procedure as outlined in the scientific method.

We should always be on the alert to question any conclusion that cannot stand the test of reason. What effect could the breaking of a mirror have upon your luck for the next seven years? Test all your pet superstitions by a scientific examination of all angles of the situation, always remembering that one instance does not prove a case any more than "one swallow makes a summer."

An attempt has been made to use this method in other fields than science. Hence we have studies in social science and political science. They have not approached the true scientific procedure of the exact sciences, but they have made a definite step in the right direction. When social and political units were very small, the problems were simpler. Everyone could know all the facts and have a true scientific method of arriving at the proper solution of the problem.

Today, with our complex civilization, even the simplest problems have so many inter-relationships with other problems that the ordinary citizen cannot arrive at an intelligent answer. There are two courses for us to choose. We can use the outworn trial and error method, which may make the problem more difficult to solve by introducing complications, or we can use the scientific method.

If we work scientifically, we will collect all the facts that can be assembled from every available source. Then we shall be able to say, "Here is the problem and here are the facts. How shall we act?" If we follow this plan we shall be in a better position to make political decisions. Of course, even then, we may have to use the trial and error method, if two courses of action seem equally desirable. But at least we shall base our decision on information and not emotions.

Even though the scientific method has not worked perfectly in other than the scientific realm, it has greatly affected the life of the race. There is no branch of human endeavor that has escaped its influence. Art, literature, philosophy and religion have all been greatly changed by it. In conclusion, we must think of science, not as a tangible thing, but as a method of acting and thinking. By means of this method, all the fields of science have been developed. Also we should place our emphasis upon what we expect from science in the future rather than upon what it has accomplished in the past. See SCIENCE AND THE SCIENCES.

Hope for the Future Through the Aid of Science

There is a tendency on the part of some young people to wish that they had lived in the "good old days" when there were discoveries to be made. To them it seems that so many wonderful things have been accomplished, there is nothing left to be done. Probably at the time George Washington lived, people had the same inclination to think that all deeds of daring and human betterment had been performed. Yet consider what has been accomplished in the last century and a half!

Today we are merely on the threshold of scientific achievement. The discoveries of the next hundred and fifty years will dwarf, by comparison, those of the past. We have been considering the accomplishments of the past and the tool which made those achievements possible. Let us now consider some of the possibilities for the morrow. No one can safely predict the future in any field, but we can consider some of the studies being made and speculate on the possibility of their success. Science is not a modern Aladdin's lamp which will fulfill all our wishes, but it offers an opportunity and a challenge to deeds far surpassing those of the past.

POWER AND ENERGY

The search for energy with which to produce power to run the wheels of industry and lighten the burden of man is an age-old quest. When our ancestors found that they could use the power of running or falling water to grind their grain or do other useful work, they had taken a big step toward lightening their labor. Next they used the power of steam and, later, the power of gasoline to run their engines. These machines depend upon the use of the energy of fuels to supply the power. We have to look forward to the exhaustion of these fuels, and then some other source of energy will have to be tapped. After all, when we use these natural fuels, we are borrowing energy from the past. The coal and oil were formed ages ago and may be thought of as stored solar energy. Let us consider some possibilities for supplying energy without borrowing from these stores.

If the plants that formed the coal, captured and stored the radiant energy from the sun, why could we not utilize the energy from the sun directly? We use electricity to make light; why not use the energy from the sunlight to make electricity?

Not much has been done toward the achievement of this goal, but it is not out of the realm of possibility. The sun is constantly bombarding us with radiant energy; in fact, enough hits the earth in a few minutes to supply all the power needed in a year if we could capture and utilize it.

The nearest to the accomplishment of this feat is the use of the photoelectric cell (sometimes called the electric eye). This cell can take light and transform it into a weak electric current. While the work that can be done with the photoelectric cell is not sufficient to run heavy machinery, it is a beginning in the utilization of the energy of light.

Scientists dream of breaking the atom and releasing the energy it contains. If this could be accomplished we would never need worry about power. If the energy in a gram of hydrogen gas could be released and controlled, it could supply the power to do the

HARNESSING A WATERFALL
Water diverted into a huge pipe sends turbine machinery spinning, causing a shaft to revolve. From the friction thus set up, electrical current is produced.

work of thousands of men. Research laboratories of the entire world are seeking means to release this energy, but nature seems to have securely hidden the secret. Some scientists think the secret will never be found, but others are more hopeful. If a method of releasing this energy is discovered it will mark the dawn of a new day for the human race.

We may also look forward to the use of the energy of moving wind to do much of our work. The wind could be used to store up energy that could be utilized when the wind was not blowing. In the same way the force of ocean waves and tides could be utilized. Our use of water power is probably not over twenty-five per cent of what it could be.

We could make more effective use of the energy of the fuels that we are now using. It has been estimated that there is enough potential energy in a gallon of gasoline to run a car 400 miles. While we can never approach that efficiency, there is no doubt we can improve automobiles to the point where we can utilize several times as much of the energy of gasoline as we do now.

Also there are undoubtedly other chemical sources of fuels of which we are unaware, or have not perfected. For example, alcohol can be made from plants and then used as fuel.

The famous "Electrical Wizard," Charles P. Steinmetz, prophesied that someday we would produce electric power so cheaply that it would be necessary for man to work only two or three days per week. When this goal is reached, man's energy will be released to seek improvement of the human family.

INCREASING HAPPINESS THROUGH BETTER HEALTH

When sufficient power is released to secure economic freedom for man, a great deal will have been done to improve his health and happiness. It is well known that much of the premature loss of health is due to overwork, worry and lack of economic security. Lack of financial means prevents a large proportion of our population from taking advantage of the knowledge we already possess. However, we cannot wait for improved conditions before we concern ourselves with the problem. There are some concrete things being done now, and more will be done in the future, to improve the health of all.

The history of Polar expeditions and the stories of men aboard ship for months has acquainted us with the dangers of malnutrition. Scurvy and kindred ailments were the expected lot of such adventurers. Research into this problem finally led to our knowledge of vitamins. We now know that a few green vegetables or a small quantity of fruit would have prevented such maladies. Today there are exploring parties in the Polar regions that live for months in a manner that previously spelled disaster. The difference is in the food they eat.

It is possible to starve at the same time that we are eating ravenously. There are certain things that the body needs and those must be supplied. The vitamins are chemical substances that are necessary for life, health, growth and reproduction. They are the health-giving agents that maintain our vitality and ward off disease.

Each vitamin has its own role to perform. If a single one is missing, in the midst of plenty, our health is impaired. Chemists and biologists are beginning to discover some of the secrets concerning these vitamins, and some have actually been prepared in the laboratory. True science knows no national boundary lines. It is working for the good of man the world over, and in the science laboratories of all civilized countries the problem of nutrition is being attacked. We know many things about the use of different types of food elements, but there is still much to be learned.

When we really know what each thing we eat does to the body, then we will know what to eat and what to avoid. We already know that the exclusive use of highly refined foods leads to impaired health and tooth decay. Eating polished rice robs us of vitamins that might be secured by eating the rice in its natural state. Exclusive use of refined white flour has similar results. There is a tendency now toward the use of flour made from the entire wheat kernel or from white flour enriched with vitamins.

When we know exactly what we should eat and can produce all the food elements and vitamins in the laboratory, it may be possible to eat synthetic foods entirely. There is a possibility that palatable foods could be made in the laboratory containing exactly the elements we need, and none of the things we ought to avoid. That day is a long way off, but it may be a reality at some future time.

Thousands of dollars are being expended annually in laboratories to attack the problem of cancer. No solution has yet been found, but information is being collected that will eventually give the scientist the answer he is seeking.

Heart ailments are the causes of more deaths than any one single disease. The causes of bad conditions of the heart are so interrelated with the problems of diet, worry and general health that no one cause can be given. For that reason the solution of economic, physical and mental problems will decrease the number of deaths due to hardening of the arteries and heart failure.

The use of proper diet and sensible methods of living will do much to increase the span of life to more than our alloted "three score and ten." Many scientists say that our span of life today could be increased by at least ten years through the proper use of the knowledge we already possess. Increasing knowledge of the function of the glands of the body will undoubtedly give us a clue to longer life.

Death is inevitable and we should not expect to prevent it. It is a natural cycle of life to go through the stages of birth, youth, maturity, old age and death. However, if we could maintain proper health until death it would be a great advantage to increase the span of life. Many men that have made great contributions to human welfare were overtaken by death in the midst of their creative work, and all mankind would have benefited by ten or fifteen years more of their work.

Chemistry also offers much promise for the future in the development of new materials other than the foods and drugs we have been discussing. The creation of new textiles and fabrics is already a fact, and we can be sure of vast improvement over those now known.

The manufacture of rayon from plant cellulose is already a well-known accomplishment. Another synthetic fiber, nylon, is made from air, coal and water. If allowed to develop to its fullest possibilities, the synthetic textile will make it possible for everyone to have sufficient clothing at a reasonable price.

The plastics industry is just in its beginning. We have materials such as cellophane, celluloid, artificial rubber and bakelite from which many useful articles are made.

One need that is likely to be filled is a substitute for glass. Such a substitute should be transparent like glass, but it should be flexible. Glass fractures easily if any pressure is applied to it; the flexible substitute would bend without breaking. This property would be an advantage not only as far as construction is concerned, but would make glass safer. Broken glass is a dangerous threat to our lives. If a person were thrown into a windshield of flexible glass, it would spring enough to reduce the danger of head injuries.

There are many people who say that science should take a holiday. We have so many inventions that have taken the place of hundreds of men that a serious unemployment problem has arisen. The whole economic world seems to be disjointed, and critics of science assume that if it took a holiday, the world would have a chance to work out a solution.

When science is evolving discoveries and inventions that take the drudgery out of existence, why should we ask it to stop while a laggard economic and social system catches up? Science moves along unhampered by tradition; it is our social and economic system that is hemmed in by traditions.

This is a changing world and no system that is perfect today will be perfect tomorrow. Let us hope that the future will give a free rein to science to develop what it may for the betterment of mankind; and that the social order will use these developments unselfishly to promote general health and happiness.

For additional reading on the points covered in this section, the following articles will be of interest:

Alcohol	Fuel
Bakelite	Nutrition
Cellophane	Nylon
Celluloid	Rayon
Chemistry	Rubber
Energy	Vitamins

General Reading List

CALDWELL, O. W. *Science Remaking the World.* Doubleday, Doran & Co.

CRESSY, E. *Discoveries and Inventions of the 20th Century.* G. Routledge & Sons.

DARROW, F. L. *The New World of Physical Discovery.* The Bobbs-Merrill Co.

DAVIS, W. *The Advance of Science.* Doubleday, Doran & Co.

DE KRUIF, PAUL. *Seven Iron Men.* Harcourt, Brace & Co.

DIETZ, DAVID. *Story of Science.* Allen & Unwin, Ltd.

EDDINGTON, A. S. *The Nature of the Physical World.* The Macmillan Co.

GAIL, O. W. *Romping through Physics.* Alfred A. Knopf.

GARBEDIAN, H. G. *Major Mysteries of Science.* Covici-Friede.

GREGORY, R. A. *Discovery, or the Spirit and Service of Science.* The Macmillan Co.

HARDING, F. S. *Popular Practices of Fraud.* Longmans, Green & Co.

HARROW, B. *Eminent Chemists of Our Time.* D. Van Nostrand Co.

HART, I. B. *Makers of Science.* Oxford University Press.

HARVEY-GIBSON, R. J. *Two Thousand Years of Science.* The Macmillan Co.

HOGBEN, L. *Mathematics for the Million.* W. W. Norton & Co

———. *Science for the Citizen.* Alfred A. Knopf.

HOLMYARD, E. J. *The Great Chemists.* Methuen & Co.

JAFFE, B. *Crucibles.* Simon & Schuster.

———. *New World of Chemistry.* Silver, Burdett & Co.

KALLET, A. *Counterfeit.* Vanguard Press.

PHILLIPS, M. C. *Skin Deep.* Vanguard Press.

RICHARDS, H. *The Universe Surveyed.* D. Van Nostrand Co.

SCHLINK, F. J. *Eat, Drink and be Wary.* Covici-Friede.

SKILLING, W. T. *Tours Through the World of Science.* McGraw-Hill Book Co.

SLOSSON, E. E. *Creative Chemistry.* D. Appleton-Century Co.

———. *Snapshots of Science.* D. Appleton-Century Co.

VAN LOON, H. *Man the Miracle Maker.* Liveright Publishing Co.

RECREATION

Overview for Recreation

Carving a living out of the wilderness in the New World left the early settlers of our country little leisure for recreation. Indeed, diligence was so looked upon as a virtue that anyone who took time off for amusement was frowned upon as an idler or loafer. The Puritans of New England attempted to suppress the theater, card playing, horse racing, dancing and other forms of recreation; only the more well-to-do planters of the South were not stopped by their consciences from indulging in these amusements.

Early in the nineteenth century, a great economic change came over the country. Heretofore civilization in the colonies had been predominantly agricultural; people had come together at harvest time, for barn raisings and for quilting parties, making even their social gatherings productive. Now, however, came the industrialization and the resultant urbanization of the United States. People flocked to the cities and worked for long hours in factories. But not until the trades unions had succeeded in cutting the hours of the workers was there leisure for recreation and self-improvement. A people unaccustomed to free time and lacking the opportunities for wholesome pleasures afforded by an agricultural society turned then for their amusement to the fraternal orders and other forms of entertainment that sprang up during this period.

Shorter working hours do not account for all the leisure time of the present-day industrial society. Inventions have also played their part; labor-saving devices, for instance, have freed from drudgery many thousands who have only to turn to other mechanical devices for their diversion.

Unemployment has given an enforced leisure to countless numbers; and public and private social agencies have turned serious attention to the needs of this group. There are also the many boys and girls released from work by child-labor and school-attendance laws whose free time must be provided for.

There is danger to both individual and society from misspent or wasted leisure. Thus we find in modern society a greater need for recreational opportunities and the constructive use of leisure time than at any other period in the nation's history. We also have greater means for supplying this need, and a more enlightened public conscience regarding the control of these facilities and their availability to the people.

In the following pages these problems and the means for meeting them are discussed in greater detail.

How the Modern World Plays

PIONEER PLAY

The early settlers in America were deeply concerned with the business of making a living. From dawn to dark the entire family was engaged in needful tasks, stopping only for meals. Only in the evening would the members pause for brief relaxation, and even then the women would busy themselves with knitting or mending. But bedtime came early for these hard-working people; candles and firewood must not be wasted, and the next day's labors must find them rested.

The religious preoccupation of the early colonists led them to forbid play on Sunday, their one day of rest. Even in school no time was allowed for play. It is not to be marveled at, then, that the people looked forward with great pleasure to the barn raising, the quilting party, the husking bee and the sugaring-off, when whole families would gather to help a neighbor in a task that needed many hands. These affairs were made occasions for frolicking, for square dancing, games and other pastimes. Spelling bees, church revivals, weddings and christenings were other social gatherings.

On the Western frontiers, where the men far outnumbered the women, amusement took the form of such physical contests as rail splitting and tree chopping. Lumbermen indulged in "log birling"—a contest which consisted of riding rapidly-turning logs. Roping contests, bull-dogging steers, riding bucking horses and shooting matches offered diversion to the cowboys. Miners and cowboys drank and gambled in the saloons of the mining camp and "cow town."

RECREATION OF A LATER PERIOD

With the settlement and urbanization of the country the communities became less dependent upon their own resources for recreation. Schools, halls and churches opened their doors to lecturers and entertainers from the city. For a week in the summertime the Chautauqua would offer a variety of entertainment. The annual county fair brought friends from miles around to enjoy the exhibits and to savor the varied entertainment that the occasion provided. The medicine show was a popular itinerant amusement in the nineteenth century, the circus was popular with people of all ages and horse races were an enjoyable pastime. There

THE PIONEERS LOVED SINGING

were also the opportunities for social life provided by the lodges, clubs and farmers' organizations of the period.

Organized sport as a means of recreation developed somewhat later. Baseball, a popular pastime for both armies during the Civil War, grew afterward into the popular American game that it is today. Croquet was universally played, giving place toward the close of the nineteenth century to the more strenuous game of tennis. In this same period, roller skating had a considerable vogue with persons of all ages.

In the "gay nineties" bicycling was extremely popular, particularly among city dwellers. The vogue declined as the automobile became general, only to revive after World War I, when bicycle clubs and youth hostels gave new impetus to the sport of "wheeling."

Consult the following references for further information on the subject of early recreation in America:

Barnum, Phineas
   Taylor
Baseball
Bicycle

Chautauqua Institu-
   tion
Circus
Fraternal Societies

Bibliography

BARNUM, P. T. *Struggles and Triumphs.* The Macmillan Co.
CLARKE, J. S. *Circus Parade.* Charles Scribner's Sons.
JAMES, WILL. *Lone Cowboy.* Charles Scribner's Sons.
LUTES, DELLA. *Country Kitchen.* Little, Brown & Co.
McLAREN, GAY. *Morally We Roll Along.* Atlantic Monthly Press.
MITCHELL, E. V. *Horse and Buggy Days in New England.* Coward-McCann.

RECREATION AND THE INDUSTRIAL AGE

Labor-saving machinery and the resultant legislation governing hours of labor have released men, women and children from a workday of about fourteen hours, and have given them a leisure never before enjoyed. At the same time the Machine Age has put at their disposal many mechanical devices for their enjoyment. Small wonder, then, that the man of today is confronted with the need of using this leisure time wisely.

Many forms of recreation are needed to meet the needs of modern life. It is apparent that one whose work is dull or monotonous needs mental stimulation when his workday is done. On the other hand, a laborer whose work is nerve-racking should not be stimulated; he should instead find recreation that is relaxing and refreshing to mind and body. Workers who are physically inactive during the day need to join in active games and not be mere spectators.

Unemployment is an aspect of modern industrial life to present its problems in the wise use of leisure time. To counteract the mental and nervous strain attendant upon long periods of enforced inactivity, social and welfare agencies have long devoted much thought to providing constructive activity, regardless of the little immediate financial return. This purpose prompted the Federal government, during the financial depression of the 1930's, to establish such agencies as the Work Projects Administration, the Federal Writers' Project and the Federal Theater.

Adult education provides profitable activity in times of enforced leisure. Many forms of entertainment, too, are available to everybody—open-air concerts, community singing, plays and dancing. Modern living has made recreation a necessity; and it is an interesting fact that today everyone, rich and poor alike, has at his disposal more opportunities to meet that need than had the wealthier classes in the pioneer period.

Invention has played a vital part in modern recreation. Consider, for example, the automobile, which made it possible for everyone, limited only by his time and means, to seek recreation away from home. It opened up for his pleasure places that could not easily be reached by railroad—forest areas, parks, hunting and fishing areas. In normal times it carries thousands of Americans annually to spots of scenic or historic interest, mountains, seashores and neighboring countries—principally Mexico and Canada.

As a peacetime industry the American moving-picture business ranks only after steel, agriculture and automobile manufacture. The social influence of an amusement of such universal popularity is apparent in more than the interest taken in the costumes, manners and interior decorations portrayed on the screen. Recognition of the emotional appeal of the moving pictures, particularly on young people, has led to concerted action on the part of civic and church organizations to improve the quality of pictures.

When at its best, the motion picture instructs through the newsreels and the fictional delineation of historic events and the lives of great people. As entertainment, it offers an escape from monotony.

Like the moving picture, radio entertains millions of people of every age. Except in the emergency of war, there is no formal censorship of radio. The broadcasting companies voluntarily maintain a consistently high standard. The social values of radio are indeed far-reaching. Trappers and traders in the frozen North receive messages and programs broadcast to them from outside. Radio sets have been installed in prisons that provide entertainment for the convicts for purposes of reform. And radio has brought untold cheer and amusement to shut-ins.

Indeed, radio has done more to dissipate sectionalism than is possible for the motion picture or automobile, or for any other device known. Everyone—in congested city and remote rural district alike—may hear at the same time a concert of fine music, a good play, a variety program or a speech from the White House. Sports announcers have helped to increase public interest in athletics by their play-by-play accounts of the game. Amateur radio fans have found a community of interest in what is at once a profitable hobby and a source of entertainment.

The following articles offer further information on the social effects of invention, enforced leisure and mechanical devices for entertainment:

Adult Education
Athletics, subhead
  Work and Play
Automobile
Electricity, subhead
  The Future of Electricity

Industrial Revolution
Invention
Moving Pictures
Radio, subhead
  Social Implications
  of Radio

Bibliography

FLOHERTY, J. J. *On the Air.* Doubleday, Doran & Co.
GANNETT, L. S. *Sweet Land.* Doubleday, Doran & Co.
KIMBALL, W. A. *Touring with Tent and Trailer.* McGraw-Hill Book Co.
LOWELL, MAURICE. *Listen In; an American Manual of Radio.* Dodge Publishing Co.
NAUMBURG, NANCY. *We Make the Movies.* W. W. Norton & Co.
O'BRIEN, H. V. *Folding Bedouins; or, Adrift in a Trailer.* Willett, Clark Co.
SAERCHINGER, CÉSAR. *Hello America! Radio Adventures in Europe.* Houghton, Mifflin Co.
SELDES, GILBERT. *The Movies Come from America.* Charles Scribner's Sons.
WING, PAUL. *"Take It Away, Sam!"* Dodd, Mead & Co.

LEISURE-TIME PLAY

The increasing public interest in outdoor recreation since the turn of the century has naturally accompanied the shorter working day, the rising standard of living and the greater emphasis on social welfare.

Many find the greatest relaxation and refreshment in camping trips. Fishing, hunt-

EYES ON THE BALL
Golf calls for coördination of mind and muscle.

BASEBALL—GREAT AMERICAN GAME

ing, canoeing, swimming and hiking are a few of the activities of camp life. Other outdoor recreations that enjoy a long season are golf, tennis, baseball and sailing. Some sports belong specifically to wintertime—skating, hockey, ice yachting, coasting, tobogganing and skiing.

Athletic contests, such as organized football and baseball, polo games, horse races and regattas, provide recreation for thousands of enthusiastic spectators. And through advertising, journalism, radio and newsreel, vast numbers of absent "fans" also enjoy these games.

Indoor play, also, offers recreation for leisure hours. Bridge and other card games, chess and checkers, backgammon and a great many parlor games are popular home recreations. More active indoor sports include basket ball, billiards, bowling, boxing, fencing and wrestling.

These games and sports encourage teamwork and good sportsmanship, and provide healthful exercise and wholesome enjoyment for leisure hours that might otherwise be wasted or misspent.

There has been some speculation as to whether the athletic contest does not tend to make Americans a nation of spectators rather than participants. But the increasing interest in golf, tennis and swimming and the rising number of community facilities for baseball and other sports show that Americans like to play the games themselves.

Consult the following articles for information on games, sports and other leisure-time activities:

Archery	Hearts
Association Football	Hockey
Athletics	Ice Yachting
Backgammon	Indoor Baseball
Baseball	Kites
Basket Ball	La Crosse
Billiards	Lawn Tennis
Boxing	Marbles
Bullfighting	Olympic Games
Camps and Camping	Physical Culture
Canoes and Canoeing	Ping Pong
Cards, Playing	Polo
Checkers	Pool
Chess	Race
Coasting	Rodeo
Cribbage	Rowing
Cricket	Sailboat and Sailing
Croquet	Shuffleboard
Curling	Skates and Skating
Dancing	Ski
Entertaining	Solitaire
Fishing, or Angling	Swimming
Football	Tennis
Game	Tobogganing
Games and Plays	Trapping
Golf	Whist
Gymnasium	Yacht and Yachting
Handball	

Bibliography

CALAHAN, H. A. *Ship's Husband; a Guide to Yachtsmen.* The Macmillan Co.
CHELEY, F. H. *Camping Out and Woodcraft.* Halcyon House.
HUGHES, W. L. *Book of Major Sports.* A. S. Barnes & Co.
JACOBS, H. H. *Improve Your Tennis.* Methuen & Co.
MASON, B. S. *Primitive and Pioneer Sports for Recreation Today.* A. S. Barnes & Co.
REYNOLDS, H. A. *Game Way to Sports.* A. S. Barnes & Co.
ROBERTSON, LAWSON. *Modern Athletics; How to Train for the Various Events.* Charles Scribner's Sons.

ORGANIZATIONS AND LEISURE TIME

Underprivileged sections of large cities, where opportunities for wholesome leisure-time activities are lacking, have been found to be breeding places for crime. Consequently, philanthropic individuals and both private and public agencies are striving to provide playgrounds, recreational equipment and trained play leaders in as many communities as possible. Today, settlement houses, community centers and public libraries are helping to supply this need. Farm organizations, such as the Grange, and such religious organizations as the Y.M.C.A. and the Y.W.C.A. supply worth-while companionship and activities for leisure time.

Youth groups, such as the increasingly popular youth hostels, and fraternal societies and clubs of all kinds are other private agencies working toward this end.

The Federal government has also enlisted in this recreational program. The Forest Service of the Department of Agriculture is turning the national forest areas in their charge into pleasant vacation playgrounds by cutting roads and trails and providing camp sites, outdoor fireplaces and wood for fuel. The Agricultural Extension Service enriches the leisure time of rural boys and girls by providing, through the 4-H Clubs, opportunities for contests and worth-while projects of many kinds. The National Park Service, in the Department of the Interior, maintains the national parks and monuments, and many buildings and places of patriotic or historical interest, for the enjoyment of the public.

Further information on help that organizations render in the recreation program may be found in the following articles:

Boys' and Girls' 4-H Clubs	Hull House Library
Boy Scouts	Parks, National
Camp-Fire Girls	Social Settlements
Canning Clubs	Young Men's Christian
Club	Association
Community Center	Young Women's Christian Association
Girl Scouts	tian Association

Bibliography

ALBRIGHT, H. M. "Oh, Ranger!" A Book About the National Parks. Dodd, Mead & Co.
CHOATE, A. H. Juliette Low and the Girl Scouts. Girl Scouts of America.
CLEMENS, CYRIL. Uncle Dan; the Life Story of Dan Beard. Thomas Y. Crowell Co.
KANE, J. F. Picturesque America, Its Parks and Playgrounds. Resorts and Playgrounds of America.
MATHIEWS, F. K. Boy Scouts' Book of Outdoor Hobbies. D. Appleton-Century Co.
NORTON, E. V. Play Streets, and Their Use for Recreational Programs. A. S. Barnes & Co.
SETON, E. T. Book of Woodcraft and Indian Lore. Doubleday, Doran & Co.

HOBBIES AND LEISURE TIME

Man's need to express himself through creative activity is an imperative one, and the mass-production methods of the modern factory system do not give him the opportunity to satisfy this need. Creative activities may counteract the dulling effects of routine work; and, as his daily work fails in this respect, man must increasingly exercise his creative genius in his leisure time.

Very frequently a person's hobby interest may develop into a creative activity of profit and distinction. Such was the case with a boy who was interested in maps and places; a hobby that found expression first in making maps for friends who were planning trips ultimately developed into a full-fledged travel bureau. A woman's interest

THE SHORE AS A PLACE FOR PLAY

in miniatures prompted her to construct model rooms in which to display them; today she has a remarkable set of rooms, complete and authentic in every detail and representing many styles of architecture, which she has often exhibited.

But a creative activity need not be so extensive as this to yield the necessary satisfactions. Many people find pleasure in converting raw materials into finished form; whether or not the finished product is perfect does not detract from the satisfaction of having made something. The amateur craftsman has an almost endless variety of materials to work with—wood, clay, wax, soap, stone, leather, cloth, rope, yarn, glass, concrete or linoleum. He may carve, mold, shape, spin, weave, chisel or use a lathe.

Model making is a leisure-time activity of increasing popularity. The Federal government capitalized on this interest in World War II by having children of school age make models of airplanes for use in aircraft training classes. Model ships, coaches, houses, rooms, furniture and railroad trains and historical scenes in three-dimensional settings (dioramas) are among the objects made by the model builder.

People who enjoy growing things find pleasure and satisfaction in gardening and landscaping in their leisure time. One who combines an interest in growing things with an interest in science may now grow plants without soil, feeding the plants with chemicals mixed in the right proportions.

Weaving, pottery making and metal working may produce useful as well as artistic products, and may well develop from enjoyable leisure-time activities into profitable enterprises. Through experiments in line

SPORT IN A SNOWCLAD WORLD

and color, these crafts provide opportunities for artistic expression.

Caring for pets interests many people of all ages. It is a leisure-time activity that may be as simple and inexpensive or as extensive and costly as the individual's interest or purse may dictate. It is an activity for leisure time that can—and often does—develop into a profitable undertaking with great opportunities.

Interesting information on these and many other activities are to be found under the following headings:

Advertising	Drawing
Arts and Crafts	Floriculture
Basket and Basketry	Flowers
Batik	Gardening
Bees	Goldfish
Bookbinding	Knots
Camera	Landscape Gardening
Canary	Lathe
Carrier Pigeon	Map
Candy and Candy	Nature Study
Making	Photography
Cat	Pottery
China Painting	Printing
Cookery	Weaving
Dog	Wood Carving

Bibliography

BOWLES, E. S. *Homespun Handicrafts.* J. B. Lippincott Co.

DESCHIN, JACOB. *New Ways in Photography.* McGraw-Hill Book Co.

GREENBIE, M. L. B. *Arts of Leisure.* McGraw-Hill Book Co.

LAMPLAND, RUTH. *Hobbies for Everybody.* Harper & Bros.

LOCKREY, A. J. *"Plastics" in the Home and School Workshop.* Governor Publishing Corporation.

PERRY, E. K. *Art Adventures with Discarded Materials.* Wetzel Publishing Co.

SPITZ, CARL. *Training Your Dog.* Marshall Jones Co.

THE COLLECTING HOBBY

Collecting appeals to children and adults alike. It may find expression through a wide array of interests, and from the inexpensive pleasure in collecting natural objects to the more costly hobby of collecting priceless masterpieces and rarities. Presidents and kings have found relaxation in this hobby; George V of England, for example, had one of the world's greatest collections of stamps of the British Empire. A famous American collection sold for $875,000.

Stamp collecting (philately) has become a hobby of such universal appeal that many books have been written on the subject, and many shops deal exclusively in stamps and stamp-collectors' supplies. The Federal Postoffice sells blocks of its new and unusual issues of stamps to stamp collectors.

Book collecting is another hobby that has a wide following. First editions, rare books and books autographed by the authors or other important people are particularly prized. Some people strive to build up comprehensive libraries on a particular subject or field of interest, and still others collect books as examples of beautiful or unusual printing and format.

There are also collectors of antiques—period furniture, old glass, dishes, engravings or lamps. Others collect coins, dolls, woodcarvings, guns, musical instruments or gems. And still others collect such oddities as canes, travel posters and match books. However, the collector must beware of those who, honestly or otherwise, would take advantage of the collecting interest. Dishonest persons, for instance, have artificially "antiqued" objects to meet the public demand for antiques. And manufacturers have issued pennants, stickers and similar items in sets for collectors, thus defeating the purpose of a hobby whose satisfaction lies in collecting objects with discrimination, and not in buying them.

The type of collection that has most value to the collector is the one that brings him the richest returns in knowledge and information. A collector of Indian relics, for instance, learns interesting facts about how the Indians came to make and use the articles; why and how similar articles differ among different tribes and in different parts of the country. His interest has given him material for a book that would add to the field of Indian lore, or for a lecture that would interest both children and adults. This hobby has real value.

Additional information of interest to those whose hobby is collecting may be found in such articles as the following:

Autograph	Glass
Bibliomania	Numismatics
Furniture	Postage Stamps

Bibliography

CLIFFORD, C. R. *Junk Snupper.* The Macmillan Co.
COLLINS, A. F. *Collecting Stamps for Fun and Profit.* D. Appleton-Century Co.
HORNADAY, W. T. *Taxidermy and Zoölogical Collecting.* Charles Scribner's Sons.
McMILLER, WHEELER. *Young Collector.* D. Appleton-Century Co.
MOORE, N. H. W. *Collector's Manual.* Tudor Publishing Co.
Stamp Collector's Round Table. Ed. by F. W. Loso. Frederick A. Stokes Co.
WEST, H. F. *Modern Book Collecting for the Impecunious Amateur.* Little, Brown & Co.

LEISURE-TIME READING

Many people have become authorities on certain subjects through their leisure-time reading and study; others find in their recreational reading the mental stimulation and relaxation necessary to offset the dullness or tension of their regular employment. But whatever their purpose, they may become more interesting companions for others as a result of their reading. The ability to enjoy good books may be cultivated, and everyone may profit by suggestions as to what to read.

Mother Goose is a universal favorite with small children, as are such tales as "Henny Penny," "Goldilocks" and "The Little Pig That Wouldn't Go over the Stile." As they grow older, they enjoy such simple little stories as "Peter Rabbit" and "The Three Little Pigs." When imagination plays an important part in their development, fairy tales and the ever-popular *Alice's Adventures in Wonderland* delight them. And then, when physical energy abounds, their taste turns to tales of adventure that range from bloodthirsty stories of pirates and brigands to tales of knighthood—from the story of Ali Baba and the Forty Thieves to the adventures of King Arthur and his Knights of the Round Table.

The horizon of their interests expands, as they grow older, and opens up to them a new world of adventure in books of travel, science, history or biography, as their interest dictates. They read of Indians and cowboys, sports and the work of men in almost any occupation.

Although most of us prefer our drama acted out for us, there are many who enjoy drama as literature. For those young people

READING CAN BE FUN
Good books entertain and instruct.

who like to read plays, there are collections that range from one-act playlets to the well-loved works of Shakespeare.

Those who are not familiar with poetry have missed the joy of reading some of the finest works of mankind. There are so many different types of poems and so many different verse forms that there are poems to fit every mood and literary taste.

Some books have a universal appeal that causes them to live on long after others, written at the same time, are forgotten. The appeal of great books is lasting because they seem as real to the reader as real life. Often a great piece of literature has been spoiled for the young reader because he has read it before he was old enough to appreciate it. Usually it is the books whose spirit we caught at first reading that we enjoy owning and rereading from time to time.

The articles LITERATURE and DRAMA give a general survey of each of these subjects. The following titles may be referred to for additional information on great writings and literary types:

Aeneid	Fable
Alice's Adventures in Wonderland	Fiction
	Figures of Speech
Ancient Mariner	Folklore
Autocrat of the Breakfast Table	Grail, The Holy
	Gulliver's Travels
Ben-Hur	Hamlet
Bible	Harun-Al-Rashid
Biography	Hiawatha
Blank Verse	History
Bluebeard	Homer
Canterbury Tales	Iliad
Charge of the Light Brigade	Language and Grammar
Cinderella	Les Miserables
Comedy	Library
Courtship of Miles Standish	Limerick
	Lyric Poetry
Epic	Macbeth
Essay	Man without a Country
Evangeline	

INSTRUMENTS OF THE ORCHESTRA AND BAND

Strings: (1) harp; (2) piano; (3) violin; (4) viola; (5) violoncello; (6) bass viol; (7) guitar; (8) ukelele; (9) mandolin; (10) banjo. *Wood Winds:* (26) fife; (27) piccolo; (39) flute. *Brasses:* (28) bugle; (29) alto horn; (30) trumpet; (32) baritone horn; (33) cornet; (34) bass tuba; (35) mellophone; (36) French horn; (37) sousaphone; (38) slide trombone. *Reeds:* (22) alto saxophone; (23) oboe; (24) clarinet; (25) bassoon. *Reed Organ:* (21) piano accordian. *Percussion Instruments:* (11) snare drum; (12) bass drum; (13) Chinese wood block; (14) tambourine; (16) crash cymbal; (17) cymbal; (18) triangle; (19) rattle; (20) marimba xylophone; (40) kettle drum.

Masque
Melodrama
Minstrel
Miracle Play
Morality Plays
Morte d' Arthur
Mother Goose
Mystery
Mythology
Novel
Odyssey
Paradise Lost
Pastoral Poetry
Poetry

Poor Richard's
  Almanac
Reading
Rip Van Winkle
Robin Hood
Robinson Crusoe
Romance
Romanticism
Sonnet
Story Telling
Swiss Family
  Robinson
Tragedy
Ulysses

Bibliography

BECKER, M. L. *First Adventures in Reading.* Frederick A. Stokes Co.

DREW, E. A. *Enjoyment of Literature.* W. W. Norton & Co.

EASTMAN, FRED. *Books That Have Shaped the World.* American Library Association.

EATON, A. T. *Reading with Children.* The Viking Press.

HALLECK, R. P. *Romance of American Literature.* American Book Co.

HAPGOOD, NORMAN. *Why Janet Should Read Shakespeare.* D. Appleton-Century Co.

MARSHALL, H. E. *English Literature for Boys and Girls.* Frederick A. Stokes Co.

MOORE, A. C. *My Roads to Childhood.* Doubleday, Doran & Co.

THE ARTS AND LEISURE

Through the arts—painting, sculpture, architecture, music, dancing—man has always found creative expression for his love of the beautiful. But art has the further value to man of emotional release.

There has been a definite trend in America toward a greater interest in and appreciation of art in all its forms, influenced largely by the effect of Europe on the United States since the turn of the century. In the prosperous decade after World War I, for instance, men and institutions of wealth purchased valuable works of art, financed musical organizations and erected beautiful buildings. The increased leisure time allowed thousands of Americans to study art as a recreational activity, to visit museums and art galleries and to hear the compositions of great composers.

One does not need to be a painter or sculptor to appreciate art; nevertheless, more people than ever before are studying art in their leisure time, experiencing thus the joy of creative self-expression and lightening the monotony of daily living. The satisfaction that comes from a profitable leisure-time activity, the personal enrichment that comes from being able to enjoy beauty without owning it and the ability to reflect that appreciation in one's personal surroundings are other benefits of artistic study.

In the same way, one does not have to be a musician to enjoy good music. He can cultivate high musical standards by listening to and learning to appreciate fine music as recorded for the phonograph or broadcast on the radio, and he can attend concerts and read books about music, composers and instruments. However, the ability to play an instrument doubles one's enjoyment of music. Those who can play the piano or violin—or even a mouth organ—need not know boredom or loneliness.

Dancing has in recent years become a favorite recreational pastime, an interest stimulated largely by moving pictures and the revival of ballet dancing. Increasing numbers of students are studying dancing for pleasure; ballroom, folk and tap dancing are especially popular. Besides the enjoyment derived from the activity, dancing has the added value of contributing to one's grace of movement, good posture and social poise. Dancing is but one of the arts that have been encouraged by the schools, Federal and local projects and social organizations to the end that schools and other public buildings have been beautified and interest has been aroused in things American.

The articles on ARCHITECTURE, MUSIC, PAINTING and SCULPTURE give general information on these subjects. Further information may be found under the following titles:

Archaeology
Art and the Arts
Dancing
Drawing
Fine Arts

Instrumental Music
National Music of the
  United States
Painting
Sculpture

Bibliography

ADAM, T. R. *Civic Value of Museums.* American Association for Adult Education.

BURRIS-MEYER, ELIZABETH. *Color and Design in the Decorative Arts.* Prentice-Hall.

DREW, E. A. *Discovering Drama.* W. W. Norton & Co.

McKINNEY, H. D. *Discovering Music.* American Book Co.

TOLMAN, BETH. *Country Dance Book.* Farrar & Rinehart, Inc.

VAN DE WALL, WILLEM. *Music of the People.* American Association for Adult Education.

VAN LOON. H. W. *The Arts.* Simon & Schuster.

High-School List

BARTON, F. B. *Photography as a Hobby.* Harper & Bros.

DULLES, F. R. *America Learns to Play; a History of Popular Recreation, 1607-1940.* D. Appleton-Century Co.

JOSEPH, MRS. H. H. *Book of Marionettes.* The Viking Press.

LAMPLAND, RUTH. *Hobbies for Everybody.* Harper & Bros.

LOOMIS, ANDREW. *Fun with a Pencil.* The Viking Press.

MENKE, F. G. *Encyclopedia of Sports.* Frank G. Menke, Inc.

MAY, E. C. *Circus from Rome to Ringling.* Duffield & Green, Inc.

THORP, MRS. M. F. *America at the Movies.* Yale University Press.

NAUMBURG, NANCY. *We Make the Movies.* W. W. Norton & Co.

RICKETT, E. W. *Let's Do Some Gilbert and Sullivan; a Practical Production Handbook.* Coward-McCann.

READ THESE BOOKS FOR PLEASURE

INTRODUCTIONS TO GREAT LITERATURE

Adler, Mortimer J. .... How to Read a Book
Auslander, Joseph & Hill, Frank E. .... The Winged Horse
Canby, Henry Seidel & others.......... Designed for Reading
Jessup Alexander..................... Representative Modern Short Stories
Macy, John Albert.................... The Story of the World's Literature
Neilson, William Allan............... Roads to Knowledge
Stauffer, R. M. .... The Progress of Drama Through the Centuries
Tinker, H. L. .... Essays—Yesterday and Today
Woollcott, Alexander................. The Woollcott Readers

FICTION

Austen, Jane......................... Emma; Pride and Prejudice
Blackmore, Richard Doddridge......... Lorna Doone
Bronte, Charlotte.................... Jane Eyre
Cather, Willa........................ My Antonia
Churchill, Winston................... Richard Carvel
Cooper, James Fenimore............... Leatherstocking Tales
Davis, W. S. .... Gilman of Redford; Friend of Caesar
Dickens, Charles..................... David Copperfield; Tale of Two Cities
Dumas, Alexandre .... The Three Musketeers
Eliot, George........................ Adam Bede; Mill on the Floss
Gaskell, Mrs. .... Cranford
Goldsmith, Oliver.................... The Vicar of Wakefield
Hawthorne, Nathaniel................. The Scarlet Letter; The House of Seven Gables
Masefield, John...................... Bird of Dawning; Lost Endeavor
Melville, Herman..................... Omoo; Typee; Moby Dick
Scott, Walter........................ Ivanhoe; The Heart of Midlothian
Stevenson, Robert Louis.............. Black Arrow; Treasure Island
Thackeray, William Makepeace........ Vanity Fair; Henry Esmond
Tolstoi, Lyoff Nikolayevitch......... War and Peace
Wells, Herbert George................ Joan and Peter
Wharton, Edith....................... Age of Innocence

POETRY ANTHOLOGIES AND COLLECTIONS

Grover, Edwin Osgood................. The Nature Lover's Knapsack
Monroe, Harriet .... Poets and Their Art
Palgrave, F. T. .... Golden Treasury
Untermeyer, Louis .... Yesterday and Today
Wells, Carolyn .... Nonsense Anthology
Wilkinson, Bonaro .... Poetic Way of Release
Yeats, William Butler............... Oxford Book of Modern Verse

DRAMA

Murray, Gilbert .... Ten Greek Plays
Shakespeare, William................ Complete Plays, edited by W. G. Clark
Smith, A. M. .... Short Plays by Representative Authors
Whitman, C. H. .... Representative Modern Dramas

ESSAYS AND HISTORY

Beard, Charles Austin, and Beard,
 Mary Ritter........................ The Makings of American Civilization
Carlyle, Thomas .... Heroes and Hero Worship
Eastman, Fred .... Books That Have Shaped the World
Holmes, Oliver Wendell............... Autocrat of the Breakfast Table
Irving, Washington .... Knickerbocker's History of New York
Lamb, Charles........................ Essays of Elia
Parsons, Geoffrey.................... The Stream of History

BIOGRAPHY

Addams, Jane .... Twenty Years at Hull House
Clemens, Samuel L. .... Joan of Arc
Eaton, Jeannette .... Leader by Destiny
Franklin, Benjamin................... Autobiography
Ludwig, Emil .... Napoleon
Myers, C. L. .... Readings in Biography
Plutarch .... Lives
Sandburg, Carl....................... Abraham Lincoln: The War Years
Strachey, Lytton..................... Queen Victoria

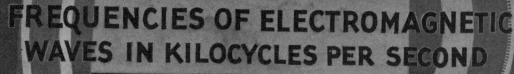

COSMIC RAY	1,000,000,000,000,000,000
	100,000,000,000,000,000
GAMMA RAY	10,000,000,000,000,000
	1,000,000,000,000,000
X-RAY	100,000,000,000,000
	10,000,000,000,000
ULTRA VIOLET	1,000,000,000,000
VISIBLE RAYS	100,000,000,000
HEAT RAYS	10,000,000,000
	1,000,000,000
$\varepsilon = h\sqrt{}$ PLANCK 1900	100,000,000
	10,000,000
HERTZ	1,000,000
$\dfrac{d^2y}{dt^2} = v^2 \dfrac{d^2y}{dX^2}$ D'ALEMBERT 1747	100,000
	10,000
RADIO BROADCASTING	1,000
	100
	10
	1